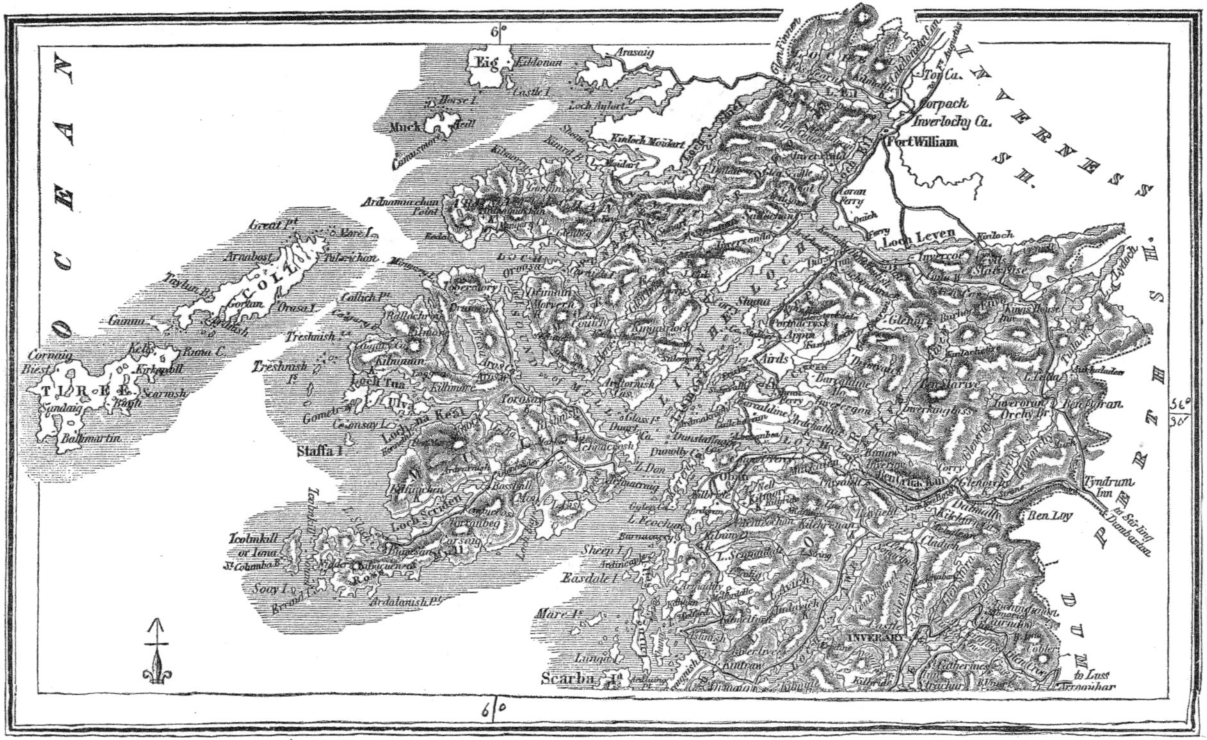

O C E A N
INVERNESS SH.
PERTH SH.
DUM
Eig
Muck
Staffa I
Scarba
Loch Leven
Fort William
Inverlochy Ca.
Corpach
Arasaig
Tyndrum Inn
Ben Loy
INVERARY
Oban
Easdale I
Sheep I
Mare I
Lunga
Soay I
Icolmkill or Iona
Ulva
Treshnish
Tiree
Coll
Gunna
Cornaig
Ballmartin
Arnabost
Great Pt
to Luss

From rocky Duard, from Mingarry grey,
The terror of the clans has passed away.
They sleep, the plaided warriors of MacLean,
Where dust of battle may not rise again.
Sheathed is the claymore, vanished from the sea
The white-winged pride of Ocean Chivalry;
Hushed is the slogan, bloodless flow the waves,
And Death seems buried in those island Graves!
—*Mosse MacDonald.*

Mull, thou art fairest of all isles
    That gem the breezy West,
And oft my thought floats back to thee,
    When sweet peace holds my breast!

Thy rich-embowered, green-cinctured bays,
    Thy gently sloping hills,
Thy proud far-viewed sky-cleaving Ben,
    Thy sweetly tinkling rills.
—*Professor John Stuart Blackie.*

A HISTORY of the
CLAN MACLEAN

FROM ITS FIRST SETTLEMENT AT DUARD CASTLE, IN
THE ISLE OF MULL, TO THE PRESENT PERIOD

INCLUDING

A GENEALOGICAL ACCOUNT OF SOME OF THE PRINCIPAL FAMILIES

TOGETHER WITH

THEIR HERALDRY, LEGENDS, SUPERSTITIONS, ETC.

by
J. P. MacLean

ILLUSTRATED WITH MAPS, PORTRAITS, VIEWS OF BATTLE-FIELDS, CASTLES,
TOMBS, RUINS, AND ARMORIAL BEARINGS

Mar mhadadh ag òl eanruich ainmeaunan Chlann 'ill-Eathain
—*Eachann, Lachann; Eachann, Lachann.*—
MacLean Proverb

HERITAGE BOOKS
2008

HERITAGE BOOKS
AN IMPRINT OF HERITAGE BOOKS, INC.

Books, CDs, and more—Worldwide

For our listing of thousands of titles see our website
at
www.HeritageBooks.com

A Facsimile Reprint
Published 2008 by
HERITAGE BOOKS, INC.
Publishing Division
100 Railroad Ave. #104
Westminster, Maryland 21157

Copyright © 1999 Heritage Books, Inc.

Originally published
Cinncinnati
Robert Clarke & Co.
1889

— Publisher's Notice —
In reprints such as this, it is often not possible to remove blemishes from the original. We feel the contents of this book warrant its reissue despite these blemishes and hope you will agree and read it with pleasure.

International Standard Book Numbers
Paperbound: 978-0-7884-1316-2
Clothbound: 978-0-7884-7168-1

PREFACE.

This record is largely confined to the events that occurred during the growth and decadence of the clan. There are many questions just as important and interesting as historical events that are intimately connected with the family, and which should be particularly set forth. The origin of the race, its migrations, manners, customs, and many other characteristics must be of intrinsic value. Whoever studies or desires to become acquainted with his ancestry never tires of prying into all the various related subjects. The very nature of them demands a separate treatise, and as they are necessarily extensive, a volume must be required for their consideration. In order to set forth fully these related subjects, I have collected the material, and at an early day I hope to be able to give it to the reading public; however treating it in a more general than special manner.

In the preparation of this work, for a basis I have relied on the "Account of the Clan MacLean," published in 1838, and the Pennycross and Ardgour MSS, frequently using the exact language used by their compilers. Donald Gregory's "History of the Western Highlands" has been of great assistance, and deserves to be specially mentioned; for it would be difficult to write concerning the West Highland clans without recourse to this invaluable publication. I have not depended upon such material as may be found in printed volumes, but present many important facts heretofore inaccessible to the public. For a large part of the hitherto unpublished matter, I am greatly indebted to Sir Fitzroy Donald MacLean, Bart., the present hereditary chief, who very obligingly placed at my disposal copies of such parts of the official state papers of Scotland as bore directly upon the subject. Archibald John MacLean of Pennycross, not only gave me a complete copy of the Pennycross MS, but rendered other assistance of much value. For a copy of the Ardgour MS, I am indebted to Alexander Thomas MacLean, present laird of Ardgour. In the mansion house at Lochbuie I spent four pleasant and profitable weeks, during which time Captain Murdoch Gillian MacLean of Lochbuie kindly gave me full access to all the papers in his Charter Room, from which I made liberal extracts. To him I am indebted for many courtesies. I found

(iii)

Rev. Alexander MacLean Sinclair, not only fully informed on the history of the clan of which his maternal grandfather was a worthy and honored member, but also ever ready and willing to impart his knowledge along with many valuable suggestions.

It will be observed that this volume is almost wholly confined to the MacLeans of Scotland. The family histories of whatever branch must necessarily begin with the clan itself; and as the clan history does not extend outside of Scotland, the foundation must necessarily be laid in the land of its birth. To treat of the MacLeans in other countries would require several volumes—America alone would demand a large one. Having presented the clan proper, the other histories could readily find a beginning. The various cadets or septs have been presented as fully as it was possible. In some instances an account could not be obtained owing to the carelessness in preserving the records; and hence, unwillingly, I have been forced to pass them over. In some of those given, it was found next to impossible to reach the descendants now living.

Instead of an Index a copious Table of Contents is given. Owing to the repeated recurrence of the same name an index would not be of so much value as a full table of contents; and it is believed that in the latter, the reader will experience no difficulty in finding the desired information.

I am fully aware of the many imperfections contained in this volume. Due effort has been made to remedy them; but this in some instances has been found impossible owing to the want of accurate information. Being removed a distance of four thousand miles adds also to the perplexity. In some respects this may be regarded as an advantage; for a judgment might be formed more correctly when not influenced by the pressure of immediate surroundings.

This history is not written under the patronage of any one, neither was it suggested by any one. I had an anxiety to learn of my ancestry, in which I took a deep interest. The results of my investigations I desired to lay before those who belong to the same worthy lineage. If there is any word of censure to be bestowed, or any financial loss sustained, I must bear the burden alone.

MARCH 4, 1889.

TABLE OF CONTENTS.

CHAPTER I.
PRELIMINARY REMARKS.

Importance of clan history—Essential requirements—MacLeans deserving of honorable mention—Sir Walter Scott, Professor Blackie, and William Allan on—How styled—Political history—Traditionary—Under Lords of Lorn—Under Lords of the Isles—Independence of—Adherence to the house of Stuart—Religious stages—Druidism, Culdeeism, Catholicism, and the Reformation—Development—Growth—Zenith of power—Decline—Skene on Argyle family—Policy of the government—Compact between Huntly, Argyle, and Lachlan MacLean—Harpers—Physicians and Genealogists. 21–26

CHAPTER II.
THE HOME AND ORIGIN OF THE CLAN.

Isle of Mull—Location—Description—Geology—History—Dalriad Scots—The Norsemen—Ceded to Somerled—Angus Og MacDonald obtains possession—Charter from Robert Bruce—Edward Balliol grants to John, First Lord of the Isles—Donald, Second Lord of the Isles, grants to Lachlan MacLean in 1390—Charters of 1495, 1409, and 1390—Origin of the name MacLean—Skene's list—Tables of Drs. Beaton and Kennedy—Ancient genealogists not always reliable—Culture of genealogists—Relationship of MacLeans to MacKenzies—Old Dougall of Scone—Three clans from—Gilleain, founder of Clan MacLean. 26–32

CHAPTER III.
FIRST PERIOD OF THE CHIEFS.
FROM A. D. 1250 TO A. D. 1400.

Gilleain—Origin of the crest—Possessions in Mull—Gylen Castle—The first chief and founder—Gille-Iosa, second chief—Followers of Alexander III.—Norwegian invasion—Battle of Largs—Gille-Iosa at—Death of—Malcolm, third chief—Ragman Roll—Malcolm heads the clan at Bannockburn—Battle of—Death of Malcolm—Sons of—Donald and Neil in Exchequer Rolls—Sons of—John, fourth chief—Lachlan and Hector—Feud with MacKinnon—Seizure of Lord of the Isles—Lachlan's demands—Marries Lady Margaret—Friendship of the two brothers—Lachlan becomes fifth chief—Sons of—Death of—Called first of Duard. 33–39

CHAPTER IV.
THE MACLEANS AS VASSALS OF THE LORDS OF THE ISLES.
FROM A. D. 1365 TO A. D. 1493.

Charter of 1390—Hector Roy, sixth chief—A celebrated swordsman—Kills the Knight from Norway—Expedition to Ireland—Island and castle of Cairnburg—Hector

(v)

marries daughter of earl of Douglas—Hector's faithfulness—Expedition of the Lord of the Isles—Checked by Angus Dhu—Battle of Harlaw—Hector slain—Buried at Iona—Anniversary of MacLeans and Irvins—Lachlan Brounach, seventh chief—Prisoner at Harlaw—Marries daughter of earl of Moray—Warlike character of—Treachery of James I.—Imprisonment and murder of Highland chiefs—Vengeance of Alexander, third Lord of the Isles—Inverness burned—Royal army summoned—Alexander surprised—Deserted by Camerons and Clanchattan—Surrenders and imprisoned—Lachlan imprisoned—Rebellion of Donald Balloch—Royal army defeated at Inverlochy—Donald flees to Ireland—King comes to Dunstaffnage—Wholesale executions—A great pestilence—Lachlan MacLean and Murdoch Gibson ravage Lennox—Death of Lachlan—Marriages of—Sons of—Demands of Donald MacLean—Slays MacMaster—Takes Ardgour and becomes first laird of—Neil MacLean, first of Lehire and Ross—Demands of John Garbh—Receives Coll—Imprisons Clanranald—Warlike character—Deprived of his castle—Goes to Ireland—Frees the laird of MacLeod—Slays MacNeil—Again rescues MacLeod—Lachlan Og, eighth chief—Fourth Lord of the Isles—Treason of—Purchased by Edward IV. of England—Rebellion of, suppressed—Commission of earl of Argyle against—Sues for pardon and despoiled of certain lands—Rare judgment of Lachlan MacLean—Marries Argyle's daughter—Argyle's unkindness—Lachlan's heirs—Marriage—Daughters of—Charter to Celestine MacDonald—Witnesses charters—Charter to John Davidson—Hector Odhar, ninth chief—Rebellion of Angus MacDonald—MacLeans loyal to the Lord of the Isles—Expeditions against Angus—Battle of Bloody Bay—Lord of Isles and Hector Odhar prisoners—Feud between Kenneth MacKenzie and MacDonald of Lochalsh—Kenneth's cruelty to his wife—Church at Contin burned—Battle of the Park—Death of Lachlan MacLean—Heroic conduct of—Duncan Mór—Final forfeiture of the Lord of the Isles—MacLeans divided into four principal septs.   39–55

CHAPTER V.

The MacLeans Become an Independent Clan.

FROM A. D. 1493 TO A. D. 1598.

Laudable object of the king—Corresponds with principal chiefs—Effective measures of—Court at Mingarry castle—Submission of chiefs—Imprisons chief of MacKenzie and young MacIntosh—Strong measures by lords of council—Chiefs commanded to be peaceable—Feud between MacLeans and Camerons—Possession of lands of Lochiel in dispute—MacLeans carry off cattle—Perfidy of the king—Argyle lieutenant of the Isles—Inhabitants expelled—Argyle enriched—Rebellion of Donald Dhu—Imprisoned forty years—The throne shaken—Clans united—Country ravaged—Efforts of the king—Confederacy broken up—Submission of the chief of MacLean—Other chiefs submit—Some remain in rebellion—Rebellion suppressed—Rights maintained —Donald again prisoner for forty years—Feud between MacLeans and Camerons again breaks out—Feud between the MacLeans of Duard and Lochbuy—Uncertain point in the history—Facts stated—Defects in the records—Death of Hector Odhar prior to 1500—A suppressed chief—Evidence concerning Lachlan, the suppressed chief—Recognized by official archives—Testimony of Tytler and Keltie—Discrepancies—Reasons for suppressing—Possessions inherited by Lachlan—Popularity of James IV.—Summons the whole array of his kingdom—Battle of Flodden—Lachlan MacLean slain at—Lachlan Catanach, eleventh chief—Difficulties involved in his history—Meaning of Catanach—A great chieftain—Leads the rebellion of Donald Gallda—Captures Cairnburg and Dunskaich—Sir Donald proclaimed Lord of the Isles—Efforts at suppression—Rebellion suppressed—Lachlan receives remission—

Table of Contents.

Sir Donald again in rebellion—Deceives MacLean and MacLeod, who attempt to arrest him—Petitions of Argyle and Lachlan—Decision in regard to Lochbuy and MacLeod—Lachlan's petition treated with severity by historians—The facts stated—Argyle's character—MacLean and MacLeod respited—King's lands in Mull and Morvern—Lachlan commissioned to arm his tenants—Lachlan's remission—Precept for lands of Tiree—Letter in favor of Alexander MacLean and Alexander MacLeod—Episode of the Lady's Rock—Version by Gregory, by legendary account, and by Pennycross MS—Lachlan marries daughter of Achinbreck—Marries Marian, daughter of Treshnish—Sons of—Lives at Cairnburg—Obtains charter—Procures letters of protection—Murdered by John Campbell—Duplicity of Argyle—Murder of Lachlan avenged—Argyle's distress—Hector MacLean and other chiefs submit—Hostages—Argyle deprived of certain powers—Hector Mór, twelfth chief in 1527—Noble conduct of—Private character—Receives king's protection—Feud between Duard and Lochbuy—James V. visits Western Isles with a fleet—Chiefs of Clan MacDonald visit him—Seizes Hector Mór and other chieftains—Terms extorted—Death of James V.—Rebellion of Donald Dubh in 1543—Negotiations with Lennox—Statement made by chiefs—Illiteracy of—King of England sends money to the Isles—Oath of allegiance to England—Death of Donald Dubh—MacLeans oppose James MacDonald's pretensions—Argyle orders a force against Hector Mór—Action of Campbell of Duntroon—Argyle visits Duard—Double marriage—Hector Og weds Janet Campbell—Estrangement of clans—Feud between Duard and Coll in 1561—Injustice to Coll—Dispute with MacDonald of Islay—Beginning of a long and bloody feud—Action of Privy Council—Hector Mór assigns his estates to Hector Og—Lands of Ardgour—Of Ulva—Charter to Janet Campbell—Donald Monro's description of Western Isles—Duard castle—Additions made by Hector Mór—Aros castle—Hector Mór's marriage and sons—Daughters of—Story of Ailean nan Sop—Death of—Sons of—Patrick MacLean—Hector Og, thirteenth chief—A spendthrift—Agreement with John Dubh—Son and daughters of—Sir Lachlan Mór, fourteenth chief—Character of—Testimony of Spottiswoode, Blackie, Skene, Gregory, and Tytler—Educated in Edinburgh—Attempt to deprive him of his estates—Complaint against Argyle—Rights his wrongs—Argyle's advantage—Lachlan visits Edinburgh—Proposed marriage with Athol's daughter—Weds daughter of Glencairn—Feud breaks out with MacDonald of Islay—Peace declared—Angus weds sister of Lachlan—Feud renewed in 1585—Cause of—League of the MacDonalds—Desperate straits of the MacLeans—King interferes—Angus imprisoned in Duard castle—Released—Spottiswoode's version—Treachery of Angus—MacLeans beheaded—Escape of Lachlan—John Dubh beheaded—Summary vengeance of son of—Lachlan's vengeance—Islay ravaged—MacDonalds combine—Mull invaded—Signal service of Borreray—Flight of MacDonalds—Exasperation of—Land on Bachca—Defeat of—King interferes—MacIan of Ardnamurchan—Weds mother of Lachlan—Unfortunate quarrel—MacDonalds slaughtered—MacIan imprisoned—Petition of—Arrival of the Florida—Agreement between Lachlan and Spanish captain—Rum, Eig, Canna, and Muck ravaged—Mingarry castle beseiged—Treachery of Spanish captain—Donald Gorm MacLean—Destruction of the Florida—Tales of—Feud with MacDonalds unabated—King interferes—Lachlan and Angus brought to trial—Extracts from official records—Remission to Lachlan in 1588—Description of Western Isles in 1590—Lachlan's expedition to Ireland in 1591—Harmony between MacLeans and MacDonalds—Regarded with disfavor at court—Lachlan summoned—Rebellion of Huntly, Angus, and Errol—Battle of Glenlivat—Heroic conduct of Lachlan Mór—Testimony of Tytler, Gregory, Scott, Spottiswoode, Browne, Keltie, Cromb, and others—Conduct of Lochnell—Lachlan enlists in the cause of England—Tytler's account of—Queen Elizabeth enlists Lachlan's forces—His power over the Islesmen—Lachlan disbands his forces—The fleet of the Islesmen sails for Ireland—Lachlan defeats nine hundred of Clanranald's force—Imprisons Clanranald, Knoydart, MacIan, and others—John Achinross—Letter of, to Nicolson—Elizabeth expresses her gratitude—The Islemen dispersed—Letter of Lachlan to Bowes—Rebellion in Ireland continued—Bowes consults with Lachlan—Parsimony of Elizabeth—Elizabeth shamed into a settlement—King determines to increase his revenues—Proceeds against chiefs—Commands them to meet at Dumbarton—Lachlan submits—Received into favor—MacDonald of Sleat pardoned—Rhinns of Islay bestowed upon Lachlan—Oppresses Coll—Coll's complaint—Lachlan visits Linlithgow—Lachlan gives security—Difficulty between Lachlan and Lochiel—Battle—James MacDonald seizes his father's estates—Inhumanity of—Indignities to his father—James seeks strife with Duard—Rhinns of Islay in dispute—A friendly meeting fixed upon—Perfidy of Sir James—Battle of Tra-Ghruinnaird—Heroism of Sir Lachlan—Is slain—Dubh-Sith—Account of the battle, by Gregory, Skene, and Tytler—Legend—Burial of Sir Lachlan—A tragedy — Epitaph by Dr. Johnson—Sir Lachlan's character—A protestant—His sons—Daughter. . . 55–137

CHAPTER VI.

THE MACLEANS AS PARTISANS OF THE HOUSE OF STUART.

FROM A. D. 1598 TO A. D. 1746.

Hector Og, fifteenth chief—Obtains commission of fire and sword against Sir James MacDonald—Summons MacKinnons, MacLeods, and MacNeils—Joined by Lochiel — Battle of Benbigrie — Islay ravaged — Lochiel captures Lochbuy — The last conflict with the MacDonalds—In '1599 the king again decides to mulct the chiefs — Commission of lieutenancy granted — Charged in 1601 to augment the king's rents — Hector defrauded by Huntly out of lands in Lochaber—Meeting at Stirling—Chief of Kintail asks assistance of Hector—Ardnamurchan invaded—Argyle interferes—Hector sends Kintail home in his great galley—A stratagem—Character of Argyle—Statements concerning, by Gregory and Keltie—Machinations of Argyle in 1603—Hector gives surety in 1604 to deliver up Duard castle—Capriciousness of the king—Certain chiefs ordered to give obedience to lord Scone—Only Angus MacDonald complied—Inhuman order of extirpation granted by king to Huntly—Thwarted by the jealousy of the Presbyterians—Terms demanded against the chiefs—An expedition arrives at Duard castle—Treachery of the Bishop of the Isles and imprisonment of chiefs—Terms extorted—Chiefs released—Meet at Icolmkill—Celebrated statutes of—Practice of handfasting—Oppressive proclamation—Chiefs give surety for appearance in 1611—Bishop of Isles becomes steward and justice—Commotion among the MacNeils of Barra—Evils of handfasting—Hector settles with exchequer in 1613—Roving commission—Titledeeds—Kingerloch's warning—Argyle plots for Islay—Stirs up MacDonalds to rebellion—Patronymics—Preparations for defense—Hector sympathizes with MacDonalds—Renders assistance—Called to an account—Argyle obtains Islay and Kintyre—Hector's alliances—Feuds now of rare occurrence—Beneficial effects from king's removal to London—MacLeans and others summoned before council in 1616—Demands made of them—Hector committed to ward—Released—Appearance in 1617—Death of Hector Og in 1618—Marriages—Sons and daughters—His possessions—Hector Mór, sixteenth chief—Inactivity of—Becomes involved in debt—Marriage—Dies without issue in 1626—Sir Lachlan MacLean, first Baronet, seventeenth chief—Possesses king's favor—Cunning of Argyle—Statements of Browne, Hume, and MacAulay—Unseemly conduct of at death of Montrose—Conduct of Archibald—Report of bishop Knox in 1626—Sir Lachlan visits London in 1631 and is created Baronet of Morvern—Character of Charles I.—Fisheries of the Isles—

TABLE OF CONTENTS.   ix

Commission on—Report of—Rebellion against the king—In 1641 the king visits
Edinburgh—Argyle's duplicity—Tries to involve Sir Lachlan—Argyle throws off the
mask—Montrose proceeds to Scotland—Raises an army—Joined by Sir Lachlan—
Battle of Inverlochy—Slaughter of the Campbells—Cowardice of Argyle—Campbell
of Skipness saved by Ewen MacLean—MacLean of Brolass arms other MacLeans,
the MacQuarries, and MacNeils, to the number of eleven hundred—Join Sir Alexander MacDonald—Progress of Montrose—Sir Lachlan's complete forces join Montrose after battle of Alford—MacLean of Treshnish with twelve men puts three
hundred of Baillie's army to flight—MacLeans burn castle Campbell—Indignation
of Lochiel—Battle of Kilsyth—Heroic conduct of MacLean of Treshnish—Highland army disbanded—More plots against the king—Montrose surprised at Philiphaugh—Highlanders rally to the support of Montrose—MacLean of Coll—Charles
deceived by the Scottish nobles—Sold to the English parliament—David Leslie
marches against the Islesmen—Murder of MacDonalds—Mull overrun—Career of
blood and plunder—Duard castle besieged—Castle surrendered to Leslie—Murder
of the Irish gentlemen—Remarkable escape—Savage brutality—Argyle secures a
claim against the lands of Sir Lachlan—Sir Lachlan thrown into prison—Death of
in 1648—Sons and daughters of—Sir Hector Roy, eighteenth chief of MacLean—
Evil times—Charles II.—Argyle harrasses the MacLeans—Sir Hector resents the injuries—Sir Hector honors the bond extorted from his father—Pays a large part of
it—Renewal of feuds—Sir Hector avenges the murder of Kingerloch—Murder of
MacLean of Muck—At the command of Charles, Sir Hector enters the field at the
head of eight hundred MacLeans—Battle of Inverkeithing—Sir Hector and nearly
all his clansmen slain—Devotion to their chief—Sir Allan MacLean, nineteenth
chief—Donald of Brolass and Hector of Lochbuy manage the estates—Argyle aug-
ments his claims—Argyle agrees to subjugate his native country for £12,000—Executed for his many crimes—Archibald, his successor, prosecutes his claims against
MacLean—Sir Allan attempts a settlement—Sir Allan goes to London in 1672—Argyle assisted by Lauderdale—Duplicity of Argyle—Sir Allan agrees to payment—Sir
Allan's marriage—Sir John, twentieth chief—Lachlan of Brolass and Lachlan of
Torloisk become guardians—Brolass proposes to arbitrate with Argyle—Argyle invades Mull—Possesses Duard and Aros castles—Depredations—Inhumanities—Lord
MacDonald promises the MacLeans assistance—Argyle prepares for another invasion—The fleet driven back by a hurricane—The state of the dispute and the
debts given in a document drawn up by Brolass and Torloisk—Original cause of the
debt—The debt manipulated—Allies of MacLeans assault a Campbell frigate—Raids
by MacLean of Lochbuy—Campbells suffer depredations—MacDonalds become party
to the MacLeans—Argyle obtains a commission against—In lieu of his claim Argyle
is given Tiree—Unsavory Lauderdale—In 1679 Argyle invades Coll—Capitulation—
Sir Ewen Cameron deserts, by purchase, the MacLeans—Argyle obtains commission
for Cairnburg—Argyle executed in 1685—MacLeans burn castle Carnassary—Death
of Brolass and Torloisk—Sir John manages his estates—Appoints overseers—Travels
in England and France—Goes to Ireland with James II.—At the seige of Derry—
Returns to Scotland—Sacheverell's description of the people of Mull—James's cause
upheld by Dundee—Cause of Highland uprising—Argyle's insignificance and un-
popularity—Sir John joins Dundee—Lochbuy fights the battle of Knockbreck—Sir
Alexander MacLean relieves MacNeil of Callechilly—Duard castle assaulted—Athol
the seat of war—Battle of Killiecrankie—Sir John commands the right—Death of
Dundee—Incompetency of General Cannon—Attack on Dunkeld—Battle of Cromdale—Sir John protects Cannon—Compact of the chieftains—Characteristic letter to
MacKay—Argyle represents Sir John to William as an enemy—Procures letters of
fire and sword against the MacLeans—Sir John retires to Cairnburg—By order of
James capitulates—Goes to London—Argyle seeks to ruin Sir John—Proceeds to

St. Germains—Marries—Arrested in London—Sent to the Tower—Granted a pension of £500 sterling—Escapes from the governor of Fort William in 1714—George, elector of Hanover, becomes king—Character of—Highland chiefs address him—Meeting of the MacLeans in Mull—Harsh treatment of the Highlanders—Earl of Mar raises the standard of James—Joined by Sir John—MacLeans assault Fort William—Battle of Sheriffmuir—Mar's incapacity—Council of war—Highland army disbanded—Sir John dies at Gordon castle in 1716—Description of—Character of—Argyle receives his estates—Sir Hector, twenty-first chief—Born in 1703—Tutored by Coll—His education—In 1721 goes to France—In Scotland in 1725—Goes to France in 1728—Highlanders disarmed—Alarm in 1719—Revolution of 1745—Résumé—Charles of Drimnin leads the MacLeans—Join Charles just after battle of Falkirk—Battle of Culloden—Charles of Drimmin slain—Ferocity of Cumberland toward his prisoners—President Forbes—Repulsed by the king—Great atrocities—Clan system broken up—Sir Hector's part in the revolution—Documents relating to—Arrested—Taken to London—Set at liberty—Dies at Rome in 1750—Description of—Character. 137–224

CHAPTER VII.

The House of Brolass.—From Donald to the Present.

FROM A. D. 1600 TO 1889.

Allan of Brolass succeeds to Sir Hector's titles—Donald, first of Brolass—At Inverkeithing—Tutor of Sir Allan—Marriage—Issue—Lachlan, second of Brolass—Character of—Tutor of Sir John—Member of parliament—Marriage—Died in 1687—Donald, third of Brolass—Served in the revolution of 1715—Marriage and issue—Died in 1725—Sir Allan becomes twenty-second chief—Serves in Holland—In America—Retires with family to Inch Kenneth—Entertains Dr. Johnson—Lawsuit with Argyle—Recovers lands—Dies in 1783—Beloved by all—Buried at Inch Kenneth—His tomb—The old chapel—Sir Hector, twenty-third chief—His lineage—Died in 1818—Sir Fitzroy Jeffreys Grafton MacLean, twenty-fourth chief—Enters the army—Rises to the rank of general—Engages in several battles—Governor of St. Thomas and St. John—His sound government—Married in 1794—Also in 1838—Died in 1847—Sir Charles Fitzroy, twenty-fifth chief—Educated at Eton and Sandhurst—Retired from the army in 1846—Described—Married in 1831—Died in 1883—Sir Fitzroy Donald, twenty-sixth chief—Served in the Crimea—Becomes colonel—Receives medal—In America—Described—Character—Married in 1872—Issue—Lady MacLean described. 224–232

CHAPTER VIII.

The House of Lochbuie.

Picturesque scenery—Site of Moy castle—Difficulties in tracing history of—Hector, first of Lochbuie—Legend of—The castle described—Sons of—Murdoch, second of Lochbuie—John, third of Lochbuie—Hector, fourth—John Og, fifth—Notable character—Principal lands of—Engages in rebellion of 1503—Feud with Camerons in 1513—Feud with Duard—Helps avenge the murder of Lachlan Catanach—Killed in a feud with Duard—Murdoch Gearr, sixth laird—Legend of—Contest with Scallasdale—Enters rebellion of Donald Dubh in 1543—Dies 1586—John Mór, seventh laird—High character of—Kills an Italian swordsman on the stage—Imprisons John Roy—Marriage and death—Hector, eighth laird—Assists MacDonalds—Buys lands of Lochiel—Sells to Argyle—Present at enactment of Statutes of Icolmkill—Entry of lands—Hector Odhar, ninth laird—Receives charter in 1612—Appears before council—Dies about 1628—Murdoch Mór, tenth laird—Served heir, 1630—Conforms to the kirk—Appears at Inverary in 1634—Dies without issue—Lachlan Mór, eleventh laird—Becomes heir in 1668—Receives charter in 1670—Died about 1684—Hector, twelfth laird—Attempt to assassinate—Joins the revolution of 1689—Victor at Knockbreck—Gives up Moy—Gives over estate to his sons—Dies in 1707—Murdoch, thirteenth—Letters to—Dies in 1727—John, fourteenth—Lachlan, fifteenth—Hector, sixteenth—Receives lands in 1742—John, seventeenth—In full possession in 1750—Builds residence—Contract for—Heavy debts of—Imprisons three of his vassals—Statement of the case—Visited in 1773 by Dr. Johnson—Contents of his charter chest—Dies in 1778—Account of his son Archibald—The last piper—Murdoch, eighteenth, raised tories in American revolution—Commands Newcastle Jane—In 1791 brings action against trustees of his estate—Builds Lochbuie House—An attempt to sell the estate—Memorializes duke of York—His issue—Murdoch, nineteenth—Enters army—Retired in 1812—Died in 1844—Donald, twentieth—MacLeans of Batavia—Purchases the estates—Marriage—Character—Died in 1863—Murdoch Gillian, twenty-first—Educated at Edinburgh—Enters army—War correspondent "London Times"—Improves the estate—Enterprise—Marriage—Issue. 232-250

CHAPTER IX.

CLANN THEARLAICH O'BUIE.

Origin of—Glen Urquhart—Sir Charles, first of—First to bear a distinctive title—Builds Castle Bona—Defeats Clan Chattan near Ruthven castle—Marriage and issue—Sir Ewen constable of Urquhart in 1421—Marriage and issue—Sir Charles succeeds in 1439—Marriage and issue—Donald captain of Cairnburg—Hector Buie succeeds about 1450—Battle with the Camerons—Barbarities—Battle with MacIntoshes—Heroic conduct—Hector Buie enters Clan Chattan confederacy—Hector Buie slain—Marriages and offspring—Ewen succeeds as fifth of Urquhart—Strife about lands of Urquhart—Ewen killed at Flodden—Offspring of—MacLeans of Dochgarroch—Infringement of Dunean—Revenge—Before Huntly—John, first of Dochgarroch—Purchases lands—Fined by Mary of Guise—Killed in Lochaber—Farquhar, a bishop—Killed at Pinkie in 1547—Roderick, deputy governor of Inverness in 1556—Invades Caithness—Massacre at Bowrie castle—Donald joins the Reformation—Battle at Loch End—Sir Alexander at Battle of Glenlivat—Created knight—Killed in 1635—Issue—David, a soldier of fortune—Killed at Red-castle—Lachlan joins Dundee—John, sixth, at Inverlochy, Auldearn, and Kilsyth—At Inverkeithing—Obtains a new charter—Issue—John Og, seventh—At Killiecrankie and Dunkeld—Marriage—John, eighth—Character—At Sheriffmuir—Kills a Hessian—Changes spelling of name—Issue—Charles, ninth—Retires from the army—Asserts his claims to the estate—Marriage—John, tenth—Estate managed by his brothers—William, eleventh—Captured by Spaniards—Retires in 1796—Estate becomes involved—Estates sold in 1832—Marriage and issue—Allan, twelfth—Lives near Inverness—William, the present head—Allan. 251-261

CHAPTER X.

THE MACLEANS OF KINGERLOCH.

High position—Patronymic—Supports Lochbuie—Genealogy imperfect—Charters of 1625 and 1627—Lands—Branches—Sir Charles, first of Kingerloch—Dean of Morvern—Donald a baron in 1540—Prominent—Hector confirmed in lands during Mary's reign—Donald registered lands in 1609—Donald succeeds in 1675—Denounced rebel in 1680—Espoused the cause of the Stuarts in 1689, 1715, and 1745—

Lachlan flees to Holland—Hugh, laird from 1759 to 1780—Letters of—Donald successor—Hector removes to Nova Scotia—Sells estates in 1812—Murdoch, head of the family, dies in 1865—Issue—Robert, the present head—Marriage and issue. 261-263.

CHAPTER XI.

THE MACLEANS OF SCALLASDALE.

District of—Early history unknown—Murdoch becomes tutor to his nephew—Later family of—Gillean—Family of—Coppurnach, Gruline, Kilmory, Pennygowan, Tapull, Killran, and Knoch, cadets of Lochbuie.   264

CHAPTER XII.

THE MACLEANS OF LEHIRE.

Oldest branch of Duard—John Dubh—Neil—Neil nan Ordag—John—John Og—Slain by Allan nan Sop.   265

CHAPTER XIII.

THE MACLEANS OF ARDGOUR.

Family seat—Description—Donald, first—MacMasters not extirpated—Ewen, second—Seneschal to earl John in 1463—Allan, third—Man of importance—John, fourth—Handfasting—A son John famous for his strength—Signalized in all Sir Lachlan Mór's wars—John the laird died about 1545—Allan, fifth—Ewen, sixth—Noted for agility—Killed by the MacDonalds—Allan, seventh—Estates managed by Charles—Attempt to defraud Allan — Allan asks assistance of Argyle — Argyle demands lands of Ardgour—Charles taken by stratagem—Montrose empowers Allan to hold lands from the king—Lived to a great age—John, eighth—Lived to a great age—Ewen, ninth—His character—Allan, tenth—Born in 1668—Represented the family in evil times—Estate in bad condition—Managed by trustees—Dies in 1756—John, eleventh—Died in 1739—Hugh, twelfth—MacLachlans attempt to possess the estate—Torloisk took the management and recovers the estate from ruin—Died in 1768—Alexander, thirteenth—Enters army—Daring rider—Died in 1833—Issue—Alexander, fourteenth—Enters service of East India Company—Marriage—Died in 1872—Alexander Thomas, fifteenth—Educated at Harrow—Entered service East India Company—Judge of high court at Fort William—Marriage and issue—Character of—Possessions.   265-272

CHAPTER XIV.

THE MACLEANS OF BORRERAY.

Neil Ban—History imperfect—John, Alexander, Archibald, Donald, and Nial Ban, lairds—Family of Nial Ban—Descendants—Sons of Charles—John, seventh laird—Archibald, eighth—Family.   273-275

CHAPTER XV.

THE MACLEANS OF TRESHNISH.

Captains of Cairnburg—John, first of—Donald, second of—Character of Donald, third of—Ewen, fourth of—Character—Family—Ewen, fifth of—Lands—John, sixth of—

TABLE OF CONTENTS. xiii

Ewen, seventh of—Favorite of Montrose—Warlike character of—Hector, eighth of—
Ewen, ninth of—Family of—John, tenth of—Deprived of his lands. . 275-278

CHAPTER XVI.
THE MACLEANS OF INVERSCADELL.
First of—Charles, fifth of—Family of—Allan, sixth of—Sells lands. . . 278

CHAPTER XVII.
THE MACLEANS OF BLAICH.
Two periods of—First of—Second family of—William becomes master of revels. 279

CHAPTER XVIII.
THE MACLEANS OF ROSS.
Third branch of the MacLeans—Lands of—Lachlan's talents—Sons killed at Inverkeithing—Descendants of—Hector of the Leda frigate—Ewen, brother of Lachlan—Sons of. 280

CHAPTER XIX.
THE MACLEANS OF COLL.
Description of Coll—Breachacha castle—Early description of—The fourth branch—John Garbh, first of—Character of—Lands of—John Abrach, second of—Killed by Camerons—John, third of—In possession in 1493—Receives respite—Charter granted—Hector, fourth of—Learning of—Poet—Feud with Duard—Hector Roy, fifth of—Lachlan, sixth of—Prominent character of—Possessions of—Appears before privy council in 1616—A principal landlord—Charter for Muck—Avenges murder of his son—John Garbh, seventh of—Wisdom of—Composer of music—Anecdote of—Morals of—Son Hector—Lachlan, eighth of—Drowned—John Garbh, ninth of—Death of—Donald, tenth of—Hector, eleventh of—Described—Judicious—Opposes revolution of 1745—Last Harper of Mull—Lachlan, twelfth of—Hugh, thirteenth of—Family of—Popularity of Donald—Drowned—Alexander, fourteenth—Character of—Hugh, fifteenth of—Character of—Residence—Anecdote of—Possessions sold—Alexander, last of Coll—Sisters. 281-292

CHAPTER XX.
THE MACLEANS OF ACHANASAUL.
Cadet of Coll—Allan at battle of Gruinart—Character of John—Anecdote of—Lachlan, a physician. 292

CHAPTER XXI.
THE MACLEANS OF MUCK.
Isle of Muck—Character of Hector—In Montrose's army—Murdered—Hector, second of—Lachlan, third of—At Sheriffmuir—Hector, fourth of—Donald, fifth of—Lachlan, sixth of—Served in America—Lieutenant of Tower. . . . 294

CHAPTER XXII.
THE MACLEANS OF DRIMNACROSS.
Neil, first of—In civil wars—Wounded at Inverkeithing—Hector killed at Dunkeld—Allan at Grisiboll—Family of. 295

CHAPTER XXIII.
THE MACLEANS OF TOTARANALD.
John in civil wars—Heroism of Hugh at Inverkeithing—Account of—John fails to be rewarded—Family of. 296

CHAPTER XXIV.
THE MACLEANS OF CROSSAPOL.
Allan, first of—Neil succeeds in 1832—John. 297

CHAPTER XXV.
THE MACLEANS OF HAREMERE HALL.
Origin of—John of Muck—Alexander of Haremere Hall—Family of—Descendants—Burial grounds. 298

CHAPTER XXVI.
THE MACLEANS OF KINLOCHALINE.
Morvern—History of—Antiquities—Conference of 1462—Ardtornish castle—Killundine castle—Castle of Dogs—Kinlochaline castle—Burned in 1664—Loch Aline—Fifth branch of Duard—John Dubh—Family of—Hector, first of Kinlochaline—Charter of lands—John, second of—At Inverkeithing—Hector, third of—Angus, fourth of—At Sheriffmuir. 299–302

CHAPTER XXVII.
THE MACLEANS OF DRIMNIN.
Location—Castle—John Garbh, first of—Family of—Allan at Killiecrankie—Killed at Sheriffmuir—John Diurach wounded at Inverkeithing—Descendants of—Charles, first of Ardnacross—Allan of Drimnin—John, second of—Allan, third of—Charles, fourth of—Naval officer—Commands MacLeans at Culloden—Killed—Anecdote of—Allan, fifth of—Family of—Family of Lachlan of Calgary—Of Allan of Gruline—Of Donald of Aros—Of Hector—Of Ewen. 302–309

CHAPTER XXVIII.
THE MACLEANS OF PENNYCROSS.
Residence—House of Morvern—Alexander, first of Pennycross—Archibald, second of —Family of—Alexander, third of—Archibald John, fourth of—Described—Sells Carsaig. 309–311

TABLE OF CONTENTS. xv

CHAPTER XXIX.
THE MACLEANS OF TORLOISK.

Family seat—Lachlan, first of—At Gruinnart—Prominence of—Hector, second of—Lachlan, third of—Prudence of—Alexander, fourth of—Donald, fifth of—At Sheriffmuir—Died in 1748—Hector, sixth of—Lachlan, seventh of—Marianne succeeds—cadets of Torloisk.   312–315

CHAPTER XXX.
THE COUNTS MACLEAN OF SWEDEN.

Sir John goes to Sweden—Changes his name—Marries in Gothenburgh—Descendants of.   315

CHAPTER XXXI.
IONA.

Description of—Druids—St. Columba—The Culdees—Romanism—Nunnery—Monastery bombarded—MacLeans of Duard possess lands—Description of ruins—Reilig Odhrain—Burial place of MacLeans—MacLean of Coll—Niel of Ross—Ailean nan Sop—Grulin—Duard—Lochbuie—The rider—Dr. John Beton—Unknown—Prioress Anna—MacLeans' cross—Prioress Mary—Patrick MacLean—Last Romish bishop—Hector MacLean—Family of—Charter of 1390—Lands in 1561—Contract of 1580—Rentals—Restored in 1635—Result of reformation—Moore on.   317–329

CHAPTER XXXII.
SUPERSTITIONS.

Mull witches—Power of—Celebrated witch of 1588—Spanish princess—Women tortured in 1662 by Chisholm—Sir Allan MacLean interferes—A tale of Dunstaffnage—Story of Eoghann a'chinn bhig—Divination—Story of Allan and Lachlan MacLean—MacLean Leug—A bishop's folly—Legend of St. Oran—Personal experience.   330–336

CHAPTER XXXIII.
LEGENDS OF MULL.

Allan nan Sop—Feud between Allan MacRuari and Duard—Feud between MacKinnon and the MacLeans—Story of the harp—Sir Allan, nineteenth of MacLean—Allan MacDonald of Moydart and Duard's daughter.   336–341

CHAPTER XXXIV.
MARKS OF DISTINCTION.

Coat of Arms—On Duard castle—Stoddart's representation—Keltie's—Lochbuie—Dochgarroch—Ardgour—Brolass—Pennycross—Coll—Badge—War-cry—March—Tartan—Lochbuie brooch.   342–347

CHAPTER XXXV.
CHIEFTAINSHIP.

A chief—His character—Lachlan Lubanach and Hector Reganach—The claim of the house of Lochbuie—Claim considered—Claims of Duard—Statement of Hugh of Kingerloch—Claims of house of Coll—Considered—Gregory's statement—Houses feudally independent. 347–351

CHAPTER XXXVI.
ON THE NAME OF MACLEAN.

Changes in—Origin of—Mac-Gille-sheathain—Mac-Ghille-athain—Mac-Ghille-eoin—Variations in Gaelic—Official records of Scotland—14th century, McGilhon, Makgilleone—15th century, McGillane, Makgilleon, McGilleon, McGilleoin, Makgillane, McGillan, McGilleone, Makgilleone, Maklane, MakGilleoin, McClan, McClean—16th century, Maklane, McClane, Makclane, Makclain, Makalane, Makgilleon, Makgillane, McGillane, McGilleon, MacGilleon, Macklane, McClayne, Makillan, McLane, Makclayne, Makgilleoun, McGilleoun, MakYllean, McLean, MacGullayne, McGellayne, McGillayne, Maclane, McClene, McGillan, McClaine, McClein—17th century, McClayne, McClane, McCleane, Mᶜclean, McLeane, McLene, Mᶜclaine—18th century, McLean, Maclaine, McLaine, MacLain, MacLeane—19th century, MacLaine, MacLean, McLean, McLaine, McLain, McClean, McClain, McLane, MacLane. 351–359

CHAPTER XXXVII.
DR. SAMUEL JOHNSON AND THE MACLEANS.

Johnson and Boswell's tour—Donald MacLean—Party arrives at Coll—Hector MacLean's interview with Johnson—At Breachacha—Kindness of Coll—Fosterage—Sail for Tobermory—Dr. Hector MacLean—Manuscript of poems—Miss MacLean's learning—Arrives at Inch Kenneth—Sir Allan—Go to Iona—Incident—At Lochbuie—Incident—Leave for the mainland. 359–364

CHAPTER XXXVIII.
THE CLANSMEN AFTER CULLODEN.

Brutality after Culloden—Abolishing Highland garb—Owners of the soil—Deprived of rights—Heartless clergy—Evictions—Dispersion of MacLeans—MacLeans oppressed—Unpleasant statistics—Horrors from Coll—Ardgour and evictions—Sufferings of MacLeans by exorbitant rents—Lady Matheson—Martyrdom of John MacLean—The press-gang—William MacLean—Strange story. 365–373

CHAPTER XXXIX.
DISTINGUISHED MACLEANS.

Gen. Francis MacLean—Gen. Allan—Lieut.-Gen. Sir Hector—Lieut.-Gen. Sir Joseph—Lieut.-Gen. Sir John—Gen. Sir Archibald—Lieut.-Gen. Allan Thomas—Maj.-Gen. John Hector Norman—Chief Kaid Harry—Lieut.-Col. Alexander—Governor George—Bishop John—Rev. Dr. John—Dr. Adam Clarke—Hector MacLean—Colin A. MacVean—Rev. A. McLean Sinclair. 373–281

TABLE OF CONTENTS. xvii

CHAPTER XL.
MacLean Poets.

Eachunn Bacach—Iain MacAilein—Andrew—Iain MacGilleain—Hector of Coll—Catriona—Mairearad—Am Cùbair Colach—Gilleaspuig Làidir—Am Bard MacGilleain—Dòmhnull—Tearlach—Rev. Duncan—Mary—Malcolm. . . 382-385

CHAPTER XLI.
MacLean Authors.

Lachlan—John—Finley—C.—Neil—Rev. John—Dr. R.—Kate S.—Dr. Donald—Rev. Arthur J.—Rev. Alexander—Sir John—Rev. Archibald—Rev. Dr. Archibald—John—John, supreme justice—Rev. Dr. John—Rev. Dr. W. W.—Sallie Pratt—Mary Webster—Alexander—John J.—John Patterson—Account of Clan, pub. 1838—Clan Tarlach O'Buie, 1865—Genealogical Account, pub. 1872—Pennycross MS—Advocates' Library—Vatican—Celtic Magazine—Other MSS—Strange fatality. . 385-392

CHAPTER XLII.
The Family of John MacLean.

Number of MacLeans—Attainments—Geographical names—John—Account of—Issue—Sarah—John—Margaret—Stephen—Elizabeth—William—Joseph—Mary — James—Descendants—Facts concerning the family. 392-400

APPENDIX.

Note A.—Account of the Florida. 401

Note B.—Letters of John Achinross and Sir Lachlan Mór MacLean. . . 402
    Letter of John Achinross. 402
    Letter Sir Lachlan Mór to Sir R. Cecil. 403
    Letter Sir Lachlan Mór to Bowes. 403
    Letter John Achinross to George Nicholson. 404

Note C.—Poetry on the MacLeans. 406
    No. 1.—The Island of Mull. 409
    No. 2.—The Last Harper o' Mull. 410
    No. 3.—Chieftain MacLean. 410
    No. 4.—MacLean's Child. 410
    No. 5.—MacLean's Child. 411
    No. 6.—Wild Revenge. 413
    No. 7.—MacLean's Child. 416
    No. 8.—Callum o' the Glen. 418
    No. 9.—Inch Kenneth. 419
    No. 10.—Nine Noted Chiefs of MacLean. . . . 419
    No. 11.—War Song of Lachlan. 419

No. 12.—Coronach on Sir Lachlan.	420
No. 13.—The Lady of Duard's Vengeance.	420
No. 14.—Burial of Sir Lachlan Mór.	421
No. 15.—The Battle of Knockbreck.	422
No. 16.—MacLean's Welcome to Prince Charlie.	423
No. 17.—Gathering of the Clan.	423
No. 18.—The Isle of Inch Kenneth.	424
No. 19.—A Lay of Clan MacLean.	424
No. 20.—Courtship of Hector MacLean.	425
No. 21.—Glenara.	439
No. 22.—The Lady of the Rock.	439
No. 23.—The Family Legend.	452
LIST OF SUBSCRIBERS.	477

ERRATA.

Page 361, sixth line; for "layers," read "players."
Page 396, third line from bottom; for "1886," read "1866."
All other errors will readily be detected.

LIST OF ILLUSTRATIONS.

TITLES.	DRAWN BY.	PAGE.
Map of Mull and adjacent Territories		Frontispiece.
Geological Map of Mull	J. P. MacLean	27
Flodden-Field	Mrs. H. C. MacLean	64
Ruins of Duard Castle	" "	86
Duard Castle in 1677	Sir Fitzroy D. MacLean, Bart	87
Inverlochy Castle and Battle-Ground		167
Pass of Killiecrankie		202
Battle Field of Sheriffmuir		211
Plan of Battle of Culloden		217
Battle of Culloden		218
Battle Field of Culloden	Mrs. H. C. MacLean	220
Sir Allan MacLean		226
Tomb of Sir Allan MacLean	Colin A. MacVean	228
Ruins on Inch Kenneth	" "	228
Side View of Chapel on Inch Kenneth	" "	229
Sir Fitzroy Donald McLean, Bart		231
Lochbuie House and Castle Moy	Mrs. H. C. MacLean	233
Murdoch Gillian MacLean	W. R. Grant	250
Urquhart Castle	Mrs. H. C. MacLean	251
Alexander T. MacLean	W. R. Grant	272
Front View Breachacha Castle	Mrs. H. C. MacLean	282
Landside View Brachacha Castle		282
Archibald John MacLean		310
Iona Cathedral and St. Oran's Chapel		316
Tombs of the MacLeans in Reilig Odhran	Mrs. H. C. MacLean	320
Tomb of MacLean of Coll	J. P. MacLean	322
" " " (Side view)	" "	322
" " " Ross	" "	322
" Ailean nan Sop	" "	322
" MacLean of Grulin	" "	322
" " Duard	" "	323
" " Lochbuy	" "	323
" the Rider	" "	323
" Dr. John Beaton	" "	324
" a MacLean	" "	324
" Prioress Anna	" "	324
MacLean's Cross		325
MacLean Leug (two views)	Colin A. MacVean	335
Coat of Arms Duard Castle		342
" Combined	J. P. MacLean	343
" MacLeans		343
" Lochbuie		344
" Dochgarroch		344
" Ardgour		344
" Brolass		345
" Pennycross	A. J. MacLean	345
" Coll		345
Hector MacLean and Dr. Johnson		361
Hector MacLean	W. R. Grant	380
John P. MacLean		389
James MacLean	Mrs. H. C. MacLean	396
Dunolly Castle and Fingal's Stone		438

(xix)

PRINCIPAL AUTHORITIES CONSULTED;

FROM BOOKS IN THE AUTHOR'S PRIVATE LIBRARY.

Alexander (W.L.) Iona. London. No date.
Blackie (J.S.) Altavona. London, 1883.
Blackie (J.S.) Language and Literature of the Scottish Highlands. Edinburgh, 1876.
Boswell (James). Tour to the Hebrides. London, 1852.
Browne (James). History of the Highland Clans. Glasgow, 1843. 4 vols.
Burke (Bernard). Landed Gentry of Great Britain and Ireland. London, 1871. 2 vols.
Chambers (Robert). Rebellions of 1689, 1715. Edinburgh, 1829.
Chambers (Robert). Rebellion of 1745-6. London and Edinburgh, 1869.
Collectanea de Rebus Albanicis. Edinburgh, 1847.
Cromb (James). Highlands and Highlanders. Dundee, 1883.
Ewing (Alexander). Iona. London, 1866.
Gordon (I.F.S.) Iona. Glasgow, 1885.
Graham (H.D.) Antiquities of Iona. London, 1850.
Gregory (Donald). History of the Western Highlands and Isles. London, 1881.
Hogg (James). Jacobite Relics. Paisley, 1874. 2 vols.
Hume (David). History of England. Boston. No date. 6 vols.
Johnson (Samuel). Journey to the Western Islands. London, 1876.
Johnston (T.B.) Geography of the Clans of Scotland. Edinburgh, 1873.
Johnstone (James). Haco's Expedition against Scotland. Edinburgh, 1882.
Keltie (John S.) History of the Highland Clans. Edinburgh, 1882. 2 vols.
Logan (James). The Scottish Gaël. Hartford, 1849.
Logan (James). The Scottish Gaël. Inverness, 1876. 2 vols.
MacAulay (T.B.) History of England. Boston. No date. 5 vols.
MacCallum (Duncan). History of the Ancient Scots. Edinburgh, 1858.
MacKenzie (Alexander). Celtic Magazine. Inverness, 1876-1888. 13 vols.
MacKenzie (Alexander). Highland Clearances. Inverness, 1883.
MacKenzie (Alexander). History of the MacDonalds. Inverness, 1881.
MacKenzie (Alexander). Isle of Skye. Inverness, 1883.
MacKenzie (John). Beauties of Gaelic Poetry. Glasgow, 1841. 2 vols.
MacLaughlan (Thos.) Celtic Gleanings. Edinburgh, 1857.
MacLean (John). Clachnacuddin. Inverness, 1886.
MacLean (John). Sketches Highland Families. Dingwall, 1848.
MacLean (Lachlan). Iona. Oban, 1841.
Monro (Donald). Description Western Isles. Glasgow, 1884.
Robertson (J.A.) Historical Proof of Highlanders. Edinburgh, 1865.
Scott (Walter). Lord of the Isles. Edinburgh, 1871.
Scott (Walter). Tales of a Grandfather. Boston, 1852.
Sinclair (A.M.) Glenbard Collection. Charlottetown, 1888.
Sinclair (A.M.) Clarsach na Coille. Glasgow, 1881.
Sixth Report Royal Commission. London, 1877.
Skene (W.F.) Celtic Scotland. Edinburgh, 1886. 3 vols.
Skene (W.F.) Dean of Lismore's Book. Edinburgh, 1862.
Skene (W.F.) Highlanders of Scotland. London, 1837. 2 vols.
Spottiswoode (John). History Church of Scotland. Edinburgh, 1851. 3 vols.
Statistical Account of Argyleshire. Edinburgh, 1845.
Tytler (P.F.) History of Scotland. Edinburgh, 1887. 4 vols.

A HISTORY

OF

THE CLAN MacLEAN.

CHAPTER I.

PRELIMINARY REMARKS.

The MacLeans have every reason to be proud of their history and ancestry, even though it be judged in the light and civilization of this age. This clan history is written wholly for the benefit of the descendants of the brave men who once wielded the claymore on behalf of Scotland, and also in defense of their own individual rights. Clan histories are written especially for the benefit of those who wish to pry into the acts of their forefathers, thus making the subject one of personal value. But this class of histories serves another purpose, in that it is of intrinsic value to those who desire to make a critical study of the Highlands of Scotland. Individual actions when combined with others make history. When one family, united by ties of kinship, has continued together for centuries, especially during times of civil commotions, or revolutionary periods, and if that family be numerous, it must of necessity have played a very important part in the creation of its country's history.

To set forth a clan history in all its faithfulness requires two essential qualifications: The historian must be in full sympathy with his subject, and at the same time be rigidly just in the narration of his facts. The deeds of a people of a past age are not to be judged in the light of the nineteenth century. In forming accurate and just opinions, their surroundings, habits, enlightenment, political government, and predominant religion must be considered.

Of all the clans of Scotland none is more deserving of honorable mention and having its history carefully recorded than that of MacLean. For centuries it held a conspicuous place for independence of bearing and disinterested loyalty in the history of Scotland. It rapidly grew in influence and power until it reached its zenith, at which time, during the reign of James VI., it was accounted the most powerful of any in the Hebrides.* At the date of the final forfeiture of the Lords of the Isles (1493) the lands belonging to the clan comprised the greater part of Mull, the whole of Coll and Tiree, portions of Islay, Scarba, districts in Morvern, Lochaber, and Knapdale, not to mention some of the smaller islands. No clan has received more honorable mention. Sir Walter Scott † has sung concerning it:

> " May the race of Clan-Gillian, the fearless and free,
> Remember Glenlivat, Harlaw, and Dundee."

They were "a bold and hardy race." ‡ Professor John Stuart Blackie has seen fit to record ‖ that "there were mighty men in Mull in those days, and the MacLeans were amongst the mightiest. . . . They were amongst the most loyal of the loyal at Largs and Bannockburn, and they could not fail to share the sorrows of the discrowned monarch at Inverkeithing and Culloden. The MacLeans, if not always wise in action, were generous in purpose and noble in conduct." William Allen, the Scottish poet, in a letter to the author,§ says: "The MacLeans were all brave men, all Hectors, and the finest swordsmen of the Highlands."

The history of this family—sometimes called Clan Gillian and Clan Lean, in Scottish history—may be subdivided in three different ways, the first being its political history. It might result in some degree of interest to trace the relationship existing between the MacLeans and the McDougalls, or the proud Lords of Lorn, during the traditionary history of the former. If they were at one time subjects of the Lords of Lorn, as asserted by Skene,** the grip could not have been very strong, as may be testified by the MacLeans espousing the cause of Bruce. It is possible that at one time they owed some allegiance to the McDougalls of Lorn, but it does not appear that it was regarded as of any binding force. During the traditionary period they existed more as a tribe than as a clan, and we know of it almost wholly from the feats of daring and bold position taken by the chief, who generally managed to distinguish himself. The history becomes clear, positive, and satisfactory in what might be termed the second period, which lasted from the year 1366 to 1493, or when the MacLeans were vassals of the Lords of the Isles. The renunciation of allegiance to the Lord of Lorn, and the attachment to the Lords of the Isles

---

* Gregory's *Western Highlands*, p. 419; Brown's *History of the Highland Clans*, Vol. IV., p. 491. † *Flora McIvor's Song*. ‡ *Tales of a Grandfather, Second Series*, p. 59. ‖ *Allavona*, pp. 168, 178. § Dated June 12, 1888. ** *The Highlanders*, Vol. II., p. 205.

was a most fortunate one. The latter had befriended Bruce in his dire extremity, while the former pursued him with great ferocity. The latter, at the time of espousal of the MacLeans, was rapidly acquiring supremacy over the other descendants of their great progenitor, Somerled, which was greatly increased when Bruce ascended the throne. Favors bestowed upon the Lords of the Isles operated for the benefit of the MacLeans, in so much so that their possessions rapidly increased, especially during the time of John, Fourth Lord of the Isles. The third period commenced in 1493, when the MacLeans became independent, and numbered four powerful branches—Duard, Lochbuy, Ardgour, and Coll. As these various branches had received charters direct from the Lords of the Isles, they were consequently feudally independent of each other. After they ceased to be vassals they continued for a while to support the MacDonalds, and for a long time might have been allies of that house if jealousy had not taken possession of them, which led them to unite all their forces for the purpose of effectually crushing the growing power of the MacLeans, which happened at the close of the sixteenth century, but which was averted through the consummate skill of Sir Lachlan Mór MacLean. This period may be said to end with the year 1598. The fourth and last period in the history of the clan marks its blind adherence to the house of Stuart, which ends with the battle of Culloden, in 1746. During this period the clan was forced to undergo great vicissitudes, the lands nearly all alienated, and the House of Duard became practically extinct. The remaining history is wholly that of individuals.

The religious aspect may resolve itself into a division. The earliest records of the Gaëls present them as believers in Druidism, a form of religion having some excellent qualities. In some respects it was simple—a belief in one God, the immortality of the soul, an altar of either turf or stone, and an offering from the increase of the fold. In the Highlands, Druidism found a peaceful and protected home, and there its last rites were solemnized. The ancient inhabitants placed a high value on liberty, and preserved their country from the yoke of Rome; and on her Bens and in her Glens no altars were erected to idols. This had much to do with preserving the original character of its inhabitants. This religion may date its final overthrow from the advent of St. Columba in the Island of Iona, A. D. 563. It is not claimed that the MacLeans, as a tribe, were under the influence of Druidism, but, being pure Gaëls, their ancestors were, and this had something to do in the formation of their character. Hence, it can be truthfully asserted that in no period of their history were the MacLeans idolators. The Culdee form of the Christian religion was established, in Scotland, by St. Columba, and was not overthrown until about 1150. The Highlanders were converted to Christianity through the missionary labors of the Culdees, whose principal seat was at Iona. The third period was that of Romanism, which ended about 1560, when the Reformation gained control of the law-making power, and ordered the cathedrals and monasteries to be destroyed. It is very doubtful if the chiefs of MacLean ever became ardent Roman Catholics. There is no evidence of it. It is well known that Culdeeism was taught by individuals long after Catholicism had supplanted it in Iona. We find, during the fifteenth century, four bishops, of the family of MacLean, repudiating celibacy, and thus showing their predilection for the Culdee creed. The last period is marked by the entire clan embracing the doctrines of the Reformation.

The third division is an interesting one from a purely anthropological standpoint. In it can be seen the development into a tribe from stalwart progenitors, until the clan has been fully formed. This period might end with John Dubh, fourth chief of MacLean. The growth then is rapid, until the chieftainship of Sir Lachlan Mór, or down to about 1580. The zenith of power was reached during the reign of that chieftain, although others would have it as late as the first baronet, Sir Lachlan, sixteenth of MacLean, or to about 1630. After the last-mentioned date the decline can easily be traced. The causes which led to it are manifold. The seeds of decay were sown during the long feud with the MacDonalds. The adherence to the house of Stuart was all loss—no profit having accrued from it. Add to this fact that on the west was the ocean, and on the east the powerful house of Argyle, chief of the Clan Campbell, which early had its eyes on the possessions of the MacLeans. The chiefs of the Campbells, called lords, earls, marquises, and dukes, were not the best disposed of neighbors. Skene, the greatest of all historians of Keltic Scotland, in speaking of the Argyle family, says[*] its history "consists principally of the details of a policy characterized by cunning and perfidy, although deep and far-sighted, and which obtained its usual success in the acquisition of great temporal grandeur and power. Of the duplicity and greed of this family numberless instances could be cited, and many authorities quoted; but ample evidence will be given in its proper place."

Unscrupulous men, who become powerful, use such arts as appear to belong to them. Most of the feuds recorded of the clans can be traced to the ma-

---

[*] *The Highlanders*, Vol. II., p. 284.

chinations of some earl, or other powerful personage at court, who wished, by the disturbances he created, to increase his power or possessions. Nor was this all. It was the constant policy of the government to divide the Highland clans as much as it possibly could, and by their disunion prevent that legitimate influence in the affairs of the nation to which they were justly entitled. As evidence of this statement the following copy of a contract is given, which is taken from the "Acts of the Lords in Council," Vol XXIX, folio 77 : "At Edenburgh the IX day of Marche the yeir of God 1516 yeires. It is appointit and aggreit betwix my lordis of counsale specially deput thairto at the comand of my lord governouris in the Kingis name and for his hienes service on the ta pairt and my lordis of Huntlie, Ergyle and Lauchlane McClane of Dowart personaly present on the tother pairt in maner and forme as eftir followis. That is to say gif the Clanquhattane or ony otheris within my lord of Huntlys boundis failzeis to the Kingis grace intymis cuming makand misreulle upon his liegis or dissobey and to his lawis the said Erle of Ergile and Lauchlane and otheris within the boundis of the said Erle of Ergilis lieuetenandry sall outhald the said Glenquhattane and utheris that falzeis under the said Erle of Huntleis boundis fra all boundis within the said Erle of Ergilis lieuetenandry And attour thai sall assist and supple the said Erle of Huntlie againis the said Clanquhattane and utheris that happinnis to falze within the said Erle of Huntlies boundis. And the said Erle of Huntlie sall outhold Donald of the Ilis and utheris that falzeis within the Erle of Ergilis lieuetenandry fra all boundis under his reule and attour sall assist and supple the said Erle of Ergile in persute of the said Donald and utheris. In witnes herof the saidis Erlis of Huntlie, Ergile and Lauchlane McClane has subscrivit this writ with thair handis yeir, day, and place foirsaidis. ALEXR ERLE OF HUNTLIE
ERLE OF ERGILE
LAUCHLANE MCCLANE OF DOWALD
touchand the pen."

This compact is easily explained. The Clan Chattan—that is, the MacPhersons and MacIntoshes, with some smaller tribes—had refused to comply with Lord Huntly's demands, and through the government interest got the promise of assistance of the MacLeans and Campbells. The name of Donald of the Isles was undoubtedly introduced by Argyle for two reasons: first, he hoped to have Donald forfeited in order to possess his lands; and secondly, MacLean could not have been prevailed upon to fight against his mother's clan without some just reason. As Donald had abused his confidence, by the insertion of his name, the assistance of MacLean could be procured.

It is worthy of record that the chiefs maintained the dignity of the family. In every sense of the word, the clansmen as well as the chiefs were true Highlanders, preserving the manners, customs, and sympathies that characterized the Gaël. Whatever was regarded as essential for dignity and hospitality, the MacLeans were the peers of all. In the choice of men for certain pursuits, the best were always chosen. The MacNeils, a celebrated race of bards, were the hereditary harpers of the MacLeans of Duard. For their physicians, the Beatons, the most famous of Scotland, were chosen, who also became the family seanachaidhs, or genealogists, in which lore they were equally noted. To them much of the clan history owes its preservation.

CHAPTER II.

THE HOME AND ORIGIN OF THE CLAN.

The home of the MacLeans is the island of Mull, and here the clan originated. This island is one of the inner Hebrides, situated between 5° 40′ and 6° 20′ longitude west from Greenwich, and between 56° 18′ and 56° 40′ north latitude. It is separated from the mainland of Scotland by the Sound of Mull on the north and the Firth of Lorn on the east. In shape the island is very irregular, owing to the great indentations formed by the sea-water lochs. Speaking generally, it is thirty miles long by twenty-five in breadth. Its coast line may be roughly estimated at three hundred miles, and its whole area at four hundred and fifty miles. The general surface is rugged. Ben More, the highest mountain, rises to a height of three thousand, one hundred and seventy-two feet, but, like the other mountains of the island, is wanting in bold outlines. All of the hills and mountains have the softness of a pastoral range, which, consequently, makes the scenery remarkable for a quiet and solemn beauty. Its valleys, outlines of mountains, purple moorlands, and lochs have charms seen in no other isle. It thus affords varied attractions for the geologist, artist, and tourist. The greater part of the surface indicates varied geological disturbances. Ben More is an extinct volcano, and from it came the molten mass that formed the stupendous columns seen in the southern part of the island. Also, those wonderfully symmetrical pillars found on the island of Staffa, and forming Fingal's Cave, were belched forth, in a molten mass, from the crater of Ben More. The dolerite and basaltic rocks are interbedded with volcanic ashes, clay beds, and lignite, belonging to the vast bed of Miocene lavas. Here and there may be seen the outcroppings of the Miocene beds. The extreme point of the Ross of Mull is of granite formation.

Perhaps no part of Scotland affords better grazing than this island. The higher grazings are occupied by black-faced sheep and deer. The Mull ponies, noted for certain characteristic points, and supposed to have been mixed with

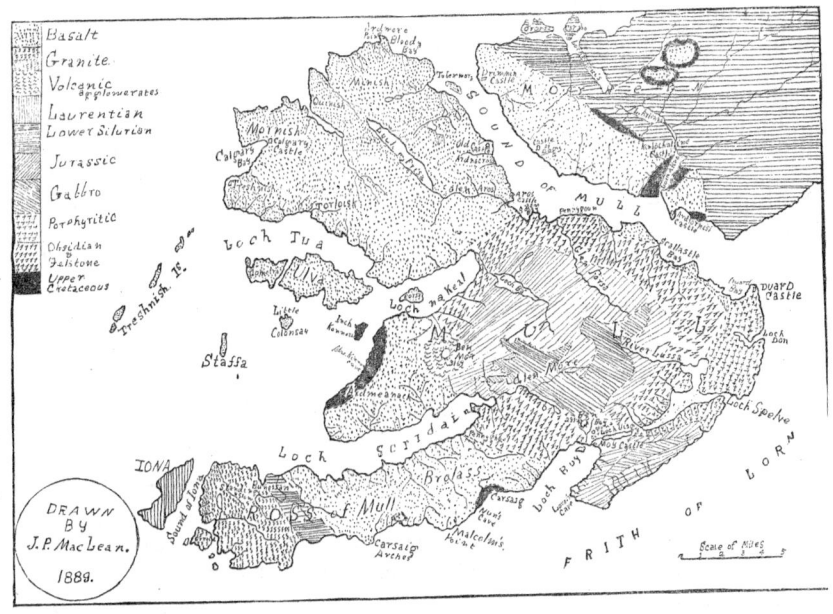

Spanish horses brought to the island by the ill-fated "Florida"—a vessel belonging to the Spanish Armada, in 1588—and which were particularly sought for, have almost disappeared.

At the present time, the island is divided into seven districts: Mishnish, at its northern extremity; Mornish and Aros, to the south of Loch-na-Keal; Torosay and Gribun, to the east of the same loch, and Brolass and Ross of Mull, to the east and south of Loch Scridain.

Of the ancient history of the island but little is known. On the high mountain that separates the North from the South are two cairns, called Carn Cul ri Erin, or, the cairn with its back to Eire, *i. e.*, Dalriada, and the other Carn Cul ri Allabyn, or, the cairn with its back to Alban, which seem to mark some ancient boundary, and believed to be the line between the Dalriad Scots from Erin and the Cruithne of Alban. This conclusion appears to be probable from the fact that about the year 503 the Dalriad Scots occupied the south part of Argyleshire, consisting of the districts of Cowall, Kintyre, Knapdale, Argyle proper, Lorn, and probably Morvern, Islay, Iona, Arran, and the small adjacent islands. The boundary which separated them from the Cruithne extended from the island of Colonsay through Mull to the center of the district of Morvern on to Luine Loch, opposite Appin.*

In later years, the island fell into the possession of the Norsemen, for we find that, in the year 888, Harald Harfagr added the island to his kingdom of Norway. In the year 1156, a bloody engagement took place between Somerled and Godred, which resulted in the latter ceding to the former Bute, Arran, Islay, Jura, Mull, and several smaller islands, as well as the district of Kintyre. It is also recorded that the "Danes were put to flight; many of them were lost in the sea endeavoring to gain their ships; the land of Mull and Morvern being freed at that time from their yoke and slavery."† From this it would appear that the Norsemen made no permanent settlement in Mull, but simply held the country, and probably did not intermarry with the natives.

Angus Og MacDonald, fifth in descent from Somerled, was a faithful and uncompromising friend of Robert Bruce in his attempt to free his native land from the harsh grasp of England. He sheltered this monarch, after the disastrous defeat at Methven, in his castle at Dunaverty, August, 1306. In all his subsequent actions, Angus bore an important part, and at the battle of Bannockburn commanded five thousand Highlanders under sixteen of their own immediate chiefs. As a reward for his great services, Bruce conferred upon him, in 1314, the lordship of Lochaber—forfeited by the Comyns, and the lands of Duror and Glencoe, and the islands of Mull, Jura, Coll, and Tiree, which had belonged to the family of Lorn. Angus Og died in Islay, about 1329, and was succeeded by his son John, First Lord of the Isles, who became an important factor in the turbulent times in which he lived, being one of the ablest and most sagacious of chiefs. Instead of attaching himself to the house of Bruce, he became an important adherent of Edward Balliol in his claims for the crown of Scotland. For this service, Balliol, in 1335, conferred on John the whole of the territories which his father Angus possessed, besides Kintyre and Knapdale, and the isles of Skye and Lewis. In order to unite the whole force of his kingdom against the English, King David Bruce,

---

* Skene's *Dean of Lismore*, p. xxiv.; *Celtic Scotland*, Vol. I, 228.   † *Collectanea de Rebus Albanicis*, p. 324.

in 1344, confirmed John in the following possessions: the isles of Islay, Gigha, Jura, Scarba, Colonsay, Mull, Coll, Tiree, and Lewis, and the districts of Morvern, Lochaber, Duror, and Glencoe. According to Skene,* John died about 1386, and was succeeded by his son Donald, Second Lord of the Isles.

On the 12th of July, 1390, dated at Ardtornish, Donald granted to Lachlan MacLean the custody and constableship of the Castle of Duard. This charter was confirmed at Glasgow in 1495:

"At Glasgow, July 13, 1495. King James IV. confirms a charter granted by King James I. by which these charters were confirmed:

(1) Charter granted by Donald of the Isles to Hector Makgilleon lord of Doward, constable of the castle of Karnaborg, and his heirs male of the lands of Tyrvughafeal in the island of Coll, in the place of victuals, meal and cheese, which used to be given by inhabitants of Tyriage to the constable of the said castle yearly. Dated at the castle of Ardtornish 1 November 1409.

(2) Charter by the same Donald to Lachlan Makgilleone of the custody and constableship of the castle of Doward with the enceinte land of Torosay, lands of Glenleues, Broylos, Burglands in Ardineaganach, Akranbegan as far as to Ulwalch; half of the constabulary of the Castle of Deunconail and Deunkerd with the islands of Garbealeach, Garbealean and Scealda; lands of Ardlavach in Luing, lands of Moylburg in Scarba; the upper half of Dura, lands in Morvarn, lands of Achugnaha, Achagranache, Achaglain, Ulgadall, Dubgeare, Nasrone, Achagtesege McRuslaag. Dated at Ardtornish 12 July 1390.

(3) Charter by the same Donald of the Isles to Lachlan Makgilleone and his heirs, of the constabulary and keepership of the castles of Kernaborg and Isleborg, with the small ones Floda and Lunga; lands of Godmadray, Aencangboge, Bedlich; office of Fragramanache and Armanache in the Isle of Hy. Dated 12 July 1390.

(4) Charter by the same Donald to the said Lachlan Makgilleone and his heirs, of the office of bailiery of all the lands of Tyriage, with lands of Mannawallis, Hindebollis, and office of steward of the house of the said Donald of the Isles. Dated at Ardthorannis 12 July 1390." [*Registrum Magni Sigilli*, Lib. XIII., No. 300.]

The above shows that the MacLeans possessed a portion of Mull, by charter, as early as 1390.

The MacLeans take their name from, and trace their origin as a clan to, Gilleain, who flourished about the year 1250. Skene,† following the manu-

---

* *The Highlanders*, Vol. II., p. 70.   † *Celtic Scotland*, Vol. III., p. 480.

script of MacFirbis and MacVurich of 1647, gives the genealogy commencing with the grandson of that Lachlan MacLean who received a charter for Duard Castle in 1390. "Lachlan son of Eachduinn (or Hector) son of Lachlan son of John son of Malcolm son of Maoiliosa son of Gilleeoin son of MacRath son of Maolsruthain son of Neill son of Cuduilig, Abbot of Lismore, son of Raingce son of Old Dougall of Scone."

Doctor John Beaton, the last seanachaidh of the MacLeans of Duard, and Doctor Kennedy, in his "Dissertation on the Royal line of Stuarts," trace the line back to Erc, an Irish chieftain, and through Erc to Aonghas Turmhi Teamhrach, an ancient Irish monarch. The two tables thus appear in parallel columns:

Dr. Beaton's Catalogue.	Dr. Kennedy's Catalogue.
Gilleain mac	
Crath mhic	
Mhaolsuthin mhic	
Neil mhic	
Condueli mhic	
Cealli mhic	
Fhraine mhic	
Shean Dughaill Scóinne	
Mhic Jeril Duerbh mhic	
Ferghuis mhic	
Neachduin mhic	
Colls mium mhic	
Baoghain mhic	
Esche mhic	
Mhurehuidsh mhic	
Loghairne in hóir mhic	Loghairne Már mac
Ferghuis Abhraruoidh, eadhorn Righ Alba* Mhic Eri mhic	Eri mhic
Eochi bunream hair mhic	Eochi anureamhair mhic
Inoghuis valaich no Inaghuis fiar mhic	Inaghuisyalich be mhic
Ferghuis mhic	Ferghuis mhic
Eochi Tuamhil mhic	Feachra mhic
Felim lamdoid mhic	Felemlamdoid mhic
Cine mhic	Cinta mhic
Guori mhic	Guori mhic
Fuinduin mhic	Fuinduin mhic
Cairbre riad mhic	Eocha mhic
Conoir mhóir mhic	Conoir mhic
Alloid mhic	Mogna laimhe mhic
Cairbre Chromchinn mhic	Luig alltach mhic
Dári Dornmhor mhic	Cairbre chromachinn mhic
Cairbre ffuinmhov mhic	Dári Dórmhor mhic
Conoir mhóir mhic	Cairibri ffuinmhov mhic

*Fergus I., King of Scotland.

The Home and Origin of the Clan. 31

Edir Sceoil mhic
Eodnin mhic
Eri mhic
Olloil mhic
Deadhi mhic
Shine mhic
Truen mhic
Rothreun mhic
Earnali mhic
Manimhoir mhic
Ferghie mhic
Olloilerm mhic
Frachri fravray mhic Aonghuis

Tuirmhich teainrich righ
Eran or the 75th monarch of Ireland, vide Peter Welsh.

Conoir mhoir mhic
Edir Sceoil mhic
Eoghm mhic
Olloil mhic
Eri no hior mhic
Deadhe mhic
Shine mhic
Rothm mhic
Iruen mhic
Rothreun mhic
Mani mhor mhic
Fergo mhic
Feradich mhic
Alloil Erin mhic
Ferchar Fiarvain mhic
Aonghus Fairmhic Jeam mhic

As heretofore noted, it was the custom of the greater families in the Highlands of Scotland to keep their family historians, who recorded the exploits of the great men of the clan, their marriages, and other notable transactions. As the chieftains were often illiterate, they sent the seanachaidh to Ireland, who was there instructed in the Irish language, and returned home freighted with incredible romances, flatteries, and panegyrics upon the Irish kings; and as no history was so well known among the Highlanders as that of Ireland, by the continual intercourse between them and that nation, from which several of them came, and the connection between their languages, might have given their genealogists cause to derive their origin entirely from that country. The seanachaid is not always to be relied upon. He desired to flatter his master, and readily traced out such a genealogy as was desired; hence, to genuine Highland families has been assigned an Irish, a French, or Norman origin, or just such an origin as flattered the fancy of the chief, who thought it more honorable to be descended from a Danish pirate, a Norman adventurer, a French wanderer, or an Irish princeling, than from an honest man of his own glens. It may be regarded as an unquestionable fact that the MacLeans are of a purely Highland origin. It can not be proved that Gilleain was or was not descended from any of the sons of Erc. So far as Aongas Tuirmeach Teamhrach is concerned, he may have been a very good king, and ruled over Ireland for the long period of sixty years, as asserted by the Irish annalists; and, again, there may never have been such a man. If there ever was such a king, he must have ruled over a very small principality, having been more the chief of a tribe than a king.

The remote genealogists, whether from indolence, incompetency, or else from the turbulent times which wrought disaster every-where, have left but little information concerning the ancestry prior to the beginning of the fourteenth century. However, information is gained here and there which affords some assistance in unraveling the history.

It has been claimed that the MacLeans and MacKenzies are descended from a common ancestor. This is based on the following grounds: 1. The tradition in the families is to that effect. 2. Comneach, the founder of the clan MacKenzie, was a descendant of Gilleain. 3. There was a close friendship which always existed between the two clans, which was particularly exemplified by Sir Lachlan Mór MacLean sending his son, Hector, to be educated in the house of Cailean Can, and in Sir John MacLean, when a child, being sent for protection from the Campbells to the Earl of Seaforth, with whom he lived several years. It does not follow that all Gilleains were the same. The Gilleain of the MacKenzies was known as Gilleain na h'Airde, proving that he lived either in Aird Mhic Shimi in Inverness-shire, or else in Aird Rois, the name by which the mountainous region in the center of Ross-shire was designated in early times. The founder of the Clan MacLean was Gilleain na Tuaighe, or Gilleain of the Battle-ax, who lived in Argyleshire.

The MacLeans can trace their origin with precision to Old Dougall of Scone, who must have flourished about the year 1100, and has been described as an influential, just, and venerable man.* In some genealogies he is made the son of Mocche, and again the son of Fearchar Abraruadh, who must be placed four centuries earlier. Raingce, son of Old Dougall, had three sons, Cucatha, Cusidhe, and Cuduilig. Cucatha, or Dog of Battle, was the progenitor of the Clan Conchatha, in the district of Lennox, by whom it is possible the Clan Colquhoun is meant. Cusidhe, or Dog of Peace, was the progenitor of the Clan Consithe, in Fife. What clan is here referred to is not known. Cuduiligh, from whom the Clan Conduilig, that is, the Clan MacLean, in the island of Mull, became lay-abbot of the Monastery of Lismore, in Argylshire. His son was called Niall, and Niall's son was named Rath, or MacRath. Rath is said to have married a sister of Somerled, Sombairle Mór MacGillebride, who was slain at Renfrew in 1164. He had a son named Gilleain, or Gille-Eoin, the founder of the Clan MacLean, or more truly Mac-Ghilleain.

---

* Skene's *Celtic Scotland*, Vol. III., p. 343.

CHAPTER III.

FIRST PERIOD OF THE CHIEFS.

From a. d. 1250 to a. d. 1400.

I. Gilleain flourished about the year 1250. He was known as Gilleain na Tuaighe, from his carrying, as his ordinary weapon and constant companion, a battle-ax. He was a man of mark and distinction. The following anecdote is related of him, which probably accounts for the origin of the Mac-Lean crest, which consists of a battle-ax between a laurel and cypress branch, and is still used on the coat-of-arms: He was on one occasion engaged, with other lovers of the chase, in a stag-hunt on the Mountain of Bein 'tsheatá, and having wandered from the rest of the party in pursuit of game, the mountain became suddenly covered with a heavy mist, and he lost his way. For three days he wandered about, unable to recover his route, and on the fourth, exhausted by fatigue, he entered a cranberry bush, where, fixing the handle of his battle-ax in the earth, he laid himself down. On the evening of the same day his friends discovered the head of the battle-ax above the bush, and found its owner, with his arms round the handle, stretched, in a state of insensibility, on the ground.

The evidence, so far as it is now attainable, goes to show that Gilleain, as well as his father, Rath, held large possessions in Upper-Mull, and along the whole northern coast of that island. It also appears that the island of Kerrera was part of his property, and at its southern end he established himself, and there built a castle, which still bears his name, Gylen, or Gillean. It afterward became one of the strongholds of the MacLeans of Duard, and in it, at one time, was kept the famous Brooch of Lorn, belonging to King Robert the Bruce. The lofty ruined tower of Gylen Castle, covered with ivy, rests on the edge of a cliff, over a beach where the Atlantic has rent the rocks into fantastic shapes.

As Gilleain was the undoubted founder of the clan, to him has justly been ascribed—The First Chief of MacLean. He had three sons, Bristi, Gillebride, and Maoliosa.

II. Gille-Iosa, second chief.

Maoliosa, or Malo-Iosa, or Gille-Iosa, means the servant of Jesus. He was a distinguished follower of Alexander III. of Scotland, and was conspicuous in expelling Haco. From the Norwegian account,* we learn that Alexander III. sent an embasssy to King Haco, requiring him to give up the territories in the Hebrides, which Magnus Barefoot had unjustly wrested from Malcolm, predecessor to the Scottish king. Haco refused; then the embassy offered to purchase the territory; this was also refused. In 1263, King Haco assembled a numerous host, declaring the expedition was intended against that part of Scotland which bordered the western seas, and the object was to revenge certain inroads made by the Scotch into his dominions. The expedition was commanded by Haco in person. The armament is described as mighty and splendid; the ships being many, large, and well appointed. When the expedition arrived at the island of Kerrera, it was joined by King Dugal, predecessor of the MacDougalls of Dunolly, with other Hebrideans. This increased the armament to one hundred vessels, for the most part large, and well provided with both men and arms. There the forces were divided, fifty ships being sent south to the Mull of Kintyre to plunder. Haco then sailed south to Gigha, where he anchored, but soon after proceeded to the Mull of Kintyre. The Norwegians committed great depredations, both in the islands and on the mainland. The Scottish monarch, however, was not idle. He assembled his forces, and proceeded against the invaders. The two armies met at Largs, on the coast of Ayrshire, on October 2, 1263. The Norwegian army, although very large, could not all be brought into action, because a violent tempest arose, which prevented the greater part of the army from being brought ashore. In the Scottish army was a body of fifteen hundred horsemen, mounted on Spanish horses, armed, both horse and man, from head to heel, in complete mail. The foot-soldiers were well-accoutered, and in addition to the long spears of the Saxons, they carried the Norman bow. This memorable engagement was commenced by the Scots. The right wing, composed of the men of Argyle, Lennox, Athole, and Galloway, was commanded by Alexander, Lord High Steward, while Patrick Dunbar, Earl of March, commanded the left, composed of the men of Fife, Stirling, Berwick, and Lothian. The king, in person, commanded the center, which was composed of the men from Ross, Perth, Angus, Mar, Mearns, Moray, Inverness, and Caithness. Haco also commanded his center, which brought the kings close together in combat. The High Steward turned the enemy's left, and by an adroit maneuver wheeled back on the rear of Haco's center, which forced

---

* *Haco's Expedition.* Translated by Johnstone, 1782.

First Period of the Chiefs—1250 to 1400.

Haco to retreat from the field, leaving from sixteen to twenty-four thousand of his men on the field, while the Scottish loss did not exceed five thousand.

Gille-Iosa, or, as it has been written, Gillise MacGillean, must have performed prodigies of valor in this action, for he has received honorable mention. This distinguished warrior died in the year 1300, and was succeeded by his son—

III. Malcolm, third chief of MacLean.

Malcolm's name has been written Maol-Calum and Gille-Calum, which means Servant of Columba. He was married to Rioghnach, daughter of Gamail, Lord of Carrick.

The name of Gille-Moire MacGilleain is attached to the Ragman Roll in 1296. It appears to be the same as Gille-Calum of the genealogists. This is a point by no means certain, but is more than probable.

Malcolm, at the head of his clan, fought at the battle of Bannockburn, on Monday, June 24, 1314. It was at this battle that the power of the English Edwards was broken, and the sovereignty of Scotland once more recognized. Robert Bruce's army consisted of thirty thousand men, while that of Edward has been estimated at over one hundred thousand. The English lost thirty thousand, and that of the Scots did not exceed ten thousand. With Edward were all the great English nobles and barons, and their followers, all well equipped. The engagement was commenced by the English, who poured forth their arrows, until they fell like flakes of snow. The Scottish army was arranged in a line consisting of three square columns, the center commanded by the Earl of Moray, the right by Edward Bruce, and the left by Sir James Douglas and Walter, the Steward of Scotland. The reserve, composed of the men of Argyle, Carrick, Kintyre, and the Isles, formed the fourth line of battle, and was commanded by Bruce in person. In this reserve were five thousand Highlanders, under twenty-one different chiefs, commanded by Angus Og MacDonald, father of John, first Lord of the Isles. The following clans, commanded in person by their chiefs, have the distinguished honor of fighting nobly: Stewart, MacDonald, MacKay, MacIntosh, MacPherson, Cameron, Sinclair, Drummond, Campbell, Menzies, MacLean, Sutherland, Robertson, Grant, Fraser, MacFarlane, Ross, MacGregor, Munro, MacKenzie, and MacQuarrie. The Clan Cumming, MacDougall of Lorn, MacNab, and a few others, were present, but unfortunately on the wrong side. As already observed, the MacLeans were under the immediate command of their chief, Malcolm. After the battle was fully on, Bruce brought up the whole of his reserve, which completely engaged the four battles of the Scots in one line. The noise of the battle, as described by an eye-witness, was awful; there was the clanging of arms, the knights shouting their war-cry, the flight of the arrows maddening the horses, the banners rising and sinking, the ground covered with gore, the shreds of pennons, broken armor, and rich scarfs soiled with blood and clay; and amidst the din was heard the groans of the wounded and dying. Step by step the Scots gained ground, and fortunately, in a critical moment, the camp-followers, desiring to see the battle, appeared over the hill, and were taken by the English for Scotch re-inforcements. Immediately dismay spread through the English ranks, which, the Scots noticing, made a fearful onslaught, which broke the English army into disjointed squadrons. The flight at once became general, and the slaughter fearful to behold. In the thickest of the fight the Highland clans plied their battle-axes with terrible effect. This did not escape the attention of the watchful Bruce; and, to show his appreciation for the great service, he assigned to Angus and his descendants, forever, the honorable position of the right flank of the royal army.

Malcolm, who died in the reign of King David Bruce, had three sons, Donald, Niall, and John. Donald and Neil appear in the Exchequer Rolls of Scotland. In an account rendered by the constable of Tarbart, on July 13, 1325, of his disbursements from April preceding, these entries occur: (1) "And to the men who came round the Mull with a ship belonging to Donald McGilhon, by four codri of cheese, value 2 shillings, 8 pence. And for watching the same ship at Westa Tarbart for 15 days, 5 shillings. And of eight men of John and Neil, sons of Gilhon, staying by the king's command for one month, 28 codri of cheese, value 16 shillings and 4 pence." [Exchequer Rolls, Roll II., Vol. I., p. 57.] In an account rendered by John of Logan at Scone, 24th August, 1329, from 17th February, 1327-8, this item occurs: (2) "And to Neil McGillon by the king's gift one chald." [Ibid., Roll XI., p. 201.] In account rendered by Sir Robert of Peblis, Chamberlain of Scotland, at Scone, 9th December, 1329, this entry occurs: (3) "And to Neil McGillon in part of payment for keeping the castle of Scraburgh,* by letter of precept of the keeper, and his receipt, 10 pounds." [Ibid., Roll XII., p. 238.]

Donald had two sons—Maoliosa, or Malise, and John—two daughters, Beatag, or Beatrice, and Aithbric. Neil had two sons, Diarmad and Maol-Calum, or Malcolm.

IV. John, Fourth chief of MacLean.

John succeeded his father as chief of the clan. He was known as Ian

---

* Supposed to be Cairnburgh, on one of the Treshnish Isles.

Dubh, or Black John. He married a daughter of Cumming, Lord of the Braes of Lochaber. He died during the reign of Robert II. He undoubtedly had large possessions, particularly the lands of Duard and Lochbuy, of which the Lords of the Isles were feudal superiors. He had two sons, Lachainn Lùbanach, or Lachlan the Wily, and Eachann Reaganach, or Hector the Stern.* It would appear that John designed the lands of Duard for Lachlan, and those of Lochbuy for Hector. Such, at least, was the way in which they were disposed of.

These two brothers made a considerable figure during the reigns of Robert II. and III. The prominence of their father, as well as their own affable behavior and pleasing manners, gained for them the friendship of John, First Lord of the Isles, in so much so, that it excited the jealousy of the courtiers, among whom the chief of MacKinnon, the master of the household, became a most inveterate enemy. In order to accomplish his revenge, or satiate his jealousy, he determined to cut the brothers off by taking their lives, while they were hunting with Lord John. Having been warned of MacKinnon's designs, the brothers easily thwarted his plans. Shortly afterward MacDonald (Lord of the Isles) started on some expedition from his castle at Aros in Mull to the mainland, intending to remain for a season at his castle of Ardtornish in Morvern. MacKinnon, having been unavoidably detained, was to follow after, but, meeting the two brothers, he renewed the quarrel between them. Both parties were well armed, and had their retainers. In the affray which took place MacKinnon was killed while in the act of mounting into his galley, and his followers dispersed. Skene calls this "one of the most daring actions which has ever been recorded of any Highland chief." † His version, however, is somewhat different from the above. Not knowing how the Lord of the Isles would take the death of the master of his household, they resolved to apply heroic measures, and keep by force that friendship which they thought might now be forfeited. They now proceeded to follow up their act by one still more daring.‡ Immediately they manned MacKinnon's galley with their own men, and started in pursuit of John, whom they overtook a short distance from Ardtornish, captured his vessel, and carried him prisoner to one of the Garvelloch islands. Here he was detained until he solemnly promised them to remain their true friend. Not satisfied with this, they con-

---

* It is one of the mysteries past finding out why Hector should be made the equivalent of Eachann. The former means an *anchor*, and the latter *lord of horses*.

† *The Highlanders*, Vol. II., p. 207. ‡ *Ibid.*

veyed him to the island of Iona, and placing him on the Black Stone, held sacred in those days, and used to confirm binding agreements, he vowed indemnity, not only for the death of MacKinnon, but also for the violence done his own person. He, moreover, obligated himself to give his daughter, Margaret, in marriage to Lachlan, and would use his influence with MacLeod of Lewis to obtain the hand of a daughter of that chief for his brother Hector. Still Lachlan was not satisfied, for he demanded of the captive chief: "I shall have your daughter," said he, "yet it is but meet you should give her a dowery." "Speak out and let me hear the price of your demands," said MacDonald. "Eniskir with its isles," replied Lachlan. This was promised him, as well as voluntarily appointing him lieutenant-general in war, and gave to him and his posterity the right hand of all the clans in battle, which was never once disputed with them. On first view, it appears singular why Lachlan gave pre-eminence to the small but towering rock of Eniskir. It is probable he already possessed about all the land he desired; but as Eniskir occupies a central position in the sea, and commands an extensive view of the large isles by which it is surrounded, it was deemed a valuable acquisition. Considering all the circumstances, in this transaction, it is probable that MacDonald was not as anxious as his captors, for he exhibited no disposition to resent their harsh treatment, but appears to have treated the whole affair in a good-natured manner. According to the MacDonald MS, the Lady Margaret married Lachlan of her own inclination and yielding. From this it would appear that Lachlan only took the precaution to maintain what he had doubtless gained by fair means. The events just narrated occurred about the year 1365. In the year 1366, Lachlan married the Lady Margaret, daughter of John, First Lord of the Isles. There must have been a close relationship existing between the two families prior to this marriage, for Lachlan was forced to obtain a dispensation for marriage with Margaret from the Pope. Professor Munch, in a communication to the Society of Antiquaries of Scotland, states he had seen this dispensation in the Vatican.*

Lachlan and Hector were two affectionate brothers, faithful in their friendships, but fearful in their resentments. Hector was a man less imperious and more conciliating in his ways than his brother Lachlan. By the assistance of his brother Lachlan he extended his possessions, acquiring lands in Lochaber and other places. They engaged in desperate feuds with the Clan Dugall, or MacDougall, and the Clan Cameron, the details and

---

* Robertson's *Historical Proofs*, p. 297.

causes of which have not been preserved. Hector was the founder of the house of Lochbuy and that of Urquhart, in Inverness, which for several centuries was one of great power.

V. Lachlan Lùbanach, Fifth Chief of MacLean.

The date of the beginning of Lachainn Lùbanach as fifth chief of MacLean, and successor to his father, John Dubh, is not known. It, in all probability, antedates 1365. His feuds with the MacDougalls and Camerons were during that period after he became chief. John, First Lord of the Isles, lived until 1386, when he was succeeded by his son Donald. Under the Second Lord of the Isles, Lachlan took due precaution to have his lands confirmed by charter, which occurred in 1390, as already noticed on page 29. He had five sons, Hector, his successor in Duard, John, Lachlan, Neil, and Somerled. He lived to a great age; the date of his death is not known, but it must have been before 1405, for on January 28th, of that year, at Dundonald, Hector was a witness to a charter confirmed by the king in favor of James Kennedy. [*Registrum Magni Sigilli*, Lib. IV., No. 56.] Lachlan Lùbanach is generally regarded as the first MacLean of Duard. This is doubtless owing to the fact that the oldest recorded charter in existence is in his favor. But that does not imply that he was the first possessor.

CHAPTER IV.

THE MacLEANS AS VASSALS OF THE LORDS OF THE ISLES.

FROM A. D. 1365 TO A. D. 1493.

This period, which may be denominated the second, probably begins with the marriage of Lachlan Lùbanach with the Lady Margaret MacDonald, for at that time it is known he came into possession of territory belonging to the First Lord of the Isles. Perhaps a clearer and happier choice would fix it in 1390, when the charter from Donald was secured. As the history of Lachlan was set forth in the previous chapter, it is now necessary to proceed to the chieftainship of his son and successor, who appears in the annals as—

VI. Eachann Ruadh nan Cath, Sixth Chief of MacLean,

Or Red Hector of the Battles. He is sometimes called Hector Rufus Bellicosus, and also Hector Roy. He early distinguished himself by daring exploits, and was noted as being one of the best swordsmen of his time. He became so celebrated as a swordsman, that many knights who had gained for themselves renown came from distant parts to measure weapons with him. One of these was a renowned knight of Norway, who challenged Hector Roy to mortal combat. The challenge was accepted. They met at Salen, in Mull, where they fought, and where the Norwegian fell. A green mound and cairn on the sea-shore mark the spot where Hector had his antagonist buried.

There was an old Gaelic poem, which affirmed that Hector commanded a great fleet to the coast of Ireland, and there defeated some of the ships of the king of England. He landed his troops; placed the city of Dublin under contribution; carried fire and sword into the country; destroyed many of his enemies, and burnt their houses. This must be the expedition hinted at in Hollingshed's "Chronicle of Ireland," where it is recorded that "in the year 1400 at Whitesuntide, the first year of King Henry IV., the constable of Dublin, and divers others at Stanford in Ulster, fought by sea with the Scots, where many Englishmen were slain and drowned."

As noted on page 29, Hector received a charter from Donald, Lord of the Isles, dated 1409, for certain lands, and is there described as " lord of Duard and constable of the castle of Cairnburg."

As the island of Cairnburg will be mentioned several times, and in different places, it will be necessary to give it more than a passing notice. This small island is the most northerly of the Treshnish Isles, situated about two miles from the nearest point on the coast of Mull, and about three miles from Ulva. The whole circumference exhibits a wall of rock perfectly perpendicular, and at its base is surrounded by a very deep sea, which there forms a furious current; thus surrounded, it is rendered by nature almost inaccessible. The only landing-place consists of steps cut in the face of the rock, which are continued in a winding staircase to the top. For over a thousand years it was used as a royal garrison. The defenses at the summit are partly cut in the solid rock and partly masonwork; the ruins of the keeper's house, the watch-tower, and guard-house are on the level within; it altogether forms a most interesting specimen of an ancient stronghold. It is said to have been originally built by one of the kings of Norway for a royal residence.

Hector Roy's marriage to a daughter of the Earl of Douglas greatly enlarged his influence. That nobleman made many overtures to induce Hector to withdraw himself from his dangerous connection with his uncle Donald, Lord of the Isles and Earl of Ross, now on the brink of open war with Robert, Duke of Albany and regent of the kingdom. Hector firmly withstood the blandishments of his father-in-law, for his duty as hereditary Lieutenant-General of the Isles was to his uncle Donald, and the approaching contest afforded a new field for the display of his valor.

Donald MacDonald, Lord of the Isles, claimed that the earldom of Ross, which included the isle of Skye and a district on the mainland equal in extent to a little kingdom, belonged lawfully to him in right of Margaret, his wife. Albany resisted the claim, and the property was granted to the Earl of Buchan. This forced Donald to raise the flag of rebellion, and he exhibited a capacity and power which shook the very foundations of the government. He possessed all the pride and power of an independent island prince. He mustered the whole array of the Isles, consisting of ten thousand men, fully armed, as was the fashion of the Islesmen, with swords fitted both to cut and thrust, bows and axes, short knives, and round bucklers formed of wood or strong hide, with bosses of brass and iron. This army was commanded by Donald in person, with Hector MacLean and the chief of MacIntosh as principal leaders and heads of their respective septs, besides other innumerable chieftains, all being animated by that old and deep-seated animosity which existed between the Keltic and Saxon races. With this large army, the insular prince burst like an avalanche upon the earldom, sweeping every thing before him until he reached Dingwall, where he encountered a formidable opponent in Angus Dhu, who attacked him with great fierceness. The check thus given was but temporary, for Angus was made prisoner and his army cut to pieces. The army then assembled at Inverness, and a general summons was issued to levy all the fighting men in Bayne and Enzie. The army next swept Moray, thence through Strathbogie, and from there into the extensive district of Garvyach, which belonged to his rival, the Earl of Mar, and which was given up to cruel and indiscriminate havoc. The army of the regent, under Mar, advanced from Aberdeen to meet the Highland host, which was descried resting at the village of Harlaw, on the water of Ury, not far from its junction with the Don. Mar's army, although small, yet consisted of the bravest barons of Angus and Mearns, and, after long experience, believed that one knight in steel was equal to a whole troop of *ketherans*. Immediately, Mar formed his army in battle array, intrusting the leading of the advance to Sir James Scrymgeour, constable of Dundee and hereditary standard-bearer of Scotland, and to Sir Alexander Ogilvy, the sheriff of Angus, who had with them a small but compact band of men-at-arms; whilst Mar himself followed with the main army, composed of the Irvings, Maules, the Morays, the Straitons, the Lesleys, the Stirlings, the Lovels, headed by their respective chiefs. The Highland army was drawn up in the cuneiform order, Hector Roy MacLean commanding the right wing and the chief of MacIntosh the left. "The shock between two such armies may be easily imagined to have been dreadful; the Highlanders, who were ten thousand strong, rushing on with the fierce shouts and yells which it was their custom to raise in coming into battle, and the knights meeting them with leveled spears and ponderous maces and battle-axes. In the first onset, Scrymgeour and the men-at-arms who fought under him with little difficulty drove back the mass of Islesmen, and, cutting his way through their thick columns, made a cruel slaughter. But though hundreds fell around him, thousands poured in to supply their places, more fierce and fresh than their predecessors; whilst Mar, who had penetrated with his main army into the very heart of the enemy, found himself in the same difficulties, becoming every moment more tired with slaughter, more encumbered with the numbers of the slain, and less able to resist the increasing and reckless ferocity of the masses that still yelled and fought around him. It was impossible that this should continue much longer without making a fatal impression on the Scots; and the effects of fatigue were soon seen. The constable of Dundee was slain; and the Highlanders, encouraged by his fall, wielded their broadswords and Lochaber axes with murderous effect, seizing and stabbing the horses, and pulling down their riders, whom they dispatched with their short daggers. In this way were slain some of the best soldiers of these northern districts. Sir Robert Davidson, with the greater part of the burgesses who fought around him, were amongst the number; and many of the families lost not only their chief, but every male in the house. The sheriff of Angus, with his eldest son George Ogilvy, Sir Alexander Irvine of Drum, Sir Robert Maule, Sir Thomas Moray, William Abernethy, Alexander Straiton of Lauriston, James Lovel, Alexander Stirling, and above five hundred men-at-arms, including the principal gentry of Buchan, shared their fate; whilst Mar himself, and a small number of the survivors, still continued the battle till nightfall. The slaughter then ceased."* According to Buchanan, "there fell so many eminent and noble personages as scarce ever perished in one battle against a foreign enemy for many years before." In the midst of the carnage, the renowned chief of MacLean performed prodigies of valor. His massive sword, wielded by an arm of great strength, laid prostrate every foe it encountered. In the afterpart of the day, while victory yet weighed the balance with an even hand for either side, he and Sir Alexander Irvine of

---

* Tytler's *History of Scotland*, Vol. II., p. 41.

Drum singled out each other by their armorial bearings on their shields. "Ha! chief of Duard, follower of a rebel vassal, have I at length the satisfaction to see thee within reach of my sword's point?" exclaimed the knight of Drum. "Time-serving slave," replied MacLean, "thou hast, if it be satisfaction to thee; and if my steel be as keen as my appetite for life of thine, thou shalt not have time to repeat thy taunt." The result was not of long duration, for such was the fury with which the heroic rivals fought, that they fell dead foot to foot on the field, ere a friend had time to assist either. The body of Hector was carried from the field of battle by the Clan Innes and Ilvurrich, upon their shields, to Iona, where it was entombed.

In this battle, fought July 24, 1411, the Highlanders lost nine hundred men, a small loss compared with that of the Lowlanders. During the night, the island lord retreated, checked and broken, but neither conquered nor very effectually repulsed. The battle made a deep impression on the public mind, and fixed itself in the music and poetry of Scotland. While the battle was not decisive, and neither could well claim the victory, yet the insular prince kept possession of the earldom of Ross, which after his death was conceded to his son Alexander by King James I.

The anniversary of the battle of Harlaw was for many generations observed by the houses of Duard and Drum; and on such occasions an exchange of swords took place between the respective successors of MacLean and Irvine, as a token of respect to the memory of their brave ancestors, and as a bond of perpetual friendship between themselves.

The traditions of the country speak affectionately of Hector Roy, and what has been preserved represents him generous as well as brave. He left two sons, Lachlan, who succeeded him, and John Dubh.

VII. Lachlan Bronnach, Seventh Chief of MacLean.

Lachlan, seventh chief of MacLean, received the sobriquet of Bronnach, or swag-bellied, on account of his corpulency. He was with his father on the fatal field of Harlaw, where he was made prisoner by Alexander Stewart, Earl of Mar. During his captivity, he became acquainted with the earl's daughter, the Lady Margaret, whom he afterward married. According to some accounts his estates were managed by his uncle John during his captivity, while others state it was his brother, John Dubh. This confusion results from the names of the two being the same. It is not probable that he remained in confinement for any considerable length of time. He did not possess the same war-like character that distinguished his father. He appears neither to have sought nor avoided war, but was ready for action when the time arrived. His name, however, does not come prominently forward until the year 1427, when a useless war was brought on through the treachery of King James I. This monarch summoned a parliament to meet him at Inverness, in 1427, at which the Highland chiefs were invited to attend. As the chiefs entered the hall in which parliament was assembled, each was immediately arrested and placed in irons in different parts of the building, not one being permitted to communicate with any of the others. Among the number was Alexander, Third Lord of the Isles, and his mother, the Countess of Ross. Some of the great chiefs were immediately beheaded, and the rest sent to various prisons, where after a time some were liberated, and the rest put to death. On his liberation, the young Lord of the Isles set about to avenge this unparalleled outrage, for he keenly felt the indignity of his imprisonment. In 1429, he summoned all his vassals in Ross and the Isles, and advanced against the town of Inverness, which he burnt to the ground, besides wasting the crown lands, in revenge for the treacherous treatment he had received there two years before from the king. King James immediately placed himself at the head of a large army, and came upon Alexander unexpectedly. The Clans Cameron and Chattan now deserted the island lord, who was immediately attacked and defeated. Alexander was forced eventually to surrender unconditionally, when he was imprisoned in Tantallon Castle, and his mother confined in Inchcolm, in the Firth of Forth. Along with him we find in prison Lachlan MacLean * and other chieftains.

Donald Balloch, in 1431, a cousin of Alexander, enraged beyond measure at the pusillanimous submission of his kinsman, collected a fleet and an army in the Hebrides, ran his galleys into the neck of sea that divides Morvern from the island of Lismore, and disembarking at Lochaber, swept over that district with all the ferocity of northern warfare. At Inverlochy he met a superior force of the king's army, commanded by Alexander, Earl of Mar, and Alan Stewart, Earl of Caithness. With their broadswords and battle-axes, the Islesmen commenced a furious attack upon the well-armed and disciplined Lowland knights. The royal army was cut to pieces; the Earl of Caithness, with sixteen of his personal retinue, and many other barons and knights, were left dead on the field. Mar, although severely wounded and barely escaping being made prisoner, succeeded in rescuing the remnant of his army. In the engagement, Donald Balloch made a main battle and a front of his men. The front was commanded by MacIan of Ardnamur-

---

* Skene's *Celtic Scotland*, Vol. III., p. 297.

chan and John Dubh MacLean, brother of Lachlan Bronnach, and the main battle by Ranald Bán. The royal army sustained a loss of nine hundred and ninety, while that of Donald was but twenty-seven men.

Donald Balloch carried off as much plunder as he could collect, re-embarked in his galleys, and retreated to the Isles. Against him the king now brought a superior force, and after several encounters Donald fled to Ireland. The king established himself at Dunstaffnage Castle, received the submission of most of the chiefs engaged in the rebellion, and apprehended and executed about three hundred principal men.

In 1439, Lachlan Bronnach exhibited a warlike character. James II. was then on the throne, and engaged in practicing dissimulation among his nobles, who were contesting with one another, each engaged in accomplishing his self-purposes. " The people were afflicted by almost every scourge which could be let loose upon a devoted country : by internecine feuds, by a severe famine, and by a wide-spread and deadly pestilence. The fierce inhabitants of the Western Isles, under the command of Lachlan MacLean* and Murdoch Gibson, two leaders notorious for their spoliations and murders, broke in upon the continent; and, not content with the devastation of the coast, pushed forward into the heart of the Lennox, where they slew Colquhoun of Luss in open battle, and reduced the whole district to the state of a blackened and depopulated district." †

The date of the death of Lachlan Bronnach is unknown. He was living as late as the year 1463, for on the 12th April of that year, both he and his son Lachlan witnessed a charter confirmed by the king to Thomas Younger, of Dingwall, of Usuy in the earldom of Ross.‡

Before his marriage he had a son by a daughter of MacLean of Kingerloch, Mac-Mhic-Eachainn Chinnghearloch, called Donald, of whom the families of Ardgour and Borreray are descended. By his first wife, Margaret, daughter of the Earl of Mar, he had Lachlan Og, his heir and successor. By his second wife, Fionnaghal, daughter of William MacLeod of Harris, he had two sons, Neil of Ross and John Garbh of Coll.

Donald, the first son, possessed some of the spirit of his great-grandfather, Lachlan Lùbanach. He determined, though his father was bound to submission, to show that he was not. With the consent of his father, he armed a number of followers, crossed over to MacDonald's Castle of Ardtornish, and

---

* It is possible, and even probable, that this Lachlan was other than Lachlan Bronnach.
† Tytler's *History of Scotland*, Vol. II., p. 128.   ‡ *Reg. Mag. Sig.*, Lib. VI., No. 116.

demanded of that chief of the Isles an inheritance. The island lord, either admiring the gallantry of the young MacLean, or else not willing to fall out with him, answered: "Falbh! nach leum thu'n garreadh far is ioshlae." (Begone! Canst thou leap the fence where 'tis lowest?) Immediately comprehending that the hint applied to MacMaster, chief of Ardgour, who did not at the time stand high in the good graces of the imperious lord, MacLean started off to Kingerloch, where, arming an additional number of men, he proceeded to Ardgour, attacked and routed the MacMasters, pursued their chief to the Corran ferry, where he was overtaken in a parley with one of his boatmen in the attempt to escape. He and his son were instantly dispatched. The boatman, with a view to ingratiate himself with MacLean, related how he had retarded the progress of his late master in his purpose to escape, by starting difficulties in venturing across the Corran, the day being rather stormy. "Thou art a faithful hind, truly," sarcastically replied Donald, "and 't is but meet that so trustworthy a vassal should follow his chief;" and, lifting his battle-ax, yet reeking with the blood of MacMaster, he swept the treacherous servant's head off at one blow.

The lands of Ardgour were immediately confirmed by charter from the Lord of the Isles to Donald, and the same charter was afterward ratified by King James I. The estate thus acquired has passed for centuries, in regular order, from Donald the first possessor through a succession of honorable descendants, to the present laird.

Neil, or Niall, another son of Lachlan Bronnach, who appears to have been of a peaceable nature, received from his father a grant of the lands of Lehire, in Mull. His descendants, particularly in the Ross branch, *Sliochd a Chlaimbh Iaruin* (the race of the Iron Sword), were at one time very powerful, though the elder line was early cut off by the daring hand of the notorious Allein na Sop, who killed Neil, third laird of Lehire, in his house of Torloisk, and seized upon his estates.

John Garbh, second son of the second marriage of Lachlan Bronnach, an enterprising character, and well worthy of being the grandson of Hector Roy, appears to have hit upon a similar plan, in the acquisition of landed property as his brother Donald, for he demanded an inheritance from the Lord of the Isles, and obtained the island of Coll, in addition to the lands of Quinish, in Mull, already conferred on him, and held both of MacDonald as his feudal superior. It is stated he afterward acquired by purchase the island of Rum of Allan MacRuarrie of Clanrannold, but Clanrannold, for some reason, not mentioned, refused to confirm the sale. John Garbh succeeded in obtaining possession of his person, and carried him prisoner to his castle of Breachacha, located in the south-eastern part of Coll, where he detained him for nine months, when the right of the disputed possession was fully conceded. Before his captive was released, he demanded his " bond of future friendship and perpetual amity."

John Garbh had more than one opportunity for the display of his warlike disposition. The Lady MacLean, widow of Lachlan Bronnach and mother of John, having married MacNeil of Barra, that chieftain, assuming to himself an unjust authority over the possessions of his step-son, came to Coll and occupied the castle of Breachacha (*Breachd* or *Breac*, spotted, and *achadh*, a field or meadow, so called because in summer it is enameled with clover and daisies), in defiance of the young proprietor's remonstrances; and his intrusion would have cost MacNeil dearly, had it not been for the influence the mother exercised over her son, by whom she was always regarded with the most filial affection. He chose rather to retire out of the country for a time, than administer during his mother's life the chastisement on his step-father which he so justly merited. After a voluntary exile of some years in Ireland, receiving intelligence that his maternal uncle, Alastair,[*] laird of McLeod, was detained prisoner for some unexplained reason by the Lord of the Isles, his native boldness, now nurtured to maturity, could not brook the insult thus offered to the brother of his beloved mother. He returned to Scotland with a few armed followers, resolved at once to avenge his own and his uncle's wrongs. He immediately proceeded to the castle of Ardtornish, where MacDonald was engaged in council; and ere that island prince had time to recover from the surprise caused by the sudden appearance of MacLean on the floor of the council chamber, armed from head to foot, with his great battle-ax in his hand, John Garbh, in one breath, and in a tone that made the old walls of Ardtornish sound the note of death as the result of the least resistance, demanded the cause of detention and the immediate and unconditional release of his uncle. MacDonald, undoubtedly not admiring the bold intrusion of his threatening visitor, thought it best to comply with his demand, and instantly set the Laird of MacLeod at liberty. MacLean now, attended by his uncle and a trusty band of fifty armed men, proceeded to Coll, where he received intelligence that MacNeil was, with six score men, building a house at Grisipoll, about the

---

[*] There must be some mistake in the personage. MacKenzie, in his "History of the MacLeod," gives but two brothers of John's mother, viz., Malcolm and William. I do not find that either was held prisoner by MacDonald. The Pennycross MS says it was Alastair Crottach; but he was the eighth laird of MacLeod, and flourished about 1498.

middle of the island, and that the castle of Breachacha was garrisoned with about twenty of Barra's men. Making his way directly for Grisipoll through private roads, he surprised MacNeil, who, with all his followers, was put to the sword, not one escaping. MacNeil was a bold, resolute man, for he singled out John in the conflict; and, notwithstanding MacLean's great strength and dexterity, he was like to be overcome by MacNeil, who wounded him in the head through his helmet with his battle-ax, and as Barra was about to give John another stroke, which would have ended him, a servant of the latter, named Gilireamhack, came behind MacNeil, and with one stroke killed him. His mother, who was then at Grisipoll, came to lament the havoc that deprived her of her husband and almost her son, and then began to upbraid the latter with cruelty; to which he replied that in future he would care for her. The garrison at the castle at once surrendered. Pursuing his victory, John Garbh landed in Barra, subdued the whole island, built a castle upon Loch Inhaistye, and kept possession of the whole for seven years, and then turned the island over to his half-brother, young MacNeil.

He rescued his uncle a second time, who had been imprisoned by Clanranald at Castle Tirimm Moidart.

VIII. Lachlan Og, Eighth Chief of MacLean.

Lachlan Og, or Young Lachlan, so called in order to distinguish him from his father, was lord of Duard and chief of MacLean during that eve when great political changes were about to take place in the Western Isles. The western chiefs had thought themselves practically independent of the king, and were obedient only to the Lord of the Isles, who ruled in princely style. In 1448, John MacDonald became Fourth Lord of the Isles, and soon evinced himself as one of the strongest opponents of the king's party. In 1462, he entered into a compact with the banished house of Douglas and the commissioners of England, in which it was stipulated that John, with his vassals and such auxiliaries as would be furnished by Edward IV., and the assistance that might be given by the Douglases, should enter upon the conquest of Scotland; that John, Donald Balloch, and John, the sons and heirs of MacDonald, upon the payment of a stipulated sum of money (John, £200 sterling annually in time of war, and one hundred marks in time of peace; to Donald Balloch, £40, and to John, his son, £20, in time of war, and in times of peace half these sums respectively), should become forever the sworn vassals of England, and assist in the wars in Ireland and elsewhere. In the event of the conquest of Scotland, then that kingdom should be equally divided between John, Donald Balloch, and the Earl of Douglas. While these negotiations were still pend-

Vassals of the Lords of the Isles—1365 to 1493.   49

ing, the Lord of the Isles assembled a large force, captured the castle of Inverness, and commenced to assert authority over Inverness, Nairn, Ross, and Caithness. How this extraordinary rebellion was suppressed is uncertain. He was summoned before parliament for treason; and that on failing to appear, the process of forfeiture against him was suspended for a time, and he was allowed to retain undisturbed possession of his estates for about fifteen years. The treaty of 1462 did not come to light until 1475, when the Scottish government determined to proceed against John as an avowed traitor and rebel. Commission was given to Colin Campbell, first Earl of Argyle, to prosecute a decree of forfeiture against him; and on the appointed day, failing to appear, sentence was passed upon him. So great were the preparations now made against him, that MacDonald sued for pardon, and with much humility surrendered to the king's mercy. He was pardoned and restored to his forfeited estates on July 1, 1476. Soon after, the earldom of Ross and the lands of Kintyre and Knapdale became inalienably annexed to the crown. This caused great dissatisfaction on the part of Angus, the bastard son of MacDonald, a man who was early accustomed to rebellion. The division of the lands also divided the vassals of the Lordship of the Isles, the MacLeans, MacLeods, and MacNeils adhering to John, while the various branches of the Clan MacDonald made common cause with the turbulent heir of the lordship.

Lachlan Og was called upon to pilot the clan during these troublous times, being beset both within and without. The seanachaids have recorded but very little of his life; but they declare him " to have been a good and pious man." Enough is recorded to show that he was possessed of rare judgment, and maintained a peaceful demeanor. He lived and died one of the most peaceful of his race.

He was married to Catherine, daughter of Colin Campbell, first Earl of Argyle. His father-in-law and his accomplices were successful in involving the Lord of the Isles in difficulties, and although he did not scruple to misrepresent his son-in-law and brand him as a recreant chief, yet Lachlan's judgment and skill warded off every blow Argyle attempted to inflict.

Unfortunately, the records do not show when he became chief and when he died. He was living in 1478, for in that year, at Edinburgh, on December 22d, he was witness to a charter confirmed by the king to David, Earl of Crawford.* He probably died soon after. By his wife, Catherine Campbell, he had Hector, his heir and successor; Fionnaghal, who was married to

---

* *Reg. Mag. Sig.*, Lib. IX., No. 15.

Celestine MacDonald, lord of Lochalsh and Lochcarron; and Anne, who was married to Sir Robert Munro of Fowlis. The marriage of Fionnaghal must have taken place in 1462, for in that year (at the castle at Dingwall, February 2d), John of the Isles grants to his brother "Celestine de insulis of the lands of Lochalsh, etc., to hold to the said Celestine and the heirs to be gotten between him and Finvola, daughter of Lachlan McGilleone of Dowart." *

The records † show that Lachlan McGilleain was witness to a "charter granted by Alexander, lord of the Isles, to his esquire, Gilleownan of Roderic of Murchard, Makneill, of the island of Barra, etc., and failing the said Gilleownan, then to the surviving brother of him gotten between the said Roderic Makneill and the daughter of Ferchard Makgilleoin. Dated at the Isle of St. Finlagan in Isla, on the vigil of St. John the Baptist, 1472."

Rolland Makclane of Dowart and Hector McClane of Carnlochboy are witnesses to a charter "granted by John lord of the Isles to John Davidson, of the lands of Grenare in Carrick. Dated at Isla 20th August 1746." ‡ This same charter appears to have been duplicated in 1478, with "Rolland Maklane of Dowart" ‖ again as a witness.

IX. Hector, Ninth Chief of MacLean.

This chieftain has been called Eachuinn Odhar, or Hector the Swarthy, and sometimes Eachuinn ni num-bristion, on account of his brave and warlike disposition. The times were favorable for the display of his inclinations. Angus MacDonald, bastard son of the Lord of the Isles, a man of great natural violence, succeeded in establishing a supremacy over his father, among the chiefs descended from the family of the Isles. These chiefs were easily drawn off, because John, Fourth Lord of the Isles, in 1476, gave up the earldom of Ross and the lands of Kintyre and Knapdale, and had made improvident grants of lands to the MacLeans, MacLeods, MacNeills, and some smaller tribes. Angus placed himself at the head of the various branches of the Clandonald, and raised the standard of revolt against his father. John went to Stirling, and there, on account of his son's disobedience, resigned all his possessions to the king, except the barony of Kinloss in Murray, of Kinnaird in Buchan, and of Cairndonald in the West, which he reserved to support his own grandeur during his lifetime.§ Angus determined not to surrender any of the hereditary possessions to the king, or even to his father himself. Several expeditions sent by the king against Angus proved unsuccessful. The first,

---

* *Reg. Mag. Sig.*, Lib. VI., No. 16.   † *Ibid.*, Lib. XIII., No. 188.   ‡ *Ibid.*, Lib. VIII., No. 1.
‖ *Ibid.*, Lib. IX., No. 30.   § MacKenzie's *History of the MacDonalds*, p. 98.

under the Earl of Athole, assisted by the MacKenzies, MacKays, and Frasers, was defeated with great slaughter at Lagebread. The second expedition, under the Earls of Crawford and Huntly, made no impression. A third, under Argyle and Athol, accompanied by John, succeeded, through an accommodation, in persuading several tribes to join the royal forces. The two earls appeared to be afraid of attacking Angus, and this expedition resulted in failure. " John, the father, however, undismayed by their pusillanimity, proceeded onward through the Sound of Mull, accompanied by the MacLeans, MacLeods, MacNeills, and others, and having encountered Angus in a bay on the south side of the promontory of Ardnamurchan, a desperate combat ensued, in which Angus was again victorious."* This place is near Tobermory, and has since been known as Badh-na-fola, or the Bloody Bay. Hector Odhar not only headed his clan, but also took his hereditary post of lieutenant-general under the Lord of the Isles. This naval engagement was fought with the most rancorous animosity, and prodigious slaughter was committed on both sides. Angus succeeded in taking prisoner both his father and the chief of MacLean. The result of this battle (fought in 1482), was to establish Angus completely in possession of the extensive territories of his clan.

It can not be said that the Isles were at peace long at a time, for the clans continued to be more or less involved in feuds with one another, as the following instance illustrates:

Kenneth, chief of the MacKenzies, married Margaret, daughter of John of Islay, in 1480. Some time after, Alexander of Lochalsh, Margaret's cousin, came to Ross, and presuming upon his relationship with the family of MacKenzie, took possession of Balcony House and adjacent lands, and then provided a great feast, and to it invited most of the powerful chiefs, among them his cousin, Lord Kenneth MacKenzie. In order to provide accommodations for all his distinguished guests, he was forced to put some of the out-houses in order. Kenneth came late, accompanied by forty able-bodied men, but without his lady, which gave umbrage to MacDonald. One of the MacLeans of Duard had chief charge of the arrangements of the house. On Kenneth's arrival, MacLean informed him that, owing to his connection with the family, they had taken the liberty of providing lodgings in the kiln. Kenneth, being a powerful man, and maddened at the supposed insult, instantly struck Mac-

---

* Brown's *History of the Highland Clans*, Vol. IV., p. 440.

Lean a blow on the ear which felled him to the ground. This aroused the household of MacDonald, who flew to arms. Kenneth, noticing the transports of the guests on the shore, seized some, sank the rest, and with his followers passed over to the other side. Four days later, he degraded his wife by sending her in the most ignominious manner to Balnagown. She was blind of an eye, and in order to insult her brother in the grossest manner, he sent her mounted on a one-eyed horse, accompanied by a one-eyed servant, and followed by a one-eyed dog. At the time she was in a very delicate state, having shortly before borne a son, the only issue of the marriage. The inhumanity heaped upon her was so great that she never wholly recovered her health.

MacDonald was very much exasperated on account of Kenneth's conduct, and the insult heaped upon his sister. Immediately he dispatched MacLean, his great steward, to collect his followers in the Isles, and request the aid of his relatives on the mainland. The force raised amounted to fifteen hundred men. As they advanced through Lochaber and Badenoch, they were joined by the Clan Chattan, and at Inverness by the young Laird of Kilravock and some of the Frasers. After reducing the castle at Inverness, they plundered the lands of Sir Alexander Urquhart, Sheriff of Cromarty, and then ravaged the lands of the MacKenzies. On arriving at Contin, MacDonald found the people in great terror and confusion. The able-bodied men were with MacKenzie, and the aged, the women and children—the day being Sunday—took refuge in the church, thinking they would be secure within its sacred precincts. MacDonald, having little or no scruples on the score of religion, ordered the doors closed and the church burnt. The priest, helpless, aged, men, women, and children alike were burnt to ashes. From there MacDonald marched against MacKenzie, who was at Kinellan, not far from Contin. Kenneth's force, six hundred in all, was posted in a strong position, yet so conveniently situated as to attack MacDonald if a favorable opportunity occurred. At midday, MacDonald drew up the Islemen on the moor, distant about a quarter of a mile from the position of the MacKenzies, the forces separated from each other by a peat moss full of deep pits and deceitful bogs. Kenneth placed a body of archers in ambush, commanded by his brother Duncan, intending to make a sally and then retreat, in order to induce the Islemen to pursue him, and thus entangle them in the pits and bogs of the moss. Having made all his arrangements, he boldly marched to meet the foe in the direction of the intervening moss, avoiding, from his intricate knowledge of it, all the dangerous pits and bogs. " MacLean of Lochbuy,* who led the van of the enemy's army, advanced and charged him with great fury. MacKenzie, according to his pre-arranged plan, at once retreated, but so masterly that in so doing he inflicted ' as much damage upon the enemy as he received.' The Islesmen soon got entangled in the moss, and Duncan observing this, rushed forth from his ambush, and furiously attacked the MacDonalds in flank and rear, slaughtering most of those who entered the bog. He then turned round upon the main body, who were taken unprepared. Kenneth seeing this, charged with the main body, who were well instructed in their chief's design, and before the enemy were able to form in order of battle, he fell on their right flank with such furious impetuosity, and did such execution amongst them, that they were compelled to fall back in confusion before the splendid onset of the small force which they had so recently sneered at and despised. Gillespie, stung at his nephew's taunt before the engagement commenced, to prove to him that ' though he was wary in council, he was not fearful in action,' sought out MacKenzie, that he might engage him in single combat, and followed by some of his bravest followers, he with signal valor did great execution among his opponents as he was approaching Kenneth, who was in the hottest of the fight; and who, seeing Gillespie coming in his direction, advanced to meet him, killing, wounding, or scattering any of the enemy that came between them. He made a signal to Gillespie to advance and meet him in single combat; but finding him hesitating, Kenneth, who far exceeded him in strength while he equaled him in courage, would ' brook no tedious debate, but pressing on with fearful eagerness, he at one blow cut off Gillespie's arm and past very far into his body, so that he fell down dead.'" In this action, known as the battle of Park, MacDonald was taken prisoner, "and MacLean of Lochbuy (*Lachlainn MacThearlaich*) was killed by Duncan Mor, MacKenzie's ' great scallag,' or ploughman. What remained of the MacDonalds were completely routed and put to flight, but most of them were killed, ' quarter being no ordinar complement in thos dayes.' "

The death of Lachlan MacLean, who lead the MacLeans into the engagement, as well as commanding the van, is thus described: "A raw, ungainly,

---

* I do not know who this MacLean of Lochbuy was. At the time this battle was fought (1488), John Og, son of Hector MacLean, was Lord of Lochbuy. It might have been a brother or uncle. But further along he is called *Lachlainn MacThearlaich*. The Clan Thearlaich was the MacLeans of Urquhart and Dochgarroch, a branch of the house of Lochbuy; but I fail to find a Lachlan there of this period.

but powerful-looking youth from Kintail was seen looking about, as they were starting to meet the enemy, in an apparently stupid manner, as if looking for something. He ultimately fell in with an old, big, rusty battle-ax, set off after the others, and arrived at the scene of strife as the combatants were striving with each other. Duncan (for such was his name), from his stupid and ungainly appearance, was taken little notice of, and was going about in an aimless, vacant, half-idiotic manner. Hector Roy, noticing him, asked him why he was not taking part in the fight and supporting his chief and clan? Duncan replied, '*Mar a faigh mi miabh duine, cha dean mi gniomh duine*' (Unless I get a man's esteem, I shall not perform a man's work). This was in reference to his not having been provided with a proper weapon. Hector answered him, '*Deansa gniomh duine's gheibh thu miabh duine*' (Perform a man's work and you will receive a man's share). Duncan at once rushed into the strife, exclaiming, '*Buille mhor bho chul mo laimhe, 's ceum leatha, am fear nach teich romham, teicheam roimhe*' (A heavy stroke from the back of my hand (arm) and a step to (enforce) it. He who does not get out of my way, let me get out of his). Duncan soon killed a man, and drawing the body aside he coolly sat upon it. Hector Roy noticing this extraordinary proceeding, as he was passing by in the heat of the contest, accosted Duncan, and asked him why he was not still engaged with his comrades. Duncan answered, '*Mar a faigh mi ach miabh aon duine cha dean mi ach gniomh aon duine*' (If I only get one man's due I shall only do one man's work. I have killed my man). Hector told him to perform two men's work and that he would get two men's reward. Duncan returned again to the field of carnage, killed another, pulled his body away, placed it on the top of the first, and sat upon the two. The same question was again asked, and the same answer given, ' I have killed two men, and earned two men's wages.' Hector answered, ' Do your best, and we shall not be reckoning with you.' Duncan instantly replied, '*Am fear nach biodh ag cunntadh rium cha bhithinn a cunntadh vis*' (He that would not reckon with me I would not reckon with him), and rushed into the thickest of the battle, where he mowed down the enemy with his rusty battle-axe like grass, so much so that Lachlan MacThearlaich, a most redoubtable warrior, placed himself in Duncan's way to check him in his murderous career. The heroes met in mortal strife, but MacThearlaich, being a powerful man, clad in mail, and well versed in arms, Duncan could make no impression on him, but being lighter and more active than his heavily mailed opponent, he managed to defend himself, watching his opportunity, and retreating backwards until he arrived at a ditch, where his opponent, thinking he had him fixed, made a desperate stroke at him, which Duncan parried, and at the same time jumped backwards across the ditch. MacThearlaich, to catch his enemy, made a furious plunge with his weapon, but it instead got fixed in the opposite bank of the ditch, and in withdrawing it he bent his head forward, when the helmet, rising, exposed the back of his neck, upon which Duncan's battle-axe descended with the velocity of lightning, and such terrific force as to sever MacThearlaich's head from his body. This, it is said, was the turning point in the struggle, for the MacDonalds, seeing the brave leader of their van falling, at once retreated and gave up all for lost."*

This insurrection cost the MacDonalds the lordship of the Isles, as others had the earldom of Ross. At a parliament held in Edinburgh in 1493, the possessions of the Lord of the Isles were declared to be forfeited to the crown. In the following February, John MacDonald, the aged Lord of the Isles, made his appearance before King James IV., and made a voluntary surrender of every thing, after which, for several years, he remained in the king's household as a court pensioner.

On the final forfeiture of the Lords of the Isles, the MacLeans became independent. Also, by charters for lands granted, the clan became divided into several heads, the principal families being Duard, Lochbuy, Coll, and Ardgour, each branch receiving charters direct from the king, which was but a confirmation of those previously possessed from the Lord of the Isles.

CHAPTER V.
THE MacLEANS AS AN INDEPENDENT CLAN.
FROM 1493 TO 1598.

On the final forfeiture of the Lords of the Isles, the king determined to reduce the wild and remote districts of the Highlands to a more regular form of government. In order to accomplish this, he sought "to attach to his interest the principal chiefs of these provinces; to overawe and subdue the petty princes who affected independence; to carry into their territories, hitherto too exclusively governed by their own capricious or tyrannical institutions, the same system of a severe but regular and rapid administration of civil and criminal justice which had been established in his Lowland domin-

---

* MacKenzie's *History of the Clan MacKenzie*, in *Celtic Magazine*, Vol. III., pp. 161–169.

ions, was the laudable object of the king; and for this purpose he succeeded, with that energy and activity which remarkably distinguished him, in opening up an intercourse with many of the leading men in the northern countries. With the captain of the Clan Chattan, Duncan MacIntosh; with Ewan, the son of Alan, captain of the Clan Cameron; with Campbell of Glenurcha; the MacLeans of Duard and Lochbuy; MacIan of Ardnamurchan; the Lairds of MacKenzie and Grant; and the Earl of Huntly, a baron of the most extensive power in those northern districts—he appears to have been in habits of constant and regular communication, rewarding them by presents, in the shape either of money or of grants of land, and securing their services in reducing to obedience such of their fellow chieftains as proved contumacious, or actually rose into rebellion."* The king believing that his personal presence would have a salutary effect, visited the Highlands twice during the year 1493, and proceeded as far as Dunstaffnage and Mingarry in Ardnamurchan; and in the succeeding year, such was the indefatigable activity with which he executed his public duties, he thrice visited the Isles.

"In 1495, after making extensive preparations for another expedition to the Isles, the king assembled an army at Glasgow; and on the 18th of May we find him at the castle of Mingarry, in Ardnamurchan, being the second time within two years that he had held court in that remote castle. John Huchonson, or Hughson, of Sleat; Donald Angusson of Keppoch; Allan MacRuari of Moydert, chief of Clanranald; Hector MacLean of Duard; Ewin Allanson of Lochiel, captain of the Clan Cameron, and Gilleonan MacNeill of Barra, seem to have made their submission in consequence of this expedition. In this year, too, Kenneth Og MacKenzie of Kintail and Farquhar MacIntosh, son and heir of the captain of Clan Chattan, were imprisoned by the king in the castle at Edinburgh. This may have been partly owing to their lawless conduct in 1491, but was more probably caused by a dread of their influence among the Islanders. The measures now taken by the king were soon after followed up by an important act of the lords of council (1496), which merits particular notice. This act provided, in reference to civil actions against the Islanders—of which a considerable number were then in preparation—that the chief of every clan should be answerable for the due execution of summons and other writs against those of his own tribe, under the penalty of being made liable himself to the party bringing the action. This, although undoubtedly a strong measure, was in all probability rendered necessary by the dis-

---

* Tytler's *History of Scotland*, Vol. II., p. 257.

turbed state of the Isles after so many rebellions, and could hardly fail to produce a beneficial effect; for in these wild and remote districts the officers of the law could not perform their necessary duties in safety, without the assistance of a large military force. At the same time that this important regulation was made, five chiefs of rank—viz., Hector MacLean of Duard, John MacIan of Ardnamurchan, Allan MacRuari of Moydert, Ewin Allanson of Lochiel, and Donald Angusson of Keppoch—appearing before the lords of council, bound themselves 'by the extension of their hands,' to the Earl of Argyle, on behalf of the king, to abstain from mutual injuries and molestation of each, under a penalty of five hundred pounds."*

In the year 1500, the long-existing feud between the Camerons and MacLeans broke out. On the forfeiture of the chief of the Clan Cameron, the lands of Lochiel were granted by Alexander, Lord of the Isles, to John MacLean of Coll; and, afterward, for some reason which does not appear, were conferred by John, Lord of the Isles, in 1461, to John MacLean of Lochbuy, and again to Celestine, Lord of Lochalsh. All of these claims were properly resisted by the chiefs of the Camerons. John MacLean, second Laird of Coll, held the lands for a time by force, but was at length killed in Lochaber by the Camerons, which for a time checked the claim of the MacLeans. But now the whole of the Clan MacLean became involved in the feud, some in order to avenge the death of Coll, and others who had been placed under obligations to support the claim of John of Lochbuy. The chief of the Camerons, in order to strengthen himself, acknowledged the claims of Lochalsh, who thus became bound to maintain Cameron in possession against all agressors. The MacLeans broke in upon the lands of Lochaber with renewed violence, and carried away a great prey of cattle, but failed to maintain possession of the territory.†

The policy of leniency which had governed the king up to 1499 was suddenly changed, and all his promises grossly violated, and "the moderate and wise measures already adopted were succeeded by proceedings so severe as to border on injustice. The charters which had been granted during the last six years to the vassals of the Isles, were summarily revoked. Archibald Campbell, second Earl of Argyle, was installed in the office of lieutenant, with the ample and invidious power of leasing out the entire lordship of the Isles. The ancient proprietors and their vassals were violently expelled from their

---

* MacKenzie's *History of the MacDonalds*, p. 117.　† Gregory's *History of the Western Highlands*, pp. 70, 76, 95.

hereditary property; whilst Argyle and other royal favorites appear to have been enriched by new grants of their estates and lordships. We are not to wonder that such harsh proceedings were loudly reprobated: the inhabitants saw, with indignation, their rightful masters exposed to insult and indigence, and at last broke into open rebellion. Donald Dhu, grandson of John, Lord of the Isles, had been shut up for forty years,* a solitary captive in the castle of Inchconnal. His mother was a daughter of the first Earl of Argyle; and although there is no doubt that both he and his father were illegitimate, the affection of the Islesmen overlooked the blot in his escutcheon, and fondly turned to him as the true heir of Ross and Innisgail. To reinstate him in his right, and place him upon the throne of the Isles, was the object of the present rebellion. A party, led by the MacIans of Glencoe, broke into his dungeon, liberated him from his captivity, and carried him in safety to the castle of Torquil MacLeod in the Lewis; whilst measures were concerted throughout the wide extent of the Isles for the destruction of the regal power." † Although the king labored to break up the union among the confederated chiefs, despite his efforts it broke forth with destructive fury. Badenoch was wasted, Inverness given to the flames, and so widely had the contagion of independence spread throughout the Isles, that it fairly shook the power of the king. The king assembled his forces, and "in April, 1504, the royal army had its rendezvous at Dumbarton, and from that place artillery and warlike stores of every description available, including 'gun stanes,' were sent forward for the siege of Cairnburgh, a fort on an isolated island on the west coast of Mull. The Earl of Arran received two commissions against the Islanders, and, at the same time, the Earl of Argyle, MacLeod of Harris and Dunvegan, and MacIan of Ardnamurchan, favored and were in regular correspondence with the king, who did not on this occasion proceed in person to the Isles. The rebellion turned out a more formidable affair than was anticipated, and very little progress was made to repress it in this campaign. In the following year, the insurrection becoming still more alarming, the king determined to lead his army in person. He invaded the Isles with a powerful force from the South, while Huntly attacked them from the North and took several prisoners, none of whom, however, were of distinguished rank or influence. At the same time the royal navy was employed under Sir Andrew Wood and Robert Barton. This expedition resulted in breaking up the confederacy of the Island lords; many of them submitted to the royal authority, among the first

---

* Carried off from Islay when an infant. † Tytler's *History of Scotland*, Vol. II., p. 272.

being the powerful chief of the MacLeans, Lord of Duard, which act upon his part also implied the submission of MacNeill of Barra and of MacQuarrie of Ulva, two chiefs who, since the forfeiture of the lordship of the Isles, had followed the banners of their powerful neighbors, the MacLeans. MacLean of Lochbuy soon followed the example of his chief, while the MacDonalds of Largie, a powerful sept of the MacDonalds of Islay, also came in. Ranald MacAllan, heir to the chief of Clanranald, was already in high favor at court, so that the power of the Islanders was almost completely shattered. Some of the great chiefs still held out, the principal of whom was Torquil MacLeod of Lewis, though his chief, MacLeod of Harris, had all through been loyal to the crown. He had taken an active and leading part in the rebellion of the Islanders under Donald Dubh; and it is extremely probable that he entertained little hope of obtaining remission for his offenses, which probably determined him in his resolution to hold out after the other leaders had made their submission." *

The tedious rebellion was at length suppressed, but the process of expelling the inhabitants from their ancient possessions did not make any progress, and the clans of the Isles and the adjacent coasts continued to occupy, many of them perhaps contrary to law, their ancient domain. Donald Dhu, for whose sake the Island chieftains had made such great sacrifices, was again taken prisoner, and remained committed in the castle at Edinburgh for nearly forty years after this period, when he escaped the second time, under the regency of Arran, when the faithful Islanders again assumed his cause.

After the suppression of the insurrection of 1506, the West Highlands and Isles generaly enjoyed a repose for a period of eleven years, when, in 1511, the old quarrel between the Camerons and MacLeans, regarding the lands of Lochiel, was resumed. Also, a feud between the MacLeans of Duard and Lochbuy, about the same time, was carried on with much bitterness, regarding their conterminous lands in Morvern and the Isle of Tiree. These feuds were checked through the attentive care of the king.†

Before proceeding farther, it is necessary to stop at this point and consider a serious difficulty that besets us in presenting the line of chiefs. The previous chapter closed with Hector Odhar as chief of the MacLeans, and the presumption is that this chapter opens during the lordship of the same

---

* MacKenzie's *History of the MacDonalds*, p. 129. See also Gregory's *Western Highlanders*, p 96; Brown's *History of the Clans*, Vol. IV., p. 443; and Keltie's *History of the Highland Clans*, Vol. II., p. 224. † Gregory's *Western Highlands*, p. 110.

chieftain. The principal cause of the difficulty arises from the fact that all the MacLean manuscripts state that Hector Odhar fell at the battle of Flodden Field, in 1513. As the defect in the history has never been pointed out or considered before, it should here be fully set forth:

1. The MacLean manuscripts are all agreed that Hector Odhar not only fell at Flodden Field, but that he was succeeded by his son, Lachlan Catanach.

2. That Lachlan Catanach lived to be a very old man, when he was murdered.

The evidence shows that he was murdered in 1527. The Pennycross manuscript says he lived to be nearly ninety. Then he must have been born about the year 1437. If so, then his father, Hector Odhar, should have been born not later than 1417, which would have made him not less than ninety-six at the time he was killed at the battle of Flodden Field. A fact so remarkable would not have escaped notice. Nothing, however, is recorded as to his age. It is probable that Hector Odhar did live to a good age, and this fact has been, by some negligence on the part of a seanachaidh, attached to Lachlan Catanach. It is more than probable that Hector Odhar did not live as late as the year 1500, and the chieftainship was entailed to an illegitimate son, named Lachlan, who became the

X. Tenth Chief of MacLean.

That there was such a chieftain, and that his name should be restored to the list and no longer suppressed, I produce the following evidence:

1. There was an illegitimate son who had the property entailed to him. In *Registrum Secreti Sigilli*, Volume I., folio 29, may be found the "legitimation to Lauchlane McGilleon son natural to Hector McGilleon of Doward. October 1496." In the same records, same volume and folio, may be found a "Precept for charter of resignation to the said Lauchlan, of lands of Torresay, Castle of Doward, lands of Browhes, & Merkland in Ardmanach etc. in free barony to him and his heirs male; whom failing, to the said Hector Makgillane, and his heirs male; whom failing, to Donald McGillan brother of the said Hector, and his heirs male; whom failing, to the heirs male whatsoever of the said Hector bearing the arms and surname of McGillan. To hold in ward, relief and marriage. 8 October 1496."

2. In the next place, I purpose to show that the said Lachlan was recognized as Lord of Duard, on and after the year 1499. In the same records, same volume, folio 115, may be found a "respite to Lachlan McClean of Doward, John McClean of Coil, Donald McClean 'Eym' to the said Lachlan. 27 February 1499."

AN INDEPENDENT CLAN—1493 TO 1598.

In the same records, Volume III., folio 1, is a "remission to Lachlan Maklane of Dovarde and his complices, for various faults. 31 May 1505."

In the same records, same volume, folio 36, is a "letter to Lauchlane Makgilleon of Doward and 9 other landit men in the Isles, charging them not to intromit with the Kirk rents pertaining to the Bishop of the Isles, and so help him to gather them in. 23 January 1506."

In the same records, same volume, folio 208, is a "letter of Licence to Lacklane Makgillane of Dowart to sell his lands of Carrequhoull, Auchnadalyn, etc. in the Lordship of Badenoch, to Alexander Earl of Huntly. 2 January 1508."

Same date, records, and volume, folio 209, is a letter of regress to the said Lachlan to the same lands of reversion.

In the same records, volume, and folio, date of January, 1508, is a protection to "Lady Agnes daughter of Donald Makgillane, Prioress of the nuns" in Iona, charging "Lauchlan McGillane of Dowart," and others.

In the same records, Volume IV., folio 58, is a "letter of safe conduct to Lauchlan McGillane, his kinsmen and servants to come to the king's presence at Stirling, to be of force for 40 days. 12 April 1510."

Same records and volume, folio 72, may be found a "precept for charter of apprising to Duncan Stewart of Appin, over the lands and castle of Dowart, apprised from Lachlan McGilleon of Dowart for 4500 merks due to the said Duncan: reserving to the said Lachlan power to redeem within 7 years. 8 April 1510."

3. Testimony of writers. The testimony of impartial writers, who have made the official records of Scotland a special study, is of some weight. By far the best and most authentic history of Scotland is that written by P. F. Tytler, which originally appeared in eight volumes between the years 1828 and 1843. In Volume II., page 294,* he states it was Lachlan MacLean that fell at Flodden. Keltie, in *History of the Highland Clans* (Vol. II., p. 224), says, "Lachlan MacLean was chief of Dowart in 1502;" and again, "Lachlan MacLean of Dowart was killed at Flodden." MacKenzie, in his *History of the MacDonalds* (p. 126), names Lachlan MacLean as chief of Duard in 1502. On page 136, he mentions Lachlan MacLean as being killed at Flodden; but on the opposite page (137), he says it was "the brave Hector Odhar, chief of the MacLeans."

The seanachaidhs involve us in another difficulty. From the death of

---

* Nimmo's edition of 1887.

Hector Roy MacLean at the battle of the Harlaw, in 1411, to the death of Hector Odhar at Flodden, in 1513, we have only the following chiefs: Lachlan Bronnach, Lachlan Og, and Hector Odhar, or three chiefs covering a period of one hundred and two years, and one of them not too old for battle. The average of the lordship would be thirty-four years, which would be rather extraordinary for feudal times.

To offset the above records, facts, and conclusions, we have only the word of the seanachaidhs, and those who have quoted from them without investigation.

It comes with considerable force that the chieftainship of the brave Lachlan has been purposely suppressed. We can account for it only upon the assumption that he was born out of wedlock. This need not necessarily throw doubt on the marriage of Hector Odhar; for, as the seanachaidhs claim, he married a daughter of MacIntosh, chief of the clan Chattan, and by her there was no issue. The chieftainship of his illegitimate son, Lachlan, being suppressed, his marriage would likewise share the same fate. To cover up these facts might have pleased the immediate successors of Lachlan.

Lachlan inherited the whole domain that had been confirmed to his father, Hector Odhar, in 1495, which gave him possessions in Mull and Tiree, with detached lands in the isles of Islay, Jura, Scarba, etc., and certain districts in Morvern, Knapdale, and Lochaber. And moreover, he was heritable keeper of the following castles: Duard, in Mull; Cairnburg, in the Treshnish Isles; Dunconnell, in Scarba; Dunkerd, in the Garvelloch Isles; and Isleborg, the locality of which is uncertain.*

After the suppression of the rebellion of Donald Dhu, in 1506, justice was administered throughout the kingdom with great impartiality, and in the Highlands, in a manner before unknown, which lasted during the remainder of the reign of James IV. The king became very popular among the leading Islanders.

In 1513, James IV. determined upon an invasion of England, and summoned the whole array of his kingdom to meet on the common moor of Edinburgh. In obedience to the command, an army of one hundred thousand men assembled. On August 22d, with this great force, James crossed the border; but instead of advancing and at once achieving success, he lingered in the neighborhood of the Tweed until his force was reduced by desertion to thirty thousand men. On September 6th, he took up his position on Flodden Hill,

---

* Gregory's *Western Highlands*, p. 69.

the last and lowest eminence of the Cheviots toward the north-east. On the morning of the 9th, the English army, numbering thirty-two, thousand, under the Earl of Surrey, advanced from the south-east, and by a skillful movement cut off all communication between James and Scotland. The Scottish army advanced against the English in battle array, each army drawn up in a similar manner, which consisted of a center, a right and left wing, and a reserve placed behind the center. The left wing of the Scottish army, commanded by the Earls of Huntly and Home, charged the English right and entirely defeated it. Instead of following up the success, Home's borderers gave themselves up to pillaging both armies; and Huntly, after the first charge, is said to have deserted the field. In the center, the king placed himself in front of his lancers and billmen, surrounded by his nobles. The first consequence of this was so furious a charge upon the English center that its ranks were broken. "On the right the divisions led by the earls of Lennox and Argyle were composed chiefly of the Highlanders and Islesmen; the Campbells, MacLean, MacLeods, and other hardy clans, who were dreadfully galled by the discharge of the English archers. Unable to reach the enemy with their broadswords and axes, which formed their only weapons, and at no time very amenable to discipline, their squadrons began to run fiercely forward, eager for closer fight, and thoughtless of the fatal consequences of breaking their array. . . . They found, however, an enemy in Sir Edward Stanley, whose coolness was not to be surprised in this manner. The squares of English pikemen stood to their ground; and although for a moment the shock of the mountaineers was terrible, its force once sustained became spent with its own violence, and nothing remained but a disorganization so complete that to recover their ranks was impossible. The consequence was a total rout of the right wing of the Scots, accompanied by a dreadful slaughter, in which amid other brave men, the earls of Lennox and Argyle were slain. Yet, notwithstanding this defeat on the right, the center, under the king, still maintained an obstinate and dubious conflict with the earl of Surrey. The determined personal valor of James, imprudent as it was, had the effect of rousing to a pitch of desperate courage the meanest of the private soldiers, and the ground becoming soft and slippery from blood, they pulled off their boots and shoes, and secured a firmer footing by fighting in their hose. No quarter was given on either side; and the combatants were disputing every inch of ground, when Stanley, without losing his time in pursuit of the Highlanders, drew back his division, and impetuously charged the rear of the Scottish center. It was now late in the evening, and this movement was decisive. Pressed on the flank by Dacre and the admiral, opposed in front by Surrey, and now attacked in the rear by Stanley, the king's battle fought with fearful odds against it; yet James continued by his voice and his gestures to animate his soldiers, and the combat was still uncertain when he fell pierced with an arrow and mortally wounded in the head by a bill, within a few paces from the English earl, his antagonist. The death of their sovereign seemed only to animate the fury of the Scottish nobles, who threw themselves into a circle round the body, and defended it till darkness separated the combatants." The Scots withdrew from the field during the night, leaving their artillery behind them. The English loss was eight thousand, and the Scottish ten

FLODDEN-FIELD.

thousand men. Of the Scottish loss, "a great proportion were of high rank; the remainder being composed of the gentry, the farmers, and landed yeomanry, who disdained to fly when their sovereign and his nobles lay stretched in heaps around them. Amongst the slain were thirteen earls—Crawford, Montrose, Huntly, Lennox, Argyle, Errol, Athole, Morton, Cassillis, Bothwell, Rothes, Caithness, and Glencairn, the king's natural son; the archbishop of St. Andrews, the bishops of Caithness and the Isles, the abbots of Inchaffray and Kilwinning, and the dean of Glasgow. To these we must add fifteen lords and chiefs of clans: amongst whom were Sir Duncan Campbell of Glenurcha, Lachlan MacLean of Duard, Campbell of Lawers, and five peers' eldest sons, besides La Motte, the French ambassador, and the secretary of the king. The names of the gentry who fell are too numerous for recapitulation, since there were few families of note in Scotland which did not lose one relative or another, whilst some houses had to weep the death of all. It is from this cause that the sensations of sorrow and national lamentation occasioned by the defeat were peculiarly poignant and lasting."*

As noted in the foregoing, the chief of MacLean, who had become the most powerful in the Hebrides since the forfeiture of the Lords of the Isles, mustered his forces and was with the army on the fatal field of Flodden. The Pennycross manuscript says that this brave chief, "seeing the king in danger from the English archers, interposed himself and received in his body the arrows leveled at his sovereign." If this account be correct, then after the defeat of the Scottish right wing, of which Lachlan and his clansmen formed a part, he, with his forces, must have hastened to the assistance of the center. The account published by Seneachie (1838, p. 25), states: "It is said, before he fell, that the dead bodies of his clansmen, who flocked about their chief to shield him from the overwhelming numbers by which he was assailed, literally formed a wall around him."

XI. Lachlan Catanach, Eleventh Chief of MacLean.

The death of Lachlan at Flodden placed Lachlan Catanach at the head of the clan. Owing to a want of clearness on the part of the documents in the official archives of Scotland, and looseness of statement on the part of the seanachaidhs, we are in some difficulties relating to this chieftain. Some of these difficulties are necessarily cleared up in the statements offered in the previous section. It may be assumed that he was a legitimate son of Lachlan, the illegitimate son of Hector Odhar. On the assumption that he was the son of Hector, it has been declared that he received the appellation *Catanach* from his mother's people, and with them—Clan Chattan—he lived a great many years. I think what I have stated in the previous section, already referred to, does away with this assumption. The word *catanach* not only means "one of the Clan Chattan," but also *hairy, rough, shaggy;* hence he was called Lachlan the Shaggy. He was cradled in troublous times; but whether he took any part in the expeditions of his father or grandfather, the seanachaidhs have borne no testimony. As they have passed so lightly over the lives of Lachlan Bronnach and Lachlan Og, and preserved so little about Hector Odhar, and nothing whatever concerning Lachlan, who fell at Flodden Field, it is not singular that Lachlan Catanach should fail to receive due attention at their hands. What they have preserved presents difficulties which are hard to

---

* Tytler's *History of Scotland*, Vol. II., pp. 292-4.

unravel. But fortunately, we are not left to their mercy; for the official records of Scotland, and what has been preserved in the history of other clans, leave us a full account from the time of his chieftainship to that of his death, although some parts are far from being clear. The official archives and contemporary history show him to have been active, brave, and fearless, yet possessing a degree of cunning not usually given to man. His influence over the clansmen was as great as that possessed by any of his predecessors, and which never wavered.

In the rebellion which immediately broke out after the battle of Flodden, Lachlan Catanach appears to have been the prime mover, as well as the principal leader. The design of this rebellion was to place Sir Donald Gallda on the Island throne. Donald, while still a youth, had been seized by James IV. in one of his northern expeditions, and retained in the royal household, where he became a favorite of that monarch. Having escaped from the field of Flodden, he returned to his northern home, where immediately a plan was formed to restore the ancient principality of the Isles in the person of Sir Alexander MacDonald of Lochalsh, Donald's brother. During the month of November, Sir Donald, with a large body of Highlanders, marched to Urquhart, expelled the garrison from the castle, seized the stronghold, and laid waste the surrounding country. While these operations were going on in the North, Lachlan Catanach, assisted by the MacLeans of Lochbuy and Ardgour, stormed and seized the castle of Cairnburg, and put the garrison to the sword. Soon after, with the assistance of Alexander MacLeod of Dunvegan, possessed himself of the castle of Dunskaich, in Skye, and afterward demolished it as a place of protection. Its gray ruins may still be seen, bearing evidence of its ancient greatness and strength.

All who resisted the authority of the new Lord of the Isles were threatened with the extremity of fire and sword. The successes so rapidly accomplished drew other clans into the rebellion, and soon after Sir Donald was proclaimed Lord of the Isles. To suppress this rebellion, Colin Campbell, Earl of Argyle, received a commission to convocate as many subjects as might be necessary to proceed against MacLean and his associates.* Other individuals were commissioned to act in the northern shires. Letters were addressed by the council to all the chiefs on the mainland adjacent to the Isles, commanding them to resist with their utmost power all Islanders who should land within their territories with hostile intent. Notwithstanding the preparations made

---

* Gregory's *Western Highlanders.* p. 115.

by the government, many of the most powerful families, especially the MacLeans, MacLeods, and the Clan Ian Mhor of Islay, resolutely persisted in their efforts to establish an independent sovereignty. However, after much delay, consisting of an interval of tumult and predatory warfare, the insurgents submitted, and, upon assurances of protection, came to court and arranged in person the terms upon which they were to be pardoned and restored to favor. On 6th September, 1515, Lachlan MacLean received a respite for taking the castle of Cairnburg, which was good until the following January.* Colin Campbell, third Earl of Argyle, having ravaged the island of Bute, and MacKenzie of Kintail, having seized the royal castle of Dingwall, took out remissions. Apparently all disturbances were at an end. The reconciliation of Sir Donald, who still retained much power in the Isles, appeared complete, in so much so that, on the 24th September, 1516, he was summoned to join the royal army, then about to proceed to the borders. Some months afterward, he fell under suspicion of the government. Through the intrigues of English emissaries, he fell into the treasonable practices of Lord Home, which brought that nobleman to the block.

In 1517, Sir Donald was again in rebellion, with Lachlan Catanach MacLean and MacLeod of Lewis for leaders. He gave out to the Islanders the false impression "that the lieutenancy of the Isles, and various other offices belonging to the crown, had been bestowed upon him by the regent and council. Sir Donald succeeded at first in raising a considerable body of men, with which he expelled MacIan from Ardnamurchan, and took possession of the castle of Mingarry. Although repeatedly charged, by order of the council, to deliver up the castle and lands to the rightful owners, he not only refused, but, in defiance of the government, he razed the castle of Mingarry to the ground, and ravaged the whole district of Ardnamurchan with fire and sword. Meantime, his chief leaders found that he had deceived them, and that his intention was to lay waste, instead of protecting, the lands of which he professed to have received the control. They became disgusted, too, with his refusal to follow their advice, and with the reckless character of his proceedings (for the dangerous consequences, either to himself or his followers, however obvious they might be, could not terrify him, or divert him from his insane projects), and at length, taking the matter into their own hands, determined on apprehending him, and delivering him up to the regent. Sir Donald, however, being made aware of their design, effected his escape; but his two

---

* *Registrum Secreti Sigilli*, Vol. V., fol. 12.

brothers were made prisoners by MacLean of Duard and MacLeod of Dunvegan, who hastened to offer their submission and palliate their own conduct." *

Early in 1517, the MacLeans of Duard and Lochbuy, MacLeod of Harris, and the Earl of Argyle presented petitions to the privy council, and making suggestions and certain offers regarding the affairs of the Isles. These petitions are separate and distinct, but must have been made after mutual consultation, for all are uniform regarding the suppression of the rebellion. These state papers are important, because they throw much light upon the history and manners of that period, and merit particular notice. Argyle demanded that he should be invested with very high powers over the men of the Isles, " for the honor of the realm and the common-weal in time coming." He desired a commission of lieutenandry over all the Isles and adjacent mainland, on the grounds of the vast expense he had previously incurred, of his ability to do good service in the future, and of his having broken up the confederacy of the Islanders. The commission was granted to him, with the exception of the territories belonging to Huntly in Lochaber, the Clan Chattan, and Ewin Allanson, and the isles of Bute and Arran. The commission was limited to three years, or further at the regent's pleasure. He further claimed and obtained authority to receive into the king's favor all the men of the Isles who should make submission, except Sir Donald of the Isles, his brothers, and the Clandonald. He further demanded and received power to pursue the rebels with fire and sword, to expel them from the Isles, and use his best endeavors to possess himself of Sir Donald's castle of Strome in Lochcarron.†

As so many animadversions have been cast upon Lachlan Catanach MacLean's petition, I herewith give the record, which is the first time it has ever been printed in full, with decision of the council:

"To Lauchlane Makclanis desiris of Dowfart. In the first anent the remissioun desiryt be him to his self kynnismen seruandis frendis and portakars that is Donald Makalane Gillonan Makmaknele of Barry Nele Makynnon of Mesnes Dwnsleif Makcura of Ulway and Lauchlan McEwin of Ardgour for all crimes be past.

The lordis counsalis that my lord governour grant this remission and gif the samyn the said Makclane gevand plegis sufficient sic as the governour and counsale sall devise and mene be thair names for gude reule in tyme cuming.

Anent the hundreth merk landis of the Ile of Tery and utheris landis in the Mule to the said soume desirit be Makclane for the inbringing of the Kingis malis in all placis within the Row, Ardnamurquhan, exceptand samekill as partenis to Makcane for quhilk he sall answer.

The lordis understandis that the Kingis landis may nocht be givin in heretage

---

*Gregory's *Western Highlanders*, p. 118. † *Acta Dominorum Concilii*, Vol. XXIX., fol. 82; also, Gregory's *Western Highlanders*, p. 121.

notycles for the gude service done be the said Lauchlane McClane and to be done counsalis the governour to suffer the said Lauchlane to intromett and uptake the proffeitis pertenyng to the King of the said Ile of Tere to his awn *utilte* induring my lord governouris administration with condition that the said Lauchlane answer and caus the Kingis servitouris to be answerit zerlie to the Kingis grace and his servitouris according to his Rentale of the said boundis and gevand cautioun tharfor.

Anent the service of the tennentis of the Kingis Grace desirit be the said Lauchlane the lordis counsalis my lord governour grant to him the service of thai tennentis of the Kingis quhilk his forbearis as he had grantit to thame of befoir of the King and to do him service in his just materis the Kingis grace my lord governour and the Erll of Ergile lieutenent exceppit.

Anent the generall acquittans desirit be the said Lauchlane of all malis fermes and dewiteis pertenyng to the King oure Souerane of Tere Mul Ylay and Germarry intromettit be the said Lauchlane.

The lordis thinkis and counsalis the governour to gif this discharge with condition that gif the said Lauchlane failzeis hereftir to the Kingis grace or inbringing of his malis and answering thairintill according to the kingis rentale the samyn discharge to stand of nane avale to him.

As to the landis of Mul and utheris landis that the said Lauchlane had of befoir of the Kingis grace now desirit in fewferm be him.

The lordis counsalis my lord governour to latt thame stand in tak to the said Lauchlane as he had thame sen the Kingis landis may nocht be gevin in heretage the said Lauchlane fynd and cautioun for payment of the malis and dewities of the said landis.

As to the jvstifying of Donaldis twa brethir and forfactour aganis the said Donald the temporale lordis will shaw my lord governour thair mynde quhilkis temporale lordis that is to say Huntlie Levinax Drummond Ogelby Balwery and Kers referris to my lord governour quhat he thinkis to be done with the saidis personis. And the remanent of my saidis lordis temporale that is to say Ergile Cassillis Erskin Borthnick Avendale Lees Kincavil Capitan of the Castel Comptrollare and Otterburn deliveris the saidis personis to be justifyt eftir thair demeritis.

The lordis counsalis my lord governour to admit any resignatioun of landis or officis maid in his handis be resignatioun personaly maid be the possessouris in favouris of the said Lauchlane and to gif him infeftment thairof referrand the samin resignatioun and infeftment to my lord gouvernouris plessour.

LACHLANE MAKLANE OF DOWARD
Wt my hand on ye pen." *

John MacLean of Lochbuy and Alexander MacLeod of Harris demanded and received remission for themselves and for their followers on giving up hostages; but MacLeod demanded in addition a heritable grant of the lands of Trouterness, in Skye, but was continued as king's tenant as formerly.

The extensive power granted to Argyle and MacLean was more nominal than real.

The severity cast upon Lachlan Catanach for his demand for the execution of Sir Donald's brothers is inconsiderate, in singling him out and placing the entire censure upon him. Let the following points be fully considered:

---

* *Acta Dominorum Concilii*, Vol. XXIX, fol. 130.

1. Let it be admitted that the demand was cruel, yet Argyle should be brought under the same censure, for he demanded and received power to grant remission to all rebels except "Sir Donald of the Ilis his brethir and clan and clan-donale," and the last he was to pursue with "fire and sword." 2. The lords of council away from the scene of action, and uninfluenced by any personal injury, recommended that the two brothers of Sir Donald should be put to death. Of this matter Gregory says :* " In regard to the execution of the two brothers the council were divided in opinion; the majority being in favor of capital punishment, while the others wished the matter to be left entirely to the regent; and, although it can not be positively affirmed, there is reason to think that the opinion of the majority prevailed." If Lachlan should come under the ban, the others should not be spared. 3. Lachlan MacLean labored under great provocation. Sir Donald had intentionally deceived him, as already noted, and besides had refused to take counsel regarding his insane and reckless proceedings. Under pretense of obeying the government, Lachlan went innocently into rebellion. It was enough to exasperate the leaders, and cause them to resort to strong measures. 4. Was the demand of Lachlan any worse than many a sober act perpetrated by the throne, or in the name of the regent, and by those in close intimacy with the government, not only during that particular period, but later, as well as in former times? 5. Lachlan was unable to write his own name, thus being constantly exposed to deception by designing men. The whole document shows the handiwork of Colin Campbell, third Earl of Argyle. How far he may have deceived Lachlan will never be known; that he was capable of it his character amply testifies. Proof of this will be adduced in its proper place.

The official records show that on September 6, 1515, "Lachlane Makclane of Doward and Alister Makcloid of Dunvegan, and their people, received a respite, for besieging and taking of the King's castles of Carnebog and Dunskaith, and assisting Donald Ilis of Lochalsh, and other treasonable deeds; to endure till 1st January next." †

" Tack to Lauchlen Maklane of Doward of the King's lands of Mull and Murwerne for 11 years. 8 March 1516–17." ‡

" Letter in favor of said Lauchlan giving him power to raise and gather all the tenants who obeyed him before in the time of the late King, for the weal of the Kingdom, and the just quarrels of the said Lauchlan, excepting

---

* *Western Highlands*, p. 123. † *Registrum Secreti Sigilli*, Vol. V., fol. 12. ‡ *Ibid.*, Vol. V., fol. 100.

the King, the Governor, and the earl of Argyle, his lieutenant. 10 March 1516–17." *

" Precept of Remission to Lauchlan Makclane of Doward, Donald Makclane, Gillenwin Makneil of Barra, Dulleis Makwidy of Ulva, Neil Makkynna of Moisnes, and Lauchlane Makclane of Ardgowr, their kin and servants, for all that passed before the date thereof. 12 March 1516–17." †

" Precept for gift in favour of Lauchlan Makclane of Doward, of the fermes of the lands of Teree, for his good and faithful service to the King, and to bring in the King's fermes on the south of Ardmurch, except the lands which belonged to John Makclane of Ardnamurchane, for which the said John shall be answerable. 14 March 1516–17." ‡

There is also a " respite to Alexander Makillan of Duford and Alexander Makcloid of Dunvegane, and their kin and friends to the number of 100 persons, to come to Edinburgh or elsewhere in the realm, on lawful business, to last till 15 March next. Edinburgh 6 January 1516." ‖ The above Alexander MacLean must have been one of the principal men living in Castle Duard.

There is an episode in the life of Lachlan Catanach which has been variously told, and of such a nature as to be the subject of poesy and dramatic art, and particularly made notorious in Joanna Baillie's " Family Legend." Notwithstanding the different versions, the ground-work of the story has never been denied. Lachlan's first wife was Elizabeth, daughter of Archibald Campbell, second Earl of Argyle. The account of the story, as given by Gregory,§ is as follows: " Either from the circumstance of this union being unfruitful, or more probably owing to some domestic quarrels, he (Lachlan) determined to get rid of his wife. Some accounts say that she had twice attempted her husband's life, but whatever the cause may have been, MacLean, following the advice of two of his vassals, who exercised a considerable influence over him from the tie of fosterage, caused his lady to be exposed on a rock, which was only visible at low water, intending that she should be swept away by the return of the tide. This rock lies between the island of Lismore and the coast of Mull, and is still known by the name of the 'Lady's Rock.' From this perilous situation, the intended victim was rescued by a boat accidentally passing, and conveyed to her brother's house. Her relations, although much exasperated against MacLean, smothered their resentment for a time, but only to break out afterward with greater vio-

---

* *Registrum Secreti Sigilli*, Vol. V., fol. 100.   † *Ibid.*, Vol. V., fol. 101.   ‡ *Ibid.*   ‖ *Ibid.*, Vol. V., fol. 80.   § *Western Highlands*, p. 128.

lence; for the Laird of Duard, being in Edinburgh, was surprised, when in bed, and assassinated by Sir John Campbell of Calder, the lady's brother."

The above is generally considered as the authoritative account. The following differs materially, and never has been printed before. It was related to me by the present chief, Sir Fitzroy Donald MacLean, Bart., who heard it in Mull. Argyle's daughter did not desire to marry MacLean, for she had a youthful lover at Inverary. But having considered the matter fully, she thought by marrying the Lord of Duard she might gain such an influence over him as in the end would succeed in enriching the estates of her brother. With this view she consented to become the wife of Lachlan. From her lover she would not be parted, so he was disguised as a monk, and passed for her confessor. In the passage across the Firth of Lorn, an attendant, belonging to the house of MacLean, suspicioning something from their actions, pulled off the cowl from the head of the would-be monk, and thus exposed the youth. When the birlinn arrived at Duard Castle, MacLean was in the midst of his orgies. He was accustomed to sleep with a sharp sword by his side; to this she strongly objected, which made him very angry. She now commenced to plot for the betrayal of the lands of MacLean into the hands of Argyle. This, as well as the youth disguised as a monk, was duly reported to the Lord of Duard, which caused much disturbance. MacLean was called one day away from the castle, and while he was gone his two foster-brothers, thinking to do him a favor, seized Elizabeth, and left her on the rock to perish. From this perilous position she was rescued by a passing boat of the MacLeans, and who, knowing the domestic infelicity of the couple, carried her to Inverary.

The version as preserved by the Pennycross manuscript differs from all others: "Lachlan was a few years married, but had no child by her, on which she made every attempt to alienate the estate of Duard from the family in favor of her brother John, who a little before then had married Marellia, daughter of Calder of Calder by whom he got that estate. Lady Elizabeth, finding her husband not to be wrought upon to transfer his family estate, made an attempt to poison him with cavalle she had made for him. On account of this, she was left on the rock, known still by the name of 'Lady's Rock.' Her brother, Colin, earl of Argyle, ever after kept her under a sort of confinement, and she was even struck out in the family genealogy* from amongst her sisters." This statement doubtless is the most authentic.

---

* George Crawford's notes on the MS genealogy of the family of Argyle.

An Independent Clan—1493 to 1598.

The date when this occurrence took place, judging by Lachlan's other marriages and other events, must have been between the years 1490 and 1495.

Lachlan afterward married Margaret, daughter of Sir Dugald Campbell, of Achinbreck,* by whom he had no issue. His third wife was Marian, daughter of John MacLean of Treshnish, commonly called the Captain of Cairnburg. By her he had two sons, Eachann, or Hector Mór, his heir and successor, and the notorious Ailean na Sop. He also had a bastard son, Patrick, by one Catherine Kay, who became bishop of the Isles.

Lachlan's marriages must all have taken place before he became chief of the clan, for his oldest son was of sufficient age to become chief on his father's death; and besides that, with both Hector and Ailean grown, or nearly grown, he resided for several years with his family at Cairnburg, having made himself master of that stronghold, where he received visits from those friendly chiefs near him—MacNeil of Barra and his family being the most frequent guest.

In 1526 he obtained a charter under the great seal from King James V.: "Lachlan MacLean de dowart terarum de Torosay cum Castro Baronie de Dowart Broloss, &c." †

In 1527, Lachlan Catanach, having procured for himself letters of protection ‡ from the king, and thereby believing himself secure, repaired to the city of Edinburgh. While in bed, and entirely unprotected, he was stabbed to death by Sir John Campbell of Calder, a brother of the Earl of Argyle. This murder occasioned an old song, a fragment of which still remains:

> " Fie John, for shame yer sare to blame
> For sic an ugly prankit,
> To steal so weighty to his bed
> And prick him in his blankets.
> Had ye sae thick been wi auld Nick,
> Afore ye got the Calder,
> Ye might hae gaen hame to your den
> Without Marella Calder."

The reason for this murder is easily traced. Some have asserted that it was because of the exposure of Campbell's sister on the rock; but that occurrence happened over thirty years before, and since then Argyle and MacLean had acted in concert. Neither could it have been because John Camp-

---

* *Vide* Pennycross and Ardgour MSS. † *Pub. Archives*, Lib. XX., No. 49. ‡ Tytler's *History of Scotland*, Vol. II., p. 349.

bell failed to obtain the estate of MacLean through treachery of his sister; for an opportunity for assassination had presented itself before. The character of Argyle points to him as either leader or privy to the assassination. It is undeniable that it was considered by the Argyle family that Lachlan must be put out of the way. Hence, assassination was resorted to. That Colin Campbell, third Earl of Argyle, was capable of resorting to this, is proved by his general character. Gregory says* that in 1529 it dawned upon the king and council that Colin, third Earl of Argyle, who held the office of royal lieutenant, had secretly fomented the disturbances in the Isles, in hopes of benefiting by the forfeitures which were expected to follow. Tytler † says: "The Earl of Argyle, who, holding the high office of governor of the Isles, was frequently tempted to represent any attack upon himself or his adherents as a rebellion against the authority of the sovereign."

The murder of a chief so popular as Lachlan Catanach, of necessity would not go long unavenged. About this time Alexander MacDonald of Islay, smarting under the sense of injustice done him by Argyle, through an invidious attempt to appropriate his lands, was ready for open rebellion. The two clans—MacLean and MacDonald—readily joined together; the former to avenge the death of their chief, and the latter to resent a gross injustice. The combined clans, equipped for war, made a descent upon Roseneath, Craignish, and other lands belonging to the Campbells, which they ravaged with fire and sword, killing at the same time many of the inhabitants. The Campbells, on the other hand, retaliated with equal ferocity, and the isles of Mull, Tiree, with the wide district of Morvern, were abandoned to indiscriminate plunder. The Campbells, however, were worsted, for by August of 1529 Sir John Campbell, the murderer of Lachlan, on behalf of his brother, the Earl of Argyle, appealed to the council for powers of an extraordinary nature, to enable him to restore the peace of the country. He wanted all the substantial householders in the shires of Dumbarton and Renfrew, and the bailliaries of Carrich, Kyle, and Cunningham commanded to meet Argyle, with provisions for twenty days. The council refused to issue the order, on account of the harvest, but gave direction for a cannon, two falconets, and three barrels of powder to be forwarded from Dumbarton, should it be necessary to besiege any of the strongholds of the Isles. The council, having its suspicions fully aroused concerning Argyle, sent a minion to Alexander of Islay, to summon him and his followers to lay down their arms under

* *Western Highlands*, p. 139.   † *History of Scotland*, Vol. II., p. 349.

pain of treason; and also to treat with that chief about coming under protection. The mission was unsuccessful, and but little progress was made during the next six months; but in the spring of 1530, preparations were made on an extensive scale for bringing the clans into subjection. "The tenants of the Isles, according to a roll of them placed in Argyle's hands, were to be summoned to come to the king's presence, upon the 24th of May, 'to commune with his majesty for good rule of the Isles.' They were likewise to be prohibited from giving any assistance to the rebels, or from convocating the king's lieges in arms, under the pain of treason; which the men of Carrick, Kyle, and Cunningham, of Balquhidder, Braidalbane, Rannoch, Apnadull, Athole, Menteith, Butt, and Arran, were to be charged, under high penalties, to join the king's lieutenant at such places as he should appoint, and to continue with him in the service for a month; and the burgs of Ayr, Irvine, Glasgow, Renfrew, and Dumbarton, were to send their boats with provisions for the army, for which payment was to be made. In case any of the Islemen should be afraid to trust themselves in the low country, they were offered protections for their coming to the king, and for thirty days additional, to admit of their returning home safe.

"These preparations produced some effect. In the month of May, nine of the principal Islanders—Hector MacLean of Duard, John MacLean of Lochbuy, John Moydertach, captain of the Clanranald, Alexander MacIan of Ardnamurchan, Alexander MacLeod of Harris, the Laird of Coll (MacLean), John MacLeod of Lewis, and Donald Gruamach of Dunskaich—sent by the hands of Hector MacLean of Duard, one of their number, offers of submission to the king, who immediately granted them a protection against Argyle and any others, provided they would come to Edinburgh, or wherever the king should happen to be holding court, before the 20th June, and remain as long as his majesty should require their attendance; it being always understood that the protection was to last for twenty days after their departure from the Highlands. As an additional security for their safety in coming and going, the king promised to take two of the following hostages from the Earl of Argyle: Duncan Campbell of Glenurchy, Archibald Campbell of Auchinbreck, Archibald Campbell of Skipnish, and Duncan Campbell of Ilangerig, who were to be confined in Edinburgh Castle. Colin, Earl of Argyle, dying in this year, was succeeded by his son Archibald, fourth earl, who immediately took the oath of allegiance to the king, and was appointed to all the offices held by his father and grandfather. Meantime, owing to the sickness and death of the late earl, the king's service in the Isles had remained stationary; and, in the month of November it was resolved that the king should proceed in person against the rebels in the following April, which term was afterward altered to the first of June; and, in contemplation of the royal expedition, various important arrangements were made. . . . Finally, a parliament was summoned to meet at Edinburgh on the 24th of April, to pass sentence of forfeiture against the Islemen who should then continue disobedient.

"Alexander of Islay hastened to open a communication with the king, as soon as he became aware of the magnitude of the royal expedition; and, having received a protection and safeguard, he came to his majesty at Stirling, made his submission, and was received into favor upon certain conditions. The same course was pursued by Hector MacLean of Duard; and, as these chiefs had been the principal leaders of the insurgents, the rebellion might now be looked upon as nearly at an end." *

The king found it necessary to deprive Archibald Campbell, fourth Earl of Argyle, of the chief command of the Isles, and confer the same upon Alexander of Islay, which caused Argyle, with the whole strength of his vassals and retainers, to throw himself into the arms of England.†

XII. Hector Mór, Twelfth Chief of MacLean.

Lachlan Catanach was succeeded as chieftain and Lord of Duard by his son Eachann, better known as Hector Mór, or Hector the Great, in 1527. He is described by the seanachaidhs as being good, kind, affectionate, and brave, an accomplished politician and an approved warrior; and that in him the clan realized all it desired in a noble chieftain. To most of his vassals he granted extended leases, by way of encouragement in the improvement of lands and the building of more comfortable dwellings. He lived altogether, while permitted to do so by his troublesome neighbors with which he was surrounded, more like a noble of modern times than a feudal baron. He made many improvements on the demesne of Duard; and was the founder of that noble addition to Duard Castle called the Great Tower. His alliance was courted by many of the powerful lords; and the king thought it of importance to secure his loyalty by calling him into his council. Hence, we find him taking his seat in parliament as one of the lords of the kingdom.

In private life his character was above reproach, and in his warlike pursuits he acted upon that system which had legal sanction. His domestic establishment was conducted with becoming splendor; he provided handsomely

---

* Gregory's *Western Highlands*, pp. 132–136; see Mackenzie's *History of the MacDonalds*, pp. 159–162; also, Tytler's *History of Scotland*, Vol. II., p. 350. † See Tytler's *History of Scotland*, Vol. II., p. 352.

for his daughters, who were all married to leading men in the kingdom; and he left to his son and heir an unburdened estate, with a considerable amount of money.

However much inclined Hector Mór may have been to the arts of peace, yet in feudal times, with invidious foes and warlike preparations around him, it was impossible for the chief of MacLean to be an idle spectator. It has already been narrated how he avenged the murder of his father. For the part he took in burning the houses of Roseneath, Lennox, and Craignish, he received a remission on June 8, 1531.* He had previously received a letter (Edinburgh, June 1, 1827), "charging the Sheriff of Inverness to command Colin Campbell, earl of Argyle, Sir John Campbell of Calder, Knight, his brother, and their accomplices, that they make no hosting, convocation of the leiges, or invasion upon the said Hector, his kin and friends." †

For some reason, the nature of which is now unknown, a feud broke out between the MacLeans of Lochbuy and those of Duard, about the year 1537, during which John Og MacLean of Lochbuy and his two elder sons were killed. The old feud between the Camerons and MacLeans was renewed, but could not have been of much moment, for we only receive a trace of it.

The Western Isles were not only subjected to the strifes of the avaricious at court, but also to unwise actions upon the part of rulers. In 1540, James V. determined upon an imposing expedition to the Western Isles. During his minority, the northern districts and western islands had not only been grievously neglected, but, in a measure, had been reduced to a deplorable state. So the king determined to visit the territory in person, overawe the rebellious chiefs, enforce obedience to the laws, and reduce within the limits of order and good government that portion of his dominion; and to accomplish this purpose, he fitted out a fleet of twelve ships, amply furnished with artillery, provided for a long journey, and commanded by the most skillful mariners in the kingdom. This powerful fleet quitted the Firth of Forth toward the end of May. After passing the Orkneys, the expedition sailed "to the coast of Sutherland for the purpose of seizing Donald MacKay of Strathnaver, which was effected with difficulty. Thence the fleet proceeded to the isle of Lewis, where Ruari MacLeod, with his principal kinsmen, met the king, and were made to accompany him in his further progress. The west coast of the isle of Skye was next visited, and Alexander of Dunvegan, lord of that part of the island, was constrained to embark in the royal fleet.

---

* *Reg. Sec. Sig.*, Vol. IX., fol. 18.   † *Ibid*, Vol. VI., fol. 66.

Coasting round by the north of Skye, the king then came to the district of Trouterness, so lately desolated by the chief of Sleat. Here various chieftains, claiming their descent from the ancient lord of the Isles, came to meet their sovereign—particularly John Moydertach, captain of the Clanranald, Alexander of Glengarry, and others of 'MacConeyllis kin.' These chieftains probably hoped to secure the royal favor by coming to meet the king before the course of his voyage led him to their own districts. From Trouterness, James proceeded, by the coast of Ross, to Kintail, where he was joined by the chief of the MacKenzies; and then sailing southwards by the Sound of Sleat, he visited, in succession, the isles of Mull and Islay, and the districts of Kintyre and Knapdale, taking with him, on his departure, Hector MacLean of Duard, and James MacDonald of Islay, the two principal leaders of the South Isles. He then landed at Dumbarton, but sent the fleet, with the captive chiefs on board, back to Edinburgh, by the route followed in coming to the Isles." Having the chiefs in his power, he exacted such terms from them as he thought would be necessary to maintain obedience. Some of the chiefs were liberated by giving hostages, but others were detained until after the king's death, "and were then only liberated by a piece of state policy." *

As might have been anticipated, this violent seizure of the chieftains would necessarily result in exasperating them, although they might repress their resentment for a time. Two years afterward James V. died in the flower of his age, and was succeeded by his infant daughter, the unfortunate Mary, during whose reign, and the regency preceding, Scotland was distracted by foreign aggression, domestic feuds, and unscrupulous factions.

In 1543, Donald Dubh, who had been in hopeless captivity for nearly forty years, again managed to effect his escape. On his arrival in the Isles, he was received with enthusiasm by the same clans which had supported him in 1506; and, with their assistance, he at once commenced preparations for the expulsion of the Earls of Argyle and Huntly from their unholy acquisitions in the lordship of the Isles during his long imprisonment.

In all the documents illustrative of the proceedings of Donald, we find that Lennox was acknowledged by the Islesmen to be the true regent and second person of the realm of Scotland; and, on this account, they became entangled in the interests of England.

With the advice of the chieftains, Donald opened negotiations with the

---

* Gregory's *Western Highlands*, p. 147; see also MacKenzie's *History of the MacDonalds*, p. 171; also, Tytler's *History of Scotland*, Vol. II., p. 366.

Earl of Lennox through Rory MacAlister, bishop elect of the Isles, and Patrick MacLean. The document, dated July 28, 1545, is a diplomatic curiosity, and presents the interesting fact that not one of the signers was able to write his own name. It also shows what gross injustice they were forced to labor under:

> "Quhairfor, your Lordships sall considder we have beyne auld enemys to the realme of Scotland, and quhen they had peasche with ye kings hienis, thei hanged, hedit, presoned, and destroied many of our kyn, friendis, and forbearis, as testifies be our Master, th' Erle of Ross, now the king's grace's subject, ye quhilk hath lyin in presoun afoir he was borne of his moder, and is not releiffit with their will, bot now laitlie be ye grace of God. In lykewise, the Lord Maclain's fader was cruellie murdressit, under traist, in his bed, in the town of Edinbruch, be Sir John Campbell of Calder, brudir to th' Erll of Argyle. The capitane of Clanranald, this last zeir ago, in his defens, slew the Lord Lovett, his son-in-law, his three brethren, with xiii scoir of men; and many uther crewell slachter, burnying, and herschip that hath beyn betwix us and the saidis Scottis, the quhilk war lang to wryte. Hector Maclane, lord of Doward; Johne Macallister, capitane of Clanranald; Rorye Macleod of Lewis; Alexander Macleod of Dumbeggane; Murdoch Maclane of Lochbuy; Angus Maconnill; Alane Maclane of Turloske, brudir germane to the Lord Maclane; Archibald Maconnill, capitane of Clan Houston; Alexander Mackeyn of Ardnamurchane; Jhone Maclane of Coll; Gilliganan Macneill of Barray; Ewin Macinnon of Straguhordill; Jhone Macquorre of Ulway; Jhone Maclane of Ardgour, Alexander Ranaldsoun of Glengarrie; Angus Ranaldsoun of Knwdort; Donald Maclane of Kengariloch." *

The commissioners were well received, and the terms offered by them were accepted by the King of England, who, as a proof of his sincerity, soon remitted a considerable sum of money to the Isles, which was placed in the hands of the chief of MacLean to enable him to carry on the war with vigor. Considerable assistance otherwise, in the way of men as well as of money, appears to have been afforded by the English king.

"On the 5th of August, the lords and barons of the Isles were at Knockfergus in Ireland, with a force of four thousand men, and a hundred and eighty galleys; when, in presence of two commissioners, sent by the earl of Lennox, and of the constable, mayor, and magistrates of that town, they took the oath of allegiance to the king of England, 'at the command of the said earl of Lennox.'" †

The death of Donald Dubh, in 1545, left no claimant to the Lordship of the Isles. The Islanders, after a while, chose James MacDonald of Islay, as their leader—a chieftain whose pretentions to the Lordship of the Isles were much inferior to those of Donald Gorm of Sleat. However, he was opposed by many who had been the strongest supporters of Donald Dubh—such as the

---

* Tytler's *History of Scotland*, Vol. II., p. 349. † Gregory's *Western Highlands*, p. 170.

MacLeans (with the exception of Ailean nan Sop of Gigha and Torloisk), the MacLeods, the MacNeills of Barra, the MacKinnons, and the MacQuarries. All of these now endeavored, and, with success, to effect their reconciliation with the regent, the Earl of Arran. This defection of the Island lords toward James MacDonald may be accounted for on the ground that he had hitherto strenuously opposed the whole movement of his brother chieftains in favor of Donald Dubh.

In the year 1557, while Hector Mór was engaged in constructing his additions to Duard Castle, Archibald Campbell, fourth Earl of Argyle, ordered an armed force against him. This grew out of an engagement between Ailean nan Sop and some of Argyle's people, in which the latter were defeated. Ailean, it appears, was bent on having more revenge on account of the murder of his father. Argyle ordered all his vassals to meet him at Clachan-Soal, on an appointed day, for the purpose of going to invade the island of Mull, and to have their birlinns or galleys ready for that purpose; Campbell of Duntroon, who was a great friend of MacLean, told Argyle he had no birlinn, and that he could get none at so short a warning; but Argyle would take no excuse, and go he must. The day before Argyle was to sail for the intended expedition, Duntroon went to Duard, and, on arriving there, MacLean invited him into the castle, but Duntroon excused himself, as he was in a hurry, being obliged to meet his chief next morning early; but that he had come to ask a favor of him, which was that he (MacLean) should give him one of his birlinns, as he was ordered by Argyle to meet him next day at Clachan-Soal with one, and he had none. MacLean asked him what expedition they were going on. Duntroon answered: "To invade yourself." "Very well," returned MacLean, "you shall have one, and welcome." A birlinn was ordered completely equipped for Duntroon. Just before leaving, he asked MacLean what he should say to Argyle if he questioned him. "You may tell him," replied MacLean, "if he comes in peace and friendship, he shall be received with a hearty welcome; but, if he comes otherwise, I am equally ready to receive him." Early next morning, Duntroon went to Clachan-Soal, where Argyle and all his vassals were assembled. Argyle, seeing a fine birlinn coming to harbor, went to see who it was. Finding it was Duntroon, he asked him where he had been, as he noticed he had come from Mull. Duntroon replied that he had told his lordship he had no birlinn, and, since he would not take that for an excuse, he had gone to Duard to ask one of MacLean, which he had given him, and was now ready to go whatever way his lordship was pleased to order him. "Does MacLean know that it is against himself I am going?" "He does, my lord; I told him," replied Duntroon. "And what said he?" "He was looking over his masons building an addition to his castle," replied Duntroon; "and he said, if you came in peace and friendship, you and your friends would receive a hearty welcome; but, if you came otherwise, he was equally prepared to receive you." For some time Argyle was silent; but, finally, asked Duntroon what his advice would be. Duntroon, in substance, answered that, if his advice should be taken, his lordship had no business to keep up a quarrel on account of his aunt's and uncle's bad behavior, which, in justice, should be consigned to oblivion; that the earl should marry one of MacLean's beautiful daughters; and that Janet, the earl's daughter, should be given to MacLean's handsome son and heir. The earl thought the advice good, and, taking some of his friends along with him, repaired to Duard. They were well received at the castle, and, before departing, the double marriage took place, Argyle marrying Catherine, second youngest daughter of Hector Mór, for his third wife. His daughter, Janet, at the same time, was married to Hector Mór's eldest son and heir, Eachann Og.*

The repeated failures of the western clans to re-establish, in any shape, the old lordship of the Isles, proved to them the futility of making another attempt. Having no longer a common object, the clans, by degrees, became estranged from each other, and the less powerful ones were forced to contend against the aggressions of their stronger neighbors. This caused many disturbances throughout the Highlands, which often called for redress on the part of the government. The MacLeans took their share in these broils. Among the first to receive any note was "the dispute between MacLean of Duard and MacLean of Coll (in 1561), which is chiefly remarkable as indicating the progress of the feudal system in the Isles. Duard, who was generally acknowledged as chief of his clan, insisted that Coll should follow and serve him in all his private quarrels, like the other gentlemen of the tribe. Coll, however, who held all his lands direct from the crown, declined to follow this haughty chief, claiming the privileges of a free baron, who owed no service but to the sovereign as his feudal superior. Irritated at the independent tone assumed by Coll, and determined to assert what he conceived to be his just claims, the lord of Duard, taking advantage of the other's temporary absence, caused his lands to be ravaged, and his tenants to be imprisoned. Such, indeed, was the tyranny exercised by Duard over his weaker neighbor, that

---

* *Vide* Pennycross MS.

the family of Coll, from being in a prosperous condition, was reduced, in a short time, to the brink of ruin. Nor was it till after the lapse of several years, that the sufferer by these violent and illegal proceedings succeeded in drawing the attention of the privy council to his situation; so great was the power and influence of his oppressor. The decision of that tribunal was, as might have been expected, adverse to the claims of Duard; who was ordered to make reparation to Coll for the injuries done to the property and tenants of the latter; and, likewise, to refrain from molesting him or his followers in future. At a later period we shall find that the feud between these families was only suspended, not concluded, by this decision of the privy council.

" The next dispute was between the MacLeans on the one part, and MacDonalds of Islay on the other. This affair demands our attention, not so much on account of its origin, which was merely a quarrel as to the right of occupancy of certain crown lands in Islay, as because it was the commencement of a long and bloody feud between these tribes, in which both suffered severely, and which led eventually to the utter ruin of that powerful branch of the Clandonald. Of the early details of this feud, which was aggravated by previous disputes regarding the island of Gigha, little is found in the usual sources of information. The Isles of Mull, Tiree, and Coll were invaded (1562) by the Clandonald of Sleat; and it may be supposed that the MacLeans and their allies were not backward in similar hostilities. It is uncertain which side was the aggressor; but from the tenor of certain proceedings before the privy council, it appears probable that the MacLeans were to blame —a fact which, indeed, is distinctly asserted by a historian, himself a privy councillor in the reign of James VI. According to this writer, the Rinns of Islay (the lands in dispute) were actually occupied by the MacLeans, who claimed to hold these lands as crown tenants; but the decision of the privy council established that James MacDonald of Islay was really the crown tenant, and that the MacLeans, if they continued to remain on the lands, must hold them of MacDonald, under the same conditions of personal and other services as the rest of MacDonald's vassals in Islay held their lands. Such a decision must have been, no doubt, very galling to a powerful and high-spirited tribe like the MacLeans; and we can scarcely be surprised at the deep-rooted hostility which so long prevailed between them and the Clandonald, when we consider the point of honor which was involved in their dispute. Such was the inveteracy with which the rival chiefs pursued their quarrel, even after the matter had been brought before the privy council, that, in 1565, they were compelled to find sureties each to the amount of ten thousand pounds, for their abstinence from mutual hostilities. It deserves to be remarked, that Archibald, fifth earl of Argyle, was one of the sureties for each chief, he being connected by marriage, with both; as it proves that this nobleman did not contemplate extending his power and influence in the same unscrupulous manner that some of his successors afterwards did, at the expense both of the MacDonalds and MacLeans."*

Under the chieftainship of Hector Mór, the MacLeans put forth their last efforts in behalf of the Lords of the Isles; also, under the same chief, the two clans became estranged, and entered upon a long course of strife, which was detrimental to the interests of both.

The lover of exact history is always interested in official records. Concerning Hector Mór, the following facts have been culled:

On January 9, 1539-40, Hector passes over a charter in favor of his son and heir the lands of Torosay, castle of Duard, lands of Brolass, Tiree, with office of bailliery thereof, lands in Knapdale, Jura, Morvern, and Lochaber, but reserving life rent for the same.†

February 11, 1539-40, he obtained a respite "for all crimes past, to endure for 19 years." ‡

November 12, 1542, received a charter for lands of Kilmichell and More, in Islay.||

"Precept for charter under the great seal, to Hector McClane of Doward, heritably, of the lands and barony of Argour, which belonged before to John McCarlych of Argour, but now to the Queen as *ultima* hæres, because the said John died without lawful heirs; to hold of the crown on the same terms as Doward, being included therein. 4 February 1548-9." §

June 23, 1553, he received charter for the lands of Ulva and Laganvalsagary, in the shire of Terbert.**

January 26, 1557, he gave a charter to Janet Campbell, daughter of Earl of Argyle, of the lands of Dunnowlycht, Rannochquhen, etc., in Knapdale and Lochaber.††

The earliest description of the Western Isles made from personal ob-

---

* Gregory's *Western Highlands*, pp. 190-192. It is not to be understood by the above quotation that Gregory intends to give Argyle generally a good character. Tytler expressly calls him "a venal baron" (*History of Scotland*, Vol. III., p. 203). Tytler farther says (*Ibid.*, 244), that Argyle was a participant in the murder of Lord Darnley. See also pp. 231, 237, and 241, same volume.

† *Reg. Sec. Sig.*, Vol. XIII., fol. 43.   ‡ *Ibid.*, fol. 54. || *Ibid.*, Vol. XVI., fol. 77.   § *Ibid.*, Vol. XXIII., fol. 37.   ** *Ibid.*, Vol. XXV., fol. 84.   †† *Ibid.*, Vol. XXIX., fol. 15.

servation is that by Donald Monro, High Dean of the Isles, who traveled through most of them in 1549. As it was during the lordship of Hector Mór, it will be of much interest to those interested in the Clan MacLean. What he says in reference to the lands of this clan is here given in the same order as in the original: "Nairest that iyle (Gigha) layes Duray, ane ather fyne forrest for deire," owned in "pairt be MacGullayne of Douard, pairt be McGellayne of Kinlochbuy," etc. "Lunge is possist be McGillayne of Doward, in feu fra the earl of Ergile." In Ila is a castle "callit Lochgurne, quhilk is biggit in ane iyle within the said fresche water loche far fra land, pertaining of auld to the Clandonald of Kintyre, now usurped by McGillayne of Doward." "Twelfe myle northward from the iyle of Colnansay lyes the iyle of Mull, ane grate rough ile, noch the les it is fertile and fruitful. This ile contains in lenth from the northeist to the southweste twenty-four myles, and in breid from the eist southeist to west northwest uther twenty-four myles, with certain woodes, maney deire, and verey fair hunting games, with maney grate mertines and cunnings for hunting, with a guid raid fornet Colmkill, callit Pollaisse. There is sevin paroche kirks within this iyle, and thre castles, to wit the castle of Doward, a strenthey place, bigged on a craige at the sea syde; the castle of Lochbowy, pertaining to McGillayne of Lochbowy; the castle of Arose, which in former time pertinet to the lord of the iyles, and now is bruked be McGillayne of Doward. In this ile there is twa guid fresche waters, ane of them are callit Ananva, and the water of Glenforsay, full of salmond, with uther waters that has salmond in them, but not in sic aboundance as the twa forsaid waters. This ile hath alsa salt water loches, to wit, Loch Ear, ane little small loche, with guid take of herringes: this loche layes in the southwest of the countrey. Then is Loch Fyne, quherin ther is a guid take of herrings. Northwest fra this loche, lyes Loche Seaforte, guid for the herring fishing. Lykwayes on the east pairt of the countrey layes ane loche, callit Lochepetit. Narrest this loche, in the southe southeist, layes Lochbowy, a fair braid loche, quherin there is grate take of herring and uther fishings. This iyle pertains pairtly to McGillayne of Doward, pairtly to McGillayne of Lochbowy, pairtly to McKynnoun, and pairtly to the Clandonnald of awld." "Upon the narrest coste of Mull lays ane iyle callit Calfe, ane myle of lenthe, full of woods, with ane sufficient raid for shipes, perteyning to McGillayne of Doward." "Befor the castel of Aross lyes twa iles, perteyning to McGillayne of Doward." "The ile of Knightsness (near Aross) perteining to McGillayne of Doward." "Ellan Madie (south from Duard) pertains to McGillayne of Doward." "Ellan Moir perteining to

McGillayne of Lochbuy." "Scalpay in heritage perteines to McGillayne of Dowarde." This work gives a brief description of two hundred and nine isles.

Reference has been made to the building of the addition to Duard Castle by Hector Mór. It is probable that all the additions to the ancient tower were made at this time. The castle is located on a point of land forming the extreme north-eastern part of the island of Mull. The point of land projects into the Sound of Mull, with Duard Bay on the west and the Firth of Lorn on the east. It is two miles from the southern extremity of Lismore, and three miles from the nearest point of Morvern. The castle is located upon a perpendicular rock, facing the sea, which rises to a height of about one hundred feet. The castle may be approached from the land on the eastern and southern sides. The northern and western sides present the face of the perpendicular rock. The castle derives its name from *Dubh*, meaning black, and "Aird," a height, or promontory; and hence the word means Black Promontory. Anciently it was generally written *Doward*, and recently it has been shortened, but improperly, into *Duart*. It should be written *Duard*, thus preserving its etymology. Originally the castle consisted of a single tower composed of three stories about fifty feet in height. This tower, with the exception of the roof and various floors, is still in a perfect condition. The tower or oldest part corresponds to the architecture of the thirteenth century. Its walls on two sides are fourteen feet thick, and the other sides ten feet, the interior being forty-four by twenty-two feet. The stair, still entire, winds up through the wall, which separates it from the center square or court-yard. In this wall, along the course of the stair, are crenells opening into the outer court or square. The tiers or apartments were supported by beams resting upon corbels. The windows are deep recesses, forming acute angles toward the entrance of the light, and on either side of the window is a long flat stone, resting upon rubble work, raised to a height of an ordinary chair. The first story is now filled with debris. On the north side of the tower a platform was left on the rock. This platform was walled in by Hector Mór, at the same time he added the ample court-yard on the east. The eastern wall is seventy-nine feet long, and the north and south walls one hundred and twenty-six feet and three inches. The northern part of the new structure was separated from the court-yard by a wall, and used for a dwelling. The space on the rock inclosed by a wall was used for soldiers. The dungeon was on the first floor of the new structure, and the magazines in the court-yard. The castle was entered by a doorway

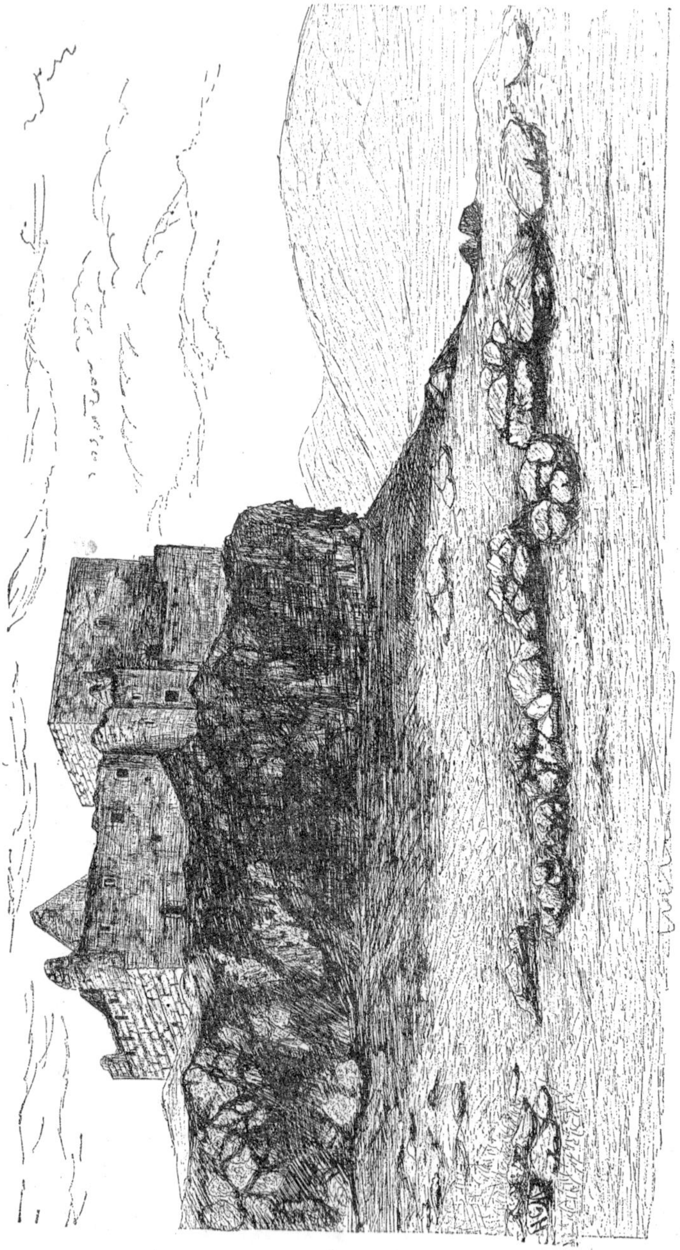

RUINS OF DUARD CASTLE.

An Independent Clan—1493 to 1598.

at the south four and one-half feet in width, protected by an iron gate. Originally it was defended by a postern gate, with portcullis, and defended by a barbican. The moat protecting the eastern wall may still be traced. The walls of the new addition are neither so thick nor so high as those of the high tower. Nothing is being done to protect these additional walls. Even a superficial view shows the site to have been well selected, and the castle one of great strength, and very formidable for the times in which it was built.

Aros Castle was another stronghold of the MacLeans. It is located on the shore of Aros Bay, an inlet of Salen Bay. It was a royal castle of the Lords of the Isles, by one of whom it is said to have been built, but undoubtedly is of much older date. It rests in a very picturesque manner on

Duard Castle in 1677.

the summit of a steep rock facing the sea, and bears evidence of being a place of strength, and on the land side secured by a moat and drawbridge.

Hector Mór married Mary, daughter of Alexander MacDonald of Islay and the Glens, by whom he had two sons and seven daughters: Eachann Og, his heir and successor, and John Dubh, predecessor of the family of Kinlochaline; Marian, married to Norman MacLeod of Harris; Mary, to Donald MacDonald of Sleat; Catherine, died unmarried; the second Catherine, first to Archibald Campbell, fourth Earl of Argyle, and secondly to John Stewart of Appin—Catherine was a high-spirited woman, and was distinguished for her beauty and culture; Julian, married first to Calvagh O'Donnell of Tirconnell, and secondly to the great O'Neill, in Ireland; Una, to Cameron of

Lochiel; and Janet, to MacDonald of Keppoch. Hector Mór died about the year 1568.

Hector Mór's brother, Ailean, second son of Lachlan Catanach, but better known as Ailean nan Sop, or Allan o' the Wisp, because he set fire to buildings with straw, was a very noted character. Many legends have been told concerning him, some of which can not be true, although they may contain a grain of truth. The best known legend is that related by Sir Walter Scott, in his "Tales of a Grandfather;"* but it is wholly wrong in several essential particulars. It is so mixed with Patrick MacLean and Sir Lachlan Mór MacLean, that it would be difficult to reconstruct it. It is, however, so well told that others have seen fit to copy it bodily.† Notwithstanding Scott's assertion to the contrary, all the MacLean manuscripts are agreed that Ailean was born in wedlock, was the younger brother of Hector Mór, and second son of Lachlan Catanach, by his wife Marian. Ailean, or Allan, first comes into notice during the time when his father resided at Cairnburg. During that time, a daughter of MacNeill of Barra, who was a young lady of great beauty, was visiting the chieftain's family, and Allan, being captivated with her, made honorable love, which met with discouragement at her hands. This marked a turning-point in his career. Allan, thus repulsed in his advances, meditated the most brutal insult to the family's guest, and taking advantage of the absence of his father and mother, who were on a brief visit to the mainland, he violently seized his intended victim. She, however, succeeded in escaping from him, and in her alarm rushed toward the brink of a precipice, as if intending to throw herself off. She was closely pursued by Allan; and the scene being in the immediate neighborhood of the guard-house, a domestic on duty there, suspecting the wrong intention, with great quickness rushed forward, and seizing hold of the lady with one hand, with the other dexterously hurled Allan headlong over the precipice. Fortunately for Allan, he was caught on a projection which at that point formed a shelf. Here he remained, and was not extricated until he begged the lady's forgiveness and vowed pardon to the intrepid domestic who had so unceremoniously hurled him into his awkward position. This is the origin of the familiar modern phrase, "putting a lover on the shelf." The spot is still called *Urraigh Ailean nan Sop* (Allan na Sop's Shelf).

According to the feudal laws, he did not inherit any of his father's es-

---

*Second Series, Vol. I., pp. 59–63. † Keltie's *History of the Highland Clans*, Vol. II., p. 263; *New Statistical Account* of Argyleshire, p. 343; *Book of Scottish Story*, p. 738, etc.

tates, so he took to the seas for a living, and became a freebooter. Having learned by experience that he must have a permanent abode, and having quarreled with Neil MacLean of Torloisk, a weak man, he murdered him and took possession of his lands of Torloisk. He engaged in so many expeditions by sea, which were always attended with success, and exhibiting a high degree of desperate courage, his influence became widely felt, which he did not fail to use to good account. In all the disturbances then taking place in the Isles, he never failed to perform an important part. Sometimes he espoused the interests of his brother Hector Mór, and again he is found on the opposite side. He was one of the eighteen principal barons in the cause of Donald Dubh, in 1543. When Sir James MacDonald was put forward by the Islanders, after the death of Donald Dubh, that crafty chieftain saw the necessity of attaching Allan to his interests. To gain him over he granted him the island of Gigha in 1539; and the Earl of Argyle purchased his friendship by a grant of the lands of Kilcharmaig in Knapdale, and MacDonald of Islay by gift of Tarbert Castle. The influence arising from the friendship of these powerful leaders, his being the brother of the Lord of Duard, together with his consummate address and daring, made Allan a valuable acquisition to any of the parties now struggling for supremacy in the kingdom. The Earl of Lennox, in his treasonable alliance with the King of England, during the Earl of Arran's regency, and in the minority of Queen Mary, succeeded in attaching Allan to his interests. He accompanied the Earl on a certain mission to England in the character of an ambassador from James MacDonald of Islay, who was then styled Lord of the Isles. For this and other treasonable practices he, however, succeeding in receiving a pardon from Queen Mary.

While Allan has been represented as a notorious freebooter, and that neither high nor low escaped his rapacities, yet the stories preserved of him prove that he was often swayed by gentle influences. Once Allan made a descent on Coll and carried off the lord (Hector, fourth MacLean of Coll) a prisoner. "Coll was a poet and musician, and when in prison he composed a tune, still, I believe, preserved, under the name of 'Allan nan Sop's March,' which having sung with much grace, his stern enemy was so moved that he immediately gave him his liberty." *

Allan died in 1551, in bed, at an advanced age, and during his last moments he was reminded that during his life he had engaged in nineteen suc-

---

* Logan's *Scottish Gael*, Vol. II., p. 300.

cessful campaigns. He replied that if he had known that, he should have made it a score. He was buried at Iona, where his tomb may still be seen.

I have no evidence that he was ever married. He had two bastard sons, Hector and John, who were legitimized August 3, 1547.*

July 28, 1539, he received a gift "of the non-enty maills of Geya, Comeravoch, Terbert and other lands for all terms since the death of Malcolm McNele, last possessor thereof, and until the entry of the rightful heir." †

Of Patrick, bastard son of Lachlan Catanach, but little is known. He was "Justicias of the Isles and Bailie of Icolmkill." In 1545 he served as one of the plenipotentiaries of Donald Dubh to the English court.‡

The records ‖ seem to make Patrick a bishop: "Gift to Mr. Patrick McClane of the temporality of the diocese of the Isles, and Abbey of Icolmkill, vacant by decease of Ferquard, last bishop thereof. 7th August, 1547." According to Gregory, it was Roderick MacLean who was put forward by the regent to the vacant bishopric. Spottiswoode says: "Ferquhard, the forty-fourth bishop, is said by Keith to have procured from the pope license to resign the bishopric in favor of Mr. Roderick MacLean, who was at that time archdeacon of the Isles, but appears not to have obtained possession of the see till after the year 1549, at which time, according to Keith, it was vacant." §

XIII. Hector Og, Thirteenth Chief of MacLean.

Hector Mór was succeeded by his son Eachann Og, or Hector, the Younger. He should have been called Eachann Struidhear, Hector, the Spendthrift. Hector Og survived his father not longer than five years, during which short period he not only spent, by his improvident conduct and profligacy, all the ready money left by the late noble chief, but burdened the estates with debt. He appears to have inherited nothing of the qualities which distinguished his father, but lived at peace in the free enjoyment of his pleasures. He was the only worthless chief of MacLean. He appears to have built for himself a residence at Iona, situated near the head of Port-a-Churraich, where traces of the house are still shown. It is called "Garadh-Eachann Og," or Garden of Young Hector.

Hector Og entered into the following agreement with his brother John Dubh: "Contract between Hector Makclayne of Dowart and John Dow Mak-

---

* *Reg. Sec. Sig.*, Vol. XXI., fol. 28. † *Ibid.*, Vol. XIII., fol. 16. ‡ Gregory's *Western Highlands*, p. 172. ‖ *Reg. Sec. Sig.*, Vol. XXI., fol. 29. § *History of the Church of Scotland*, Vol. I., p. 261.

clayne, his brother germain. Whereby the said Hector sets in tack to the said John the 25£ 6s. 8d. land in the dominion of Morvarn, 25 merk land in Glennoherry in Islay, and other lands therein mentioned, with the office of bailie over these lands, and also the office of bailie over certain other lands belonging to the said Hector Makclayne. The inhabitants of these lands are to rise with the said John Dow at MacLean's command, and have liberty to move from place to place on these lands. John Dow McLane is content to 'live on his own particular living' and to avoid all oppression, and if he should commit any manner of crime against any of Hector's 'native men, tenants and freeholders,' it shall be fully redressed. Hector is to accept John as a principal counsellor in all weighty matters, and if Hector should send his forces to Ireland or Scotland, John is to have preeminence over the rest of his kin, &c., in the absence of Hector. Hector consents that John resort not to the earl of Argyle till further favors be obtained. Hector MacLean also consents to his brother's marrying the laird of Coll's daughter, if he can do so lawfully without slander or offense to the kirk of God; if he can not lawfully marry her, he may do with her as he please, independent of the said Hector 'till God provide remeid.' Dated at the head of Loch Alyne, 14th May, 1573." *

As previously noticed, Eachann Og married Janet, daughter of the Earl of Argyle, in the year 1557, by whom he had one son, Lachlan Mór, his heir and successor, and three daughters: Mary, married to Angus MacDonald of Islay; Janet, to Roderick MacLeod of Lewis; and Marian, to Hector Roy, fifth MacLean of Coll. He died during the latter part of 1573, or the beginning of 1574.

XIV. Sir Lachlan Mór MacLean, Knight, Fourteenth Chief of MacLean.

Eachann Og was succeeded by his son Lachainn Mór, or Big Lachlan, or Great Lachlan, afterward Sir Lachlan Mór MacLean, Knight. He was called "Big Lachlan," both on account of his stature and the greatness of his mind. He was the most accomplished and warlike chief that ever held sway in Duard. His military talents were of a very high order; his chivalrous character commanded the respect of his most inveterate foes, and his personal interest for and kindness toward his followers endeared him to his clansmen. So great were his qualities that historians have been forced to pay tribute to his memory. "A brave and gallant soldier, as he proved himself by his conduct at

---

* *Sixth Report Royal Commissioners on Hist. Manuscripts*, Part I., p. 625.

Glenlivat, in 1594."* "He was one of the most remarkable men connected with the Highlanders of Scotland in his days." † "By his education in the continent, he had learned civility and good manners, and living accordingly, was in great respect both with his own people and all his neighbors about." ‡ "It is good for the MacLeans to cherish in their heart of hearts Lachlan Mór and Hector Mór, and the other worthies of their genealogical tree. Lachlan Mór, or Big Lachlan, who was mighty both in soul and body, and had to make a big business of blood with the MacDonalds of Islay, the days when keeping his next door neighbors stoughtly at bay, was a necessary part of each man's manhood." ‖ "Lachlan Mór was a person well fitted by his great talents and military genius to meet the emergency upon which the fate of his clan seemed to depend." § "The powerful family of MacLeans had now for their chief a young man of an active and energetic spirit, under whom this tribe exercised a great influence in the Isles." ** "Amongst the chief leaders, who assumed the state and independence of little princes, were the earl of Argyle, Lachlan MacLean of Duard, Angus MacDonald of Dunyveg, Donald Gorm MacDonald of Sleat, and Roderick MacLeod of Harris, known in traditionary song as Ruari Mór. Of these chiefs, the lord of Duard, commonly called Lachlan Mór, was by far the most talented and conspicuous. He was, in all respects, a remarkable person; by no means illiterate, for he had received his nurture in the low country, and had married a daughter of the earl of Glencairn. But in war and in personal prowess he had then no equal: an island Amadis of collossal strength and stature, and possessing, by the vigor of his natural talents, a commanding influence over the rude and fierce islesmen." ††

At the time of his father's death, Lachlan was a minor, and his mother having married Hector, son of Ailean nan Sop, his stepfather became tutor of the estate. King James VI. became very much interested in the youth, so had him sent to Edinburgh and brought up in his court. At the age of eighteen, or in 1576, Lachlan repaired to Duard, in order to take possession of the estate. Hector, his stepfather, had managed the estate with consummate ability, and being a bold, daring man, had kept the neighboring clans at peace, owing to their fear of his resentment. But he had determined to gain full possession of the property, by putting Lachlan out of the way, and expecting to make his peace with his wife, the mother of Lachlan. His plans

---

* *Collectanea de Rebus Albanicts*, p. 43. † *Book of Scottish History*, p. 638. ‡ Spottiswoode's *Hist. Church of Scotland*, Vol. III., p. 344. ‖ *Altavona*, pp. 169, 180. § Skene's *The Highlanders of Scotland*, Vol. II., pp. 210. ** Gregory's *Western Highlands*, p. 217. †† Tytler's *History of Scotland*, Vol. IV., p. 235.

were frustrated, owing to Lachlan being at court and continuing there until he was grown. Hector went so far as to make proposals to the chieftains, or principal gentlemen of the clan, to exclude Lachlan altogether, who was represented by his ambitious kinsman and guardian as of too effeminate a character, arising from the nature of his education in the Lowlands, to be fit for so important a station as chief of the warlike MacLeans. When the young heir returned home to take the management of his estates, he was much caressed by his tutor, who at the same time endeavored to cause the clan to have a bad impression of him, pretending that he was an idiot. Yet, young as he was, he easily penetrated his tutor's designs, and looked upon himself as a prisoner, where he ought to have been master, surrounded only by the tutor's creatures. He was fully cognizant that they only waited a favorable opportunity for cutting him off. Lachlan counter-plotted him, and with the assistance of his uncle, John Dubh, and Master Lachlan MacLean, a son of Lochbuy, he, being favored by the porter, who opened the door of Castle Duard to them by night, surprised Hector Ailean nan Sop in bed, carried him to the island of Coll, and there caused him to be beheaded.

Having gained full possession of his estate, Lachlan at once commenced to set things in order, and right such wrongs as had been done to his clansmen during the years of his minority. Colin Campbell, sixth Earl of Argyle, thinking a favorable opportunity had come to accomplish the purposes of his family, already formed, of seizing the estate, sent a party of his clan to the island of Luing, which they plundered, and committed other depredations, the nature of which is set forth in Lachlan's petition to the king and the lords of the privy'council. "The complaint sets forth that the earl of Argyle had 'cruellye conspirit the slaughter' of the complainant, and especially in March 1577, had 'perswadit and conducit with' the uncle of the latter, John Dubh MacLean, by promising him great rewards for the performance of his 'malicious and weikit interpryiss' upon him, and his sister's son, and for taking and spoiling of his (Lachlan's) place of Duard. This conspiracy was frustrated by the confession of John Dubh, but the earl was not by this turned from his purpose, and had stirred up Angus MacDonald of Dunyveg, to carry it into effect. Angus, assisted by some of Lachlan's enemies from Ireland, and others, to the number of twelve hundred, besieged the house of Lochgorme with fire and sword. In this and other depredations he was assisted by the earl with a land-force of two hundred, and also by sea with a galley and men, and had promise of other support. On another occasion Lachlan's servant, while on his way through Argyle to the Lowlands, was imprisoned by Campbell of Lochgoilhead at the special command of the earl; and every hindrance was given to the kin and friends of Lachlan in trading with the Lowlands, all access through the country of Argyle being denied to them, and their persons imprisoned till payment of ransom. The earl has also, by two hundred of his servants, visited the island of Luing, driven thence a large number of cows, horses, and sheep, and despoiled the women and children of their clothing. Various other complaints are made against the earl." * The earl was powerful enough to have action put off, and a decree was not rendered until 29th December, 1578, when the earl and his accomplices were ordered to return answer. Dated Stirling Castle.†

The youthful Lord of Duard was not one who would brook unnecessary delay, so he summoned his clansmen, and at the head of a powerful force poured into Argyle's country. Not satisfied with this, he transferred some of his forces to Ireland, and laid waste the lands of Schayne O'Dochtrie of Glach, in retaliation for the assistance rendered Argyle. So sudden and so effective was the work of Lachlan, that Argyle hastened to compromise the difficulty, by fully indemnifying the people of Luing for their loss. But Argyle waited his opportunity, for on August 27, 1579, at that time being chancellor and justice of Scotland, thus taking advantage of his position, he compelled Lachlan to deliver pledges for abiding trial at a future date for damage done to O'Dochtrie of Glach; and on May 27, 1580, caused him to give to him (Argyle) lands to the amount of two hundred merks yearly value, in payment for the invasion of Glach.‡

During the month of December, 1577, Lachlan paid a visit to court, where he was received in a very flattering manner by most of the nobles there assembled, who, having been informed of the gallant check recently given to the authority of Argyle in the west, vied with one another in the endeavor to secure the friendship of so powerful an adherent as the spirited young Lord of Duard had proved himself to be. The king proposed and received consent of all parties that the chief of MacLean should espouse Dorothea Stewart, daughter and heiress of the Earl of Athol. Preliminaries having been settled among the parties, Lachlan started for the Highlands, in order to make ready for the wedding, and on his way visited William Cunningham, Earl of Glencairn, at his castle on the banks of the Clyde. Cards were introduced in the evening, and MacLean's partner was one of the earl's daughters. In the course of the evening the game happened to be changed, and the company

---

* *Appendix to Sixth Report Royal Commission on Hist. MSS*, p. 630, 1877.   † *Ibid.*   ‡ *Ibid.*

again cut for partners, on which another of the daughters whispered in her sister's ear that if the Highland chief had been her partner she would not have hazarded the loss of him by cutting anew. The chief overheard the remark, and was so well pleased with the compliment, and so fascinated with the charms of Margaret Cunningham, that a match was made up between them, which happened December 30, 1577, and soon after they were married. This action on the part of MacLean gave great offense to the king, besides losing the richest heiress at that time in Scotland, as well as an earldom.

Lachlan now found himself in the full enjoyment of domestic happiness, and possessing great influence and power, besides being at the head of the most powerful of West Highland clans, and in the very zenith of its strength. But Lachlan's life was not destined to be one of repose. The old feud which commenced in the time of his grandfather Hector Mór, again broke out, and mutual aggressions became common among the MacLeans and Angus MacDonald of Dunyveg and the Glens, on account of the Rhinns of Islay. MacDonald would carry fire and sword into some district belonging to MacLean; the latter would retaliate by laying waste certain lands belonging to the former. These depredations were kept up with the most rancorous animosity on both sides. This state of affairs having been made known to the government, the belligerent chiefs were commanded to subscribe, within a certain limited period, assurances of indemnity to each other, under penalty of treason.* This led to a temporary suspension of hostilities between the two clans, and in order to bind the two families together, Angus MacDonald of Islay married Mary, sister of Lachlan Mór. This marriage was hailed with great satisfaction by both the MacLeans and MacDonalds, and the principals looked upon it as affording some hope of permanent peace and concord between them. A friendly intercourse was now kept up between the two clans, without interruption, for several years, with the most happy results; and from inveterate enemies they became the most cordial friends.

Peace now reigned on the island until the autumn of 1585, when an unfortunate circumstance plunged the Clan MacLean into a conflict with the Clan MacDonald, from which the former never fully recovered, and marked the decline of the MacDonalds of Islay. Donald Gorm MacDonald of Sleat, being on a voyage from Skye, to pay a visit to his relative Angus MacDonald of Dunyveg, in Islay, and accompanied by a retinue befitting his rank, was forced by stress of weather to take shelter on the north-west coast of Jura,

---

* *Record Privy Council,* 12th January, 1578–9.

on that part of the island belonging to Sir Lachlan Mór MacLean. At the same time, two gentlemen of Donald Gorm's clan—Hugh, nephew of Donald, and MacDonald Terreagh—from the same cause, sought shelter in another harbor, in the immediate vicinity of that occupied by the chief of Sleat. The two individuals above mentioned having recently quarreled with Donald, and learning that he was then in the adjacent harbor, embraced the opportunity to gratify their feelings of revenge by an act which they hoped might involve Donald Gorm and his party in destruction, by drawing upon them the vengeance of the chief of MacLean. In order to accomplish their design, they seized some of the cattle belonging to MacLean's tenants, and immediately put to sea. Neither any of the inhabitants nor Donald Gorm had knowledge of the presence on the island of the party who planned and executed this malicious plot. Their nefarious design unfortunately took immediate effect. The MacLeans, missing their cattle, at once attributed the loss to MacDonald of Sleat's followers; and without delay reported the matter to the chief of Duard. Lachlan, being bound to protect his vassals, and not waiting for an investigation, immediately summoned such of the clansmen as lay nearest, and without delay proceeded to Jura, that he might inflict such punishment as he thought Donald's party merited. Early in the following morning, the MacDonalds were surprised at a place called Innir-Chnochd-Breachd, and fell an easy prey to their assailants. Sixty of the MacDonalds were slain, and their chief only escaped the same fate from the circumstance of his accidentally sleeping on board his galley on the night of the attack. Immediately he returned to Skye, much exasperated at what he had reason to believe was an unprovoked attack and a wanton determination to renew hostilities. He vowed vengeance against the MacLeans, and the feeling of revenge spread among all the branches of the MacDonalds and their allies. Besides the MacDonalds of Skye and Islay, who were particularly involved, there rallied the Clanranald, the Clanian of Ardnamurchan, the Clanleod of Lewis, the MacNeills of Gigha, the MacAllisters of Loup, the MacPhees of Colonsay, and other tribes of lesser note.

Before the forces had gathered, preparatory to a descent on Mull, the original cause of the rupture (the malicious conduct of the MacDonalds of Skye) had become fully known; but the desire for revenge was so great that the MacDonalds would listen to no terms for peace until they had fully avenged the fate of their clansmen. Sir Lachlan was forced to meet this powerful league single-handed, and in the conflict which at once ensued he was reduced to such straits, that in the month of September the king deemed it necessary to write a letter, under his own hand, to the chief of the MacLeods, earnestly entreating him to give all the aid in his power to the chief of MacLean against the MacDonalds.* The chiefs of MacDonald, thus finding that the king was disposed to interfere in behalf of MacLean, felt a disposition to accommodate matters, and suggested that the disputed lands in Islay should be conceded to MacLean; and the Lord of Islay promising that this should not stand in the way of the desired reconciliation, proceeded, against the advice of his followers from Skye, to Duard Castle, in order to effect an amicable arrangement of all their disputes. In taking this step, MacDonald calculated on his private influence with MacLean, whose sister he had married a few years before. He was at first hospitably received and sumptuously entertained by his brother-in-law, but the Lord of Duard determined to improve the chance which put his powerful enemy within his grasp; and, knowing the vacillating character of MacDonald, he resolved that the fulfillment of the terms offered should not depend solely upon a mere promise. On the second day after his arrival, Angus, together with those who accompanied him, were placed in close confinement, within the walls of Duard Castle, and there continued until all the demands of MacLean were acceded to. For the performance of the agreement, Angus was obliged to give his son James, then a boy, and his brother Ranald as hostages; whereupon he was set at liberty with his attendants. He then returned to his castle of Dunyveg, exasperated against his brother-in-law, and determined to obtain full revenge for the injuries inflicted upon himself and his kinsman, Donald Gorm.†

The version of this affair as given by Archbishop Spottiswoode is different from the above, and is entitled to some credit, for he was contemporary (about seven years younger than Sir Lachlan) and an impartial witness: "MacDonald out of an emulation made many quarrels to the other, and in end laid a plot to murder him (though he had married his sister), which he went about in this manner. He sent a message to MacLean, offering to visit him at his home, and to stay some days, providing he would come back, and make merry with him in his country, that the world might see all injuries were forgotten, and that they loved one another as brethren and good neighbors ought to do. MacLean answered, that he should be welcome, but for his going back with him they should talk at meeting. MacDonald receiving this answer, came the next day, and was received very kindly by MacLean. Some

---

* Original letter in the charter chest of Dunvegan, dated September 18, 1585. † Gregory's *Western Highlands*, p. 231.

four or five days he staid, using the fairest shows of amity that could be wished, and being to part homewards, entreated MacLean to go with him, saying, that he would leave his eldest son and a brother-german pledges for his safety. MacLean upon his importunity yielded to go, but refused the pledges, lest he should seem to distrust him, and so went, taking with him of the trustiest of his kindred and servants some forty-five."*

Some time after MacDonald had left Duard Castle, Lachlan Mór came to Islay, to receive performance of the promises made by Angus regarding the Rhinns of Islay, bringing with him his nephew James, one of the hostages, the other being left behind in the castle. MacLean took post at the ruinous fort of Elan-Loch-Gorm, in the Rhinns of Islay, where he was detained three days on account of some affairs of his tenants, during which time he received repeated invitations from MacDonald to come to the latter's house at Mullintrea; and the better to lull MacLean into security, he directed his wife—MacLean's sister—to write an invitation by her own hand, expressive of surprise at her brother's tardiness in visiting them, and of sorrow at his apparent suspicion that any injury could be contemplated against him. The amiable and obedient wife, believing that no harm could befall her brother under the roof of which she was mistress, added her own assurance that an affectionate reception should welcome him and his retinue. After the most solemn and repeated protestations of MacDonald that no hostility was meditated, MacLean at length was prevailed upon to comply with the request. Accordingly, he came to Mullintrea with eighty-six of his clan and servants, in the month of July, 1586, and was sumptuously entertained on his arrival. During the evening, however, as it approached to the time of retirement, the Lady MacDonald noticed something suspicious in certain messengers who suddenly arrived at the castle, and, after holding a hasty interview in private with her husband, as suddenly took their departure. Being unable to communicate these suspicious circumstances to her brother, she took the opportunity to say to him: "In so stormy a night, the shepherd should well guard his flock." The hint was not lost on the island chief, who, on retiring, preferred for his resting-place for the night an out-house, in which accommodations were made for his friends, instead of the apartments in the castle previously provided for him; and, for additional security, took to bed with him his little nephew James. About midnight, between three and four hundred of the MacDonalds, with their treacherous chief at their head, surrounded the houses in which the MacLeans

---

* *History of the Church of Scotland*, Vol. II., p. 344.

were lodged. Angus summoned the chief of MacLean "to come forth and drink." MacLean answered that of drink they had already too much, and that it was time to rest. "Yet it is my will," said Angus, "that ye arise and come forth." On hearing this, MacLean began to suspect some bad dealing, and dressing himself, after ordering his men to prepare themselves, opened the door, where, perceiving a large company in arms and Angus at their head with a drawn sword, asked what the matter was, and if he intended to break his faith. "No faith," said he; "I gave none; and must now have an account of you and your friends for the wrong I have received." MacLean, with his companions, rushed out into the midst of the MacDonalds, and holding in his powerful grasp the boy James, in the manner of a shield, commenced an immediate attack. The poor child cried piteously, now beseeching his uncle, then his father. The stern MacDonald, seeing that the immediate destruction of his son might be the result of his perseverance in the slaughter he contemplated, at length solemnly pledged his "honor and faith" for MacLean's personal safety, and quarter to his followers, if he would deliver up the child. Lachlan, realizing he was surrounded by a force five times greater than his own, and no prospect by further resistance, complied with the terms offered, and yielded up his arms. He was at once conveyed by some keepers to another house. All the rest yielded on like promise, gave up their arms, and were bound two by two, and then thrown into prison. But there were two that Angus, seeing that he had now all in his power, refused quarter. One was a brave youth of the Morvern MacLeans, whose powerful arm had, in previous conflicts, laid many a bold MacDonald in the dust; the other was that MacDonald Terreagh, of whom mention has already been made as being the original cause of the slaughter in Jura, and who, since that time, had attached himself to the MacLeans. These two men defended the door of the house in which they had taken shelter so desperately that neither Angus nor his men could enter; whereupon, fire was put to the house, and the two heroic youths were consumed in the flames.

 MacDonald had no idea of keeping his pledge; so the very next day, two of the MacLeans were brought forth and executed in the presence of their chief. On Lachlan remonstrating against this atrocity and reminding Angus of the solemn pledge he had given, the latter replied: "I have you now in my power, and will hold to no pledge until my revenge is as complete as it is my will it should be." In this manner, two of the MacLeans were brought out every day, until they were all put to death except Lachlan Mór and his uncle, John Dubh of Morvern; and they escaped only by an accident that happened to the sanguinary Angus, who fell from his horse on the very eve of their intended execution.

In the meantime, Raonuill MacColla,* an individual of rank and a near kinsman of Angus, and another prominent MacDonald, had been taken prisoner by the MacLeans, and were now confined in Duard Castle. On learning this, Angus was disposed to come to some terms; so he at once agreed that the chief of MacLean should return, and the release of John Dubh MacLean should immediately follow the restoration of the two MacDonalds confined in Duard Castle; and for the fulfillment of certain conditions, to which Lachlan was forced to subscribe, he must have placed in his hands the following hostages: Hector MacLean, Duard's eldest son; Alexander, brother of William MacLeod of Dunvegan; Lachlan and Neill, sons of Lachlan MacKinnon of Strathordell; John and Murdo, sons of Ruari MacNeill of Barra; Allan, son of Ewin MacLean of Ardgour; and Donald, son of Hector MacLean, constable of Cairnburg. This decision was also hastened from the action of the king, who, hearing of these atrocities, employed the chiefs of the Campbells, who governed the earldom of Argyle during the minority of the seventh earl, to mediate between the contending clans. Angus also demanded, through the king's agents, free pardon for his crimes.

A few days after MacLean had been released, MacIan of Ardnamurchan came to MacDonald and informed him that, as soon as Lachlan had arrived in Mull, he caused the two imprisoned MacDonalds to be executed; upon which, and within an hour, and without deliberation, Angus caused John Dubh to be beheaded. Lachlan Mór, in the meantime, made all haste to liberate his captives, who reached their homes the day the murder of John Dubh of Morvern was committed.

A son of John Dubh (Allan of Ardtornish), a stripling of the age of sixteen years, upon learning that MacDonald of Ardnamurchan was instrumental in the death of his father, immediately mustered his followers, and entering that chieftain's possessions, seized upon such portions of his estate as lay nearest his own; and with such severity did the young warrior pursue his avenging course, that MacIan was at last glad to purchase peace with him at the expense of a considerable part of his estates; and believing it best to make the reconciliation lasting, gave young Allan his daughter Una in marriage.

---

* This establishes the fact that MacLean had not originally demanded hostages, and the version of Spottiswoode is correct, though I have followed versions less favorable to Sir Lachlan Mór.

The wanton destruction of so many of MacLean's near relations, friends, and leading men of his tribe, and the more recent execution of John Dubh, a tried and true adviser, could result only in harboring such feelings as would call for deep revenge. When the intelligence reached Mull that MacLean of Morvern had been beheaded, Lachlan Mór at once called together all his clansmen, vassals, the MacNeills of Barra, the MacKinnons, the MacQuarries, and the Clanleod, and without delay fell upon the greater part of Islay, and wasted it with fire and sword, and put to death between five and six hundred men; or as the account says, " all the men capable of bearing arms belonging to the Clandonald of Islay." Angus himself was hotly pursued and forced to take shelter in his castle of Dunyveg, where he was closely besieged. At length, on the intercession of his lady, and on his resigning free and unconditionally the one-half of Islay to his victorious foe, a truce was entered into, and MacLean returned to Mull.

The victorious career of Lachlan Mór, and the death of so many of their clansmen in Islay, roused the vengeance of the MacDonalds generally, and they now formed a combination, in which all the chieftains of that name bound themselves not to lay down their arms until the ravages committed by the chief of MacLean in Islay should be fully and satisfactorily punished. This league consisted of the MacDonalds of Kintyre, Skye, Clanranald, and Ardnamurchan; the subordinate clans of MacNeil of Gigha, MacAllisters of Loupe, and MacPhees of Colonsay. They also had the assistance of MacLean of Borreray, who on this occasion was forced to enlist under the banner of his feudal superior, Donald Gorm of Sleat; and so suddenly did they assemble together and enter Mull, that the chief of MacLean had no force whatever in readiness sufficient to repel this invasion. He was therefore obliged to summon all the inhabitants to withdraw themselves from the valleys and sea-coast, and take shelter with their property in the mountains, where he himself took post with them. While Lachlan was thus engaged in looking after the security of his people, the invaders sailed up Loch-nan-gall (on the map Loch na Keal), on the west coast of Mull, and landed between Derryguaig and Knock, at the foot of Ben More: from hence they pushed forward their outposts as far as Sron-na-Cranalich, within three miles of a small valley called Lichd-Lí, where the MacLeans were encamped. Lachlan Mór gave strict orders that no one should advance beyond a certain pass, at which it was his intention to dispute the progress of his enemies when they attempted to force it. Contrary to his instructions, however, John of Inverscadell, son of Mac-

Lean of Ardgour, a bold and spirited youth, who commanded the detached parties, and whose bravery on this occasion overmatched his prudence, could not witness the advance of the MacDonalds without some attempt to check them, so he removed from the post to which he had been assigned, and with a few followers attacked the advanced party at Sron-na-Cranalich. The result was the loss of almost every individual of his faithful band, one of whom was Allan, son of MacLean of Treshnish, a youth of much promise, and whose death was greatly felt. Early on the following morning the invaders moved forward with the intention of attacking the MacLeans in their position. On the march, and as they were approaching the pass already mentioned, MacLean of Borreray placed himself near MacDonald of Sleat, and presuming on the credulity and superstition of the times, and in order to affect his purpose, appeared to be very dull and melancholy. MacDonald noticing this, inquired of him if the cause of his particularly thoughtful mood did not arise from a reluctance to fight against his clan and kinsmen; and if so, he was welcome to fall back and pass to the rear, and resign his "post to such as might not be deterred from doing their duty by such treacherous scruples." "*Treacherous* scruples," replied MacLean, "I entertain not; more care for *thee* and thy followers makes me in a melancholy mood;" and in a half-suppressed tone, as if addressing himself, added, "That horrid! and, I fear, ominously fatal dream!" MacDonald, in great anxiety, exclaimed, "What dream?" "Listen," said Borreray, "you shall hear: At the middle hour of night, as a peaceful slumber came o'er me, a voice distinctly repeated the following lines to me:

> An Lichd-Li sin, O! Lichd-Li!
> 'S ann ort-sa bheirear an dith!
> 'S iad Clann-Ghilleain a bheir buaidh,
> Air an t' shluagh a thig air tir;
> An Gearna Dubh sin, 's i 'n Gearna Dubh,
> 'S ann innte dhoirtear an fhuil;
> Marbhar an Ridire ruadh,
> Mu'n teid clardheamh 'n truaill an diugh."
> Feared Lichd-Lee,* ah! dread Lichd-Lee!
> Direful are the deeds the fates have doomed on thee!
> Defeated by the sons of Gillean the invading multitude shall be.
> On thee, Gearna-Dubh,† streams of blood shall flow;
> And the bold Red Knight shall meet his death ere a sword is sheathed.

---

* Lichd-Lee was the spot where the MacLeans were encamped, and was so named from the ground being partially covered with a pavement of smooth, flat rocks. † A projecting rock or precipice, forming the key of the position occupied by the MacLeans.

Borreray's dream worked with the most happy effect upon the superstitious credulity of the Red Knight of Sleat; for, finding the MacLeans in full force, and most advantageously posted at the pass of Gearna-Dubh (the dreaded spot where the fates had prophesied his downfall), MacDonald turning to his men said: "I know that you are faithful and true followers; you have hitherto been so, and that you have exemplified by your gallantry and bravery in action. I predict, however, that should we go to battling against the MacLeans to-day, we would come out of it with dirty hands; and I, your commander, would fall under the heavy sword of MacLean! And now we will do a very prudent thing if we at once set sail from Mull." Instantly the retreat was sounded, and pursued as they were by the MacLeans, aided by the artful but worthy Borreray, who now took his opportunity, accompanied by his followers, to change sides, the best MacDonald was he who could first make to the vessels. They were overtaken at the very spot, where on the night before they were seen sharpening their broad-swords on a flag-stone, near where they were encamped (and the impressions made on the stone by the sharpening may still be seen); and so panic-stricken were they, that hardly any resistance was made to the merciless attack of the MacLeans, great numbers being slain, without the assailants on their side losing a single individual. The heads of the dead were cut off and thrown into a well, at the head of Loch-na-Keal, which has ever since been called "Tobar-nan Ceann," or The Well of Heads.

This defeat served only as additional feul to the rage of the MacDonald's, and exasperated to the utmost against the MacLeans, as the whole clan now was, a fresh levy was immediately made amongst the vassals of those chiefs who headed the late invasion, and the place of rendezvous was appointed at a small fortified island south of Kerrera, on the coast of Lorn, called Bachca. This formed a convenient post, as being situated in a central position between the MacDonalds of the North and those of the South. The chief of MacLean, however, did not witness these symptoms of renewed hostilities against him without due preparation on his part; and he lost no time in summoning to his aid all the chieftains of his own name, and those of MacNeil, MacKinnon, and MacQuarrie. Thus prepared, Lachlan Mór did not think it advisable to stand on the defensive only, as regarded the threatened invasion, but determined at once on attacking his enemies in their stronghold at Bachca; and the necessary preparations for this purpose being completed, he crossed over to the coast of Lorn early in the morning, his van being commanded by the gallant MacLean of Borreray on the right, and by MacNeil of Barra on the left. The main body was led by Lachlan Mór in person. Borreray and Barra concentrated their line, consisting chiefly of archers, at the principal landing place on the west of the island, where they found the MacDonalds in strong force prepared to dispute their landing. The attack was immediately commenced, and with such rapidity and fatal precision were the showers of arrows from the galleys directed, that the defenders were soon forced to make a precipitate retreat into their interior works. The MacLeans, following up their advantage, pursued the MacDonalds into the center of the island, where a terrible slaughter ensued, three hundred and forty of the MacDonalds and their adherents being either killed or wounded. The victors also took many prisoners, among whom were the chief of Sleat, the chief of Ardnamurchan, MacLeod of Lewis, and MacPhee of Colonsay. The victory was not only of great importance from the fact that only two common soldiers were killed and one gentleman of the Morvern MacLeans wounded, but also because the principal leaders had been captured. In the battle of Bachca the advantages were in every respect in favor of the MacDonalds; they were in possession of an island strongly fortified, and at the commencement of the action numbered two thousand five hundred men, whereas MacLean's followers did not exceed twelve hundred. About eighteen hundred of the defeated host made good their retreat by having taken the precaution to have their boats in readiness, in case of reverse, on the opposite side of the island. The victorious MacLeans, satisfied that their enemies could not again soon be assembled to make head against them, returned to their peaceful occupations.

A conflict so severe in the Western Isles, and so detrimental to good government, could not pass without due notice from the king; and for the more effectual suppression of similar disorders in the future, MacLean was called upon to give hostages for his quiet behavior toward the MacDonalds, which were to be placed at the disposal of the sovereign. The hostages in possession of Angus MacDonald were ordered to be transferred to the king, and kept where he should appoint, till the final settlement of the dispute between the Clandonald and the Clanlean. MacLean was required forthwith to release the chiefs captured by him at the battle of Bachca, and the heads of both tribes, their principal supporters and allies, were charged to remain quiet, and to abstain from all conventions or gathering in arms, and from all attacks on each other; so as not to hinder or disturb the king in his attempts to bring about a settlement of their various disputes.* To all these conditions Lachlan Mór submitted, was received into favor, and shortly afterward the king conferred upon him the honor of knighthood as an *eques auratus*. MacDonald failed to liberate the hostages according to the decree, and was in consequence outlawed.

It has been mentioned that, in the feud between the MacLeans and MacDonalds, the Clanian (MacDonalds of Ardnamurchan) not only assisted their kinsmen, but the chief, John, was the immediate cause of the death of the faithful John Dubh. A favorable opportunity presented itself for redress on the MacIans, of which Sir Lachlan was not slow to avail himself. John MacIan of Ardnamurchan, chief of that sept, had, before the breaking out of the late feud, been a suitor for the hand of Sir Lachlan's mother (formerly Janet Campbell, and sister of the late Earl of Argyle), who enjoyed a considerable jointure in her own right, which had been conferred on her by Hector Mór, twelfth chief of MacLean, but who, on account of his previous policy, had incurred the displeasure of Sir Lachlan, now renewed his suit, without any objection from the warlike chief of MacLean, although well aware that MacIan could have no motive in seeking the hand of a woman of his mother's age but the possession of wealth and influence. Sir Lachlan viewed the proposed alliance with disgust rather than approbation, but concluded to tolerate the ambition of MacIan, that it might work out its own ruin. The mother gave her consent to the proposed marriage, and the chief of Ardnamurchan, with a train becoming the occasion, proceeded to Mull for the purpose of claiming his bride, who at that time resided at Torloisk House, one of the seats of the chief of MacLean, where the ceremony was performed. Sir Lachlan was present, with many gentlemen of the clan, and the day passed in much conviviality and apparent friendship. During the evening, however, after the newly-mated pair had retired to rest, one of MacIan's company introduced the subject of the late feud, and in the argument thereby engendered, one of the MacLeans maintained that the matter was introduced with a view of breeding a quarrel, and that it ill became the MacDonalds to complain of results of the feud, as, were it not for the generosity of their (the MacLean's) chief, few leaders would have remained to the Clandonald at the battle of Bachca. Heated with wine, the parties came to high words; some of the gentlemen of MacIan's retinue jeeringly boasting that their chief only married the "old lady" for the sake of her wealth. "Drunkards ever tell the truth," vociferated a kins-

---

* *Record Privy Council*, April 16, 1587.

man of the chief of MacLean, as he plunged a dirk into the body of the inconsiderate MacDonald. The most barbarous slaughter now ensued; in the moment of exasperation, nearly all the followers of MacIan were killed. The cause of the quarrel being explained to Sir Lachlan, who was not present at the above occurrence, he made use of a Gaelic phrase, having for its meaning, "if the fox rushes upon the hounds, he must expect to be worried." His followers, comprehending by this that he was quite indifferent to the fate even of MacIan himself, and having imbibed enough wine to make themselves reckless, broke into the nuptial chamber and dragged the unhappy bridegroom from his bed, and would have instantly dispatched him, had not the lamentations of his mother for once moved the rugged nature of her imperious son. MacDonald and his two remaining followers, Allaster and Angus MacIan, were then seized and thrown into the dungeon of Duard Castle.

Having given the version of this affair as presented by the MacLean seanachaidhs, it is but just to give MacIan's account, as presented by his advocate, David MacGill, to the privy council. This petition avers: " Lauchlane of Dowart having of a lang tyme bigane conspirit" " the cruell murthour and slauchter causles of Johnne McKane of Ardmurchin and his freindis," and as Lachlan could not prevail by force, " he travillit be craft and policie," and pretended great friendship, " offering for the better mantenance of friendship amangis thame thaireftir the mariage of Jannet Campbell moder to the said Lauchlane; quhilk boing lykcit of be the said Johnne McKane, at last, at the said Lauchlane's eirnist desyre and requeist, the said Johnne repairit to the toun and place of Torluisk upon the twelft day of Aprile last bipast, quhair" the marriage took place; "and at nycht the said Johnne McKane wes convayed be the hand be the said Lauchlane to his moderis awne chalmer and bed, purpoislie to cullour his mischeiff, and that the said Johnne McKane, and his freindis quhilkis beheld the same, mycht be cairles of thair awne suretie, as indeid thai depairtit immediatlie thaireftir to tak the same nychtis rest in ane uthir house or barne ewest to the parte quhair the said Johnne McKane wes, loukeing for na harme nor injurie of ony persone, and chieflie of the said Lauchlane or ony of his, in respect of his former behaviour actioun foirsaid. Nevirtheles, immediatlie eftir thay haid fallin on slep, the said Lauchlane and his compliceis, armed with havirshonis, swerds and durkis, enterit perforce within the said house or barne, and in maist cruell and barbarous maner, without pitie or compassioun, unmercifullie murdreist and slew thame to the nowner of auchtene personis, gentlemen besydis utheris; and not satisfeid thairwith, repaired immediatlie thaireftir to the chalmer quhair the said Johnne

McKane wes lyand, and with the like crueltie persewit him, like as thai at the same tyme, had bereft him of his lyff, wer not his awne bettir defens, and the lamentable crying oute and eirnist sute of the said Lauchlanis moder, for quhuis caus at last thay spaired his lyffe detening him nochtwithstanding sensyne, with Allaster McKane, and Angus McKane, his page, in strait firinance and captivitie, putting his persone to dalie tortour and panis, and on nawise will putt thame to liberty without he be compellit." To answer this complaint, Lachlan was duly summoned; but failing to make appearance, he was, at Dumfries, June 18, 1588, " denounced rebel." *

Soon after the above occurrence, the " Florida," commanded by Captain Don Fareija, one of the scattered ships of the celebrated Spanish Armada, was forced by stress of weather and want of provisions into Tobermory Bay, in Mull. The captain, arrogantly presuming on his floating power, sent peremptory orders to Duard Castle, commanding Sir Lachlan MacLean to supply his ship with such provisions as he might require, or as the island could afford; but his mandate not meeting with attention at the hands of him to whom it was addressed, he threatened to use the means within his power to help himself. The chief of MacLean was now aroused to indignation by the presumption of the foreign straggler, and returned answer to the effect "that the wants of the distressed stranger should be attended to after he had been taught a lesson of more courteous behavior; and in order that he might have such lesson as speedily as his wants seemed pressing, he was invited to land and supply his wants by the forcible means threatened; for it was not the custom with the chief of MacLean to pay ready attention to the wants of a threatening beggar." The Don thought it the wisest course to decline the invitation of the Lord of Duard, and now promised payment for all such necessaries as might be supplied him. On this condition, the people of Mull were given permission to furnish such supplies as were required.

In the meantime, MacIan's treatment on his nuptial night had aroused the Clanranald, who were not slow to provoke hostilities with the chief of Duard. MacLean delayed not in his preparations to meet the coming aggression by a counter expedition; and for this purpose entered into an agreement with the Spanish commander, by which he was to have the assistance of a hundred marines from the "Florida," partly in return for the provisions supplied by the inhabitants. With these auxiliaries in addition to his own clan, Sir Lachlan proceeded against the MacDonalds, whom he defeated in every engage-

---

* *Register of Privy Council*, Vol. IV., p. 290.

ment. He first proceeded to ravage and plunder the isles of Rum and Eig, then occupied by the Clanranald, and the isles of Canna and Muck, belonging to the Clanian. Having burned and subdued these islands, he then, with his foreign auxiliaries, made a descent upon the mainland of Ardnamurchan, and for three days laid close seige to MacIan's castle of Mingarry, his sanguinary followers, at the same time, spreading themselves in every direction throughout the lands belonging to that chieftain, laid it waste with fire and sword. In the midst of these successes, Sir Lachlan received a message from the commander of the "Florida," requesting the return of the Spanish force, as the ship was prepared to take her departure. MacLean of Treshnish at the same time sent a communication to his chief that the Spaniard was about to take his leave without settling with the people for the provisions supplied. Sir Lachlan remonstrated with Captain Fareija on the injustice thus contemplated, and the wily Don promised every satisfaction should be given ere he left the country; at the same time, he urgently requested the return of his men. Sir Lachlan, determined that his cunning ally should not, if possible, escape without discharging the obligations upon him, thought it proper to detain three of the principal officers as hostages, but permitted the rest of the Spaniards to return to the ship; at the same time, he sent Donald Glas, son of John Dubh MacLean of Morvern, on board the "Florida," to receive an adjustment of the demands of his people. No sooner, however, had Donald Glas set foot on board the "Florida," than he was disarmed and made prisoner, and cautioned, at the peril of his life, to attempt any communication with his friends. Exasperated to the utmost fury by such treatment, and finding that the Spaniard was making preparation for immediate departure, Donald at once resolved that he should not escape unpunished, even though the fearful step he was about to take for this purpose was destruction as certain to himself as to his foes. Finding the cabin in which he was confined to be in the immediate vicinity of the powder magazine, he found an opportunity in the night time to force his way into it, and laying his train in as concealed a position as possible, he waited the period when the final decision of Don Fareija might force him to the desperate step contemplated. At daylight on the following morning, Donald Glas was, in derision, summoned on deck to take a last farewell of the towering hills of Mull and Morvern, the beloved mountains of his native soil. Finding by the preparations going on that his own abduction and treachery to his kinsmen was in reality meditated, he requested a few attendants that accompanied him on board to make the land as speedily as possible; and slipping a letter for his chief into the hand of one of them, he returned below, under pretense of mental suffering at this forcible separation from his native land. Allowing sufficient time for his friends to reach a safe distance, he set himself to accomplish his dreadful purpose; and immediately firing his train, this remnant of the ill-fated Armada, with upward of three hundred souls on board, was blown to pieces in the bay. Of the Spaniards, only three escaped the immediate fate of their countrymen; one of these was so mutilated in the explosion that he died the next day.* The name of Donald Glas MacLean nowhere occurs in the popular histories of Scotland; yet he was just as brave, just as heroic and self-sacrificing, as any hero that ever fell upon the field of battle.

Many traditional tales have been related in Mull concerning Captain Fareija and his *loingeas* (ship)—one of them relating to a dog belonging to one of the Spanish officers, and which the people seem to have regarded with superstitious reverence as long as it lived. The poor animal was thrown ashore upon a fragment of the deck to the distance of a mile and a half, and was discovered in an apparently dying state by one of the inhabitants; but by attention it recovered, and no sooner did the faithful creature revive, than the shore opposite to where the wreck of the "Florida" sunk became its constant resort. Here it would sit looking toward the spot, howling most piteously, and by force alone could it be removed from the place. The remarkable manner displayed by this dog so wrought upon the superstitions of the people that it has formed a more lasting impression, through the ages that have since elapsed, than the retribution which swept over three hundred of their fellow-creatures.

The Spanish officers in the hands of the chief of MacLean were immediately set at liberty, and permitted to leave the country; but as they held Sir Lachlan to be connected with the destruction of their companions, they proceeded to Edinburgh, and there lodged complaint against him before the king and council.

The feud between the MacDonalds and MacLeans, during this time, suffered no relaxation, but was carried on with deep-seated hostility. The MacDonalds of Islay and Sleat joined with their kinsmen of Clanranald and Ardnamurchan against the MacLeans, and for a time the most barbarous destruction was carried on by both parties. The lands of the MacLeans were also ravaged, their adversaries having employed English mercenaries. At last the hostile clans became tired of their fruitless barbarities, and by mutual agree-

---

* For some interesting particulars concerning the "Florida," see Appendix, Note A.

ment MacLean released John MacIan and the other prisoners held by him, and Angus gave up the eight hostages formerly placed in his hands by Sir Lachlan.

About the same time the government took notice of these commotions, and the impecunious James found it entirely too favorable an opportunity to lose the advantage of filling his depleted exchequer. "Instead, however, of resorting to force, and thus compelling them and their followers to submission, a less manly course, although one, perhaps more suited to the disposition of the sovereign, was followed on this occasion. Remissions, under the privy seal, were granted to the MacLeans and MacDonalds, and their principal adherents, for all the crimes committed by them during their late feud; and, by these and similar means, Lachlan MacLean of Duard, and Angus MacDonald of Islay, and Donald Gorm MacDonald of Sleat, were at length induced to come to Edinburgh, on the pretense of consulting with the king and council for the good rule of the country. While there, by a breach of faith on the part of the government which no circumstance can excuse, and which only proves the weakness of the executive at this period, the three island chiefs were seized and imprisoned in the castle. After some time, MacLean and Angus MacDonald were brought to trial for the crimes already pardoned by the remissions under the privy seal; one of the principal charges against them being their treasonable hiring of Spanish and English soldiers to fight in their private quarrels. Both these chiefs, however, refused to plead or to go to a jury; but submitted themselves absolutely to the king's mercy, placing their lives and lands at his disposal." * This action on the part of MacLean flattered the vanity of James, and further aided as Sir Lachlan was by the powerful influence of his father-in-law, the earl of Glencairn, he made his peace with the king; not, however, without paying a heavy pecuniary fine into the hands of the money-loving monarch. MacLean and the chief of Islay were each amerced in the sum of twenty thousand pounds. MacLean was discharged on his promise to present hostages within a certain time after his release; but Islay was not released until he had placed his two sons as hostages in the hands of the king, besides a near relative, for his appearance on a certain fixed day; and even if he should then appear, his hostages should be detained until Donald Gorm of Sleat—who was fined four thousand pounds—should give hostages from among his own kinsmen for the performance of the conditions prescribed to him. After all the arrangements had

---

* Gregory's *Western Highlands*, p. 240.

been made, the chieftains returned to their estates, which was in the year 1591.

Relative to the above narrative of events the following is of interest as taken from the official records:

Dated at Holyrood House, April 16, 1587, is the decree relative to the imprisonment of Lachlan MacLean and Angus MacDonald. It remits the great crimes of Angus McConeill of Dunnyveg and Glennis and his accomplices, " and causit satisfie all things that mycht stay thair intendit rigour agains Lauchlane McClayne of Dowart, then detainit in maist strait captivitie," and the eight hostages placed in Angus's hands should be delivered to Archibald, earl of Argyle, or any of his tutors who should convey the same to the king, and all parties commanded to live in quietness.*

At Edinburgh, January 3, 1588, before the privy council Lachlan MacLean is charged that in the previous October, " accumpayed with a grite nowmer of thevis, brokin men and sornaies of Clannis, besydis the nowmer of ane hundreth Spanyeartis, come, bodin in feir of weir to his Majesties propir ilis of Canna, Rum, Eg, and the Ile of Elennole, and eftir they had soirned, wracked and spoiled the saidis haill Illis, they treasonablie rased fyre, and in maist barbarous, shamefull and cruell maner, byrnt the same Illis, with the haill men, wemen and childrene being thoir intill, not spairing the pupillis and infantis, and at that same tyme past to the Castell of Ardnamurchin, assegeit the same, and lay abowte the said Castell three dayis, using in the meantyme all kynd of hostilitie and force, baith be fyre and swerd," from which they were forced by " gude subjectis," and the " like barbarous and shamefull crueltie has sendle bene hard of amangis Christeanis in any kingdome or age." Lachlan making no appearance, it was recommended that he be denounced rebel.†

" On the 20th March 1588 King James granted a remission to Lachlan MacLean of Duard for the cruel murder of certain inhabitants of the islands of Rum, Canna and Eig. From the remission was excepted the plotting of felonious burning and flaming up, by sulphurous powder, of a Spanish ship, and of the men and provisions in her, near the island of Mull." ‡

In Skene's *Celtic Scotland* (Vol. III., pp. 428–440) is a description of the Western Isles appended, which has all the appearance of an official report, and written about the year 1590. Skene says it must have been written between 1577 and 1595, which would bring it during the chieftainship of Sir

---

* *Register of Privy Council*, Vol. IV., pp. 159, 160. † *Ibid.*, pp. 341, 342. ‡ *Appendix Sixth, Report Royal Commission Hist. MSS*, p. 609.

Lachlan Mór. It is particularly valuable, at this time, for it gives an idea of the strength of the MacLean forces. It begins with the information that "the haill Isles of Scotland were devidit in four pairts of auld, viz. Lewis, Sky, Mule, and Yla, and the remanent haill Isles were reknit but as pertmets and pendicles of the said four Iles." "Perteining to the Ile of Mule were Lismoir, Tuahannais, Ulloway, Commatra, Inschkennycht, Sanct Colmisinche, *alias* Colmkill, Tircich, and Coll." Mull "is all 300 merk land, and will raise 900 men to the weiris. McClane Doward, callit Great McClane, hes the maist pairt thairof, extending to aucht score merk land and ten, and will raise on it with the pairt he hes of the Bischop 600 men thairupon. McClane of Lochbuy hes thriescore merk land, and will raise 200 men thairon. The Bischop has 30 merk land thair, but McClane Doward hes it in his possession occupiet be his kin. The Laird of McKynvin hes 20 merk land, and the uther 20 merk land pertenis to the Laird of Schellow (Coll), but they will raise 100 thairon. . . . In everie pairt thairof are mony deires, raes, and wild foullis. McClane of Doward hes twa castellis in this Ile, the ane named Doward, the uther callit Aross, quhilk sumtime perteinit to McConneill. McClane of Lochbuy hes ane castell thair intill callit the Castell of Lochinbuy. Ilk merkland in this Ile payis yeirlie 5 bollis beir, 8 bollis meill, 20 stanes of cheese, 4 stanes of buttir, 4 mairtis, 8 wedderis, twa merk of silver, and twa dozen of pultrie, by cuddiche, quhanevir thair master cummis to thame." "Scalpa is four merk land perteining heritablie to McClane. It is mair fertile and commodious for deir and hunting nor it is ather for corns or store. It will raise 20 men." "Coamatra is four merk land, and pertenis to McClane of Dowart; it is plane, fair, and verie commodious for corns and catell of sa mekle. It payis yeirlie as Mull payis. It will rais 16 or 20 men." "Inschenycht is an Ile perteining to the said McClane, holding payment and commodities in all sortis as the said Ile of Coamatra." "Collow (Coll) is 30 merk land, and pertenis to the Laird of Collow; is very fertile alsweill of corns as of all kind of catell. Thair is sum little birkin woodis within the said Ile. Ilk merk land payis yeirlie as is declarit of the Ile of Mule, and will raise seven score men." "Tierhie (Tiree) is commodious and fertile of corns and store of gudes. It is 140 merk land, and will raise to the weiris 300 men. It pertenis to great McClane of Doward, and is all teillit land, and na girs but ley land, quhilk is maist nurischand girs of any other, quhairthrow the ky of this Ile abundis sa of milk that thai are milkit four times in the day. The yeirlie dewtie thairof is sa great of victuall, buttir, cheis, mairtis, wedderis, and other customes, that it is uncertain to the inhabitants thairof quhat thai should pay, but obeyis and payis quhatevir is cravet be thair maister for thair haill deuties, only to tak so mony firlotts as micht stand side be side round about the haill Ile full of victuall, half meill, half beir, and it wes refuseit." "Ila is 18 score merk land and will raise 800 men. McClane of Doward hes the half thairof. This Isle is plenteous of woodis, quhairin are mony deir, raes, and wild foullis. It is commodious for all kind of fisches, and in all the small burnis of this Ile are multipill of salmond and other fisches. McClane hes one strengthie castell thairin, quhilk standis in ane niche within ane fresche-water loch callit Lochgormen. The merk land in this Ile payis yeirlie three and ane half mairtis, 14 wedderis, 28 geis, 4 dozen and 8 pultrie, 5 bollis malt with ane peck to ilk boll, 6 bollis meill, 20 stane of cheis, and twa merk of silver. And ilk merk land man sustein daylie and yeirlie ane gentleman in meit and claith, quhilk dois na labour." "Jura is 30 merk land, the half pairt thairof pertainis to the said McClane. The haill will raise, with the Ile of Scarba 100 men. The land is excellent, and very fertile for corns; but is fair the maist part wilderness and woodis, quhairin is mony deir, raes, and other wild beistis. Sa mekle labourit land as is in this Ile, it payis alike to Ila of dewties." "McClane of Doward hes Layng of my lord Argile for service. It has na set rentall of dewtie, because it is everie yeir alterit or set." "Scarba is 4 merk land, and pertenis to McClane of Lochbuy in heritage. It is all woodis and craigis, except twa tounis. It payis zeirlie, samekle as is labourit thairof, as the remanent Iles payis, and will raise 17 men." This description does not relate to possessions on the mainland.

The life which Sir Lachlan had been leading made him restless, and his desire for war grew upon him. Immediately after his release in 1591, he offered, through Bowes, to Elizabeth, Queen of England, his services in aid against the chiefs of Islay and Sleat, as well as O'Rourke and other Irish barons, who were then in rebellion against her authority. In terms of his engagement, he proceeded to Ireland at the head of eighteen hundred of his followers, and, by his assistance, the queen's deputy soon suppressed the rebellion.

The suspension of the desolating feuds of the powerful chiefs of MacLean and MacDonald was an event of the utmost importance to their followers, and one of which they had every reason to feel more than ordinary gratitude. Peace appeared to be fully established, and the prospects for growth and prosperity brightened every day; and between the clans a friendly intercourse was maintained. This state of affairs continued uninterrupted for a considerable time; but this universal harmony now existing between parties so long at enmity and so deadly hostile to one another, was looked upon more with jealousy than satisfaction by the government. The government was so weak and impotent that its principal strength, as regarded the Isles, lay rather in the dissensions of those chiefs who were powerful and restless; and the growth of friendship between the MacLeans and MacDonalds was regarded with great disfavor. King James had long believed that there was great wealth in the Isles, and he constantly turned his eye in that direction, when not begging a pension from the queen of England, in hopes that money might be extracted for his coffers. Money could be realized by the arrest, imprisonment, and threatened forfeiture of the most influential chiefs. Where the will was so disposed, it was not difficult to find a pretext for the exercise of arbitrary power. A decree was issued on 8th of June, 1592,* commanding Lachlan MacLean of Duard to appear personally before the king and his council upon 13th July next, and to find surety for the thankful payment of the king's " rentis of his propir landis in the Ilis possest be him and his freindis, in conformity with the said Act of Parliament." This act of parliament (Acts III., 561, 562) required Lachlan to give obedience before the 1st August next, under pain of forfeiture of life, lands and goods. This act had been passed against him because all the terms of his late remission had not been complied with. But James cared not for that, as his own statement in the decree shows it was money. From the decree, it appears he had failed to give hostages and enter his own person in ward at the castle of Edinburgh. About the same time, many others were peremptorily brought before the king.

On the 16th March, 1592-3,† at Edinburgh, the king, with advice of his council, ordains letters to issue to relax the following persons from the horn for " ony cause bygone," receive them to the king's peace, and " giff to thame the wand thairof,—Lauchlane McGillane of Dowart, McGillan of Lochboy, McClaine of Coll, McCloyd, tutor of Harrick, Lauchlane McFingoun, alias McKynnoun, of Strathoradell, Hector McQueine or McCorrey of Ullovay, Chairlis McGilleane, tutor of Ardgour, John Oig McGillane of Ardnamurcho, Allane McGillane, bailie of Morveane, Johnne McGilleane, bailie of Rosie, Neil McGillecallum, captain of Arros, McGilleawne, captain of Carnybreigh, McNeill of Barry."

Three of the leading earls of Scotland were strong Catholics, and possessed considerable influence; these were Huntly, Angus, and Erroll. They formed a conspiracy with Philip of Spain for the restoration of the Catholic religion

---

* *Register Privy Council*, Vol. IV., p. 755. † *Ibid.*, Vol. V., p. 54.

in Scotland. So bold did they finally become, that in June, 1594, they were declared forfeited by parliament. The commotion stirred up by these papists had a corresponding result in the Isles, and the chiefs there pursued the even tenor of their way. As Sir Lachlan Mór remained contumacious, or for some misdemeanor, the same parliament also declared him forfeited. This was undoubtedly caused by the want of money, for on Lachlan offering the king a considerable amount of money, the forfeiture, so far as he was concerned, was reversed. It may have been that the king only desired to humiliate such powerful chiefs, and their obedience flattered his vanity. Such proceedings were certainly calculated to alienate the good will of MacLean, for the unwarrantable procedure and its object were plainly visible. But the Catholic earls resorting to open rebellion, James found that the assistance of the MacLeans was necessary, not only to preserve the peace of the kingdom, but the throne itself. For some unaccountable reason, unless it was the mere accident of birth, the command of the royal forces was bestowed upon Archibald Campbell, seventh Earl of Argyle, an individual of no experience and but eighteen years of age. The folly of this appointment was fully made manifest. Under this earl, Sir Lachlan was asked to serve with his clansmen. The army was composed partly of Campbells, but particularly of MacLeans, MacNeills, MacGregors, MacIntoshes, and Grants; in all, between six and seven thousand men. Three thousand were chosen men, bearing harquebuses, bows, and pikes; the rest were more slenderly equipped, both as to body armor and weapons. Argyle made many boasts, and sent a challenge to Huntly, and that within three days he would sleep in Strathbogie. He ordered "the herald to proclaim the royal commission by sound of trumpet in the marketplace, and appointed Sir Lachlan MacLean of Duard to the chief command under himself." The army marched into Badenoch, and laid seige to the castle of Ruthven, which the MacPhersons strongly defended. Failing here, Argyle next led his army through the hills to Strathbogie, intending to carry fire and sword through Huntly's lands. On his arrival at Glenlivat, Argyle found that Huntly and Erroll were in the vicinity with fifteen hundred men, principally of cavalry. In this army were also Highlanders—the Clan Cameron, the MacPhersons, and Clanranald. On October 3d (1594) Huntly marched against Argyle, and opened fire; "and on the first discharge, which was directed at the yellow standard of Argyle, struck down and slew MacNeill, the Laird of Barra's third son, one of their bravest officers, and Campbell of Lochnell, who held the standard. This successful commencement occasioned extraordinary confusion amongst the Highlanders, to many of whom the terrible effects of artillery were even at this late day unknown; and a large body of them, yelling and brandishing their broad-swords and axes, made some ineffectual attempts to reach the horsemen; but receiving another fire from the little ordnance train of Captain Gray, they took to flight, and in an incredibly short time were out of sight and pursuit. Still, however, a large body remained; and Argyle had the advantage not only of the sun, then shining fiercely in the eyes of his opponents, glancing on their steel coats and making the plain appear on fire, but of the ground; for his army was arrayed on the top of a steep hill covered with high heather and stones, whilst the ground at the bottom was soft and mossy, full of holes, called in that country peat-pots, and dangerous for cavalry. But all this did not deter Huntly's vanguard, under Errol and Auchendown, from advancing resolutely to the attack. Errol, however, dreading the marsh, made an oblique movement by some firmer ground which lay on one side, and hoped thus to turn the flank of the enemy; but Sir Patrick Gordon of Auchendown, urged on by his fiery temper, spurred his horse directly toward the hill, and getting entangled with his men in the mossy ground, was exposed to a murderous fire from the force under MacLean of Duard. This chieftain was conspicuous from his great stature and strength; he was covered with a shirt of mail, wielded a double-edged Danish battle-ax, and appears to have been a more experienced officer than the rest, as he placed his men, who were mostly 'harquebusiers,' in a small copsewood hard by, from which they could deliver their fire, and be screened from the attack of cavalry. Auchendown, nevertheless, although his ranks were dreadfully thinned by this fire of the enemy's infantry, managed to disengage them, and spurring up the hill, received a bullet in the body, and fell from his horse; whilst his companions shouted with grief and rage, and made desperate efforts to rescue him. The Highlanders, however, who knew him well, rushed in upon him, dispatched him with their dirks, and, cutting off his head, displayed it in savage triumph; a sight which so enraged the Gordons, that they fought with a fury which alike disregarded discipline and life. This gave an advantage to MacLean, who, inclosing the enemy's vanguard, and pressing it into narrow space between his own force and Argyle's, would have cut them to pieces had not Huntly come speedily to their support and renewed the battle; attacking both Argyle and MacLean with desperate energy, and calling loudly to his friends to revenge Auchendown. It was at this moment that some of the Gordons caught sight of Fraser, the king's herald, who rode beside Argyle, and was dressed in his tabard, with the red lion embroidered upon it, within the double tressure. This ought to have been his protection; but it seemed rather to point him out as a victim; and the horsemen shouting out, 'Have at the lion,' ran him through with their spears, and slew him on the spot. The battle was now at its height, and raged for two hours with the utmost cruelty. Errol was severely wounded with a bullet in the arm, and by one of the sharp-barbed arrows of the Highland bowmen, which pierced deep into the thigh. He lost his pennon or guidon also, which was won by MacLean. Gordon of Gicht was struck with three bullets through the body, and had two plates of his steel coat carried into him—wounds which next day proved mortal. Huntly himself was in imminent danger of his life; for his horse was shot under him, and the Highlanders were about to attack him on the ground with their knives and axes, when he was extricated and horsed again by Innermarkie; after which, he again charged the enemy under Argyle, whose troops wavered, and at last began to fly in such numbers that only twenty men were left around him. Upon this, the young chief, overcome with grief and vexation at so disgraceful a desertion, shed tears of rage, and would still have renewed the fight, had not Murray of Tullibardine seized his bridle and forced him off the field. Seeing the day lost, MacLean, who had done most and suffered least in this cruel fight, withdrew his men from the wood, and retired in good order; but seven hundred Highlanders were slain in the chase, which was continued until the steepness of the mountains rendered pursuit impossible. Such was the battle of Glenlivat." * The loss of Huntly did not amount to over seventy.

All historians who have recorded the battle of Glenlivat have been loud in their praise of the conduct of Sir Lachlan Mór MacLean. Among these, the following are selected: Gregory says: "The conduct of Lachlan MacLean of Duard, who was one of Argyle's officers in this action, would, if imitated by the other leaders, have converted the defeat into a victory. That chief acted the part of a brave and skillful soldier, keeping his men in their ranks, and employing with good effect all the advantages of his position. It was his division which inflicted the principal loss on the rebels; and, at the close of the action, he retired in good order with those under his command. It is said that, after the battle, he offered, if Argyle would give him five hundred men in addition to his own clan, to bring the Earl of Huntly prisoner into Argyle's camp. This proposal was rejected; but having come to the ears of

---

* Tytler's *History of Scotland*, Vol. IV., p. 223.

Huntly, incensed him greatly against MacLean, whose son afterwards, according to tradition, lost a large estate in Lochaber through the animosity of that powerful nobleman."* Sir Walter Scott uses the following language: "The chief of MacLean alone, a man of uncommon strength and courage, dressed in a shirt of mail, and armed with a double-edged battle-axe, defied the efforts of the assailants for some time, but was at length compelled to flight." † Spottiswoode says: "In end, the Argyle men were disordered and put to rout. The earl himself labored all he could to rally them again together, but it would not be; so amazed they were, as, without once looking back, down they went the other side of the hill with all the speed they could make. MacLean, with a few isles-men, stood long unto it after the rest were gone, and retired in good order with the small company he had." ‡ In the *Spottiswoode Miscellany* (Vol. II., p. 261), is the following: "The Islanders made strong resistance and stood long after the main body had betaken them to flight, especially their leader MacLean, who was so pertinacious and headstrong that but with strong hands by his friends, and others he was told of the lieutenant's retreat, could not be withdrawn from the fight. In the lieutenant's army were 12,000 men, whereof above 500 were killed, many prisoners and the colors taken." The author of the *Conflict of the Clans*, written during the reign of James VI., says: "In end, Argyle with his main battle began to decline, and then to flee apace, leaving MacLean still fighting in the field; who, seeing himself thus destitute of succors, and his men either fled or slain, retired in good order with the small company he had about him, and saved himself by flight; having behaved himself in the fight, not only like a good commander, but also like a valiant soldier." || Browne records that, "after a hard contest the main body of Argyle's army began to give way, and retreated towards the rivulet of Altchonlachan; but MacLean still kept the field and continued to support the falling fortune of the day. At length, finding the contest hopeless, and after losing many of his men, he retired in good order with the small company that still remained about him." § Keltie says: "The earl of Errol was directed to attack the right wing of Argyle's army, commanded by MacLean. . . . The fall of Auchindun so exasperated his followers that they set no bounds to their fury; but MacLean received their repeated assaults with firmness, and manœuvered his troops so well as to succeed in cutting off the earl of Errol, and placing him between his own body and that of Argyle,

---

* *Western Highlands*, p. 259. † *History of Scotland*, Vol. II., p. 349. ‡ *History of the Church of Scotland*, Vol. II., p. 459. || *Celtic Magazine*, Vol. XI., p. 119. § *History of the Highland Clans*, Vol. I., p. 225.

by whose joint forces he was completely surrounded. . . . MacLean still kept the field, and continued to support the falling fortune of the day. At length, finding the contest hopeless, and after losing many of his men, he retired in good order with the small company that still remained about him." * " Huntly won the day, but the MacLeans were the only party that won honors on that occasion." † The *Book of Scottish Story* (p. 640) declares that, " on this occasion Lachlan Mór was greatly distinguished for bravery and for prudence, having acted the part of an experienced commander, and gained the applause of both armies." The Pennycross MS, in harmony with the various MSS of the MacLean family, says, that Lachlan Mór drew up his men at a short distance from the main body, as a reserve, kept his ground, and when the Gordons began to attack him, they poured such a shower of arrows upon them that they were glad to give them no more trouble. The MacLeans, standing their ground till evening, retired in good order, and joined Argyle at night. Lachlan Mór offered to Argyle, if he would allow him to choose five hundred men out of the army, together with his own clan, he would bring the Earl of Huntly, either dead or alive, to him. This proposal the Earl of Argyle rejected; and Huntly, having heard of it, studied revenge, which was afterward effected, as shall be told in its place.

Archibald Campbell of Lochnell, commander of one of the divisions of Argyle's army, had opened up a traitorous correspondence with the confederated earls. " This ambitious baron, whose previous machinations for the destruction of his chief and his own advancement to the earldom had not yet come to the knowledge of Argyle—thought the present an excellent opportunity of accomplishing his long-cherished views. He therefore sent a private message to Huntly, desiring him to attack the Highlanders, and promising, in the course of the engagement, to aid him with the division under his command. He likewise suggested that some pieces of artillery which accompanied Huntly's army should be fired at Argyle's banner; hoping thus to get rid of that nobleman by an apparent chance shot, and to discourage the faithful Highlanders, who were many of them unacquainted with artillery. The advice of Lochnell was followed; but the result was unexpected." The missiles struck down the treacherous Lochnell.‡

The triumph of the Popish earls for their success at Glenlivat was of short duration. The king with a sufficient force proceeded against them and

---

* *History of the Highland Clans*, Vol. I., p. 109.   † *The Highlander* (Inverness), June 27, 1874.   ‡ Gregory's *Western Highlands*, p. 258.

demolished their fortresses. Huntly was forced to flee abroad, and Angus lurked as a fugitive in the wilds of Douglasdale.

We are next introduced to Sir Lachlan Mór as an important personage in the cause of England, during the reign of Elizabeth. This has been so well told by Tytler* that his language is here adopted : "The queen of England began bitterly to repent her neglect of Scotland, and to look with alarm to a storm which threatened her on the side of the Isles. She was now trembling for her empire in Ireland, where Tyrone had arisen in formidable force, and, assisted with Roman gold and Spanish promises, threatened to wrest from her hands the fairest provinces of her kingdom. In these circumstances, both Elizabeth and the Irish prince looked for assistance and recruits to the Scottish Isles. These nurseries of brave soldiers and hardy seamen were now able to furnish a formidable force ; a circumstance not unknown to the English queen, as her indefatigable minister, Burghley, whose diplomatic feelers were as long as they were acute and sensitive, kept up a communication with the Isles. From a paper written in the end of the year 1593, by one of his northern correspondents, it appears that the Isles could, on any emergency, get out a force of six thousand hardy troops, inured to danger both by sea and land, and equipt for war on either element. Of these, two thousand wore defensive armor, actons, habergeons, and knapsculls; the rest were bowmen or pikemen; but many, adds the island statist, had now become harquebusiers. This force, it is to be observed, was independent of those kept at home to labor the ground; the whole of the Isles being different from the rest of feudal Scotland in one essential respect, 'that they who occupied the ground were not charged to the wars.' . . . Of these chiefs, the Lord of Duard, commonly called Lachlan Mór, was by far the most talented and conspicuous ; and, Elizabeth well knew, had the power of bridling or letting loose that formidable body of troops which Donald Gorm and Ruari Mór were now collecting to assist her enemies in Ireland. . . . It is curious to trace Elizabeth's connection with this man. The lord of Duard's confidential servant happened to be a certain shrewd Kelt, named John Achinross; he, in turn, was connected by marriage with Master John Cunningham, a worthy citizen and merchant of Edinburgh. This honest bailie of the capital, forming the link between savage and civilized life, corresponded with Sir Robert Bowes; Bowes with Burghley or Sir Robert Cecil; and thus Elizabeth, sitting in her closet at Windsor or Greenwich, moved the strings which could

---

* *History of Scotland*, Vol. IV., pp. 234-7.

assemble or disperse the chivalry of the Isles. This is no ideal picture, for the letters of the actors remain. As early as March, 1594-5, Achinross informed Bowes that MacLean and Argyle were ready, not only to stay the Clan Donnell, who, under Donald Gorm, were then mustering to assist Tyrone, but that MacLean himself would join the English army in Ireland, if Elizabeth would dispatch three or four ships to keep his galleys whilst they attacked the enemy.* As the summer came on, and the fleet of Donald and his associates waited only for a fair wind, Cunningham hurried to the Isles, had a conference with MacLean, and thence rode post to London, where, in an interview with Sir Robert Cecil, he urged the necessity of instant action and assistance.† The bridle which the laird of Duard held over the Islemen was simple enough; being a garrison of six hundred mercenaries, well armed, and ready to be led by him, on a moment's warning, against any island chief who embarked in foreign service, and left his lands undefended at home.‡ The support of this force, however, required funds: Elizabeth demurred; MacLean was obliged to disband his men; and the most part of the fleet weighed anchor, and bore away for Ireland.‖ It consisted of a hundred sail, of which fifty were galleys, the rest smaller craft; and the number of soldiers and mariners was estimated at about five thousand.§ Nine hundred men, however, under the captain of the Clan Ranald,** still remained; and as they passed Mull had the temerity to land for the night; running their 'galleys, boats, and birlings,' into a little harbor, where they imagined themselves secure. But MacLean, by what Achinross termed a 'bauld onset and prattie feit of weir,' took the whole company prisoners, threw the chiefs into irons, sent them to his dungeons in his different castles, appropriated their galleys, and transmitted the common men to the mainland.†† Amongst the chief prisoners then taken, were the captain of Clan Ranald and three of his uncles, the laird of Knoydart, MacIan of Ardnamurchan, Donald Gorm's brother, and others; and an account of the surprise was immediately transmitted by John Achinross to Nicholson, the English envoy at the court of James. We can pardon the enthusiasm and abominable orthoepy of this devoted Highland

---

* MS State-paper Office, March 25, 1595, contents of John Achinross's letter to Robert Bowes. † MS letter, State-paper Office, John Cunningham to Sir R. Bowes, June 25, 1595; also, MacLean of Duard to Sir Robert Cecil, July 4, 1595; also, same to Sir R. Bowes, July 4, 1595; also, ibid.. Nicolson to Bowes, July 5, 1595. ‡ MS letter, State-paper Office, John Achinross to George Nicolson, July 22, 1595. ‖ Ibid., Nicolson to Bowes, July 26, 1595. § Ibid., Mr. George Areskine to Nicholson, Dunoon, July 31, 1595. ** Ibid., same to same. †† MS letter, State-paper Office, Achinross to Nicholson, July 31, 1595.

servant when he exclaims: 'My maister is acquaentit with thir prattie onsettis, without respect to number find and vantage: for divers tymis he plaid this dance heir aganis his enemies. I assuir you, thir men that are tane and in captivity, ar the maist doubttit and abil men in the Ilis. Lat your guid maister and Sir Robert comfort thame with this gude luke, done be ane vailyeant man of weir, and ane man of honor, in beginning of her majestie's service.' *

"Elizabeth was delighted with this exploit of Lachlan Mór, assured him of her gratitude and friendship, and sent a more substantial proof than words, in a present of a thousand crowns: an 'honorable token of her favor,' as he called it in a letter to Cecil, in which he promised all duty and service to the queen. She wrote, at the same time, to the earl of Argyle; flattered him by some rich token of her regard; and ordered Nicholson, her resident at the Scottish court, to deliver it and her letter to him in person, at Dunoon in Argyle. All this was successfully accomplished; and so cordially did MacLean and Argyle co-operate, sowing distrust and division amongst the chiefs and leaders who had followed the banner of Donald Gorm and MacLeod, that their formidable force only made the coast of Ireland to meet the English ships, which were on the watch for them, enter into a friendly treaty, and disperse to their different ocean nests, before a single effort of any moment had been made. This sudden arrival, and as sudden disappearance of the fleet of the Islesmen, appears to have puzzled the chroniclers of the times, and even their more acute modern successors. A black cloud had been seen to gather over Ireland; and men waited in stillness for the growl of the thunder and the sweep of the tempest, when it melted into air, and all was once more tranquillity. This seemed unaccountable; almost miraculous; but the letters of honest John Cunningham, and his Keltic relative Achinross, whose epistles smack so strongly of his Gaelic original, introduce us behind the scenes, and discover Lachlan Mór as the secret agent, the Keltic Prospero, whose wand dispersed the galleys and restored serenity to the ocean. The reader may be pleased with an extract from a letter of this brave lord of Duard to Sir R. Bowes, although his style is a little ponderous, and by no means so polished as the Danish steel axe with which it was his delight to hew down his enemies: he is alluding to the future plan of the campaign intended by Tyrone and O'Donnell against Elizabeth, and to the best way to defeat it:

"'The earl is to pursue you on one side, and O'Donnell is to pursue your

---

* MS letter, State-paper Office, Achinross to Nicholson.

lands presently on the other side. They think to harm you meikle by this way. If my opinion were followed out, the earl and O'Donnell shall be pursued on both the sides: to wit, by your force of Ireland on the one side, and by the earl of Argyle's force and mine, with my own presence, on this side. To the which, I would that you moved the earl of Argyle to furnish two thousand men; myself shall furnish other two thousand; and I would have six or eight hundred of your spearsmen, with their *buttis*, and four hundred pikemen. If I were once landed in Ireland with this company, having three or four ships to keep our galleys, I hope in God the earl should lose that name ere our return. . . . In my name your lordship shall have my duty of humble service remembered to her majesty, and commendations to good Sir Robert Cecil, with whom I think to be acquainted. Your lordship will do me a great pleasure if you will let me know of any thing in Scotland that may pleasure Sir Robert. I am so *hamely** with your lordship, that without you let me know hereof, I will think that your lordship does dissimull with me. I am here, in Argyle, at pastime and hunting of deer. I am hamely with your lordship, as ye may perceive. At meeting (for the which I think long), God willing, we shall renew our acquaintance.'" †

"The continuance of the rebellion in Ireland, and the intrigues of Tyrone with the Western Isles, had greatly annoyed Elizabeth; and Bowes was ordered to communicate with the king, and with MacLean of Duard, on the subject. He found that James had resolved to adopt speedily some decided measures to bring the Isles into order; and hoped to succeed by employing in this service the earl of Argyle, MacLean, and MacKenzie, to whose sister MacLean had lately married his eldest son. The ambassador had been, as usual, tutored to spare his mistress's purse, whilst he sounded MacLean's 'mind, power and resolution;' and exerted himself to the utmost to drive a hard bargain. He was alarmed, too, with the din of warlike preparations then sounding through the western archipelago: Donald Gorm was mustering his men, and repairing his galleys; MacLeod of Harris had lately landed from Ireland, and was ready to return with fresh power; and Angus MacDonald, another potent chief, was assembling his galleys and soldiers.‡ MacLean himself was in Tiree, then reckoned ten days' journey from Edinburgh; and Argyle, so intent in investigating the murder of Campbell of Calder, now traced to Campbell of

---

* Hamely, familiar. † MS letter, State-paper Office, Lachlan MacLean of Duard to Sir R. Bowes, Garvie in Argyle, August 22, 1595. ‡ MS letter, State-paper Office, March 6, 1595–6. Memorial to John Cunningham, February 22, 1595–6. Answers by MacLean to the questions proposed by Sir R. Bowes, March 30, 1596.

Ardkinglass, that Bowes could have no immediate transactions with either. He set, however, Cunningham and Achinross, his former agents, to work; and when these active emissaries got amongst the Highlanders, the storm of letters, memorials, contracts, queries, answers and estimates, soon poured down on the unhappy head of Bowes, who implored Cecil, but with small success, to send him instructions, and some portion of treasure, to satisfy Elizabeth's Keltic auxiliaries, who clamored for gold. MacLean was perfectly ready, as before, to attack Tyrone; and confident that the plan of campaign, which he had already communicated, if carried into vigorous effect, would reduce the great rebel. But he made it imperative on the queen to furnish two thousand soldiers, and advance a month's pay to his men. He himself, he said, had neither spared 'gear nor pains in the service; and yet her majesty's long promised present of a thousand crowns had not yet arrived.' * These remonstrances produced the effect desired. Elizabeth was shamed into some settlement of her promises; and MacLean, with his island chivalry, declared himself ready to obey her majesty's orders with all promptitude and fidelity." †

It is uncertain whether or not Sir Lachlan performed any service for the English queen after this. His death soon after probably prevented it. Tyrone's rebellion was not suppressed until 1602.‡

Early in the year 1596, the king, by the advice of the privy council and of the estates of parliament, then in session, and in order to increase his revenues, determined to proceed in person against such chiefs as he deemed remained contumacious. A proclamation was issued, by which all earls, lords, barons, and free-holders, worth over three hundred merks of yearly rent, should meet the king at Dumbarton, on the first day of August, well armed, and with forty days' provisions, and likewise provided with vessels to carry them to the Isles. This proclamation caused Sir Lachlan and Donald of Sleat immediately to repair to court. It is recorded,‖ and dated at Holyrood House, June 15, 1596, that Lachlan MacLean of Duard, having lately, in order to "testifie his humble obediens and dewitie to his Majestie," repaired to the king's presence, submitted himself to his clemency and grace, and satisfied the lords auditors of exchequer "anent all thingis quhilkis wer layed to his charge;" and the said Lachlan, "expecting now in end his Hienes favourable

---

* MS letter, State-paper Office, February 24, 1595–6; *Ibid.*, Bowes to Sir R. Cecil, March 6, 1595–6; *Ibid.*, Bowes to Cecil, March 16, 1595–6; *Ibid.*, MacLean to Bowes, Coll, March 18, 1595–6; *Ibid.*, MacLean's answers to Bowes, March 30, 1596. † Tytler's *History of Scotland*, Vol. IV., p. 240. ‡ For some of Achinross's and Sir Lachlan's letters, see Appendix, Note B. ‖ *Register of Privy Council*, Vol. V., p. 295.

countenance, pardoun and mercy aganis the proces of foirfaltour led aganis him," his majesty, with advice of his council, receives the said Lachlan into his favor, and reposes him to all his lands, living, and honors, as freely as if the said process and doom had never been led, declaring that the effect thereof shall cease in time coming, at least until his highness may "establishe and perfyte quhatsoevir may be tend or be thocht convenient for the full and sufficient suirtie of the said Lauchlane with advise of his Esteatis in Parliament; quhilk his Majestie, in his princelie worde promissis to caus be effectual to the said Lauchlane, with the ratification of thir presentis, in the nixt Parliament." Intimation hereof is ordered to be made by open proclamation at all places needful, with charge to the lieges not to "sklander, murmour, reproche or backbyte" the said Lachlan for any cause or crime bygone, under all highest panis and offence; and officers of arms are required to relax the said Lachlan from any process of horn used against him at any time bygone, and to give him the wand of peace.

MacDonald of Sleat made submission also, and was pardoned. But Angus MacDonald of Islay remained contumacious, at which the king's displeasure was so marked that he bestowed upon MacLean the Rhinns of Islay, so long disputed between that chief and the MacDonalds.* Angus, however, submitted during the month of October.

During the same year Sir Lachlan came nearly losing the advantage he had gained with the king by having previously taken advantage of the death of Hector MacLean of Coll, and the minority of Lachlan, the son and successor of that baron, by seizing the castle and island of Coll, and the other estates of that family, and expelling all their adherents. Lachlan MacLean of Coll, now arriving at the age of maturity, entered complaint before the privy council, alleging that in the possession of his lands he is now "maist havelie molestit, troublit and opprest" in the possession of the said lands by Lauchlane McClayne of Dowart, and Rory Beg McClayne, his deputy and servant, who, shortly after the decease of the complainer's father, "takand the advantage of his minoritie, seirit thameselffis upoun his landis foirsaidis, possest thameselffis thairwith, and with the said complenaris place and castell of Bretach, quhilk house they intend to dimoleis and cast doun, and hes detenit the said place and landis, and intromettit with and uptakin the mailles, fermis and dewities thairof continuallie sensyne, and be way of deid, forceablie detenis and with-holdis the same fra the said complenair." Both parties appear-

---

* Gregory's *Western Highlands*, p. 265.

ing personally, the king, with advice of his council, ordains the chief defender to find caution that he shall deliver the portalice of Bretach to Sir William Stewart of Howstoun, his majesty's lieutenant of the Isles and Highlands, for the better "furthsetting" of the king's service, when required upon twenty-four hours' warning, and also that he shall enter the complainer to the possession of his said lands within thirty days hereof, and suffer him and his tenants to "peaceablie brouke, labour and manure the same; conform to his infeftments, under the pain of 10,000 merks." Dated at Linlithgow, December 23, 1596.*

Sir Lachlan must have remained for several days in Linlithgow, for on December 25th, together with Lord Hereis, he became surety for Duncan MacDougall of Dunnoldycht, in the sum of five thousand merks.†

During the same year there must have been some symptoms of the renewal of the feud between the MacLeans and the MacDonalds, for the records show a registration by the principal and Thomas Craig as procurator for the sureties, of a bond of caution in twenty thousand merks by Lauchlane Macklane of Dowart as principal, and Archibald, earl of Ergyle, as surety for him, in manner and to the effect foresaid,—Kenneth MacKenzie of Kintale becoming surety in relief. "This bond not to extend to any action or quarrel that may fall out between the said principal and his friends and the Clan Donald, Clan Renile, Clan Eane, and their friends and partakers, till the principals and chiefs of the said clans find caution on the like conditions. Subscribed at Edinburgh and Striveling 13th and 14th June, before Kenneth Makkenzie of Kilcreist, Mr. Johnne McKenzie, parson of Dingwall, Allister McKenzie, Johnne Auchinros, Mr. George Erskin, Mr. Donald Campbell, and the earls of Mar and Merschell as curators for the earl of Ergyle." ‡

. In the year 1598 the following unfortunate circumstance took place, which broke the friendship between Sir Lachlan and Allan Cameron of Lochiel: "Donald MacIan of Ardnamurchan, who had been betrothed to one of Lochiel's daughters, was basely murdered by his own uncle, while he was providing himself with a suitable equipage for his wedding, which, according to custom of the times, he was to have celebrated with great magnificence. The murderer, commonly known as 'Mac Mhic Eoghainn,' was a man of gigantic size and strength, and possessed the district of Suainart on lease from his nephew, MacIan, whom he killed; not, it is said, in resentment of any injury done to him, but with the view of succeeding him in his estate and

---

* *Register of Privy Council,* Vol. V., p. 354.   † *Ibid.*   ‡ *Ibid.,* p. 740.

command of the clan as the next heir. For MacIan, Lochiel had the highest esteem on account of his many excellent qualities, and he no sooner heard of his death than he determined to revenge it. The murderer, in dread of Lochiel's resentment, fled with all his goods and cattle to the Island of Mull, to place himself under the protection of Lachlan Mór MacLean of Duard, who was his near relative on his mother's side. Lochiel, getting information of his precipitate flight, pursued him with the few men he had about him, not exceeding sixty, and captured his goods, but notwithstanding the haste he had made, Mac Mhic Eoghainn himself escaped across the Sound of Mull. MacLean, seeing all that had passed, from the opposite shore, dispatched his eldest son, Hector, with two hundred and twenty men, with Mac Mhic Eoghainn at their head, to recover the goods. Lochiel, now finding himself obliged to fight, posted his men in an advantageous position, which largely made up for his deficiency in numbers. Mac Mhic Eoghainn, armed cap-a-pie, advanced with an air which indicated the highest contempt for his enemy; but, feeling warm under the weight of his armor, he raised his helmet to admit the fresh air. One of Lochiel's archers at once observed this, and, taking his unerring aim, he pierced him in the forehead with an arrow, killing him on the spot. The death of Mac Mhic Eoghainn so dispirited his followers that Lochiel secured an easy victory over them. Hector MacLean and twenty of his followers were taken prisoners, but Lochiel immediately released them without ransom. Lachlan Mór himself crossed the Sound of Mull during the action, and pursued Lochiel with a much larger force than his own, but he managed to escape without much loss." *

In the same year, Angus MacDonald's son James, who had been knighted by the king, although never having exhibited any military capacity, and still quite a young man, and of a very violent temper, presuming on the favor that had been shown him while a hostage at court, determined to deprive his father of his influence and seize upon the estates. "A quarrel among the Mac-Allasters of Loupe favored his designs, and seems to have suggested to him the idea of procuring his father's death, as if by accident. The young Laird of Loupe, Gorrie MacAllaster, who had succeeded to the estate when a minor, had lately, since he was come of age, a serious dispute with his tutor or guardian, in the course of which he killed the latter. The sons of the tutor took refuge with their chief, Angus MacDonald of Dunyveg; whilst the Laird of Loupe, who eagerly sought their lives, procured the support of Sir James MacDonald

---

* MacKenzie's *History of the Camerons*, Celtic Magazine, Vol. VIII., p. 372.

on the arrival of the latter in Kintyre. Understanding that the tutor's sons were with Angus MacDonald, at his house of Askomull in Kintyre, Sir James and his associates, to the number of two or three hundred armed men, surrounded the house in the dead of night, and on the refusal of the MacAllasters to surrender themselves prisoners, the house was immediately set on fire. Although perfectly aware that his father and mother were in the house, Sir James savagely refused to let the fire be extinguished; and at length, his father, endeavoring to make his escape, was made prisoner, after being severely burnt and suffering many indignities from Sir James's servants. He was then carried to Smerbie in Kintyre, and confined there in irons for several months. The other inmates of the house likewise fell into the hands of Sir James, and were treated with various degrees of severity; but he does not appear to have caused any of them to be put to death. Sir James now took command of his clan, and neglecting his promises to the king, conducted himself with such violence in his new capacity, that in the month of June, 1598, it became necessary to issue a proclamation for another royal expedition or raid to Kintyre. . . . Early in August, Sir James MacDonald had contrived to procure from the king a letter approving of his late proceedings in Kintyre, and particularly of his apprehension of his father." *

The royal expedition did not proceed against the recusant James, for the reason that news was received at court that a feud had broken out between the MacDonalds and MacLeans. Sir James, now fully in possession of the estate, burned for an occasion to measure swords with his uncle, the Lord of Duard, for the numerous injuries he conceived his clan to have suffered in former years at the hands of the MacLeans. As has been previously noted, the lands in dispute (the Rhinns of Islay) were recently confirmed to Sir Lachlan by the crown, and in so far as this particular point was concerned, the nephew does not appear to have felt disposed to oppose his possession of them; only that he still claimed his right of feudal sovereignty over the possessor. While this point was in agitation, another subject became the cause of an immediate rupture. A certain farm on the sea-side, called Portaskaig, which formed the boundary line between their estates, and which, from its convenience as a landing-place, was deemed of considerable importance by each party, was claimed by Sir Lachlan as being within the limits of his grant. This was disputed by Sir James, and after many fruitless endeavors to settle the matter between themselves, it was suggested by Sir Lachlan that the point

---

* Gregory's *Western Highlands*, p. 281.

should be submitted to the arbitration of mutual friends, and in the event of their determination proving unsatisfactory, that it should finally be left to the decision of the king. To this MacDonald seemingly gave a willing consent, and a day and place were appointed for a future conference and for naming the arbitrators. The 5th of August, 1598, was the day appointed for this purpose, and Tra-Ghruinnaird, or Gruinnart Shore, in Islay, was fixed upon as the place of meeting.

In the meantime both parties, evidently doubtful of a favorable result, and influenced moreover by want of mutual confidence, made their preparations rather with a view to a hostile meeting than a friendly conference. Sir James MacDonald mustered together about fifteen hundred of his clansmen and vassals in Islay and Kintyre, and Sir Lachlan, with about six hundred followers, among whom were his two sons, Hector Og and Lachlan Og, arrived at an island called Elleniamh,* on the day appointed. Here he left the greater portion of his followers in the care of his eldest son, Hector Og, while with his younger son Lachlan and one hundred and forty kinsmen, he proceeded to attend the expected conference at Gruinnart; and at once sent his proposals to MacDonald. Sir James in the meantime, the better to deceive his uncle, had concealed his men in the rear of the neighboring hills, but met the messengers with a few followers, and returned answer by some gentlemen of his clan, with instructions to observe how MacLean was guarded. MacDonald's messenger, ascertaining the comparative weakness of Sir Lachlan's party on shore, and satisfied that no assistance could be afforded him by his friends on the island, from the circumstance of the galleys being shored at high water, and the impossibility, from their weight and bulk, as well as the length of the shore and softness of the sand surrounding the island, to float them before the return of the tide, went back to their chief, reported accordingly, and counseled MacDonald that "now or never was the time to be revenged on MacLean." Young MacDonald instantly issued from behind the hills at the head of eight hundred followers, and drawing them up in hostile array on an eminence overlooking the position of the MacLeans, tauntingly sent word to his uncle that he was "come with his friends to the conference, and that his demands were an unconditional surrender of the point in dispute."

The action and warlike manners of young MacDonald revealed to the chief of MacLean the treacherous intention of his nephew, and though illy-

---

* Properly *Eelean-Thianan*, or St. Finnan's Island, off the eastern shore of Islay.

prepared to chastise the insolent tone assumed by him, and enraged at his arrogance, he instantly summoned his friends around him, and finding them all eager to encounter the MacDonalds, the brave Sir Lachlan Mór drew his trusty claymore from its scabbard, and stretching it out in his firm grasp, cried, "He who sees the setting sun can tell his son this steel had done its duty;" and then, with a smile upon his countenance, and pointing to the hill occupied by the MacDonalds, he added, "Follow me; let us salute my nephew in his exalted station with due respect." The MacLeans rushed forward, and swept the foremost of the foe from off the hill. The MacDonalds with a re-enforcement returned to the attack and again were driven from off the field before the impetuous attack of Sir Lachlan and his clansmen. The MacLeans now found opportunity to take a good position on the hill, from which it now became the object of Sir James to dislodge them; with this object in view, he ordered a retreat in the direction of a neighboring eminence, in the rear of which he had placed a strong force of the Kintyre men, in the hope to entice the MacLeans from the advantageous position gained by them. In this maneuver, however, the military experience of his uncle proved too much for him. Having gained a position which promised every advantage in case of attack, and in which he hoped to be able to maintain himself against his enemies until the state of the tide enabled his friends from the islands to join him, Sir Lachlan suffered the MacDonalds to practice their stratagem unmolested. Sir James finding that his foes were not to be beaten by stratagem, and knowing that delay might prove as dangerous to him as it was of importance to the MacLeans, determined on attacking them at once with a force which he hoped would be irresistible; so, placing himself at the head of nine hundred of his followers, he made a furious attack upon the position held by the MacLeans. Here the veteran warriors of Glenlivat and other well-fought battles, formed by the skillful management of their intrepid leader into an impregnable phalanx, bid defiance to their assailants, until the presumptuous daring of Sir James, who, surrounded by his personal friends, advanced within a hundred yards of the spot whereon his uncle stood, so roused the indignation of the latter, that he rushed forward, observing to those around him that he would "pluck a feather out of that eaglet's plume or perish in the attempt," and, followed by his devoted band with the rapidity of a mountain torrent, he hewed a path through the MacDonalds to within a sword's length of their chief; and for a moment beholding his nephew with a look of furious indignation, mingled with affection, this cool and collected warrior and greatly accomplished soldier merely observed, "*A Shemish! a Shemish! a mhic mo pheàther fág mo radhad"* (James! James! son of my sister, avoid my path), and at the same instant the massive weapon, raised perhaps with a different intent, fell with fatal effect upon another assailant. At this moment a shot from an insignificant follower of the ungrateful nephew brought the heroic chief of MacLean to the ground.

The man who killed Sir Lachlan Mór was a diminutive creature named *Dubh-sith*, whose surname was Shaw. Traditions still preserved in Islay state that he was a native of Jura and noted as being a superior archer and brave soldier. He lived in that part of Jura belonging to the MacLeans, and was a great admirer of Sir Lachlan Mór, and much attached to the clan. He went to Sir Lachlan and asked permission to fight for him, but was bluntly refused and told that his company would disgrace the men. His pride stung to the quick and his former love turned into hate, he went to Sir James MacDonald and proffered his services. Sir James sneeringly remarked to him, "Yes, indeed, I wish I had five hundred of the like of you!" Shaw immediately started off, but was called back, by Sir James, "Fight with my men, but be careful not to harm my uncle." To this he made no reply, but shook his head and set off. Shaw was armed with a gun, and climbing a tree waited for the opportunity when Sir Lachlan should be thrown in his way. As Sir Lachlan was ascending a rising ground not far from where Shaw was concealed, he bent so that there was an opening between the joints of his armor. Shaw noticing this took aim and wounded him mortally. This act was not only execrated by the MacLeans but also by nearly every member of most of the other clans also.*

The MacLeans, maddened to desperation by the fall of their beloved chief, fell furiously upon the MacDonalds, and making Sir Lachlan's body their rallying point, fought around it under the influence of such uncontrollable fury that no regard to the overwhelming numbers opposed to them could induce a single individual to accept the quarter now offered by Sir James; who, notwithstanding that the force already at his disposal outnumbered the MacLeans more than four to one, had to call up his reserve of Kintyre men to his aid; and it was almost by utter annihilation that the MacDonalds were able to overcome the devoted followers of the chief of MacLean. All the MacLeans were killed save about twenty, and of these a dozen left the field at an early period to escort Lachlan Og, who was severely wounded, to a place of safety. The few who survived the dreadful conflict could not retreat to the island where

---

* Extract from a letter by Hector MacLean of Islay to the author, March 22, 1888.

their boats and friends were, but were forced to fly to other places where they might obtain safe passage home.

The MacLeans, on the island of Elleniamh, under Hector Og, for the reasons already stated, could only be idle spectators of the disastrous fate of their chief and friends on shore; and unable from their reduced numbers to make head against the MacDonalds, when the tide rolled in, they took to their galleys and returned to Mull.

The above account, as preserved by the MacLean historians, differs materially from that given by Gregory, who says, "Sir Lachlan MacLean of Duard had succeeded in procuring from the king a grant of part of the island of Islay, forfeited by his old rival Angus MacDonald. Taking advantage of the dissensions of Clandonald, and calculating on the youth and inexperience of his nephew, Sir James, he levied his vassals and proceeded to Islay, in order to expel the MacDonalds, and put himself in possession of his new acquisitions in the island. Sir James MacDonald was not, however, disposed to yield to the pretentions of MacLean, and had already collected a number of his clan in Islay to oppose his uncle's proceedings. The mutual friends of both parties, desiring to spare the effusion of blood, labored to effect a mediation between them. A meeting was accordingly agreed to be held at Lochgruinart, in Islay, to arrange their differences, to which place the rival chiefs repaired, each with a considerable number of his followers, but the MacDonalds were inferior in force. To the pressing entreaties of the mediators, Sir James MacDonald yielded so far as to offer his uncle the half of the island for his life— denying at the same time the validity of the title on which MacLean founded his pretensions—provided he would agree to hold it, as his predecessors had held the Rhinns of Islay, for their personal service to the Clandonald. Moreover, Sir James offered to refer their disputes to the decision of any impartial persons MacLean might choose to name; and, in case of their differing, to the decision of the king. But MacLean, much against the opinion of his friends, who advised him to accept these offers, would hear of nothing but an absolute surrender, on the part of Sir James, of all title or claim to the island. Upon this, both parties resolved to settle the dispute by the sword. They encountered at the head of Lochgruniart, and a desperate conflict ensued. Sir James in the beginning of the action caused his vanguard to make a detour, as if they intended to retreat, but really with the object of gaining the top of an eminence near at hand, which Sir Lachlan was also desirous to possess. By this stratagem Sir James succeeded in gaining the height first, from which he charged the MacLeans with great vigor, and, forcing their van back upon their main body, threw the whole into confusion, and finally routed them. Sir Lachlan MacLean, with fourscore of his kinsmen and two hundred common soldiers, were killed; and his son, Lachlan Barrach MacLean, being dangerously wounded, made his escape with difficulty, with the survivors, to their boats. Sir James MacDonald was himself severely wounded, and, for a time, his recovery was doubtful; whilst thirty of his followers were killed and sixty wounded." *

Gregory relies on the statement of Sir R. Gordon, in his "History of Sutherland," for the truth of the above. While some parts of it may be true, yet as a whole it is evidently incorrect; for Gregory says (p. 265), and already quoted (p. 125), that the king granted to Sir Lachlan the Rhinns of Islay, which he already possessed, and the chiefs of MacLean before him, and which the MacDonalds claimed the MacLeans held of them as feudal superiors. In a foot-note Gregory says, "The MS History of the MacLeans gives a somewhat different account of this affair, throwing the chief blame upon the MacDonalds. Anderson's History of Scotland and Birrel's Diary agree in the censure of Sir James MacDonald." Gordon must have mixed his account with the vengeance Hector Og took on Sir James for the loss of his father.

Skene has the following account: "On the death of Angus of Islay,† this grant produced some negotiations between MacLean and James MacDonald, Angus' son, and in order to settle their difference a meeting was agreed upon between them, but MacLean coming unadvisedly with a small attendance, and his boats being stranded by the retiring tide, he was surprised by James MacDonald and killed after a brave resistance. And thus fell the greatest chief whom the MacLeans ever had, a victim to the treachery of the MacDonalds of Islay." ‡

Tytler, who based his investigations upon original documents, gives a different account, which appears to have been derived from a letter written August 10, 1598, by Nicholson to Cecil. He says Lachlan MacLean of Duard was "treacherously slain in Islay, by his nephew, Sir James MacDonald, who persuaded him to visit the island; alleging, as a pretext, his desire to make an amicable settlement of their differences. So little did the brave lord of Duard suspect any foul play, that he came to the meeting without armor, in a silk dress, and with only a rapier at his side. Along with him were his sec-

---

* *Western Highlands*, pp. 283–5.   † Skene is mistaken about the death of Angus. This did not happen until 1613.   ‡‡ *Highland Clans*, Vol. II., p. 212.

ond son, and the best of his kin, in their holiday garb, and with little other arms than their hunting-knives and boar spears; but, although set upon by an ambush of nearly seven hundred men, they made a desperate defense. MacLean, a man of herculean strength, slew three of the MacDonalds at the first onset. When he saw there was no hope, he commanded his son, who fought beside him, to fly, and live to avenge him; but the chief himself, and a little knot of his clansmen, stood shoulder to shoulder, and were not cut down till after fifty of their assailants had fallen. The death of this great chief was little resented by the king, for James had long been jealous of his dealings with Elizabeth." *

There is a legend preserved by Sir R. Gordon which declares that Sir Lachlan consulted with a witch as to the result of his expedition. The hag advised him in the first place not to land upon the island of Islay on a Thursday; secondly, that he should not drink of the water of a certain well near Gruinnart; and lastly, she told him that one MacLean should be killed at Gruinnart. The first of these injunctions MacLean transgressed unwillingly, being driven into the island of Islay by a tempest on a Thursday; the second he "transgressed negligentlie, haveing drunk of that water befor he wes awair, and so he was killed ther at Groinard, as wes foretold him, but doubtfullie." †

The remains of Sir Lachlan Mór MacLean was left on the battle-field. A day or two after the battle, "it is said that two females, of whom different accounts are given—some calling them strangers, some clanswomen, some relations of the dead—grieving to think that the body of so notable a chief as Sir Lachlan Mór should be unburied and uncared for on the moorland, came from a distance in search of it. They hired a rude vehicle—the only one to be had in the neighborhood—and having found the corpse, proceeded to carry it to the nearest burying-grounds, about six miles distant. The way was rough, and the driver looking behind him saw the head of the great chief, which extended beyond the car, nodding to him at every jolt, as if it had life, and were giving him directions. Boor, or perhaps enemy, as the fellow was, he laughed when he saw this. At the next heavy rut he looked again to please his savage soul with the same ferocious enjoyment. But this time the elder female, who had watched him, acted as described in the ballad.‡ She killed

---

* *History of Scotland*, Vol. IV., p. 267. † Quoted by Cromb, *Highlands and Highlanders*, p. 83; Keltic, *History Highland Clans*, Vol. I., p. 111; Author of *Conflicts of the Clans*, "Celtic Magazine," Vol. XI., p. 220. ‡ See Appendix, Note C, No. 14.

the brutal driver with the chieftain's dagger. Then, along with her companion, she brought the mortal remains of Sir Lachlan to the place where they still lie buried." *

Sir Lachlan Mór MacLean lies buried in the churchyard of Kilchoman, Islay, near the south wall of the church, and over his grave is laid a great stone. There is a churchyard, Kilnave, near the battle-field; but the body was taken to Kilchoman that it might be more honored, for he was buried inside the church, and when a new church was built there, about sixty years ago, the wall was so constructed that the grave was left outside.

Dr. Johnson, an Aberdeenshire man, and physician to Charles I., wrote a Latin epitaph as follows:

"Lauchlanus Maclanus Dowardius excelsus prorsus animo et heroica corporis dignitate puriter et robore, cum nobilissimus heroum veterum virtutis laude comparandus ex insidiis per sororis suæ filium indignissimus morte peremptus est anno Christi 1598.

    Heroum veterum nova gloria fama novorum
    Fama vetus pariter gloria prisca, recens.
    Objice fela neces et mille pericula rerum
    Deficiunt citius tela pericula neces,
    Quam MacLano animi est animus suo barbara dexter
    Pectora putoribus conciliive vigor
    Nusquam hæc; tuta fides ferit impice dextra nepotis
    Heroum hac nullum secula ferre valent."

The above quotation I have copied from the Pennycross manuscript. The whole of it is manifestly incorrect, and it is evident that Johnson's works were not before the annotator; but taken from a corrupt text. The meaning of the prose appears to be as follows: "Lachlan MacLean of Duard was very tall and of heroic bodily dignity, and in like manner of physical strength, comparable with the noblest of ancient heroes, in praise of worth. He was slain most ignominiously through the treachery of his sister's son, in the year of Christ 1598."

The verse is wild and irreducible to exact sense. It probably means, *first*, that the fame and glory of the moderns may equal the ancients; *second*, place no reliance on weapons, slaughter and fear, nor perils; for all these

---

* Pattison's *Gaelic Ballads*, p. 219. Pattison also adds, "A spirited gentleman of the clan recently endeavored to raise a sum sufficient to erect a monument over the grave of the chief—the most famous and ablest the MacLeans ever had; but, unfortunately, he did not succeed to his satisfaction."

things fail sooner than courage to MacLean, or strength to his spirit. In whose breast has there been such vigor of counsel? Sure faith might bring, but the impious right hand of his nephew. Not any age avails to bring the hero.

Whoever has followed the career of this noble chieftain, must feel sad over his fate. His death was deeply lamented, not only by his own people, but by the Highland clans generally. His chivalrous character, his indomitable spirit in defense of his own rights, his readiness to redress the wrongs of his people, his stern and cool behavior on the field of battle, his affable and kind bearing toward his friends and vassals, and his commanding presence, make him an ideal chieftain, and one which even the present age is forced to admire. Brought up at the court of James VI., his early education biased him in favor of the reformed religion, which he ardently embraced from a conviction of its truth, and thus became the first Protestant of his name. Notwithstanding his activity in clan feuds, he was sincerely attached to his religion and his people. Into his possessions he introduced clergymen of exemplary piety, and so great were his efforts in this direction and so successfully performed, that even to this day, although three hundred years have elapsed, yet in the whole Highlands, there is not another district where the principals of the Reformation are more tenaciously held, than in that dominion once ruled by the proud lord of Duard. By example, as well as by precept, he demonstrated to his people that he had no faith in the teachings of the Romish church. Illustrative of this fact the following tradition has been preserved: It was the practice of his Catholic ancestors to walk thrice in procession around the shores of a small island lying in Lochspelvie, invoking success on the expedition on which they were about to engage. Just before the fatal battle of Tra-Gruinnart, he showed his contempt for Catholic superstition by walking thrice around the island, but in the opposite direction, for his ancestors had walked right about, or in the direction of the sun.

As an active upholder of the reformed religion, we find him so recognized by the government. For in a "Renewal of Acts against the Jesuits and seminary priests; with reconstitution of the commission for putting the Acts in force, and appointment of a new commission of select clergy in the shires to co-operate in the work, and promote subscription to the Confession of Faith and Covenant, over the whole kingdom," the name of "Lauchlane McClayne of Dowart," appears in the roll of commissioners for executing the said Acts henceforward, given in the general assembly of the kirk of Scotland. Dated at Edinburgh, 6th March, 1589-90.*

If it be objected that Sir Lachlan's excessive love of military exploits does not comport with an active religious character, it may be replied, that not only has many a warrior been a devout worshiper, but the times and the system of government under which he lived had a tendency to produce such anomalies in character. Sir Lachlan lived under a feudal system which existed in full operation in the Highlands, and the princely privileges it conferred on the leaders of powerful clans were not likely to remain a dead letter in the hands of one so ardent a lover of exploits as this chief of MacLean. The state of the kingdom in his lifetime, torn as it was by the dissensions of contending parties, made it impossible for one possessing so much influence as Sir Lachlan Mór to be an idle spectator of events; and whether on behalf of the king, or in the vindication of his people's rights, his powerful sword was ever ready to aid the cause of justice. He at last fell with that sword in his grasp, and in the forty-first year of his age, leaving a name revered and beloved as long as his paternal protection is remembered and duly appreciated, or his undaunted courage continues to be spoken of with the admiration it can not fail to command.

His issue by Margaret, daughter of William Cunningham, sixth earl of Glencairn, was Eachann Og, his eldest son and successor, Lachlan Og, of whom the family of Torloisk was descended, Gillean, married to Mary the elder, Allan, married to Mary the younger, both daughters of John Dubh of Morvern, and Charles. The only daughter married Hector MacLean of Lochbuy, the first Protestant of his family also.

CHAPTER VI.

THE MacLEANS AS PARTISANS OF THE HOUSE OF STUART.

From A. D. 1598 to A. D. 1746.

XV. Eachann Og, Fifteenth Chief of MacLean.

The death of Sir Lachlan Mór MacLean raised his son Eachann Og, or Young Hector, then twenty years of age, to the chieftainship of the clan. His

---

* *Register Privy Council*, Vol. IV., p. 463.

first act was to adopt retaliatory measures upon the MacDonalds for the death of his father and kinsmen at Tra-Gruinnart. He obtained a commission of fire and sword against the MacDonalds of Islay, and at once summoned the chief of the MacKinnons, MacLeod of Dunvegan, and MacNeil of Barra to his assistance. The chief of the Camerons of Lochiel joined this force with his clan. Although Sir Lachlan MacLean had so recently crossed swords with Lochiel, yet when the report was brought to the latter that the former had expressed his grief that he had so much offended his nephew, Lochiel, "for," said he, "he is the only chief in the Highlands of sufficient courage, conduct, and power to revenge my death, and I am confident that, if I had not injured and provoked him in the manner I have done, he would not have allowed himself much rest until he had effected it;" the chief of the Camerons immediately put himself at the head of his clan and joined the forces of Hector. The united clans, fully equipped, proceeded to Islay. Sir James MacDonald, in anticipation of this movement on the part of the young lord of Duard, mustered together the whole gathering of Islay and Kintyre, and prepared himself for a conflict which he had reason to believe would be of a sanguinary nature. The hostile parties met at a place called Benbigrie, and as neither felt disposed to offer nor to accept terms, the result was an immediate battle. The followers of the chief of MacLean, upon this occasion, considerably outnumbered the MacDonalds; but Sir James, well aware that he need hope for no reconciliation with his enraged kinsman, told his followers that in a resolute resistance alone existed any hope of safety to themselves or of protection to their homes. The MacDonalds, goaded to desperation by a knowledge of these facts, fought with uncontrollable fury, and it was not until the heights of Benbigrie were covered with their slain, and their chief carried off the field dangerously wounded, that their assailants succeeded in routing them. Overwhelmed by numbers the unfortunate MacDonalds were at length obliged to give way and fly in the utmost confusion, not knowing whither, neither mountain nor valley afforded them shelter from their victorious pursuers. A few, however, carrying with them their wounded chief, made their way to Kintyre, leaving Islay a prey to the ruthless invaders. For three days the allied clans pursued the work of destruction with remorseless barbarity throughout the island. Every human habitation was burned to the ground; and the poor inhabitants were left to seek their only shelter in caves and clefts of rocks among the mountains, without fuel and without food. The career of the merciless victors only ceased when the work of destruction was complete.

Lochiel had the satisfaction of taking "Hector MacLean of Lochbuy, who aided the MacDonalds against his own chief, with several of his followers, prisoners of war, and detained them in chains for six months. Lochbuy, however, soon after had ample opportunity of being even with Lochiel." *

Of all the conflicts between these two clans, this, *the last*, was the most sanguinary and destructive. The MacLeans and their confederates no doubt felt themselves justified in executing signal vengeance upon their enemies, for the treachery displayed at Tra-Guinnart, and the loss there of so distinguished a chief. They were also forced to make the destruction as complete as possible, for the conduct of Sir James MacDonald had made him popular with his clan, and his actions had met their approval. However deplorable may have been the loss of life, and the sufferings endured by the innocent and helpless, the result was to put a final and effectual end to the struggle between the contending clans. Ever after the battle of Benbigrie the MacLeans and MacDonalds laid aside their animosities, and lived on the happiest terms of friendship and reciprocal good will.

In the year 1599, King James, finding the royal exchequer still in a depleted condition, again turned his eyes toward the Western Isles, and decided that the chiefs should be mulcted in a sufficient amount to meet his demands; so he appointed a new commission of lieutenandry over the whole Isles and Highlands of Inverness-shire, which was granted to the duke of Lennox and earl of Huntly, the latter having been recently restored to favor. Although the official document, which sets forth the reasons for the action of the king, gives a shocking picture of the Islesmen, yet this clause establishes the true import of the commission: "And besides all their other crimes, they rebelliously withhold from his Majesty a great part of the patrimony and proper rent of the crown, deprive the country of the benefit which might redound thereto, by the trade of fishing, and of other commodities which these bounds render. And now, at last, a great part of them have banded, conspired, and daily practice, by force and policy, in their barbarous and rebellious form, to disappoint his Majesty's service in the Lewis." †

As to the extent which this lieutenandry was acted upon is now uncertain. It is positive, however, that as a matter of justice, but little was due the crown from rents, and the amount demanded was beyond the ability of the chiefs to meet.

In 1601, another commission of lieutenandry was granted to the same

---

* MacKenzie's *History of the Camerons*, "Celtic Magazine," Vol. VIII., p. 374. † Gregory's *Western Highlands*, p. 287.

parties; the South of Argyleshire Isles included under the immediate charge of Lennox. These lieutenants were charged to assist certain colonists who would be better *able greatly to augment* the king's rents. Power was given them to use force and pursue the Islesmen with fire and sword. Rewards were offered these commissioners for the faithful performance of the duty assigned to them.*

Acting upon his authority, Huntly, who had charge of the northern districts, summoned a convention of estates, to meet at Stirling within a given period, under a penalty of forfeiture against an absentee; but many of the northern chiefs, from the distance they had to travel, and the limited period allowed for their appearance, were unable to be in attendance on the day appointed. As Hector MacLean of Duard owned the lands of Garbhghambluch, in Lochaber, he started at once for Stirling. On arriving there, he met Huntly on the street early on the morning that his name was to be called. After Huntly had saluted him, MacLean asked him if he thought he would have time to change his clothes before the roll would be called. Huntly answered he had plenty of time. On repairing to his lodging, MacLean learned the convention was in session, and immediately hurried to the assembly, and on arriving there found his name had been called. On parting with Hector in the street, Huntly went direct to the convention, and determined at once to put in execution the threat he had uttered against Sir Lachlan Mór MacLean, on account of the latter's proposal to bring Huntly dead or alive, the night after the battle of Glenlivat; so he ordered MacLean's name called at once, and as the latter was not present, Huntly immediately applied for the forfeit, procured it, and is still in the possession of the duke of Gordon. All the friends and interest that Hector could make, or bring to bear on the king, were never able to reverse the sentence, as Huntly always made great opposition. Thus he felt himself amply revenged on the son of Sir Lachlan Mór.

The Pennycross manuscript informs us that Hector Og got the estate in its best condition and before the sentence of forfeiture of the Lochaber portion amounted to five hundred mark land. The Lochaber estate which he lost by Huntly was twenty pound land.†

---

* *Record of Privy Council*, 16 June, 1601.

† The extent of the possessions of Duard at this period is of interest. From *Inquisitionum ad Capillam Domini Regis*, published in 1811, Vol. I., under Argyle, we read: "1603, April 1. Hector McClayne de Doward, haeres Hectoris McClayne, avi,—in Terris de Torosay cum castro et molendino:—Terris de Brolos; 8 mercatis terrarum in Ardmamachburg, Glenkynnuir,

In 1602, MacKenzie of Kintail engaged in a feud with the Clanranald of Glengarry, regarding their lands in Wester Ross. The violence between the clans became so great that the chief of Kintail repaired to Duard castle for assistance; for he had discovered that the MacDonalds of Islay, Ardnamurchan, and Glencoe were on the point of lending aid to Clanranald. Hector MacLean at once agreed to hold these clans in check, and if found necessary

Gomodra, Trisnis, jacentibus in Mule:—Galgray (vel Collozray) Inewry, Colleschlay, Sonepoil, Kilchreis, Tennomoir, Ardorenis, jacentibus in Morevis:—Mandulon Crossepoill, et Keren jacentibus in Terrigh, cum officio balliatus de Terrigh: Kearnburgh cum insulis ejusdem. Dunchonill cum insulis ejusdem et Molway, jacentibus in Skarby. Troig, Buangell, Glenamuk, Ardskalenis, Cannis, Egistill, Ardvegnis, jacentibus in Iuray Dowanultache, Ranachan, Achytymolen, jacentibus in Knapdaill:—Tarrislay jacentibus in Illay, infra vice comitatum de Tarbirt, cum quibusdam aliis terris in vice comitatu de Inverness A. E. 228 in N. E. 114 m."

"1615, July 1. Hector Maklane de Doward avi in terris et Baronia de Doward continente terras de Torresay, cum castro de Doward et molendino terras de Brolas: 8 mereatas terrarum jacentis in Ardmanuachburg Glenkynneir, Gomadra, Cresems, jacentes in Mule Colloyray, Ineway, Caliochlay, Sonepoile, Gilchrist, Pememare Ardirenis jacentes in Mariens—Mandalon Crossipoill et Keren, jacentes in Tierig, cum officis balliatus de Tierig—Kearnburgh cum insula ejusdem et Moluay jacentes in Scarbay. Troaig Owanagell, Glenamuk, Ardskaleins, Eamunis Equistill Andnagenil, jacentes in Dowray. Downnamultich, Ranaguhan Aithtay et molendius, jacentes in Knapdale:—Torlisay in Ilay, infra vice comitatum de Tarbet; in 20 libratis terrarum antiqui extentus subscriptus, viz.: terris de Distunmull Cartomoci, Kilmichael Ardnaleig; terris de duobus Fannemorcis, Torloisk, Cascar, Ardesgony, Burbeg, Buymoir, Rendill, Glekewgary, Ewinsay, Crossopolle Langavill, Knokawy, Kildony Drunziga, Ducharen, Dromolkyn, Tunadill cum molendius et piscatione jacentibus in insula de Mull et infra vice comitatum de Tarbat—20 Libratis, 6 solidatis et 8 denariatis terrarum antiqui extentus subsquentibus, viz., juarteres terrarum de Coall juarteria terrarum de Setrynmul; juartaria terrarum de Archalick et Fairland juar: Ter: de Carspellan, juar. ter. de Garrinsay et Kilnallan juar. Ter: de Garbols et Duach juari: ter: de Dall: jr. ter. de Robols et Kepols jr. ter. de Killiegan et Skanlastill: dimidietate octavæ partis terrarum de meglene, dimi: act: partis ter; de Owo: et oct: part. ter. de Bow et 6 Solidatarum et 8 denariatarum terrarum de Stanlastill cum molendino in insula de Ilay et vincomitatu de Tarbat annecatis ad Baroniam de Doward. Terris de Illway, Lagan, Walsagaray, infra vin comitatum de Tarbat extendentibus per se ad 20 mereatas terrarum antqui extentus cum juibusdam aliis terris in vincomitate de Inverness."

In the same work, under the head of *Inverness*, may be found the following: "1603, April 1. Hector McClayne de Doward, 'haeris' Hectoris McClayne avi—in terris de Auchnakay, Auchalane, Dugerre Keanboch, Auchranick, cum lie Stratum lie Clariche, et lie Claschbraik Auchtedonil, onladill cum lie slow (srow) Achetawer, Annisky, Coulek, Doway, Correchenley cum Suknanock, Auchichterre, Thomguharrig, jacientibus in Lochabir:—4 mereatis terrarum de Scalpay, viz: Tarm et Skeodin infra vincomitatum de Inverness; advocatione ecclesiarum infra terras et insulas antedictas cum officio balliatas: omnibus cum terris in Argyle unitis in Baroniam de Doward."

would invade their territory. To fulfill this agreement, the chief of MacLean was soon compelled to invade Ardnamurchan, and into those parts carried fire and sword, as well as the adjoining territories of the MacDonalds. Archibald Campbell, seventh earl of Argyle, claiming the MacDonalds to be his vassals, procured criminal letters against MacLean. Hector and MacKenzie repaired to Inverary, when the latter informed Argyle that "he should rather be blamed than MacLean, and the king and council than either of them, for he having obtained, on good grounds, a commission of fire and sword against Glengarry and such as would assist him, and against these men's rebellion and wicked courses, which frequently his lordship seemed to own, that he did charge, as he did several others of the king's loyal subjects, MacLean to assist him." After considerable discussion all parted good friends, Argyle agreeing to molest MacLean no farther. MacLean and MacKenzie immediately proceeded to Duard, where the former with his kinsmen and immediate friends sumptuously entertained the latter. Both chiefs consulted as to the best and safest means for the homeward journey of MacKenzie. Hector offered him all his chief and best men to accompany him by land, but this he declined, saying, that he would not put him to so much inconvenience, but would return in the boat in which he came. MacLean persuaded him that the boat would not be safe, and induced him to take his own great galley. So he sailed in his friend's great birlinn, under the command of Hector MacLean, constable of Cairnburg, accompanied by several other gentlemen of the MacLeans. "In the meantime the MacDonalds, aware that MacKenzie had not yet returned from Mull, convened all the boats and galleys they could, to a certain island which lay in his course, and which he could not avoid passing. So, coming within sight of the island, having a good prospect, a number of boats, after they had ebbed in a certain harbor, and men also, making ready to set out to sea. This occasioned the captain to use a stratagem, and steer directly to the harbor, and still as they came forward he caused lower the sail, which the other party perceiving made them forbear putting out their boats, persuading themselves that it was a galley they expected from Ardnamurchan, but they had no sooner come for-gainst the harbor but the captain caused hoist sail, set oars and steers aside, immediately bangs up a bag-piper and gives them shots. The rest, finding the cheat and their own mistake, made such a hurlyburly setting out their boats, with their haste they broke some of them, and some of themselves were bruised and had broken shins also for their prey and such boats as went out whole, perceiving the galley so far off, thought it was folly to pursue her any further, they all returned wiser than they came from home." MacKenzie was carried home, and landed there, without any mishap, late at night.*

Hector Og, for a neighbor, had Archibald Campbell, seventh earl of Argyle, a man unscrupulous in his dealings and given to much plotting. Of this man Gregory says: " In after life Sir James MacDonald blamed Argyle and Calder as the prime movers of all the severities exercised against him and his clan. It was the opinion, too, of one of the contemporary officers of state for Scotland (Sir Alexander Hay)—a man of much sagacity and experience—that the frequent insurrections in the South Isles which occurred in the first fifteen years of the seventeenth century were encouraged, if not originated, by Argyle and the Campbells for their own purposes. In the following pages undoubted evidence will be found of such underhand proceedings, on the part of the earl of Argyle, in one of the most prominent of these insurrections." † Keltie says Argyle used his influence to stir up the MacGregors " to acts of violence and aggression against his own personal enemies, of whom the chief of the Colquhouns was one; and it is further said that he had all along meditated the destruction of both the MacGregors and the Colquhouns, by his crafty and perfidious policy." ‡

In 1603, Argyle's machinations against the house of Duard come to light. He succeeded in obtaining letters from the king in which it is set " forth the need for furtherance of authority, and repressing the insolence of ' the broken men of the Isles.' For this end the letter commands the king's messengers in that part to charge Angus MacDonald of Dunyveg, and Hector MacLean of Duard, the keepers of these fortalices respectively, to render and deliver the same to Archibald, earl of Argyle, ' to whom we have given some speciall directiouns anent the matteris of the Isles.' The said Angus MacDonald and Hector MacLean are to remove themselves and property from the fortalices whithin 24 hours after being charged to do so, under the pain of treason. Failing delivery of the castles, the keepers shall be held traitors, and sentence of forfeiture pronounced on them. Given at Holyrood House, 20 September 1603." ‖

This document does not contain the signature of James but has the cachet of " James R " at the head of the letter in place of the sign manual. James had proceeded to London on the 5th of April previous. It is probable that Argyle did not attempt to use the authority thus procured.

---

* MacKenzie's *History Clan MacKenzie,* "Celtic Magazine," Vol. III., p. 363. † *Western Highlands,* p. 289. ‡ *History of the Highland Clans,* Vol. II., p. 182. ‖ *Appendix to Sixth Report Royal Commission,* p. 615.

In the year 1604, "Hector MacLean of Duard, who, among other offenses, had failed to pay the crown rents for his possessions, was obliged to give security to the privy council that his castle of Duard should be delivered up to any person whom the king and council should authorize to receive it, on twenty days warning."*

The state of the islands during this period would have been satisfactory had King James pursued an honorable course; but the capricious manner of that vacillating monarch kept affairs too much in jeopardy. It was well known that many of the Highland proprietors were very indifferent about the formality of registering their estates, and others looked with contempt upon the formality of holding their lands by virtue of "a scrap of parchment." This gave a favorable opportunity to the monarch, and certain noblemen high in authority of enriching themselves. Consequently, during the summer of 1605, Sir David Murray (Lord Scone), Comptroller of Scotland, was directed to repair to Kintyre to receive the obedience of the principal men of the clans in the South Isles, with surety for the payment of the king's rents and duties. Hector MacLean of Duard, Angus MacDonald of Dunyveg, and all the principal chiefs and gentlemen in the Isles, south of the point of Ardnamurchan, together with Cameron of Lochiel, MacRanald of Keppoch, MacIan of Ardnamurchan, MacIan of Glencoe, Stewart of Appin, MacDonald of Largie, and MacAllaster of Loupe on the mainland, were summoned to appear personally before Lord Scone at Lochkilkerran, in Kintyre, on the 20th day of July, to give their obedience, to find sureties for the payment of the crown rents, and to bring with them and exhibit the title-deeds to all lands claimed by them in the Highlands and Isles. If any of them should fail to obey the proclamation, their title-deeds at once should be declared null and void; and power was given to the comptroller to pursue them with fire and sword as rebels to the king. In order that this might not be an empty threat, an officer was sent to the Isles to receive from their respective owners the castles of Duard in Mull and Dunyveg in Islay; and in order to prevent the escape of the islanders, the inhabitants of Kintyre and the West Iles were ordered, by proclamation, to deliver all their boats to this officer; and moreover forbidden to use boats without his special authority.† The record shows that only Angus MacDonald, and the heads of his vassals, attended the meeting; and Lord Scone was unable to compel the attendance or even punish the more distant chiefs. Angus MacDonald paid up all the arrears due for his lands in Kintyre and

---

*Gregory's *Western Highlands*, p. 306.   † *Record Privy Council*, June, 1605.

Islay, and also gave his son Archibald as a hostage for his future obedience. Notwithstanding this fact, the privy council, in 1606, influenced by the earl of Argyle,* gave the latter a charter of the lands in north and south Kintyre, and in the isle of Jura, in consideration for a large feu-duty, a great proportion of which he induced parliament to remit.

The sense of justice and humanity of the king and ruling class of this period, is exemplified in the commission given in 1607 to Huntly. "That the marquis should undertake the service upon his own private means alone—that he should conclude it within a year, and have no exemption from paying rent but for that space—*that he should end the service, not by agreement with the country people, but by extirpating them*—that he should take all the North Isles, except Sky and the Lewis, in feu from the king, as being in his majesty's hands by forfeiture of the present possession, or otherwise—and that he should pay for these isles such a rent as should be fixed by the comptroller of Scotland, according to the principles observed in the rental of the South Isles. The marquis of Huntly, to his shame be it recorded, accepted nearly all these conditions undertaking *to end the service, by extirpation of the barbarous people of the Isles, within a year.* He declined, however, to leave the fixing of the rent as feu-duty to the comptroller, but offered to pay four hundred pounds a year, of which three hundred were to be for Uist, and the remaining hundred for the other isles specified. This rent the council refused to accept, as being ' a very mean dewtie' for the isles which were to be granted to Huntly, but left this point to the decision of the king as the party chiefly concerned. Before, however, this difference was finally settled, and the vassals of Huntly let loose to massacre the barbarous Islemen, the jealousy entertained by the Presbyterians of any increase to the power of the marquis, who was an adherent of the church of Rome, caused this enterprise to be abandoned altogether. When Huntly appeared before the privy council on the 23d of June, to hear the final determination of the king regarding the amount of rent to be paid for his grants in the Isles, he was, on a complaint by the more violent of the Presbyterians, ordered by the council to confine himself within the burgh of Elgin, and a circuit of eighteen miles round it; and while in this durance he was enjoined to hear the sermons of certain Presbyterian divines, that so he might be reclaimed from his errors. This accident—for it does not bear the appearance of a scheme concerted to save the Islanders—seems alone to have prevented the reign of James VI. from being stained by a massacre which, for

---

* Gregory's *Western Highlands,* p. 310.

atrocity and the deliberation with which it was planned, would have left that of Glencoe far in the shade. But whether the interference of the Presbyterians was accidental or intentional, the Islanders of that day owed nothing to their prince, whose character must forever bear the stain of having, for the most sordid motives, consigned to destruction thousands of his subjects." *

"The king, having experienced the inutility of trusting to the Scottish militia alone for the furtherance of his projects in the Isles, now determined to employ, in addition, some regular troops and ships of war from Ireland. In the month of March, 1608, this intention was announced to the lieges in Scotland by a proclamation, which (as a sufficient number of troops could not be spared from the Irish garrisons) summoned to the aid of those intended to be sent, the militia of the shires of Dumbarton, Argyle, Torbert, Ayr, Renfrew, and Galloway, directing them to meet at Islay, on the first of June, with the forces from Ireland. No lieutenant was yet named to have the chief authority over the expedition; but it was contemplated, at this time, that there should be two of these officers—one for the South another for the North Isles. Another proclamation was made at the same time, forbidding the chiefs on the mainland opposite the Isles to harbor or give supplies to any of the Islesmen, under the highest penalties. The Scottish privy council seem to have neglected nothing which might tend to facilitate the execution of an enterprise implying so much cost and such lengthened preparations. They granted a commission to Andrew, lord Stewart of Ochiltree, and Andrew Knox, bishop of the Isles, to meet and confer with Angus MacDonald of Dunyveg and Hector MacLean of Duard, and to receive offers from these chiefs. A month later, this commission was renewed, with the addition of Sir James Hay of Beauly, comptroller to the commissioners, who were required to report the result of their conference on or before the 20th of May. Very minute instructions were given by the council as to the terms to be demanded from the Islanders by the commissioners. These terms comprehended—*First*, Security for his majesty's rents; *Secondly*, Obedience to the laws by the chiefs and all their followers; *Thirdly*, delivery by the chiefs of all 'houses of defense, strongholds, and *crannacks*,' to be placed at the king's disposal; *Fourthly*, Renunciation by the chiefs of all jurisdiction which they claimed, heritably or otherwise, and submission to the jurisdiction of sheriffs, bailies, justices, or other officers appointed by the crown; *Fifthly*, That they

---

* Gregory's *Western Highlands*, p. 314. These facts are taken from *Records of Privy Council* from 26th March to 30th April, 1607, and letters of Huntly.

should be satisfied with such lands and possessions, and under such conditions as the king might appoint; *Sixthly,* That their whole birlinns, lymphads, and galleys should be destroyed, save those required for carrying to the mainland his majesty's rents paid in kind, and other necessary purposes; *Seventhly,* That they, and such of their kinsmen as could afford it, should put their children to school, under the directions of the privy council; *Lastly,* That they should abstain from using guns, bows, and two-handed swords, and should confine themselves to single-handed swords and targes. A mandate was issued to Angus MacDonald, his son, Angus Og, and all others, keepers of the castle of Dunyveg, charging them to surrender that fortress to the officer bearer of the mandate, within twenty-four hours after his arrival. At the same time, a new proclamation was made, adding to the militia formerly summoned to meet at Islay on the first of June the array of Edinburgh and the other southern counties, and of Stirling, Fife, Kinross, Perth, Clackmannan and Torfarshire." The change caused the day of meeting at Islay to be postponed to the first of July. Preparations for service in the Isles proceeded with great vigor. Vessels were ordered to be in readiness to transport the Lowland militia, and the burghers of the West commanded to prepare boats, well furnished with buscuit, ale, wine, beer, and other victuals, for the support of the army. Lord Ochiltree was appointed lieutenant over all the Isles, and a council was appointed to assist him, of which the bishop of the Isles was the head. Full power was given to the lieutenant to treat with all or any of the Islanders, and encouraged to obedience. All castles were to be demolished save such as the commission thought should be garrisoned. The preparations for the expedition were not completed till early in the month of August, when Ochiltree was joined off the island of Islay by troops from Ireland under Sir William St. John, and at a later period the armament was further increased by the arrival of an English galley and another vessel, the latter of which carried a battering train with its necessary ammunition.

"The castle of Dunyveg, in Islay, was delivered to the lieutenant by Augus MacDonald without hesitation, along with the fort of Lochgorme in the same island. The latter was instantly demolished; but a garrison of twenty-four men was placed in the former. On the 14th of August, the armament sailed from Islay, and on the 15th, after a very tempestuous voyage, reached the castle of Duard in the Sound of Mull. This fortress having been summoned in the regular manner, was surrendered by its proprietor, Hector MacLean of Duard, to Lord Ochiltree, by whom it was garrisoned and furnished on the 17th. Ochiltree had previously proclaimed that, as royal lieutenant, he would hold a court at the castle of Aros in Mull, to which all the chiefs in the Isles were summoned, and at which he proposed, among other things, to carry into effect in Mull that part of his commission relating to the destruction of the lymphads, birlinns, and Highland galleys. But in the meantime, having ascertained that this would be attended with great injustice to the Islanders, unless the galleys and other vessels on the adjacent coasts of the mainland were likewise destroyed, so as to secure the Isles from molestation on the part of their neighbors, he wrote to the council for further instructions on this point, requesting permission also to deal with the mainland castles as he should think proper.* The powers he requested were immediately granted to him, under a reservation which saved from destruction the boats and vessels belonging to ' obedient subjects.' At Aros the following Islesmen assembled to attend the lieutenant's court, viz.: Angus MacDonald of Dunyveg; Hector MacLean of Duard ; Lachlan, his brother ; Donald Gorm MacDonald of Sleat; Donald MacAllan, captain of the Clanranald; Ruari MacLeod of Harris; Allaster, his brother; and Neill MacIlduy, and Neill MacRuari, two gentlemen in Mull, followers of MacLean of Duard; who all, if we may believe the report of Lord Ochiltree, placed themselves at his disposal without condition as promise. It appears, however, from a contemporary author, that this report can not altogether be depended on. According to this writer, Ochiltree conferred at length with the Islanders, ' giving them fair words, promising to be their friend, and to deal with the king in their favor.' Having taken very strict order with Angus MacDonald for his future obedience, he suffered that chief to depart home. But not finding the others so ready to accede to all his proposals, the lieutenant, by the advice of his chief counsellor, the bishop of the Isles, invited them to hear a sermon preached by that prelate on board the king's ship, called the Moon, and afterward prevailed upon them to dine with him on board. Ruari MacLeod of Harris alone refused to enter the vessel, suspecting some sinister design. When dinner was ended, Ochiltree told the astonished chiefs that they were his prisoners by the king's order, and weighing anchor, he sailed direct to Ayr,† whence he shortly proceeded with his prisoners to Edinburgh, and pre-

---

* Letter from Ochiltree to the Privy Council, dated at Duard, in Mull, 18th August, 1608.

† It is evident that the bishop did not feel at ease on account of the part he took in kidnaping these chiefs. In a letter sent to James VI., dated 17th September, 1608, the bishop says, " My credeit amangis thir folkis be the forme of this last actioun practischit amangis thame, sum what (as apperis) deminischit, that it mycht pleas your Majestie to appoynt sum uther of yonger aige, gritter curage, bettir discretioun and credeit in thois cuntries," etc. Given in full in *Collectanea de Rebus Albanicis*, pp. 113, 114.

sented them before the privy council, by whose orders they were placed in the several castles of Dumbarton, Blackness, and Stirling. In the report of his proceedings which Ochiltree on this occasion gave in to the privy council, he assigned the lateness of the season as an excuse for his not having proceeded against MacNeill of Barra and MacLeod of Lewis, intimating at the same time that the former of these chiefs was a depender upon MacLean of Duard, who would answer for his obedience. He stated, likewise, that he had, in compliance with a letter from the comptroller, restored to MacLean the castles of Duard and Aros, upon the promise of that chief to surrender them when required; that he had taken surety for the delivery of the castle of Mingarry in Ardnamurchan; and that he had broken and destroyed all the galleys and other vessels he could find in those parts of the Isles which he visited." The imprisonment of so many chiefs at one time afforded the king a better opportunity to accomplish his long cherished projects; nor was he backward in availing himself of it. These powerful chiefs finding themselves wholly at the king's mercy, presented humble petitions, and submitted themselves entirely to his pleasure, and made many offers in order to procure liberation, and taking credit for having come willingly with the lieutenant. A commission was appointed to receive the offers of the Islesmen, and to consult and deliberate upon all matters connected with the civilization of the Isles and the increase of the king's rents. Minute instructions were given for their guidance, and all their deliberations should be submitted to the king. At this time James VI. was engaged in expelling the Irish inhabitants from Ulster, " and granting their lands to settlers from England and Scotland, yet he now hesitated to treat, with like severity, the same Scottish Islanders whom, in the preceding year, he had actually proposed to extirpate. His chief object now seems to have been to curtail the power of the great proprietors, by procuring from them the voluntary surrender of considerable portions of the estates which they claimed as their inheritance.* In this, as in many of his projects, which sounded well in theory, James was disappointed; but other suggestions made by him at this time, favored as they were by circumstances, and followed up with zeal by the commissioners, were productive of so much benefit that from this time we may trace a gradual and permanent improvement of the Isles and adjacent Highlands." †

---

* Royal Commissions and Instructions, dated 6th December, 1608.   † Gregory's *Western Highlands*, pp. 318–326.

The bishop of the Isles was sent by the commissioners to London to report their deliberations to the king. He returned with instructions that he and the comptroller should, during the summer (1609), visit and survey the Isles, being accompanied, both going and coming, by Angus MacDonald of Dunyveg and Hector MacLean of Duard, who should be released for this purpose. The other prisoners should be retained in confinement until the bishop's return. But availing himself of a discretionary power given him, the bishop, accompanied by all the chiefs and gentlemen recently kidnaped, set sail on his mission about the middle of July, and before the end of that month almost all the Islesmen met him in the celebrated island of Icolmkill, or Iona. Determined to take advantage of the unanimity he had gained, the bishop held a court in which, with the consent of the assemblied chiefs, he enacted nine statutes of the utmost importance for the improvement of the Isles. These enactments are known as the famous "Statutes of Icolmkill," and are worthy of the particular attention of every lover of Highland history:

"The court of the South and North Illis of Scotland holdin at Icolmekill be ane Reverend fader in God, ANDRO BISCHOP OF THE ILLIS haveand speciall pouer and commissioun to that effect of his Majestie and Counsell the twentie thrie day of August the yeir of God 1609 yeiris; the suitis callit and the court lauchfullie affirmit be

THE QUHILK DAY in presence of the said Reverend fader, the speciall Baron's and Gentilmen of the saidis Yllis underwritten viz. Angus McDonald of Dunnoveg; Hector McCleane of Doward; Donald Gorme McDonald of Slait; Rorie McCloyd of Hareiss; Donald McAllane vc eane of Ilanterame; Lauchlane McCleane of Coill; Lauchlane McKynnoun of that ilk; Hector McCleane of Lochbowie; Lauchlane and Allane McCleanes brothers germane to the said Hector McClane of Doward; Gillespie Mcquirie of Ullova; Donald Mcfie in Collonsaye; Togidder with the maist part of thair haill speciall freindis, dependaris and tennentis compeirand judiciallie:—

AND UNDERSTANDING and considering the grite ignorance unto the quihilk not onlie thay for the maist pairt thame selffis, bot alsua the haill communalitie, inhabitantis of the Illandis hes bene and ar subject to, quihilk is the caus of the neglect of all dewtie to God and of his trew worship to the grite grouth of all kind of vice proceiding partly fra the laik of pastouris plantit and partly of the contempt of these quha as alreadie plantit:—For remeid quhairof thay haif all aggreit in ane voce, Lyke as it is presentlie concludit and inactit, That the ministeris alswele plantit as to be plantit within the parochynnis of the saidis Illis, sal be reuerentlie obeyit; thair stipendis dewtifullie payit thame; the rwynous kirkis with reasonable diligence repairit; the Sabothis solemplie kepit; adultereis, fornicationis, insest and sic uther vyle sklanderis seveirlie punist; *marriageis contractit for certane yeiris* * simplicitir dischargeit and the committaris thairof repute and punist as fornicatouris."* † The *second* statute ordained the establishment of inns at such places as were most convenient in the several islands; which was designed not only for the accommodation of travelers, but to relieve the burden from the tenants and laborers. The *third* statute was intended to diminish the number of idle persons, for the expense of keeping them fell principally upon the tenantry, in addition to their usual rents. A limit was put to the number of individuals of each household, and the chiefs were to support their households from their own means. The *fourth* statute provided against such persons who were not natives found sorning, or living at free quarters on the poor inhabitants, an evil which had reached a great height. The *fifth* statute declared that one of the chief causes of poverty in the Isles, and of the cruelty and inhumanity practiced in their feuds, was the inordinate love of strong wines and aquavite. It was therefore decreed that imported liquor should be destroyed, and a fine of forty pounds to any one who, for the first offense, purchased it from a mainland trader; one hundred pounds for the second, and for the third offense the loss of his entire possessions. It was, however, provided that any individual could brew as much aquavite as his own family required; and the barons and wealthy gentlemen might purchase in the lowlands such liquors as were required for their private consumption. The *sixth* statute declares " that the ignorance and incivilitie of the saidis Ilis hes daylie incressit be the negligence of gaid educatioun and instructioun of the youth in the knowledge of God and good lettres: For remeid quhairof it is enactit that everie gentilman or yeaman within the saidis Islandis or ony of thame having children maill or famell and being in goodis worth thriescoir ky, sall putt at the leist thair eldest sone or, having na childrene maill, thair eldest dochtir to the scuillis in the lawland and interteny and bring thame up thair quhill thay may be found able sufficientlie to speik, read and wryte Inglische." ‡ The *seventh* statute

---

*This evidently shows that the practice of handfasting (as it was called) was not yet abolished. Upon this strange practice John Mac-Vic-Ewin, fourth Laird of Ardgour, had handfasted with a daughter of MacIan of Ardnamurchan, whom he had taken on a promise of marriage if she pleased him. At the expiration of two years he sent her home to her father, but his son by her (the gallant John of Inverscaddel, already noticed at p. 101) was held to be a legitimate offspring, by virtue of the handfast ceremony. †*Collectanea de Rebus Albanicis*, p. 118.
‡ *Ibid*.

forbade the use of firearms of any description, for any purpose whatever. This was "awing to their monstrous deadly fueds." The *eighth* provided against bards and other idlers of the class, who were first threatened with the stocks and then with banishment. The *ninth* contained some necessary enactments for the enforcement of the preceding.*

Taken as a whole, the "Statutes of Icolmkill" were wise and salutary. Notwithstanding the fact that the Highlanders suffered much from the capricious conduct of James VI. and his predecessors, yet it is true, however startling may be the fact, that the first traces of that unwavering and overflowing loyalty to the house of Stuart, for which they have been so highly and so persistently lauded, are to be found in that generation of their chiefs where education was conducted on the high church and state principles as laid down by Andrew Knox, bishop of the Isles. These measures must have been considered by the assembled chiefs as promising beneficial results, for it does not appear that they attempted the least opposition to their operation.

At the time the bishop returned from the Isles a complaint was made to the lord commissioners by MacLean of Duard and MacDonald of Islay, and other chieftains, on account of a certain oppressive proclamation against the Western Isles. It does not appear by whom this proclamation was made; but it was well calculated to cut off the king's revenues in the Isles. The privy council passed the following act, in response, dated at Edinburgh, 28th September, 1609. "Forsamekle as Hector McClayne of Dowart, Angus McConeill of Dunyvaig and certane utheris chiftanes of the Yllis who ar addebtit to the Kingis Majestie in the maillis and dewyteis of thair landis, hes of lait meanit thameselffis unto the Lordis Commissionaris, that thay ar verie far prejugeit and maid unable to pay his Majesties dewyteis of thair landis, be ressoun of a Proclamatioun and Prohibitioun maid within the boundis of Ergyle that no mercheantis or utheris sall buy ony mairtis,† horses, or utheris goodis within the boundis of Mule or ony utheris of the West Yllis; The saidis yllismen having no utheris meanes nor possibilitie to pay his Majesteis dewyteis bot be the sale of thair mairtis and horsses; and the buying of such commoditeis being in all tymes begane a free, constant, and peceable trade to the merchandis alsweill of Ergyll as of the incuntrey, without ony restrent, trouble, questioun, or impediment moved or intended in the contrair at ony tyme heirtofoir; Quhairby as the makaris of that Proclamatioun hes commit-

---

* See Gregory's *Western Highlands*, pp. 329–333.   † *Marts*; cattle fattened for winter consumption.

tit a verie grite errour and oversicht in usurpeing upon thame such a soverane power and auctoritie noway competent to a subject; and thairwithall hes defraudit and prejugeit his Majesteis goode subjectis of the benefite of thair lauchfull trade and intercourse of their goodis wairis and merchandice,—so have thay very far hinderit his Majestie in the tymous and thankfull payment of his dewyteis; in heich contempt of his Majesteis auctoritie and lawis: Thairfoir," * the said proclamation is annulled, and all leiges strictly prohibited from interfering with the trade of the Isles.

The proceedings of the bishop of the Isles met with the king's approval, and in order to hear his pleasure declared to them, six of the principal Islanders assembled in Edinburgh, on the 28th of June—MacLean of Duard, MacDonald of Sleat, MacDonald of Dunyveg, MacLeod of Harris, the captain of Clanranald, and MacKinnon of Strathordell, together with Cameron of Lochiel and Allan Cameron MacIandy of Lochaber. All were compelled to give sureties to a large amount for their appearance before the council in May, 1611 next, obliged to promise to concur with and assist the king's lieutenants, justices, and commissioners, in all matters connected with the Isles; that they should live together in peace and friendship; and any question which should rise among them should be decided according to the ordinary course of law and justice. A month later the bishop of the Isles received a life commission as steward and justice of all the North and West Isles (except Orkney and Shetland), and all former commissions of lieutenandry over the Isles were recalled. He was likewise made constable of the castle of Dunyveg in Islay.†

A commotion of some magnitude broke out in the year 1613 among the MacNeills of Barra. Ruari MacNeill, the chief of that clan, had for several years enjoyed the society of a lady of the name of MacLean, according to an ancient practice not then altogether disused in the Isles, called *handfasting* or in other words, taken a wife *on trial*, and by her had several sons. Subsequently he married a sister of the captain of the Clanranald, and deprived his former children of their inheritance. The latter, however, maintained their claims until forced to yield to the younger members of the family, by the captain of the Clanranald. The eldest son of the senior family having taken part in an act of piracy on a ship of Bordeaux was apprehended in the Isle of Barra, by Clanranald, and taken to Edinburgh, where he died before the time

---

* *Collectanea de Rebus Albanicis*, p. 153. † *Record Privy Council*, from 8th May to 27 July, 1610.

for trial. In revenge for this, his brothers-german, aided by Hector MacLean of Duard, seized Neill MacNeill, the eldest of the junior family, and sent him to Edinburgh to be tried for the same offense of piracy, but through the influence of his uncle, Clanranald, was liberated. The surviving sons of the first family seized the old chief, their father, and placed him in irons. Having refused to exhibit him before the privy council, they were proclaimed rebels, and a commission against them was given to the captain of Clanranald, who used his powers in such a way as to secure the peaceable succession of his nephew to the Barra estate on the death of the old chief, which occurred soon after.

Hector MacLean of Duard, Donald Gorm of Sleat, Ruari MacLeod of Harris, and Donald MacAllan, captain of Clanranald, are mentioned as having settled with the exchequer, in the year 1613, and as continuing in their obedience to the laws.

In the same year, at the suggestion of Archibald Campbell, earl of Argyle, who was determined to appropriate some of the MacLean estates, and who had been in London paying attendance upon the king, a roving commission, composed chiefly of his followers, was appointed by the government to demand the title-deeds of certain chiefs. The estates of the MacLeans in Morvern became the first object of attack. These, though in possession of the chief of MacLean as feudal superior since the forfeiture of the Lord of the Isles, in 1493, had, it would appear, never been registered; notwithstanding this commission, however, MacLean was for ages acknowledged as the legal proprietor; but the king, without consulting either honor or justice in the matter, agreed to have a charter of the Morvern estates drawn up in favor of Campbell of Lawers, a relative of the earl. But fearing that the injustice thus done to the MacLeans might rouse that clan to acts of insubordination, the king made it conditional upon Lawers and the earl that they should take and maintain possession of the lands at their own risk alone. The experience of the commissioners on their first visit to one of the proprietors (MacLean of Kingerloch) afforded them a lesson of what they might expect in their proposed spoliations in Morvern. When the commissioners asked Kingerloch to satisfy them as to the tenure by which he held his lands, the indignant chieftain replied, "I can produce no sheepskin nor crotchets upon parchment to satisfy you, but the tenure by which I and my forefathers have held these lands are at your service;" and so saying, he made a sign to his piper, who instantly set up the clan gathering, and out issued from different places of concealment about one hundred warriors all armed. " Such, messieurs com-

AN INDEPENDENT CLAN—1598 TO 1746.

missioners," said Kingerloch, "is the tenure by which my forefathers have hitherto held these estates, and by the same tenure, *if it please you*, it is my purpose still to hold them. Tell your employers this is the answer of *Machd-Mhichd-Eachuinn-Chingherloch*." * The commissioners of Argyle importuned Kingerloch no farther, but after partaking of the hospitality of his table for that night, they contented themselves by withdrawing from Morvern on the following day.† This affair having been noised abroad the MacLeans flew to arms, determined to resist this maneuver of Argyle, who, realizing that he had been thwarted, thought it best to proceed no farther.

Argyle still pondered over the problem of how to possess himself of Islay. In 1614, he stirred up the MacDonalds of Islay ‡ to rebellion, in hopes thereby to profit by what must eventually be their disaster. The escape from prison of Sir James MacDonald, in 1615, and the consequent excitement it produced, complicated matters very much. In the midst of these commotions, Argyle made a precipitate journey to London without any prospects of an immediate return. The privy council set about to place the Isles and adjacent mainland, from Skye to Kintyre in a posture of defense, and to deter the MacDonalds, under Sir James, from landing; as it had been communicated that they had set sail from Eig. The Campbells were to defend Argyle proper, Knapdale and Kintyre; to the lairds of Duard, Lochbuy, Coll, and MacKinnon, two hundred men for the defense of the coasts from Lorn to the point of Ardnamurchan; to the earl of Enzie, one hundred men, to defend the coast of Lochaber; and to Clanranald, MacLeod of Harris and MacDonald of Sleat, each two hundred men, for the defense of their own coasts. Notwithstanding all the precautions made, Sir James MacDonald, on June 18th, landed on the isle of Colonsay with several hundred men, and soon after made himself master of the castle of Dunyveg. As Islay and Kintyre had been given to Argyle, on condition that he should hold them at his own expense, the privy council requested the king to have the conditions fulfilled. But Argyle succeeded in having the government to take hold of the matter with renewed efforts. Sir James was very active and succeeded in enter-

---

* The patronymic of the head of the Kingerloch MacLeans was Mac-Vic-Eachuinn Kingerloch, or the son of Hector's son of Kingerloch. MacLean of Duard was called *MacIlleathan*, The MacLean. The Lochbuy branch *Sliochd Mhurchaidh Ruaidh*, the descendants of Red Murdoch. The Ardgour family as *Mac-Mhic-Eoghin*, the son of Ewen's son.

† Gregory (*Western Highlands*, p. 348) gives a short account of this affair, taken from an Original Memorial, dated April 13, 1613, preserved in the General Register House.

‡ See Gregory's *Western Highlands*, pp. 354, 365.

ing into a bond of friendship with Donald Gorm of Sleat, the captain of Clanranald, and Ruari MacLeod of Harris; "and that Hector MacLean of Duard, if not actually engaged in the rebellion, had announced that, if he was desired to proceed against the Clandonald, he would not be very earnest in the service. These disheartening reports were confirmed to a certain extent by Ardchattan's spies, who declared to him that vassals of the three first mentioned chiefs formed a considerable part of Sir James' force; whilst MacLean's brother had already taken part with the rebels in expelling Calder's men from Islay." * It is true that the chief of MacLean permitted his brother Allan to render assistance to Sir James MacDonald, but to what extent does not appear. The rebellion was suppressed during October of the same year, and Sir James MacDonald, deprived of the inheritance of his forefathers, and his lands, through cunning and treachery possessed by Argyle and Campbell of Calder, fled to Ireland, where he was sheltered for a time by his kinsman Randall MacDonald of Dunluce, first earl of Antrim; but Argyle's enmity followed him to this retreat, and Sir James knowing that his life was in perpetual danger from the emissaries of his despoiler, escaped to Spain. He was afterward pardoned and died in London in 1626.

On the suppression of this rebellion Hector Og MacLean of Duard, as chief of the clan, was called upon by the government to account for the share his brother Allan and others of his kinsmen had taken in the late proceedings. Parliament, however, contented itself with demanding the appearance of Allan and of Hector Roy of Coll before the council to give in their submission and swear allegience to the king. This being done, sureties were then granted them for all acts of past disobedience, and they were permitted to return to their homes.

The acquisition of Islay and Kintyre appears to have appeased the longings of the Argyle family for their neighbors' property, at least for a time. The records do not show that at this period they made any attempts upon the lands of the MacLeans. This must be attributed to the influence of the chief, arising from his numerous connections at this time amongst the highland barons by his marriage alliances. His first wife was the daughter of the chief of Kintail; his second marriage to a daughter of Sir Archibald Acheson of Gosford, then Secretary of State for the kingdom, caused his influence to receive additional weight. This secured him protection against Argyle in that

---

* Gregory's *Western Highlands*, pp. 370–377.

quarter where alone a MacLean could fear his power, namely, in the secret councils of the state, or in the private closet of an erratic sovereign.

The removal of King James from the court of Edinburgh to that of London, on the whole, had a beneficial effect on the Isles. The laws now enacted, from time to time, for the better government of the Isles, began to be felt with good effect throughout the Highlands generally. The deadly family feuds, so inimical to the happiness of the people, were now of rare occurrence, and the chiefs themselves became more and more reconciled to such measures as were deemed advisable for the permanent welfare of the inhabitants.

The government issued a summons in the year 1616 commanding the attendance before the privy council (Scottish) of Hector Og, chief of MacLean; Lachlan MacLean of Torloisk, brother of Duard; Hector MacLean of Lochbuy; Lachlan MacLean of Coll; Sir Ruari MacLeod of Harris; Sir Lachlan MacKinnon of MacKinnon, and Sir Donald MacDonald, chief of the Clanranald; and as these chiefs had not made their appearance during the previous year, on account of the insurrection, very strict measures were now taken in order to insure their obedience in the future. "They were obliged to bind themselves mutually, as sureties for each other, to the observance of the following conditions: *First*, That their clans should keep good order, and that they themselves should appear before the council, annually, on the 10th of July, and oftener if required and on being legally summoned. *Secondly*, That they should exhibit annually a certain number of their principal kinsman, out of a larger number contained in a list given by them to the council. Duard was to exhibit four; MacLeod, three; Clanranald three; and Coll, Lochbuy and MacKinnon, one of these chieftains, or heads of houses, in their clans respectively. *Thirdly*, That they were not to maintain in household more than the following proportions of gentlemen, according to their rank, viz.: Duard, eight; MacLeod and Clanranald, six; and the others three each. *Fourthly*, That they were to free their countries of *sorners* and idle men having no lawful occupation. *Fifthly*, That none of them were to carry hackbuts or pistols, unless when employed in the king's service; and that none but the chiefs and their household gentlemen were to wear swords, or armor, or any weapons whatever. *Sixthly*, That the chiefs were to reside at the following places respectively, viz.: MacLeod at Dunvegan, MacLean of Duard at that place, Clanranald at Elanterim, MacLean of Coll at Bistache, Lochbuy at Moy, and MacKinnon at Kilmorie. Such of them as had not convenient dwelling-houses corresponding to their rank at these places were to build without delay, ' civil and comelie' houses, or repair those that were decayed. They were likewise to make 'policie and planting' about their houses; and to take *mains*, or house-farms, into their own hands, which they were to cultivate, 'to the effect they might be thereby exercised and eschew idleness.' Clanranald, who had no *mains* about his castle of Elanterim, chose for his home-farm the lands of Hobeg in Uist. *Seventhly*, that at the term of Martinmas next, they were to let the remainder of their lands to tenants, for a certain fixed rent, in lieu of all exactions. *Eighthly*, That no single chief should keep more than one birlinn, or galley, of sixteen or eighteen oars; and that in their voyages through the Isles they should not oppress the country people. *Ninthly*, That they should send all their children above nine years of age to school in the Lowlands, to be instructed in reading, writing, and speaking the English language; and that none of their children should be served heir to their fathers, or received as a tenant by the king, who had not received that education. *Lastly*, The chiefs were not to use in their houses more than the following quantities of wine respectively, viz.: Duard and MacLeod, four tun each; Clanranald three tun; and Coll, Lochbuy and MacKinnon, one tun each; and they were to take strict order throughout their whole estates that none of their tenants or vassals should buy or drink any wine. MacLean of Duard, and his brother Lachlan, having delayed to find the required sureties, were committed to ward in Edinburgh castle, whence he was liberated in a very short time, and allowed to live with Acheson of Gosford, his father-in-law, under his own recognizance of £40,000, and his father-in-law's for 5000 merks, that he should remain there until permitted by the council to return to the Isles. Duard's brother was not liberated until the following year, when his own bond was taken for the conformity of himself and his son Hector to the obligations imposed upon the other Islanders in July 1616. His dwelling-place was to be at Ardnacross in Mull; and he was allowed to keep two gentlemen in his household. Donald Gorm of Sleat, having been prevented, by sickness, from attending the council with the other chiefs, ratified all their proceedings, and found the required sureties, by a bond dated in the month of August. He named Duntullim, a castle of his family in Trouterness, as his residence; and six household gentlemen, and an annual consumption of four tun of wine, were allowed to him; and he was annually to exhibit to council three of his principal kinsmen. These proceedings being communicated by the council to the king, were approved by his majesty; who, at the suit of the Islanders, ordered that the chiefs, and some of their immediate relations, might have licence to use fire-arms for their own sport within a mile of their dwellings."*

In the following year, 1617, Hector MacLean of Lochbuy, Lachlan MacLean of Coll, Lachlan MacLean of Torloisk, Sir Ruari MacLeod of Harris, Sir Donald Gorm of Sleat, the captain of. Clanranald, and Sir Lachlan MacKinnon of Strathordell, made their appearance before the council in the month of July.†

Hector Og died in the year 1618, in the fortieth year of his age. He was twice married: first, to Janet, daughter of Cailean Cam, 11th MacKenzie of Kintail, by whom he had Hector Mór, his heir and successor, and Lachlan; also one daughter, Florance, who married John Garbh, 7th MacLean of Coll. His second wife was Isabella, daughter of Sir Archibald Acheson of Gosford, by whom he had Donald, first MacLean of Brolass, John Dubh, predecessor of the counts MacLean of Sweden, and a daughter, Isabella, who died unmarried. The marriage of Florance to John Garbh affords an insight into marriage customs as practiced by the MacLeans. She was given a dower which consisted of a hundred and eighty kine, with the stipulation that if she became a widow, her jointure should be three hundred and sixty. Doubtless the number was reckoned according to the wealth of the contracting parties.

XVI. Eachann Mór, Sixteenth Chief of MacLean,

Or, Big Hector, the sixteenth chief of MacLean, eldest son of the first marriage of Hector Og, succeeded to an extensive and unincumbered estate, and at a period when the family had great influence, owing in part to its

---

* Gregory's *Western Highlands*, pp. 392-6. Taken from *Records Privy Council*, from 11th July, 1616, to 22d March, 1617.

† Under the year 1622, Gregory says: "Since the year 1617, the Islanders have continued (with the exception of Hector MacLean of Duard) to make their annual appearance before the privy council with tolerable regularity. In July, 1619, the time for their yearly appearance was, at their own request, altered from July to February; but, in 1621, it was again altered to July, owing to the uncertainty of the weather in spring. In the following year, Sir Ruari MacLeod of Harris, Sir Donald Gorm of Sleat, John MacDonald, captain of the Clanranald, and the lairds of Coll, Lochbuy and MacKinnon, made their obedience to the privy council, as usual, when several acts of importance relating to the Isles were passed. By the first of these they were bound to build and repair their parish churches to the satisfaction of the bishop of the Isles; and they promised to meet the bishop at Icolmkill, whenever he should appoint, to make the necessary arrangements in the matter. The bishop, at this time, promised to appoint a qualified commissary for the Isles—complaints having been made on this head. By another act, masters of vessels were prohibited, under the penalty of the confiscation of the article, to carry more wine to the Isles than the quantity allowed to the chiefs and gentlemen by the act of 1617."—*Western Highlands*, p. 404.

matrimonial alliances. The judicous management of the possessions and the policy pursued by his father secured to him a strong protecting influence throughout the country. By nature, Hector Mór was inactive and inclined to a peaceful life, being content with his position and surroundings. His character was not one that was likely to embark in any measure that might prove disadvantageous. For some reason, not now known, he became indebted, as the following, taken from an act of the privy council, March 28, 1622, sets forth: " Sir Rory McKenzie of Cogache hes action aganist Sir John McDougall of Dunnolich, narrating That quhair Hector McClane of Dowart his brother in law being put at as weill for his Majesteis dewteis as for debts to his creditors quhairby his house wes lyke to be ruined ; and Sir Rorie out of regaird to him and standing of his house having not only tane on him the burden of the said Hector's debts but the yeirlie payment of his Majesteis dutie extending to tua thousand fyve hundred merkis, for quhilk he had got a rycht to the said Hector's estate : And the said Sir John MacDougall having caused his officiers and servants quho attendit at Ferreis opposite to the Isle of Mull quhair the Tennents of Mull wer accustumed to land with thair goodis to be sold in the country to mak (provisioun) for payment of his Majesties dutie, exact a certane tole for the saidis goodis, molesting and invading them if they refuised. Sir Johne and his officiers ar ordained to be denunceit (rebels) thairfoir." *

Hector Mór was married to Margaret, eldest daughter of Sir Roderick MacLeod of MacLeod, and died without issue in 1626. His widow married Æneas MacDonnell, 7th of Glengarry.

In the person of Hector Mór occurred the first failure in the direct and immediate succession, from father to son, among the chiefs of MacLean ; the eldest son of every preceding chief having regularly succeeded to his father's titles and estates for upward of four hundred years, from Gillean, the founder of the clan, to Hector Mór.

XVII. Sir Lachlan MacLean, Bart., Seventeenth Chief of MacLean.

Hector Mór was succeeded by his brother Lachlan, seventeenth chieftain, and first baronet, who came into possession under the most favorable circumstances. The clan had long been at peace, all its forces well recruited and just as loyal to its chief as at any time in its previous history. Lachlan had power and influence sufficient to guard him against open attack from any enemy in his immediate neighborhood, possessing the favor of the king

---

* *Collectanea de Rebus Albanicis*, p. 154.

(Charles I.) as some security against treacherous misrepresentations at court, he had nothing to fear from open or secret enmity; and his irreconcilable foe, Archibald Campbell, who became eighth earl of Argyle in 1638 (although he enjoyed the estate for many years before, as his father had been proclaimed an outlaw), and afterward marquis, but known as *Gillespie Gruamach* (Archibald the morose), made many attempts to entrap him in his coils. This Argyle was by far the ablest of his family that has ever lived, and a man greatly to be feared. As he is a prominent figure in this period of Scotland's history, it will be of importance to give an estimate of his character, especially when it is considered what two successive chiefs of MacLean had to contend against. Browne says of him: "There is nothing in his conduct which can be justified by the impartial historian. Duplicity, cunning, cowardice, and avarice, were his characteristic traits. His zeal for religion and the covenant was a mere pretence to enable him to obtain that ascendency among the covenanters which he acquired, and his affected patriotism was regulated entirely by his personal interests." * Again: "Argyle's talents were more fitted for the intrigues of the cabinet than the tactics of the field." † "A man equally supple and inflexible, cautious and determined, and entirely qualified to make a figure during a factious and turbulent period." ‡ "Argyle was the head of a party as well as the head of a tribe. Possessed of two different kinds of authority, he used each of them in such a way as to extend and fortify the other." || This Argyle not only asserted the cause of Charles II., and placed the crown on his head (January 1, 1651), but afterward assisted in the ceremony of proclaiming Cromwell Protector, and signed an engagement to support the usurper's government. On the restoration of the monarchy, he again faced about and hastened to London to congratulate Charles on his success. When James Graham, the great Montrose, was led to execution, and while the people were weeping at the sight of fallen greatness and invoking the blessings of heaven upon the head of the illustrious

---

* *History of the Highland Clans*, Vol. II., p. 93. † *Ibid.*, Vol. I., p. 355. ‡ Hume's *History of England*, Vol. V., p. 106.

|| Macaulay's *History of England*, Vol. III., p. 288. This author also adds: "A peculiar dexterity, a peculiar plausibility of address, a peculiar contempt for the obligations of plighted faith, were ascribed, with or without reason, to the dreaded race. 'Fair and false like a Campbell,' became a proverb. It was said that MacCallum More after MacCallum More had, with unwearied, unscrupulous, and unrelenting ambition, annexed mountain after mountain and island after island to the original domains of his house. Some tribes had been expelled from their territory, some compelled to pay tribute, some incorporated with the conquerors."

captive, Argyle "surrounded by his family and the marriage party of his newly wedded son, Lord Lorn, appeared publicly on a balcony in front of the earl of Moray's house in the Canongate, from which he beheld undaunted the great Montrose, powerless now to do him personal harm. To add to the insult, either accidentally or on purpose, the vehicle which carried Montrose was stopped for some time beneath the place where Argyle and his party stood, so that they were able to take a leisurely view of the object of their hate and fear, and it would appear that they took advantage of their fallen foe's position to indulge in unseemly demonstrations of triumph and insult." * While Argyle did not witness the execution of Montrose, yet his son Archibald, afterward ninth earl, did, and of his conduct it is recorded that he entertained his new bride with the spectacle of that execution, and "mocked and laughed in the midst of that weeping assembly; and, staying afterward to see him hewn in pieces, triumphed at every stroke which was bestowed upon his mangled body." †

Soon after Lachlan's accession to the chieftainship, Thomas Knox, bishop of the Isles, made his report (1626) on the state of his diocese. Of the Isles belonging to the MacLeans he says, "Mull belongethe to Hector M^{c}cleane ‡ of Dowart, Hector M^{c}cleane of Lochbowie, Sir Lachlane McKinnon and Lachlane M^{c}clean of Coill; 24 mylles in lenth and 24 mylles in breid. Peyis to the Bischope for his awin pairt of the teind 500 merkis oute of McLeane of Dowartis parte. McLene of Lochbowie his teindis ar yitt unsett. The teindis of 40 merk land belonging to McKinnon and Coll ar sett with uther teindes as heirafter sall be insert. This Ile is servit [be] M^{c}clean, persone of Killane, Mr. Johne Campbell and Niniane McMillan. Coll belonging to the Laird of Coll is 8 mylles in lenth, 4 in breid, peyis to the Bischope with the thrid of the teind of his tuentie merk land of the Quynische in Mull 100 merkes yeirlie. This Yle is servit yeirlie be Mr. Hew M^{c}cleane. Tiry belongeth to Hector M^{c}cleane of Dowart; is 8 mylles in lenth 2 in breid. Peyis to the Bischope, sex chalderis beir yeirlie; and is servit be Martine M^{c}illura. Muck ane small Iland conteining onlie tua tounes, belonges to the Laird of Coll, peyis ane chalder of beir." ||

The first visit of Lachlan to court since the death of his brother was in

---

* Keltie's *History of the Clans of Scotland*, Vol. I., p. 271. † *Ibid.*, Vol. I., p. 277.

‡ This is positive evidence that Hector Mór was living in 1626. The "Account of the Clan," published in 1838, says he died in 1624. The Ardgour MS says he was still living when Lachlan received the title of Baronet. || *Collectanea de Rebus Albanicis*, p. 124.

1631, and while there Charles I. created him a baronet of Nova Scotia, by the title of Sir Lachlan MacLean of Morvern, with remainder to his heirs male whatsoever. It is dated September 3, 1631, and recorded in the General Register House. The original is in Latin. The reception tendered him by the king made a lasting impression upon the generous nature of Lachlan, in so much so that it confirmed him in that steadfast loyalty from which in the cause of that unhappy sovereign he never swerved. But this unfortunate prepossession laid the foundation of many disastrous results to his race, and, as will appear, ultimately threatened the total extinction of his powerful family. For an era in British history was now approaching which put the test to blind adherence to kingly prerogative on the one hand, and the inalienable rights of the people on the other. Charles I. succeeded his father in 1625 to the throne. He inherited the most extreme notions of the power of the throne, and deeply imbibed his father's notion that an Episcopal church was the most consistent with the proper authority of kings; and mistook the general movement in the public mind for an agitation amongst a few disaffected persons. By his arbitrary acts he more and more embittered public feelings. Charles was not unmindful of his duties to the Isles during the gathering of the storm.

During the month of May, 1634, he wrote to the privy council of Scotland directing an inquiry into the exactions of the heritors of the Isles from those engaged in the fisheries; and the bringing in of foreigners by the heritors. A commission was appointed, consisting of Archibald, Lord Lorn (afterward eighth earl of Argyle) and the bishop of the Isles, to inquire into the matter. They made their report on the 29th August, 1634, and as it throws much light on the customs of that epoch it is here inserted. They convened at Inverary the landlords and heritors of the Isles, viz:

"Sir Donnald McDonnald of Sleat, Knight Barronet; Johne M^{c}cleod of Herreis; Johne McRannald of Ilantirum, captane of Clanrannald; Neil McNeill of Bara; Sir Lauchlane M^{c}claine of Morverne, Knight Barronet; Murdoch M^{c}claine of Locbuy; Lauchlane M^{c}claine of Coill; and Lauchlane McCharles v^{c}fingon for the Laird of M^{c}kynnon: And the foresaid Commissioun being publictlie read over in all their audiences, Thereafter the saids Commissioners did interrogat and examine everie one of the saidis Ylanders in particular, what dewteis they exact of his Majesteis subjects of the associatioun resorting there; and the saids Sir Donnald McDonnald, Johne McCleod, Johne M^{c}rannald, and Neill McNeill of Bera *viva voce* gave the answer and declaratioun following vizt *That it wes the ancient custame* befoir the dait of the Contract afterspecifeit (quhilk they think to be about fourteene yeeres since or thereby) to everie ane of thame in whose boundis the herring fishing fell oute, *to exact of* everie barke and ship resorting thereto, for ankorage or ground leave *ane barrell of aill or meill* in the owner's optioun; and for ilk anker layed on shoare, *sax shillings aucht pennies;* and out of every last of herring slaine there, *thrie pundis* *money*; Togedder *with the benefite of everie saturdayes fishing*: And *that now they exact onlie* frome his Majesteis subjects of the Associatioun for ilk ship and barke that comes to the herring fishing, *threttie sax shillings* Scottish money; and for ilk ship that comes to the gray and white fishing *twenty markis*: And this for ankorage and ground leave conforme to ane Contract past betwix the said Sir Donald, Johne M^{c}rannald and umquhile Sir Rorie McCleod and some others of the Ylanders on the ane part, and certane of the Burrowis in the East countrie on the other part in anno 1620 or thereby; Quhilk they say is registrat in the bookes of Counsell:—They being interrogat what is the ground leave of the saids dewteis quhilk they now lift, they say they can make no division, because the same is payable to thame be the said contract for ane ankorage and ground leave, quhilk they refer to the contract itselffe:—Being demandit by what warrand they uplift the saids exactions and dewteis foresaids, they answer that they ar heretours of the ground and so may lawfully take up satisfactioun for ground leave and ankerage; it being ane ancient custome and in use to be done past memorie of man:—Being demandit how they can exact the particular exactions and dewteis foirsaids from ane of his Majesteis subjects of the associatioun who have not contracted with thame, They ansuer that they take no more aff thame than aff these who have contracted; wherein they think they doe thame favour, Becaus they thinke they might uplift frome thame the foresaid ancient dewtie and exactions that they war in use to gett before the dait of the said Contract, in respect of the antiquitie of the custome and that they are heretours of the lands and that they have made no conditions with thame:—Item the saids Sir Lauchlane M^{c}claine, Murdoch McClaine of Lochbuy, Lauchlane McClaine of Coill and Lauchlane McCharles v^{c}fingon being all examined anent the premisses, They and ilkane of thame declared that there is no fishings within their boundis, wherethrow they may exact aniething frome his Majesteis subjects of the associatioun; But if the fishings were in these bounds they would be content to exact no more nor the saids north Ylanders doe:—And the saids haill ylanders being demandit how and by whome strangers wer brought in and their vessellis loadned with fisches and uther native commoditeis; They all in one voice ansuered that nane of thame nor anie within thair bounds does anie such thing; onlie the said Sir Donald McDonnald declares that the last yeere there came into Lochmadie to the herring fishing in his bounds ane Dutche ship having the Deputie of Ireland his warrand, and some Frenche shippis with some men of Air who transported no commoditeis away bot herring and uther fishes:—Upoun the trueth of the quhilkis ansueres and declarations above written, the said ylanders and ilk ane of thame for thair awne parts to give their oaths of veritie:—In witness whereof the saids commissioners and ylanders have subscribed thir presents day yeer and place foresaid. Sic subscribitur, A. Lorne; Neill Isles; Sr. Donald MacDonald of Sleat; L. M^{c}clane Moruerne; J. McLeod of Dunvegane; J. McC. rannold. Us Neill McNeill of Bara, Lauclane McClaine of Coill and Lauchlane McCharles v^{c}fingon abone written at our commands becaus we cannot write our selffes."*

Public feeling ran so high against the king on account of his extravagant acts that the murmurings broke out into rebellion, which in 1640 had assumed such proportions in Scotland that an army commenced the invasion of England, and defeated the royal army at Newburn-Upon-Tyne. This advance met with the sympathy and good wishes of no small part of the English people. The parliament of 1640 was resolute in its opposition to the king's despotism, and began by the impeachment of the ministers and high officers of

---

* *Collectanea de Rebus Albanicis*, p. 109.

state. Charles was ultimately (January 27, 1649) condemned to death as a tyrant, murderer, and enemy of the nation; and three days later was beheaded in front of the palace of Whitehall.

In the year 1641 the king visited Edinburgh for the settlement of some Scottish affairs, much about the period that his disputes with his English parliament were agitating the kingdom. On this occasion none appeared more forward to offer obsequious court to the king than the eighth earl of Argyle. All his professions of attachment and his seemingly sincere declarations of fealty were received by the unsuspecting monarch with good will, who, ere he returned to England, created him marquis of Argyle. At the very moment the king was heaping honors upon him he was making traitorous proposals to the Western chiefs to seduce them from their allegiance; and Sir Lachlan MacLean was one of the first he atttempted to engage in his course. The object of this, then well guarded, is now plainly revealed. Had he succeeded in his attempt to incite the chief of MacLean to open rebellion, or had he entangled the unsuspecting Lachlan, the long cherished purpose of his race would have been accomplished, and the inheritance of MacLean would have become his prey. There is no evidence that MacLean saw the true import of the intrigue; but, fortunately, his devotion to Charles saved him from the snares artfully set to entrap him. The proposals were rejected with scorn, and the honest chieftain declined any further correspondence with his covert enemy. About the same time Sir Lachlan received a letter from the king expressing confidence in the well known fidelity of his house in the cause of the reigning family. Argyle attempted a reconciliation with Sir Lachlan, and evinced much anxiety to learn the nature of the king's communication; but the chieftain, becoming more and more convinced of Campbell's designs, only repeated his former resolutions to hold no correspondence with him. Campbell became convinced that nothing could shake the loyalty of Sir Lachlan; and equally satisfied that his own ambitious views to rule the conduct of the island chiefs in regard to the approaching struggle could not be accomplished while the most powerful of them seemed thus disposed resolutely to thwart him. MacLean now became the object of his determined hostility. Anxious to form a party which might arm him with influence in the contention between the king and his parliament, Campbell continued for some time to watch the progress of events without declaring for either; but holding himself in readiness to throw his influence into the preponderating scale whenever circumstances promised safety to his purpose. When, therefore, the affairs of the king in England enabled him to throw off the mask with seeming safety, he hesitated no longer; and that monarch, who had but a short time before heaped honors upon the head of Archibald Campbell, the first marquis of Argyle, found, in 1644, one of the most avowed of his enemies.

In the spring of 1644, James Graham, the first marquis of Montrose, known for his uncompromising character and warlike genius, by command of the king, proceeded to Scotland to raise the royalists in the North. After the battle of Marston Moor, he threw himself into the Highlands, and after a time placed himself at the head of the Irish auxiliaries and a body of Highlanders under Sir Alexander MacDonald. To this body the clans rapidly gathered, and soon after (September 1st) gained a victory at Tippermuir, near Perth. Soon after, he dispatched couriers to the Western chiefs, calling upon them to join the royal standard without delay. Sir Lachlan MacLean instantly prepared to obey the summons, but finding all the roads through the county of Argyle shut against him by the Campbells, aided in strong force by a body of Lowlanders, he did not think it prudent to hazard, with his clan, an immediate march through the county; but, leaving instructions with his brother Donald of Brolass to assemble the MacLeans and the other clans subordinate to him as soon as practicable, he took his departure from Duard castle, accompanied by about thirty of his kinsmen, of whom were MacLean of Coll and Ewen of Treshnish, the latter recently returned from Ireland, where he had been in command of a detachment of MacLeans from the massacre of the Protestants in 1641. Sir Lachlan, passing through Morvern, was joined by MacLean of Kinlochaline, Allan MacLean of Ardgour, and MacLean of Kingerloch; with this small band he joined Montrose on the day before the battle of Inverlochy. In the meantime Montrose had defeated a force of Covenanters near Aberdeen (September 13th), and taken' possession of that city. The approach of Argyle with a force of four thousand caused him to retreat into the wilds of Badenoch. Having received a large accession from the Highland clans, the great marquis suddenly appeared in the country of the Campbells, frightfully devastated it, drove Argyle himself from Inverary castle, and then turned North intending to attack the Covenanters, who were posted in strong force at Inverness. While marching through Glen Mór—the great glen of Scotland—he heard that Argyle was following him in force. He wheeled upon his pursuer, fell upon him unexpectedly at Inverlochy, February 2, 1645, and utterly routed his forces.

As already noted, Sir Lachlan joined Montrose the day before the battle, and was received by the marquis with much cordiality, and publicly thanked

AN INDEPENDENT CLAN—1598 TO 1746.   167

for the promptitude with which he answered the summons. His followers immediately had parts allotted to them about Montrose's own person, and were to continue in such positions until the levies from Mull and Morvern arrived. On the following morning Montrose took up a position to the southward of the river Lochy, about two miles north-east of Fort William. About sunrise the battle was commenced by the Athol men, led on by Montrose in person. In this charge Argyle's right was turned, and the retreat cut off by the only path open to them, the western road by Balachulish. "By break of day Argyle betook himself to his galley, and, rowing off shore, remained a spectator of the combat, when, by all the rules of duty and gratitude, he ought to have

INVERLOCHY CASTLE AND BATTLE GROUND.

been at the head of his devoted followers." * Having thus witnessed the destruction of his army, from a safe distance, he fled to the Lowlands. The Campbell leaders did all that brave men could do to check the impetuous assault of the royal forces, but at last, disheartened by the furious attack and the desertion of their leader, they threw down their arms and attempted to gain their boats. Their victorious pursuers rendered this attempt abortive, by fiercely attacking them at the place of embarkation, where about fifteen hun-

---

* Scott's *Tales of a Grandfather*, Second Series, p. 127. For accounts of Argyle's cowardice at the battle of Inverlochy, see Stewart's *Sketches of the Highlanders*, p. 386; Keltie's *History of the Clans*, Vol. I., p. 196; Brown's *History of the Clans*, Vol. I., p. 362, etc.

dred were killed, and over one thousand taken prisoners. Montrose had only three privates killed, but quite a number wounded. In the attack by the Athol men, Campbell of Skipness, one of the bravest of Argyle's leaders, was brought to the ground by the sword of a gentleman of the Clan Stewart, who was in the act of repeating the blow with fatal effect, when his sword was arrested by that of Ewen MacLean, the captain of Cairnburg, whose companion in arms Skipness had been in the suppression of the late Irish rebellion. Campbell of Skipness' life was saved, but at the expense of a severe wound to the generous laird of Treshnish, who, in the act of protecting Campbell, received the blow aimed at him. Skipness, on being brought before Montrose, declared, had he entertained the least suspicion of the cowardly character of Argyle, he would that morning have placed himself in the ranks of the royal army. The generous conduct of MacLean of Treshnish had its reward in the approbation of his chivalrous leader. During the brilliant achievements that followed, Treshnish had invariably some post of honor assigned him under the special direction of Montrose.

The result of the battle of Inverlochy roused the chiefs of the Isles in every direction to active exertion in the royal cause. Donald MacLean of Brolass, in the absence of his brother and chief, marshaled together the MacLeans, with the subordinate clans, the MacQuarries and MacNeills. At the head of these, amounting to eleven hundred men, seven hundred and fifty of whom were MacLeans, with Brolass as his lieutenant-colonel, Sir Lachlan placed himself, and advancing immediately into Lorn, formed a junction with Sir Alexander MacDonald, the celebrated hero and commander under Montrose. The chief of MacLean and Sir Alexander, in their progress to Montrose's camp, cleared the county of Argyle of such parties of the enemy as still lurked there.

In the meantime Montrose, having considerably augmented his forces, resumed his march toward Inverness. Directing his course to the east, he carried fire and sword into Elgin, Banff, and Aberdeenshire. The city of Dundee was captured and pillaged; and on May 9th he attacked and routed Hurry at Auldearn, near Nairn, leaving upward of three thousand of the enemy dead upon the field. On July 2d he inflicted a more disastrous defeat on Baillie at Alford, in Aberdeenshire. Shortly after this battle the forces of Sir Lachlan MacLean joined the main army, which now amounted to five or six thousand men, and at once proceeded south, followed by Baillie, who picked up re-enforcements on his way. During the march toward Auchterarder Baillie detached about three hundred of his cavalry to harrass Montrose, who was marching on a parallel with the enemy by the foot of the mountains west of Crieff. Montrose, annoyed at the attacks of the troopers, called for MacLean of Treshnish and told him to select a dozen of the best marksmen, and " check the gasconading swaggerers." The gallant Treshnish made his selection from among the MacLeans and Camerons, and watching his opportunity, turned upon the hovering horsemen, and by the first fire brought five of their number to the ground; a whole troop composing the advanced guard of the cavalry instantly took to flight, followed by their elated pursuers into the open plain. Panic-struck, and in their terror creating their pursuers into the formidable mass, not of twelve, but of twelve hundred, they galloped on in the most fearful confusion, never looking behind until they reached Auchterarder, where they reported the narrow escape they had.

During the march of a portion of Montrose's army toward Stirling, the MacLeans laid waste the parishes of Muchort and Dollar, of which the marquis of Argyle was superior, and burnt castle Campbell, the principal residence of the Argyle family in the Lowlands, in requital of similar acts done by Argyle and his followers in the country of the MacLeans. In speaking of a part of this affair, MacKenzie says: " When Montrose attacked castle Campbell, a stronghold on the border of Fifeshire, then in possession of Argyle, a party of the MacLeans, who were out with Montrose, marched up to the very walls of the castle. Though the garrison was six times the number of the Islanders, the inmates of the castle 'had not the courage so much as to fire a gun, or even to look them in the face.' Young Lochiel (afterwards the famous Sir Ewen Cameron), who was present, was so disgusted with the cowardly conduct of the governor of the castle that he turned upon him and told him to his face that he and every one of the garrison ought to be hanged; and then turning to Argyle he exclaimed, ' For what purpose, my lord, are these people kept here? Your lordship sees the country destroyed; and that they may be easily cut to pieces, one by one, without their being capable to unite and help one another; but your fellows are so unfit for the business for which they were brought here, that they have not courage so much as to look over the walls. Argyle made scarcely any answer at the time, but he soon after dismissed the governor, making him the scapegoat for what had actually occurred before his own eyes, while he was present in the castle and could have assumed the command himself." *

Montrose crossed the river Forth four miles above Stirling, marched

---

* *History of the Camerons, Celtic Magazine,* Vol. VIII., p. 469.

through Kippen, and passing the Kilsyth Hills by Fintry, encamped at the village of Kilsyth, where he now resolved upon waiting his antagonists. Here he was followed by Baillie, Argyle, and others, who took up a position three miles to the eastward of Kilsyth; and observing that Montrose had greatly narrowed his field of operations by concentrating his forces upon the village of Kilsyth, determined to surround him and cut off all the avenues for escape. Montrose immediately comprehended the intention of his enemies, and perceiving that, in their eagerness to prevent his retreat, they had weakened their center by the extension of their wings, he strengthened his own center, of which he took immediate command; and then forming his wings so as to exhibit a battle front both east and south, he closed up his enemies as near as possible. By this arrangement, his center formed also his reserve, ready to aid either wing, as occasion might render necessary. In the progress of these preparations, he sent for his favorite follower, MacLean of Treshnish, and ordered him to select a hundred men and occupy certain cottages and small gardens in advance of his left. "Captain of Cairnburg," said the great Montrose, "in sending you upon this service, I feel it my duty to tell you that the post I assign you is of such importance as to require all your courage and tact to overcome your danger." "Danger! my lord," replied MacLean, "the more dangerous the more honorable: call it desperate, so is my resolution." Treshnish proceeded to his post, which he had not occupied many minutes before he was furiously attacked (August 15th) by the enemy; but his chosen band of valiant Kelts soon made their foes recoil. Every shot took effect, and the advancing column, confused by this determined resistance to its first essay, stood still for a few minutes, unresolved whether to retreat or advance. Encouraged by the apparent irresolution of his enemies, the fearless MacLean rushed forward at the head of his devoted followers and attacked the column sword in hand. The chief of MacLean, observing the danger to which Treshnish exposed himself, exclaimed, "My brave kinsman will be cut to pieces," and rushed forward to his relief without waiting, in the ardor of the moment, for the necessary orders to do so. The whole of Sir Lachlan's division, stripped to their shirts, and throwing aside every thing likely to encumber them, instantly followed him. Several of the clans, in their eagerness to engage, immediately followed the example of the MacLeans, and the battle now became general throughout the whole lines. These attacks were wholly without orders, and must have deranged the plans of Montrose, but that generous commander merely remarked, on the Earl of Airley expressing himself strongly against the Highland chiefs acting in so disorderly a manner, "Speak them fair, my lord, they are brave and true gentlemen, and withal right loyal; and if they willed it so, could fight and win a battle even if you and I were asleep. They now need only your support and mine, and support they shall have." So saying, he immediately divided his center into two divisions, one of which under lord Airley be sent to support the left, while with the other he himself in person attacked the weakened center of the enemy and broke through it. The enemy thus dissevered became one mass of confusion. In this state the royalists fell upon their foes with uncontrollable fury, in the exasperation of the moment quarter being totally unheeded. The MacLeans, MacDonalds, and the men of Athol here distinguished themselves most conspicuously. Fighting shoulder to shoulder, those brave clans carried on the work of death with a seeming determination not to leave an enemy alive to "relate the disaster of Kilsyth." The Covenanters were defeated with frightful loss, not less than six thousand being left dead upon the field. Only three hundred of the foot escaped the carnage, but the dragoons, more fortunate, escaped with the loss of about four hundred men. Archibald Campbell, or as he is better known as the marquis of Argyle, imitated the example he had set at Inverlochy, by running toward the Frith of Forth, where another friendly galley was in readiness to receive him. He was most terribly frightened, nor did his fear subside until the ship, on board of which he took refuge, was, at his earnest supplication, got under weigh and put out to sea.

The cause of Charles was for the moment triumphant, and Montrose master of the situation. He had been appointed lieutenant-governor of Scotland, and commander of the royal forces. All the principal cities in the West hastened to proclaim their fidelity, and the blame of the recent trouble was laid on the unfortunate Presbyterian clergy.

On the disbandonment of the Highland army the chief of MacLean and Sir Alexander MacDonald, with their followers, started for home, and on the way encountered a party of seven hundred of Argyle's men, who still lurked at a place called Laggan Mór, in Lorn, and with their advanced guard, consisting of two hundred men only, totally routed them.*

Sir Lachlan MacLean and his brave clansmen now hoped to enjoy permanent peace and live at home free from anxiety. Soon again summons came from the royal lieutenant, and the chief of MacLean made ready to join Montrose.

---

* See Whishart's *Life of Montrose*, Chap XII.

The partial disbanding of the royal army once more gave hopes to the factious leaders of Scotland. David Leslie, who commanded on the borders, was secretly invited to return to Scotland and proceed against Montrose, whose army did not exceed fifteen hundred men. By forced marches Leslie passed into Scotland through Selkirkshire, and with six thousand troops surprised Montrose at Philiphaugh, September 13th. Here Montrose lost the fruit of six splendid victories. The defeated royalists fell back on Perthshire, where Montrose summoned the clans to rendezvous at Strathearn. To this point the faithful Highlanders began to assemble, and among the foremost were the MacLeans of Coll, which was acknowledged by Montrose in a letter to John Garbh, the seventh laird of Coll.* While the faithful friends of the royal cause were gathering to the standard, the deceived monarch was prevailed upon by the members of the Scottish council to command Montrose to cease from his warlike preparations *under the penalty of high treason!* Montrose retired abroad; and Sir Lachlan MacLean did not proceed farther after his clansmen responded to the call.

The king was now completely in the possession of his enemies in Scotland, who compelled him to submit to certain propositions. There were two he refused to agree to, one of which was the establishment of the directory and the recognition of the Westminster confession. The earl of Loudon (John Campbell of Lawers), the marquis of Argyle (Archibald Campbell), and the earl of Dunfermline offered the king that they would go to London and treat with parliament for a mitigation of the propositions. After their arrival in London, it was observed by the royalists " that their treating would end in a bargain ;" for, " although professing themselves great sticklers for the freedom, honor, and safety of the king, they not only offered to concur in any measures that parliament might propose, should the king remain obstinate, but offered to withdraw the Scots' army from England, on receiving payment of the arrears of pay due to the army for its services. Such an offer was too tempting to be withstood; and a committee having been appointed to adjust

---

* The letter is as follows:

"Sir, I must heartily thank you for yr willingness and good affect to his mas service, and particularly the sending along of yr sons (John and Hugh), to whom I will have ane particular respect. Hope we also that you will continue ane good instrument for the advancing thereof, the king's service; for which and for yr former loyal carriages be confident that you shall fynd the effect of his mas favor, as they can be witnessed by

"Your very faithful friend,

"STRATHEARN, 20th *Jan.*, 1646.   MONTROSE."

the balance due to the Scots, it was finally agreed by the latter, after many charges on both sides had been disallowed, to accept of £400,000 in full of all demands." * It appears that £200,000 of this money was paid on the delivery of the person of the king into the hands of parliament, which was consummated January 28, 1647. The Scottish intriguers now threw off all disguise, and without delay prepared an army of horse and foot, so as to overawe the royalists, who might attempt to save their king. At the head of this army was placed the notorious David Leslie, and afterward to it Argyle was assigned. The army marched into Banff, thence into Perthshire, and from there into the Western Isles, and succeeded in surprising Sir Alexander MacDonald in Kintyre. Leslie laid siege to Dunaverty castle, which was well defended by three hundred men. Sir James Turner, Leslie's adjutant-general, says that after the surrender " they were put to the sword, every mother's son, except one young man, Maccoul, whose life I begged to be sent to France, with a hundred followers which we had smoked out of a cave, as they do foxes, who were given to Captain Campbell, the chancellor's brother." "This atrocious act was perpetrated at the instigation of John Nave or Neaves, 'a bloody preacher,' but, according to Woodrow, an 'excellan man,' who would not be satisfied with less than the blood of prisoners." † This deed was one of the charges against Argyle when brought to trial at a subsequent period for his numberless atrocities. The evidence appears that he privately advised it. Certain it is, he took no steps whatever to prevent it. The father of Sir Alexander, Colla-Kittoch MacDonald, was seized in Islay, turned over to Argyle, and afterward hanged in a cleft of a rock, near Dunstaffnage castle, amidst the fiendish yells of his enemies.

With five thousand troops, Leslie and Argyle passed from Islay into Mull, and overran it from one end to the other, committing the most disgraceful outrages that diabolical ingenuity could invent. These wanton cruelties were the more inhuman because no resistance of the inhabitants had been offered on this occasion to the invaders. Sir Lachlan MacLean, knowing that resistance would be fruitless, had instructed his people to remain at home in pursuit of their domestic concerns, lest by appearing in arms they might afford a plea to the enemy to desolate the island altogether. Notwithstanding this defenseless position Argyle and Leslie had Sir James Turner to let loose the army, who commenced a career of blood and plunder all over the island, who

---

* Browne's *History of the Highland Clans*, Vol. II., p. 2.   †*Ibid.*

stated that for himself he did not care if the whole clan were put to the sword.*

Duard Castle was now besieged by this army, the leaders of which threatened to put every human being within to the sword if they were obliged to take it by force. On the march through Dumbarton, Argyle had the son and heir of the chief of MacLean seized at an academy which he was attending there, and took him along with him in the expedition. He threatened to take the life of the son, in the presence of the father, if Duard Castle was not given up. It also reached the ears of Leslie that within the castle were eight Irish gentlemen, followers of Sir Alexander MacDonald; these were especially demanded. Sir Lachlan peremptorily refused to deliver them, and prepared to defend the castle to the last; and on account of this refusal it was that Turner was sent on his expedition of rapine and blood. The people were forced to abandon their homes and seek refuge in the defenses of the mountains. Sir Lachlan, finding that a defense was useless, and knowing the atrocity committed at Dunaverty, accepted of the best terms offered. He agreed to place the castle at the disposal of Leslie on condition that they recalled the detachments which were sent out under Turner and Sir Donald Campbell of Ardnamurchan, and that the lives of the inmates of the castle be spared. In this condition the chief of MacLean distinctly mentions "eight Irish gentlemen, his friends, who are enjoying the hospitality of the Lady of Duard." The castle was surrendered, but the conditions were disregarded by Leslie and Argyle. The Irish guests were seized, and carried a short distance from the castle, where seven of them were shot. The rock where this barbarous action occurred is still called Creag nin Erenich, or the Irishmen's Rock. The circumstance under which the only survivor escaped the fate of his companions is both curious and interesting. Just as the victims were brought out to prepare for death, Marian, youngest daughter of the chief of Duard, accompanied by a kinsman on horseback, was taking her departure from the castle for Moy, the seat of MacLean of Lochbuy, and happening to pass the very spot where the late happy guests of her father's halls were at that instant preparing to meet their doom, overcome by the distressing sight, she fainted away and fell to the ground. Her kinsman immediately jumped off his horse and flew to her aid. At the same moment her fall caught the attention of one of the gentlemen in the melancholy group, who, exclaiming, "Ye heartless murderers, will none of you save the lady?" rushed forward, and vaulting with the

---

* Browne's *History of the Clans*, Vol. II., p. 5.

quickness of thought into the deserted saddle of the lady's kinsman, he galloped off, and was soon out of the reach of pursuit among the mountains. Whether the fit and fall of the maiden were a premeditated design or the result of accident may be determined from the fact that by the instrumentality of the same lady the gallant fugitive had a boat provided for him on the south side of Mull, by which he finally escaped. There was no reason whatever for the execution of these prisoners. They had simply obeyed the call of their sovereign to put down a rebellion. The savage ferocity of the Covenanters in this deed of blood is well illustrated by the account of Sir James Turner of the conduct of Sir Donald Campbell of Ardnamurchan: "Here I can not forget one Donald Campbell, fleshed in blood from his very infancy, who with all imaginable violence pressed that the whole Clan MacLean should be put to the edge of the sword; nor could he be commanded to forbear his bloody suit by the lieutenant-general and two major-generals; and with some difficulty was he commanded silence by his chief, the marquis of Argyle." *

The success of the parliamentary party, and the execution of the king, which took place soon after, brought to the front the ambitious and unscrupulous, the result of which was that law and justice were trampled under foot. The time had now come when the long cherished desire of the house of Argyle against the MacLeans might be realized. Since the commencement of the civil war the estate of MacLean had paid none of the public dues, Sir Lachlan estimating the amount of those dues as a remuneration trifling enough to indemnify him for the expense of maintaining a thousand armed followers at his own expense on behalf of the king during Montrose's campaigns; and, from conscientious reasons, he now felt less disposed to pay them into the hands of those whom he believed had usurped the sovereign's authority. Non-compliance on the part of Sir Lachlan was just what Argyle desired. He instantly set himself about purchasing up all the debts, both public and private, which he could find against the chief of MacLean; and these debts, together with certain alleged to be owing on account of his ecclesiastical revenues to the bishop of the Isles, and some old debts for the payment of which he pretended to be security, enabled Argyle to establish a claim of £30,000 against the chief of MacLean. His next step was to have Lachlan decreeted before the exchequer, which he had no difficulty in accomplishing owing to the influence he exerted there. This was all accomplished before Sir Lachlan had the least intimation of the existence of any proceedings against him.

---

* Browne's *History of the Clans*, Vol. II., p. 7.

When apprised of the fact he made all haste to proceed to Edinburgh in hopes that the committee of estates would listen to him. Even this resource, frail hope as it at best promised, was debarred him; for his persecutor had, of his own authority, issued a writ of attachment against the person of Sir Lachlan, who was taken prisoner at Inverary, and thrown into Argyle's castle of Carrick *for a debt due to Archibald Campbell, marquis of Argyle.* For upward of a year Sir Lachlan suffered imprisonment rather than sign a bond in acknowledgment of the debt, demanded by Argyle. His health at length declining, and seeing no hope of relief by legal measures in a country now prostrate, Sir Lachlan was induced to listen to the affectionate protestations of his friends, who, alarmed at the state of his health, advised his signing the bond, as the only condition upon which his release could be obtained. By this time he was in a dying condition, and submitted himself to the wishes of his friends, by signing the bond. His liberation immediately followed, and he returned to his castle of Duard, in Mull, where on the 18th of April, 1648, he expired. His remains were carried to Iona, where amongst the noble line of Duard's chiefs he lies buried.

Sir Lachlan MacLean was married to Mary, second daughter of Sir Roderick MacLeod of MacLeod, by whom he had issue two sons and three daughters—Hector, his heir and successor, and Allan. His daughter Isabella married Sir Ewen Cameron of Lochiel; Mary married Lachlan MacKinnon, and the youngest daughter, Marian, died young and unmarried.

XVIII. Sir Eachann Ruadh, Eighteenth Chief of MacLean.

Red Hector, or as he has been called, Hector Roy, or Hector Rufus, succeeded his father as eighteenth of Duard and second Baronet of Morvern. His lines were cast upon evil times. The civil commotions continued during the period of his chieftainship. King Charles I. was brought to the block, and his son Charles II. was offered the crown by the Scots in 1650, and in the beginning of 1651 was crowned at Scone. Archibald Campbell, first marquis of Argyle, was head of the committee of estates of Scotland, and whose character has already been set forth. With such a man at the head of affairs, and the deplorable condition into which the country had fallen, what good could befall the young chief of Duard? Although warlike, chivalrous, brave, and generous, he had upon one side the ocean, and upon the other, Argyle, who could muster five thousand claymores. The power of oppression possessed by Argyle soon exerted itself over the MacLeans. His clan and dependants, actuated by his own desires, began to harrass and provoke the MacLeans of Morvern by continued aggressions upon their property. The

MacLean proprietors in Morvern, not willing to hazard their own safety with a government at whose hands they could not hope for much justice, felt an unwillingness to commence hostile measures of retaliation against the depredators; at length, however, after many sufferings, they entered into a bond of self-defense, and consulted their chief as to the measures of protection most advisable to be pursued. In a foray of the Campbells of Ardnamurchan, into Morvern, in the year 1651, they carried off a considerable number of cattle belonging to the MacLeans. Sir Hector complained to Argyle of the depredatory conduct of his people, and demanded peremptory and immediate satisfaction. Campbell not showing due willingness to give the required satisfaction, Sir Hector called together his people, and, entering Ardnamurchan, seized upon two of the principal offenders, whom he immediately ordered to be hanged at the castle of Drimnin, in Morvern; and after forcing the plunderers to make ample restitution for their depredation upon the MacLeans, and terrifying them into a promise of honest behavior for the future, the young chief marched into Lorn, where he also made such reprisals upon the Campbells as compensated his people for the injuries suffered by them so long. While these reprisals were being inflicted, the marquis was at Inverary, and gathering a force marched westward toward Lorn, and meeting Sir Hector on Lochawe-side, imperiously inquired how he dared to enter his lands, or commit the injuries upon his people of which he was lately guilty. " Daring, my lord Argyle," answered the young chief, " is a quality to which I well know *you* are a total stranger, and of which it does not, therefore, become you to speak. But as *I dare* be an honest man myself, I dare also to punish the dishonest; and since it appears you dare not or will not keep your unruly robbers in order, I am resolved they shall keep clear of my people, or the district of Lorn shall within a month exhibit the spectacle of a Campbell thief hanging to every tree in it."

Although Sir Hector might well dispute the validity of the bond thus extorted from his father, as already noticed, his extreme notions of honor would not permit him to argue its illegality or refuse its payment. It appears to have sufficed the noble young chief to see his father's name attached to that unsavory document to authorize him to pay it. He at once set about doing so, and in one payment advanced Argyle £10,000 to account. Yet even in this transaction Argyle managed to dupe the youthful lord of Duard, by giving him a common receipt, instead of indorsing the amount on the original bond. This receipt, as was generally believed, was purloined with other papers from Duard Castle by some emissary of Argyle at a future period, not a farthing of which was credited of the £10,000. In after years, Argyle's successor sued for the full amount of the original bond, without any deduction being allowed on the score of this installment.

As already noticed, the unsettled state of the kingdom brought about a renewal of the ancient clan feuds and forays which formerly existed, and those disgraceful barbarities, so destructive to the best interests of society, became at this time, in the Highlands, as common as ever. Those disposed toward it, unchecked by law and unawed by any controlling power, led only a life of murder and rapine. The MacLeans and other clans that remained loyal to the house of Stuart continued to suffer severely from the plundering excursions of the opposition hordes which infested the country, the suspended state of law and justice enabling them to pursue their depredations with perfect impunity. It became the duty of the well-disposed chiefs, as a matter of necessity, summarily to suppress and punish these irregularities; so that the country continued for a considerable period in the most deplorable state of disorder.

Among the many disturbances, the following may be mentioned: Some Camerons, who lived in Morvern, having killed MacLean of Kingerloch and wounded his son, made good their escape. Sir Hector, with great promptitude, entered the field with a sufficient force, and succeeded in destroying all their cattle, to the number of three or four hundred, and was resolved on a further prosecution of them, declaring that he would make a greyhound carry a purse of gold through Lochaber, if he lived for any length of time. About the same time, the MacIans of Ardnamurchan resolved to avenge the injury done them, as they conceived it, by Sir Hector's father, who brought so many of them to justice; and being privately instigated by Sir Donald Campbell, a number of them landed by night near Isle of Muck's house, and began to drive away his cattle. Hector MacLean—Isle of Muck—happened to be out with one servant only, but attacked them, his gun missing fire. He was shot dead by one of the theives, who was called Gillespic MacIan Shaor, a most notorious robber, whose character is still fresh in the neighborhood. The murderers escaped, but two of them were afterward apprehended by the earl of Seaforth's orders and hanged. The laird of the Isle of Muck was a brother of MacLean of Coll, a gentleman who was much respected, and whose death was greatly lamented.

With the news of the murder of the laird of Muck also came the orders of Charles II., who was now in Scotland, and organizing an army for the purpose of opposing Cromwell, who at this time was pursuing his victorious career into the very heart of the kingdom. Charles had his headquarters at Perth, but on the approach of Cromwell from the east, the royal army marched southward upon Stirling, and took up a position at the Torwood, some miles south of the town. Here the royalists received large reinforcements; among others, Sir Hector MacLean, recently appointed colonel of foot for Argyleshire, who brought to the field fifteen hundred followers, of whom eight hundred were MacLeans. The MacLeans, officered by the principal gentlemen of that name, were under the immediate command of Donald of Brolass, uncle to the young chief, as lieutenant-colonel. This division was composed of the better classes, and their military bearing, as well as their respectable appearance, generally called forth the admiration of the whole army. Little time passed ere the courage of this band was put to the test. Cromwell, on approaching Falkirk, found the royalists so strongly intrenched in their position that he did not deem it safe to attack them; but after a series of maneuvres, in which he succeeded in deceiving the royalists, he managed to send over the Frith of Forth, at Queensferry, the larger portion of his army, under General Lambert, with the intention to throw himself into the rear of Charles's army.

When the news of Cromwell's movement was received in the camp of Charles, Holburn of Menstrie was dispatched with the cavalry, Sir Hector MacLean with a division of the Highlanders, and Sir John Brown with some Lowland regiments, for the purpose of opposing Lambert's advance to the North. Lambert had not advanced beyond Inverkeithing, within three miles of North Queensferry, before he found himself intercepted by the royalists. On the morning of July 20, 1651, he drew up his army in battle order, on the rising ground immediately south of Inverkeithing. As soon as Holburn saw the Highlanders fairly engaged in the struggle, he drew off his cavalry, a thousand strong, without firing a shot, and thus left the remainder of the army to the mercy of treble their number. A song, familiar to the generality of MacLeans, expresses the conduct of Holburn:

"Dhág e dèodh Mhachdghilleain cuir a chàthà na ónhreachd."
(He left the undaunted son of Gilleain alone to fight the foe.)

The brave Sir Hector witnessed the flight of the craven dragoons with pity and contempt, though not with dismay. He instantly called to him the laird of Buchanan and Sir John Brown, to whom the young chief addressed a few words expressive of his resolution, even with the small force they had, to continue the battle. "They are double our number," added he, "but what of that; let them come to the sword's point, there is not a MacLean in my gathering but will undertake two." Sir John Brown remarked, that they were engaging their enemies, not only under great numerical disadvantages, but the position of the enemy was another important advantage they had over them. Sir Hector quickly replied: "What would you have me do? Would you have me fly, like that cowardly old horseman, Holburn, and be forever the scorn of honest men? Our honor and our loyalty demand that we do our best." And striking his sword into the ground on the spot on which he stood, he observed: "Let the English traitor's deputy march on; here, surrounded by his faithful clan, he will find Duard's chief ready to receive him."

The battle commenced from Lambert's left, where, from a battery planted on the brow of the hill, the firing was fearfully destructive to the MacLeans and Buchanans, whose exposed position on the lower ground it completely swept. Sir Hector noticing that the MacLeans and their brave allies were becoming furious from the destructive effect of the enemy's artillery, and were every moment more and more eager to be within the claymore's length of their foes, threw himself into the midst of them and led them up the hill. Here the overwhelming numbers of Lambert enabled him literally to encircle the devoted Highlanders. Sir John Brown, with about two hundred cavalry and two battalions of foot, had to withstand the whole weight of the enemy's right, and was therefore unable to afford any relief to Sir Hector. Borne down by numbers, after repeated conflicts in which they behaved with honor and suffered severely, Sir John's division took to flight, leaving their gallant leader prisoner in the hands of the enemy and mortally wounded. The desperate purpose of the chief of MacLean, "neither to yield nor fly," was still his fixed resolve. He formed his undaunted band into a solid body, exhibiting a front in every direction, so as to be better prepared to repulse the attacks which, surrounded at every point as he was, could be directed against him on every side. Even thus encircled, and having with him not more than eight hundred MacLeans and about seven hundred Buchanans and others, the daring young chief bid defiance to the whole of Lambert's veteran army, led by the most experienced general under Cromwell. The successive charges made upon Sir Hector's determined band by this mass of overwhelming veteran troops was fearfully destructive. No idea of asking for quarter was dreamed of by this band in so great peril. Under these disadvantages, even terrible to contemplate, did the chief of MacLean maintain the unequal contest for four hours, repulsing not only the attacks of the foe, but repeatedly charging him in return. In these charges both the MacLeans and Buchanans were slaughtered in great numbers; their foes, also, for some hours, suffering equally as severely. At length the diminished numbers of the Highlanders rendered them an easy prey; still to yield was deemed a dishonorable alternative by the chivalrous chief of MacLean. His body literally hacked with wounds, he still continued to oppose the foe and to encourage his faithful followers to persevere, telling them that the cause of their king was worthy a greater sacrifice. The last and decisive charge made by Lambert's cavalry could only be met by the exhausted Highlanders with the last efforts of despair. The enemy in this charge directed his attacks more particularly against the spot occupied by Sir Hector. His noble and heroic clansmen now seeing that the principal object was to cut off their beloved chief, the few that still survived flocked around his person, and numerous were the attempts upon the life of Sir Hector which a MacLean rendered abortive by the sacrifice of his own. In their devotion for their young chief, those fearless spirits offered their own breasts to the weapons aimed at him, and as each in succession rushed forward for this purpose, his resolution was evinced, as he threw himself upon the enemy to shield the person of his chief, by the exclamation of *Feàr eil airson Eachainn!* (Another for Hector!) * Under the influence of this extraordinary feeling of devotion, no less than eight gentlemen of the name of MacLean lost their lives at Inverkeithing. With life only ended the resistance of the fearless Sir Hector Roy.† His body, already covered with numerous deadly wounds, received the immediately fatal one from a musket shot; the ball penetrated his breast, and he fell dead on the spot. The few who survived the carnage of the sanguinary day being all severely wounded, fell into the hands of the victors, but after a short detention, and when able to travel, they were restored to their homes.

In this battle one house alone, the MacLeans of Ross, or the "Race of the Iron Sword," lost no less than *one hundred and forty men*, chiefly of the better class. This highly respectable and brave race were, by this disaster, almost totally annihilated. Of the eight hundred MacLeans who engaged at Inverkeithing, not more than forty escaped alive, and even those to the day of their death exhibited in the mutilated state of their persons palpable proofs

---

* "This phrase has continued ever since as a proverb or watch-word when a man encounters any sudden danger that requires instant succor." Stewart's *Sketches of the Highlanders*, p. 63.

† For notices of Sir Hector's noble conduct at Inverkeithing, see Stewart's *Sketches of the Highlanders*, p. 63; Blackie's *Altavona*, p. 182; Keltie's *Highland Clans*, Vol. I., p. 324; Vol. II., p. 226.

of their sufferings upon this dreadful day. The killed and wounded among the officers of the clan were:

KILLED.

Sir Hector MacLean of Duard and Morvern, Colonel of Foot for the County of Argyle, and chief of the Clan MacLean.

Lachlan, son of MacLean of Torloisk.

John and Donald, } sons of MacLean of Ardgour.

Hugh,* son of MacLean of Coll.

Murdoch, Allan, Lachlan, Ewen, and John, } Sons of Lachlan Odhar of Ardchraoishnish, of the MacLeans of Ross.

Hugh, son of MacLean of the Isle of Muck.

Allan, son of MacLean of Drimnin.

Archibald, son of MacLean of Borreray.

Charles, son of MacLean of Inverscadell.

Several other gentlemen of the Lochbuy and Ross families met their deaths at Inverkeithing, but their names are not mentioned.

SEVERELY WOUNDED.

Donald MacLean of Brolass, uncle of the chief, and Lieutenant-Colonel commandant of the clan MacLean.

John MacLean of Kinlochaline.

Ewen MacLean of Treshnish; the gallant Captain of Cairnburg, frequently mentioned in the preceding pages.

John of Totteronald, son of MacLean of Coll.

John Diurach MacLean of the Ardtornish family.

Neil MacLean of Drimnacross.

The death of the brave Sir Hector Roy, in his twenty-seventh year, threw

---

* This gentleman, with a heroic devotion and desperate daring of which the history of military prowess has perhaps never afforded a more extraordinary instance, seeing a number of bayonets directed against the breast of his chief, before whom but an instant before Hugh fell with both legs shattered by a cannon shot, with one desperate effort threw himself forward upon the points of the bayonets, averting, for a short period at least, the fate of his chief.

a sad gloom over the affairs of his house and clan. From his resolute and honorable character every hope was entertained that his affairs would soon be rescued from the fangs of Argyle; but the tender years of his brother Allan afforded an opportunity to Argyle to accumulate additional embarrassments upon the house of MacLean.

As Sir Hector never married, he was succeeded by his brother Allan, at that time six years of age. This made the second failure in the direct line of succession, and that within a period of twenty-five years.

XIX. Sir Allan MacLean, Bart., Nineteenth Chief of MacLean.

During Sir Allan's minority, the estates were judiciously managed by his uncles, Donald MacLean of Brolass and Hector MacLean of Lochbuy. The guardians managed to pay off a portion of Argyle's claims; but the latter, learning that the late chief had contracted some debts in fitting out his clan for service during the late campaign, prevailed upon the creditors to dispose of their claims. Possessing himself of these debts, Argyle was enabled to augment his claims considerably; but finding, after the battle of Worcester, there was a likelihood of a pecuniary reward for those who adhered to Cromwell's government, left his persecution of the house of MacLean, to be pursued at some future time, and turned his attention to the prospective grant. Cromwell entered into negotiations with Argyle to bring about the submission of Scotland, and for a consideration of £12,000 the latter agreed to do all within his power for the subjection of his native country. This was one of the charges against him on his trial.*

It will be necessary here to add that the restoration of the royal authority (1660) sealed the fate of Archibald Campbell, first marquis of Argyle. For his many crimes he was beheaded at the Cross of Edinburgh, May 27, 1661; and the fact is extraordinary that the pike upon which was fixed, ten years previously, the head of the great Montrose, had now received that of his malignant enemy.

With the exception of some acts of depredation on the part of the Ardnamurchan Campbells against some families of the MacLeans, it does not appear that the tranquility of the Western Isles had been materially disturbed for a number of years. These petty aggressions Sir Allan was at all times able to punish summarily, and he took his opportunities to do so; but the old arrogance was to commence again by the same hereditary foe of the house of MacLean.

---

* See Browne's *Highland Clans*, Vol. II., p. 92.

Archibald Campbell, son of the late marquis, was, at the intercession of his friend John, duke of Lauderdale, restored to the forfeited estates and the title of earl of Argyle by the king. At once he commenced the prosecution of his father's well-matured design against the chief of MacLean. Sir Allan endeavored to affect an arrangement, and agreed at once to come to a final settlement by making over to Argyle so much of the estates as would pay the balance due, on credit being given for the large amount already paid on the original bond. Argyle pretended not to be quite certain as to the amounts paid, and upon pretenses put off from time to time the arrangement proposed. Sir Allan, seeing no likelihood of any satisfactory arrangement being made with Argyle, agreed to refer the matter to the arbitration of the Scottish council. Argyle, although pretending to entertain this proposition, yet, in order to make this arrangement more and more difficult, actively engaged in purchasing every claim, both real and fictitious, he could find against Sir Allan. As there was no alternative but to represent the whole matter to the king, Sir Allan, in the year 1672, proceeded to London. Charles II. listened with particular attention to the relation given by the young chief of the original cause of the debt, of the means whereby the late Argyle obtained the bond upon that debt, and of the subsequent methods practiced to augment the claim. The Scottish commissioner, the duke of Lauderdale, happened to be in London at the time; was sent for, and in the presence of Sir Allan the king detailed the facts to him. The king soon discerned by the equivocating manner of Lauderdale how his favor leaned, would listen to none of the arguments advanced on behalf of Argyle, but " sternly and peremptorily ordered Lauderdale to see MacLean have justice."

Regardless of the strict command of the king, Lauderdale on his return to Scotland at once admitted the validity of Argyle's claim, and ruled that the rent of the estates should be made payable yearly to Argyle, until such time as the amount of the bond was finally settled, reserving to Sir Allan the sum of £500 sterling per annum for maintenance. To this arrangement the chief of MacLean, under the impression that a very few years would release him entirely from the annoyance, readily consented. Argyle's purpose was to conceal the amount of his claim, both real and fraudulent, from the unsuspecting Sir Allan. While, therefore, MacLean thought he had to pay little more than the original bond with its interest, subject to a deduction on the score of the different payments from time to time made to account of it, amounting to more than half its original consideration, Campbell's demand considerably exceeded £100,000, prior to the period of the collusion between him and Lauderdale; but these two "lord justices," for such were their offices, easily managed to swell the amount to the enormous sum of £120,000. So artfully was this matter handled that Sir Allan remained a stranger to it to the day of his death. The arrangement to which Sir Allan consented, that of allowing the rents of the estate to liquidate the claim, was only in its second year, when the death of the young chief, in 1674, in his twenty-eighth year, left the MacLeans, who could hardly be prevailed upon to pay the rents to Argyle even for a day, free to pursue other measures than those of tacit obedience to his plundering purposes.

Sir Allan was not free from inroads made by irresponsible persons, under the care of Argyle. Some of the miscreants he pursued into Lorn, and dealt summary justice upon them. Argyle made complaint to the king, who, on November 5, 1672, ordered Sir Allan to appear before the privy council at Edinburgh and answer the complaint.* In this summons the chief of MacLean is styled, "Sir William Allan McLain of Dowart." The name of "William" is not given to him by any of the MacLean seanachaidhs.

Sir Allan MacLean, at the age of nineteen, was married to Julian, daughter of John MacLeod of MacLeod, by whom he had issue, John, his heir and successor.

XX. Sir John MacLean, Bart., Twentieth Chief of MacLean.

Sir John MacLean, twentieth chief of MacLean and fourth baronet of Morvern, was four years old when he succeeded his father. The appointment of his two near kinsman, Lachlan MacLean of Brolass, and Lachlan MacLean of Torloisk, men of profound judgment and determined minds, gave unbounded satisfaction to the whole clan, who resolved that the Argyle–Lauderdale collusion claim should now be resisted with the sword. Brolass, however, rather than go to extremes, proposed to Argyle to clear off the debt by resigning over to Campbell such portion of the estates as by arbitration might be deemed adequate to satisfy his demand; but as a preliminary condition to this proposal, the guardians required Argyle distinctly and openly to give full credit for the various payments which had been made at different times on account of the debt, and to exhibit a clear and satisfactory balance preparatory to the settlement. Campbell agreed to do so, but on various pretexts managed to postpone the proposed arrangement from time to time, and finally, to the surprise of the guardians, declined its terms altogether. But two avenues were now open to the guardians, either recourse to the sword, or else an appeal to the

---

* *Appendix Sixth Report Royal Commission*, p. 632.

king. They resolved not a farthing of the rents should be paid, and this determination being intimated to the claimant, he immediately proceeded to Edinburgh to solicit the interference of his friend, Lauderdale. He succeeded in gaining government assistance of five hundred men, to be raised in the counties of Lanark and Renfrew, and with these, joined to eighteen hundred of his own followers, he commenced his preparations to invade Mull. The MacLeans, not yet recovered from the disastrous effects of the battle of Inverkeithing, were upon this occasion illy prepared to resist the invasion of such a force. The Campbells landed in Mull in three different places, without opposition, the inhabitants contenting themselves with removing into the mountains and fastnesses of the island for protection, with their cattle. The young chief, to shield him from personal harm, was sent to the castle of Cairnburg, and afterward to Kintail, under the care of the earl of Seaforth.

At last, the earl of Argyle was able to take quiet possession of the inheritance of the chief of MacLean. Duard and Aros castles were taken possession of and garrisoned by the invading army. Not satisfied with this, the soldiers spread themselves over the island, committing depredation and offering personal insult and violence to the unresisting inhabitants. One of the chief officers, lord Neill Campbell, for the sake of pastime, was in the habit of leading a party of his followers now and then into the mountains, where the poor inhabitants sought shelter, and after plundering them of the necessaries of life, employed himself at what he facetiously called "a game of houghing" (that is cutting off the hind legs of all the cattle they fell in with), and leaving the poor animals to die in that mutilated condition. Argyle made no attempt to restrain his followers in the barbarities performed on man and beast. Having the MacLeans at so great a disadvantage, he exacted a promise that thenceforth they should pay the rents to his agent, left the island, leaving the castles above mentioned strongly garrisoned.

The inhumanities perpetrated upon the defenseless people, and the occupation of the halls and demesnes of their chief by one whom they had learned to loathe, was galling to the proud race, and, as might have been expected, only waited for a favorable opportunity to execute a severe retaliation upon the intruders. By the time the rents became due, there was not a tenant of Sir John MacLean's but resolved at all hazards to treat Argyle's pretended right to them with scorn; and in order to strengthen themselves, in case coercion was resorted to, the guardians formed an alliance with lord MacDonald and other chiefs, who promised them one thousand men. These preparations were communicated to Argyle by the commander of Duard castle, and the earl lost no time in using his influence with the privy council, from whom he obtained such assistance as he required, with full authority to "carry fire and sword into the MacLean district." During the month of September, 1675, he embarked with a force of two thousand two hundred men; but this force never reached the island, for a dreadful hurricane, which lasted for two days, drove back the ships, some of which were lost and the rest totally disabled.* This misfortune, and the intelligence he received from Mull that the MacLeans were in great force there, caused Argyle to postpone his attempt. He took the precaution to guard the coast with five hundred men, and three hundred more to protect his lands against the incursions of the MacLeans. The earl then proceeded to Edinburgh and sought additional aid from the government, but receiving no encouragement he started for London, where he expected, by the aid of his friend, Lauderdale, to obtain such assistance as he required. Lord MacDonald and other friends of the MacLeans, hearing of Argyle's departure, also set out for London, and laid the state of the dispute before the king, who, in February, 1676, remitted the matter to three lords of the privy council of Scotland for adjudication, to which both parties submitted, and for the first time the MacLeans were enabled to bring the matter publicly before the council, where the claim of Argyle being heard, the guardians, Brolass and Torloisk, made their reply. As this document explains the whole matter so fully, and as it is of importance to those interested in the history of the family, it is here given in full:

ANSWER OF THE MACLEANS TO THE COMPLAINT GIVEN IN BY THE EARL OF ARGYLE AGAINST THEM TO THE LORDS OF HIS MAJESTY'S PRIVY COUNCIL, A. D. 1676.

"The earl of Argyle having convened the defenders before your lordships of his majesty's privy council to answer to his complaints, which he has founded upon so many laws and acts of Parliament importing the pains and punishments of treason, capital punishments, and several other punishments; and having subsumed against them, the contravention of these laws by the committing of crimes and deeds mentioned in the complaint, and conquested in the specialities thereof to a voluminous and great length; concluding that to the treasonable and capital crimes it ought to be found and declared that they have been actors or art and part therein, in high and manifest contempt of his majesty's authority; and that thereby they have tent and omitted the benefit and indulgence contained in the commission granted to the earl of Seaforth, and thro' the contravention thereof deemed to have incurred the certification therein contained; and tnat they also ought to be discerned to repossess the earl of Argyle in the estate of Dowart, and to deliver up the garrison of Cairnburg, and to refund the rents of the estates

---

* "A rumor went that there was a witch name Muddock who had promised to the MacLeans that, so long as she lived, the earl of Argyle should not enter Mull; and, indeed, many of the people imputed the rise of that great storm under her paction with the devil, how true I can not assert."—Law's *Memorials*, p. 83; quoted by Browne, *Highland Clans*, Vol. II., p. 95.

unwarrantably intromitted with by them, and to pay the earl's particular damages and losses, extending to the sum of £200,000, and that they ought to be exemplarily punished for the crimes libelled.

"Before the defenders can make particular defenses to the present ground of this complaint, which for the most part is made up of very heinous and atrocious crimes whereof they are not guilty, they humbly conceive that its fit for them to give your lordships a true and just account of the grounds and occasions of the great and many troubles and difficulties wherein the marquis and this earl, now complainer, have involved them and driven them to, merely to prove the hazard of their lives, ruin of their fortunes, and extinction of their name and family.

"It is not unknown to your lordships that the lairds of MacLean, with their friends and followers, have constantly adhered to his majesty's interest and service in the worst of times, and particularly during those most unhappy troubles in this kingdom from which, by the mercy of Almighty God, we were delivered by his majesty's happy restoration. That family did appear in his majesty's service, having joined with the late marquis of Montrose as soon as he appeared in the field with his majesty's commission, and constantly continued with him, exposing their lives and fortunes in that service, until his majesty's father, of blessed memory, having recalled the commission he gave the marquis of Montrose, they returned home, and lurked for the preservation of their lives, and could not peaceably enjoy their fortunes; for the late marquis of Argyle, finding that from the beginning of the troubles he was not able to prevail with them to join with him against his majesty's interest and authority, he took occasion to bring in forces to the island of Mull a few days after the MacLeans, under the marquis of Montrose's command, had forth the battle of Kilsyth, and taking advantage of their absence, burnt, wasted, and destroyed their possessions. After recalling Montrose's commission, he prevailed with the authority for the time to impute a garrison in the house of Dowart, under the oppression and slavery of which garrison they continued until his majesty came to Scotland in the year 1667, at which time Sir Hector MacLean did, with his friends and followers, come to his majesty to Stirling to the number of 800 well armed men of his name, and appointed upon his and their own proper charges. Having gone to Inverkeithing by his majesty's command to oppose the landing of the English usurper, Sir Hector and most part of the principal gentlemen of his name, with all of his followers, were killed upon the place valiantly fighting in defense of his majesty and the liberty of the kingdom; so that the whole 800 only 40 ever returned. After his death Sir Allan, his brother, being a child, succeeded; but how soon any persons appeared for his majesty's interest the friends of that family were ever ready as formerly; and the late chancellor, the earl of Glencairn, having his majesty's commission, the tutor of MacLean, with his name and followers, were the first that joined with him and the earl of Middleton thereafter; until that attempt for the freedom of his kingdom from the usurper proved unsuccessful, whereupon they were forced to scatter and retire. And because his name and family were known to be so forward and jealous in his majesty's service, the English, to repress them, did again garrison the home of Dowart, and keeping them in constant trouble and bondage until his majesty's happy restitution. Which garrison, as is notoriously known, was planted there by the advice of the late marquis of Argyle, who came to Mull and assisted to settle them in the house and island. All which they have represented to your lordships, not from vanity and ostentation, their greatest sufferings and mean services being but the cost of their duty, and thereof they would have been silent, if treason, rebellion, and open opposition to his majesty's authority were not loudly charged upon them in this complaint. But immediate ground of the troubles and difficulties of this family is, that in the year 1642, the late marquis, considering the aversion Sir Lachlan MacLean had to the courses of those times, and how ready he would be on every occasion to appear for his majesty's interest, the said marquis, upon pretence of some debts wherein he was cautious for him, and upon pretence of few duties payable by MacLean to the bishop of the Isles, for uplifting whereof the marquis had commission, and upon pretence of some by-gone feu duties owing to his majesty, and some other pretences of ammunition, contribution money, taxation, and the like, did by his power at the time necessitate Sir Lachlan to give him a bond for 14,000 pounds Scots, and to subscribe on account 16,000 pounds, bearing an obligement to pay that sum and annual rents. But, thereafter, Sir Lachlan having joined Montrose, and his lands being burnt and destroyed for his opposition to the public for the time, he was neither in condition to quarrel the said debts nor to pay the same, and having died under these distresses, Sir Hector, his son, being very young and unacquainted with his father's affairs, he, in the year 1650, did pay to the marquis 10,000 pounds, and, notwithstanding, gave him a bond of corroboration for 60,000 pounds, in which the foresaid 30,000 pounds and annual rents were accumulated. But Sir Hector having been killed in his majesty's service, as is above mentioned, albeit Sir Allan was minor, and that the friends of that family were altogether ruined in their fortunes by their constant adherence to his majesty's interest, yet from the year 1652 to 1659 they paid of this debt to the late marquis of Argyle, and to the lady Ann, his daughter, who was assigned thereto, 22,000 pounds. Notwithstanding, whereof, in anno 1659, the marquis pursued Sir Allan, who was then a minor, and when neither he nor his friends, in regard of the troubles, durst safely appear to defend themselves; and upon Sir Allan's announcing to be heir to Sir Hector, he intended adjudication, and for not reproduction of the process, obtained a decreet of adjudication of MacLean's estate for 85,000 pounds, without any regard or reduction of the sums of money that had been paid. After his majesty's happy restoration, MacLean and his tutor did apply to the Parliament, complaining of the great losses which they had by the late marquis, who burnt and destroyed their lands for concurring in his majesty's service, and procured garrisons to be put in the house of Dowart, and adduced witnesses, who distinctly and clearly proved that they were demnified in great and considerable sums. But the marquis' forfeiture having in the meantime proceeded, his majesty's advocate for the time stopped the sentence and constitution of the debt by authority of parliament, and which they intended for no other use but to compensate decreet of adjudication accumulated upon the family. This adjudication having fallen under the forfeiture, his majesty was pleased to give the forfeiture to the earl of Argyle and his father's creditors, in this manner, viz., in so far as extended to 15,000 pounds of yearly rent, in favor of the earl himself in the first place; for paying proper woodsetters in the next place; and for payment of the debts wherein the earl was debtor *propio nomine* and as cautioer for his father, in the third place, and for security of the lady marchioness her life rent, and of the provisions of his brother, the lord Neill, and of his sisters, in the fourth place; and, thereafter, the remainder of the estate was appointed to belong to and be proportionally divided among creditors of the late marquis, and commission was directed for taking trial of the rental and said settlement of the estate according to his majesty's gift. By the report of which commission there remained nothing to be divided among the creditors but this debt of MacLean's, which is stated to amount to £121,000 at Martinmas, 1665, and another debt of the captain of Clanranal's, £20,000; and by the report of the commissioners discern these sums to belong to the creditors.

" The earl declared himself willing to denude himself of any right he had thereto in favor of the creditors. But notwithstanding of this report appointing the sum to belong to the creditors, the earl, to expede an infeftment in his own name as donatory to the forfeiture upon the first adjudication, and intended actions of removing, and mails and duties against MacLean's tenants, obtained decreet of removing in absence; and in the meantime Sir Allan died, leaving a child of four years of age to succeed him. Upon this decreet the earl having charged, and having immediately raised letters of ejection, upon pretence that some servants of the deceased MacLean were in the house (castle of

Dowart), and would not give him admittance to that house, he convened a great many of MacLean's friends before his own justice court for treasonable convocation in arms, and keeping garrisoned houses, and making of leagues among themselves, charging them to find caution to underlie the law upon six days, and to find landed men cautioners. Whereupon the parties cited, knowing that the earl or his deputies were to be the judges in that affair, and that it would be difficult for them to find caution, especially landed men, the time being so short, resolved to send to Edinburgh to advocate the pursuit and to suspend the charge for finding caution; but thereafter being denounced in the earl's court for not finding caution, and an act of adjournal made declaring them fugitives for not compearance, they durst not adventure to pass thro' the country of Argyle; the earl having issued forth (by his own authority in his own name, as judiciary of the Isles, under a signet bearing his coat of arms) letters for denouncing them rebels to his majesty for not appearance, and upon production of his procedure procured letters of intercommuning and commission of fire and sword from your lordships of the council; and thereupon levied considerable forces, invaded the island, and having commission from your lordships to indemnify the defenders, he did accordingly indemnify them, and received possession of the house of Dowart. But in regard the tutor of MacLean would not renounce any interest of kindness and blood he had to the family of MacLean, and would not accept a charter of the lands of Brolass, containing extraordinary clauses of service and marriage, he thereupon of new convenes the tutor and several others of the name of MacLean in his justice court, proceeding against them upon the former crimes for which they were indemnified, and upon new pretensions of sorning and spulzeing his tenants, he declares them fugitives, denouncing as aforesaid, obtains letters of intercommuning and a new commission of fire and sword. And it being impossible for the defenders either to come to Edinburgh or to send, but necessarily they behaved to pass thro' the Earl of Argyle's bounds, which safely they could not do, and whereof they had a recent instance in the violent seizing of the person, they had sent with information and instructions to their agents and lawyers at Edinburgh; so that being debarred from access to the ordinary and legal remedies, and being surprised with this new commission of fire and sword after the earl had attained possession of both the houses of Dowart, Morvern, and other parts of MacLean's estate; and having grounds to suspect that the earl intended the extirpation of their name and race altogether, they resolved to continue without doing wrong, but to defend their lives until they might have an opportunity to send some persons by a compass about to represent their sad and distressed condition to the lords of his majesty's privy council. Which accordingly they did, and whereof the lords of his majesty's privy council were graciously pleased so far to take notice, that they granted them suspension of the letters of denunciation and inter-communing, and assigned them a day to compear, commanding them to disperse and lay down their arms; which they instantly did upon your lordships' command, and do now appear before your lordships. And having really represented the rise and progress of their troubles, and which have been occasioned by this pretense of debts alleged due to the late marquis in anno 1642, and which, if duly considered, will be found unjust at the beginning; and albeit it had been just yet in great part satisfied, and as to which the earl needed not have interposed himself betwixt MacLean and the creditors, with whom he would have transacted and have satisfied them of what in law and reason should have been found due; and as to any other debts which the earl has lately acquired, they were ever ready and willing to have satisfied the same by payment of the true sums which the earl paid for acquiring the same; which being promised, the defenders' answer to this complaint is as follows:—

"First. As to the pretended convocations and being in arms in August and September, 1674, and the garrisoning of the house of Dowart, they deny that they were otherways in arms than they usually are when they meet about their chief's affairs, to treat about the letting of his lands or other settlements of his estate; and as for all the diligence done against them in the earl's court, they do repeat their reasons of suspension thereof, principal eiked, contained in and eiked to the letter of suspension raised before your lordships.

"Secondly. Albeit they had been guilty of such enormous crimes as were then libelled, as they were not, yet they ought to be assoilzed for all deeds alledged committed by them preceding the 8th of September 1674, in regard by warrant from his majesty's council the earl did indemnify them, whereupon he attained to the possession of the house of Dowart and the possession of the lands of Morvern.

"Thirdly. As to the convocation, bands and leagues continuing together in arms, they the defenders humbly represent to your lordships the bad grounds before mentioned; viz., that they were unwarrantably and in a most summary manner proceeded against by the earl in his own court of justiciary; and although he had been judge competent to those high crimes and points of treason, as he was not, and no judge in the realm can be judge competent thereto but the highest court of justiciary or the court of parliament yet the letters were most inorderly executed, in regard the same being letters of treason, whereby they were charged to find caution to underlie the law for the points of high treason libelled, and to compear to answer for the same under the pain of treason, such letter by the undoubted law and practice of the kingdom, and particularly by the 125 Act, January 6th, are appointed to be executed by the ordinary heralds and pursuivants bearing coats of arms; otherwise the executions are declared null and void, and of no avail. But so it is, that the said letters were not so executed, and consequently they were unwarrantably and unjustly proceeded against, and declared fugitives for crimes of treason, and denounced rebels and traitors; upon which ground they have suspension, and thereupon the hail procedure and all that has followed thereupon should be declared null and void.

"Fourthly. As the procedure was most unorderly and unwarrantably, so it is a new and great surprise to the defenders. In regard to the earl having attained to the peaceable possession of the house of Dowart and of the lands of Morvern, and within a very few months thereafter having of new again convened them before his justice court for their actings, and some other new pretences, without acquainting them wherein they had done any wrong, they could not but think that the earl, by this procedure and his preparations to invade them, did intend their utter extirpation, which they acknowledge made them stay together until they had opportunity to acquaint the council; which they could not otherwise do but by sending their petition inclosed to a privy councillor to have the same presented, not daring to adventure their persons through the earl's country until the letters of inter-communing and fire and sword were suspended; and immediately after intimation of the council's commands they dispersed. And whereas it is pretended that since the council's orders they continue a garrison at Cairnburg, they humbly represent to your lordships that some of the earl's followers, after his first attempt upon Mull, were so cruel and inhuman to the laird of MacLean (who is but an infant of six or seven years of age) that they stripped him naked and took all his clothes from him; whereupon his friends, when the earl intended to come to Mull in September last, being apprehensive that they might proceed to cruelty against the infant, they sent him to a little rock in the sea which has no fortifications but the natural inaccessibleness of the place, and sent two or three persons with him to preserve his person against injuries; and within some few weeks after the council's orders he came forth thereof, and now stays in Airdnancross. And to the other pretended deed of riots and oppression alleged committed by them since the intimation of the council's order, they altogether deny them; but, on the contrary, they have lived in a peaceable manner, sustaining great and very considerable losses by the depredations committed upon them by the earl's friends and followers, for which they have a complaint raised and depending before your lordships. And not to trouble your lordships with any further answer to this large complaint and specialities, whereof they humbly pray your lordships to consider this affair not only with regard to their service and sufferings for his majesty and his father, of blessed memory, but also with regard to the manifold and great oppressions committed upon them by the late marquis, which are so notorious to all their neighbors and a great many of the kingdom as nothing is more evident; and also to consider what advantage has been taken against them upon account of this pretended debt of 30,000 pounds in the year 1642, whereof the grounds were unjust, and for which the deceased marquis never paid 10,000 pounds upon MacLean's account, as can be clearly instructed if your lordships shall think fit to inquire therein; and which is now amassed up, notwithstanding the sums which have been paid as is above related, to 200,000 pounds; and whereupon these advantages of legal diligence were taken against the lairds of MacLean in the time of their great distress and sufferings for his majesty; and in regard the laird of MacLean and his friends can not but think it hard to be driven from their ancient possessions by such severe advantages of law upon grounds which materially are unjust; and that, without vanity, they might have expected from his majesty upon the forfeiture of the late marquis a discharge of these pretences, and that upon material and just grounds, in regard of the devastations which were committed upon them by him and the forces under his command, or by his procurement, upon no other account but their constant adherence to his majesty's service and interest; and though the minority of Sir Allan MacLean at the time of his majesty's restoration and negligence of his friends, did occasion that they did not apply to his majesty; and that the benefit of this sum was discerned to belong to the creditors; and in regard that notwithstanding thereof the earl has not only interposed between them and the creditors, and so frustrated them of the opportunity of the easy transactions which they might have made with the creditors, albeit the debt had been just, but also has so severely followed his legal diligence that upon pretence of this debt he intended to root out their very name and memory; and seeing it could not be expected that the earl, who has tasted so bountifully of his majesty's liberality, and whereof the defenders do not envy him, would have been so rigid towards those who to his own knowledge have so eminently suffered for his majesty, by driving them to these necessities, either to lose all their fortunes and die in misery,—to run to causes for their self preservation which they abhor and detest, desiring nothing so much as to live in obedience to his majesty's laws: that, therefore, your lordships would seriously enquire into this affair from the original thereof, and to take such courses thereanent toward the settling and composing thereof as to your lordships in justice shall seem fit and expedient."

It will not be out of place again to state that the original debt was incurred by Sir Lachlan MacLean in arming his clan on behalf of the monarchy at the outbreak of the civil war; that during a part of that period he paid no revenue to the government. Argyle bought up all the claims against Sir Lachlan for a trifle, and extorted a bond for £30,000. This amount was swelled by other debts, both real and fictitious, until the whole amount did not cost the Argyle family over £10,000. The amount of £10,000 was paid in cash on the account by Sir Hector, just before the battle of Inverkeithing. Besides the above amount, between 1652 and 1659, there was paid in cash on the account £22,000. The whole amount paid on the debt up to 1676, including rents, is at this day difficult to tell; but, including rents, the actual amount would not fall below £100,000. This does not include spoliations and other sufferings forced upon the MacLeans. Notwithstanding the small amount of the actual debt and the great amounts paid on it, through the manipulations of the eighth and ninth Earls of Argyle and Lauderdale, it rapidly reached the amount of £200,000, exclusive of previous payments.

During the time of the negotiations relating to the settlement of this debt, there were instances of some interest which transpired that should not fail to be recorded. Archibald Campbell, ninth earl of Argyle, was anxious that lord MacDonald should not assist the MacLeans in their struggles against his persecutions. On September 10, 1675, he addressed MacDonald a flattering letter, and, among other things, states he had received a commission of fire, and was "ready to go about the business;" and farther adds: "I am confident you will not make their word good who say that you will assist the outlaws of the MacLaines in opposing his majesty's commission."* But the MacDonalds did lend assistance. During the same month, the MacLeans, the MacDonalds of Glengarry, and the Brae of Lochaber and the Camerons, to the number of three hundred men, in fourteen boats, assaulted one of Argyle's frigates, sent from Leith and becalmed near an old castle in Ardnamurchan. After the frigate had received one hundred and four shot in her mainsail, she succeeded in beating off her assailants.†

The MacLeans of Lochbuy were not idle spectators of the stirring scenes around them. On October 18, 1675, Lochbuy, with the brothers of MacLean of Kingerloch and three score men, in three birlinns, during the night landed in the isles of Garvelloch, and either destroyed or carried away fifty-two cows; twelve stirks; one hundred and twenty sheep; several clothes chests; brass and iron work to the amount of £436; one great cauldron, £40; four pans, £12; iron pots, £40; iron work, £12; twelve silver spoons, £80; four silver dishes, £100; one six-oared boat, £100; thirty stones of butter; forty balls of victuals, besides leaving the inhabitants, thirty-two in number, destitute.‡ In the same year, MacLean of Lochbuy, Lauchlan MacLean of Brolass, Major David Ramsay, and others, raided the island of Kerrera, and carried off "many cattle, stirks, kye," etc., for which they were charged to appear in Edinburgh.||

Campbell of Inverawe, writing to Argyle, states that, on February 24, 1677, a party of Argyle's men, who were garrisoning Duard Castle, seized a boat with Irish victuals in Lochiel, six miles from Duard, and brought her to the castle; but before the boat could be unloaded, the laird of Kingerloch's brother and Ardgour's brother, with about seventy men, got between the castle

---

* *Appendix to Sixth Report Hist. MS Commission*, p. 617.   † *Ibid.*   ‡ *Ibid.*, p. 628. || *Ibid.*

and the boat, and, concealed by a rock, hindered the unloading of it, and succeeded in seizing the boat and victuals and carrying them away, and retained possession.

On the 23d of May, 1677, the same writes to the same that, within the last few days, there were frequent meetings between the MacLeans and MacDonalds; that the former expected a vessel with guns from Lord MacDonald; that a trench had been constructed near Tobermory, in order to hinder vessels from entering the sound; and that, on the following day, Brolass was to meet Lochiel in Morvern.*

Between 1676 and 1677, both the MacLeans and Camerons of Lochiel committed depredations on the Campbells, on account of the wrongs they were then receiving. Ewen Cameron of Lochiel, Lachlan MacLean of Brolass, and others, raided the lands of Migharie and Carwallan, and carried off thirteen hundred sheep, one hundred and sixty-one horses, five hundred goats, two hundred and thirty balls corn, and twenty-four bear. At the same time, they carried away from Ardnamurchan sixty-six sheep, twelve horses, and fifty goats, amounting in all to £5,000 Scots.† The amount of damages done by the MacLeans and MacDonalds in Glenshire, during May and June, 1679, was estimated at £2,158; by the same at same time in Brae Lochfine, £764 Scots; and the whole amount in various parts of the shire of Argyle for the same time, about £10,000.‡

In the meantime, Argyle was not inactive; and being powerful at court, he obtained a commission to disarm and reduce Lord MacDonald, Archibald MacDonald of Keppoch, MacLean of Torloisk, MacLean of Brolass, MacLean of Ardgour, and other parties suspected of popery, or rebels. April 24, 1679, he commanded all such to deliver up to the sheriff deputy all manner of arms and ammunition in their possession.‖ During the month of November of the same year, he contrived to have a commission granted to the earl of Caithness, lord Lorn, lord Neill Campbell, Sir Hugh Campbell of Caddell, Sir Duncan Campbell of Auchinbreck, Sir James Campbell of Lawyers, Colin Campbell of Ardkinglass, the laird of MacLeod, Alexander Campbell of Lochinnell, and others, granting them jointly and severally full power to convene the king's lieges in arms, to pursue or apprehend to the death Lachlan MacLean of Brolass, and Hector, his brother, John MacLean of Ardgour, Hugh MacLean, fiar of the same, Allan MacLean of Inverscadell, John Mac-

---

* *Appendix to Sixth Report Hist. MS Commision*, p. 618.   † *Ibid.*, p. 628.   ‡ *Ibid.*, p. 629.
‖ *Ibid.*, p. 628.

Lean of Kenlochaline and his son Hector, and others, who were denounced rebels for not appearing in the tolbooth of the burgh of Inverary on June 23, 1675, before John Campbell, sheriff deputy; and there to answer the charge of convocating four hundred men in arms in April, 1675, by sending fiery crosses through the isle of Mull, Morvern, and other places; for remaining upon the lands of Knockmartin in a warlike posture on the 20th of that month; for convocating one hundred men at Gaderly and Glenforsay; for garrisoning Cairnburg; and for seizure of corns, horse, and swine upon the lands in Tiree. If in their defense they should flee to strongholds, fire, force, and all kinds of warlike engines were to be used for their reduction.*

This process was only a makeshift to ward off the settlement of the debt held against the estate of MacLean; but the threat of fire and sword could not have deterred the MacLeans, for, on the 6th of November, same year, Argyle received a commission against Ardgour and Torloisk, to be continued until March 1, 1680. Ardgour was charged with the violent possession of Argyle's property in Ardnamurchan and Sunart, in plundering all the MacLeans that submitted to the earl. Torloisk is charged with having joined Brolass in 1675.† These charges relate to the time when Argyle took forcible possession of Mull, and were brought at this late day solely to harass the MacLeans, and ward off the settlement of his claims. On the other hand, the MacLeans determined that the forcible possession should be attended with trouble. We find that lord MacDonald directed Donald MacDonald of Inveroy, Archibald MacLean, brother of Ardgour, John MacLean, brother of Torloisk, Donald MacLean of Sheba in Mull, to invade the lands of Colin Campbell of Inveresrigane, which they did, on May 24, 1769, and carried off sixteen horses, one hundred and six cows, besides other goods, all of which, including the destruction of property, amounted to six thousand, six hundred and sixty-two merks.

After the submission of the whole matter to the three members of the Scottish council, the guardians of the young chief were anxious for a decision. Through one pretext and another, including the charges against the MacLeans, above mentioned, and through the instrumentality of powerful friends, Argyle prolonged the suit until 1680, when complaint again was laid before the king. The king wrote a peremptory order to the council for an immediate adjustment of the suit; and the final issue was that Argyle should have the island of Tiree given to him in full compensation for his claim. From a letter dated at

---

* *Appendix to Sixth Report Hist. MS Commission*, p. 628.   † *Ibid.*, p. 629.

Windsor Castle July 10, 1680, King Charles proposed to purchase so much of Tiree as would make to the chief of MacLean the sum of £500; but earl Murray writing to the king October 1, 1681, thought it not advisable to purchase so much of Tiree, for MacLean only desired £300 yearly out of Argyle's feu duties. King Charles then (October 19, 1681) authorized the Scottish council to draw yearly on Argyle £300 for the laird of MacLean.*

In this final setttlement Archibald Campbell's old friend, John Maitland, or duke of Lauderdale, proves true to the unsavory reputation which historians have given him. In a letter to the earl of Argyle, dated at Windsor Castle July 13, 1680, he says : " The matter was condescended to both by his majesty and his royal highness ; but by the high and mighty papers that were thereafter given in on behalf of MacLean there was a stop put to the despatching of it for two days. Those papers pressed exceedingly the restoring of Mull and the Castle of Duard to MacLean ; but I said I could not, for I was sure your lordship would not grant either the one or the other: yet at last (after struggling enough) I procured the letter to be signed by his majesty, with his royal highnesses good likeing, in the very terms you will read in this copy. My Lord, I know not whether you will be pleased with what I have done in this matter, but I do assure your lordship there was nothing in my power wanting to have it settled in the most advantageous method for your service." †

The aggressions that Campbell of Argyle continued to make upon the MacLeans prove that he had no idea that there would be a settlement, at least at the time mentioned. He carried his depredations into the isle of Coll, and forced a surrender of the castle of Breachacha on July 2, 1679. There were six articles of capitulation signed by both Argyle and Donald MacLean, in which it is stipulated that the MacLeans should deliver up all arms and ammunition ; become obedient subjects and abstain from the committal of crimes; not to hinder the execution of the law ; to raise no forces ; to hold no convocations, and to purchase no arms without a warrant from Argyle. On the 30th same month Lachlan MacLean, son of the laird of Ardgour, surrendered the castle of Kinlochaline, with all its arms, on condition of being discharged from all criminal processes. On the 11th August an agreement was entered into by which Lachlan MacLean of Brolass, John MacLean of Ardgour, John MacLean of Kinlochaline, Allan MacLean of Inverscad, and others, agreed to dismiss all the prisoners taken by them ; and

---

* *Appendix to Sixth Report Hist. MS Commission,* p. 633.   † *Ibid.,* p. 621.

PARTISANS OF THE HOUSE OF STUART—1598 TO 1746.   197

they should not invade the earl's lands to effect this purpose commissions were granted to lord Neill Campbell, Ewen Cameron of Lochiel, and three others.*

It must have been about this time that Sir Ewen Cameron of Lochiel, who had been well pensioned by the MacLeans in order thereby to strengthen themselves against the Campbells, deserted them, although bound by oath and ties of relationship, by Argyle discharging him of a debt of four thousand merks; which gave rise to the saying then and still in use: " Chail Eoin a dhia s'chail T'iarl an' targiod"—Ewen has lost his God, and Argyle his money. So far as I have been able to ascertain, lord MacDonald remained faithful to the MacLeans during their hour of adversity.

At Edinburgh, December 22, 1680, Argyle had a commission to have delivered to him the crag and fort of Cairnburg, at that time garrisoned by order of Lachlan MacLean of Brolass, Hector Og, his brother, John MacLean of Ardgour, Allan MacLean of Scuvorscavadill, John MacLean of Kinlochaline, Lachlan MacLean of Torloisk, Donald MacLean of Kingerloch, Hector and John MacQuarrie, uncles to MacQuarrie of Ulva, Hugh MacLean, son of Keanlochallan, Charles MacLean of Ardnocraish, Lachlan MacCharles in Morinish, Allan MacCharles in Missineish, Donald MacCharles in Aros, Hector and Hugh, his sons, Hector and Alexander MacLean, brother of Kingerloch, Hugh MacLean of Carnae and Hector his son, Allan MacLean in Killintyn, and Hugh MacLean, late baillie in Tiree, who were denounced rebels and put to the horn for not appearing before the privy council to answer certain charges.†

But by this time Argyle had about run his course. The government laid heavy hands upon him for his treachery and treason. He was indicted and condemned to death by a jury of his peers. The devotion of his wife enabled him to escape from Edinburgh Castle, in the disguise of a page. He fled to Holland, but returned in 1685, and took part in the revolt of Monmouth; but after a series of misfortunes was seized and beheaded, June 30, 1685. In the streets of Edinburgh, and in his progress to the place of execution, he suffered a measure of degradation, the very counterpart of that over which he himself, thirty-five years before, exulted when undergone by the gallant and noble Montrose.

During the rash and ill-advised rebellion of Monmouth, in 1685, Argyle attempted to head the insurrection in Scotland, and sent the fiery cross

---

* *Appendix to Sixth Report Hist. MS Commission*, p. 632.   † *Ibid.*, 624.

through his estates, and summoned the Clan Campbell to his support. The MacLeans rallied to the support of James II. (of England), who had recently ascended the throne, and without delay commenced an invasion of the country of the Campbells, and under Lachlan MacLean of Torloisk, assisted by Lachlan MacLean of Coll, Ardgour, Kinlochaline, Lochbuy, and others, he seized Castle Carnassary, which was forced to surrender, and afterward burned to ashes. For this, when William became king, they were summoned, in 1690, to appear before the lord commissioners and make answer.*

On the forfeiture of Argyle, 1682, Tiree was restored to MacLean. The same year the king appointed Sir George Gordon of Haddo lord chancellor; lord Queensbury, lord treasurer; marquis of Athol, earl of Perth, lord justice general; earl of Seaforth, Sir George MacKenzie of Tarbet, and Sir George MacKenzie, overseers of MacLean's estates. The faithful and able guardians, Brolass and Torloisk, died respectively in 1686 and 1687, when Sir John MacLean began the management of his own affairs. Having appointed John MacLeod of Mishinish, Archibald MacLean of Ardtown, Lachlan MacLean of Calgary, and Allan MacLean of Grulin, his agents, he started on his travels; first to England, thence to France, whence he returned to Ireland with king James II. He returned to Scotland from the siege of Derry with Sir Alexander MacLean of Otter, son of the bishop of Argyle.

A description of the people of the isle of Mull is given by William Sacheverell, governor of the isle of Man, who was employed in 1688 in the attempt to recover the stores of the Florida, which was blown up and sunk one hundred years before, by Sir Lachlan Mór MacLean in the harbor of Tobemory, and who, in that year, made an excursion through Mull. In 1702 he published an account of this excursion, and thus describes the dress, armor, and general appearance of the people as he saw them in the isle of Mull in 1688:

"During my stay, I generally observed the men to be large-bodied, stought, subtle, active, patient of cold and hunger. There appeared in all their actions a certain generous air of freedom, and contempt of those trifles, luxury and ambition, which we so servilely creep after. They bound their appetites by their necessities, and their happiness consists, not in having much, but in coveting little. The women seem to have the same sentiments with the men; though their habits were mean and they had not our sort of breeding, yet in many of them there was a natural beauty and a graceful

---

* *Statistical Account of Argyleshire*, p. 556.

modesty, which never fails of attracting. The usual outward habit of both sexes is the plaid; the women's much finer, the colors more lively, and the squares larger than the men's, and put me in mind of the ancient Picts. This serves them for a veil, and covers both head and body. The men wear theirs after another manner, especially when designed for ornament; it is loose and flowing, like the mantles our painters give their heroes. Their thighs are bare, with brawny muscles. Nature has drawn all her strokes bold and masterly; *what is covered is only adapted to necessity*—a thin brogue on the foot, a short buskin of various colors on the leg, tied above the calf with a striped pair of garters. What should be concealed is hid by a large shot-pouch, on each side of which hangs a pistol and a dagger, as if they found it necessary to keep those parts well guarded. A round target on their backs, a blue bonnet on their heads, in one hand a broad-sword and a musket in the other. Perhaps no nation goes better armed; and I assure you they will handle them with bravery and dexterity, especially the sword and target, as our western regiments found to their cost at Killiecrankie." *

Almost immediately after the accession of James II. (February 6, 1685) he violated the fundamental laws of the constitution, and soon after was at war with his parliament. The breach widened, until at last, in 1688, seven of the leading politicians dispatched an invitation to William, Prince of Orange, to come and occupy the English throne. Finding himself deserted by the army and other classes, James retired to France, but the following year came to Ireland with a small force, was defeated at the Boyne, July 1, 1690. The affairs of the dethroned monarch were ably upheld by James Graham, Viscount Dundee, in Scotland, who rallied the Highland clans and resisted the government of William and Mary.

Dundee possessed the confidence of the Highland clans, and he looked to them for support in his attempt to restore the exiled monarch. There were others who believed that the clans were not jealous for James, but were actuated largely by their hatred toward the house of Argyle. Others have joined in this impeachment of the sincerity of the clans. MacAulay goes so far as to say: "It does not appear that a single chief who had not some special cause to dread and detest the house of Argyle obeyed Dundee's summons. There is indeed strong reason to believe that the chiefs who came would have remained quietly at home if the government had understood the politics of the Highlands. . . . If the Camerons, the MacDonalds, and the MacLeans

---

* Quoted in *Collectanea de Rebus Albanicis,* p. 44 of the Transactions.

could be convinced that, under the new government, their estates and their dignities would be safe, if MacCollum More (Argyle) would make some concessions, if their majesties would take on themselves some arrears of rent, Dundee might call the clans to arms, but he would call to little purpose." * Viscount Tarbat, conceiving this to be true, suggested to General MacKay that all clans which were in debt to Argyle should be discharged from the claim, " and that a separate offer should be made to the chief of the MacLeans to make good a transaction which had been in part entered upon between him and the late earl for adjusting their differences. This plan was approved of by the English government, but the affair is said to have been marred by the appointmant of Campbell of Cawdor as negotiator, who was personally obnoxious to the chiefs. MacKay attempted to open a correspondence with Cameron of Lochiel on the subject, but could obtain no answer, and MacDonald of Glengarry, to whom he also made a communication, heartily despising the bribe, advised the general, in return, to imitate the conduct of General Monk, by restoring James." † While the clans could not be bribed, they had every reason to look with distrust upon the ascendency of Archibald Campbell, tenth earl of Argle, and afterward first duke. Of him MacAulay is moved to say, that in personal qualities he was most insignificant, and "had even been guilty of the crime, common enough among Scottish politicians, but in him singularly disgraceful, of tampering with the agents of James while professing loyalty to William. Still Argyle had the importance inseparable from high rank, vast domains, extensive feudal rights, and almost boundless patriarchal authority." ‡ Keltie says, " he was too dissipated to be a great stateman." ||

Early in 1689, Dundee set out for the Highlands, and around his standard gathered the Camerons of Lochiel, Stewarts of Appin, MacDonalds of Glengarry and Glencoe, the clan Ranald, MacDonalds of Keppoch, and the MacLeans. In obedience to the summons Sir John MacLean immediately sent Hector MacLean of Lochbuy as his lieutenant-colonel, with three hundred men, to join Dundee. On his march Lochbuy was attacked by five troops of horse, sent by the enemy to intercept him, under command of a major of MacKay's army. When the MacLeans saw the enemy was upon them, they threw aside their loose garments and took position upon a ridge, called Knockbreck, in Badenoch, and after a severe conflict, Lochbuy put the horse to flight and

---

* *History of England*, Vol. III., p. 302. † Keltie's *History of the Clans*, Vol. I., p. 353.
‡ *History of England*, Vol. IV., pp. 281-2. || *History of the Clans*, Vol. II., p. 183.

killed the commander, with the loss on the side of the MacLeans of only one ensign and a few private soldiers. The action happened about daylight, and Lochbuy's force was partly concealed by a fog. Dundee, alarmed by the furious firing to the northward of him, the noise of which was greatly increased by the echo of the mountains, and doubtful of the result, prepared, in anticipation of a general engagement, to march to the relief of the MacLeans; when, immediately after, Lochbuy himself, at the head of his warrior band, was seen issuing from among the hills and approaching the camp, driving before him a considerable number of prisoners, and enriched with the spoil of the vanquished. At the battle of Knockbreck the first blood in Scotland was shed for king James.*

Sir John continued to make preparations to join Dundee at the head of his clan, during which time he received intelligence that his friend MacNeill of Callechilly was surrounded in the island of Gigha by some English ships of war. He dispatched Sir Alexander MacLean of Otter to his assistance, who relieved MacNeill, with the loss of but one man. His preparations having been completed, Sir John marched to join Dundee, leaving castle Duard well garrisoned, which was furiously assaulted during his absence by Sir George Rooke and the men-of-war under his command, which, without effect, withstood the cannonading for several days.

Circumstances conspired to make Athol the seat of war, and around Blair Castle the first and last grand struggle of Dundee in behalf of James was to be waged. The contingent from Ireland, long and anxiously expected, proved to be only three hundred ill-fed, ill-armed, and ill-disciplined men under Colonel Cannon. Dundee saw that his sole reliance was on his faithful Highlanders, who amounted to but little more than three thousand men, five hundred of whom were MacLeans under Sir John.

The continued possession of Blair Castle was a matter of great importance to Dundee, and as it was in danger of being assaulted by lord Murray, a light party of Highlanders under Sir Alexander MacLean was sent to give it succor. Soon after it was ascertained that MacKay was marching to Blair, which made it necessary for Dundee to direct all his strength to that point. While at Blair castle Dundee learned that MacKay's army had taken possession of the pass of Killiecrankie. He immediately dispatched Sir John MacLean, with a party of four hundred men, to reconnoitre; but being informed that the enemy was there in full force, he found it necessary to

---

† For description of this battle, see Appendix, Note C., No. 15.

strengthen Sir Alexander with all the force he had with him. Before engaging the enemy he inquired fully into the nature of the ground and from the hill of Shierglas took a distant view of the foe. The two armies did not come together until toward the close of the day, July 27, 1689. The army of Dundee, about eighteen hundred strong, occupied the high grounds about Wizard house; MacKay's, numbering about thirty-five hundred, stood upon a lower platform of the same range of hills. The right of Dundee was commanded by Sir John MacLean, composed of his clan and those of subordinate chieftains, divided into two battalions, because confronted by two regiments.

PASS OF KILLIECRANKIE.

On the left was Sir Donald MacDonald's regiment, commanded by his son and Sir George Berkley, assisted by a battalion under Sir Alexander MacLean. The main body was composed of the clans of Lochiel, Glengarry, and Clanranald, with the Irish auxiliaries and a troop of horse commanded by Sir William Wallace. It was about eight o'clock when the clans made the charge with all the impetuosity of a Highland onset. For the sake of lightness, they were stripped almost to the kilt, stooped low, and holding their targets before their heads, they rushed swiftly upon the enemy, who were partially intrenched. When they were near the foe, they stopped a moment, fired, threw away their guns, and then flew headlong upon the enemy, using their claymores and Lochaber axes. Dundee seemed to be every-where. He flew from clan to clan, and animated them to action. MacKay's army, by the sudden onslaught, was pierced in every part toward the left of its center. Within seven minutes, that wing was shattered and driven off by the MacLeans, who chased some of them into the coils of the Pass, and others across the river Garry, where the greater part were slain. The left of the Highland army was not quite so successful; for the enemy, after sustaining the fury of the first onset, forced the MacDonalds to retreat. "The MacLeans were now wholly engrossed in the pursuit and its concomitant attendants. The chief, however, who seems to have been an uncommonly brave man, with a few gentlemen of his clan, made a wheel to the left; and joining with Sir Ewen Cameron of Lochiel, they advanced briskly along the verge of the valley, and attacked the Dutch and Hastings's brave regiment in the flank."* This movement of the Camerons and MacLeans gave the MacDonalds time to rally, and that wing of the enemy, now attacked both in front and flank, was forced to retire. Few of the enemy who fled first made their escape, for those not cut down by the claymores of the MacLeans were waylaid in the pass of Killiekrankie by the Athol men. The army of MacKay was almost annihilated; the wreck, consisting of about four hundred, reached Stirling the next day. The Highlanders' loss was about eight hundred, including Dundee, their great commander. The dreadful effect of the slaughter made by the Highlanders was made apparent the next day. The enemy lay in heaps, almost in the order in which they were posted, and so mutilated that the victors gazed upon them with surprise and horror. Some had their skulls cut off above their ears, by a backstroke of the claymore, and others had their heads divided in halves by one blow. But few Highlanders fell after they drew their swords, and a majority of those who were slain fell within a few paces of the enemy.

The victory at Killiecrankie aroused the apathetic, who hastened to swell the ranks of the victorious army. But the death of Dundee was greater than a defeat. The command now devolved on General Cannon, an old, inactive, and inexperienced man, wholly unsuited in almost every respect, who led the army from one disaster to another, until it was totally ruined. He marched the army toward Perth, and then to Aberdeen. He had not less than four thousand men, and was followed by MacKay, who had raised about fifteen hundred dragoons. From Aberdeen he marched into Banff and Moray. A regiment of religious enthusiasts, known as Cameronians, had taken up a position at Dunkeld. Cannon determined to attack the place, although he had

* Hogg's *Jacobite Relics*, Vol. I., p. 196.

nothing proper for the reduction of the place. Having spent all their ammunition, and finding they could maintain their position no longer, the Highlanders withdrew. In this action, Hector MacLean of Torrestan, of the family of Coll, and Hector MacLean, son of Kingerloch, were slain, and Sir Alexander MacLean had his leg broken. Several private soldiers of the name of MacLean were also killed and wounded.

After this action, Sir John MacLean sent Captain Allan MacLean, his cousin, and Captain John MacLean, brother of Sir Alexander, with a detachment to the north under Cannon, who, with other Highlanders, were attacked at Cromdale. Here Cannon and Buchan suffered themselves to be surprised in bed by Sir Thomas Livingston, and, though at the head of fifteen hundred brave Highlanders, were utterly defeated and scattered, which occurred May 1, 1690. In this action, the detachment under Sir John MacLean's officers stood their ground till surrounded by the enemy, when the soldiers threw away their arms and made their escape; but Captains Allan and John MacLean, indignant at the conduct of their men, fought until, overwhelmed by numbers and wounded, they were taken prisoners. Cannon fled to Mull, where he was protected by Sir John MacLean.

The repulse sustained at Dunkeld convinced the chieftains of the incapacity of Cannon; so they entered into a compact to assemble on the following September, day and place not specified, each agreeing to bring the following number of men: " Sir John MacLean 200, Sir Donald MacDonald 200, Sir Ewen Cameron 200, Glengarry 200, Benbecula 200, Sir Alexander MacLean 100, Appin 100, Inveray 100, Keppoch 100, Lieut.-Col. MacGregor 100, Calochele 50, Strowan 60, Barra 50, Glencoe 50, MacNaughton 50, Large 50; but in case any of the rebels shall assault or attack any of the above named persons betwixt the date hereof and the said day of rendezvous, we do all solemnly promise to assist one another to the utmost of our power, as witness these presents, signed by us at the castle of Blair, the 24th of August, 1689." *

Seven days before the date of this compact, these associates, and other friends, sent a very characteristic letter to MacKay, in answer to a friendly invitation to lay down their arms. In this they say : " We scorn your usurper, and the indemnities of his government;" " we will die with our swords in our hands before we fail in our loyalty and sworn allegiance to our sovereign." *

Archibald Campbell, tenth earl of Argyle, was not slow in taking advan-

---

* Browne's *History of the Clans*, Vol. II., p. 183. † *Ibid.*

tage of the disasters which followed so rapidly after the battle of Killiecrankie. In a letter dated October 22, 1690, to the tutor of Torloisk, he empowers the latter to show to the lairds of Ardgour, Lochbuy, Kinlochaline, and others of the name of MacLean, who were on treaty to lay down their arms, that they were granted above date to consider it, and that he will not receive them under protection unless they deliver them up under oath and surrender their forts; in which case he will, if need be, go to London and procure their remission for life.* He also instructs John Campbell, bailie of Jura and governor of Aros, to march with all speed and fortify the old castle of Aros; to seize upon the person and goods of all in Mull, Coll, and Tiree who continued in rebellion. Colin Campbell of Bragleine is instructed to receive the house of Lochbuy, and garrison it with twenty-four men.†

Notwithstanding this activity on the part of Argyle, Sir John. MacLean returned home and retained possession of his estates until the former represented him to King William as an enemy to his cause, and procured a commission from him to bring the MacLeans to obedience, which he began to do with fire and sword. He came to Mull with twenty-five hundred men, but Sir John being unprepared for resistance in consequence of the desertion from his cause of Glengarry and Lochiel, who had faithfully promised to assist him, he did not deem it prudent to offer opposition, all friends, save his own clan, having forsaken him; and knowing that although he should get the better of Argyle, yet, being in arms against the existing government, and his wily enemy being in favor, his ultimate ruin was inevitable. He therefore, having the good of his people at heart, advised them to take protection from Argyle, while he himself with a number of his armed followers went to the garrison of Cairnburg, where he captured several ships belonging to King William, one of which was laden with necessaries for the army in Ireland. He staid in this fortress until March, 1692, when he received an order from King James to capitulate with the government. It appears he surrendered Duard castle and Cairnburg on the 31st of March,‡ and was allowed a pass to go before King William unmolested. On the 26th of April he received an order from the chancellor of Scotland which permitted him and his two servants to travel from the place of his residence to any place in England or Flanders, that he might throw himself upon his majesty's mercy.||

Sir John went to London and was well received by the king, who offered

---

* *Appendix Sixth Report Hist. MS Com.*, p. 629. † *Ibid.*, p. 634. ‡ *Ibid.*, p. 618. || *Ibid.*, p. 634.

him a regiment, which was declined. He then desired him to go as a volunteer to the next campaign, and when he returned justice should be done to him. In the meantime the king directed Johnson, the secretary of state for Scotland, to see that no injustice was done Sir John in his absence. Sir John came to Edinburgh to put his affairs in order before he went abroad, but the secretary, who was influenced by Argyle, and an enemy of MacLean, denied the king's order and threatened to imprison him in the castle. Upon this Sir John proceeded to London with the intention of following the king to Flanders. When he arrived in London the queen told him that she had received letters from Scotland informing her that he had gone into the Highlands to raise a rebellion; but Sir John succeeded in assuring her that there was no truth in the report; upon which she wrote to the king on his behalf, and he proceeded on his way to Holland. On his arrival at Burges, he met some friends of the exiled king, among whom a report was in circulation that a counter-revolution had just taken place in England, and that William was dethroned. With a fatal credulity Sir John listened to this report, and unfortunately acted upon it; for instead of joining king William, he immediately proceeded to the court of James at St. Germains, where he remained until Anne's accession to the throne. He there married Mary, daughter of Sir Æneas MacPherson of Esky.

Upon queen Anne's accession to the throne (March 8, 1702), there was an indemning offer to those who had gone abroad with king James. Sir John availed himself of this opportunity to return to Britain, but on his way his wife was taken ill at Calais, where she gave birth to a son. This retarded his progress, so that the day prefixed in the indemnity elapsed before he came to England; yet trusting to the queen's clemency, he embarked as soon as his family could bear the sea. On his arrival in London he was arrested and sent to the Tower, and soon after brought to trial before the privy council for taking part in the celebrated Queensberry plot, but was acquitted. On his liberation the queen gave him a pension of £500 sterling per annum, which he enjoyed during the remainder of his life; the greater part of which he spent in London, and occasionally was seen in the Highlands.

At the time of the death of queen Anne, August, 1714, Sir John was at Achnacarry castle in Inverlochy with some other gentlemen. The governor of Fort William had received accounts of the death of the queen, but kept it a secret. Sir John invited the governor and officers to dine with him, and during the meal they appeared very happy. Lachlan MacLean of Grulin, on going out, discovered the house surrounded with soldiers under arms; and returning spoke to Sir John in Gaelic, who with the company arose from the table. The governor attempted to take both Sir John and Lochiel prisoners, but they succeed in passing the guard and making good their escape.

On the death of queen Anne, the English parliament called George, elector of Hanover, to the throne. He was narrow and bigoted. To him Britain to the last " was a foreign country, for which he had no love, and of the language, feelings, and thought of which, he was profoundly ignorant. His affections remained with Hanover." * He made no attempt to conciliate the factions who he thought were opposed to him, but violently turned his back upon them, and threw himself into the arms of the whigs, who alone shared his favor, and who were not slow to extend their interests and connections. If he had been wise and prudent, he might have avoided some of the calamities which followed. There was a general disposition to acquiesce peaceably in the selection of him for a sovereign. The leading Highland chiefs addressed to him a letter in which they expressed their readiness to serve him. This was signed by Sir John MacLean, MacDonald of Glengarry, Cameron of Lochiel, MacDonald of Keppoch, Sir Donald MacDonald, MacIntosh of MacIntosh, MacKenzie of Fraserdale, MacLeod of Contulick, Grant of Glenmoriston, Chisholm of Comer, and MacPherson of Cluny.†

The conduct of George, elector of Hanover, excited the most violent discontent throughout the kingdom, and the populace raised tumults in different parts of the kingdom. In the month of January, 1715, he issued an extraordinary proclamation, calling a new parliament. In the midst of these disorders, James, brother of queen Anne, and son of James II., but better known as the Chevalier de St. George, proclaimed his right to the throne, from which he had been excluded, and assumed the title of James III.

The whole tendency of the MacLeans at this time was to remain quiet. During the month of December, 1714, Sir John MacLean was at the house of Auchinbreck. On the 27th of December, Campbell of Glendaruel came to Mull and called a meeting of all the MacLeans, save Lochbuy, at Grulin. To them Glendaruel presented an address to the king which he desired them to sign, which they refused, until he prevailed upon some of them by urging that Sir John had no way of living but by favor of the king, who might be prevailed upon to continue his pension. At a meeting held January, 1715, at Kilmichell, there was present Sir John MacLean, Auchinbreck, Lochnell, MacLachlan, MacDougall, and all other gentlemen of Kintyre, it was decided

---

* Chamber's *Encyclopœdia*, Article George I.   † Keltie's *Highland Clans*, Vol. I., p. 422.

to send an address to the king. On January 18, 1715, James Campbell, sheriff deputy of Argyleshire, writes to John Campbell, duke of Argyle, that he had signed a warrant to search Sir John MacLean and Glendaruel. On the next day he writes to the same that Lochbuy had just come from Mull, and stated that when there he heard of no address to the Chevalier, but had seen the address of the clans to king George, which had several sheets of subscribers.*

It will thus be seen that Sir John MacLean and some other chieftains were not allowed to be loyal to the new ruler. An arrest was attempted by the governor of Fort William, and now he is harassed by the duke of Argyle, although the latter was in possession of all his estates. For all this persecution they had no other ground than that of suspicion. It is no wonder that Sir John's face should be turned to the Chevalier, whom, there is no doubt, he believed was the rightful sovereign. If there be any shadow whatever for the doctrine of the divine right of kings, then James III. should have been proclaimed king of Great Britain. There was no justice in the act of his exclusion; that is, to people believing in a monarchy. In a republic, all doctrines of a monarchy are simply abhorrent.

John Erskine, the eleventh earl of Mar, was dismissed from the office of secretary of state for Scotland by the king on his succession. Even before he had seen him he had conceived a great dislike for Mar, although the latter did all in his power to ingratiate himself into the sovereign's favor. He was abruptly and unceremoniously dismissed because he was a tory. The studied insult which he continued to receive from the king drove him into rebellion. He proceeded to the Highlands and placed himself at the head of the Jacobites, as the followers of James III. were called. On the 6th of September, 1715, the earl of Mar assembled at Aboyne the noblemen, chiefs of clans, gentlemen, and others, with such followers as could be brought together, and proclaimed James, king of Great Britain. The insurrection, both in England and Scotland, began to grow in popularity, and would have been a success if a strong military man had been at its head. Nearly all the principal northern chiefs were drawn into the movement. Sir John MacLean raised a regiment of his own name in Mull, which numbered eight hundred men. Both the MacLeans and Camerons of Lochiel were late in arriving at the theater of war, owing to many obstructions placed in their way by the Argyle Campbells. They broke through by going up Glenmore, and on their

---

* *Appendix Sixth Report to Hist. MS Com.*, p. 619.

way, assisted by some MacDonalds, they made an assault upon Fort William. They carried, sword in hand, two of the outworks, in each of which were a lieutenant, sergeant, and about twenty-five men; but were obliged to abandon the enterprise for want of cannon, and proceeded toward Inverary. The MacLeans joined the main body of Mar's army at Achterarder, some days before the battle of Sheriffmuir. At Achterarder, during the night of November 10th, the whole clan Fraser, amounting to four hundred men, deserted the Highland army, which was followed by two hundred of the earl of Huntly's followers. The army thus diminished marched off their ground in the following order: "The master of Stair with the Fife-shire squadron, and two squadrons of Huntly's cavalry, formed the advance of the whole. The west clans then followed, being, first, the MacDonalds, under their different chiefs of Clanranald, Glengary, Sir Donald MacDonald, Keppoch, and Glencoe. The next were Breadalbane's men, with five regiments, consisting of the following clans: the MacLeans, under Sir John MacLean, their chief; the Camerons, under Lochiel; the Stewarts, commanded by Appin; and those who remained of Huntly's followers from Strathdon and Glenlivat, under Gordon of Glenbucket. This chosen body of Highlanders were in high spirits, and so confident of success, that they boasted that their division of Mar's army only would be more than enough to deal with the duke of Argyle, and all the force he commanded." *

The rest of the army, commanded by Mar in person, followed the advanced division. The army numbered about eight thousand men, and was confronted by the duke of Argyle with about thirty-five hundred veteran troops. These two armies came together on Sunday, November 13, 1715, at a place called Sheriffmuir, an elevated and uneven waste, skirted on the west by the high road leading from Stirling to Perth. Mar marshaled his army into two lines; the center of the first line being composed of ten battalions of foot, consisting of four thousand men, commanded by the captain of Clanranald, Sir John MacLean, the laird of Glenbucket, Brigadier Ogilvie, and the two brothers of MacDonald of Sleat, all of whom were under the direction of General Gordon. On the right of this line were placed two of the Marquis of Huntly's squadron of horse, and the Stirling squadron. The left wing was composed of the Perthshire squadron. The center of the second line consisted of eight battalions of foot, composed of divisions from Seaforth's, Huntly's, Panmure's, and Tullibardine's followers. Two squadrons of horse

---

* Scott's *Tales of a Grandfather*, Vol. I., p. 165, Third Series.

formed the right and one squadron the left wing. Both armies marched to the crest of the hill, and when they were brought face to face some confusion occurred, and the clans under General Gordon were thrown to the right of Mar's line, which was hastily formed, and as already noted consisted of the western clans, MacDonalds, MacLeans, and the followers of Breadalbane. During a moment of hesitation, "old Captain Livingstone rode up, a veteran soldier, who had served in king James' army before the revolution, and with several oaths called to General Gordon, who commanded the right wing, instantly to attack. The general hesitated, but the chiefs and clans caught the enthusiasm of the moment. A gentleman by the name of MacLean, who lived to a great age, thus described the attack of his own tribe; and there can be no doubt the general onset was made under similar circumstances. When his clan was drawn up in deep order, the best born, bravest, and best armed of the warriors in front, Sir John MacLean placed himself at their head, and said with a loud voice, ' Gentlemen, this is a day we have long wished to see. Yonder stands Mac Callum Mór for king George. Here stands MacLean for king James. God bless MacLean and King James! Charge, gentlemen!' The clan then muttered a brief prayer, fixed the bonnet firm on the head, stripped off their plaids, which then comprehended the philabeg also, and rushed on the enemy, firing their fusees irregularly, then dropping them, and drawing their swords, and uniting in one wild yell, when they mingled among the bayonets." * The duke's left wing being so violently assaulted by the Highland right was completely routed, and the fugitives fled with all speed to Stirling, carrying the news that Argyle was totally defeated. Argyle succeeded in driving Mar's left back a distance of two miles, but the right and center returning from the pursuit struck Argyle's right wing in the rear. From this difficulty Argyle succeeded in extricating himself, then retired to Dunblane, and from there to Stirling. About five hundred men were slain on either side. The victory was with the Highlanders, but Mar's military talents were not equal to the occasion.

In a council of war, held some time after the battle of Sheriffmuir, Mar drew up an instrument, in which it was agreed that the subscribers should continue in arms, and accept of no conditions except under the royal authority. During the discussion which followed after the presentation of the bond, the master of Stair demanded to know what persons were allowed to vote, as constituting the majority of the gentlemen in arms. "Sir John MacLean

---

* Scott's *Tales of a Grandfather*, Vol. I., p. 170, Third Series.

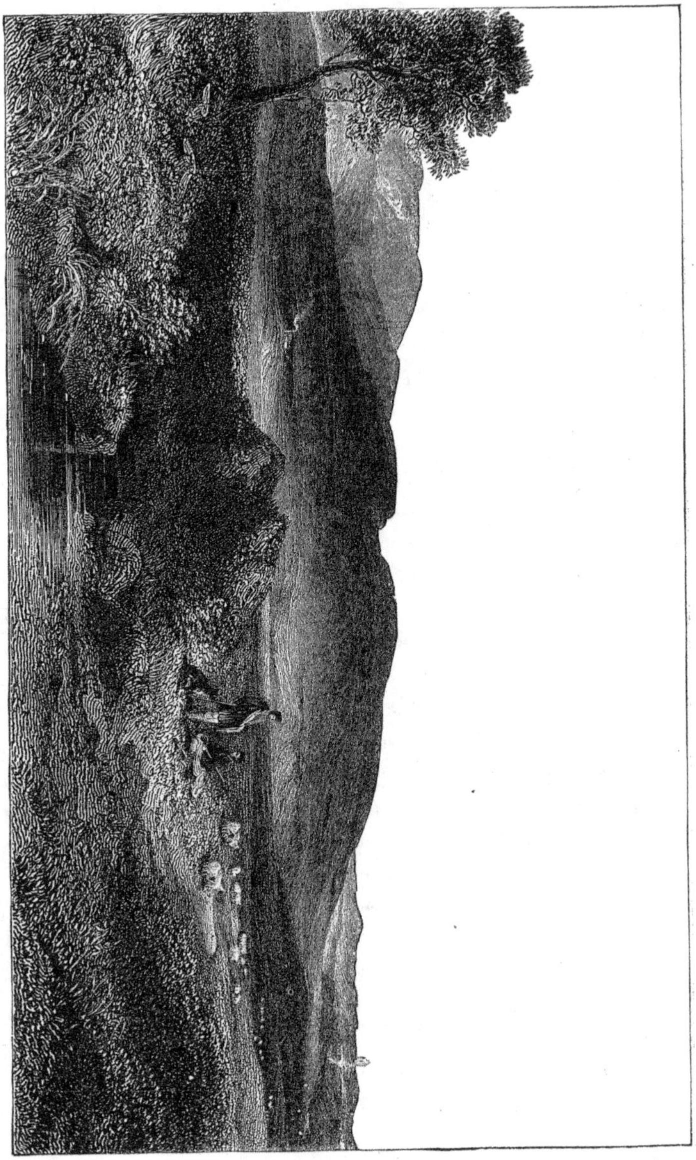

Battle Field of Sheriffmuir.

haughtily answered, that unless some such power of selection were lodged in the commander-in-chief, all his regiment of eight hundred men must be admitted to vote, since every MacLean was a gentleman." * Mar endeavored to soothe those who were disaffected, and endeavored to press on the dissentients the dishonor of deserting the king. The Highlanders at this time were confronted by ten thousand well disciplined troops, while their own army had been weakened by desertions. The chiefs who still remained keenly felt their position. They complained that they had been induced to enter the field by promises of troops, arms, ammunition, and a general of military talent. The council of war broke up without coming to any resolution. The Highlanders remained true to the cause long after the Lowlanders had become dejected and dispirited. The remnants of the army were marched to Aberdeen, and there disbanded in February, 1716.

When the Chevalier de St. George and Mar abandoned the faithful Highlanders, Sir John MacLean was offered accommodation in the Chevalier's ship, but refused it. He parted with his men at Keith, and went to Gordon castle. The night of his escape from the governor of Fort William at Achnacarry castle, Sir John caught a severe cold, which from frequent exposure developed in consumption, and at Perth he became very ill. At Gordon castle, this brave but unfortunate man breathed his last, on the 12th of March, 1716, in the forty-fifth year of his age. He was the last of the powerful lords of Duard. He was buried in the church of Raffin, in the shire of Banff, in the burial-place of the Gordons of Buckie. By his wife Mary, daughter of Æneas MacPherson of Esky, he had one son—Sir Hector, and five daughters—Louisa, Isabella, Mary, Ann, and Beatrice. The last named died at Glendaruel, in the fourteenth year of her age, and is buried there. Isabella married a MacQuarrie of Ormaig in Ulva, where some of her descendants were living as late as 1840. No record has been preserved concerning the rest.

Both the Ardgour and Pennycross manuscripts pay the following tribute to his memory: Sir John MacLean was in every respect a fine gentleman. He was tall, rather above the ordinary size, though well proportioned; his countenance was cheerful, his actions agreeable, his manners graceful, and commanded both love and respect. His complexion was ruddy and his face symmetrical. His polite address and courteous behavior showed he had spent most of his time at court. He was well educated, and spoke Gaelic, English, and French fluently; he was sincere and honest, studying always to do as he

---

* Scott's *Tales of a Grandfather*, Vol. I., p. 199, Third Series.

would wish to be done by. This part of his character laid him open to be deceived, which frequently happened, from a belief that those great men whom he came in contact with were honest like himself. He was unalterably steady to what he believed to be his duty, and through this he lost his estates, the rank he had in his country, and became an exile. If he had been flexible and induced to change sides, he might have made his fortune with king William, or with the Whig party in queen Anne's reign; but a steady honesty was the leading characteristic of his family, and from that standard he never departed. His gallant behavior at Killiekrankie, when but eighteen years of age, supplemented at Sheriffmuir and other places, showed he was brave. His generosity often straitened him; he was humble and affable, an affectionate friend and a generous enemy. From what has been said, he was a poor politician, and in that respect hardly adapted for the times.

The character of Sir John MacLean, taken as a whole, is one to be admired. His great weakness consisted in that supposed duty he thought he owed to a line of monarchs. His life is a living monument in attestation of the Biblical injunction, "Put not your trust in princes." Queen Anne was the favorite of her father, James II.; and although it was in her power to restore to him his forfeited estates, there is no evidence that she even proposed justice to Sir John. The race of MacLean was ever true to the house of Stuart, and thousands of them perished in its support. In return, they were persecuted and neglected. On the other hand, the family of Argyle, that fomented strife and discord, that engaged in rebellion and treason, that plotted the overthrow of the reigning dynasty, although it met with some severity upon two of its members, yet from those sovereigns it had abused it received honors, powers, and enlarged estates. It presents the anomaly that princes do not reward faithful servants, but those who fawn upon them and pander to their desires. As a matter of policy, fairness, justness, and good judgment, there was no reason for giving the estates of Sir John MacLean to Archibald Campbell, tenth earl of Argyle. It may be a matter of some consolation and gratification that these estates have nearly all slipped from the fingers of this grasping family. That portion of the Morvern estates belonging to Sir John MacLean passed out of the Argyle family in 1819, and in 1845 it was owned by eleven different landlords. Many years ago, Duard castle and its adjacent lands also passed into other hands. The Ross of Mull, Kilfinichen parish, the islands of Iona and Tiree, are still possessed by that family.

XXI. Sir Hector MacLean, Bart., Twenty-first Chief of MacLean.

Sir Hector MacLean was born at Calais, November 6, 1703. At the age of four he was brought to England, and from thence to the Highlands, and delivered to the care of Donald MacLean of Coll, his near relation and fast friend. In that gentleman's family he remained until he was eighteen, having been instructed by good preceptors, and under their care laid that foundation for letters which he afterward improved to so great an advantage. Afterward, he studied in Edinburgh, where he made great progress in philosophy, the mathematics, and civil law. In 1721, he went to France, to complete his studies in belles lettres and civil law. He returned to Scotland in 1725 to visit his relations, but went back to France in 1728, where he remained, sometimes in Boulogne, and at other times in Paris. He left France just before the revolution of 1745 broke out in Scotland.

During this period, we gain but little information concerning the clan MacLean. Although their chief was deprived of his estates, his people remained true to him. This is clearly proved by the loyalty shown to Sir John MacLean during the insurrection of 1715. After Mar had left the country, the next step was to disarm the clans. Duncan Campbell, who appears to have been in charge of Duard castle, in a letter dated at Duard, April 12, 1716, states, the people of Appin, Glencoe, Lochiel, and Keppoch had delivered up their arms, and it was said that Glengarry was ready to do so, and if such was the case, there would be no difficulty in disarming the Highlands. In the region of Duard, most of the arms had been secured, except what had been taken to Cairnburg, "which was the best of their arms. Whither they may be soe wise as to deseart that rock or not, I cannot well tell you. As yett the number of arms got does not at all agree with the number that was in rebellion." Officers were to go from that district to Morvern, thence to Ardnamurchan, thence to Coll, in order to disarm all in that shire.*

There was considerable alarm in the West Highlands during the year 1719, for fear the disaffected clans would join with certain Spanish ships in a fresh outbreak. Writing at Inverary, May 4, 1719, James Campbell, sheriff deputy, says that, on the Friday previous, there was to have been a gathering of all the MacLeans in Mull, where it was thought that Glendaruel was to be, *incognito*. Ten days previous to that time, he (Campbell) had sent word to Brolass, the leading man among the MacLeans, advising him to beware of involving himself and others in new difficulties, for it would be harder to extri-

---

* *Appendix Sixth Rep. Hist. MS Com.*, p. 619.

cate themselves than it was the last time. From the information received, it does not appear whether or not this great meeting really took place, and if it did, whether the object was to discuss the best interests of the clan, or to decide what course should be pursued should another revolution be inaugurated. Although thirty years elapsed between the outbreak of the revolution of 1715 and that headed by Prince Charles Stuart, it does not follow that the clans rested easily during that time. The changed order of affairs, to some, must at least have been very irritating.

George II. became king in the year 1729. The revolution under Prince Charles Edward Stuart broke out in 1745. There was much disaffection throughout the British Isles with the reigns of the electors of Hanover. If a free, untrammeled vote of the people could have occurred, it is probable that the exiled Stuarts would again have been on the throne. Charles Stuart, grandson of James II., sailed from France, July 12, 1745 (O. S.), in a small vessel of eighteen guns, and landed on the mainland of Scotland on the 25th of the same month. On the 19th of August, in the vale of Glenfinnan, he raised his standard. With the small force he had there collected, he commenced his march through the Highlands, every-where trying to raise the clans, which rallied to his support from every side. The mountainous districts of Badenoch were traversed, and the 30th of August, the army arrived at Blair castle. On the 4th of September, the army reached Perth, and on the 16th the city of Edinburgh was captured without a struggle. On the 19th Sir John Cope, commander-in-chief of the royal forces in Scotland, was surprised at Prestonpans by the Highlanders and utterly routed, leaving baggage, cannon, and camp equipage on the field. With a force of only sixty-five hundred men Charles advanced into England. Carlisle surrendered at his approach, and unmolested, he proceeded as far as Derby. Three English armies, each larger than his own, were prepared to meet him. He had expected that his army would be constantly reinforced as he proceeded south. Having been disappointed in this, he commenced a retreat into Scotland by way of Carlisle, Glasgow, and Stirling. On January 17, 1746, the battle of Falkirk was fought. Each army was composed of eight thousand men—the royal forces under General Hawley consisted of the best troops in the English army. Hawley was ignominiously routed in the brief space of twenty minutes, leaving an immense quantity of baggage, provisions, and ammunition, besides seven cannon on the field. The Highland army retreated to Perth, from there north, and on April 16, 1746, fought the famous battle of Culloden.

The clan MacLean still remained steadfast to that dynasty which always appeared to them as the only legitimate one, and made this conspicuously manifest in the bold enterprise of Prince Charles. Although deprived of their chief, Sir Hector, they called to the front the brave and chivalrous Charles MacLean of Drimnin, who nobly and efficiently commanded them. No sooner had Charles summoned the clans than the fiery cross was seen flying over the mountains and through the valleys of Mull and Morvern, summoning the faithful followers to aid the enthusiastic aspirant in his attempt to gain the crown of his ancestors. In obedience to the call five hundred MacLeans responded, all ready to prove that in every respect they were worthy descendants of a noble, devoted, and brave ancestry. Efforts were made to dissuade them from their undertaking, and those who had great influence and foresaw what would be the inevitable result, warned them to remain peaceably at home. The more prudent obeyed the summons. But the band, principally composed of the MacLeans of Duard, actuated largely by chivalry, determined to shed their last drop of blood, if necessary, along with the other loyal clans. They found themselves almost thoroughly hemmed in by powerful enemies who kept them from joining Prince Charles' army. Finally they succeeded in breaking through and joining Prince Charles just after the battle of Falkirk, and at a time when the cause of the prince was almost hopeless. They were ready and did their duty at the battle of Culloden.

On the morning of April 16th, the Highland army found itself worn out with its long night's march and greatly overcome by hunger. When they arrived in camp at five in the morning, many went off in search of provisions. The cannon was fired and the pipes played the "Gathering" of the various clans, but many were now out of hearing. The army was drawn up in the following order: The right wing, consisting of the Athol men, Lochiel, Appin, and Cluny, was commanded by lord George Murray. The center, under lord John Drummond, was composed of Lovat, MacIntosh, Farquharson, and MacLeod. The left, under the duke of Perth, composed of MacLean, Clanranald, Keppoch, and Glengarry. Behind the first line were the French and Irish picquets, lord John Drummond's regiment, the Perthshire squadron of horse, and a few hussars. The second line was made up of Roy Stuart's regiment, Gordon's and Glenbucket's men, and Kilmarnock's guards. The duke of Perth and Ogilvy's men formed the reserve. A plan of the battle, showing the position of the two armies, is given in the accompanying illustration. The formidable appearance of the duke of Cumberland's army by no means dismayed the exhausted Highlanders, but were impatient to begin the battle. The attack commenced by a continuous fire of the artillery, which continued for nearly an hour. The artillery was galling to the Highlanders and fast depleting their ranks, and unable to endure it any longer, the MacIntoshes, who were very near the center of the first line, broke forth and rushed upon the enemy. The men under lord George Murray then advanced with a shout, and broke through the first line of the enemy, capturing two cannon; but upon reaching the second line, such a destructive fire was poured upon the clansmen that they recoiled, and retreated in confusion. The MacIntoshes and others of the clans in the center succeeded in piercing the first line, but

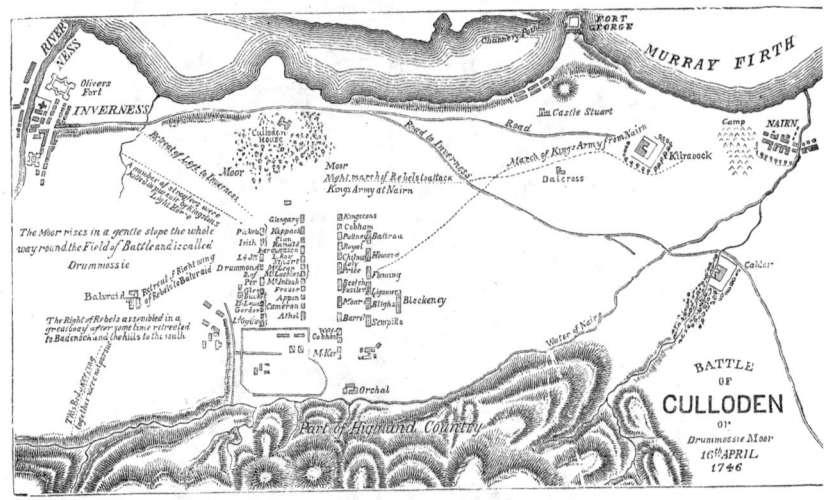

PLAN OF BATTLE OF CULLODEN.

were repulsed by the steady fire of the reserve. The left wing, consisting of the MacDonalds—Glengarry, Keppoch, and Clanranald regiments—refused to take part in the fight. In vain did the valiant captain of Keppoch exclaim, "My God! Have the children of my tribe forsaken me?" And rushing forward trying to induce them to follow, he fell mortally wounded. The MacLeans were among those who broke forward with sword in hand and routed the left of the duke of Cumberland's army. In this attack, though for a brief period victorious, they suffered fearfully; the whole of their front line, consisting chiefly of the gentlemen of the clan, being swept away before they came within sword's length of their foes. When the center of the enemy turned upon them in support of the defeated left, the brave assailants, over-

BATTLE OF CULLODEN.

whelmed by numbers, were forced to retire. In the act of doing so, while rallying his men, MacLean of Drimnin missed one of his sons, and inquired of an immediate attendant if he saw any thing of him. "Sir," said the attendant, "I fear he has fallen." "If he has, it shall not be for naught," replied the father; and instantly turning upon the ranks of the enemy, with his pistol in one hand and his sword in the other, he rushed again into the conflict. His faithful attendant attempting to remonstrate with him for uselessly throwing away his life, Drimnin ordered him out of his way, addressing him at the same time with his usual kindness in the Gaelic language: *Allein! comma léat missé, mas toil léat do bhéatha thoir 'n arrigh dhuit fhéin*—Allan! Heed me not; if thou value thy life, take care of thyself. Chambers gives the following account, saying after MacLachlan, colonel of the MacLean regiment, which included a body of his own name, was slain, "his lieutenant-colonel, MacLean of Drimnin, who then assumed the command, was bringing off his shattered forces, observed two of his sons, who had fought by his side, severely wounded, and heard that a third had been left dead on the field. Exclaiming 'It shall not be for naught,' this brave old gentleman, without bonnet or wig, rushed back into the fight, attacked two dragoons, killed one and wounded the other, but was at last cut down by other three, who came up to the assistance of their comrades." *

Out of the five regiments which charged the English—the Camerons, Stuarts, Frasers, MacIntoshes, and MacLeans—almost all the leaders and front men were slain. The Highlanders lost a thousand men out of the five thousand that went into action, from which number eleven hundred and fifty must be deducted, who were MacDonalds, and refused to fight. The duke's army consisted of nine thousand of the best disciplined and appointed troops in the English service.

The MacLeans, MacLauchlans, and MacGillivrays, who fell in this battle, are buried in one trench, which is fifty-six feet long, the tomb in the foreground of the battle field marking the spot. *See page* 220.

The ferocity exhibited toward the prisoners, the sick, the wounded, and the dying, by the duke of Cumberland, beggars all description. He superintended with evident satisfaction the murder in cold blood of the unfortunate prisoners and wounded that fell into his hands, many of them being gentlemen of high standing and great courage. On the other hand, Prince Charles Stuart cared with gentleness those who had, on previous occasions, fallen into

---

* *History of the Rebellion of* 1745–6, p. 310.

his hands. He never forgot they were his countrymen; the duke forgot they were human beings. In the massacre which followed the battle of Culloden, the MacLeans, as well as other clans, suffered severely.

President Forbes of Culloden, who did more to preserve the throne of George the II. during this revolution than even the army of the duke of Cumberland, exerted all his influence and ingenuity to save the lives of those who had fallen into the hands of Cumberland, but his efforts were not always successful. Again and again he raised his voice against the massacre, and entreated the victor to spare the lives of his victims, but the work of vengeance went on. Even near his own house of Culloden eighteen wounded officers

BATTLE FIELD OF CULLODEN.

were captured, then tortured for two days, and on the third huddled into carts, carried into the court-yard, ranged in a row against the wall, and all shot to death. He went to the duke and firmly declared that the wholesale slaughter that was going on was not only inhuman, but also contrary to the law of the land and against the laws of God. "The laws of the country, my lord," answered the duke, with a sneer, "I'll make a brigade give laws, by God!" It must be remembered that this duke of Cumberland was the second son of the reigning monarch. Shortly afterward, President Forbes visited London, and being asked by the king if the reports of the atrocities following the battle of Culloden were true, he replied, "I wish to God I could consistently with truth assure your majesty that such reports are destitute of foundation." The king in great displeasure abruptly left him; in consequence of which his accounts with the government were with difficulty passed, and an immense balance was left unpaid. In this way the house of Hanover discharged its debt of gratitude to its most loyal, its greatest of servants.*

The barbarities did not stop with the massacre of the Highlanders who fought at Culloden. Cumberland spread his army over the disaffected district, burned houses, destroyed castles, killed cattle, and committed such atrocities, the details of which are sickening to relate. Not satisfied with the destruction which was carried into the very houses of this gallant, brave, and generous race of people, the British parliament passed an act that, on and after August 1, 1747, any person, man, or boy, in Scotland, who should on any pretense whatever wear any part of the Highland garb, should be imprisoned not less than six months; and on conviction of second offense, transportation abroad for seven years. The soldiers had instructions to shoot upon the spot any one seen wearing the Highland garb,† and this as late as September, 1750.

This law and other laws made at the same time were unnecessarily severe. The abolition of the Highland garb affected the clans that fought for George II., as well as those which were disaffected. The former had great reasons for complaint, and their petitions were of no effect. The law was not abolished until 1782. The estates that were forfeited were not returned until the year 1784. This bill passed the house, but met with violent opposition from the lord chancellor in the house of lords. To its credit let it be said that notwithstanding the opposition it passed by a large majority.

The English government took every step necessary to break up the clan system, and the battle of Culloden may be said to end that system. The loyalty of the people remained the same to their chiefs. While Sir Hector MacLean lived to see the end of a system that had been maintained for ages by mutual affection and loyalty, yet as long as he lived, although in foreign lands, he was regarded as the father of his clan.

The reason he did not act a prominent part in the rebellion of 1745 may be briefly set forth. Before the outbreak, he was taken into the councils of the select few. The available records show that the king of France had promised to make him a lieutenant-colonel in the army in the forthcoming war; but through some meddling of lord John Drummond, a difficulty arose as to

---

* See John MacLean's *Historical Sketches of Highland Families*, p. 82. † Letter from Lochgarry to Sir Hector MacLean, in Browne's *Highland Clans*, Vol. IV., p. 74.

this appointment, which threatened complications, and the king was anxious to prevent the result which might follow by depriving Sir Hector of his rank.*

The Chevalier de St. George, writing June 22, 1745, says: "I am glad to find Balhady was so far safe on his journey. I hope and believe he will be returned on this side of the sea, before Sir Hector MacLean's going to Scotland could possibly make any noise, which I hope it will not, though I wish some other expedient could have been fallen upon, to keep him and lord John Drummond at a distance from one another, which was the chief, if not the only motive of his going thither." †

From Sempil, date June 28th, we learn that "Sir Hector MacLean is arrived in Scotland, and that upon his arrival lord Elcho, who had been some time at London, was immediately sent for, and set out accordingly, in all haste, for Scotland, from whence" Erskine, Traquair and Balhady infer that something rash will be attempted, which is strengthened by the part John Murray has acted since he returned thence, and some things reported as coming from Sir Thomas Sheridan. "From this connection of Murray with Sir Thomas Sheridan, and lord Elcho's sudden call upon Sir Hector MacLean's arrival, the three gentlemen I have named above dread a deal of mischief; they are persuaded Sir Hector's journey was concerted, or rather directed, by Sir Thomas, and they think nothing but a letter from the prince to Murray can prevent the bad consequences of it;" and a request is made that the Chevalier should command all to remain quiet and give no cause of suspicion to the government.‡ From these disclosures, it would appear that Sir Hector intended to head the revolution before the landing of Prince Charlie, but was prevented by lord Drummond (Balhady) and others.

In Edinburgh, Sir Hector took up his lodgings with one Blair. Here, by the treachery of his host, who hoped to reap a handsome reward by his baseness, caused him to be arrested and sent to the castle. But all he accomplished by his officiousness was the loss to himself of a kind and liberal lodger, for which, it is said, Maggie Blair gave many a sound rating during the remainder of his life to her "gowk of a husband." Sir Hector was arrested on the 5th of June, and with him were apprehended his servant, Lachlan MacLean, and George Bleau of Castlehill. The grounds of this arrest were suspicion of being in the French service and of enlisting men there. By the

---

* Sempil's letter, March 22, 1745. See Browne's *History of the Clans*, Vol. II., p. 456.
† *Ibid.*, p. 463. ‡ *Ibid.*, p. 465.

king's solicitor and some army officers, the prisoners were examined for several hours, and then Sir Hector was committed to the castle, Mr. Bleau to the jail, and Lachlan MacLean to that of the Canongate. All were afterward sent under a strong guard to London, where they again underwent a long examination, and were remanded back into the messenger's custody.* While Sir Hector was held in confinement, an order came from the court of France giving him unlimited credit.† In May, 1747, he was set at liberty as a French prisoner, and at once returned to France.

The long confinement nor the defeat at Culloden did not cause him to lose hope in the Stuart cause. In a letter dated at Paris, January 24, 1750, and supposed to be addressed to Mr. Edgar, he shows his familiarity with the state of affairs:

"*Sir :*—By accounts I have from very good hands, I think myself obliged to put you upon your guard about any informations you may receive about affairs in Scotland, that you might not for some time give too high credit to them. I hope in a little to be able to lay an exact state of these things before his majesty; but in the meantime think it my duty to give you this hint, to hinder other people's imposing, or the bad effects of their being imposed on themselves. I hope to write soon to you again, and am in the meantime, most sincerely,

Sir, your most humble and most obedient servant,

MACLEANE." ‡

From Paris Sir Hector went to Rome, where, during the month of July, he had an apoplectic fit, but partially recovered. During the month of October, he had a second attack of apoplexy, from which he died, 1850.

Sir Hector MacLean was of middle stature, and lame in one leg; yet he walked, danced, and performed all his exercises with strength and agility, his body being strong and capable of bearing fatigue. He was a graceful horseman; his countenance was grave but pleasing; his manners and address polite; his complexion was fair, his eyes large and piercing; he was brave and too generous; he was affable and affectionate. He was well versed in divinity, history, politics, civil law, and mathematics. He spoke English, Irish, Gaelic, French, and Italian, and understood Latin well. He possessed a remarkable memory, with a solid and ready judgment, so that he could not be defeated in

---

* See Hogg's *Jacobite Relics*, Vol. II., p. 317. † Glengarry's letter to Cardinal York, Browne's *Highland Clans*, Vol. IV., p. 61. ‡ *Ibid.*, p. 67.

an argument. In matters of moment he was knowing, discreet, and secretive, in consequence of which he was much trusted and depended upon by his friends. He was honest, sincere, and steady, far above the arts of hypocrisy, and never departed from the rules of honor and probity.

Sir Hector MacLean died without issue, never having been married. In him occurred the third break of the line of chieftains, and the first failure in the family of the chieftains. It is befitting that such should be the case. The clans were no more; the last effort had been made for the house of Stuart, and the oppression of the clansmen was being carried on with great violence, which was to end in cruel evictions, the recital of which brings sorrow and sadness of heart. The whole line of chieftains were much respected in their country, loved by their friends, feared by their enemies, never betrayed their trust, and whose peculiar characteristic was more brave than politic. Sir Hector was a fit ending for such a glorious line.

CHAPTER VII.

THE HOUSE OF BROLASS, FROM DONALD TO THE PRESENT TIME.

A. D. 1600 TO 1889.

On the death of Sir Hector MacLean, the title of baronet devolved upon Allan MacLean of Brolass. Sir Allan MacLean was fourth laird of Brolass, and a descendant of Donald, first laird, who was the first son of the second marriage of Hector Og, fifteenth chief of MacLean, and from his father acquired the lands in Brolass, Mull. Donald was at the battle of Inverkeithing with his chief, who was killed, and then became the tutor of Sir Allan, the nineteenth chieftain. Donald was married to Florence, daughter of John Garbh, seventh laird of Coll, by whom he had three sons, Lachlan, who succeeded him, Hector Mór and Hector Og, who married Janet, daughter of MacNeil of Barra. He left two sons, Donald, who died young, and John, married to Florence, daughter of Allan MacLean of Gormony, whose issue was Donald, a merchant in Glasgow, and Hector, a merchant in Jamaica.

Donald, first MacLean of Brolass, lived to an advanced age, and was succeeded by his eldest son,

Lachlan, Second MacLean of Brolass, who was a good and prudent man, of a solid judgment and excellent temper. He was slow in action, and on account of this weakness contrived to associate with him Lachlan of Torloisk, a man full of spirit and activity. He was appointed tutor to Sir John MacLean, and associated Torloisk with him in the management of the estates, and kept Argyle from getting any solid footing in the estates of MacLean, till Argyle was glad to take Tiree in compensation for his whole claim. He was member in parliament for the shire when the duke of York was commissioner for Scotland, and though he was much caressed by the duke, who desired to reconcile Brolass to his celebrated measures for abrogating the penal statutes, but refusing to vote against what he believed to be his duty, he absented himself from parliament when those measures were being discussed. He was married to Isabella, daughter of Hector MacLean, laird of Torloisk. He died in the year 1687, in the thirty-seventh year of his age, and was succeeded by his son,

Donald, Third MacLean of Brolass, who was left fatherless at a very early age, and burdened with many distresses, both in his own private affairs and those of his clan; yet by the greatness of his mind and prudent management he overcame them all. He entered the army and served for some time as lieutenant during the reign of Queen Anne; but in the attempt made by her brother for the recovery of the crown of his ancestors, in the year 1715, MacLean of Brolass served as lieutenant-colonel under his cousin, Sir John, at the battle of Sheriffmuir, where he received two severe wounds on the head from a trooper's saber. He was married to Isabella, daughter of Allan MacLean of Ardgour, by whom he had Allan; Catherine, married to Lachlan, son of Donald MacLean of Coll; Isabella, married to John MacLean of Lochbuy; and Anna, married to Allan MacLean of Drimnin. Donald also had a natural, or illegitimate son, called Gillian, who became a lieutenant in Guernsey, was married, and had issue. Donald's brother Allan was a lieutenant in the British service, and was in the Spanish war betwixt Philip of Spain and the emperor. He died at Stirling in 1722. Donald died in the year 1725, and was succeeded by his son Allan, who became the *Fourth Laird of MacLean,* and on the death of his third cousin, Sir Hector MacLean, as already mentioned, Allan became

XXII. Sir Allan MacLean, Bart., Twenty-second Chief of MacLean, And the Sixth Baronet of Morvern. Sir Allan in his youth embraced a military life. The first notice of his military career is as captain under the earl of Drumlanrig in the service of Holland. On the peace of Aix-la-Chapelle the regiment was reduced, and Sir Allan returned home on half pay. He then married Una, fourth daughter of Hector MacLean of Coll. He then obtained a commission in the Montgomery Highlanders, and was captain-commandant of the nine additional companies sent to reinforce the three Highland regiments then in America, where he staid until the final conquest of Canada, which occurred in 1760. He then returned to Britain on leave of absence, and obtained a major's commission in a corps raised by Colonel Charles Fitzroy (afterward lord Southampton), in which he served until the close of the "Seven Years' War," in 1763. The regiment

SIR ALLAN MACLEAN.

then being reduced, he retired on half pay, but subsequently attained the rank of colonel. With his three daughters, his wife having died while he was in America, he leased the island of Inch Kenneth, and there took up his residence. With their servants, they comprised the only inhabitants of the island. Here Sir Allan maintained the dignity and authority of his birth, living in plenty and with elegance.

It was here that he entertained the celebrated Dr. Samuel Johnson from October 17 to 19, 1773. At that time he was engaged in an expensive and tedious law-suit with John Campbell, fifth duke of Argyle. This family, not content with the seizure of the estates of Duard, had also possessed themselves of the lands of Brolass.* For the recovery of his rights, Sir Allan commenced his law-suit. Dr. Johnson's sympathies were enlisted in his behalf. His attorneys were Boswell and MacLaurin. Boswell, writing to Dr. Johnson from Edinburgh, July, 1777, says: "Sir Allan MacLean has carried that branch of his cause, of which we had good hopes; the president and only one other judge were against him. I wish the house of lords may do as well as the court of sessions has done. But Sir Allan has not the lands of Brolass quite cleared by this judgment, till a large account is made up of debts and interest on the one side, and rents on the other. I am, however, not much afraid of the balance." † There are many of Sir Allan's letters, addressed to John MacLean of Lochbuy, in the Lochbuie Charter Room. In one of them, dated Inch, September 13, 1779, he speaks of his "tedious, expensive law process with the duke of Argyle" as nearly ended. He gained a portion of his ancient patrimony, and lived to settle up his affairs. He died on Inch Kenneth, December 10, 1783. Sir Allan's only son died in infancy. His daughter Maria was married to Charles MacLean of Kinlochaline; Sibella married John MacLean of Inverscadell, by whom she had a son and daughter; and Ann died unmarried.

The name of Sir Allan MacLean is still spoken of with great respect in Mull and the adjacent islands. He was particularly noted for his hospitality to strangers, amiability of disposition, methodical manners, and courteous bearing. He was thoroughly beloved by the MacLeans, who looked upon him as their chief, and were obedient to his desires.

Sir Allan lies buried near the spot where he explained to Doctor Johnson his American campaign. The grave is at the north-east corner of the old ruined chapel, and surrounded by a low stone wall. The grave is covered

---

* In a petition of Archibald MacLean of Pennycross against lord Armidale's interlocutors, dated February 16, 1808, I learn that Sir Allan's law-suit grew out of a contract entered into between Sir Lachlan MacLean and lord Lorn, in 1634, whereby Sir Lachlan agreed to become a vassal of Lorn's in certain lands, and among others, those of Brolass. These lands were afterward erected into the Barony of Aros, and afterward adjudged from the MacLeans by the marquis of Argyle. In the year 1783, by a decree-arbitral, Sir Allan gained possession of the lands in dispute. Sir Allan was succeeded in these lands by his son-in-law, Charles MacLean of Kinlochaline; but the latter allowing his affairs to fall into confusion, the estates were judicially sold, having been divided into three lots, one of which was purchased by Archibald MacLean of Pennycross.

† Boswell's *Life of Johnson.*

228   HISTORY OF THE CLAN MACLEAN.

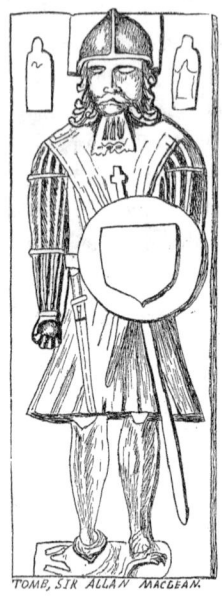

TOMB, SIR ALLAN MACLEAN.

by a sculptured sand-stone, seven feet long by two feet six inches wide, and probably removed from Iona. The engraving of it, as well as the sketch of the chapel, showing the stone inclosure, was made on the spot, at my request, by Colin A. MacVean, F. R. G. S. The figure is in high relief and dressed in the old quilted armor used in the Highlands some three or four hundred years ago. By the side of the head are two figures representing a monk and nun praying. The feet rest upon a hound, as was customary on the tombs of chiefs. The right hand grasps a ball and the left supports a shield, which, unlike those on the chiefs' tombs in Iona, is without device. The arms are the old two handed broad-sword and the dirk. The hair is shown long and curling, and the upper lip covered by a mustache. The left foot has been broken off. The grave needs some repairs, and the MacLeans should see to it.

The old chapel remains the same as when seen by Dr. Johnston in 1773, save a portion of the east wall has been thrown down, and the altar and bell have been removed. This venerable structure is sixty feet in length and thirty in breadth. We have no knowledge when it was built; doubtless it was constructed under the indefatigable labors of the monks of Iona. Dean Monro, who visited the island in 1549, speaks of it.

RUINS ON INCH-KENNETH.

XXIII. Sir Hector MacLean, Bart, Twenty-third Chief of MacLean.
Sir Allan MacLean having died without male heirs, he was succeeded in his

THE HOUSE OF BROLASS—1600 to 1889.   229

titles by his nearest of kin, Hector MacLean, the immediate descendant of his grand-uncle, Hector Og, second son of Donald, first MacLean of Brolass. As already noted, Hector Og married a daughter of MacNeill of Barra, by whom he had two sons, Donald, who died young, and John. Hector Og lost his life in crossing the sea from Mull to Barra in a small open boat, and was succeeded by his only surviving son,

John MacLean, married to Florance, daughter of Mac-

RUINS OF INCH KENNETH CASTLE.

Lean of Garmony, brother of Lochbuy, by whom he had one son, Donald MacLean, married first, Mary, daughter of John Dickson, of Glasgow, by whom he had several sons and daughters. His sons by this marriage all died young, except Hector; his daughter, Janet (who died in May, 1836), was married to General Allan MacLean, son of Donald MacLean of Torloisk; her sisters died unmarried. His second wife was Margaret, daughter of James Wall of Clonea castle, in Waterford, by whom he had Fitzroy Jeffreys Grafton.

Sir Hector MacLean became seventh Baronet of Morvern. In his earlier years he served for some time in the army, but during the greater portion of his days he lived a retired life. He died without issue, November 2, 1818, and was succeeded by his half brother,

XXIV. Sir Fitzroy Jeffreys Grafton MacLean, Bart, Twenty-fourth Chief of MacLean.

This is an exceedingly strange name for the chief of MacLean. The previous chiefs had but one, and they were content with the good old names of Lachlan, Hector, Allan, and John.

Sir Fitzroy Jeffreys Grafton MacLean in early years made the profession of arms his choice. September 24, 1787, he obtained his commission as ensign in the twenty-ninth regiment, and rapidly rose to the rank of General, passing through the following grades: Lieutenant, June 19, 1788; Captain, July 15, 1793; Major, March, 1795; Lieutenant-Colonel, November 18, 1795; Colonel, September 25, 1803; Major-General, July 25, 1810; Lieutenant-General, June 4, 1814; General, January 10, 1837. In 1793, he was at the capture of the island of Tobago and in the attack on Martinique. In 1803, he was appointed commandant of the Batavians, who were received into the

15

British service on the surrender of the Dutch West India colonies. In the expedition for the capture of Surinam, he commanded the advanced corps of the army. In 1805, he was at the capture of the Danish islands of St. Thomas and St. John, the government of which was conferred upon him in 1808, and continued as such until 1815. His administration of the affairs of those islands, his impartial conduct, mild sway, and kind disposition, were such as to endear him to all classes of the inhabitants, and when he took his departure, it was amidst the universal regret of the people. For his gallant behavior at the capture of the island of Gaudaloupe, in 1810, he received and was permitted to wear a medal. In June, 1815, he returned to Europe, after passing, with very little interval, a period of twenty-eight years on active service in the hot climate of the West Indies. On his return he resided chiefly in London. In 1794, he married the widow of John Bishop, of Barbadoes, and only child of Charles Kidd, and by her had several children, all of whom died in childhood except Charles Fitzroy and Donald. His wife dying in 1832, he married, September 17, 1838, Frances, widow of Henry Campion, of Sussex county. Sir Fitzroy J. G. MacLean died July 5, 1847. His son Donald became a barrister at law and a member of parliament. He married, in 1827, Harriet, daughter of General Frederick Maitland, and died in 1874.

XXV. Sir Charles Fitzroy MacLean, Bart, Twenty-fifth Chief of MacLean.

Charles Fitzroy succeeded to the titles of his father, and became the ninth Baronet of Morvern. He was born October 14, 1798. He was educated at Eton College and the Royal Military College, Sandhurst. In 1816, he entered the Scots Guard, and afterward commanded the 81st regiment. For some time he was military secretary at Gibraltar. In 1846, he retired from the army, being at that time Colonel of the 13th Light Dragoons. In person he was tall, of a manly appearance and pleasing address. He took a lively interest in the historical details of his family in past times. On the attempt to abolish the Highland garb in the army, Sir Charles was prominent among those of his countrymen who opposed the change.

May 10, 1831, Sir Charles married Emily Eleanor, fourth daughter of the honorable and Rev. Jacob Marsham, D.D., canon of Windsor, who died April 12, 1838, and by her had Fitzroy Donald, his heir and successor; Emily Frances Harriet; Louisa Marianne, married July 12, 1860, to Hon. R. P. Nevill, second son of the earl of Abergavenny; Fanny Henrietta, married October 2, 1855, to Admiral Sir A. W. A. Hood, R. N.; and Georgina Marcia, married October 20, 1868, to John A. Rolls of The Hendre.

Sir Charles died at West Cliffe House, Folkestone, December 27, 1883. The character of the deceased baronet was highly appreciated by his neighbors, and one of the local journals, in noting his demise, said: "A more liberal-minded gentleman, one more generally respected, we shall not have to reside with us again, and whilst his advanced age rendered death a visitor that must be expected, the community will feel that it has sustained a loss in this high souled gentleman which will not soon be replaced."

XXVI. Sir Fitzroy Donald MacLean, Bart., Twenty-sixth Chief of MacLean,

And tenth Baronet of Morvern, was born May 18, 1835. He entered the Thirteenth Light Dragoons as cornet, and in 1852 promoted a Lieutenant; 1854, Captain; 1856, Major; 1861, Lieutenant-Colonel; in 1871, commanding Thirteenth Hussars; Colonel commanding West Kent Yeomanry Cavalry in 1880. In 1854-5, he served in Bulgaria and the Crimea, and was with his regiment at the landing at Eupatoria cavalry affair of Bulganak, battle of the Alma, and siege of Sebastapol. May 18th, 1855, he received the Crimean medal for his gallant conduct in the Crimea. He also received two clasps and the Turkish war medal. In 1859 was aid-de-camp to field-marshal lord Seaton, and in 1860 the same to general Sir George Brown. In 1865 he was selected to report on the French cavalry manœuvres, and was frequently in conversation with the French emperor.

SIR FITZROY D. MACLEAN, BART.

Besides being a man of soldierlike qualities, a keen sportsman, both on the moor and across country, and an excellent horseman, Sir Fitzroy is a fine linguist and an extensive traveler. He has visited most European cities, especially those in Norway, Denmark, France, Italy, Turkey, etc. Soon after the American civil war he was stationed with his regiment in Canada; and part of his leave of absence was spent in traveling in the United States, when he visited most of the battle fields. He looks back with the greatest pleasure to the courtesy he received in the United States.

In person, Sir Fitzroy is rather tall and spare; in manners affable and polite, and possesses all the elements of a cultivated gentleman. In his family he is kind and affectionate, and in all respects a model husband and father. He has hosts of friends every-where. He loves Scotland, and visits it every summer. He is proud of his noble line of ancestors, and has a kind word and an affectionate grasp of the hand for every member of the clan MacLean.

Sir Fitzroy married, January 17, 1872, Constance Marianne, younger daughter of George Holland Ackers, Esq., of Moreton Hall, Cheshire, and by her has Hector Fitzroy, an Eton volunteer in training for the army, born in 1873; Charles Lachlan, in training for the navy, born in 1874; Fitzroy Holland, born in 1876, died April, 1881; John Marsham, born in 1879; and Finovala Marianne Eleanor, born in 1887.

Lady MacLean is of fair complexion, light hair, an expressive and intelligent countenance. She is very much interested in the history of the clan, and is in every respect worthy of the place she gracefully occupies. Did she live in olden times, she would be noted for her affection for her people, and would, in turn, be loved by all. She loves and honors the name of the race as much as if she had been a daughter of an ancient warrior chief of MacLean.

CHAPTER VIII.

THE HOUSE OF LOCHBUIE.

The Western Isles have ever been, and will continue to be, noted for their picturesque and romantic scenery. No other place in Scotland affords so enchanting a view as that commanded by Lochbuie House and Moy castle. Whether viewed from the castle, the mansion, the plain, the summit of Ben Buy, or any other point of observation, the eye is delighted and the mind enraptured with the mighty power of grandeur and beauty that lies before him. Even if divested of the works of man, the beauty is not apparently lessened. Taking the summit of Moy castle as the point of observation, the eye beholds the great plain, called Magh, spreading out from the loch to the north-west, reaching to the foot of Ben Buy and Ben Magh. Over this plain may be seen many houses, and the ruins of a druidical circle. To the north, Loch Uisg rests between precipitous mountains, with its outlet flowing along the base of the castle. A projecting spur of a neighboring ben divides Magh from the plain of Laggan, where are other houses and the ruins of a chapel, now used for a mausoleum, and said to have been founded by St. Columba. These

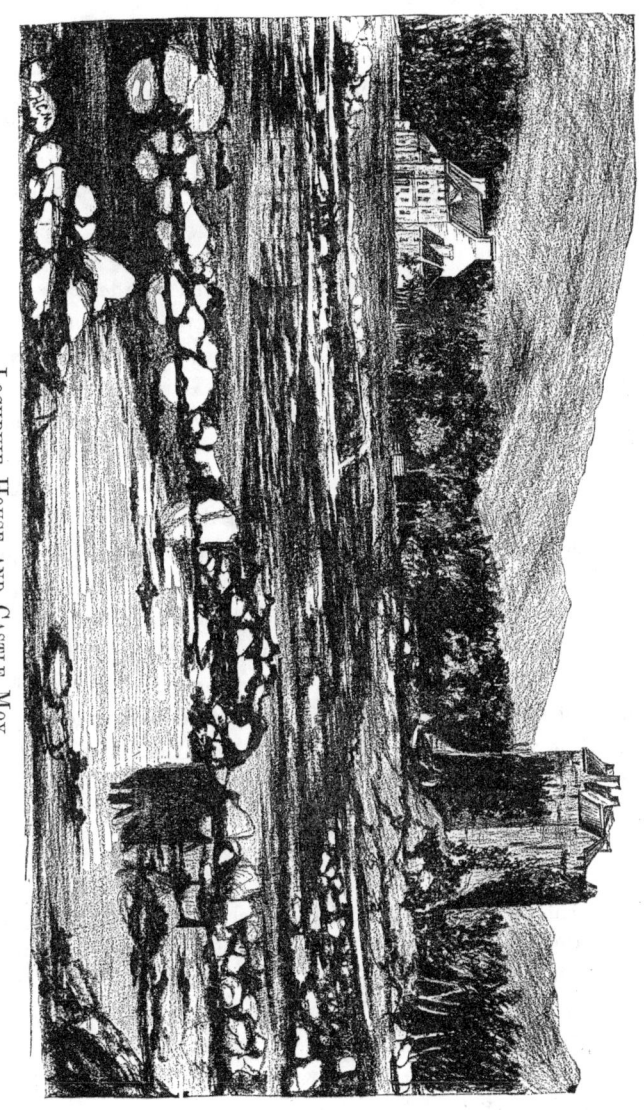

Lochbuie House and Castle Moy.

plains are under a high state of cultivation and produce abundantly, notwithstanding the fact that they have been tilled for over five hundred years. Looking south, is that beautiful sheet of water called Loch Buy, three miles long by two miles wide, hemmed in by mountains on the right whose altitudes vary from thirteen hundred to twenty-three hundred and fifty-four feet. On the left, the point of Laggan varies from nine hundred and sixty-seven to thirteen hundred and twenty-nine feet above the level of the sea. At the head of the loch and on the plain of Magh, the MacLeans of Lochbuy established their seat five hundred years ago.

The choice of this place for a home was one of great wisdom; for it is not only inviting, but its somewhat secluded position afforded a great natural shelter in days of danger and of war. The family who was allotted this territory has been fortunate, for amidst the stormy commotions which from age to age overwhelmed so many powerful houses in the Highlands, it has retained its original inheritance unimpaired, and maintained a high and independent position among the families of the Isles.

Unfortunately, most of the history of this family has been lost. In other histories, here and there, we catch glimpses of the bravery of the intrepid warriors of Lochbuy. I spent nearly four weeks, during the months of June and July, 1887, and much of the time in the charter room, and examined all the old documents belonging to the family. While there is much valuable material, there are but few documents that antedate 1750. There is but little material there that goes to make up a history of the family prior to the above date. The most valuable paper is an inventory of documents, made in 1761, but none of them are there now. There is also an inventory of charters from 1493 to 1630, and still another of the charters found among the documents of John and Archibald MacLean in November, 1785.

The word Lochbuy has been variously spelled, but the correct way is Lochbuidhe, and means Yellow lake. In the earlier documents it is spelled Lochbowie, Lochbowy, Lochboy, Lochbuye, Lochboyg, and by the family, until quite recently, almost uniformly Lochbuy. The method now adopted, and the one best suited to the pronounciation, is Lochbuie. In the inventory of 1761 I find both Lochbuy and Lochbuie used. This is the earliest date I have found for the use of the latter method. It will, however, be used in the remainder of this chapter. As to the spelling of the name MacLean, that is treated in Chapter XXXVI.

I. Eachann Reaganach, First MacLean of Lochbuie,

Or Hector the Stern, was the first laird and the founder of the family of

The House of Lochbuie.

Lochbuie. He was a son of John Dubh MacLean, fourth chief of Duard. He was a noted warrior in his day, and between him and his brother Lachlan always existed a strong affection, and were never separated in their warlike expeditions. Some of his exploits have already been noticed.

It is related that when Hector went to Lochbuie he found the lands possessed by the chief of MacFadyean, and obtained permission to build a fortalice or keep at the head of Lochbuie. When it was completed Hector ascended to the top, and, taking a bow and arrow, took aim at a bone MacFadyean was then eating from, and pierced it with the arrow. MacFadyean simply remarked, "It is time I was leaving;" took his departure, and gave Hector no trouble.

It is possible that Hector built in part Moy castle.* In the lower part it bears marks of a high antiquity, and at the time it was possessed by Hector may have been in a ruined condition. It is now one of the best preserved castles in the Hebrides, and until within the last few years its roof was kept entire. It is located on a low rock nearly midway across the head of the bay, and at high tide its base is washed by the sea. For the most part it is built of flat stones, thoroughly cemented together, being broadest at the base. The gate or door-way faces the north, and was formerly protected by a fosse. The gateway is protected by a wooden door, which swings inward; and in turn is guarded by an iron grating on hinges, which again is secured by a wooden beam built into the wall, which may be moved at will, but can not be taken out of the wall. In the wall, to the west, is a recess, where the gateman was constantly stationed. The floor of the interior of the first story is a solid rock, in the center of which is a basin four feet in depth, which is always full of water, but never overflows. Where the water comes from is unknown. In the east wall is a passage-way leading to the stairs, which passes through the east wall to the south-east corner of the second story. From that point upward the stairway is spiral, all of the steps composed of stone. Over the first passage-way, and in the wall, is the vault which held the dead during the funeral obsequies. The second and third floors are formed of solid stone arches. The second story was the judgment hall, and just off from it, and within the east wall, is the chapel, which is reached by a door-way from the spiral stairs. In the south-west corner is the dungeon, which extends from the second floor down to the level of the ground floor. It does not admit of a ray of light, and so constructed as to contain water, and

---

* In Gaelic, Caisteal nan Maoidh, Castle of Threatening.

on the floor is placed a single stone, upon which the prisoner must stand, or else drown. Where the water comes from is unknown. There is an escape to prevent an overflow. The third floor was the banqueting hall. The fourth and fifth stories had their floors composed of wood. Here chimneys, fireplaces, and windows may be seen. On the summit, at the north side, is a parapet, where a watchman was constantly on duty. The height of the castle is fifty-five feet, and on the north and the south sides the walls, on the exterior, are thirty-two feet; on the east and west sides, thirty-seven feet. At all places the walls are seven feet in thickness.

Hector Reaganach received his charter from the lord of the Isles, and hence was feudally independent of Duard. He married Christina, daughter of Malcolm MacLeod of Glenelg and Harris. He had six sons, Charles, settled in Glen Urquhart, Murdoch, Donald, Ewen, Thomas, and Malcolm. The date of his death is not preserved.

II. Murdoch, Second MacLean of Lochbuie.

Hector was succeeded in his estates by Murdoch. I have been unable to learn any thing concerning him. He was succeeded by his son,

III. John, Third MacLean of Lochbuie.

"In 1461 John of Yle, earl of Ross and Lord of the Isles, granted to his kinsman John the son of Murdac McGilleoin of Lochboyg the following lands in Locheale in his lordship of Lochaber."* The lands were twenty-one in number. John had a daughter, who was married to William, seventh MacLeod of Harris. He was succeeded by

IV. Hector, Fourth MacLean of Lochbuie.

Hector is mentioned as laird of Lochbuie in 1475,† and called Hector McGilleoin of Lochboyg. At Edinburgh, December 22, 1478, he witnessed the confirmation of a charter by David, earl of Crawford, to David Lindsay of Buky, of lands in Forfar. His name occurs as Hector Makgilleon of Loichbowe. He married Marian, daughter of Alastair Crotach, eighth MacLeod of Harris. He died about 1480, and was succeeded by his son,

V. John Og, Fifth MacLean of Lochbuie.

John Og, or young John, appears to have made a great figure in his time. He was of such prominence that James IV. attempted to win him, and further appears to have been a favorite of that monarch. Previous to his lairdship the principal lands were those of Glenforsay and Moloras, held from the Lord of the Isles. Those of Lochiel were only nominally held. Dated

---

* *Origines Parochiales Scotiæ*, Part 1, Vol. II., pp. 181–183.   † *Ibid.*

August 1, 1492, at Oransay, John received a charter of the office of bailliary of the south half of the island of Tiree, from John, Fourth Lord of the Isles, and Alexander of Lochalsh.* On the final forfeiture of the Lord of the Isles, in 1493, John MacLean made his submission to the king. At Edinburgh, March 22, 1493–94, the king confirms charter to his esquire, John Makgilleoun of Lochboye, of the lands of Growding, Culchelle, Kelbeg, Rengoun, etc., in the Isle of Mull and others forfeited by John, Lord of the Isles. He also receives lands in Inverness also forfeited by the Lord of the Isles.† At Stirling, November 10, 1495, he witnessed the confirmation by the king of a charter granted in 1409 by John of the Isles to his brother, Hugh, lord of Sleat. ‡ February 27, 1499, there was granted a respite to John McClan of Lochbo and all his accomplices for the "herschipp" of Ewin Allanson. ‖ As previously noted (page 59), he was one of the prime movers in the rebellion of Donald Dubh in 1503. After MacLean of Duard set the example, in 1505, John made his submission to the king. In 1513, he engaged in a war with the Camerons concerning the lands of Lochiel, and soon after a feud broke out with MacLean of Duard regarding their conterminous lands in Morvern and the Isle of Tiree, which was checked by the attentive care of the king. For the part he took in the rebellion of Sir Donald of Lochalsh, he received remission, March 14, 1517, for himself and all his kin and servants.§ At the time Argyle and Lachlan Catanach sent in their petitions, John also sent his. Having failed to possess himself of the lands of Lochiel, Duror and Glenco, in 1522, he sold them to Sir John Campbell of Calder. In 1528, he took part in avenging the murder of Lachlan Catanach MacLean. January 14, 1538, there is a precept for confirmation to Murdac McGillean, natural son to John McGillean of Lochboy, of the lands of Barre, Drimnin, Achzawall, and others in Morvern. It was about this time he and his two older sons, one of them the famous Eoghann a' Chinn bhig, were killed in a feud with Hector MacLean of Duard. At the time of his death his possessions comprehended lands in Mull, Tiree, and Morvern, and the islands of Jura and Scarba. He was succeeded in his estates by his illegitimate son,

VI. Murchadh Gearr, Sixth MacLean of Lochbuie.

The legend concerning Murchadh Gearr, or short Murdoch, is that his uncle Murdoch MacLean of Scallasdale desired to rob him of his estates.

* Gregory's *Western Highlands*, p. 55; Lachlan MacLean's *Iona*, p. 58. †*Reg. Mag. Sig.*, Lib. VIII., Nos. 114–116. ‡ *Ibid.*, Lib. XIII., No. 186. ‖ *Reg. Sec. Sig.*, Vol. I, fol. 114. § *Reg. Sec. Sig.*, Vol. CI.

Short or little Murdoch fled to Ireland and there ingratiated himself into the favors of the earl of Antrim. He returned with a party of resolute fellows, and landed near Moy castle after dark. He sought out his old nurse, who told him of a stratagem by which he could gain admission into the castle. She was to let loose the cattle, and when the men came out of the castle to drive them back to their inclosure, Murdoch and his men were to rush for the gateway of the castle. As the woman's husband was the gate-keeper, Murdoch protested against the plan, as it would endanger his life. As to that, replied the nurse, "Leig an tearbull leis a chraicionn," let the tail go with the hide. The stratagem succeeded, and that night the castle was in his possession. Little Murdoch next roused his friends and prepared to meet his uncle. Murdoch of Scallasdale received support from the Stewarts of Appin, and between the opponents a battle was fought in Grulin. From there the uncle marched his forces into the glen just east of Ben Buy, and almost in sight of Moy castle. Little Murdoch took a few of his followers, stole into his uncle's camp, and to his tent fastened the couples of an old kiln. Then entering the tent he thrust his dirk into his uncle's hair, pinning it to the ground. In the morning the uncle saw the warning and guessed whose work it was. Remorse seized him and he went quietly back to his own estates. In June, 1542, Murdoch was confirmed in all the estates of his father by the king, and erected into the Barony of Moy. In 1543, he espoused, along with the other MacLeans, the cause of Donald Dubh, who had again escaped from prison, and signed the petition of the Islemen in 1545, addressed to Henry VIII., and on the death of Donald Dubh, opposed the claims of Donald Gorm, in 1546. Murdoch Gearr died January, 1586. He married Anne, daughter of Sorley Buy, and by her had John Mór, and a daughter, Anne, who married John, son and heir of Sir Alexander MacNachten, who fell at Flodden field in 1513.

VII. John Mór, Seventh MacLean of Lochbuie,

Was a man of good parts, singular courage and great magnanimity, and in favor with James VI. It is related that in Scotland there was an Italian reputed to be a famous swordsman, who challenged any man in the king's army to encounter him. John Mór accepted the challenge, fought and killed him on the stage in Edinburgh, in presence of the king and court, which gave great satisfaction to the Scots. In the act of 1587, called "The General Bond," passed for the quieting and keeping in obedience the Borders, Highlands, and Isles, the name of John Mór occurs in the appended list of the landlords, along with others to the number of 136. He is ninety-ninth on the list; Sir Lachlan of Duard, seventy-sixth; Ewen MacLean of Ardgour, seventy-seventh; and Hector MacLean of Coll, ninety-eighth. On March 20, 1588, John Achinross procured authority to compel John Mór to release John Roy MacLean, whom he had imprisoned. The complaint alleges that John Roy "being desirous to visit Johnne McClayne of Lochbuy his chieff and to do unto him sic plesure and service as he wes able according to his dewitie," he had passed to Lochbuy in April 1586, expecting to have received " sic enterteynment and gude behaviour of the said Johnne as his voluntarie offer of service and obedience merite;" but the said chief "instigat and steirit up be sum personis, the said complenaris unfriendis," had immediately "putt violent handis in the said complenare, laid him in prisone in the irnis, quhairin he lies kept and detenit him sensyne," thus usurping the king's authority.* John Mór MacLean died before the year 1600. He married a daughter of MacDonald of Islay, and had two sons, Hector, his heir and successor, and Charles, progenitor of the MacLeans of Tapull.

VIII. Hector, Eighth MacLean of Lochbuie.

Hector MacLean assisted the MacDonalds of Islay, when the clan MacLean took its vengeance for the death of Sir Lachlan Mór. He was taken prisoner by Lochiel during the contest; but in turn avenged himself by buying the lands of Lochiel for a small sum; but finding, by fruitless attempts, he could not gain possession, he sold the same, in 1609, to Argyle, for four hundred marks, the same he had paid for it. In 1608, he met the bishop of the Isles at Aros castle; in 1609, signed his name, McClane of Lochbowy, to the declaration of religion,† and was present when the famous statutes of Icolmnkill were enacted in the same year. ‡ He was the first Protestant of his family. In the inventory taken in 1761 ‖ is a statement of an "original retour of service of Hector MacGilleoun as grandson and heir to Murdoch McGilleoun of Lochbuie in all and haill the lands of Mollerow as therein mentioned, viz., the penny land of Moy with the castle and lake of Lochbuie and others therein enumerated, all united into a barony called the Barony of Moy. Lands returned at one hundred and sixty marks new and eighty old extent, are held simple ward of the crown, and are returned to have been in non-entry from April, 1558, till the death of Murdoch McGilleoun, in January, 1586; and from thence, till the date of retour by reason of the time of his grandfather's death thirty years old, not having followed forth his father's

---

* *Register of the Privy Council*, Vol. IV., p. 263. † *Collectanea de Rebus Albanicis*, pp. 115–118. ‡ *Ibid.*, pp. 118–120. ‖ Lochbuie Charter Room.

right." This retour proceeds before the sheriff deputy of Argyle, and dated November 5, 1609, but not yet retoured to the chancery. The same inventory further adds: "Precept forth of the chancery for investing Hector McLaine, great grandson to Murdoch Maclaine of Lochbuie, in all and haill the lands of Mollerow as therein specified, viz., the penny land of Moy with the castle thereof and lake of Lochbuy as therein enumerated." Precept dated February 21, 1616. This would appear that Hector, eighth of Lochbuie, was now dead, although I have no other evidence, save what appears in the *Inquisitionis Generalis* (No. 15), for 1615 : " Hector McCleane de Lochbowie, hæres Murdochi McCleane de Lochbowie, *proavi*, in terris de Molorowis subscriptis." He was married to a daughter of John Gorm Campbell of Lochnell, and was succeeded by his son,

IX. Hector Odhar, Ninth MacLean of Lochbuie.

Hector Odhar, or Swarthy Hector, as already noticed, was in possession of the estates in 1616. According to Douglas's *Peerage*, on June 11, 1612, upon his father's resignation, he received a charter under the great seal, of the whole estate in Mull, in the shires of Inverness, Tarbat, and Perth. He made his appearance before the privy council in 1616, and along with other chiefs, submitted to very strict measures for his future behavior, an account of which is given on page 157. During the month of July, 1617, he made his appearance before the council. This he appears to have done every year afterward. July 23, 1622, he appeared at Edinburgh, and along with Sir Donald Gorm, Sir Rorie MacLeod, the lairds of MacKinnon and Coll, agreed to repair and build their parish kirks, and should meet the bishop of Icolmkill, and "thair confer, ressoun, resolve, and conclude upoun the forme and maner and upoun the tyme quhen and in quhat forme the saidis kirkis sall be biggit." * On December 9, 1625, he made over the lands of Moy to his eldest son, Murdoch.† In 1626, Thomas Knox, bishop of the Isles, reports "Hector M^ccleane of Lochbowie" as one of the proprietors of Mull.‡ He died about the year 1628. He married the only daughter of Sir Lachlan Mór MacLean, and by her had Murdoch, his heir, Lachlan, and a daughter, Margaret, who married Donald MacQuarrie of Ormaig.

X. Murdoch Mór, Tenth MacLean of Lochbuie.

The records concerning this chieftain are few. He was served and retoured heir to his father February 23, 1630. August 10, 1631, he obligated

---

* *Collectanea de Rebus Albanicis*, p. 122. † *General Register of Sasones;* also, Lochbuie Charter Room. ‡ *Collectanea de Rebus Albanicis*, p. 124.

himself to Martin MacGillivray, minister of the kirks of Killeane and Killenachin, that his vassals and tenants, living within said parishes, shall pay their yearly dues during the lifetime of said Martin; they shall give due obedience to the discipline of the kirk; to repair said kirks; to participate in the sacraments and to conform to the order of the kirk; they shall not convene in any other chapel; and in case either he (Murdoch) or his vassals shall fail to perform said agreement, then the said Murdoch shall pay to Martin "the sowme of ane hundrethe pundis mony foirsaid as for cost, skaith, damnage, expenss and interess to be maid and sustenit be thame thairthrow."* August 29, 1634, he appeared at Inverary, as summoned to testify before the commissioners respecting certain rights in regard to fishing, and other matters pertaining to the Isles, which has been fully set forth on page 163. Hector married Julian, fifth daughter of Sir Robert Campbell of Glenurchy, and dying without issue (about the year 1662), he was succeeded by his brother,

XI. Lachlan Mór, Eleventh MacLean of Lochbuie,

Who was served and retoured heir in the whole estate April 12, 1663, and afterward was served heir in special to his brother, January 8, 1668. In the *Inquisitiones Generalis*, No. 712, under date of January 8, 1663, occurs the following: "Lauchlanus McLeane de Lochbuy, hæres Murdochi McLeane de Lochbuy, fratris." This probably gives the actual date of the death of Murdoch, and the accession of Lachlan. The inventory of 1761 contains the following, dated March 2, 1670: "Charter under the great seal in favor of Hector McLean, eldest son of Lachlan McLean of Lochbuie, and the heirs male to be procreated between him and Margaret, daughter of Colin Campbell, Lochanell." Lachlan reserves life interest; also a portion of land to Allan, another son.† On October 18, 1675, he made a raid on the Isles of Garvelloch, and carried away much plunder. Noticed on page 193. Lachlan Mór was married to Margaret, daughter of Hector, second MacLean of Torloisk. By his wife he had Murdoch Og, John, Hector, and Mary. Murdoch married a daughter of Sir Hugh Campbell of Calder, but died before his father, and without issue. John married Isabel, daughter of MacDougall of Dunolly, and also died before his father, and without issue. Mary married Ewen, ninth MacLean of Ardgour. Lachlan also had an illegitimate son, Allan, for whom he reserved certain lands. Lachlan Mór died about the year 1684, and was succeeded by his third son,

XII. Hector, Twelfth MacLean of Lochbuie.

---

* *Collectanea de Rebus Albanicis*, p. 124.   † Lochbuie Charter Room.

The earliest notice we have of Hector is in a letter written by Alexander MacNaughtan of Dundaraw, April 1, 1671, in which he states that, the night before, Colonel Menzies, the laird of Lochnell, and young Lochbuie were at Inverary, and after cups Lochbuie offered to beat the colonel. In the midst of the difficulty the light went out, and then a pistol was fired at young Lochbuie, but, missing him, the bullet struck and killed Lochnell. All were under the influence of liquor. The blame was laid upon a MacGregor, a servant of Menzies.* He was in the revolution of 1679, on behalf of James II., and proved himself an active partisan. On March 21, 1689, James II. appointed him Lieutenant-Colonel of the regiment " whereof Sir John McLaine, Baronet is Col." † He was victor at the battle of Knockbreck, in Badenoch, which has been so forcibly and graphically described by Phillips of Amryscloss.‡ He was compelled to surrender to Argyle, October 22, 1690,‖ and soon after surrendered Moy castle, which was immediately garrisoned by twenty-four men, under Colin Campbell of Bragleine.§ On March 27, 1705, he gave over his estate to Murdoch, his eldest son, reserving to himself a life interest. At the same time, he gave a life rent of the lands of Pennygoun to John, of the lands of Garmony to Allan, and of the lands of Knockroy to Lachlan. Hector married Margaret, daughter of Colin Campbell of Lochnell, and besides the above-mentioned sons, had Margaret, Mary, and ——, " all of whom honorably married." Hector died in 1707, and is buried in the old chapel, on the estate, and now used for a mausoleum. On the headstone of his grave, he is called " Baron Sir Hector MacLean." He was succeeded in his estates by his eldest son,

XIII. Murdoch, Thirteenth MacLean of Lochbuie.

What part Murdoch and the MacLeans of Lochbuie took in the revolution of 1715, I have no information whatever. Some of them, doubtless, were with Sir John MacLean at Sheriffmuir. Their part at best could not have been much, for of the whole clan the words of MacAulay are very applicable : " The power, though not the spirit, of the clan had been broken by the arts and arms of the Campbells." ** There are letters in Lochbuie Charter Room, of date of 1720, in which Murdoch is addressed as " The Laird of Lochbuy," and also, " The Honored, The Laird of Lochbuy." Letters of similar address occur for the year 1734. In 1721, Helen, daughter of John and granddaughter

---

* *Appendix Sixth Report Hist. MS Com.*, pp. 699, 700. † Lochbuie Charter Room. ‡ See Appendix, Note C, No. 15. ‖ *Appendix Sixth Report Hist. MS Com.*, p. 629. § *Ibid.*, p. 634.
** *History of England*, Vol III., p. 301.

of Bishop Hector MacLean, served papers on Murdoch for certain moneys alleged to be due the complainant. The papers style him "Murdoch McLain of Lochbuy, eldest son of Hector McLean of Lochbuy."* Murdoch was married to Anne, daughter of Sir Hugh Campbell of Calder, by whom he had four daughters, the eldest having married Donald Campbell, of Airds. He died in the year 1727, and having no male issue, was succeeded by his brother,

XIV. John, Fourteenth MacLean of Lochbuie,

Who was second son of Hector, the twelfth MacLean of Lochbuie. John married Isabella, daughter of Duncan MacDougall of Dunolly. The inventory of 1761 states that on January 18, 1733, John disposed of his estates to his only son Lachlan.* The same document states that on December 14, 1739, "John McLean of Lochbuy becomes heir in general to his brother Murdoch." I am unable to determine the date of his death. He was succeeded by his son,

XV. Lachlan, Fifteenth MacLean of Lochbuie,

Who was married to a daughter of MacDougall of Dunolly, by whom he had Hector and Mary, the latter having married Allan MacLean of Drimmin. Lachlan was succeeded by his son,

XVI. Hector, Sixteenth MacLean of Lochbuie.

The inventory of 1761, shows that Lachlan MacLean disposed of his property to his eldest son Hector, dated February 22d, and on June 22, 1742, Hector resigns life rent to his father Lachlan. This is recorded in the Book of Sessions, January 12, 1757.* Hector was in full possession in 1744.* The MacLeans of Lochbuie took no part in the revolution of 1745-6, under Prince Charles. They had been warned that the attempt would be futile. Hector was never married, and his estates descended to a distant kinsman,

XVII. John, Seventeenth MacLean of Lochbuie.

Allan, third son of Hector, Twelfth MacLean of Lochbuie, married Julian, daughter of Lachlan MacLean of the family of Torloisk. He had several sons, all of whom died young except John. He had a daughter, Julian, who was married to Hector MacLean of Torren. On the death of Hector, Sixteenth of Lochbuie, Allan's son John became heir and successor, and the Seventeenth of Lochbuie.

It is probable that John became laird of Lochbuie a little prior to 1750. In that year we find him in full possession of the estates. Down to his time

---

* Lochbuie Charter Room.

the family resided in the castle. The following is the contract for building the new house near the castle, dated at Moy, May 22, 1750: "House to be 40 ft. long and 28 foot wide within walls, and side walls 18 ft. high, out of stone and lime, at following rates: Each rood of masonry 18£ Scots; five shillings for each foot plain hewn stone; 7 pence each foot of mouldings, and 7£ Scots for each vent to be carried up, with 12 pounds Scots for making up scaffold. One third to be paid in advance; one third when half done, and one third when completed. All materials to be furnished by Lochbuy. John MacLaine. Witnesses, Allan MacLean, Kilmory, John MacLean." * This house was completed in 1752, and since that time Moy castle has not been used for a residence. As early as 1759 John MacLean appears to have been oppressed with debts, for Hugh MacLean of Kingerloch, date June 5, 1759, speaks of "a dale of business to settle particularly upon account of my friend Lochbuy's sake."* From 1770 to 1774 the arrears on the estate were thought desperate. In 1750, Isabel MacDougall, relict of John MacLean (Fourteenth) of Lochbuie, served a summons on John MacLean, now of Lochbuy, for certain moneys from the estate alleged to be due her. It is more than probable that John inherited a considerable indebtedness along with the estates. There are many letters in the charter room which press him sorely for debts due, among which are quite a number from Brigadier Allan MacLean, then living in London.

October 13, 1758, he caused Hector MacLean of Killean and Allan MacLean of Kilmory to be locked up in Moy castle for certain misdemeanors. Afterward they brought suit against him for damages. This is the case alluded to by Boswell in his "Tour of the Hebrides." There is a very long and very interesting reply by John MacLean to the complaint presented, in the Lochbuie charter room. Briefly summed up, the answer is: *First.* Allan MacLean had irritated and threatened Lochbuie unnecessarily on divers occasions, and because a horse was refused to Hector, the latter slandered outrageously Lochbuie's daughter Peggie. For this Hector was forbid the house, on which account the complainants threatened and dogged Lochbuie, in so much so that he was forced to secure them. To prove his assertions true, Lochbuie names twenty witnesses, twelve of whom are MacLeans. *Second.* Answers the charge that he is in the habit of imprisoning men, five of whom are mentioned. Lochbuie alleges that one was a recruit for Captain MacLean of Brolass, one for stealing a cow, one for stealing a mare, and one for

---

* Lochbuie Charter Room.

fighting. Names of six witnesses given. *Third.* To the charge that he was an oppressor of his tenants and neighbors, he alleges that his tenants enjoyed more ease, were better treated, and more honest than ever before. Names nine witnesses. *Fourth.* To the charge that he protects thieves, the answer is a denial, and no thief lives on the estate, but before he became proprietor the estate suffered from thieves, and that in 1755 he returned three to Inverary. Three witnesses are mentioned. *Fifth.* To the charge that two persons live on his estate who are thieves, it is averred that they are innocent until proved guilty, and that they are as honest as their accusers. Three witnesses are given. *Sixth.* To the charge that the complainants while in the castle were exposed to the wind and weather, wanted the necessaries of life, and were confined from Friday till Sunday, it is answered that they were at large in the castle, and fared better than they did when at home, had sheets, blankets, coal, cooked meat, spirits, milk, nuts, and apples; were set at liberty at eight o'clock Saturday night, and then dined and drank punch with Lochbuie. Six witnesses are given, among whom appear the names of the mother of Sir Allan MacLean, and Alexander MacLean, surgeon. *Seventh.* To the charge that Lochbuie carried arms, it is answered that he is so entitled. *Eighth.* To the charge that Hector MacLean suffered in means and health by his being imprisoned, it is affirmed that the complainant is a bankrupt, and not worth any thing, and no complaint was made of his health until some time after. *Ninth.* To the charge that Kilmory died soon after, it is declared that after his release he was strong, and traveled through Mull and Morvern, and then took a journey into the low country, where he died. That Lochbuie had befriended him in many ways. Eleven witnesses are named. Lochbuie further alleges that when he "came to be Laird the country was wild, the people's grain destroyed and horses killed." There is also a private paper from an eye-witness, a female servant, which, if true, would have justified Lochbuie in taking summary measures on the culprits. Notwithstanding his defense, he was fined 500 marks Scots and £180 sterling of damages and expenses, or all told, $994.53.

Dr. Samuel Johnson and Boswell paid him a visit in 1773. The former called him "a true Highland laird, rough and haughty, and tenacious of his dignity;" and "a very powerful laird."[*] Boswell describes him as "a bluff, comely, noisy, old gentleman, proud of his hereditary consequence, and a very

---

* *Tour of the Hebrides*, p. 134.

hearty and hospitable landlord."* John died in the year 1785, and in the following November among his effects were found the charter of confirmation of the estates to John McGillian in 1493; charter to the estates in favor of John McGillian, 1537; charter of confirmation of estates to Murdoch MacLean, 1542; charter to Hector MacLean, 1612; charter of estates to Murdoch MacLean, 1625; and a charter in favor of Hector MacLean in 1670. John MacLean was married to Isabel, daughter of Donald, third MacLean of Brolass, and sister of Sir Allan MacLean. By his wife he had one son and three daughters, Archibald, Isabel, and Catherine. There was a daughter called Peggie. Whether or not this was one of the above, or still another named Margaret, I am unable to say. There was an illegitimate son named Gillean.

Prior to the year 1776, John made over his estate to his son, Archibald, who finding his estate so deeply involved, in above year, appointed two trustees, who in turn appointed John MacLean of Grulin, factor. About the same time Archibald obtained a captain's commission in the army, and started for America, where he joined the 84th or Royal Highland Emigrant Regiment. He possessed a harsh, quarrelsome nature. He quarreled with his commander, Brigadier Allan MacLean of Torloisk, and brought several charges against him. The court of inquiry sentenced Archibald to suspension from the army, which finding, on being presented to George III., was changed to dismissal. He left America for England in order to lay the matter fully before the king. On the way across the Atlantic he engaged in a quarrel with a traveler named Daniel Monroe, who tried his best to avoid Archibald. One day, threatening to kill Monroe, he started for his state-room, when Monroe waylaid him and ran a sword through him. For this Monroe was brought to trial in England and acquitted. The correspondence on this subject is voluminous in the charter-room of Lochbuie house. He was killed August 6, 1784.

While in Boston, Archibald married Barbara Lowther, who returned with him to England. She attempted to pacify Archibald during his quarrel with Monroe, but only received vile abuse from him, which is wholly unfit here to print. She applied to her father-in-law, John, for relief, but he refused, on the ground that not having been married one year, she was not entitled to any share in the estate under Scottish law. John, however, in various ways, spent £779 in her behalf. Barbara next petitioned the king for relief, on the grounds that Archibald had burdened himself with debt in purchasing his

---

* *Journal of a Tour of the Hebrides*, p. 270.

commission, and through this expenditure she had been left destitute. A deaf ear was turned to her.

John MacLean had his piper, and was, perhaps, the last of the Lochbuies who particularly favored this art. John MacLean, on the garrison staff, Fort William, Bengal, writing January 29, 1799, states that thirty years before " Hector MacLaine was piper to John Maclaine of Lochbooy, and was allowed to be the first in Scotland." *

Before leaving Scotland, Archibald, by will, devised all his estates to Murdoch, son of Lachlan MacLean of Knockoy, fourth son of Hector, twelfth MacLean of Lochbuie. Lachlan married Flora, daughter of Lachlan, sixteenth MacQuarrie of Ulva. He had a large family, the eldest of whom was

XVIII. Murdoch, Eighteenth MacLean of Lochbuie.

Murdoch entered the army as a lieutenant, October 21, 1761, and was connected with it for thirty-six years. In the early part of the American revolutionary war, he was engaged in raising tories for the army, and at that time was a member of the 114th regiment; and in 1775, added one hundred Highlanders to the Royal Highland Emigrant Regiment, to which he had been appointed captain June 14th, then stationed in Boston. Soon after he was placed in command of the Newcastle Jane, containing a cargo of clothing and provisions valued at £20,000, and with thirty recruits, all designed for the garrison at Halifax. On the way he was attacked by an American privateer, but succeeded in beating off his assailant, the latter having eleven killed and thirteen wounded.† In 1778, he was sent from Halifax by General Massey with dispatches to Sir William Howe, but was detained owing to the evacuation of Philadelphia. In 1782, he was sent with his regiment to South Carolina. In 1791, he was compelled to bring action against the trustees of his estate to give an account of their trust. This was not accomplished until the year 1793. It was about the same time he built the present mansion, known as Lochbuie House. He chose a most eligible site in every particular that could be desired by a proprietor of so extensive an estate. In 1793, he furnished one hundred men for the Argyleshire Fencibles. In 1794, he furnished one hundred men for the 98th Argyleshire Regiment, of which he was major. October 11, 1794, he was appointed lieutenant-colonel in the Dumbartonshire Regiment of Fencibles. February 17, 1797, he tendered three hundred men and the use of Moy castle for storing arms to the duke of York. In the same

---

* Lochbuie Charter Room.   † Letter of Major-General Eyre Massey, dated May 10, 1779, in Lochbuie Charter Room.

year, an attempt was made to sell the estate of Lochbuy on account of a debt resting upon it of £11,120. This somewhat alarmed Murdoch, and he drew up a petition to the duke of York, in which he enumerated the services he rendered the government. Besides this, he states that all the men he had raised for the Argyleshire and Dumbarton regiments were his own tenants, and at his own expense; and this expense, with a previous incumbrance on the estates, and a large family, had greatly embarrassed him. For all his services he asked for a higher rank and a position in the army for his son, Murdoch. This memorial received a curt reply from the duke, dated April 5, 1797, and referred him to the duke of Portland.* February 14, 1786, Murdoch married Jane, daughter of John Campbell of Airds, and by her had eleven children: Murdoch, his successor; John, a lieutenant in the 73d regiment, served in New South Wales, and lost his life in an engagement with the natives of Ceylon, in 1817; Jane, married to Captain Campbell, and had a numerous issue; Flora, married first to Dr. Allan MacLean, of the family of Brolass, by whom she had issue, and secondly, to Dr. Whitehead of Ayr; Margaret, married to Dugald MacDugall of Gallaneach, and had issue; Phœbe, married to Colonel Donald Gregorson of Barrichboye, and had issue; Elizabeth, married to Donald Campbell of Achnacraig, and had issue; Harriet, married to John Stewart of Fasnacloich, and had issue; Catherine, unmarried; Mary, married to John Gregorson of Ardtornish; and Jane, married to —— Scott of Ettrick Bank, county of Selkirk. I find no record of his death. He was succeeded by his son,

XIX. Murdoch, Nineteenth MacLean of Lochbuie,

Who was born August 1, 1791. He was a lieutenant in the Forty-second Royal Highlanders, and was present in some of the battles in which that regiment was engaged during the Peninsular war. He retired from the army in the year 1812; and on April 7, 1813, he married Christina, daughter of Donald MacLean, and by her had Murdoch, an officer in the Ninety-first foot or Argyleshire regiment, and died August 7, 1850, without taking possession of the estates; Donald; John Campbell; Alexander, married to Marian Palmer Sands; Lillias; Elizabeth Henrietta, married to Dr. Mackenzie; Marianne; Allan; Jane; and Margaret Maxwell, who died February 5, 1861. Murdoch died August 20, 1844, and was succeeded by his second son,

XX. Donald, Twentieth MacLean of Lochbuie,

Who was born October 26, 1816. Not expecting to come into possession

---

* Lochbuie Charter Room.

of the estate, Donald went to Batavia, Java, and there became a merchant, and succeeded in amassing a fortune. The death of his brother Murdoch revealed the deplorable state of the finances of the estates of Lochbuie, and Donald allowed them to be sold. He purchased it all in, and obtained sixty thousand acres, consisting of the original lands in Mull, possessed by his ancestors, and held them free of all incumbrance. He was married October 23, 1844, to Emilie Guillaumine, third daughter of Charles A. Vincent, and had issue, Murdoch Gillian, his heir and successor; Antoine, born in 1846; Emilie Guillaumine, married to Frederick Campbell; Rosa Elizabeth; and Christina Sarah. Donald died October 12, 1863. Donald was a man of great energy and enterprise. He commenced to improve his estates and put them under a high state of cultivation. He was very popular with all his tenants, and after his death they erected an obelisk to his memory, which stands near the roadside not far from the head of Loch Uisg. After his death, his widow repaired the ruins of the old chapel, on the plain of Laggan, and turned it into a mausoleum. In one tier of the vaults her body and that of Donald's lie side by side. He was an officer in the kirk (Presbyterian), and regularly worshiped in the little chapel that stands at the very head of Loch Uisg.

XXI. Murdoch Gillian, Twenty-first MacLean of Lochbuie.

The twenty-first MacLean of Lochbuie breaks the long record of single names, and for the first time the Lochbuie estates has a laird with a double name. But no one will have reason to complain, for both are good and honored MacLean names. Murdoch Gillian was born in Batavia, September 1, 1845, and came into possession of the whole estate on the death of his father. At the age of eight he left Batavia with his parents, and removed to Lochbuie. He was educated at Edinburgh Academy, and took a course of military training at a private school near London. In the year 1864 entered the Sixth or Carbineer regiment of dragoon guards, and rose to the rank of captain, and continued in the service for six years. During the Franco-Prussian war he was military correspondent of the "London Times," and was present at the battles of Gravelotte, Strasbourg, Metz, and Thionville. He is a large, well-proportioned man, and sandy complexioned. He has taken great pride in his estates, and added many improvements. He has built a wall around his fine gardens, and cultivates in them almost every flower that will grow in that latitude. The gardens are arranged after the English style. The crofter houses are by far the best I saw in the Highlands, and his tenants fare as well as any in Scotland. The road-ways are solid and durable. He has commenced a museum, which has already reached good proportions; established a fish-hatchery, and stocked Loch Uisg with American fish. For several years he has attempted to establish a hospital for seamen and others, and for that purpose has offered valuable donations. He has established episcopacy on the estates, and by outside assistance has erected a chapel not far from his residence. I was at his residence for four consecutive weeks, and found him, like all true Highland gentlemen, hospitable. In manner he is free, and disposed to enjoy the good things of life. He is tenacious on what he believes to be his rights, but liberal and forgiving, and his natural goodness of heart will undoubtedly lead him to prefer the native Highlander to imported help. The estate is now composed of thirty thousand acres. The present estate is bounded by Glen Mór on the north, running from the head of Loch Beg almost to Loch Spelve, thence south embracing the entire promontory south of Spelve and Uisg. The west line extends from Rudha Dubh (at the mouth of Loch Buy) across to the head of Loch Beg. On the 17th June, 1869, he was married to Catharine Marianna, youngest daughter of Salis Schwabe, Esq., of Glyngarth, Anglesey, and by her has issue, Kathlein Emilie, Mabel Julia, Edith Jane, Kenneth Douglas Lorn, and Ronald Gillian.

Murdoch G. MacLaine.

The cadets, septs, or branches of the Lochbuie family are numerous, but the records are very imperfect. Lieut.-Col. Murdoch Hector MacLean of the Seventy-seventh regiment, was the historian of the Lochbuie family, but I am unable to discover what became of his history. It is said to have been in the Lochbuie Charter room in 1839.

CHAPTER IX.
CLANN THEARLAICH O' BUI.

The Clann Thearlaich or Clan Tearlach, or offspring of Charles, sometimes spoken of as the MacLeans of the North, forms the first branch of Clann Ghilleain Locha-buidhe, or MacLeans of Lochbuie. The Clan Tearlach includes the MacLeans of Glen Urquhart and those of Dochgarroch, or Davochgarioch.

THE MACLEANS OF URQUHART.

Glen Urquhart, situated on the west side of Loch Ness, is about fifteen miles in length, and about the same distance south by west of Inverness. At the mouth of the Glen, or where the stream pours into Loch Ness, is the famous royal castle of Urquhart. The castle is of great antiquity; has a wonderful history; around it have been performed great deeds of valor; and, when thoroughly equipped for defense, would garrison six hundred men.

I. Sir Charles, First MacLean of Urquhart.

The progenitor of Clan Tearlach was Charles, eldest son of Hector Reaganach, first MacLean of Lochbuie. Charles, sometimes called Charles of Achat, was a distinguished warrior, and from his sovereign received the honor of knighthood, and thus became the first MacLean bearing a distinctive title. He was a follower of Donald, second Lord of the Isles, from whom he obtained certain lands in Glen Urquhart, one

URQUHART CASTLE.

of the loveliest vales in the Highlands. He was placed in charge of Urquhart castle by Alastair Carrach in, or soon after, the year 1394; and also, about the same time, became lord paramount of the town of Inverness, with certain privileges, among which was the right of raising one hundred armed men for the service of his sovereign. He is said to have built the castle of Bona, known as Caisteal Spioradan, or castle of spirits, near the lower end of Loch Ness. Of the many engagements in which he took a prominent part, the following, that occurred in 1386, has been preserved: The Clan Chattan, having raided Lochaber, also uplifted cattle from Kilmalew, the heritage of Hector Reaganach; whereupon Sir Charles went in pursuit, and overtook the spoilers near Ruthven castle, where he defeated Clan Chattan and rescued the cattle. In this action the MacGillimores were the principal sufferers, in consequence of the MacPhersons having refused to participate; but mortified at the discomfiture of their comrades, they rallied and pursued Sir Charles as far as Bencher, near Glen Tilt, when a second engagement took place, ending in the defeat of the MacPhersons. In the second encounter, Sir Charles was wounded. A history entitled "Clan Tarlach O' Buie" (p. 31) says mortally, and was borne off the field by his friends, and buried at Iona. He was married to a daughter of Farquhar Cumyn of Dalshangie. All authorities declare that he was succeeded by Hector Buie, but I am disposed to think that the author of "Clan Tarlach O' Buie" is correct in assigning Hector to a later period. He makes Ewen and Farquhar, Abbot of Tearne, the issue.

II. Sir Ewen, Second MacLean of Urquhart.

In 1421, Sir Ewen was confirmed by king James II. constable of Urquhart and captain of Bona or Spiritual castle. Urquhart castle was repaired and made to hold four hundred men. Sir Ewen, after a life of turmoil, died in 1439. He married lady Catherine, only child of Roderick of the Isles. By his wife he acquired the lordship of Ottar in Cowall. He left Charles, his heir, and Sween, or Simon, who inherited the estates of Ottar, and from whom Sir Alexander MacLean, who fought at Killiecrankie, was descended.

III. Sir Charles, Third MacLean of Urquhart.

Sir Tarlach, or Charles, was returned heir to his father as constable of Urquhart about 1439. In that year, he was witness to a bond given by the lord of the Isles. It is related he married a daughter of Grant of Frenchie, by whom he had issue—Hector, Alexander, Donald, and Angus. Donald was in command of Cairnburg at the time it was carried by assault by Lachlan Catanach MacLean. Donald was father of Agnes, or Annie, prioress of Iona.

IV. Hector Buie, Fourth MacLean of Urquhart.

Hector Buie succeeded to the estates of his father, and also as constable of Urquhart, about 1450. "In Hector's time, and for centuries thereafter, the herds of cattle reared on the rich pastures of Urquhart and Glenmoriston were an irresistible temptation to the cattle lifters of Lochaber, and numerous were the raids made by the Camerons and the Kennedies into the Glen, and deadly were the feuds that consequently arose. Hector Buie retaliated by marching a band of Urquhart men into Lochaber, while Lochiel happened to be in Ireland. 'Donald, chief of the Camerons,' says the old historian of Lochiel, with reference to the invasion,' was soon recalled from Ireland by the groans of the people, who were cruelly oppressed and plundered by a robber from the north, called Hector Buie MacLean, who, with a party of ruffians, took the opportunity of his absence to infest the country. Being joined by a sufficient party of his clan, he pursued the robbers, who fled before the news of his arrival, and overtook them at the head of Loch Ness. But Hector, with his prisoners, for he had taken many, and among them Samuel Cameron of Glenevis, head of an ancient tribe of that clan, escaped him by taking sanctuary in a strong house called castle Spiriten, where he barbarously murdered them. In revenge of their death, Donald caused two of Hector's sons, Donald and Hector, with others of the gang who had fallen into his hands, to be hanged in view of the father, a wretch so excessively savage that he refused to deliver them by way of exchange, though earnestly pressed to do so.' " * After Hector Buie had slain the prisoners in revenge for the murder of his two sons, he exhibited the trunkless heads from the ramparts, and then rushed out claymore in hand, when a desperate conflict ensued, which ended in the defeat of the Camerons. It must have been about the year 1452 that the following battle is said to have taken place: "We have already mentioned that the Borlum (MacIntosh) family were the terror and scourge of the neighboring lairds. However, MacLean of Dochgarroch, who had experienced much annoyance and oppression, made a bold attempt to resist Borlum's overbearing power, and set his threats at defiance, which so maddened him, that to be revenged he directed his son, and about thirty of his vassals and dependents, to proceed to Dochgarroch house, raze it to the ground, and destroy every thing belonging to his now mortal enemy. The good and worthy proprietor of Dochgarroch, being apprised of this force having marched, and the object in view, but ignorant of their number, sent twelve brave and faithful clansmen to watch young Borlum and his desperate companions in arms. On the north bank of the river, a little to the west of the ancient castle of Spirituel, the little band of the MacLeans met the more numerous one of Borlum advancing at a rapid rate; no words were exchanged, no explanation demanded; both

---

* *Transactions*, Gaelic Society, Inverness, p. 169; see also MacKenzie's *Hist. of Camerons*.

parties knew each other too well to require information as to either's mission. Undismayed by the disparity in numbers, the MacLeans, with their claymores and Lochaber axes, rushed upon their opponents. The MacLeans maintained their ground most gallantly, diminishing their foes at every blow, and ultimately forced them into the river, where, up to their middle in the water, the battle was fought with unabated fury and deadly animosity, for a considerable time. The clear stream was reddened with the blood of the slain and wounded, for some distance from the spot of combat. So brave and determined were the MacLeans, with the recollections of the wrongs and oppressions of their foes fresh in their memory, and the desperate enterprise upon which they then were, that every blow inflicted added fresh vigor to the resolute arm dealing it, and they firmly resolved, that before yielding to the laird of Borlum's son, every one should be ' with his back to the field, and his feet to the foe.' Such was the undaunted courage and deadly determination evinced by both parties, that the combatants did not separate until almost annihilated. Of the gallant little handful of MacLeans, three only survived to tell the result of this bloody fray; and among the eight of the MacIntoshes who escaped, was Borlum's wounded son. Tidings of this affair spread like wildfire through the country; and the neighboring lairds secretly rejoiced at the repulse the MacIntoshes received; and the undaunted bravery displayed by the few sons of clan Gillean was the theme of their praise." * From the general tenor of the above quotation, and the fact that there does not appear to have been any feud between clans MacLean and MacIntosh, it must relate to a conflict with the Camerons. Hector Buie entered the confederacy or union of clans known as the Clan Chattan. Hector held the lands of Davochgarrioch of the abbots of Kinloss, and the 100 merks land of Kilmalew of William Creighton. Sir Donald of Lochalsh assailed castle Urquhart, and, after a desperate resistance, Hector Buie and all the garrison were put to the sword. Hector was three times married—first to Marian, daughter of the chief of Clanranald, by whom he had Ewen, Allan, and Farquhar; next, to Margaret, daughter of Malcolm Beg MacIntosh, chief of Clan Chattan, by whom he had Neil and Charles; and lastly, to Margaret, daughter of lord Lovat, by whom he had Alexander.

V. Ewen, Fifth MacLean of Urquhart.

Ewen succeeded his father at a time when Glen Mór na Albyn was rife with feuds and rapine. On the forfeiture of the lord of the Isles, in 1475, the

---

* MacLean's *Hist. and Trad. Sketches*, p. 27.

earl of Huntly, acting on behalf of the crown, let the lands of Urquhart and Glenmoriston to Hugh of Rose, baron of Kilravock. Hostilities at once broke out between Rose and the chief of MacIntosh, the latter either desiring to have the lands for himself, or else to hold them for his relative, Ewen MacLean. The matter was finally left to "six honorable men," who, March 26, 1479, awarded the lands in dispute to Rose, which was agreed to by MacIntosh in 1481; but Ewen MacLean refused to submit, and then, on September 23, 1481, Farquhar MacIntosh granted a new bond to Rose, binding himself, in the event of Ewen continuing his resistance, "to take lawful part with the said baron, his barns (children) and party agains the said Ewine and his party." The MacLeans, thus deserted by their powerful friends, were forced to submit, and in 1482, Rose was in full possession of Glen Urquhart and Glenmoriston.* Ewen, according to tradition, was a bold and chivalrous character, and in 1503, aided in the insurrection headed by Donald Dubh; but in 1505, made his submission to the king and received pardon. He obeyed the summons of the king in 1513, and fell on the fatal field of Flodden. It is related that Ewen married a daughter of MacKay, ancestor of lord Reay, by whom he had John, Isabel, and Jannet. Isabel married William MacIntosh, chief of clan Chattan, and Jannet married John Abrach, second MacLean of Coll.

THE MACLEANS OF DOCHGARROCH.

When the MacLeans were forced to give up their lands in Glen Urquhart, they still held possession of those of Dochgarroch, of which the earl of Huntly was feudal superior, for which the MacLeans were to pay annually a chaldron of barley. The treatment they had received was not at all suited to their temper, and " in consequence of the infringements of the laird of Dunean, the MacLeans still located in Urquhart proceeded to resent the treatment of their old proprietor of Dochgarroch, after the Highland fashion, by a large body suddenly falling upon the cattle of the laird of Dunean, the tails of which they docked, and in consequence many of them ran mad, to the great terror of the neighborhood; while some of them rushed into the river Ness and were drowned. Complaint of this having been made to the earl of Huntly, he summoned MacLean to appear before him. Accompanied by fifty of his old clan from Urquhart, who volunteered their services on the occasion, and who were willing to shed their blood in defense of their clansman and leader, he proceeded to comply with the summons, which, from the well known ferocity of the earl,

---

* *Transactions Gaelic Society, Inverness,* p. 170.

would have been no pleasant excursion for the disturber of the earl's territory and the peace of his favorite, the laird of Dunean, had it not been for the desperate valor for which the MacLeans were celebrated. It happened, also, that the earl had not an available force adequate to render the exercise of arbitrary punishment upon the laird of MacLean at all advisable or safe, and as his wild and well armed mountaineers approached the castle of the earl of Huntly, the countess, who was walking in the grounds at the time, was the first to discover the advance of these warlike looking men, and precipitately retreated within the castle and announced their arrival to the earl, who having given an audience, and suitable admonition, peaceably dismissed Dochgarroch, with a direction to give an additional chaldron of barley for his lands. This was intended merely for the occasion, but the estates of Dochgarroch and Dochnalurg have ever since had to pay this compensation for the Highland revenge of docking cattle." *

I. John, First MacLean of Dochgarroch.

John succeeded his father as sixth chief of Clan Tarlach, and first of Dochgarroch. He succeeded and governed during the tumultuous times that followed the disastrous death of James IV., and the minority of James V. He purchased the lands of Dochgarroch for three thousand merks of Huntly, with the proviso to furnish the Gordon four mounted troopers whenever required. He was a man of daring character, and much courted by the leaders of the factions during this unhappy period, especially by Huntly, and also by the young king himself, after his escape from the thraldom of Angus and Douglas in 1528. Mary of Guise summoned to her court at Inverness all the Highland lairds and chiefs of clans to answer for their misdemeanors. MacLean of Dochgarroch at the time was on a hunting excursion in chase of a white deer at Mealfourvonie, and was unavoidably absent from her court, which was immediately construed into a proof of contempt and hostility, and an escheat was issued against him and all non-attendants. The earl of Huntly having secretly abetted MacLean, was fined three thousand merks, his proportion of the penalty imposed upon MacLean. John was killed in 1544 in a battle in Lochaber, having accompanied Huntly on an expedition into that district. He left an only daughter, who married MacKenzie of Gairloch, and was succeeded by his uncle,

II. Farquhar, Second MacLean of Dochgarroch,

Who was the third son of Hector Buie. It appears that this was the

---

* MacLean's *Clachnacuddin,* p. 76.

Farquhar who in 1530 was nominated bishop of the Isles. A family tradition relates that he acquired the sobriquet of *Gorach*, or foolish, because he resigned the bishopric without first having himself duly infested in the lands of Urquhart. He was killed in the battle of Pinkie in 1547. Farquhar apparently left issue, Roderick, Donald, Charles, John, James, Hector, Mary or Marion, prioress of Iona, and ———, who married MacKenzie of Kintail.

III. Roderick, Third MacLean of Dochgarroch.

Roderick, in 1548, was deputy governor of Inverness castle. In 1556 he invaded Caithness in order to collect bishop's rents and dues. While absent queen Mary arrived and ordered him to be put to the horn. The earl of Sutherland and the MacKenzies marched against him and drove him into Bowrie castle, carried the fortress by assault, and put all the garrison to the sword (composed mostly of monks and canons), and then caused Roderick's body to be hung up on the ramparts. Dying without issue, Roderick was succeeded by his brother,

IV. Donald, Fourth MacLean of Dochgarroch,

Who was brought up in the house of his foster-mother, the wife of the laird of Grant, and through her influence embraced the principles of the Reformation. About the year 1565, whilst the greater part of the clan was absent in the prosecution of a feud with the Clan Ian of Ardnamurchan, the Clan Chattan (it must have been the Camerons) seized the opportunity to plunder and ravage the estates of MacLean, and carried off two of his sons, but his wife Margery escaped with the youngest, and found protection with the laird of Grant. In the meantime MacLean returned, assembled his adherents, pursued and overtook the spoilers at the castle of Loch End, who in order to prevent rescue sacrificed their prisoners, and exhibited their heads upon the ramparts. MacLean, goaded to desperation, rushed to the assault, and although the drawbridge was lined with raw-hides, inside uppermost, and covered with sand, whereby the leaders of the assault slipped their footing, and in that prostrate state were immediately dispatched by the arrows of the defenders, yet, nothing daunted, the MacLeans ultimately carried the fortress, and reduced it to a heap of ruins. Donald married twice, first to Margery, daughter of the laird of Grant, by whom he had three sons and one daughter; secondly, to a daughter of MacKenzie of Dunachnahard, by whom he had one son, Donald. His other issue were Alexander, John, Hector, and Elizabeth, who married Walter Urquhart, sheriff of Cromarty. Donald died in 1622.

V. Sir Alexander, Fifth MacLean of Dochgarroch,

Came prominently into notice at the battle of Glenlivat, fought in 1594, where he led, in the absence of his father, his kinsmen, the MacLeans of Kingerloch and Glenevis. These composed the left wing of the forces under Sir Lachlan Mór MacLean. He was created a knight by Charles I. He met his death in 1635 at the hands of the MacDonalds of Sleat, who attacked him while he was collecting his rents. He was interred in the churchyard of Kilpeter in North Uist. He was twice married, first to a daughter of Rose of Kilravock, by whom he had issue, John his heir, Charles of Culbokie, David of Buntait, and Jannet, who in 1614 married William Baillie of Dunean; by his second wife, Annabella, daughter of Andrew Munoe of Daan, in Tarbet, by whom he had James, a physician. David married a lady of the Lovat family, and settled in the Aird. He obtained a high reputation as a soldier of fortune; that early in the civil war he joined Strachan's regiment of dragoons, and after sharing in all the checkered fortunes of the opponents of Montrose, obtained the command of a troop, with which he was ordered to reduce Red-Castle, where a remnant of Montrose's soldiers kept their ground. David summoned them to surrender, and approaching near enough to hold converse on the subject, was shot by an arrow, which so infuriated his command, that they rushed forward, stormed the castle, and reduced it to ashes. Then they carried their captain's remains to Kirk-Hill. A stone erected over the grave bore the inscription, "Here lies one of David's worthies." David had a grandson, Lachlan, who joined the "Black Watch," and was ordered to Brae-Mar at the gathering in 1689. When ordered to join MacKay, Lachlan, with many others, took off their bonnets, took a drink at the brook, then shouted aloud, "King James forever!" and forthwith joined the ranks of Dundee. After the battle of Killiecrankie, he settled at Broughty Ferry, and there vowed he would never shave until the Stuart dynasty was restored.

VI. John, Sixth MacLean of Dochgarroch,

Was a very brave man, and devoted to the house of Stuart. He fought under Montrose at Inverlochy, Auldearn, and Kilsyth. He was present at the disastrous battle of Inverkeithing, and there lost one hundred and forty of his immediate followers. In 1636 he obtained a new charter for his lands of Dochgarroch and Dochnalurg, under the great seal of Scotland. He was married to Agnes, daughter of Fraser of Strys, by whom he had eight sons and three daughters: Alexander, the eldest, died in 1671, without issue; John Og, his successor; John Ban, died in Strathdearn; Hector, fell at Killiecrankie; Allan, settled in Sutherlandshire, where his descendants became quite numerous; Donald, settled in Rosemarkie; David; Farquhar, fell at Killiecrankie; Bridget, married Angus MacQueen of Inches; Margaret, married Domald Campbell of Lopich; and Jannet married Malcolm MacIntosh of Borlern.

VII. John Og, Seventh MacLean of Dochgarroch,

Suffered greatly for his attachment to the Stuarts. Led by his chief, Sir John of Duard, he shared all the perils and glory of the short career of Dundee; was actively engaged in the battles of Killiecrankie and Dunkeld in 1689. From this ill-fated gathering he never returned; and all his kindred who did return were put to the horn, outlawed as rebels, and widely dispersed. He married Margaret, daughter of Baillie Fowler of Inverness, by whom he had six sons and two daughters: John, his successor; Alexander, an ambitious man, who took advantage of his brother's absence and difficulty in the war of 1715, by usurping the lands of Dochgarroch; David, who had a son named Alexander; Donald, settled in Argyleshire; Charles, died unmarried; Farquhar, a man of roving habits, who left his country and never returned; Jannet, married William MacIntosh; and Annie, married James Ross.

VIII. John, Eighth MacLean of Dochgarroch,

Was a man of generous sentiments and chivalrous character. He was among the first to join the earl of Mar when he unfurled the standard of the Stuarts at Brae-Mar, in 1715. He was present at Sheriffmuir, and continued in arms until he witnessed the hopelessness of the cause he had espoused. He returned home, but not to enjoy peace; for the share he had taken in the war brought him, in common with others, under the notice of the government, and a heavy fine was the result of his opposition to the successful sovereign. He was a man of uncommon strength; and it is related of him, that after his return from the war, he encountered four Hessian soldiers pillaging meal at a mill which belonged to him at Dochnalurg, when he, with one stroke of his claymore, killed one of the robbers, and forced the rest to retire without their intended booty. A strict inquiry was instituted, and although the fact was notorious in Inverness, yet he escaped with impunity, for no one was disposed to come forward and substantiate the charge against him. This John was the first to spell his name *MacLean* among the Dochgarrochs, for they had previously spelled it according to its Gaelic pronunciation, *MacGillean*. He married Jannet, daughter of William Dallas of Cantray, by whom he had John, who was killed at Culloden; Charles, his successor; William, killed at the storming of Gaudaloupe in 1753; Jannet, and Mary. John died in 1748, and was succeeded by

IX. Charles, Ninth MacLean of Dochgarroch,

Who was bred to the profession of the law, but subsequently held a commission in the Black Watch. During the rebellion of 1745, he was stationed at Ruthven in Badenoch, and was near Inverlochy when the battle of Culloden was fought ; and, it is said, though opposed to Prince Charles, he and many others with him heartily wished success to his cause. After the battle of Culloden, he retired from the army ; and on the death of his brother, asserted his claim to Dochgarroch, which he found his uncle Alexander unwilling to resign ; but after some litigation he made good his rights, and during the remainder of his life seduously strove to pay off the arrears of crown fines and other burdens on the estate. He married Marjory MacIntosh, by whom he had four sons and three daughters : John, his heir ; Phineas, who died young ; Angus, a lieutenant in the Bombay infantry, died in 1794 ; William, who succeeded his brother John ; Jannet, married Alexander MacIntosh ; Marjory, married Baillie Lee of Inverness ; Barbara, died unmarried. Charles died in 1778, and was succeeded by his son,

X. John, Tenth MacLean of Dochgarroch,

Who was educated at the University of Aberdeen, and then went to Grenada, in the West Indies, in 1775. He left home as a young man of bright promise, but in 1778 returned home permanently insane. The management of the estate devolved upon his brother Angus, at whose death, in 1794, John's affairs were administered by his brother William. John died in 1826, and was succeeded by his brother,

XI. William, Eleventh MacLean of Dochgarroch,

Who in early life served in the Forty-second Highlanders, and, on his first passage to India, was taken prisoner by the Spaniards. He returned from India in 1788 ; obtained a company in the Argyleshire Fencibles ; was subsequently transferred to the Eighty-third regiment, and retired from the service in 1796. The affairs of the estate became seriously entangled, owing to the revival of a dispute dating back to 1635. Up to 1774, the lands were held of the crown by virtue of a charter of entail granted to John in 1635 ; by virtue of the feu contract, 1623, the duke of Gordon, from and after 1774, continued to claim a feu duty. In litigating for his rights, Charles, ninth of Dochgarroch, became greatly involved. In 1832, William was forced to sell all his claims, which were purchased by Baillie of Dochfour. William married Elizabeth, daughter of Lachlan MacLean of Rochester (a branch of the MacLeans of Kingerloch), and had issue—Allan, who succeeded him ; Charles Maxwell, lieutenant-colonel of the Seventy-second regiment, who died in 1864— was married in 1823 to Sarah Amelia Marshall, and leaves one daughter, Charlotte Amelia ; and William (died in 1871), married to Elizabeth, daughter of Thomas Henderson of Dominica, leaving issue, William Thomas Henderson, Allan, Eliza, Helen, Annie, Isabella, Jessie, and Marian. William died in 1841, and his son,

XII. Allan, Twelfth MacLean of Dochgarroch,

Succeeded him in the chieftainship of Clan Tarlach, who is described as having been a dignified gentleman of military bearing. He resided near Inverness, being senior Baillie of Inverness, one of the directors of Royal Infirmary, also of the Royal Academy, and chairman of the Dispensary. He died in 1876, unmarried.

XIII. William Thomas Henderson, Thirteenth MacLean of Dochgarroch,

Succeeds his uncle in the chieftainship, and for some time was a subaltern in the Seventy-eighth Highlanders. On his death, he will be succeeded by his brother Allan, who married Marian Greville, and has issue, Allan MacIntosh, Hector, and Jessie Marian. Residence, Southsea, England.

CHAPTER X.

THE MacLEANS OF KINGERLOCH.

For generations this branch of the MacLeans maintained a high position among the families of the West Highlands. It is known under the patronymic of Mac Mhic Eachainn, or the son of the son of Hector. The MacLean manuscripts are agreed that it is a branch of the family of Urquhart, but the house appears to have possessed a predilection for the family of Lochbuie. In a letter written June 5, 1759, by Hugh of Kingerloch to John MacLean of Grulin, the following occurs: " I have a dale of business to settle particularly upon account of my friend Lochbuy's sake, who I never will desert, but am fully determined to support his interest; I mean the family, to the utmost of my power, as I have it by tradition that my predecessors always did support that family when they required it." *

To give a correct genealogy of this family would be an exceedingly difficult task; but from the records of other families, they shared in all the vicissitudes of the clan, and were ever ready to bear their part. They cared

---

* Lochbuie Charter Room.

but little for formalities, in so much so that in their early history they paid no attention to having their lands given to them by careful records, believing that the tenure could be held by the sword. Later this was rectified, for under date of May 30, 1772, Hugh of Kingerloch says his charters are two, dating 1625 and 1627.* The lands are situated in Morvern, and the seat was at the head of Loch a' choire, which empties into Loch Linnhe.

The branches of this house can not be given, but the following may serve for a guide in tracing out the genealogical history:

Sir Charles, First MacLean of Kingerloch, was the fifth son of Hector Buie, fourth chief of Clan Tarlach. Sir Charles was dean of Morvern, and there acquired the lands of Kingerloch. He was a cotemporary of Lachlan Bronnach, chief of MacLean, and maternal grandfather of Donald, first of Ardgour.

In 1545, Donald was a prominent character. In that year he signed the English petition.† He also appears as one of the barons of the *elect* of the lord of the Isles in 1540.

In the reign of queen Mary, Hector was confirmed in the lands of Kingerloch, who, in turn, was succeeded by his son Donald, who, on September 6, 1609, registered his lands as apparent of Kingerloch.‡

In 1675–8, there was another Donald who succeeded the " deceased Hector MacLean of Kingerloch, his maternal grandfather in lands of Kilmaloo and Kenloch." ‖ " Donaldus McCleane de Kingarloch, hæres Hectoris McClean de Kingarloch, *avipaternis*." § In December, 1680, Donald was one of the number denounced rebel, and put to the horn for garrisoning Cairnburg.** Donald died in 1700, and left issue, Lachlan, his heir and successor.

During the revolutions of 1689, 1715, and 1745, the Kingerlochs espoused the cause of the unfortunate Stuarts, which ruined their prospects and scattered their family. A part of the land, however, was retained. A member of the family, Lachlan, joined the MacLean battalion, under Drimnin, and fought at Culloden. From that fatal field he fled to Holland, where he found shelter until the act of amnesty of 1747 enabled him to return. He subsequently established himself in mercantile pursuits at Rochester, in Kent, where, in 1757, he married Miss Terry of Strood, and left John, Charles, Lachlan, William, and Elizabeth.

---

* Lochbuie Charter Room. † Tyler's *History of Scotland*, Vol. III., p. 85. ‡ *Reg. at Inverness*, September 6, 1609. ‖ *Reg.* Sasones for Argyle, December 8, 1676. § *Inquis. ad Capel. Dom. Regis Retornatorum*, September 9, 1675. ** *Appendix Sixth Report Hist. MS Com.*, p. 624.

THE HOUSE OF KINGERLOCH.   263

Lachlan succeeded Donald of Kingerloch in 1700, and had issue John, his heir, and Lachlan, progenitor of the MacLeans of Rochester, already mentioned as retiring to Holland after Culloden. John was succeeded by his son, Hugh, married to Mary Stewart, who was laird of Kingerloch from 1759 to 1780. A great many letters from him to John MacLean of Grulin are still preserved in the Lochbuie Charter Room. These letters contain much valuable historical matter. Hugh had five sons and four daughters: Donald, his successor, was married to Anne, daughter of Hugh, twelfth of Ardgour, but died without issue; Murdoch was educated for a surgeon, but obtained the rank of captain in the Second West India regiment, and was killed in the island of St. Vincent during the war with the Caribs; Colin, a lieutenant in the thirty-seventh regiment, was killed at the battle of Tournay in 1794; James was a planter in Jamaica, where he lost his life during the Carib war; Hector, the youngest brother, removed to Pictou, Nova Scotia; Mary married Donald Skinner, minister of Ardnamurchan; Margaret married Captain Hugh Cameron; Jane first married John MacCormick of Fort William, and then a MacLean; and —— married Hugh Dunoon of Pictou.

Donald was succeeded in the estates by his youngest brother, Hector, who having established himself in Pictou, Nova Scotia, sold Kingerloch about 1812. He was engaged in mercantile pursuits. He lies buried in the old cemetery of Pictou. He married a Miss Frasee of Inverlochy, and left issue two sons and two daughters. His second son, Simon, married a Miss Noonan, and had Fannie, Christina, and John, the last named having died in prison in one of the Southern states during the civil war of 1861–65.

Hector's elder son, Murdoch, the head of the Kingerloch family, was born March 18, 1807, and died April 4, 1865. At one time he was sheriff of the county of Guysborough. He married Elizabeth, daughter of Robert M. Cutler, and had issue: Kenneth John, born in 1844, and died in 1873; Robert Cutler; William Murdoch, born in 1849, married and has six sons; Charles Shrieve, died young; Norman, born in 1851, married and has three sons and one daughter; Francis George, born in 1853, married; Sophia, married to Peter Gruchy; and Elizabeth, married to John Sweetland.

The present Mac Mhic Eachainn is Robert Cutler MacLean, second son of Murdoch, who lives in Lynn, Massachusetts. He was born in 1846.

Robert married Emma Eliza, daughter of Alvin Austin, of Freeport, Maine, and has issue, Norman Plaice, born 1871, and died in 1874; Hattie Elizabeth, born in 1875; Wallace Stanley, born 1876, and died same year; Emma Austin, born 1880; and Helen Frasier, born in 1888.

CHAPTER XI.

THE MacLEANS OF SCALLASDALE.

Scallasdale is a district between Duard and Aros castle in northern Mull that was possessed by the house of Lochbuie. Of the earlier MacLeans of this district but very little has come down to us. One of them was known as Murchadh Scalasdail, a son, according to a traditional account, of John Og of Lochbuie, and uncle of Murdoch Gearr. He was a man of ability, but of an ambitious and grasping character. He served as tutor or guardian for his nephew, Murdoch Gearr, the heir of Lochbuie, and attempted to deprive him of his estates. He married a daughter of Stewart of Appin.

The later MacLeans of Scallasdale are descended from Gillean, son of John, seventeenth MacLean of Lochbuy. He was bred to the law, and was esteemed as a benevolent and honorable man. In 1771 he married Maria, daughter of MacQuarrie of Ulva, by whom he had five sons and five daughters: Allan, married to Marjory, daughter of Angus Gregorson of Ardtornish, by whom he had Gillean, a merchant in Java, and Angus, minister of Ardnamurchan; Archibald, a general in the army; Murdoch, twin-brother of Archibald, a captain in the army, and the only British officer killed at the battle of Maida in 1806; John, a major in the Seventy-third regiment, fell mortally wounded at the battle of Waterloo; Hector, a colonel in the army, married in 1816 Martha, daughter of William Osborne of Kingston, Gloucester, and died in 1847; Alicia, married John Wood of Edinburgh; Juliana, married Thomas Ross; Flora and Mary unmarried; and Margaret Anne, married William Craig of Edinburgh. Gillean died aged sixty-four.

There are other cadets of the house of Lochbuie of which scarcely any history has been preserved. Among them may be noted Cappurnach, Grulin, Kilmory, Pennygowan, Tapull, Killran, and Knock. The last named will be considered under the heading of Hector MacLean, bishop of Argyle. Of the MacLeans of Grulin, Hugh MacLean says, under date of January 20, 1771, in a letter to John MacLean of Grulin: "My father, who was one of the best genealogists in the clan MacLean, told me frequently of all those belonging to him in Mull and in a particular manner did tell me of your descent which was directly of Kingerloch's loins." *

---

* Lochbuie Charter Room.

CHAPTER XII.

THE MacLEANS OF LEHIRE.

The oldest branch of the Duard family is that of Lehire or Lether, descended from John Dubh, second son of Hector Roy, sixth chief of MacLean. John Dubh was quite a young man at the time of his father's death, yet old enough to take charge of his brother's estate during the latter's confinement in the castle of Mar. He was particularly noted as an active participant in the battle of Inverlochy in 1431. John came into possession of the sixty mark land of Lehire (afterward called Torloisk), and was succeeded by his son Neil. From Neil the family was called *Sliochd Neil a Lether*, or the race of Neil a Lether, in order to distinguish them from the MacLeans of Ross, who were called *Sliochd Neil a Roish*. Neil was succeeded by his son Neil, who received the name *Niall nan Ordag*, or Neil of the Thumbs, owing to the great number of thumbs he cut off as his opponents were trying to board his galley at the battle of Bloody Bay in 1482. Neil was succeeded in the estates by his son John, who in turn was succeeded by his son John Og. John Og was a weak, effeminate man; lived to an old age; was married, but had no children, and at last was killed by Allan nan Sop, who then took possession of the estates. From the Lether family are descended that of Langmull and others.

CHAPTER XIII.

THE MacLEANS OF ARDGOUR.

The family-seat, called Cuil House, of the Ardgour MacLeans, is located on the west side of the Corran Narrows, which separates Loch Linnhe from Loch Eil. The mansion is a large thick-walled stone house, furnished with all modern conveniences, and finely decorated by art. Back of the house the Ardgour mountains loom up to a perpendicular height of over two thousand feet. To the north-east the summit of Ben Nevis appears remarkably near. Between the mansion and the Loch, is a broad, fertile plain, upon which are solid carriage-ways, lined with trees on either side. Along the shore of Loch

Linnhe are quite a number of crofter huts. During the present century the people were removed from the glens to the present locality. Across the Loch may be seen the mountains of Glencoe. While Glen Mór in its course of sixty miles presents many beautiful localities, yet none will compare with this for a combination of picturesqueness, wildness, and beauty.

I. Donald, First MacLean of Ardgour.

The second branch of the Duard family, that of Ardgour, is descended from Donald, first son of Lachlan Bronnach, seventh chief of MacLean, by a daughter of MacLean of Kingerloch. Having been born out of wedlock, he was, in consequence, brought up among his mother's people. In his attack upon MacMaster's house by night, he was greatly assisted by his maternal grandfather. The MacMasters of that vicinity were not wholly extirpated, for an old woman of that tribe composed the rhyme—

"Nam biod Mac-Mhic-Eoghainn's Mac-Mhic Eachainn
Mar chombla air aon sgeir,
Cha tugainn-sa dheth Mac-Mhic-Eachinn,
'S dh' fhagainn Mac-Mhic-Eoghainn air."
If Ardgour and Kingerloch
Were together on a rock in the sea,
I would not take Kingerloch off it,
And I would leave Ardgour on it.

Donald was a bold, resolute, and cunning man. He was married to a daughter of Ewen Cameron of Lochiel, by whom he had three sons—Ewen, his heir; Niall Ban, progenitor of the MacLeans of Borreray; and John Ruadh, who served as tutor during the minority of John MacAllen, grandson to his brother Ewen. Donald also had a son out of wedlock, named Gillespig, or Archibald, of whom is descended the people called Clan Ewenraoch. Donald died before 1463, and was succeeded by his son,

II. Ewen, Second MacLean of Ardgour.

From this Ewen the MacLeans of Ardgour are said to derive their patronymic of Mac Mhic Eoghainn, which was applied even to the posterity of Neil Bàn, which is manifestly incorrect; but refers to Donald, first of Ardgour, who was the son of the son of Hector Buie. But as Eachainn was preoccupied by the Kingerlochs, Eoghainn refers to Ewen, second of Urquhart. Ewen held the office of seneschal of the household to earl John in 1463,[*] and was a witness to charters granted in 1463,[†] 1478,[‡] and 1479. He was married

---

[*] Gregory's *Western Highlands*, pp. 71, 72. [†] *Reg. Mag. Sig.*, Lib. VI., No. 116. [‡] *Ibid.*, Lib. IX., No. 30.

to a daughter of Thomas Chisholm of Cornar, chief of the Chisholms, by whom he had three sons—Allan, his heir; John, first MacLean of Treshnish; and Hector of Blaich and Achnadale. Ewen was living in 1495, for on the 24th October of that year, we find Ewen, son of Donald, son of Lachlan of Ardgour, a witness to the confirmation of the keepership of the castle of Strome to Alan, son of the captain of clan Cameron.*

III. Allan, Third MacLean of Ardgour,

Married a daughter of MacGhlasraich, a man of considerable importance in the braes of Lochaber. Allan was succeeded by his son,

IV. John, Fourth MacLean of Ardgour,

Who was very young when his father died. John Ruadh, third son of Donald, first laird of Ardgour, acted as his tutor. John, the fourth laird, first married a daughter of MacDougall of Lorn, by whom he had two sons, Allan, his successor, and Ewen, who succeeded his brother Allan. His second wife was a daughter of the chief of Clanranald, by whom he also had two sons, Charles and Lachlan. He afterward took a daughter of MacIan, or MacDonald of Ardnamurchan, to live with him, with the purpose of marrying her should she please him. After a trial of two years, he sent her home to her friends, but the two sons born to them were reputed lawfully begotten, because their mother was taken upon a prospect of marriage. The eldest of these sons was called Iain ninmher, from Inverscadell, a farm situated at the foot of the water of Scadell, in Ardgour, where he lived. This John was famous for his strength, boldness, remarkable valor and bravery. He signalized himself in all of Sir Lachlan Mór's wars against the MacDonalds of Islay. His brother was named Hector. Allan had a son born out of wedlock named John Glennich. The six sons were very prosperous and flourishing men of great substance, and nearly all had many children, whereby for several generations they formed little tribes of their own, each being called Mac Mhic Allan. John died about the year 1545, and was succeeded by his son,

V. Allan, Fifth MacLean of Ardgour,

Who died without legitimate issue, and was succeeded by his brother,

VI. Ewen, Sixth MacLean of Ardgour,

Noted for his quickness or agility. He married a daughter of Stewart of Appin, and by her had two sons, Allan, his heir, and John, who was the grandfather of John MacLean, the Mull poet. Ewen was killed upon the coast of Mamore, in Lochaber, in a long boat of his own, by a party of the MacDonalds

---

* *Reg. Mag. Sig.,* Lib. XIII., No. 203.

of Keppoch, who mistook him for Cameron of Lochiel, for whom they were in ambush; Ardgour having on a scarlet cloak similar to the one always worn by Lochiel. Ewen was living in 1587, for his name appears in the General Band.* In the same year, his son Allan was one of the hostages placed in the hands of MacDonald of Islay by Sir Lachlan Mór.

VII. Allan, Seventh MacLean of Ardgour.

Allan was a minor at the time he succeeded his father, and the estates were managed by his uncle Charles, who was a bold, daring, grasping, and unscrupulous man. During his administration, he not only lived extravagantly, but purposed to defraud his nephew out of his rights. He was emboldened to this design by his marriage to a sister of Sir Lachlan Mór, who was relict to Hector MacLean, second laird of Coll. Charles still held the estates after Allan had passed his minority, and the latter, listening to the advice of his mother's relations, the Stewarts of Appin, betook himself to the earl of Argyle for assistance, who, upon exacting a promise from Allan to resign the whole lands of Ardgour to him (which were held blench of the crown), agreed to restore him to the possession of the estate. Charles was taken by a stratagem, by the laird of Appin, and made a prisoner in the island of Stalker, where he was detained till he consented that his nephew should enjoy his estate without molestation. Through the influence of Sir Lachlan Mór, Charles obtained the lands of Inverscadell, Camuseven Craundulick, and Achidhaphubie, which were secured to him and his posterity by a feu right upon the payment yearly of the whole feu duty which Ardgour was to pay Argyle, which amounted to twenty-five merks Scots and cuidoich, or an entertainment for one night, which afterward was converted into the yearly payment of fifty merks Scots.

There is a warrant still in the family of the marquis of Montrose, dated at Kirktown of Bothwell, September 1, 1645, empowering the said Allan and his posterity to hold again of his majesty as formerly, instead of Argyle, and promising to procure a charter from the king when the troubles were ended. This warrant having been shown James VII., that monarch, upon the forfeiture of Argyle, gave a charter for the barony of Ardgour to Ardgour, dated at Whitehall, September 12, 1688, wherein honorable mention is made of the loyalty of the MacLeans in general and of the family of Ardgour in particular. Allan was an honest, plain man, meaning harm to no one, and readily believed any thing told to him with becoming seriousness. He was nicknamed "Ma grobhartidh," because in discourse he would say, "Air laimh ma grob-

---

* *Collectanea de Rebus Albanicis*, p. 37.

hartidh," in order to shun all kinds of oaths. Allan married Catherine, daughter of Allan Cameron of Lochiel, and by her had eleven sons: John, Hector, Allan, Charles, Donald, Lachlan Mór, Lachlan Og, Ewen the elder, Ewen the younger, Archibald, and John the younger. Donald and John Og were killed at the battle of Inverkeithing in 1651. There were also three daughters: Mary, married to Charles, second son of Allan MacLean of Ardtornish; Marian, married to John MacLean of Totaranald, and Christiana. Allan lived to the age of one hundred and two years, retained his faculties to the last, and left his estate free of debt after liberally providing for his sons and daughters.

VIII. John, Eighth MacLean of Ardgour.

The eighth laird of Ardgour was commonly called John Crubach, because, having broken his leg, he ever after halted a little upon it. He was a bold, daring man, lived to the age of ninety-five, and was buried on the island of Coll. He was first married to Anne, daughter of Angus Campbell, captain of Dunstaffnage, by whom he had Ewen his heir, Lachlan progenitor of the MacLeans of Blaich, Donald, Allan, and Archibald. His second wife was Marian, daughter of Hector MacLean of Torloisk, relict of Hector MacLean of Coll, by whom he had one son, John.

IX. Ewen, Ninth MacLean of Ardgour,

Was an honest, plain, well-inclined man, and very much resembled his grandfather. He married Mary, daughter of Lachlan MacLean of Lochbuie, and had by her Allan, Donald, Charles, John, and Lachlan. The last named was a lieutenant in the Spanish service, and was killed in a duel at Madrid. Donald, the second son, married Janet, daughter of Lachlan MacLean of Calgary. Ewen was succeeded in the estates by his son,

X. Allan, Tenth MacLean of Ardgour,

Who was born in 1668, and had the misfortune of being the representative of the family in evil times, on which account he and his tribe in a more especial manner were persecuted for depredations committed not only by them, but for the deeds of other clans also. In 1685 an indemnity for their past offenses was procured by Torloisk at London, but as Torloisk died soon after his return, no one knew it was in his custody until afterward accidentally discovered. While it was dormant Ardgour was judged and obliged to borrow sums of money by mortgaging considerable portions of his estate to pay these debts, which, together with other additional burdens added and contracted through misfortunes and mismanagement on his own as well as his son Donald's part, the estate sunk so low, that it was thought to be in a desperate condition. When the affairs reached their lowest point, Hector MacLean of Coll, Donald MacLean of Torloisk, John MacLean, minister in Kilninan, and Archibald MacLean, minister in the Ross of Mull, took upon themselves the management of the estate, and after passing through much trouble and changes, appointed Donald Cameron of Strontin superintendent under them. Cameron continued a few years, went to Edinburgh, took a ship at Leith, and never was heard of afterward. The management of the estate fell back again into the hands of the trustees, and in a tottering condition continued for many years. On the death of the eldest son Donald, in 1731, Allan made over the estate to John, then the oldest living son, after which John continued the management under the trustees. Allan reserved for himself a small yearly portion. He married Anne, daughter of Sir Ewen Cameron of Lochiel, and had issue, Donald, Ewen, John Archibald, Allan, James, Isabella, Margaret, and Mary. Donald never married; Ewen died comparatively young, on his way from Virginia, where he had been engaged in mercantile pursuits; Archibald died unmarried; Allan emigrated to Georgia, and died there; James was a lieutenant in Montgomery's Highlanders, and was killed at sea in an action with a privateer on June 1, 1767; Isabella married Donald MacLean of Brolass; Margaret married Angus MacLean of Kinlochaline; and Mary married John, son of Charles MacLean of Kinlochaline. Allan died in 1756, in the eighty-eighth year of his age.

XI. John, Eleventh MacLean of Ardgour,

Married Marjory, daughter of Allan MacLachlan of Corry, and had issue: Hugh, Hector, and Margaret, the last two having died young. John did not live long after his marriage, but died in 1739, seventeen years before his father, and was buried at Kilmore in Quinish, and was succeeded in the estates by his son,

XII. Hugh, Twelfth MacLean of Ardgour.

Hugh was but a child at the time of the death of his father. Together with his brother and sister, he was taken by his mother to Glasgow, where the sister and younger brother died. Hugh was left in Glasgow under the care of Lachlan MacLean, a merchant, and Doctor Hector MacLean of Grulin, both living in that city. Through the interference of the relatives of the mother, the estate fell into a bad condition in the attempt of the MacLachlans to gain possession of it. Hector MacLean of Torloisk, who was bred to the law, took the management into his own hands, and called to his assistance Colin Campbell of Clachombie, Donald Campbell of Airds, James MacLean, uncle to the minor, Doctor Hector MacLean of Grulin, and Lachlan MacLean, merchant in Glasgow, and by the vigilance, prudence, and faithful management and the indefatigable pains of Hector MacLean of Torloisk, with the joint assistance and counsel of the above named gentlemen, the estate of Ardgour was recovered from the very brink of ruin. Hugh was a captain in the first regiment of fencibles of Argyle raised in 1759. He married Elizabeth, daughter of Alexander Houston of Jordan Hill, and had issue, one son, Alexander, and Anna, who married Donald MacLean of Kingerloch. Hugh died in 1768.

XIII. Alexander, Thirteenth MacLean of Ardgour,

Was born in the year 1764. He entered the army in 1780, and subsequently obtained the rank of major in the Eighth regiment of Light Dragoons, and afterward held the rank of lieutenant-colonel in the third regiment of local militia of the county of Argyle. He was a splendid horseman and the most accomplished and daring rider in the Caledonian hunt. He became blind several years before his death, which last occurred in 1833. He married Margaret, daughter of John, second earl of Hopetoun, and by her had issue, Hugh, who died in infancy; John Hugh, educated at the Scotch bar, and died at Rome in 1826; Archibald, who died in Edinburgh in 1832 after having served as a naval officer; once severely wounded; captured by the American war vessel, The Prince of Neufchatel; and in 1822, promoted to the rank of captain and commander of the Blossom, of twenty-six guns; Alexander, heir and successor; Henry Dundas entered the army, became a major in 1832, and at different periods was resident governor of Ithaca, Cephalonia, Santa Maura, and Lante; died in 1863; James Charles entered the military service of the East India Company, and died of fever at Calcutta in 1829; Charles Hope was educated for the English bar, and died in 1839; Elizabeth Margaret; Charlotte Margaret died in 1824; Thomas entered the East India Company's service, and died in 1840; William entered the navy, changed his name to Gunston, and died in 1851; George became a colonel in the army, and married, in 1842, a daughter of Sir Colin Campbell; Robert died in 1835; Peter rose to the rank of colonel in the artillery, married a daughter of Sir Henry Somerset, by whom he had four sons and three daughters. Alexander was succeeded by his fourth son,

XIV. Alexander, Fourteenth MacLean of Ardgour,

Who was born February 11, 1799, married, February 14, 1833, Helen Jane Hamilton, daughter of Major-General Sir John Dalrymple, and died in 1872. Alexander entered the service of the East India Company and became collector of the Jaghire. On the death of his father, being the oldest living male heir, he inherited the estates. He had two sons, Alexander Thomas and John Dalrymple, born in Bengal, May 15, 1836, now of Lazenby, Cumberland.

XV. Alexander Thomas, Fifteenth MacLean of Ardgour.

The present laird of Ardgour was born in Madras, April 1, 1835; was educated at Harrow; entered the East India Company's civil service in Bengal in 1857; became judge of the high court of judicature at Fort William, which he filled with signal ability and impartiality, and retired with honors in 1884. In 1875, he was married to Selina Philippa, daughter of William S. Dicken, Esq., and has issue, Catherine Helen Dalrymple, born 1878; Margaret, born 1879; Alexander John Hew, born 1880; and Flora, born 1884.

Alexander Thomas MacLean, called Ardgour, after his estate, has naturally a judicial turn of mind. He readily weighs justice, and is as willing to obey its demands as he is anxious that others should be under its laws. He has a keen sense of right and wrong, but is naturally swayed by a generous disposition. His tendency is to forgive and forget the wrongs done by others. He is rather tall and slender, and has the student's stoop, while his face would indicate one who was thoughtful and given to literary pursuits. He is much interested in the welfare of his crofters and tenants, and when needy, assists them with a benevolent hand. What was the original extent of the Ardgour possessions, I have no means of knowing, but probably the same as to-day, which is fifty thousand acres.

ALEXANDER THOMAS MACLEAN.

CHAPTER XIV.
THE MacLEANS OF BORRERAY.

The first cadet of the family of Ardgour is that of Borreray, in North Uist, descended from Neil Bàn, second son of Donald, first laird of Ardgour. Neil obtained the lands of Borreray from Hugh MacDonald, first laird of Sleat, who was brought up in the family of Ardgour. The history of this branch is not preserved in its own records, but partially kept by the Ardgour family. At the time of its origin the distance was great, the particulars have been lost, and generally speaking only the bare names remain. Neil Bàn was succeeded by his son John, to whom succeeded Alexander, the third laird; the fourth, Archibald, son of Alexander; the fifth, Donald, son of Archibald; and the sixth, Nial Bàn, Donald's son. Nial Bàn married Ann, daughter of Alexander MacKenzie of Kilcoy, by whom he had nine sons and three daughters, viz., John, his successor; Donald, a minister in North Uist; Charles, who settled in Tiree; Archibald of Kirkibost; Murdoch; Allan; Ewen; Hector; and Alexander. Charles, the third son, known as Tearlach MacNeill Bhain, lived in comfortable circumstances, and married Florence, daughter of Neil MacLean of Drimnacross, by whom he had five sons: Neil, Archibald, Lachlan, Donald, and John. Neil, the eldest, was father of Captain Lachlan MacLean of Craigbeti; Archibald was a minister in Kilfinichin, Mull; Lachlan was a captain in Lamby's regiment in the service of Holland, raised to a lieutenant colonel for signal behavior at Bergen-op-Zoom, and died at the Brill in 1752; Donald was factor of Brolass, and afterward obtained the lands of Killmokiag in Tiree. He married Isabella Campbell of Dunstaffnage, and by her had three sons and three daughters. His eldest son, John, for many years was factor of Ardgour's estate; married Florence, daughter of John MacLean, son of Charles of Inverscadell, by whom he had three sons and three daughters—Charles, a physician, and Donald, a merchant. Killmokiag's second son, Charles, was major in the 43d regiment, and died unmarried, and his third son, Archibald, succeeded his father in the lands of Tiree. He married Catherine Campbell of Scamadall, and left a son, John, and two daughters, Mary and Annabella.

Archibald, second son of Tearlach MacNeill Bhain, and minister of Kilfinichin, married Susanna, daughter of Donald Campbell of Scamadall, by whom he had a numerous issue, nearly all of whom died young, but three sons, Charles, John, and Neil, and four daughters, Florence, Margaret, Ann, and Barbara, lived to maturity. The eldest son, Charles, known as Tearlach Mór na Sgurra, was distinguished for his great strength; married to Catherine, daughter of Lachlan MacLean of Isle of Muck, and had issue one son and two daughters, Archibald, Isabella, and Mary. The son served in the 71st regiment during the American Revolutionary War; also in the West Indies, Holland, and Egypt; became lieutenant-colonel in the 79th, and died unmarried in 1817. Reverend Archibald MacLean's second son was John, a surgeon in the army; married Anne Long, and had a son, also named John. This last John studied medicine, emigrated to America, became professor of chemistry in the College of New Jersey; married Phœbe Bainbridge, by whom he had the Reverend Doctor John MacLean, late president of the same college. Margaret, second daughter of the Reverend Archibald MacLean, married Reverend Neil MacLeod, and became the mother of the Reverend Doctor Alexander MacLeod of New York; Ann married Lieutenant Hugh MacLean; Barbara married Hugh MacLean, son of MacLean of Treshnish, and Florence married Donald MacLean of Isle of Muck.

Donald, fourth son of Tearlach MacNeill Bhain, known as Fear Chillmoluthaig, married Isabella, daughter of John Campbell of the family of Dunstaffnage, by whom he had three sons and three daughters, John, Charles, Archibald, Florence, Isabella, and Betty. John had five sons and three daughters. Charles died unmarried. Archibald succeeded his father in Kilmaluaig. Florence married Donald MacDonald of Glencoe. Archibald of Kilmaluaig had three sons, Donald, Charles, and John; the last two died in the West Indies. John, who succeeded his father, had issue, the late Sir Donald MacLean of New Zealand.

John, fifth son, was minister at Killean in Kintyre; married Ann, daughter of Hector MacNeil of Losset in Kintyre, and by her had Charles and Florence. Charles had four daughters, Catherine; Ann, married to Hector MacLean of Ballystretrish; Isabella, married to John MacLean, minister in Mull, and Mary, married to John MacLean of Treshnish.

John, the seventh laird of Borreray, succeeded his father Niall Bàn; married a daughter of Campbell of Strond, in Harris, and by her had Archibald, John, and Neil, the last named having married a daughter of Lachlan MacLean Vala, and by her had three daughters. John was minister in North Uist, and had a son, John.

Archibald, eighth laird of Borreray, was first married to a daughter of Samuel MacDonald of the family of Sleat, and by her had two sons and one daughter, Neil, his successor, and John. By his second wife, a daughter of John MacDonald of Balkany, he had Alexander, Hector, and John. He died in 1739, and was succeed by his son Neil, the ninth MacLean of Borreray, who married a daughter of William MacDonald of Ardnickolan, and had by her Donald, John, Archibald, William, and Allan; also two daughters, Marian and Margaret. Donald, the tenth laird, married a daughter of Campbell of Strond, and had issue. The estate was made over to him before his father's death.

CHAPTER XV.
THE MacLEANS OF TRESHNISH.

The second cadet of the family of Ardgour is that of Treshnish, the representatives of which held by hereditary privilege the post of captain of the royal castle of Cairnburg. Ewen, second MacLean of Ardgour, who flourished about 1473, had by his wife three sons—Allan, his successor; John, first MacLean of Treshnish; and Hector, first MacLean of Blaich in Lochaber. John, the first captain of Cairnburg, had a daughter Marian, who married Lachlan Cattanach MacLean, chief of Duard, and a son Donald, who became second MacLean of Treshnish, but dying without issue, he was succeeded by his cousin Donald, eldest son of Hector of Blaich.

III. Donald, Third MacLean of Treshnish,

Commonly called Donald Dubh a Chaistail, was a bold, rough man, but remarkably true to his chief. He brought with him his brother Ewen, who became the first MacLean of Comaig in Tiree. Donald was first married to a daughter of MacMartin of Letterfinlay, by whom he had Ewen, his successor. He next married a daughter of Clanranald, by whom he had Ewen Uaibhreach, who succeeded to his grandfather, Hector MacLean, in the three-merk property of Blaich, holden of the crown. Donald's third son, John, or Iain Odhar, of Achnadale, was baillie to the chief of MacLean of the estate of Garghambhich in Lochaber. His successors continued in that office while the chief kept possession of those lands, and some of the descendants remained there long after. When the marquis of Huntly took possession of that estate, the best of the people dispersed by the oppression of their new masters. Donald had another son, called Lachlan Fionn, who became the laird of Heighnis in Tiree. He was a bold, resolute man, became very rich, and had nine sons, whose offspring peopled a large portion of Tiree. His other brothers' names were Lachlan Og and Donald.

IV. Ewen, Fourth MacLean of Treshnish,

Was Donald's eldest son. He was a spirited, enterprising man, and loved to distinguish himself. He married Ann, daughter of John, laird of Lehire, and by her had Ewen, Hector, Lachlan, Allan, Donald, Charles, Archibald, and John. Lachlan was a wise and rich man, who became manager for Lachlan Og, predecessor of the family of Torloisk. Allan was killed at Sron-na-Cranalich, as mentioned on page 102. He was a famous warrior in Ireland in the wars between the O'Neils and O'Donnells. He was buried at Iona, or Icolmkill. All the sons of Ewen had issue, and many of them people of substance, who lived mostly in Tiree. Ewen was buried in Icolmkill, and was succeeded by his eldest son,

V. Ewen, Fifth MacLean of Treshnish,

Who was a man of chivalrous character, judicious conduct, and of much influence. He purchased a right by charter from Sir Lachlan Mór, his chief, of the lands of Treshnish, Gometra, the six-merk lands of Heighnis in Tiree, and Tolarandale in Coll, which he had renewed to him by Hector Og, Lachlan's son. This was witnessed by Rory MacLeod of Harris and Rory MacNeil of Barra. The ruins of his Gometra residence, an impregnable stronghold, are still to be seen on a conical rock called Dun-Bán, in the north end of the narrow channel which divides Gometra from Ulva. He was first married to Ann, a daughter of MacQuarrie of Ulva, by whom he had issue. His second wife was Flora, daughter of MacNeil of Barra, and relict of Charles, son of Allan nan Sop, by whom he had John, Neil, and Charles. He was succeeded by

VI. John, Sixth MacLean of Treshnish,

Who married Margaret, daughter of Charles, son of Allan nan Sop, and by her had Ewen, Lachlan, and John Og, and likewise a *natural* son, John, or Iain Ghanbhaur. He was succeeded by his son,

VII. Ewen, Seventh MacLean of Treshnish,

Already well known as the gallant favorite of the great Montrose. On account of some misunderstanding between him and his chief, Sir Lachlan, he went to France about the year 1632, leaving his wife and three sons at home under his father's care, where he remained ten years, leading a military life, being captain in the service. Having settled his difficulties with his chief, he returned home, and was sent by Sir Lachlan to Ireland, to command a company of MacLeans in Sir Duncan Campbell's regiment, commanded formerly by Hector MacLean of Kinlochaline, where he remained three years, when the regiment was recalled by the marquis of Argyle, about twenty days before the battle of Inverlochy; at which battle Treshnish saved the life of Campbell of Skipnish, having been companions in Ireland. On their return, each joined his respective chief, in consequence of which they were on opposite sides. Ewen brought Campbell, the night after the battle, to Ardgour, and the next day obtained a berlinn and carried him to Elanaflacker, where his friends, the Campbells, were, and the same day to Dunstaffnage; but no admittance was given at either place, on account of the great panic caused by so severe a defeat.

At length, he was obliged to bring him to Cairnburg, and from there went with him until he had personally delivered Campbell into the hands of his friends in Skipnish. Upon this account, an inviolable friendship existed between the families for a long time, until finally the people of Skipnish thought it beneath them to acknowledge a favor done to them by a person to whom they owed their lives and all they possessed. Ewen was a captain under Sir Lachlan in Montrose's wars, and commanded the forlorn hope at the battle of Kilsyth. He bravely fell with his chief at the fatal battle of Inverkeithing. While he was abroad, and after the death of his father, his brother Lachlan took charge of his affairs, and placed the charter of the lands of Treshnish into the keeping of Sir Lachlan, when for a long time it was lost, with the papers of the family. Ewen married Catherine, daughter of Allan, eldest son of the second marriage of Hector, first of that name of Coll. He was succeeded by his son,

VIII. Hector, Eighth MacLean of Treshnish,

Married to Margaret, daughter of John Garbh of Knocklacke in Ross, of the family of Kinlochaline, and by her had one son. Hector died in the year 1693, and was succeeded by his son,

IX. Ewen, Ninth MacLean of Treshnish,

Married to Margaret, daughter of Neil MacLean of Drimnacross, and by her had Hector, John, John the younger, and Lachlan. Hector was a minister in the island of Coll, and was married to Jennet, daughter of Hector MacLean of Knock of the family of Coll, and by her had Allan, Florence, and Margaret. Allan was a lieutenant in the army, and was lost in the passage from New York to Britain. Florence married Captain Lachlan MacLean of the Coll family; and Margaret married Alexander MacLean of Shingary. John, the third son, married Isabella, daughter of Charles MacLean of Heighnis, and left one son, Alexander, and three daughters, Ann, Mary, and Catherine. Alexander succeeded his father as parish minister of Killninan.

Both were men of exemplary piety; both carefully instructed the people under their charge, and were greatly noted for their painstaking care. Alexander married Christina, daughter of Donald MacLean of Torloisk, and had issue, John, Lachlan, Mary, and Isabella. John was a captain, and lost in the bay of Halifax; Lachlan attained the rank of major-general; Mary married John Campbell of Smithygreen; and Isabella, unmarried. Ann, John's oldest daughter, married first, John, second son to Allan MacLean of Grissipoll, by whom she had two sons and two daughters. She next married Hugh, son of Hector MacLean of Kilmory. Mary married Alexander MacLean of Calgarry in Mull; and Catherine married John, son of Archibald MacLean of Hyscer in North Uist, and had two sons, Archibald, who went to Jamaica, and Neil, a captain in the army, but finally settled in Canada. John died in 1756, and was buried with his father at Killfinan in Mull, when he was succeeded by his second son,

X. John, Tenth MacLean of Treshnish,

Who married Mary, daughter of Charles MacLean of Heighnis. He was dispossessed of his estate in 1768 by the managers of the duke of Argyle, after his predecessors had enjoyed it for nearly three hundred years. As the original charter was lost, the prey became an easy one under the forms of law. John had one son and several daughters. Hugh studied law; married Barbara, daughter of Rev. Archibald MacLean of Kilfinichin, and had issue, five sons and two daughters.

CHAPTER XVI.

THE MacLEANS OF INVERSCADELL.

The third cadet of the family of Ardgour is that of Inverscadell, descended from Charles Mac-Mhic-Allein, first son of the second marriage of Allan, fifth laird of Ardgour. Charles had two sons, Allan, his successor, and Ewen Dubh, who received the lands of Arihaulon and others from his father, and for which he obtained a charter; but in process of time this line became extinct, and the lands were recovered to the Ardgour estate. Allan, second MacLean of Inverscadell, was succeeded by his son, Ewen, who, in turn, was succeeded by his son, Allan, and whose son and successor was

V. Charles, Fifth MacLean of Inverscadell,

Married first to a daughter of Donald Cameron, by whom he had Allan, his successor. His second wife was a daughter of Archibald MacLean of Ardtur, by whom he had John. This John married Mary, daughter of Allan, laird of Ardgour, and by her had John, who, in the year 1760, went from North America to Jamaica to inherit an estate called Duard Castle left to him by an uncle, from which he realized a small independence, returned home, and married Sibella, second daughter of Sir Allan, chief of MacLean, by whom he had one son, Allan, a captain in the 60th regiment, and died in the West Indies. His daughter, Mary Anna, married Doctor MacKenzie Grieve. Charles had a brother, Allan of Killean in Mull, married to Margaret, daughter of Lachlan Og of Ardgour's family, by whom he had two sons, one of whom, Lachlan, lived in Dublin, married, and left issue. He was in good circumstances, and captain of a ship. On his return from Copenhagen, by stress of weather, he was blown upon the south-west coast of Ireland, and, after getting on shore by the long boat with most of the crew, was murdered by the barbarous inhabitants for the sake of plunder.

VI. Allan, Sixth MacLean of Inverscadell,

Married Marjory, daughter of Allan MacLean of the family of Torloisk, and by her had issue. He sold the reversion of the lands of Inverscadell to the Camerons, by which this branch of the family became extinct. The lands were purchased from the Camerons by Alexander, thirteenth laird of Ardgour, and once more added to that estate.

CHAPTER XVII.

THE MacLEANS OF BLAICH.

This family, representing the house of Ardgour, belongs to two periods. The first MacLeans of Blaich were descended from Hector, third son of Ewen, second laird of Ardgour. Hector was succeeded by his grandson, Hector, or Eoghan Uaibhreach, second son of Donald, third laird of Treshnish. The later MacLeans of Blaich are descended from Lachlan, second son of John Crubach, eighth laird of Ardgour. William, grandson to Lachlan of Blaich, was born in the isle of Mull, and was left an orphan at a very early age. In youth he applied himself to the study of music, in which he attained to such proficiency that the duke of York (afterward James II. of England), while lord commissioner in Scotland, invited him to court and appointed him master of music to the princesses Mary and Anne; and afterward to the position of " Master of Revels for Scotland." He had a son, William, who was a captain in the wars in Holland, and served under the duke of Marlborough. He married a daughter of Sir Francis Kinloch, by whom he had two sons, Francis, who attained the rank of major-general, and James, who died in 1748 in the East Indies.

CHAPTER XVIII.

THE MacLEANS OF ROSS.

The third branch of the family of MacLean inhabited that part of Mull known as Brolass and the Ross of Mull. This district is a bold headland or point of land projecting into the sea, and forms the extreme southern part of the island. The surface is very irregular, in one place attaining the height of twelve hundred and thirty-five feet. The rock, for the most part is granite, although there is a considerable sprinkling of other varieties, notably basalt. The MacLeans of Ross were known as *Sliochd a' Chlaidheimh Iaraiun*, or the race of the iron sword, on account of their remarkable bravery. The progenitor was Neil, third son of Lachlan Bronnach of Duard, by his second son, Neil, who obtained the lands in the Ross district of Mull. Neil of Ross had two sons, Donald and John, the latter being the progenitor of the family in the isle of Shuna. Donald's sons were Lachlan, Ewen, and John. The eldest of these,

Lachlan of Ardchraoshinish, surnamed Odhar, or Swarthy, was bold, daring, and brave. He was a constant follower of Sir Lachlan Mór in all his conflicts with the MacDonalds, and was made governor of Duard castle. He was principally instrumental in the recovery of the Lochbuy estate out of the hands of Murdoch of Scallasdale, whom he and Allan MacEachainn fought and defeated at Grulin. He had a numerous issue, and five of his sons, Murdoch, Allan, Lachlan, Ewen, and John, were killed at Inverkeithing; at least one hundred and forty of the Ross MacLeans fell there. Of his descendants, Lachlan of Bunessan married Mary, a daughter of Hector MacLean of Torren, and had a large family: John, Hector, Allan Charles, Sibella, Mary, Catherine, and Isabella. From Lachlan Odhar also descended Allan, Alexander, and Donald MacLean, three brothers, born in the Ross of Mull. Allan was a lieutenant in the Ninetieth regiment; Alexander resided in Glasgow;

Donald had two sons; the second, Hugh, had issue, Allan and Hector. Hector's son John was father of Donald MacLean of Killean, who married Mary, daughter of Charles Ian Garbh, of the family of Kinlochaline, and had issue, John, who married Catherine, daughter of Hector MacLean of Kilmory, a cadet of the Lochbuy family. The last named John left five sons and several daughters; Donald, the eldest, died in Holland, Hector, Neil, John, and Lachlan. Hector married Jennet, daughter of Alexander MacLean of Shuna, and had issue, Donald, Dugall, Neil, and six daughters. Donald was a lieutenant in the Seventy-fourth regiment, remained in America, and left a numerous offspring. Dugall was an officer in the Dumbarton fencibles, served in Ireland, returned home, married Susanna, daughter of Reverend Neil MacLeod, minister of Ross, and had issue. Hector, third son of Neil, was lieutenant of the Leda frigate. He undertook to cut out a French ship from her anchorage; he succeeded, took possession of his prize, but by the rapidity of the tide, which was strong against him, the ship drifted among the French vessels, was boarded and taken. He made a brave resistance, but was overpowered by numbers; yet he fought courageously, until he fell lifeless on the deck. A short time previously, he married Ann, daughter of Donald MacLean of the isle of Muck.

Of Ewen, the second brother of Lachlan Odhar, descended Doctor John MacLean, who resided in Brolass. He married Christina, daughter of captain Allan MacLean, brother of Donald of Brolass, by whom he had Allan, Donald, and Marian. Allan was surgeon of the Seventy-ninth Cameron Highlanders; married Flora, daughter of Murdoch MacLean of Lochbuy, by whom he had a numerous issue. Donald was a lieutenant in the Seventy-ninth regiment.

CHAPTER XIX.
THE MacLEANS OF COLL.

The island of Coll is distant about six miles from the extreme western point of the island of Mull. It is fourteen miles long from north-east to south-west, with an average breadth of two and a half miles. It is an undulating moorland, with fertile patches and some low hills, the highest, Ben Hogh, being three hundred and thirty-nine feet. The sea coast, for the most part, is rocky and precipitous, but indented with several inlets, some of which afford very good harbors. There are forty-eight fresh-water lochs on the island, supposed to cover about two hundred and twenty-seven acres. There are the remains of eight duns, and the foundations of three religious houses,

FRONT VIEW BREACHACHA CASTLE.

and also three upright stones near the south-western extremity of the island. The rock is gneiss, approaching to granite and hornblende slate. On the east side of the south-west part is Loch Breachacha, near the head of which is Breachacha castle, the seat of the MacLeans of Coll. This old castle is still almost entire. The castle is supposed to have been built by the lords of the Isles, but doubtless antedates their period. The earliest description of it known to me is that contained in an official document written between 1577 and 1595: "The laird of Collow (Coll) hes ane castell callit Brekauche, quhilk is ane great strenth be reason of the situation thairof

LANDSIDE VIEW BREACHACHA CASTLE.

verie neir to the sea, quhilk defendis the half thairof, and hes three walls about the rest of the castell and thairof biggit with lyme and stane, with sundrie gude devices for defending of the tower. Ane uther wall about that, within the quhilk schippis and boittis are drawin and salvit. And the third and the uttermost wall of tymber and earth, within the quhilk the haill gudes of the cuntrie are keipit in tyme of troublis or weiris."* The castle has long been deserted, and no pains are taken for its preservation. The height is about eighty feet, but there is no stairway whereby the summit may be reached.

I. John Garbh, First MacLean of Coll.

The fourth branch of the Duard family is that of Coll, descended from John Garbh, third son of Lachlan Bronnach, seventh chief of MacLean, and second son of the second marriage by Fionnaghal, daughter of MacLeod of Harris. He was called John Garbh from his gigantic stature and great strength. He was also called John Teomachd, from his cunning and craft. As already narrated, he received from the lord of the Isles a right to twenty pound land in the isle of Coll, and eighteen merk land in Quinish, in Mull; and from Allan Ruarrie, laird of Clanranald, the six merk land of Rum. Alexander, third lord of the Isles, bestowed upon him the twenty pound land of Lochiel, in Lochaber,† and also the six merk land in Drimnin and Achalennon, in Morvern. John Garbh lived feared by his enemies and respected by his friends. He married Isabella, daughter of Fraser of Lovat, predecessor of lord Lovat. He was succeeded in his estates by his only son,

II. John Abrach, Second MacLean of Coll.

John received the name Abrach on account of his living most of the time on his possessions of the twenty pound land of Lochiel in Lochaber, in defense of which he and a few of his friends were killed in an onset at Blar ni core, near Corpuck, by Cameron of Lochiel and his people, who at that time seized upon and burnt all of Coll's charters to those lands. John Abrach was married to Jannet, daughter of Ewen, fifth MacLean of Urquhart, by whom he had two sons, John and Hector, who were very young at the time their father was killed. The MacMhuloinighs (a tribe of the Camerons noted for their power and fierceness), who fought bravely for Coll at the battle of Blar ni core, took care of the two children and their mother, and conveyed them safely to the isle of Coll; for which good service there was ever after a reciprocal friendship between the two families, and in token of this amity it was cut in stone over the gate of Breachacha castle, that any MacMhuloinigh was welcome there, and should be rescued and protected against all enemies. From John, the MacLeans of Coll adopted the patronymic of MacIan Abrach.

---

* Skene's *Celtic Scotland*, Vol. III., p. 436.   † Gregory's *Western Highlands*, p. 71.

III. John, Third MacLean of Coll,

Appears to have been in possession of the estate in 1493. On February 27, 1499, he received a respite.* King James V. granted him a charter for the twenty pound land of Lochiel and the seven mark land of Drimnin and Achalennan in Morvern, confirming and ratifying a former charter granted to his grandfather, John Garb, by James II., and makes mention that the original rights to the lands of Lochiel, etc., were burned by the Camerons. This charter, dated December 1, 1528, is witnessed by the archbishop of Glasgow, the bishop of Dunkeld, and the bishop of Aberdeen. In May, 1530, John was one of the nine principal islanders who sent Hector, lord of Duard, to offer submission to the king,† and in 1545 was one of the lairds who consented to a treaty with the English king. There is no account of the marriage of John, or tradition that he ever had a son, yet the official records contain a precept for a charter to John MacLean, younger of Coll, son and heir apparent of John MacLean of Coll, of the lands of Coll, etc. It is dated December 25, 1542.‡ It is probable that he was married, and father and son died about the same time. John was succeeded in his estates by his brother,

IV. Hector, Fourth MacLean of Coll.

Hector made greater progress in letters than any other man in the country in which he lived during that period. He understood Latin well, and devoted much of his time to the writing of poetry, in both Latin and Gaelic, fragments of which are still preserved. These compositions testify that he was devout. On account of his literary character he was called Cleireach beag, or little clerk. That he was well adapted for an emergency is illustrated in the art he exhibited in appeasing the wrath of Ailean nan Sop. The official records show a "gift to Hector McClane, brother and heir of the deceased John McClane of Coll of the non-entry of Coll, 24 April, 1558." ‖ June 28, 1559, is recorded a precept for charter to Hector, son and heir apparent of Hector MacLean of Coll, of the lands of Coll, on resignation by the father.§ In 1561 a feud broke out between the families of Duard and Coll, on account of the former insisting on the latter following him in all his private quarrels, like the other gentlemen of the clan. Coll declined on account that he held his lands direct from the crown. The Coll family was brought to the very brink of ruin. Hector was first married to Méve, daughter

---

* *Registrum Secreti Sigilli*, Vol. I., fol. 115.   † Gregory's *Western Highlands*.   ‡ *Reg. Sec. Sig.*, Vol. XVI., fol. 57.   ‖ *Ibid*, Vol. XXIX., fol. 28.   § *Ibid.*, fol. 79.

of Alister Mac-Ian-Chathanaich MacDonald of Islay, by whom he had one son, called Hector Roy, and two daughters: Margaret, married to John Dubh, predecessor of the MacLeans of Kinlochaline, and Jannet, married to John Garbh, son of above John Dubh. Hector was married a second time, to Finovola, daughter of Godfrey MacAllister of Loup, by whom he had two sons: Allan, founder of the family of Achanasaul, and John, founder of the house of Grisipoll, both of which are now extinct. He was succeeded by his eldest son,

V. Hector Roy, Fifth MacLean of Coll,

Who married Marian, daughter of Hector Oig, chief of Duard. Hector Roy died young, and had but one issue, his son and successor,

VI. Lachlan, Sixth MacLean of Coll.

This laird was quite a prominent figure in his day. During Lachlan's minority Nial Mór acted as his guardian. At this time Sir Lachlan Mór renewed the old quarrel with Coll, in order to compel obedience to his chiefship. The invaders were met by Niall Mór, but on his way to the encounter found that the flag had been forgotten. After some annoyance an old warrior named Domhnall Mugach, seeing the perplexity of his leader, stepped forward, took off his bonnet, and pointing to his bald head exclaimed: "This will do for our standard, and I promise it will not go back a foot till night." The two parties met at Struthan nan Ceann, at Totaranald, where the invaders were defeated with great slaughter. Shortly after, Sir Lachlan Mór sent a more numerous force and subjugated the island. Niall Mór fled with Sir Lachlan's men in pursuit, and overtook him at Clachan Dubh, in northern Mull, where they slew him. Niall Mór is supposed to have been a son of Hector, fourth laird of Coll. He was a man of great strength and stature, and a brave, disinterested man. One of the first acts of Lachlan was to free his lands from the hands of Sir Lachlan Mór MacLean, who had taken possession of them during his minority. He petitioned to the privy council for redress, which granted his prayer. In this bill of complaint * it is stated that his possessions consisted of the twenty pound land of Coll, twelve pound land of Quinish, four pound land of Rum, four pound land of Achalennan, and Drimnin, all of which belonged to his father. This record is dated December 23, 1596. In 1601 he was one of the principal parties who effected a reconciliation between the MacDonalds and MacLeans of Skye. In 1609 he was one of the chiefs who met the bishop of the Isles at Iona, when the

---

* *Register Privy Council*, Vol. V., p. 354.

famous statutes of Icolmkill were enacted. He was one of the many chiefs summoned, in 1615, to defend the islands against the inroads of Sir James MacDonald, then in rebellion. He appeared before the privy council in 1616, which bound him to exhibit annually one of his principal kinsmen; that he should reside at his castle of Breachacha, and that he should not keep more than one tun of wine. He also made his personal appearance in the following year. In 1622 the council, along with others, bound him to certain acts which were deemed necessary for the welfare of the Isles, among which he should build and repair the parish kirk.* In the report of 1634, relative to the fisheries and other matters, he is mentioned as one of the principal landlords of the Isles.† He received a charter from the bishop of the Isles of the six mark land of the Isle of Muck, which formerly was possessed by the MacIans of Ardnamurchan, and had remained as tenants of the bishop. These people not only kept possession of the land, but became violent, and among other things murdered Lachlan's natural son, called Ian Gauld. This young man had been given by his father a farm, called Mingary, in Mull, for his patrimony. He went to Ardnamurchan upon some private business, when a party of MacIans attacked the boat in landing, and killed Ian, or John, and with great difficulty his servants carried off the body, which had thirteen arrows through it. For this and other crimes Coll caused fourteen of the principal men to be apprehended at Ardmore in Mull, and sent them to Inverary, where most of them were put to death. For this they afterward sought revenge. It must be this Lachlan who converted his tenants from popery to presbyterianism. The story is well authenticated and doubtless true. When Coll became convinced of the truths of the reformed doctrines, he passed over into Mull, and converted his tenants, by meeting them when going to chapel, and driving them back into a barn where the presbyterian clergyman was to preach; and having used on this occasion a gold-headed cane, it passed into a saying that their religion was that of the yellow-headed stick. This cane remained in the family until quite recently, when it either became lost or else purloined. While young, Lachlan was fourteen years in the laird of MacIntosh's house, and ever after the strictest friendship existed between the families. Rorie MacLeod of MacLeod committed to his keeping his two sons, Sir Rory and Sir Norman. He lived to a good old age, and was much regarded and respected by all his neighbors, who looked upon him as one of great prudence and bravery. He was married to Florence, daughter to the laird of Mac-

---

* *Collectanea de Rebus Albanicis*, p. 122.   ‡ *Ibid.*, p. 109.

THE HOUSE OF COLL.

Leod, and had issue, John Garbh, his successor, Hector of the isle of Muck, Neil of Drimnacross, Catherine, married to John, laird of MacKinnon, and Jannet, married to Farquhar Fraser, dean of the Isles.

VII. John Garbh, Seventh MacLean of Coll,

Who succeeded to the estates of his father, was a man of great wisdom and piety, a lover of men, and given to hospitality. He was a composer of music and a performer on the harp. Two of his compositions, Caoineadh Rioghail, the royal lament, and Toum Murron, are yet preserved. The following anecdote has been handed down concerning him: A captain, Wirttus, master of an English vessel, was wrecked on the island, and started for Coll's castle, where, seeing the laird sitting with a bible in one hand, and a harp placed by his side, was so struck by the venerable appearance of the old gentleman and his occupation, that he exclaimed with admiration, "Is this king David again restored to earth?" He was very temperate, as appears from his refusing to visit a friend of his in the isle of Skye, who promised to give up the evidence of a debt he had against the family if he would come but one night to his house and make merry with him. Coll's friends urged him to go, but he replied that he would not become intoxicated once for any consideration, which, if he went, he could not evade without disobliging his friend. This temperance and his piety were exhibited during the whole course of his life. He was first married to Florence, daugher of Sir Dugald Campbell of Auchnabreck, by whom he had Hector Roy, John of Totaranald, Hugh, killed at Inverkeithing, Florence, married to Donald MacLean of Brolass, Jannet, married to Alexander MacDonald of Achdir, and Una, first married to John MacLean of Kinlochaline, and again to Duncan Stewart of Ardshiel. He was a second time married to Florence, daughter of the second Hector Og of Duard, chief of MacLean, by whom he had one daughter, Catherine, married to Lachlan MacQuarrie of Ulva.

The eldest son, Hector Roy, married Marian, daughter of Hector MacLean of Torloisk. He died before his father, leaving issue two sons, Lachlan and Donald, and four daughters. Margaret, married first to Allan Stewart of Appin, and afterward to Donald MacLean of Kingerloch; Catherine, married to Hector MacLean of isle of Muck; Jannet, married to Hector, fifth son of Charles MacLean of Ardnacross; and Una, married to John MacLean of Achanasaul.

VIII. Lachlan, Eighth MacLean of Coll.

Lachlan succeeded his grandfather, John Garbh, in the estates. He was a man of a brave and warlike spirit, much regarded at home and abroad. He went to Holland and took with him a number of men at his own expense, on which account he was made captain in general MacKay's regiment in the Dutch service. Having returned home for a short visit, he was unfortunately drowned in the water of Lochy, in Lochaber, in the month of August, 1687. He was married to Marian, daughter of John Dubh Muidairteach, captain of Clanranald, by whom he had one son, John Garbh, and two daughters: Florence, married to John MacLeod of Tallisker, and Catherine, married to Norman MacLeod of Grishernish. Lachlan was succeeded by

IX. John Garbh, Ninth MacLean of Coll,

A youth of great promise. He was sent to Edinburgh to complete his studies, and was there killed by the splinter of a grenade thrown from the abbey by order of a Captain Wallace, who commanded a company and caused them to fire upon a mob which had made great disturbance. At the time the onslaught was made, John Garbh happened to be accidentally passing. He was eighteen years of age at the time of his death. He was succeeded in the estates by his uncle, Donald, second son of Hector Roy.

X. Donald, Tenth MacLean of Coll,

Was first married to Isabella, daughter of Sir Rory MacLeod of Tallisker, by whom he had one son, Hector. He was again married to Marian, daughter of Sir Norman MacLeod of Bernera, by whom he had Lachlan, John, Hugh, Neil, and one daughter, Catherine, married to Hector MacLean of Grulin. Donald died in April, 1729, aged seventy-three, and universally respected by all who knew him. To him succeeded his eldest son,

XI. Hector, Eleventh MacLean of Coll.

Hector was a tall, handsome man, with black hair and eyes and a fine complexion. His countenance was so expressive as to command attention and respect at first sight. He was polite in his address, and possessed in his behavior so much dignity and ease that even those who were no friends to his interests were prejudiced in favor of his person. He was endowed with excellent natural parts, having an excellent memory, quick perception, and a solid judgment. Although practicing great economy, he was generous. He knew how to make money and to use it judiciously. His passions were strong, but fully self-controlled. The estate had been greatly burdened with debt, but through the judicious management of his father and himself, he left it free of all incumbrance, and a handsome fortune besides. He sought to improve the estate and bring it up to a high state. Near the castle he built a handsome residence, where he lived opulently and entertained with hospitality. His influence was so great that to a certain extent he had the direction of the clan MacLean. He was opposed to the revolution of 1745; not that he opposed the house of Stuart, but knew the effort would be futile. It was through his influence there was not a general rising of the clan. In a letter dated at Tallisker, August 11, 1745, addressed to lord president Forbes, Sir Alexander MacDonald says of Coll: "Mr. MacLean of Coll is here with his daughter, lately married to Tallisker; and he assures us of his own wisdom; and as he has mostly the direction of that clan, promises as much as in him lies to prevent their being led astray." *

The last harper in Mull, and perhaps the last in the Highlands, Murdoch MacDonald, was harper to Hector MacLean of Coll. He was brought up in the family, and "studied with Rory Dall, in Skye, and afterward in Ireland, and remained with MacLean, as harper, until 1734, as appears from an account of payments still remaining, soon after which he appears to have retired to Quinish, in Mull, where he died. He is still spoken of as Murdoch Clarsair, and his son was distinguished as Eoin MacMhurchaidh Clarsair.† The MacNeils, a celebrated race of bards, were the hereditary harpers of the MacLeans of Duard." ‡

Hector MacLean was twice married: first to Mary, daughter of Alexander Campbell of Lochnell, by whom he had Isabella, married to Colin Campbell of Ballimore; Margaret, married to Alexander MacDonald of Boisdale; Mary, married to colonel John MacLeod of Tallisker; Una, married to Sir Allan MacLean, Bart., chief of MacLean; and Sibella, married to captain Allan Cameron of Glendessary. He was a second time married to Jean, daughter of Donald Campbell of Airds, who, dying soon after, left no issue. Hector died November 6, 1756, and leaving no male issue, was succeeded by his brother,

XII. Lachlan, Twelfth MacLean of Coll,

Who was married to Catherine, eldest daughter of Donald MacLean of Brolass, and by her had several children, all of whom died young. His brother John died while pursuing his studies at the college of Glasgow, and another brother, Neil, entered the mercantile business in Williamsburg, Virginia, where he died. As Lachlan left no children, he was succeeded by his remaining brother,

XIII. Hugh, Thirteenth MacLean of Coll,

Married Jannet, eldest daughter of Donald MacLeod of Tallisker, by

---

* Browne's *History of the Highlands*, Vol. III., p. 43.   † For poem, see Appendix C, No. 2.
‡ Logan's *Scottish Gael*, p. 417.

whom he had Donald, Alexander, Hector (afterward lieutenant-general Sir Hector), Norman, Roderick, Allan, Hugh, and one daughter, Marian, who was married to colonel Alexander MacDonald of Boisdale. The eldest son, Donald, was indeed a very promising young man, and held in esteem by all his acquaintances, who respected his sobriety, discretion, love of justice, affability, and activity. He was drowned in the sound of Ulva, with eight others, on September 25, 1774. I find the following account of this sad catastrophe: "Archibald Murdoch, Esq., younger of Gartincaber, Mr. MacLean of Coll, Mr. Fisher from England, and Malcolm MacDonald, drover in Mull, with five attendants, were unfortunately drowned in crossing a ferry in the isle of Mull. Mr. Murdoch had gone to Mull on a visit to Mr. MacLean of Lochbuie, and having dined at a friend's house, the melancholy accident happened on their return. The barge overset within a gunshot of the lands of Ulva and Mull. Mr. MacLean (John, seventeenth) of Lochbuie, and three young men in the barge, having got hold of the mast, continued dashing in the waves for three-quarters of an hour, and were saved by the ferry-boat of Ulva, which reached them as they were ready to sink." * Due mention of him is made in chapter XXXVII. Alexander, the second son, was for some years lieutenant-colonel of the Breadalbane fencible regiment. Norman attained the rank of major in the Sixty-eighth regiment. He was sent to the island of Grenada, where, during an insurrection of the Caribs, he signalized himself as a brave and experienced officer, and defended the post assigned him for four months against all attempts of the enemy until he was taken down with the yellow fever, of which he died within four days, immediately after which the post was captured. Roderick died on his passage from Jamaica to St. Domingo, where he was going to join his regiment. He was married to Christianna, youngest daughter of captain Allan Cameron of Glendessary, and left one daughter, Marian. Allan was captain in the Thirty-sixth regiment, and married Jean, also a daughter of Cameron of Glendessary. Hugh, the seventh son, was for some time a captain in the Sixtieth regiment. He died of consumption soon after his return from Jamaica. Hugh was succeeded in the estates by his second son,

XIV. Alexander, Fourteenth MacLean of Coll,

Who was a thorough Highlander. He was of an independent character, and greatly beloved for his benevolent and generous disposition. He treated his tenants with great kindness. For some time he studied law. He married Catherine, eldest daughter of captain Allan Cameron of Glendessary, by

---

* Boswell's *Journal of a Tour to the Hebrides*, p. 262.

whom he had one son, Hugh, and six daughters: Jannet, married to George Vere Hobart, second son of the earl of Buckinghamshire; Sibella; Catherine, married to major MacLeod of Tallisker; Maria, married to Alexander Hunter of Edinburgh; Marian; and Breadalbin, who devoted her energies to the good of her fellow-creatures in the land of her birth. Alexander died in the year 1835, and was succeeded by his son,

XV. Hugh, Fifteenth MacLean of Coll.

Mr. MacIntyre, parish minister of Torosay, who had frequently seen Hugh, fifteenth of Coll, describes him to me as having been a man of dignity, commanding appearance, kind, affable, and just. His father, Alexander, removed from Coll, in 1828, to Mull, and the family never returned to live again on Coll. In the immediate neighborhood of Tobermory is a beautiful loch, called Mary's lake, which was owned by Hugh. The spot is a beautiful one, situated between two finely wooded hills, extremely precipitous in their descent. This pleasing spot Hugh improved in a manner highly creditable to his taste and judgment, and on the banks of the lake erected the elegant mansion of Drumfin. Hugh was born in 1782, and at first preferred a military life, and rose to the rank of lieutenant-colonel, and for some time served in the Guards. In his regiment was John MacDonald of Tiree, who had neglected to perform some duty at a bridge, in consequence of which major Montgomery ordered him to be whipped. Hugh went twice to the major, and humbly pleaded for MacDonald. but to no purpose. When the flogging was to begin, Hugh cut the cords with his sword. Montgomery challenged MacLean, which was at once accepted; but as Hugh was then quite young, the soldiers feared he might be killed; so they sent word to the irate major that if he killed MacLean he would be shot. The duel did not take place.

Hugh received the estate burdened, and also added to the indebtedness. It was deemed advisable to sell the whole estate, which was done, in April, 1856. For a long time before it had been under trustees. It was related to me that the sale of Coll carried many pangs of grief to its owner. When he realized his lands must go, in an agony of despair, he seized a hatchet and aimlessly began to hack the trees in his yard. It was an evil day to the inhabitants of Coll when its laird gave up the property. The long line of lairds had been generous to those who looked to them for succor.

Hugh was first married in 1814 to Jannet, daughter of James Dennistoun, by whom he had issue, four daughters: Margaret (died in 1882), married to James Hamilton of Barnes; Catherine Cameron; Elizabeth, married Walter Griffith; and Isabella Sibella; the last three now living at Upper Norwood.

London. Hugh was again married, in 1825, to Jane Robertson, and had issue: Juliet, married to Ashe Windham, of Waken, Yorkshire; Alexander, his successor; John Hector Norman, lieutenant-general; William, died in India in 1867; Evan, a captain, died in 1870; and Jane Albane, married to George Dundas, died in 1883. During the later years of his life, Hugh lived in London, and in 1861 died at Woodville, in the house of his daughter Margaret.

XVI. Alexander, Sixteenth MacLean of Coll.

Alexander, sixteenth and last of Coll—Sliochd Iain Ghairbh—inherited in a remarkable degree the characteristics of his family, great benignity and kindliness of disposition, which made his forefathers among the most popular landlords of their day. In 1849, he emigrated to Natal, Africa, where he died, July 11, 1875, aged forty-seven. He was never married. In him the family of Coll, in the direct line, became extinct.

CHAPTER XX.

THE MacLEANS OF ACHANASAUL.

The first cadet of the family of Coll is that descended from Allan, the elder son of Hector, fourth MacLean of Coll, by MacAllister of Loup's daughter. Allan was sent by his father to assist Rory MacLeod against MacDonald of Sleat, over whom MacLeod gained a decisive victory. This was the last feud between those two families. Allan commanded a company of his father's men under Sir Lachlan Mór at the battle of Gruinart, where the latter was killed. He was married to Anne, daughter of MacIan of Ardnamurchan, by whom he had Hector, Ronald, and Donald, many of whose descendants reside in Ireland. John, second son of Coll by Loup's daughter, married Finovola, daughter of the laird of MacKinnon's, by whom he had John, who was married to Margaret, daughter of Roderick MacLean, a merchant in Glasgow, and had issue, Lachlan, John, Hugh, and Charles. Lachlan married Ann, daughter of Neil MacLean of Drimnacross, and had issue, Roderick, John, Hector, and Allan. Roderick left two sons, Lachlan and John, the former a captain in the East India Company's service, who married a daughter of his uncle, Hector MacLean, and afterward a daughter of Alexander MacLean of Sollose, and left two sons and several daughters. Of Charles, the youngest of the four sons of the above mentioned John, was

Lachlan of Killmore in Mull. John's second son, John, was first a minister of the church in Arran. Upon the revolution, he went to Ireland, where, for some time, he was chaplain to lord Masserene, and minister in Antrim. He was a man of great physical strength and profound piety. The following incident has been preserved, which forcibly exhibited his great reserve power. The bishop, in making his rounds of the diocese on one occasion, was accompanied by a number of the young clergy, and John also attended him. As John's dialogue was Scotch, it afforded much amusement to those who spoke refined English, and the latter, upon Saturday night, persuaded the bishop to appoint John to preach the next morning. John knew nothing of the decision until the following morning, and when apprized of the decision, simply remarked that time should have been afforded him. After the service was read, he took his bible, and calling to the door-keeper, asked him to take the book to the bishop who sat opposite. He then asked the bishop to point out the text, which, in some confusion, was complied with. The hearers declared that for forty years they had not heard so excellent or masterly discourse as he gave them that day. The bishop asked his pardon, and hoped he would show no resentment to those who were the cause. "No, no!" replied John, "let them keep free from my religion and my country, and they will have nothing to fear from me; but none shall attack either of these with impunity." He first married a daughter of Lachlan MacNeill of Lossett, by whom he had several daughters. His second wife was a daughter of James Cubbage, by whom he had John, minister of Clocher, Clotworthy, a physician in Belfast, James, minister in Rachry, in Antrim. John, minister of Clocher, married Elizabeth, daughter of Philip Mathews, rector of Ballymony, by whom he had Lachlan, James, and Henry. Lachlan was bred to the medical profession, went with the army to America, where he obtained particular notice and patronage from generals Forbes and Monkton. He was physician to Monkton's forces in the expedition against Martinico; and, subsequently, appointed receiver general of the customs while the island was in possession of Great Britain. Returning to Britain, he was appointed under secretary to lord Shelburne for the southern department, and afterward held an important post in the East India Company; and later agent for the Nabob of Arcot. On his return home, at the Cape of Good Hope, he transferred his passage from the ship to the Swallow packet. Neither the Swallow nor a single soul that embarked on board of her has ever been heard of. He left a son in India who held an important situation at the time of his father's loss.

CHAPTER XXI.

THE MacLEANS OF MUCK.

The second cadet of the family of Coll is that of the MacLeans of isle of Muck, a small island off the coast of Scotland, situated between the north end of Coll and the isle of Eig, distant about ten miles from the former and two from the latter. Hector, son of Lachlan, sixth MacLean of Coll, had the island given to him by his father. He is described as having been a gentleman of fine accomplishments, both in intellectual acquirements and personal deportment. He led a company of Coll's men under Sir Lachlan MacLean in Montrose's army, during the civil wars, and behaved with distinguished gallantry at the battle of Kilsyth. The MacIans (MacDonalds) of Ardnamurchan, from a feeling of revenge on account of Hector's father having brought so many of them to justice, and being privately instigated by Sir Donald Campbell of Ardnamurchan, then the possessor of the property of the chief of MacIan, landed by night near Muck's house, and began to drive away his cattle. Hector happened to be out with one servant only, yet he fired upon the thieves, but was immediately surrounded and shot dead. Hector was married to Julian, daughter of Allan MacLean of Ardtornish, by whom he had Hector, who succeeded him, and Hugh.

II. Hector, Second MacLean of Muck,

Was married to Catherine, daughter of the second Hector Roy, laird of Coll, and had issue, Hector and Lachlan. Hector married Marian, daughter of Lachlan MacLean of Calgary, but both died young and without issue. The younger brother then inherited the estate.

III. Lachlan, Third MacLean of Muck,

Was a captain in Sir John MacLean's regiment at Sheriffmuir. He married Mary, daughter of James MacDonald of Bellfinlay, and left two sons, Hector and Donald, and two daughters. He was succeeded by his eldest son,

IV. Hector, Fourth MacLean of Muck,

Who married Isabella, second daughter of Donald MacLeod of Tallisker, but dying without issue, was succeed by his brother,

V. Donald, Fifth MacLean of Muck,

First married to Florence, daughter of Rev. Archihald MacLean, minister of Ross in Mull, by whom he had one son, Lachlan. His second wife was

Florence, daughter of John MacLean of Treshnish, by whom he had one son, John, and three daughters, Florence, Mary, and Ann. John married Isabella, daughter of John MacLean of the Borreray family, and factor of Ardgour, by whom he had issue. Ann married lieutenant Neil MacLean, of the Leda frigate, who lost his life as previously mentioned. Donald was succeeded by his son,

VI. Lachlan, Sixth MacLean of Muck,

Served in the American revolutionary war, between 1775–82. He married an American lady, Hannah Barbara Cottingham, by whom he had a numerous issue. He was for some time lieutenant-colonel of the Breadalbane fencibles, and afterward held the post of deputy lieutenant of the Tower.

I have no further information concerning this family, save the descendants of John, second son of Donald. See Chapter XXV.

CHAPTER XXII.
THE MacLEANS OF DRIMNACROSS.

The third cadet of the family of Coll is descended from Neil MacLean of Drimnacross, third son of Lachlan, sixth laird of Coll. Neil accompanied Sir Lachlan MacLean during the civil wars, and, under Sir Hector Roy MacLean, was severely wounded at Inverkeithing. He married Florence, daughter of Allan MacDonald of Morrer, and had issue: Hector, Allan, Marian, Ann, ———, Florence, Margaret, and Janet. The elder son, Hector MacLean of Torrestan, was a captain in Sir John MacLean's regiment at Killiecrankie, and was killed at Dunkeld. He married Florence, daughter of Lachlan MacLean of Calgary, and by her had one son, Lachlan, who succeeded him in the lands of Torrestan. Lachlan served for some time in the war in Flanders under general Murray, but being unjustly treated on the subject of promotion, he retired in disgust from the service. He married Margaret, daughter of Rev. Alexander MacDonald, minister of the Small Isles, by whom he had several sons, all of whom died young. He also had several daughters, who were married.

Neil's second son, Allan MacLean of Grisiboll, or Grishipoll, married Catherine, daughter of Hugh MacLean of Balliphetrish, of the family of Borreray, and had issue: Lachlan, John, Neil, Allan, Florence, who married

Donald MacLean of Calgary, and Mary, married to John MacLean of Guirdhill in Rum. Lachlan, the eldest son, was a merchant in Glasgow, and was twice married. By his first wife he had several sons and daughters, all of whom died young, except Lachlan, unmarried, and Catherine, married to Daniel Burnett of Annat Hill. John, Allan's second son, married Anne, daughter of Rev. John MacLean, minister of Kilmore in Mull, by whom he had John and Archibald. John was a merchant in Norfolk, Virginia, where he was married, and left one daughter. Archibald was a merchant in Dantzig, and married Mary, daughter of Mr. Symson, one of the magistrates of Memel, and had issue: John, Lachlan, Archibald, Henry, and several daughters. Allan's third son, Neil, was bred to the medical profession; went to America, purchased lands in Connecticut, and for many years resided in Hartford, where he was married, and had issue, three sons and one daughter. Allan's fourth son, Allan, also went to Connecticut, where he was twice married, and left issue. He was a lieutenant and commissary in Connecticut.

Of the daughters of Neil of Drimnacross, Marian married Charles Bailie of Ross; Ann married Lachlan MacLean of Grisiboll in Coll; —— married Hector MacQuarrie of Ormaig; Florence married Charles MacLean of Hynish in Tiree; Margaret married Donald MacLean of Arihaullan, and afterward married Ewen MacLean of Treshnish; and Jannet married Charles MacLean of the family of Coll. It is further related, that " these daughters had many children of both sexes, and were themselves reputed women of great modesty and good sense."

CHAPTER XXIII.

THE MacLEANS OF TOTARANALD.

The fourth cadet of the family of Coll is that of Totaranald, descended from John, second son of John Garbh, seventh MacLean of Coll. John was with his chief, Sir Lachlan, during the civil wars. He and his brother Hugh were among the first that joined the standard of Montrose at Strathearn in the beginning of the year 1646. Both again were with their father's men at Inverkeithing, where the gallant Hugh fought after both his legs were shot off defending his cousin and chief's body until he was cut down by a saber. John was severely wounded in the head and body and taken prisoner. Soon after he was imprisoned an English officer came to see the prisoners, and coming to where John was, observed the latter fainting. The officer rendered him all the assistance he could, and when he revived asked him what had been the cause. John replied : " The shoulder-belt you have on is the cause ; for I am certain the owner of it never would have parted with it were he alive." The officer answered : " That is true ; for a braver youth was not that day on the field than he to whom this belt belonged." John replied : " That was my brother." The officer seeing Hugh's name was indented in silver and rich ornaments on the belt, he insisted on John's keeping it in memory of his brave brother. After the restoration John went to London, and was there introduced to the king, who acknowledged that he recollected his sufferings. Yet, as was the custom of Charles in dealing with his truest friends, the acknowledgment of his service was the only reward John ever received. John married Marian, daughter of Allan MacLean of Ardgour, by whom he had Allan, last of Totaranald. Allan was bred for the law, but forsook it, and retired to the country. He married Catherine, daughter of Roderick MacLeod of Harmar, by whom he had two sons, Hector and Allan. The latter, while young, was drowned. Hector married Margaret, daugther of Alexander MacLachlan, bailee of Tiree, and had issue, Allan and Roderick. Both went to sea, and afterward settled in Ireland, where the latter married. John of Totaranald had another son, called Hugh, whose descendants lived in Edinburgh. John also had three daughters, Margaret, Florence, and Ann ; the last married to Lachlan MacLean of Calgary.

There are other branches of the early lairds of Coll, but I do not know their history.

CHAPTER XXIV.

THE MacLEANS OF CROSSAPOL.

Among the later cadets of the family of Coll is that of Crossapol, descended from Allan MacLean, who married Mary, eldest daughter of MacLean of Langmull, by whom he had issue three sons, Neil, John, Donald, Catharine Mary, Christina, Jessie, and Julia. Neil succeeded his father in the year 1832. John was a merchant in London, and married in 1831 to Anne, daughter of Alexander MacLean of Kinnegharar, of the Kinlochaline family, and had issue, Catherine and Julia. Donald died in 1834 of pulmonary complaint at the age of twenty-two. Anne, sister of Allan, married Neil Campbell of Treshnish.

CHAPTER XXV.
THE MacLEANS OF HAREMERE HALL.

This family is descended through both the MacLeans of Coll and Ardgour. Captain John MacLean was the second son of Donald MacLean, fifth laird of Muck. He served abroad, and then in the Argyle fencibles. He married Isabella, daughter of John MacLean of the family of Borreray, by whom he had a son, Alexander Campbell MacLean of Haremere Hall, county of Sussex, who married, August 16, 1825, Mary Elizabeth Travers of Fairfield, Devon, and died October 14, 1864, having issue, Henry Travers, John Lachlan, George Francis, Alexander, Hector Coll, Morgan, and Adelaide Owen, married to lieutenant-colonel Edward H. Fisher. Henry Travers was a captain in the Bomby Indian army, married Marianne, daughter of captain Donald MacLean, and died January 22, 1863, leaving issue a posthumous son, Henry Travers. George Francis (died in 1885), younger brother of Lachlan, married a daughter of J. W. Cole, and had issue, Margaret Gavine, married to J. L. Scott; Emilie Fordyce, married to W. R. Dunstan; Alexander Henry Herbert, Rosalie Abbé, who died in 1887; Lowry Cole, now of Bencraig, Sevenoaks, and Adeline Travers. John Lachlan, now of Haremere Hall, was born February 20, 1828; married January, 1858, Mary, daughter of Henry Huttleston of New Bedford, Massachusetts, and has issue, Lachlan Perceval, born 1862; Cameron Travers, born 1865; Edmund Henry, born 1866; Hector George, born 1886; Mary Kate, Annie Travers, and Lilian Gray.

There are many other branches of the esteemed family of Coll, but they are so scattered that to trace them would be almost a hopeless task. The burial ground of the Coll family is located in Coll, on the point of land projecting between Crossapol bay and Loch Breachacha, distant about one mile from the castle.

CHAPTER XXVI.

THE MacLEANS OF KINLOCHALINE.

Morvern is a corruption of the native graphic appellation *Mhor Earrain*, or the great province, and anciently known as Ceann Albin, or promontory of Albin. This appellation was peculiarly applicable because Loch Linnhe, which bounds Morvern on the southeast, formed the line of separation between Drim Albin, the territory of the northern Picts, and Dalriada, the southern part of Argyleshire, the territory of the Scots. This country is particularly noted as being the scene of many of the tales of Ossian. It formed a part of the dominions of Somerled, which belonged to his ancestors, and which he regained from the rapacious Norsemen, in which he was assisted by the Mac-Inneses. King Robert Bruce conferred the lands on Angus Og MacDonald, and in an agreement between Edward Baliol and John of the Isles, in 1335, the latter was confirmed in the possession of this territory, and in the document is called "Terram de Ken-Albdan." On the 12th of July, 1390,* dated at Ardtornish, Donald, lord of the Isles, granted Morvern to Lachlan MacLean, lord of Duard. By this deed and others afterward ratified by crown charters, the MacLeans, with slight interruptions, held possession until about 1680, when, by machinations, it was possessed by the Argyle family, and sold from the latter in 1819. Some of the mountains of Morvern are of considerable height, that of Ben Mheon reaching an altitude of two thousand four hundred and twenty-three feet. Yet, when viewed in connection with the bold ranges of Mull and Appin, they are of a tame and undefined character. The country abounds in antiquities. Along the coasts are the remains of several small forts, belonging to the days of the Norse invasion. There are several Druidical circles, and many tumuli; the largest of the latter is that called Carn-na-Caillich, which is composed of loose stone, piled up to a considerable height, and measuring eighty-one yards in circumference. On an insulated and wooded eminence, at Loch Teacuis, are the remains of a vitrified fort. Of all the remains, the most conspicuous are the old castles, Ardtornish, Killundine, Kinlochaline, and Drimnin. Ardtornish, at one time, was a place of great importance, for it was one of the strongholds of the Lords of the

---

* *Reg. Mag. Sig.*, Lib. XIII., No. 300.

Isles, and where assembled the feudal and patriarchal vassals. It was here that the famous conference took place between the commissioners of Edward IV. of England and those of John of the Isles, October 19, 1462, which terminated in the notable treaty, by which the Lord of the Isles acknowledged himself a vassal of the crown of England, and promised aid in the subjugation of Scotland. The castle is located upon the point of a peninsula that projects into the Sound of Mull. The ruins now consist chiefly of the remains of an old tower, with fragments of outward defenses. The site of the spacious apartment in which the ancient *parliament* met is still pointed out, and in the face of the rock, overhanging the bay of Ardtornish, is the precipice over which the transgressors of feudal times were thrown. The castle of Killundine is located on the coast immediately opposite Aros castle. It is an interesting building, and evidently not very ancient. At one time it was a hunting lodge used by the feudal occupants of Aros castle; and, from this circumstance, it is yet known as Caisteal-nan-Conn, or the castle of dogs. Kinlochaline castle, situated near the head of Loch Aline, consists of a square tower built on a very picturesque spot which overhangs the estuary of Gear Abhain. Tradition says it was built by Dubh-Chal, a lady of the MacInnes tribe, who paid her architect a quantity of butter equal to the full of the castle. The castle was occupied by Colonel Kitteach and a detachment of his Irish troops in 1664, and afterward set fire to it, a proceeding which he afterward regretted. Loch Aline is two and a half miles long, and is as lovely and romantic a sea as ever was seen.

The fifth branch of the family of Duard is that of Kinlochaline, descended from Ian or John Dubh of Morvern, second son of the first Hector Mór, chief of MacLean, by Mary, daughter of MacDonald of Islay. He had Morvern given him by his father in life-rents for his patrimony. He was very active in assisting his nephew, Lachlan Mór, against Eachan Mhac Ailean nan Sop and against the MacDonalds, until he was taken by Angus MacDonald of Islay, in company with Lachlan Mór, in Kintyre, and then beheaded. He was thrice married: First, to Margaret, daughter of Eachann or Hector MacIan, laird of Coll, by whom he had one son called Donald Glas, who lost his life in the explosion of the Florida, in 1588. His second wife was Catherine, daughter of John Gorm, the first Campbell of Lochnell, by whom he had Allan, first of Ardtornish. The third wife was Margaret, daughter of Archibald Campbell of Ardintenny, by whom he had two sons, John Garbh and Charles. Allan MacLean of Ardtornish, at the age of sixteen, began to molest MacIan of Ardnamurchan for being instrumental in causing his father's death, and pressed old MacDonald so hard that the latter was glad to be reconciled to the young warrior at any cost, and to establish peace gave Allan his oldest daughter, Una, in marriage, with a considerable dowry. Allan was a constant follower of Sir Lachlan Mór in all his wars; was at the battle of Glenlivat, where, being shot in the head with a bullet, his life was saved by his helmet, but having been struck down, he was rescued from the Gordons by the valor of Lachlan Oir Mhac Dhonil Mhic Neil of the family of Ross. He was with Hector Og, Sir Lachlan's son, burning Islay and defeating the MacDonalds in the pitched battle of Bein Begrie in that island. He left issue, Hector, Charles, Donald Glas, Mary the elder, married to Gillean, and Mary the younger, to Allan, both sons of Sir Lachlan Mór; Margaret, married to Neil MacNeil of Barra; Jannet, married to Hector MacLean of Torloisk; Julian to Hector MacLean of Isle of Muck; Christianna to Christian MacLean of Kingerloch; and Florance to Martin MacGilivra of Pennyghael, minister of the gospel.

I. Hector, First MacLean of Kinlochaline.

Hector, second son of Allan of Ardtornish, was the first MacLean of Kinlochaline. He was the first who obtained a charter for those lands in Morvern, Tiree, and Mull, which made up the estate of Kinlochaline, partly held of the king, and partly from the chief of MacLean. He commanded a detachment of MacLeans in Ireland during the rebellion of 1641. He was first married to Jannet, daughter of Lachlan Og, first MacLean of Torloisk, by whom he had two sons, John and Lachlan; he was a second time married, to Margaret, daughter of Sir Robert Campbell of Glenorchy, by whom he had a son who died young. He was succeeded by his eldest son,

II. John, Second MacLean of Kinlochaline,

Who suffered severely at the battle of Inverkeithing. He was first married to Mary, daughter of John Campbell of Lochnell, by whom he had Hector, his successor, Allan, who died unmarried, and Jannet, married to John Cameron of Glendessary. John was again married, to Una, daughter of the second John Garbh, laird of Coll, but had no issue.

III. Hector, Third MacLean of Kinlochaline,

Married Jannet, daughter of Hector MacLean of Torloisk, and had issue,

IV. Angus, Fourth MacLean of Kinlochaline,

Who was a gallant and warlike character. He served in general Murray's regiment in the Dutch service for several years, and subsequently was one of Sir John MacLean's captains at the battle of Sheriffmuir. He first married

Margaret, daughter of Allan MacLean of Ardgour, and had several children, but all died young. He next married Anne, daughter of Ranald MacDonald of Kinloch Moidart. Having no children, he was succeeded by Charles MacLean of Drimnin, his nearest kinsman.

CHAPTER XXVII.

THE MacLEANS OF DRIMNIN.

The seat of the MacLeans of Drimnin was across the Sound of Mull from Tobermory. Here they had a castle called Drimnin. This structure occupied a commanding situation, but during the present century was pulled down, in order to prepare a site for a Romish chapel.

The MacLeans of Drimnin are descended from John Garbh, elder son of John Dubh of Morvern by his third wife, Margaret. John Garbh was first married to Jannet, daughter of Hector, fourth laird of Coll, and by her had one daughter, married to Martin MacGillivray of Pennyghael. His second wife was Mary, daughter of Lachlan Og, first MacLean of Torloisk, by whom he had Margaret, married to Hector MacLean of Treshnish; Jannet, married to Malcolm MacDuffie of Colonsay; Catharine, married to Ewen MacLean of Ballyphetrish, in Tiree, and Charles, married to Marian, daughter of Neil MacLean of Drimnacross, by whom he had Allan, Hector, John, and Mary. Allan was married to Catherine Stewart of Ireland, and had several daughters. He was a captain in Sir John MacLean's regiment at Killiecrankie and Sheriffmuir, and killed in the last named battle. Hector was killed in the Spanish service. John was killed in Flander's in queen Anne's wars. Mary was married to Donald MacLean of Killean. Charles, youngest son of John Dubh of Morvern, married Julian, daughter of Neil MacGillivray, by whom he had Lachlan and John Diurach. Lachlan married, and had a son, Donald, who was a merchant in Glasgow, married to Isabella MacAdam, by whom he had a son called Patrick, who was major commandant of colonel John Lamby's regiment in Holland. He died in London, unmarried, in 1752. John Diurach commanded the forlorn hope at Inverkeithing, and there received numerous wounds from which he suffered greatly. He married Elizabeth, daughter of Charles MacLean, Kilis, in Tyree, by whom he had a son, Hector, who married Mary, daughter of Hugh MacLean of Ballyphetrish, in

Tiree, of the family of Borreray, and by her had Lachlan, John, and Donald. Lachlan served with distinction in the second battalion of the Scots Guards in Spain, and subsequently commanded a company of volunteers under brigaadier MacIntosh at Preston, in the year 1715, where he was taken prisoner; but shortly afterward was liberated under the indemnity act of George the first. He died unmarried. John, Hector's second son, was a captain in MacLean of Drimnin's battalion at Culloden, and was one of the number massacred on the following morning. He never married. Donald, the third son, first married Anne, daughter of Charles MacLean of Kilunaig, and had issue, Mary, who married John MacLean of Langmull. His second wife was Mary, daughter of John MacLean of Killean, by whom he had Lachlan and two daughters. Lachlan went upon that ill-planned and worse executed expedition commanded by Major Paulson, from Jamaica to the Spanish main, where with many others he lost his life.

Charles MacAllan, commonly so called, second son to Allan MacLean of Ardtornish, is called the first of Ardnacross. He married Mary, eldest daughter of Allan, seventh MacLean of Ardgour, by whom he had Allan the elder, Lachlan, Allan the younger, Donald, Hector, Ewen, Anne, Florence, Margaret, and Mary. To Allan the elder he gave the lands of Drimnin in Morvern, which he purchased of Argyle. Allan, reputed to be the handsomest man in the country, married Mary, daughter of John Cameron of Callart, by whom he had John, who succeeded him, Donald, and Margaret, who married Allan MacLean of the family of Torloisk. Donald married Florence, daughter of Lachlan MacLean of Calgary, by whom he had Lachlan, who married in Ireland and resided at Muluchglass, near Dundalk, where he left numerous descendants. Allan MacLean of Drimnin died at the age of twenty-nine, and was succeeded by his eldest son, John, who married Mary, daughter of John Crubach, eighth MacLean of Ardgour, by whom he had Allan and Charles. John also died at the age of twenty-nine, and was succeeded by his eldest son, Allan, who never married, and died likewise at twenty-nine years of age. He was succeeded by his brother Charles, who was then serving in the navy. On his brother's death, he came home and married Isabella, daughter of John Cameron of Erracht. He was lieutenant-colonel and commander of the MacLeans at the battle of Culloden, and was there killed, along with his natural son, Lachlan, who was a captain in the regiment. The heroic conduct of brave old colonel Charles MacLean at Culloden is narrated on page 219. The following anecdote has been preserved concerning him, by John MacKenzie: "The laird of Drimnin kept an old schoolmaster in his house, in the double

capacity of tutor to his children and goer of errands. The dominie was one
day sent to a shoemaker, who lived on the laird's grounds, with a message ordering a pair of new shoes for his master. The souter declined the honor intended him, alleging as a reason that it was a standing rule with him 'never to
make a pair of shoes for any customer till the last which he had got were paid
for.' But there was another, if not rather a piece of the same, reason of the
shoemaker's unwillingness to make the shoes—the laird was a *dreach* payer;
one, in fact, who would run on an account to any conceivable length without
ever thinking it time to settle it. Well, the wielder of the ferule returned,
and reported to his master the *ipsis sima verba* of the son of St. Crispin. The
laird was so exasperated at the insolence of his retainer, that he immediately
determined to be revenged on the souter; and, lest he should have the hardihood to deny his own words, he took the schoolmaster along with him. Now,
the souter was a regular lickspittle; a mean, cringing, fawning, malicious, yet
cowardly wretch; for, when the laird said to him, 'Did you say to this gentleman,' pointing to the dominie, 'that you would make no more shoes for me till
I paid for the last I got?' 'Oh, no, no, sir,' said the shoemaker, with an air
of surprise; 'most willingly would I convert all the leather in my possession
into shoes for your honor. I have but too much time to work for those who
are not so able to pay me, and am therefore *always* at *your* service.' The
poor dominie was thunderstruck at the bare-faced impudence of the 'fause
loon;' but, ere he had time to utter a word in explanation, the laird had not
only laid the flattering unction to his own soul, but seizing the preceptor by
the throat, placed his head between his own knees in a twinkling, and clutching Crispin's foot-strap in the one hand, and lifting the dominie's philabeg
with the other, he therewithal plied him on the bare buttocks, so hotly and
heavily, that he had well-nigh expended the 'wrath' which he had so carefully
been 'nursing' for the rascally souter. How many stripes the wight received
deponent hath not said, but true it is, the number far exceeded that prescribed
by the law of Moses. Indeed, it is doubtful whether the 'man of letters'
might not have lost his 'precious spunk,' if the shoemaker's better half had
not flown to his rescue." * Charles, by his wife Isabella, left four sons, Allan,
John, Donald, and Lachlan. Allan, who succeeded his father, was first married to Anne, daughter of Donald MacLean of Brolass, by whom he had several children, all of whom died young, except Charles and Una, who married
Ewen Cameron of Erracht. Allan's second wife was Mary, daughter of

---

* *Beauties of Gaelic Poetry*, p. 75.

Lachlan MacLean of Lochbuie, by whom he had two sons and nine daughters. Charles, son by the first marriage, married Maria, eldest daughter of Sir Allan MacLean, but died without issue. The eldest son by the second marriage, Donald of Kinlochleven, in Mull, bred to the law, married Lillian, daughter of Colquhoun Grant (lieutenant of Prince Charles Stuart's body-guard), and had issue: Christina, married to Murdoch, laird of Lochbuie; Allan, lieutenant in the Seventy-ninth Highlanders, wounded at Toulouse, and died in 1818; Colquhoun, an officer in the navy, who died on the coast of Africa in 1822; Mary; Lillian; Anne; Hector, died in the West Indies in 1818; Margaret; Isabella, married to Alexander Crawford of Jamaica; John; Charles, married in 1837, Jane, daughter of captain Campbell of Kintra, and settled in Canada; Jane, died in 1822; Alexander, died in 1818; Archibald, bred to the law; Andrew, surgeon in the Sixty-fourth regiment; and Fitzroy Jeffries Grafton, bred to the law. Of Allan MacLean of Drimnin's daughters by his second marriage, Ann married captain Stewart; Mary married Doctor Hector MacLean; Marjory married MacDonald of Glenturret; Catherine married lieutenant John Campbell of the navy; Louisa married a Mr. Wood; Margaret, Sibella, Catherine, and Jean, unmarried. John, second son of Charles of Drimnin, married Margaret, daughter of Donald Campbell of Ceamadale. He was drowned in the sound of Mull, and left three sons, Donald, Charles, and Colin; Jannet, and several other daughters. Donald studied medicine; emigrated to Nova Scotia, where he married and left a numerous issue. Charles emigrated to Halifax, Nova Scotia, was married, and died there. Colin married Helen, daughter of Cameron of Callart; was a lieutenant, and died in Jamaica, where he left a son and daughter. Jannet married Hector Cameron, a merchant in Glasgow. The rest died unmarried. The third son of Charles, Donald, went to America as surgeon in Montgomery's regiment of Highlanders, settled and married in New York, where he died without issue. Lachlan, the fourth son, was a planter in Jamaica, and died there, unmarried, in December, 1764.

Charles MacAllan's (of Ardnacross) second son, Lachlan of Calgary, married first, Florence, daughter of Farquhar Fraser, dean of the Isles, by whom he had Donald, second MacLean of Calgary, and Florence, married first to Hector MacLean of Torrestan, and then to Donald, brother of John MacLean of Drimnin, and had issue. Lachlan's second wife was Anne, daughter of John MacLean of Totaranald, of the Coll family, and had issue, Charles, Allan of Grulin, Peter, and Marian, who married Hector MacLean of the island of Muck. Donald, second MacLean of Calgary, first married

Susannah, daughter of Archibald Campbell of Inveraw, by whom he had Charles, Alexander, and Allan, the last a lieutenant in the MacLean battalion and killed at Culloden. Alexander married Mary, daughter of Rev. John MacLean, minister in Mull, by whom he had Charles, Duncan, and Donald. Of these three, Charles resided for many years in Jamaica; Duncan died in the navy; and Donald, first in the navy, and afterward settled in America, and then entered the customs service in London.

Charles MacAllan's third son, Allan MacLean of Grulin, married Una, daughter of Donald MacQuarrie of Ulva, by whom he had Lachlan, who succeeded him; Charles of Kilunaig; John of Pennygoun; Margaret, married to Hector MacLean of Kilmory, of the family of Lochbuie; and Jannet, married to John Campbell of Achadhnoran. Lachlan, second MacLean of Grulin, married Jannet, daughter of John MacLeod of Contulish, by whom he had Hector and Una. The former married Catherine, daughter of Donald MacLean of Coll, and Una married Alexander MacGillivray of Pennyghael. Charles of Kilunaig studied law, but retired to the country. He married Marian, daughter of John MacLean of Tarbert, by whom he had Allan the elder, Hector of Torren, Donald, Allan the younger, John, Alexander, first MacLean of Pennycross, Lachlan, Archibald, Isabella, died unmarried, and Anne, married to Donald MacEachann-Vic-Ian Duirach. Allan, the elder, was a lieutenant in the Dutch service; married Isabella, daughter of Donald Campbell of Scamadall, by whom he had two sons, Charles, a lieutenant of dragoons in the East India Company's service, killed in the war with Hyder Ali; and Allan, a planter in Jamaica. Both died unmarried. Hector MacLean of Torren, the second son, married Julian, daughter of Allan MacLean, a cadet of the family of Lochbuie, and had issue, Allan, a merchant, who died in Kingstown, Jamaica; John, afterward of Grulin; Alexander, lieutenant-colonel of the Second East India regiment; and Archibald, a captain during the American Revolutionary War, in the New York Volunteers, commanded by Colonel Turnbull. He first married a Miss French, by whom he had one son and four daughters. His second wife was a Miss Drummond, when he resided at Nash Waak river, near Frederickston, New Brunswick. The daughters of Hector of Torren were Anne, married to Alexander MacKinnon of Derryguaig; Mary, married to Lachlan MacLean of Bunessan; Catherine, married to Alexander Sinclair in Kintyre; and Alicia, married to Archibald, second MacLean of Pennycross. Donald, Charles of Kilunaig's third son, married Mary Mean, and had James, John, Christopher, Mary, and Catherine. James was a merchant in Kingston, Jamaica, married his cousin, Mary Ann, daughter of John MacLean of Kingston, but left no issue; John never married; and Christopher married and left two sons who died young. Allan, the younger, fourth son of Charles of Kilunaig, was a surgeon, and died in the twenty-fourth year of his age. John, the fifth son, was a merchant in Jamaica, married to Maria, daughter of Fortunatus Duaris, and had issue, Charles, Thomas, Mary Ann, and another daughter. The sons died unmarried; Mary Ann married, first, her cousin James, and then Doctor Alexander Grant. Alexander, sixth son, more anon. Lachlan, seventh son, was a lieutenant in the Forty-second Royal Highlanders, and was killed at the Havana. Archibald, the eighth son, was a partner with his brother, John, in Jamaica, where he died unmarried.

Lachlan MacLean of Grulin and his brother Charles were both worthy men. They were liberally educated and respected, and beloved by all their neighbors. Lachlan died in the eighty-first year of his age, and Charles in his sixty-ninth, a true Christian philosopher.

Allan MacLean of Grulin's third son, John of Pennygoun, married Isabella, daughter of Colin Campbell, of the family of Dunstaffnage, by whom he had two sons and three daughters. Donald, the oldest son, was married to Ann, natural daughter of Lachlan MacLean of Lochbuie, and had issue, Lachlan, John, Hector, Donald, Alexander, and three daughters, Anna, Margaret, and Mary, the last married to David Fraser. Lachlan, bred a surgeon, married in the island of Jersey, went with his family to America, and settled near Nashville, Tennessee, where he made a purchase of lands. He left issue, John, Joshua, Gabriel, Charles Durell, Susan, Mary Ann, and Isabella. John became a merchant; Joshua, a physician; Charles, editor and printer of the *Nashville Gazette;* and Susan married William Banks Anthony, a gentleman of wealth. John, the second son of Donald, entered the navy, and died in the East Indies. Hector, third son, was killed at the seige of Seringapatam, having been the second who mounted the breach. Donald, the fourth son, was a physician. Alexander, the youngest son, married Christiana, daughter of John MacLean of Langmull; went with his family to America and settled at Ride river, on the lands purchased by the earl of Selkirk, where he was killed.

John MacLean of Pennygoun's other son, Allan, went to America, and was killed by the falling in of the roof of a storehouse in Casco Bay. John's daughters were Una, married Allan MacLean, brother of Kingerloch; Jannet married Duncan MacArthur; and Catherine married Donald MacDonald.

Donald of Aros, fourth son of Charles of Ardnacross, married Catherine, daughter of Donald MacQuarrie of Ulva, and had issue, Alexander, Angus, Charles, and a daughter married to Archibald Campbell, of the Lochnell family. Alexander enjoyed the universal esteem of all who knew him, and was a special favorite of his chief, Sir John MacLean. He went as a volunteer in queen Anne's Scotch guards to Spain with his friend, Captain Alexander MacLean of Torloisk. He was taken prisoner at the battle of Villa Viciaga, and meeting some of his MacDonald relations, they procured him a commission in the Spanish service. He served for several years and was promoted to major of the regiment. The colonel of the regiment and a subaltern named Linch had a quarrel, and meeting in a street in Madrid, drew on each other. Major MacLean at that moment coming down a cross street found the two engaged in combat. He drew and struck down both their swords, but Linch, taking advantage of the opportunity, ran the colonel throught the heart, thrusting under the major's arms, and immediately ran away. The crowd that immediately collected thought it was a duel between the major and the colonel. The people in the monastery, before which the affair occurred; testified to the innocence of Major MacLean; yet such were the laws of Spain, that drawing the sword upon the streets was sufficient to condemn him. The king interceded, but he was beheaded at the age of fifty and in the year 1739. The king took his wife and children under his immediate protection. He left three sons and one daughter, Zeiretta, who married a nobleman of Arragon. Angus, Donald's second son, married Anna, daughter of Allan MacLean of the Torloisk family, by whom he had one daughter. Charles, the third son, married Jean Campbell, and had issue, Hector and Margaret. Hector married Marian, daughter of Donald MacQuarrie of Ulva, and had one son, John, who settled in New York. Margaret married Alexander MacQuarrie of Laggan in Ulva.

Hector, fifth son of Charles of Ardnacross, married Jannet, daughter of Hector Roy MacLean of Coll; by whom he had John, Donald, and Mary. John was for many years a lieutenant in the navy. He settled in Lynn in the county of Norfolk, and was looked upon as one of the first mathematicians in England. He died unmarried. Donald married, but left no issue. Mary died unmarried.

Ewen, or Hugh, sixth and last son of Charles of Ardnacross, married Una, daughter of Archibald MacLean of Ardtun, of the family of Ardgour, and left issue.

The daughters of Charles of Ardnacross were, Anna, married to Alexander MacDonald of Kinloch Moidart; Florence, first married to John Mac-

Quarrie of Laggan, in Ulva, and afterward to captain Andrew MacLean, in Morvern; and Mary, married to Hugh Cameron, of the Lochiel family.

CHAPTER XXVIII.

THE MacLEANS OF PENNYCROSS.

The Pennycross family is a cadet of the house of Morvern, residing in the district of Brolass, in the Ross of Mull. It is descended from John Dubh, first MacLean of Morvern, who was the second son of the first Hector Mór, lord of Duard. John Dubh was thrice married, and by his second wife, Catherine, he had Allan of Ardtornish, who was father of Lachlan of Calgary, who by his second wife, Anne, had Allan of Grulin, who by his wife, Una, had Charles of Kilunaig, who by his wife, Marianna, was father of

I. Alexander, First MacLean of Pennycross.

Alexander was bred to the medical profession, and was married in 1760 to Una, daughter of Alexander MacGillivray of Pennyghael, by whom he had Archibald, his successor, and Catherine, married to Major Donald MacLean of the royal Scots regiment.

II. Archibald, Second MacLean of Pennycross,

Was born in the year 1761, and died February 17, 1830. He was much esteemed in the circle of his acquaintances; was for some time major of the 3d regiment of Argyleshire fencibles, and one of the deputy lieutenants for the county. He married Alicia, daughter of Hector MacLean of Torren, by whom he had nine sons and three daughters, of whom the following reached maturity: Alexander, his successor; Allan Thomas, Charles James, Mary, John, Juliana, Hector, Lachlan, and Archibald Donald. Allan Thomas became lieutenant general. Charles James in 1813 entered the service of the 79th Highlanders, and was in every engagement of that regiment from the above year to the victory at Waterloo, where he carried the colors. Afterward he became a lieutenant in the 31st regiment of foot, and died at Calcutta in May, 1837. Mary died unmarried, in 1837. John was for some time a surgeon, but afterward joined the Second West India regiment, commanded by his maternal uncle, Alexander MacLean, and attained to the rank of lieutenant. He died at Nassau, New Providence, in 1822. Juliana died unmarried. Hector was a merchant in London, and died at an early age, in 1834. Lachlan was a lieutenant in the Ceylon rifles, which he joined in 1829, and died at Colombo in 1830. Archibald Donald became deputy commissary-general at Bermuda.

III. Alexander, Third MacLean of Pennycross,

Was born May 3, 1791; August 6, 1740, married Charlotte Brodie, daughter of John MacLean of Elrick, and had issue, Archibald John, born March 6, 1843; Allan Thomas Lockhart, born January, 1851; also three daughters, Alicia, Charlotte, and Mary. Alexander was one of the deputy lieutenants and a commissioner of supply for the county of Argyle. He died March 8, 1876.

IV. Archibald John, Fourth MacLean of Pennycross,

Was educated at Edinburgh, afterward entered the mercantile profession, and on the death of his father succeeded to the estates. He is a D. L. and J. P. for the county of Argyle; was married at Crown Court Scotch Church, London, in 1868, to Isabella Alexandrina Simon, who was educated in America, and died at Pennycross in 1886; a woman of great beauty, sound judgment, excellent taste, and great goodness of heart, and much beloved by all who knew her. She was a fine linguist, and her qualifications made her at home in the best circles of society, and welcomed in the humble cottage of the Western Isles. Her interests were those of her husband's, and every detail was guarded with care. Archibald John MacLean is one of the handsomest men in Scotland—finely proportioned, and standing erect, five feet and eleven

ARCHIBALD JOHN MACLEAN.

inches. In every acceptation of the word, he is a true Highlander: speaks Gaelic fluently, gentlemanly in his deportment on all occasions, kind, generous, and hospitable, and a more popular man, with all classes, does not reside in the county of Argyle. He received the estate of Pennycross and Carsaig heavily burdened with debt. At once he devoted his energies to retrieve the debts of his predecessors, although much greater than the lands would bear, and succeeded in paying off a large percentage of the claims. During this time he added many improvements, and made his home, in the little nook of Carsaig, one of the most delightful and inviting in Scotland, and adorned it with rare taste and harmony. It became the retreat of such distinguished men as Sir Roderick I. Murchison, Professors J. S. Blackie and J. W. Judd, Dr. Giggie, James Aitken, Lennox Brown, William Black, and others, who could there feast their eyes on the beautiful scenery, improve their leisure hours in the library of well selected books, or else study the fossiliferous beds exposed at the foot of the cliff. Mr. MacLean's leisure hours have been devoted to the study of electricity, improvement of fishermen's houses, fish and meat transit appliances, and the preservation of ice, which could be done at a moderate cost, for which he received numerous diplomas, medals, certificates, etc., at various exhibitions in Great Britain and on the Continent. He looked forward to the time when he should hold his lands free from burdens, and every day pointed to a near realization of his hopes. But disaster awaited him. A long season of depression set in, coupled with a heavy decline in the value of land. Still he struggled on. The decease of his accomplished companion added sorrows and cares. He still hoped against hope. At last, fully realizing that the struggle would not end in success, in 1888 he turned over his property, and asked to be relieved. His manly struggle endeared him to his friends, who fully appreciated his efforts, and tendered him heartfelt sympathy and cheering words. He changed his residence to Tiroran House, Pennyghael, Mull. He has issue: Julian Archibald, born in 1873; Charles Alexander Hugh, in 1874; Isabel Juliet, in 1876; Norman Henry, in 1877; Allan Fitzroy, in 1880; Elsie Una, in 1882; Muriel, in 1884; and Violet, in 1885.

CHAPTER XXIX.

THE MacLEANS OF TORLOISK.

The sixth branch of the family of Duard is that of Torloisk. The family seat is located on the Mull side of Loch Tua, and is known as Torloisk House. This branch is descended from

I. Lachlan Og, First MacLean of Torloisk,

Second son of Sir Lachlan Mór. He received from his father a charter of the lands of Lehire-Torloisk, forfeited by the son of Ailean nan Sop, which was afterward confirmed by royal grant. He was present at the battle of Gruinnart, and was severely wounded. He was a witness to a charter given by his father to Martin MacGillivray of Pennyghael, and subscribed himself in the Irish characters, *Mise Lachin Mhac Gilleoin.* He was an important man in his day, and was so influential that he was compelled to make his appearance before the privy council. He was first married to Marian, daughter of Sir Duncan Campbell of Achnabreck, by whom he had Hector, who succeeded him. He was again married to Margaret, daughter of captain Stewart of Dumbarton, but had no issue. He was a third time married to Marian, daughter of Donald MacDonald of Clanranald, and had issue, Hector, Lachlan Og, Lachlan Catanach, Ewen, John Diuriach, Allan, Neil, Jannet, Mary, Catherine, Julian, and Isabella. Lachlan Og died unmarried, but left a natural son called Donald; Lachlan Catanach and Ewen were killed at Inverkeithing; Allan died unmarried at Harris; John Diuriach married Jannet, daughter of John MacLean, laird of Ardgour, by whom he had Allan and several daughters; Neil married a daughter of Lochbuie, by whom he had a daughter and Lachlan, who died a lieutenant-colonel in the British service; Jannet married Hector, first MacLean of Kinlochaline; Mary married John Garbh, eldest son of John Dubh of Morvern; Catherine married John, brother to MacNeil of Barra; Julian married Allan MacLean, brother of Lochbuie; and Isabel married Martin MacGillivray of Pennyghael. Lachlan Og lived to an advanced age, and was succeeded by his eldest son,

II. Hector, second MacLean of Torloisk,

Who was first married to Jannet, daughter of Allan MacLean of Ardtornish, by whom he had three daughters: Margaret, married to Lachlan MacLean of Lochbuie; Marian, married to Hector MacLean of Coll; and Mary, married to Duncan Campbell of Sandaig. He was a second time married to Catherine, daughter of John Campbell of Lochnell, and had issue: Lachlan, who succeeded him; Hector, who was killed by the MacLachlans, a band of robbers of Fiairt, in Lesmore, who infested the neighborhood; John of Tarbert (was married to Catherine, daughter of Donald Campbell of Comguish, by whom he had Donald, John, and Marianne, married to Charles MacLean of Kilunaig); Isabella, married to Lachlan MacLean of Brolass; and Jannet, married to the second Hector MacLean of Kinlochaline.

III. Lachlan, Third MacLean of Torloisk,

Was reputed one of the most gallant and accomplished gentlemen of his time, and well qualified for the highest station in the gift of his country. He did not aspire to state intrigue, but contented himself in looking after affairs of interest to his clan. He managed, in conjunction with Brolass, the estate of MacLean during the minority of Sir John, and was of great service in retrieving the embarrassed affairs of the chief. He married Barbara, daughter of Alexander, brother of Sir James MacDonald of Sleat, and had issue, two sons and one daughter: Hector, who died at the age of eighteen; Alexander, who succeeded to the estate; and Jannet, married to Archibald Campbell of Inverawe. It was in 1685 that Lachlan besieged, captured, and destroyed the castle of Carnassary, and, as is shown by the petition of Duncan Campbell,* he died prior to 1690.

IV. Alexander, Fourth MacLean of Torloisk,

Was captain in the Second battalion of the Scots Guards, and served in the Spanish wars. At the age of twenty-five, he had his leg broken at the battle of Brihuega, in Spain, in 1710, by a musket ball, of which he fevered and died. Dying without issue, he was succeeded by his cousin-german,

V. Donald, Fifth MacLean of Torloisk,

Who was a son of John of Tarbert, third son of Hector, second MacLean of Torloisk. Donald was noted for the urbanity of his manners and the kindness of his disposition. At the battle of Sheriffmuir, he was major of Sir John MacLean's regiment, and was commended for his prudent and gallant conduct on that occasion. He married Mary, daughter of Archibald Campbell of Sunderland, and had issue: Hector, Lachlan, Allan, Archibald, Mary, Anna, Alicia, Christiana, Betty, and Elizabeth. Allan, the third son, became a general; Archibald resided at Laggan, and never married; Mary and Betty died unmarried; Anna married Donald MacLean, a cadet of the house of Torloisk;

---

* *Statistical Account of Argyleshire*, p. 556.

Alicia married Lachlan MacQuarrie of Ulva; Christiana married Rev. Alexander MacLean, minister of Kilninan, Mull; Elizabeth first married Lachlan MacLean of Garmony, of the family of Lochbuie, and secondly, to James Park of Jamaica. Donald died August 20, 1748, and was succeeded by his eldest son,

VI. Hector, Sixth MacLean of Torloisk,

Who was bred to the law. He never married. On his death, which happened at Glasgow, May 29, 1765, he was succeeded by his immediate younger brother,

VII. Lachlan, Seventh MacLean of Torloisk,

And the last, in the male line. For many years he was captain of a merchantman (Mary), which plied between London and Jamaica. In the course of a voyage to Jamaica, and within a day's sail of the harbor, he fell in with a frigate. The French fleet being in the West Indies, he (Torloisk) thought she was one of that number, and having one gun of large caliber, he fired at her. The frigate was commanded by Sir George Clark, and being at night, he thought the merchantman was a line of battle ship, from the size of the ball that struck his ship. Both the officers met at dinner in Kingston, and when Sir George was congratulating himself in having escaped the line of battle ship, and probably the heavy guns, Torloisk asked him some particulars, which led them to realize they were the combatants. Clark then said: " Take this box; you may forget me, but I will never forget you, nor the Mary and your solitary twenty-four pounder." Lachlan married Margaret, daughter of Richard Smith, by whom he had only one daughter, Marianne, who became proprietress of the estate at his death, in 1799.

Marianne married general Douglas Clephane of Carslogie, Fifeshire, and had issue three daughters, Margaret, Anna Jane, and Wilmina Marianne. The last named, in 1831, married Wilhelm Baron de Norman, then in the diplomatic service of Prussia. Margaret, in 1815, married Spencer Joshua Alcoyne, the second marquis of Northampton. The estate passed into the Northampton family, by whom it is still held.

The cadets of the Torloisk family are very few. Donald, natural son of Lachlan Og, second son to the first MacLean of Torloisk, married a daughter of Martin MacGillivray, and had issue, Allan, Lachlan, and John. Allan was a captain in Sir John MacLean's regiment at Sheriffmuir. He married and had a son, Donald, who married Ann, daughter of Donald MacLean of Torloisk, by whom he had two sons: George, who died in the East Indies; and

Hector of Mingarry, married to Helen, daughter of Donald Campbell. John, third son, was a lieutenant in the Darien expedition, and afterward in general Murray's regiment in the Dutch service, and died in Flanders.

CHAPTER XXX.
THE COUNTS MacLEAN OF SWEDEN.

The seventh branch of the Duard family is descended from John, youngest son of Hector Mór of Duard, son of Sir Lachlan Mór. John was knighted, and employed by Charles the First on an embassy to Sweden. Before his return the civil war broke out. On his return he was forced to change his name from MacLean to Macleir, and also to leave his country, on account of his loyalty to the Stuart dynasty. He returned to Sweden in the diplomatic service of Charles, and finally settled in Gottenburg, where he married Anna Quickelberry, by whom he had six sons and three daughters. His eldest son, Charles, died young; the second, Jacob, was in the service of king Charles in England; the third, John, was president of Gottenburg, and married Anna Margaret Gordon; the fourth, Peter, was colonel and commandant in Stralsund, married to Abolla Sophia Vanplassen; the fifth, Gustavus, was colonel in the Swedish army and commandant in Gottenburg; the sixth, David, a general in the army and governor of west Gothland, married to the countess of Arenberg. Sir John's daughters were Maria, married to General David Duncan, in the service of the king of Denmark; Catherine, married, first, Colonel David Sinclair, and secondly, General Malcolm Hamilton; and Eliza, married to major Cailenkerheilm. General David left five sons and two daughters, of whom John Aldolphus Count MacLean was general in the army and colonel of the king's life guards. He died about the beginning of the present century, in Stockholm, leaving a numerous family.

Iona Cathedral and St. Oran's Chapel.

CHAPTER XXXI.

IONA.

The island of Iona is situated off the extreme point of the Ross of Mull, and separated from it by a narrow channel called the Sound of Iona. The island is about three miles in extreme length, by one and a half in breadth. The island has been variously called I, Hii, Hy, Iœ, and Aoi. To the Highlanders of the present day, it is known as Innis-nan-Druidhneach, or the Island of the Druids, and as Iicholumchille, or the Island of Colum of the Cell, from whence the English Icolumkill is derived.

I have collected the material for a history of the island; but as an account of the Clan MacLean would be very incomplete without special reference to its strange history, it becomes necessary to give a brief *résumé*.

It is believed that Iona was one of the last retreats of the druids, and here they held forth and taught their doctrines for a considerable period. There is no positive evidence on this point; but as it has been called the Island of the Druids from time immemorial, and as there are druidical remains both on that island and on Mull, it is probable that an important seat of learning of that priesthood was once here established. The great fame of the island, however, rests upon the efforts put forth by St. Columba and the monks, or his disciples. St. Columba was of the royal family of Ireland, born December 7, 521. In the year 563, with twelve companions from Ireland, he landed upon Iona, and founded that monastery which for centuries continued to be the first seminary of learning in Europe. He succeeded in converting and baptizing Brude, the most powerful monarch that ever occupied the Pictish throne, which was soon followed by the whole nation ostensibly professing the Christian faith. It is related that during his life-time, he and his disciples founded one hundred monasteries and three hundred and sixty-five churches, and ordained three thousand monks and priests. These monks or priests were termed Gillean-De, or servant of God, and afterward shortened into Culdee. This great saint died June 8, 597. The incidents surrounding his death were as remarkable as his life had been. Columba was succeeded by a long and noble line of abbots, who held sway over the religious houses of Iona, the names of whom have been carefully preserved. These monks, for the most part, kept aloof from the influence of Rome. In 796, the Scandinavian rovers who had been laying waste the islands of Britain in their piratical excursions, burnt the famous monastery of Iona, which, at that time, was the only sanctuary of real learning in Europe. They burnt it a second time, in 801, and in 806 again laid it waste, and murdered sixty-eight of its inmates, including both lay and clerical. In 818 was completed the new monastery made of stone, the previous ones having been constructed of wood. The site of the building was also changed. In 823, the fury of the Danes again broke upon the island, when the abbot Blathmac MacFlain and fifteen of his associates suffered martyrdom. On Christmas eve, 985, the Danes ravaged the island and slew the abbot.

In 1097 Magnus Berfaet, king of Norway, made a descent upon the island, but granted his peace to the inhabitants. During the following century there were considerable changes in Iona. The pure worship of God as practiced by the Culdees began to give way to the influence of the Romish church, and about the year 1164 the monastery was appropriated by monks of the Cluniac order. In the year 1203, Reginald, then lord of the Isles, determined to adopt the policy of the Scottish kings, and introduce into his territories the religious orders of the Roman church. So he established the Benedictine or black monks in Iona, and in connection founded the nunnery for Benedictine or black nuns; and it is of this Benedictine monastery that the present ruins are the remains. The rule of the Benedictine order continued until the year 1561, when an Act of the Convention of Estates was passed "for demolishing all the abbeys of monks and friars, and for suppressing whatsomever monuments of idolatrie were remaining in the realm." In compliance with this edict Iona shared the fate of nearly all the other cathedrals of Scotland. The monastery was bombarded with cannon; three hundred and sixty crosses that adorned Iona were cast into the sea; the great library over the chapter house, together with the registers of the church, was cast into the streets, and then gathered in heaps and burned, Keltic literature thus sustaining an irreparable loss; and the very sepulchers of the dead were rifled. The principal lands belonging to the monastery fell into the hands of MacLean of Duard, the most powerful of the neighboring chiefs.

Of the ruins still remaining, the most commanding is Saint Mary's Cathedral, or the Abbey Church, consisting of a nave, transepts, and choir, with sacristy on north side of choir and side chapels on the south. The figure is cruciform; the interior length from east to west is one hundred and forty-eight and a half feet, by twenty-two feet three inches in breadth, and the transepts from north to south are seventy feet three inches, by seventeen feet two inches in breadth. The tower is about seventy feet high. The walls are composed of a mixture of materials, among which the red-grained granite of Mull, resembling the syenite of Egypt, predominates. Some of the blocks are of immense size, and must have been hewn and polished with very great labor. Carved on the capitals of the pillars and pilasters are Scripture scenes. The walls are bare; not even an ivy leaf in a crevice to relieve the sharp outlines. The architecture is difficult to describe, for it presents a mixture of styles, and has been subjected to many alterations and repairs. The monastery is connected with the Abbey on the north side, and is in a very ruinous condition. St. Oran's Chapel is situated in the principal cemetery, called the "Reilig Odhrain," or burying place of Oran, to the southwest of and not far from the cathedral. It is a plain, oblong structure, twenty-nine feet eight inches long, by fifteen feet ten inches in breadth, in the interior, and for windows has two narrow lights; that in the north two feet high, and that in the south three feet. It is roofless, and has well withstood the ravages of centuries. Its principal object of interest is the Romanesque circular-headed west door, decorated with what is termed the "beak-headed ornament." This building is the oldest on the island, and belongs to the close of the 11th century, having been erected by the munificence of queen Margaret. The Nunnery (not shown in the engraving), although much dilapidated, still retains the evidence of its former elegance. The nuns were permitted to remain here for a time after the monks had been expelled.

The Reilig Odhrain is a large inclosure, and the great place of interment not only for monarchs, but also for the chiefs and potentates of the isles and their lineage, notably the MacDonalds, or Lords of the Isles, MacLeans, MacLeods, MacKinnons, MacKenzies, MacQuarries, and other powerful families. Some are buried within the chapel, and others in the cathedral, while ladies of rank and the prioresses are entombed within the chapel of the Nunnery. It would be difficult to state how many saints are buried either in or else close to the religious houses; but the records show that sixty-four kings found sepulture here. Of these two were kings of Ireland, three of Norway, one of France, and the rest of Scotland; the last to be interred was MacBeth. It would be out of place to enumerate all in this connection, for we are particularly interested in the relation the MacLeans sustained to the island.

In the description of the tombs I shall closely follow that given by Graham in his "Antiquities of Iona," and not follow the observations I made when on the island.

TOMBS OF THE MACLEANS IN REILIG ODHRAIN.

The first illustration exhibits such of the MacLean tombs as are in a row in the Reilig Odhrain, and inclosed by an iron railing. Next are four tombs shown together. That of MacLean of Coll (a side view is also given) is the handsomest on the island. The figure is boldly carved, and, similar to many others, is in armor, and in the act of drawing his sword. It is accompanied by two angels, one with a sword, a griffin, and two intricate devices. The inscription on the pillow is defaced. Near the right shoulder are the words *Pius* and *Hi*. The tomb of MacLean of Ross, or old *Niall an Roiss*, the predecessor and head of *Sliochd a' chlaidhimh iaruinn*, or the MacLeans of the Ross of Mull, lies on the floor of the cathedral. It represents an armed knight, with his hunting dog at his feet, and by his side a whilk shell, the upper part of which is carried away. The custom of drinking out of shells was very common among the ancient Gaëls. The tomb of Ailean nan Sop very appropriately represents his birlinn or galley, which carried him from island to island upon his raids. Besides the intricate net-work, it is adorned with fantastic animals. MacLean of Grulin's tomb lies in St. Oran's chapel, near the middle. The inscription is gone. In the center is his *claidheamh mór*, or broad-sword, the kind which formerly gleamed in Scotland's wars. Its belt is attached to it, and around it is a variety of beasts.

The third illustration of the tombs represents, first, MacLean of Duard, who appears in armor, a shield on his left shoulder, emblazoned with a winged dragon, a tower, and an ornamental border. In his belt is a long sword, and with his left hand he grasps a spear. Depending from his chin is a long beard. His feet rest upon a crouching greyhound. The inscription which formerly was upon the pillow is completely effaced. Next to Duard in the above order is the tomb of MacLean of Lochbuie, or the celebrated *Eoghan a chinn bhig*, or Ewen of the Little Head, whose ghost is still believed to appear whenever a member of the Lochbuie family dies. He is said to ride around Castle Moy on a black horse, amid a dismal clanking of iron chains. "The Rider," believed to be the tomb of a MacLean, because it is in the same row and near the others of the clan, is a handsome and singular stone. The sword shows him to have been a warrior, and the mounted figure indicates he fought on horseback. There is the figure of a female in the act of devotion; but the object which she appears to be facing can not be made out.

The first in the fourth illustration is the tomb of Dr. John Beton, the last of the order of a succession of learned men that existed in Mull from time immemorial. All their writings were in Gaelic, and amounted to a large chestfull. This treasure, doubtless replete with the history of the MacLeans,

322   HISTORY OF THE CLAN MACLEAN.

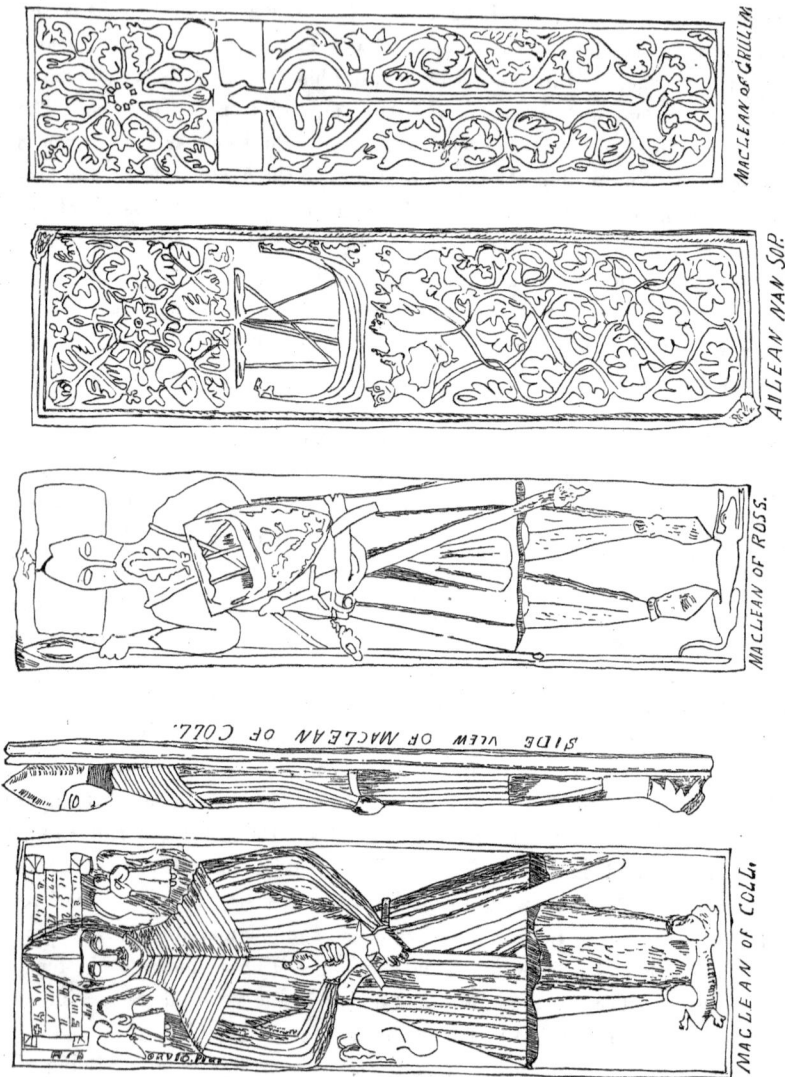

perished in the wreck of the fortunes of the duke of Chandos, about the middle of the last century. The tombstone bears the following inscription:

HIC · IACET · IOANNES · BETONVS · MACLENORVM · FAMILIE MEDIC[s] · QVI · MORTV · EST · 19 · NOWEMBRIS · ANNO · DOMINI 1657 · ET · ETATIS · SVE · 63 · DONALDVS · BETONVS · ME · FECIT 1674 · ECCE · CADIT · IACVLO · VICTRICI · MORTIS · INIQVE · QVI TOTIES · ALIOS · SOLVERAT · IPSE · MALIS · SOLI · DEO · GLORIA.

"Here lies John Beton, physician to the family of the MacLeans, who died 19th November, 1657, aged 63. Donald Beton made me, 1674. Behold!

MACLEAN OF DUART.

MACLEAN OF LOCHBUY.

THE RIDER.

he who saved so many others from ills, himself falls by the conquering dart of wicked death. Glory to God alone."

The tomb placed next in order, with the two figures at the head, is assigned to a MacLean, and is in the same row with others belonging to the clan. One figure is playing on a harp of Irish form, while underneath him is a crouching hound. The harper appears to be enchanting the praises of the stately figure mounted on horseback. Below are four figures of beasts in combination with intricate network. The most popular of the tombs is that of the prioress Anna. Her figure is cut on the face of the tomb, an angel on either side supports her head, and above them are a little looking-glass and a

324   HISTORY OF THE CLAN MACLEAN.

comb. At her feet is this address to the Virgin Mary: "Sancta Maria, ora pro me." Around the lady is inscribed: "Hic jacet Domina Anna Donaldi Terleti, filia quondam priorissa de Iona, quæ obiit ano m°d°xi°, ejus animam altissimo commendamus." (Here lies the lady Anna, daughter of Donald MacTearlach, formerly prioress of Iona, who died in 1511, whose soul we commend to the Most High.) This stone is a black marble slab, and preserved in the Chapel of the Nunnery. When the roof of the east end of the building

fell in, it broke off the lower half of the slab, upon which was carved the form of the Virgin Mary, with head crowned and mitered, the Child in her arms, and above her appear the sun and moon, to denote her the *queen of heaven*. MacLean's Cross stands between the Cathedral and the Nunnery. It is different in form, and apparently of a different era, from any other in the Highlands. It is the oldest Christian relic in Scotland, and is assigned to the period of St. Columba. The material is composed of the hardest whin-rock, and is eleven feet high, including the pedestal, and only three inches thick. It stands on solid masonry, unprotected. The face is elaborately carved with foliage, and within the circle in the upper part is represented the crucifixion of Christ. The figure is clothed in a dalmatic, girt with a girdle. On one of the arms of the cross is an hour-glass, and a small cross adorns the other arm.

Doubtless, there are other tombstones that mark the graves of MacLeans. Iona continued to be the sepulcher of the MacLeans down to a very recent period. Their bards, even in the eighteenth century, made it a matter of regret when any of the chiefs missed being interred within this sacred precinct.

MACLEAN'S CROSS.

The proximity of the MacLeans to Iona, and the influence of the latter over the clan, would lead to the supposition that the former had their representatives in the religious houses. As no records have been kept, it would be impossible to tell how many of the clan joined the orders; that some arose to the highest rank among the recluses is well known. The Prioress Anna or Agnes was a daughter of Donald, son of Charles MacLean of Urquhart. In January, 1508, king James IV. granted a letter of protection to his religious and oratrices the Lady Agnes, daughter of Donald Makgillane, Prioress of the monastery of nuns of the most blessed virgin Mary in the island of St. Columba, and specifically charges Lauchlan McGillane of Dowart, Ranold, son of Alan Makrory, and John McGillane of Lochboy not to trouble the said Prioress and convent.* The evidence shows that these chiefs had been molesting the convent in regard to its "lands, revenues, possessions, officers, tenants, families, servitors, and their movable goods." As to the time of her death, that

---

* *Reg. Sec. Sig.*, Vol. III., fol. 209.

is a matter of dispute. Most writers follow Pennant, who states the date on the tomb to be 1543; but Graham declares it is 1511.

The records also show, that on July 16, 1548, queen Mary granted a precept, to admit to the temporality of the lands, rents, and possessions of the monastery of nuns, to the Lady Mary, daughter of Ferquard, alias McGilleon, Prioress of Icolmkill, who had been promoted by pope Julius III.* Under date of February 15, 1567, the same queen grants Marian McClane (probably the grantee of 1548) the "prioressie and nunrie of the abbey of Ycolmkill now vakand throw deceis of umquhile Agnes McClane, last prioress thairof." †

The Abbey of Iona was annexed to the bishopric of the Isles about the year 1507. On the death of bishop Farquhar, queen Mary, on August 7, 1547, granted to Patrick MacLean, illegitimate son of Lachlan Cattanach, the temporality of the Isles, and Abbey of Icolmkill.‡ This position he held until his death, in 1553. A writer in the *Celtic Magazine* || says: "Patrick MacLean had been presented by queen Mary to the temporality of the bishopric and abbey of Icolmkill, and on account of his inability resigned them, in 1565, in favor of John Carswell, who became bound to pay him a yearly pension." Patrick MacLean was the last Romish bishop of the Isles. For a long time prior to his decease, the cause of religion was in an appalling state throughout the Isles and western mainland. This was partly owing to the bloody feuds which raged among the clans. The unsettled state of both civil and religious affairs which swept over Scotland produced apostasy on the part of the most influential dignitaries.

Hector MacLean became bishop of Argyle in 1680. He was first minister at Morvern, then at Dunoon, and lastly at Eastwood. He was married to Jane, daughter of Rev. Thomas Boyd, and had issue, four sons and two daughters. He was born in 1605, and died in 1687, aged 82, and is buried in the churchyard of Dunoon. Hector was unquestionably of the family of Lochbuie. According to one account, he was descended from Charles, second son of John Mór of Lochbuie. According to a letter preserved in the Lochbuie charter room, written by Hugh MacLean to John MacLean of Grulin, dated August 3, 1780, he was the son of Angus, son of John, son of Angus, son of John, son of John, a priest, son of John, son of Sir Charles of Urquhart. Andrew, the eldest son, known as Anndra Mac an Easbuig, was a captain in the army and an excellent Gaelic poet. He lived in Knock, Morvern, but was com-

---

* *Reg. Sec. Sig.*, Vol. XXII., fol. 37.   † *Ibid.*, Vol. XXXVI., fol. 22.   ‡ *Ibid.*, Vol. XXI., fol. 29. || Vol. VII., p. 415.

pelled to sell his estate owing to the depredations the Camerons made on his cattle. He married Florence, daughter of Charles MacLean of Ardnacross. Angus, his son, was a major in Castellar's regiment in Spain. After the death of Alexander, his uncle, he assumed his titles and became Sir Angus. He was married and had a son, Andrew, a captain in the same regiment as himself. Both died in the year 1780, being the last of bishop Hector's descendants in the male line.

Hector's second son was the celebrated Sir Alexander MacLean of Otter, a faithful follower of Sir John MacLean. He died at Aix-la-Chapelle. A third son of the bishop was killed at Reyzerwerts. Of the fourth son no record remains. One of the two daughters married Lachlan Og, seventh son of Allan, seventh MacLean of Ardgour.

The first positive evidence of the connection of the MacLeans with Iona, we have, is in the charter from Donald, Lord of the Isles, to Lachlan MacLean of Duard, under date of July 12, 1390, in which the latter is given the " Officium Fragramanache et Armanache in insula de Hy." * It would appear from this that the keeping of the island was given to Duard, with the title of Armanach. *Frag* means woman, and *manache* means monk. This does not give actual possession, but the interests of the monks and nuns were placed under his care or jurisdiction.

After the Act of the Convention of Estates of 1561, the principal lands belonging to the monastery fell into the hands of MacLean of Duard, who was the most powerful of the neighboring chiefs. This was the era when church property was divided among the more powerful barons and lords. Duard does not appear to have gained possession until 1574, when Mary Nikillean (doubtless Mary McClane) Prioress, with the consent of the convent, granted the lands which belonged to it in heritage to Hector McClane of Dowarde. The lands belonging to the nunnery lay in the isles of Mull, Inch Kenneth, Tiree, Canna, Coll, Skye, and Uist.†

On December 8, 1580, a contract was entered into between the bishop of the isles and Lachlan MacLean of Duard, in which the latter takes the burden of his kin, friends, and dependents upon himself to defend the immunities and privileges granted to the bishopric of the Isles and Icolmkill ; that he and his heirs shall assist and maintain the bishop in all his rights and actions, and shall collect the rents and emoluments pertaining to the bishopric within the bounds of the Isles, within six days after he has been charged so to do ;

---

* *Reg. Mag. Sig.*, Vol. XIII., No. 300.   † Gordon's *Iona*, p. 32.

that the lands of the abbey shall be freely possessed; that no Stewart-deputy shall be placed upon the lands of Ross during the present bishop's lifetime; that no person shall be suffered to oppress the lands of Icolmkill and Ross or the tenants thereon; that when the said MacLean is attending the army under the king, then only four men of Ross and four of Icolmkill shall, at their own expense, keep the castle of Cairnburg; that the duties of Mull and all other places within his dominion shall be thankfully paid yearly; that the bishop shall be obeyed the same as any other Scottish bishop; that the said Lachlan shall pay one thousand merks in part payment of deuties of kirhlands; that he shall produce his charters of such lands as he holds of the bishop before the 28th day of December following; that the said Lachlan shall give security for the deuties pertaining to the bishopric, upon which he shall be discharged from the decree obtained against him, and be reinstated as heretofore; and the bishop shall justify, maintain, and defend him; that the charter given by bishop John Carswell to Hector MacLean of Duard shall be made good. This document is signed by the following witnesses: "Jhone McLane, Baillie of the Morverne, Archibald Campble, apperand of the Otter, Jhone Campble, constable of Dunstafniche. Jhone McDonell, alias Campble, Patrick McCarthour, and James Kincaid, notar public. (*Sic subscribitur*) Jhon Bischop of the Ilis, Lauchlane McClane of Dowert; Jhone McClane, as witness, Jhone McDonald, alias Campble, witness; Jacobus Kincaid, *notarius testis in premissis.*" *

In the year 1587, king James VI., under the privy seal, granted a royal charter of novodamus, with augmentation of the rental, to Hector MacLean, son and apparent heir of Lachlan MacLean of Duard, of the island of Iona, and many other lands, formerly belonging to the abbot of Iona.† The lands enumerated in this charter comprised fifty-seven districts. For these lands the following rental was exacted by the king:

Rental of lands in Ross of Mull,	£63	8s	7½d
Rental of other lands in Mull,	21	5	10
Rental of the Island of Iona,	22	13	4
Rental of lands in Islay,	26	15	8
Rental of lands in Tiree,	28	3	4
Total yearly rent to the Crown,	£162	6s	9½d

---

* Document given in full in *Collectanea de Rebus Albanicis*, pp. 15–18; also in MacLean's *Iona*, pp. 93–100. † Given in full in *Collectanea*, with valuable notes, pp. 161–179.

Iona.

On March 14, 1635, king Charles I. writes to Sir Lachlan MacLean of Duard, desiring him to restore the island of Iona to the bishop of the Isles. "Trustie, etc. Whereas we wer informed that of late yow and your umquhile brother Hectour McCleane did without ordour or anie right violentlie intrude yourselff in the possession of the Yle of Ycolmekill which belongeth to the Bischop of the Yles for the tyme; whairof thay have bene in peaciable possession these many yeirs bypast and that yow still doe deteyne the same from the present Bischop thereof:—We holding such a violent and indirect a courss as a contempt done unto the church and consequentlie unto us; and withall taking to our princelie consideratioun the detriment thereby arising to the patrimonie of that Bischope the absolute possession of the said Yland without further hearing or delay." *

The year 1560 saw Iona full of its religious teachers, and its cathedral, monastery, and convent in a high state of repair, while culture and refinement were on every hand, and the island brought under a high state of cultivation. The reformation brought violence a year later, and left destruction every-where. In 1567 Marian MacLean, the last prioress, was living in Iona, and engaged in her religious duties, although watched on every hand. In 1790, under the power of the same reformation, all the religious houses were still in ruins, and on the island was but one religious teacher, and that was Allan MacLean, a schoolmaster. Since then these old monuments have continued in ruins, although there have been some improvements in other directions.

> "Lone isle! though storms have round thy turrets rode—
> Though their red shafts have sear'd thy marble brow—
> Thou wert the temple of the living God,
> And taught earth's millions at his shrine to bow.
> Though desolation wraps thy glories now,
> Still thou wilt be a marvel through all time
> For what thou hast been; and the dead who rot
> Around the fragments of thy towers sublime
> Once taught the world, and sway'd the realm of thought,
> And ruled the warriors of each northern clime."—*Moore.*

* *Collectanea*, p. 185.

CHAPTER XXXII.

SUPERSTITIONS.

Efforts have been made by the intelligent Highlanders of this generation to collect the legends of their country, and to study the superstitions of their countrymen. Mull has been and is still a fruitful field. All the superstitions, tales, legends, and myths, should be collected and preserved by some one living on the island. The Highland race has been a poetic and imaginative one. Some of the superstitions of the Mull people should here be recorded, although the subject can not be fully entered into.

From time immemorial, Mull has been famed as the nursery and home of a race of witches. The age and surroundings favored the belief in witchcraft. Mull has long been called "The Island of Gloom," and the teachings of the learned of the past ages made it a favored location for the disciples of the black art. Sir George MacKenzie, lord advocate of Scotland, in the reign of Charles II. and James VII., declared "witchcraft to be the greatest of crimes, and the lawyers of Scotland cannot doubt there are witches since the law ordains them to be punished." The people of Mull called the witches "Doideagan," or frizzled ones. They belonged to the clan MacLean, and took that name, and regarded themselves as retainers of the family of Duard, swearing fealty to and claiming protection from the chief. They were indigenous to the place; for Mull being an island, it was impossible that they could come from any other quarter, for the highest authority on such matters declare that

"A runnin' stream they daurna cross."

In the legends of the island these witches were of the most powerful kind. They generally inflicted their punishments by means of types: the usual method being the preparation of a clay or wax image of the person or object to be acted upon; and when the witches prick or punch these images, the persons whom these represent experience extreme torment. The most celebrated of these witches lived in 1588, and made her home on lofty Ben More. When she discovered that the Spanish Armada was about to sweep down upon England, she determined to thwart its purpose, and bring about its speedy destruction. When the vessels were announced as having entered British waters, she raised a great storm at sea, and then taking with her the clay image of a ship she went to the sea-shore, and placing her model on the water, she kept whirling it about, and, as often as it sank, down went one of Philip's invincible men-of-war. As has already been narrated, one of the vessels of the Armada was the Florida, which was destroyed by Donald Glas MacLean. On board this vessel, as the story goes, was a Spanish princess, who in her dreams had seen a warrior of great elegance, for whom she at once formed a passionate and devoted attachment. She sought long but in vain for this image of her heart's desire. So she fitted out the Florida and determined to search beyond the limits of Spain. When the vessel touched at Tobermory she saw for the first time Sir Lachlan Mór MacLean, and recognized him as the object of her search, and immediately avowed her attachment. However complimentary this avowal was to Duard's chief, it was not agreeable to his lady. Sir Lachlan became enamored of the Spanish beauty, and was much in her company. The jealousy of the lady of Duard was now fully aroused, and she determined on vengeance against the fair stranger. She sought the witch of Ben More, and implored her to use her arts in her behalf. The result of this interview is well portrayed in MacKay's "The Lady of Duard's Vengeance." * The body of the princess was washed ashore, and the remains were conveyed to Kiel-Colum-Kill, in Morvern, and deposited in a stone coffin by the side of others containing the bodies of the MacInneses. For proof of this story the coffin is pointed out. Whether this is the same witch or not Sir Lachlan is said to have consulted just before the fatal battle of Gruinart I am unable to say.

In the year 1662 a charge of witchcraft was brought against some of the MacLeans who had settled as tenants on the Chisholm's estates of Strathglass. This colony of MacLeans had come from Mull, and had been in Strathglass for several generations. Whether their repute had followed them, or their own actions had caused the charge to be preferred is not known. To the accused sundry cruel tests were applied, such as pricking their flesh with long brass pins; and then, the Chisholm of that day made application to the privy council for a commission to try them, and put them to death. The application was granted, and in all probability they would have been put to death had not Sir Allan MacLean, then chief of the clan, presented a petition to the privy council, demanding justice for them, the result of which, the commission was recalled, however not before some of the poor people who had been pricked died in prison. In commenting upon this case William Mac-

* See Appendix, Note C, No. 13.

Kay says: "In the annals of our country there is perhaps no case which illustrates better than the one now under consideration, the strength of that cord of care and confidence which, in the olden times, bound together the chief and the clan, and which the more conservative of our Highland chiefs still strive to preserve; nor do I know of any incident that more vividly reflects the best features of the old clan system. In this present age of boasted progress and cold calculating, and distant dealing between the high and the low, it affords the student of the past no small pleasure to stumble upon such kindly deeds as the exertions of Sir Allan MacLean, the knight of Duard, to shield from injustice his kinfolk and friends, . . . the poor witches of Strathglass." *

Of another class of stories is the perpetuity of animosity beyond this life. This is illustrated in the tale that a MacLean was going to dine at the castle of Dunstaffnage, when a stone from the house-top fell at his feet, thrown by some one of the clan Campbell of long ago, who still retained his grudge against the MacLeans. In the same Dunstaffnage family one of the servants married a woman of the MacLeans, but she never got rest or peace night or day, and was consequently obliged to leave the place. The clothes she would lock up would, during the night, be thrown outside the house by unearthly hands. This proceeded apparently on the theory that the dead could not rest in their graves whilst a MacLean was eating the bread of the family.

One of the best known and famous stories is that of Eoghann a' Chinbhig, or Ewen of the Little Head, which is a fair representative of the superstitions and legends of Mull. He was a celebrated warrior, noted for his bravery, besides being one of the wisest and most tender-hearted of his race. He was the eldest son of John Og, fifth son of MacLean of Lochbuie, and fell with his father in a clan battle with Duard in 1538, and then taken to Iona for interment, where his tombstone is still to be seen. He was married to a daughter of MacDougall of Lorn, an ill-tempered and penurious woman. On the night before the battle fought in Glen Cainnir, in which he was slain, and while reviewing his followers, he was approached by a Bannshee (a spirit in human flesh), who warned him of the next day's battle; being a man of playful humor, he banteringly offered her his snuff-box, but listened with full interest to what she had to communicate. She informed him that he and his followers would be defeated on the following day, and that he would be slain. He

---

* *Transactions Gaelic Society of Inverness*, Vol. IX.

replied, "Nonsense! I have never been defeated, and will defeat my enemies to-morrow as usual." "Well," said the Bannshee, "if your wife gets up early in the morning, and unsought puts butter on your plate for breakfast, before you go out to fight, you will return victorious; but if not, and you are obliged to seek the food, it will be a sure sign that you will be slain." With that warning she disappeared. He returned home, arose early, and whilst buckling on his armor, he cast many an anxious glance toward the bed whereon his wife lay pretending to be asleep. He gave many a hint, and at last he threw a shoe at her, but she did not move. "If it is food you want," she said, "you will find curds in a dish there." "Your white curds will not come out at my side to-day," said the warrior, bounding away without breaking his fast. He fell in battle, and since then has always wandered about riding on a dun horse, and the sounds of his horse's hoofs, or the crack of his whip, is sure to be heard by any one of the Lochbuie family who has a death in his family. He is always present when any one of them is in distress. He wears his old cloak about him winter and summer, with his trusty sword by his side. His horse—the same he rode at the battle of Glen Cainnir—has no equal any-where for speed; and, with equal facility, travels over land and sea. Nor does he confine his wanderings to Scotland; for he has frequently been in Ireland and Spain. The cause of this continued restlessness of this headless horseman is that he fell fasting.

A different kind of superstition is that called *taghairm*, a sort of divination. When an important question concerning futurity arose, and when a solution was desired, some shrewd person was selected to solve the problem. He was wrapped in the warm hide of a newly slain ox or cow, and then laid at full length in the wildest recess of some lovely waterfall. Here he lay for some hours, and whatever impression was made on his mind, was supposed to be the answer. The last time the *taghairm* was performed in the Highlands, was on the island of Mull, toward the close of the sixteenth or beginning of the seventeenth century, and the place is still well known to the inhabitants. Allan MacLean, commonly styled Ailean MacEachainn—Allan, son of Hector—of the family of Lochbuie, was the projector of these horrid rites; and he was joined by Lachlan MacLean, otherwise called Lachainn Odhar, who was the son of Donald, the son of Neil, the first MacLean of Ross, or the race of the iron sword. Lachlan was an exceedingly bold and warlike man, and was governor of Duard castle under his chief, Sir Lachlan Mór, and fought in all the battles of the latter. Allan and Lachlan were faithful companions in arms, and together assisted in the defeat of Murdoch of Scallasdale at Grulin, and thus secured the estate of Lochbuie to the rightful heir. At the time they resolved to perform the taghairm, both were young, unmarried, resolute, and determined. The rite then consisted in roasting cats alive one after another, as a sacrifice to the devil, during four days, without intermission or tasting of food, at the end of which they were entitled to any two boons they might crave. The ceremony commenced between Friday and Saturday, and had not long proceeded, when infernal spirits, in the form of black cats, began to enter the barn in which the rite was being celebrated. When the first cat entered, it darted a furious look at the operator and exclaimed, "Lachlan Odhar, thou son of Neil, that is bad usage of a cat." Allan, who was master of ceremonies, cautioned Lachlan that he must not fail to turn the spit, despite whatsoever he might see or hear. The cats continued to enter, and the yells of the cat on the spit, joined by the rest, were fearful. At last there appeared a cat of enormous size, and informed Lachlan if he did not desist before his great eared brother arrived, he never would see the face of God. Lachlan replied that he would not flinch until his task was concluded, even if all the devils in hell should make their appearance. By the end of the fourth day, there was a black cat at the extremity of every rafter on the roof of the barn, and their yells were distinctly heard beyond the Sound of Mull, in Morvern. At last the rites were finished, and the votaries now should demand on the spot their reward. Allan was agitated by the fearful sights he had witnessed, but was able to make use of two words which meant wealth. Lachlan, although the younger, had greater firmness, and never lost his wits, asked progeny and wealth, and each obtained literally what he asked. When Allan was on his death-bed, his pious friends advised him to beware of the wiles of Satan. The dying man replied that if Lachlan Odhar (who was then dead) and himself were to have the use of their arms, they would dethrone Satan, and take up the best berths in his dominions. When Allan's funeral procession approached the churchyard, the second-sighted persons present saw Lachlan Odhar at some distance in full armor, at the head of a party in sable attire, and the smell of sulphur was perceived by the people. The stone on which Cluase Mór—the cat with huge ears—the fiercest of the cats, sat, is still exhibited, with the mark visible in small pits upon its surface.*

The future was also inquired into by means of a Leug, or precious stone. Herewith I give two illustrations of the MacLean Leug, full size. It is a crystal set in silver, perforated in the flat edge or flang. The crystal is

---

* MacLean's "History Celtic Language," p. 264.

broken across. This was owned by the MacLeans of Duard, and then passed to the family of Ross. It is now owned by Colin A. MacVean, who received it from his mother.

Superstitions persistently inculcated for ages, produce hereditary tendencies in that direction. It must not then be surprising if more or less of it remains in Mull, and even at this late date; but to find it in a church dignitary does not speak well for his enlightenment. The present MacLean of Lochbuie was instrumental in building, near his mansion, St. Kilda's chapel. He informed me that he had decided to call the structure St. Oran's chapel. The rector related to the bishop the legend of St. Oran: That he was a companion of St. Columba; that as fast as St. Columba built the walls of his monastery on Iona, the walls, during the night, would be thrown down by some evil spirit; that the monks consulted, and then decided a human victim should be buried alive

MacLean Leug.

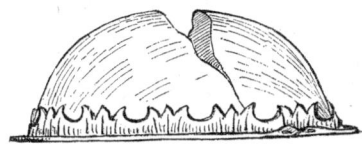

MacLean Leug.

that the evil spirit might be appeased; that St. Oran generously offered himself, and consequently was entombed alive. At the end of three days St. Columba was moved to behold his faithful companion, and caused the earth to be removed. To the surprise of all, St. Oran started up and began to reveal the secrets of the tomb, among other things, declaring that what he said about hell was a mere joke. This so shocked St. Columba that he caused St. Oran to be forcibly re-entombed. After hearing the above recital the bishop refused to dedicate the chapel to St. Oran. Lochbuie, disgusted by the credulity of both his rector and bishop, and somewhat nettled, declared firmly that its name should be St. Kilda.

While on Mull I lost my penknife, and on asking a very intelligent Highland gentleman where I could procure another, he replied: "I will sell you this one (exhibiting a three-bladed one) for a penny." It was not the penny he cared for, but the superstition of evil befalling the presentation of a sharp instrument governed him. Having neglected to comply with the terms of the bargain, he reminded me of it a few days afterward.

CHAPTER XXXIII.
LEGENDS OF MULL.

The legends of Mull are many, and all are interesting; but it is designed here to give only a few of the most characteristic. Of the many relating to Allan nan Sop (*see page* 88), the following is given as an example: The wife of MacIan was fair and vain; Allan was handsome and cunning. He, although the enemy of her husband, won her affections. She agreed to admit him to Mingarry castle upon a certain night to murder her husband, on condition that he would marry her. Allan accordingly entered the castle at night and murdered the old chief. MacIan, however, left an only son, and MacLean insisted upon the woman putting to death the son, who alone seemed to stand in the way of his subjecting the district to his own sway. The woman agreed to this, and accompanied by Allan reached the wild precipice to throw her child over into the ocean, which foamed below. The mother took the child in her arms and twice swung it in the air to cast it from her, but not doing so, she was asked why she delayed. "The child," replied the unfortunate woman, "smiles in my face whenever I attempt it." "Turn, then, your face away, and look not at its smiles," was Allan's reply. The woman did so, and the child was hurled over the rock. No sooner had she accomplished the deed than Allan turned upon her and said: "Away home, woman! You who could thus murder your husband and child might murder me."

A story is told of a feud[*] between Allan MacDonald of Clanranald—better known as Allan MacRuari—and the lord of Duard, probably Hector Odhar, ninth chief. The feuds between the MacLeans and the MacDonalds did not break out until the time of Hector Mór, twelfth chief of MacLean. Allan MacRuari was executed in 1509. Still it is possible that the chief of MacLean and Allan had become bitter foes, as narrated in certain documents. Allan was the dread and terror of all the neighboring clans, and at one time

---

[*] Partly recorded in *History of Clanranald*, pp. 82–84; MacKenzie's *History of the MacDonalds*, p. 375; MacCallum's *History of the Ancient Scots*, p. 207.

had the three powerful chiefs of MacLeod, MacIntosh, and MacKay of Strathnaver, confined in Castletirrim. At one time Allan desired to pass between Moidart and the Small Isles, and sailed with one vessel only. He was then on the very worst terms with the chief of MacLean, with whom he had been engaged in hostilities. The man on the look-out descried another large birlin coming over the point of Ardnamurchan. "Whose is she?" asked Allan. "The chief of MacLean's." "My dire foe," ejaculated Allan. "Shall we put about?" asked the steersman. "She will overtake us," said the watchman; "she is large and full of men." "Go on," said Allan; "spread my plaid over me, stretched on this beam: if hailed and questioned, say you are conveying Ailean MacRuari's remains to Iona. Play the dead march, piper." They were hailed, and answered as directed. "Let them pass with the dead," said the chief of MacLean, "we are well quit of Allan." As soon as they were out of sight, Allan arose, and said: "Row to the nearest point of Mull." He landed, and taking some of his men, ordered the rest to row to the bay of Aros. On his way across the country to Aros he set fire to the houses. In the meantime MacLean landed in Moidart, and commenced to carry off the cattle. Some who ascended the highest hills saw the island of Mull in smoke, and immediately informed their chief. "Ha!" says he, "Allan is come alive; leave the cattle, let us back and intercept our foe on his return." When Allan arrived at Aros, he boarded his galley, and said: "Row, men, to Loch Sunart, and avoid a second meeting; quick, ere he doubles the point." They landed in Salen; withdrawing the wooden pins, the birlin was soon in planks, and on the shoulders of the men, and soon launched in the water of Shielfoot, and Allan was in his castle as soon as MacLean arrived in his own; and thus saved his cattle by burning a few thatched houses.

Revenge and triumph were not always attended with bloodshed, as the following incident proves: The lower part of Mull at one time belonged to MacKinnon of Strath, and the MacLeans, who owned the rest, were anxious to obtain possession of all. Taking advantage of MacKinnon's youth and the infirmity of his uncle, MacDonald of Sleat, MacLean of Duard and Lochbuie divided the estate among their friends, and drove out the followers of MacKinnon. When MacKinnon arrived at man's estate, he went to his relative, the earl of Antrim, in Ireland, for assistance in obtaining possession of his inheritance. Forty young gentlemen volunteered to become leaders of his host. On his way to Skye, he called in Mull, and went to the hut of an old woman of his clan, whom the MacLeans had been afraid to banish, for she was reputed to be a witch. The old woman warmly welcomed her chief; and when he confided to her his intentions, she asked the number of his men. "Only forty," he replied. "It is enough," she cried, "and if you follow my advice, your revenge over the MacLeans will be complete before the morning's sun rises in the heavens. Duard and Lochbuie sleep to-night at Ledaig House without suspicion, and therefore without guard. Their men have been making merry, and are now, after much drinking, sound asleep in their birlinns. If your men are men, and if you are a true son of your father, you can slay them all without difficulty." MacKinnon resolved on a different mode of procedure. He asked his men to go with him to the woods, and there caused every one to cut off a bough and denude it of its leaves. For himself, he cut off a tall, straight branch, leaving all the foliage and twigs on it; and carrying these, they cautiously marched to Ledaig House, where they found the household asleep. At the door of the house he planted his own leafy bough, and suspended his sword above the door. At stated intervals around the house, his followers planted their bare poles, after which they quietly retired and re-embarked in their galleys. In the morning, the MacLean chiefs were greatly surprised at what had happened, and for a while were at a loss to account for it. At length Lochbuie exclaimed: "I see it all; MacKinnon has been here; that is his branch with the leaves; the bare poles represent forty men that he had with him, and that is his sword which he has left above the door to show how easy it was for him to have slain us. He has been very merciful; and we shall send for him and reinstate him in his inheritance. There shall be no war between us, for he has acted in a noble manner."

There is a proverb still current in Mull, although the circumstances which gave rise to it occurred ages ago. It is applied to a case in which one has done a favor for another, and in return receives gross ingratitude. The proverb is, "'S mairg a loisgeadh mo thiompan rithe," or, what a folly to burn my harp for her. The story begins by stating that the chief family on the island resided in a castle which was sheltered by the high hills at its back, evidently referring to the Lochbuie family. The only male representative was Neil MacLean, a lad of eighteen summers. Neil desired to see something of the world, and after repeated solicitations was permitted to go to France. No one regarded his departure with so much solicitude as his nurse, Catrina, and her beautiful granddaughter Barabel, who lived with her grandmother in a cosy hut near the castle. Neil and Barabel had ever been constant companions, and were greatly attached to each other. Soon after Neil's departure, Catrina died, and Barabel had to return to her father's cottage at the other side of the island. Five years had passed, and no word had come to her from Neil, although she had not forgotten their vows of love. Her growing beauty attracted all the youths within her vicinity, but she cared not for their attentions, because their homely manners and uncouth attempts at gallantry were not to be compared with the polished manners of Neil. Having arrived at the full zenith of her beauty, and withal a strikingly handsome woman, and coming to think that Neil was dead, she was betrothed to a very worthy man, a celebrated harper, although considerably her senior. He was a man of rare musical ability and poetic genius, combined with a gentle disposition. A few days before the time fixed for their marriage, they decided to go over the mountains to a village, to make certain arrangements for their future home. On their way home they were overtaken by a snowstorm, and soon lost their way. Barabel at last, overcome by exhaustion and benumbed by cold, sank to the ground insensible. The harper was in despair; no help was near, and no house visible—nothing but the blinding snow with which they were surrounded. The harper caught Barabel in his arms and struggled to gain the partial shelter of some overhanging rocks. Placing her in as comfortable a position as possible, he covered her with his plaid, and chafing her hands and face, he strove to restore vitality, and meanwhile bestowing words of endearment in her listless ears. He collected such material as was in his reach, and built a fire; the slight heat which it afforded soon began to revive Barabel. But the fire began to grow less and less as the sticks were consumed. There was now nothing left with which to replenish the fire but his peerless harp, which had brought him so much fame, and had been his constant companion for years, and his solace in all his vicissitudes of life. He broke his harp and placed the fragments on the dying coals, and the smoldering embers now leaped and gave forth sufficient heat to revive the insensible maiden. At the moment she sat up they heard the sound of a horn, and soon saw approaching a man followed by two dogs. The stranger explained that he had been out hunting, and seeing the fire, made toward it. Fortunately, he had a well-filled flask, which he offered to share with them. Approaching Barabel with intent to hand her the flask, he suddenly stopped and gazed intently into her face. The action of the stranger arrested her attention, and looking into his face, she gasped the name, "Neil," and fell back unconscious. The harper, during this episode, had been bending over the fire; but when he heard the cry, he hastened to restore his betrothed by pouring the fluid between her pallid lips, and by the assistance of the stranger the fair sufferer soon recovered. The embarrassment soon wore off, and they talked and smiled, while rapid glances, more expressive than words, passed between them. The harper remained unsuspicious, and when the storm abated all started together, the stranger assisting Barabel, while the harper walked in front breaking out the path. The stranger's attention now became so marked toward Barabel, that the harper became uncomfortable, but did not think it worth while to show any annoyance. When they came in sight of the sea, the stranger's boat was seen in waiting. At that moment Barabel complained of being thirsty, and begged her betrothed to go and bring her a drink from a spring some distance away. The unsuspecting harper cheerfully went to the spring, but when he had retraced his steps, he was transfixed with astonishment at seeing his faithless Barabel in full flight with the stranger, rowing rapidly from the shore. He realized that he had been robbed, insulted, and mocked. He never saw her again; but soon after received a message from her begging his forgiveness, and explaining that in the stranger she had recognized her former lover, Neil MacLean; that she was now married, and only wanted the forgiveness of her injured betrothed to complete her entire felicity. At the same time, she begged his acceptance of a fine new harp, which she had sent in place of the one he had destroyed on her account. The harper sent back the proffered present, saying he should never play on any instrument again; that his heart was broken as well as his harp; but he would freely forgive her for the wrong she had done him. He kept his word; his gentle spirit had received too cruel a blow, and he lived a solitary, listless life for a few months, and then died, a broken-hearted man.

Sir Walter Scott has preserved * the following tradition concerning Sir Allan, nineteenth chief of MacLean, although it is more befitting some of the older chiefs. "Allan MacLean, chief of that clan, happened upon a time to hear one of his favorite retainers observe to his comrade, that their chief grew old. 'Whence do you infer that?' replied the other. 'When was it,' rejoined the first, 'that a soldier of Allan's was obliged, as I am now, not only to eat the flesh from the bone, but even to tear off the inner skin, or filament?' The hint was quite sufficient, and MacLean next morning, to relieve his followers from such dire necessity, undertook an inroad on the mainland, the ravage of which altogether effaced the memory of his former expeditions for the like purpose."

Browne † preserves a letter of Æneas MacDonald, a banker in Paris, in

---

* Note to Canto III. of *The Lady of the Lake.* † *History of the Highland Clans*, Vol. IV., p. 92.

which it is alleged that Allan MacDonald, eighth of Moydart and Clanranald, in paying a visit with his lady to MacLean of Duard, "fell in love with a daughter of the said MacLean, and carried her off directly in some of his long boats, or birlinns, to Castleterrim, leaving his own lady at MacLean's house at Duard, where she did not remain long before MacDonald of Keppoch seeing her, and taking a fancy to her in her misfortunes, took her away to his house. Allan of Moydart, in the meantime, kept MacLean's daughter with him at Castleterrim, and had two sons by her, and the mother seeing that the former son which Allan had by MacLeod's daughter should be the heir, she fell upon a stratagem to put him out of the way, and make room for her own children to come in his place. It was Allan of Moydart's custom to pass with her a part of summer at a place called Keppoch, in Arisaig, which was but a few hours' rowing from Castleterrim. Near this place the sea forms a lake, called in the country dialect Loch na Keal, much frequented by vast numbers of seals. Allan's three sons often diverted themselves with shooting these animals upon the rocks, and the mother of the two younger brothers finding this apt opportunity for completing her design, gave her two sons their lesson so well, that, one day as their elder brother was taking aim at one of the seals, they shot him dead upon the spot; so that those two sons were then the only offspring of Allan. . . . Some time after the murder of Moydart's eldest and only lawful son, MacLean's daughter died, as did also MacLeod's daughter, who was in Keppoch's possession, and was properly Allan's lawful wife. Upon this, Allan, being then free of all engagements, married a daughter of MacDonald of Glengary, by whom he had a son, John," who "not being powerful enough to contend with his two brothers about the right of succession, as they were head-strong men, and he but a youth and without support, and his father, Allan, in his dotage, was obliged, after some vain attempts, to take what fortune was allotted to him, and was the first of Kinloch-Moydart." The above Allan of Moydart was chief of Clanranald from 1584 to 1593, when he died. He was prominent as early as the year 1548. This would fix the time of his visit to Duard castle during the chieftainship of Hector Mór. But that chieftain's daughters have already been accounted for; so, if the story is true, the woman must have been the daughter of one of the gentlemen of the clan.

CHAPTER XXXIV.

MARKS OF DISTINCTION.

Whatever marks of distinction, whether in the armorial bearings, tartans, or other objects, adopted by the Highlanders, the MacLeans were ever among the foremost in nurturing them, and receiving such benefits as were supposed to accrue from their use. These were adhered to with all the tenacity that characterized the clan. In the armorial bearings, the septs, cadets, or branches adopted separate ones. Duard being the parent stem, all others were necessarily more or less dependent upon it. It is not necessary to speak in detail of all, but only some of the more important ones are here given. The evidence appears to be that the Duard arms were changed during the period of the clanship. Over the doorway of the dwelling part of Duard castle, within the courtyard, is a stone built into the wall which is sculptured with the coat of arms; but it is so much defaced by the weather that it is now impossible to make out the device with certainty. The engraver has produced some of the devices more distinctly than the stone affords. The next coat of arms is taken from Stoddard's "Scottish Arms, A. D. 1370–1678" (Vol. I., page 87), and purports to comprise the whole family of MacLean, and specifies Duard, Lochbuie, Coll, and probably Morvern. It claims to be a fac-simile representation. The extreme length is nine and one-half inches, and the greater breadth six and three-fourths inches. The illustration has the following colors: The shield, divided into four parts, has the rock-arch under a silver back-ground resting upon a field of sky-blue; the arch is of vandyke brown, and the eagle's heads are green with the bills vermilion. The second part, composed of a birlinn and salmon, has the field gold, with the salmon sky-blue and the birlinn vandyke brown or sable. The quarter above contains a castle resting against a field of sky-blue, while the castle itself is silver. The fourth quarter has a hand and cross resting against a field of gold, while the upper

DUART CASTLE COAT OF ARMS.

part of the cross is silver, the lower part sky-blue, the hand vermilion, and the embroidery concealing the arm silver. The helmet is of the same pattern as that worn by kings, and is silver, save the visor and extreme part covering the left shoulder, which are vermilion. The scroll work just above the shield is sky-blue, while that on either side the helmet is gold. The castle over the helmet is silver, as also are the streamers containing the words, "I am Redie." The illustration is deficient in not giving the supporters, which were salmon.

Keltie's "History of the Clans" is Browne's rewritten. Both give the MacLean coat-of-arms, but the illustrations differ materially. The third illustration is taken from Keltie, and supposed to be the correct coat-of-arms of the MacLeans, or Duard family. Here the seals are used for supporters. The eagles and salmon, as also the hand and cross, and the mountain, rest against a field of silver, while the full-rigged birlinn is against a field of gold. Above is a tower, and below the shield, the motto, "Virtue mine honor."

MacLean Coat-of-Arms.

The shield of the coat-of-arms of the MacLeans of Lochbuie is divided, as indeed are all the others, into four parts. The salmon rests against a field of green, and the birlinn, cross, and hand against a field of gold. The birlinn, hand, and arm are red, and the cross blue. The lion rampant is red, while the field is silver. The tower is silver, resting against a field of blue. Above the shield is a helmet, over which is a battle-ax, with a laurel and a cypress branch. On the streamer below the shield should be the words, "Vincere vel Mori." The badge of this family is the Blaberry.

The coat-of-arms of the house of Dochgarroch has the blazing rock or altar resting upon blue; the birlinn, salmon, phœnix, and extended arm rest-

Maclaine of Lochbuie.

MacLean of Dochgarroch.

ing upon a field of silver; over the helmet and crest is the scroll containing the words, "Vincere Vel Mori," and underneath is another scroll containing, "Virtue mine honor."

Maclean of Ardgour.

On the shield of house of Ardgour, the birlinn rests in a field of green, in which is a salmon, and against a field of gold. The cross and hand are against a field of gold. The rampant lion is against a field of silver, and the triple-towered castle against a field of blue. Above the shield is a helmet, over which is a battle-ax crossed by a branch of laurel and cypress. Below all is the motto, "Altera Merces."

The MacLeans of Brolass, in their coat-of-arms, have the eagle heads resting with a salmon against a field of silver, as do also the hand and cross and the rock. The birlinn rests against a field of gold. The rock, the hand, and the eagle heads are red and the cross blue. The supports are ostriches. Above the shield is a helmet, over which is a tower. Below all is the motto, "Virtue mine honor." Just where ostriches come in to adorn the coat-of-arms of a sept of a Highland clan, is a mystery too great to be fathomed.

The MacLeans of Pennycross have the lion rampant, the birlinn, and the salmon resting against a field of silver. The cross and hand against gold, and the triple tower against a field of red. Above the shield is a helmet, over which is the battle-ax crossed by a branch of laurel and cypress. Beneath is the motto, "Virtue mine honor." Above the crest, "Altéra Merces."

The MacLeans of Coll in the armorial have the extended arm and the birlinn resting upon a background of silver; the eagle heads and rock resting upon gold, and the salmon on blue. The crest rests upon the shield, over which is a scroll with the words, "Altera Merces." Under the shield is

MACLEAN OF PENNYCROSS.   MACLEAN OF COLL.

a scroll with the words, "Virtus durissima Terit." The supporters consist of a hound and an ostrich.

The badge of all the MacLeans, save MacLean of Lochbuie, is the Holly. The war-cry or slogan of all is, "Bas na Beatha," Death or Life, and the march, "Caismeachd Eachuin mhic Aluin an Sop," The Warning of Hector, son of Allan na Sop. This was only played on sudden alarms, as on a hurried call to arms to repel an enemy, or on any occasion requiring immediate action. Besides this there was "The Chief's Salute," and another gathering called, Ceann na Droichide Môire. The MacLeans of Coll had still another, called, Biorlin tighearna cholla. It is impossible to reduce piobaireachds to written music, for the emphasis and the charm must be learned from man to man. The old tunes of the clans almost received their death-blow by the interdict placed upon them after Culloden.

In regard to all tartans, it is best to procure the plaid itself. A web of tartan is two feet two inches wide. If the width differs from this, then the scale of the pattern must differ also. On a scale of 54 Logan* lays down the following guide in forming the MacLean tartan: ½ black, 1½ red, 1 azure, 11 red, 5 green, 1 black, 1½ white, 1 black, ½ yellow, 2 black, 3½ azure, 2 black, ½ yellow, 1 black, 1½ white, 1 black, 5 green, 11 red, 1 azure, 1½ red, and 1 black. No chieftain of any clan could boast of a more attractive tartan than that of MacLean. In his full dress his presence was not only commanding, but the colors of his plaid lent grace to his form. But the chief was more or less renowned in the chase. The red would attract the eye of the deer, which in turn would be against the advantage of the hunters; hence it was found necessary to adopt an undress tartan. I shall give the following description, on a scale of 5½ inches by sixteenths: Commencing at the center of one block, and running to the center of the next, we have 3 black, 21 green, 3 black, 3 green, 6 black, 1 white, 6 black, 3 green, 5 black, 1 white, 6 black, 3 green, 3 black, 21 green, 3 black—first and last counted twice. This undress tartan is adopted by all the MacLeans, save the immediate family of Lochbuie. The dress tartan of MacLean of Lochbuie was adopted in 1745, and hence is very modern. Measuring from the outer edge of the center block to the beginning of the next corresponding one, we have in sixteenths of inches 34 red, 9 green, 4 blue, 1 yellow, 4 blue, and 9 green. If any one of the cadets of this house has adopted this pattern, I am unable to say.

The two most famous brooches of the Highlands are that which belonged to Robert Bruce, called the Brooch of Lorn, and the Brooch of Lochbuie. The latter was of silver ore found on the estate of Lochbuie, and made by a tinker there about the year 1500. It was handed down by the ladies of the Lochbuie family to one another, until Anna Campbell, wife of Murdoch MacLean, who had no male issue, gave it to Isabella, their daughter, on the day

---

* *Scottish Gael*, p. 505.

of her marriage. After passing through various hands it was purchased by the British Museum for £71. The workmanship is elegant. It is about five inches in diameter at the bottom; round the upper margin is a low upright rim; within that are ten obelisks, each about an inch and a quarter high, finely studded, and the top of each ornamented with a river pearl. Within these is a second rim, from which rises a neat case, whose sides project into ten demi-rounders, all neatly studded. In the center is a round crystalline ball, or magical gem. This case may be taken off, exposing within a considerable hollow.*

CHAPTER XXXV.

THE CHIEFTAINSHIP.

There has been some controversy relative to which house, by right, the chieftainship should be invested in. At this late day the question is of no importance. The clan is no more, and as a clan will never be gathered together again under any leader. The chief of a clan was one who regarded his clan with affection. He was with them in the hour of danger, and in days of adversity took their burdens upon himself. In peace, he promoted their welfare, and was always an adviser, a friend, and a father to them. He was not a chief in name, but in reality. That the chieftainship has always rested in the Duard family there is no question. No one has ever presumed to dispute this fact, but two claimants have been put forth, declaring that by hereditary right the chiftainship belongs to them, and they have been defrauded out of what in reality is their due. The first and elder of these claimants is the house of Lochbuie, who declare that of the two brothers, Lachlan Lubanach and Hector Reaganeach, the latter was the elder. For proof of this assumption the following reasons are given:

1. That Lachlan was named Lubanach because he was a cunning, crafty fellow; and through his devices he succeeded in cheating Hector, his elder brother, out of his right. 2. It has always been a tradition of the Lochbuie family that Hector was the elder of the two. 3. That it is related in old manuscripts that Hector was the elder brother. These are the only grounds that have been put forth by the Lochbuie claimants. The following answers

---

* Pennant, in his *Tour in Scotland*, gives two views of this brooch.

to the above have been given: 1. Between Lachlan and Hector there was always a bond of amity; in short, they were two loving brothers; and no evidence exists that there ever was any enmity between them. That Hector was defrauded of any right only exists in imagination, and no evidence has ever been produced. If the nickname of one is to be relied upon for an argument, then the same rule must apply to the other; for Reaganach means *stern*, and Hector's character was such that he would not brook being robbed even by his brother. 3. So far as tradition is concerned, it is equally true of the Duard family; for it not only claims to the traditionary evidence, but adjoining clans have the same. Mere tradition should not be arrayed against the simple fact that Duard always possessed the chieftainship. Then again, it must be borne in mind that these brothers were born prior to the year 1350, and the length of time must militate somewhat against tradition; and, moreover, it is not true that the Lochbuie family always had a tradition that it was the elder branch; for their claims were not set up until the impression went abroad that the Duard family was extinct. 3. The oldest manuscript which asserts the seniority of Hector is that of Hugh MacDonald, written during the reign of Charles II., or since the year 1650, and consequently more than three hundred years after the two brothers were born. Of this writer, Skene observes, that whatever he says " with regard both to the clans with whom the clan MacDonald were at feud, and to the rival branches of that great clan, must be received with great caution;" that he " perverted the genealogy " and " bastardized the heads " of rival clans.* MacKenzie says of Hugh MacDonald: He " was such an out-and-out partisan, that he scrupled not to write any thing calculated to glorify his own immediate chief and name, apparently caring little whether it was true or not." † Consequently, this testimony must be rejected.

The Duard family next proceeds to show that it is entitled to the chieftainship: 1. Lachlan obtained from the Lord of the Isles his daughter in marriage, a greater portion of the estate than Hector, and was made lieutenant-general in war, and this honor bestowed upon his posterity, besides the post of honor at the right hand of all the clans in battle. If Hector had been the elder, this gift would have been bestowed upon him. 2. MacLean of Duard has always been regarded and recognized by all authorities as chief of the clan. 3. The MacLeans of Duard have always held the leading position in the clan. In 1580 they could raise nine hundred men for war in the isle of

---

* *Collectanea de Rebus Albanicis*, p. 325.   † *History of the MacDonalds*, p. 44.

Mull, while Lochbuie could raise but three hundred. 4. All the manuscript histories of the clan affirm that Lachlan was the elder. 5. In time of war, the Lochbuies served under Duard, and no instance can be named where they aspired to full command, and without any dispute always gave up the place of honor. 6. Various cadets of the Lochbuie family always acknowledged Duard as chief. 7. In ancient times, the family of Duard is styled Laird of Mac-Lean, whereas that of Lochbuie only Laird of Lochbuie; and the former all along has used the title, of that Ilk, and the latter never has. The late Murdoch MacLean of Lochbuie, in addressing his letters to Sir John MacLean, added, "of that Ilk." And, further, for some centuries, the lairds of Duard subscribed themselves MacLean, without prefixing their Christian name, by way of preeminence, which the Lochbuies never assumed to do. 8. The chief of Duard wore the three feathers in his bonnet, which no Lochbuie, either in ancient or modern times, has ever presumed to do. 9. That the whole question of chiefship has been settled beyond controversy and doubt, is proved from the manuscript of 1450, which is the most valuable work extant on the genealogy of the Highland clans. That manuscript gives the genealogy of the MacLeans as follows: "Genealogy of the MacLeans:—Lachlan, son of John, son of ——, son of Maelsig, son of Gilleain, son of Icrath, son of Suan, son of Neill, son of Domlig, son of Ruingr, son of Old Dugall, son of Ferchard, son of Feradach, son of ——, son of Neachtan, son of Colman, son of Buadan," etc.* To this Skene (page 362) appends the following note: "This genealogy, it will be observed, commences with Lachlan, the progenitor of the Duard family, and thus proves the seniority of this branch over that of Lochbuie, descended from a brother of Lachlan. The MS. having been written during the lifetime of the two brothers, it may be held as settling this question."

The Duard MacLeans further urge upon the consideration of the Lochbuie family the following facts: 1. If it be thoroughly established that Hector Reaganach is the elder, that does not prove that the chiefship rests in the Lochbuie family, but rather in the Dochgarroch family. The Ardgour MS positively affirms that Hector's eldest son, Charles, "divested himself of the whole estate, excepting a small part, in favor of his younger brother." And, further, it is declared that the posterity of this younger brother can not show a formal renunciation from Charles. That Charles was the eldest son of Hector Reaganach is further confirmed by a letter from Hugh MacLean of Kinger-

---

* *Collectanea de Rebus Albanicis*, p. 359.

loch, under date of August 3, 1780, to John MacLean of Grulin, and now preserved in the Lochbuie Charter Room, in which he says: "From the tradition of your own family and others, it was currently affirmed that this Charles, son to Hector, first of Lochbuie, was the oldest of several sons, but contented himself with the division of Ardmeanan, and left the rest to the other brothers to divide as they thought proper." 2. If Lochbuie is the elder house, and should have the chieftainship, why should they desert the old clan tartan, and adopt one entirely different from that worn by the rest of the MacLeans?

The second claimant to the chiefship is that of Coll. It is maintained that Lachlan Bronnach was married first to MacLeod's daughter, and next to Mar's daughter; that he was taken prisoner by the earl of Mar at the battle of Harlaw, in 1411; that he was a married man at that time; that he was detained a prisoner until after the battle of Inverlochy, in 1431; that whilst he was a prisoner, his first wife died; that he then married Mar's daughter; and that for the sake of obtaining his liberty and marrying Mar's daughter, he agreed to disinherit his sons by his first marriage. To this theory the following objections have been raised: 1. The evidence rather shows that Lachlan Bronnach was not married at the time of the battle of Harlaw, for Hector, his father, could not have been born earlier than 1370, and Lachlan himself not earlier than 1392. It is possible that in 1411 he was twenty years of age, but it is not likely he was older. 2. That Lachlan was a prisoner from 1411 to 1431, is disproved from the fact that in 1427, he was at St. Finlagan, in Islay, a free man and lord of Duard. Mar took him prisoner at a battle fought in Lochaber, in 1429, and was kept in prison until 1436.* Lachlan Og's daughter, Finvola, was a married woman as early as 1463. It is reasonable to assume that her father was born at least forty years before that date, or say as early as 1423. 3. John Garbh, first of Coll, was a warrior, fearless and brave, and of such a disposition as not to allow himself dispossessed of any right. Add to this the fact that MacLeod of Harris was his uncle and the Lord of the Isles his friend, is it likely that he would tamely submit to see himself and his brother Neil disinherited, when they had such powerful and influential friends? 4. All manuscript histories agree in the statement that Lachlan Bronnach first married the earl of Mar's daughter. 5. If he was first married to MacLeod's daughter, and she died while Lachlan was a prisoner, how does she happen in later years to be the wife of MacNeil of Barra? 6. If it should be established that Lachlan Bron-

---

* Skene's *Celtic Scotland*, Vol. III., p. 297.

nach married first MacLeod's daughter, that would not justify Coll's claim to the chiefship, for then the MacLeans of Ross would have it; because of the two brothers, Neil and John Garbh, the former was the elder.

I notice that Gregory* says "that such evidence as I have seen tends to support the claim of the family of Coll to seniority." Gregory does not give any fact or reference upon which his conclusion is based. I wrote to Miss Catherine, daughter of Hugh, fifteenth of Coll, asking what evidence she possessed that John Garbh was the eldest son. I received a prompt answer stating she had none.†

It should be borne in mind that the houses of Ardgour, Coll, and Lochbuie were feudally independent of Duard, for they held their charter first from the Lord of the Isles, and then from the crown. It would appear that the Lochbuies early took upon themselves the dignity of a clan; for Dean Monro, in his "Description of the Western Isles" (page 33), written in 1549, in referring to the tombs on Iona, speaks of the "Two Clan Lynes with their lynage."

CHAPTER XXXVI.

ON THE NAME MacLEAN.

Similar to all Highland names, that of MacLean has undergone many changes. Perhaps none other can exhibit a greater variety or more curious fluctuations. As previously explained, the clan takes its name from Gilleain, known as Gilleain na Tuaidh, who flourished about the year 1250. To this name the word *Mac*, meaning *son*, is added, showing the clan is composed of the sons of Gilleain. We are informed that according to accurate Keltic orthography, the name should be spelled "Mac-Gille-Sheathain." ‡ Another authority || writes it "Mac-Ghille-athain," or "Mac-Ghille-eoin." *Mac* means *son*, *Ghille* means *servant* and *eoin*, *John*. Or taken altogether, "The Son of the Servant of St. John," referring to the apostle, John. During the period of Scottish history when Gilleain was born, it was the custom to name children after biblical characters, hence *Gilleain* was the Gaelic contraction which meant "Servant of St. John."

---

* *History Western Highlands*, p. 71. † Letter dated Glenmākra, London, December 19, 1888. ‡ MacLaughlan's *Keltic Gleanings*, p. 70. || Hector MacLean's *Tribal Names Among the Gäels*, p. 19.

The name is not uniformly spelled even in the Gaelic language. In John MacKenzie's "Beauties of Gaelic Poetry," it is thus spelled: Mac-Illeain (p. 70), Mac-Illean (p. 388), Mhac-Illean (p. 386), Mac-Ghilleain (p. 77), Mac-Ghilleoin (p. 79), and Chlan-Illeain (p. 79). In Rev. A. MacLean Sinclair's "Clarsach na Coille," I find the following methods used: Clann-Ghilleain (pp. 40, 122, 194), Mhic-Gilleain (p: 224), Mhac-Gilleain (p. 250), but in numerous other instances, Mac-Gilleain. In the same compiler's "Glenbard Collection of Gaelic Poetry," four variations are given, viz.: Mhac-Gilleain, Mhac-Gilleoin, MhicGilleain, and MacGilleain.

The official records of Scotland give many singular and curious spellings, which either prove that there was no established form, or the scribes were very indifferent as to the correctness of spelling the name. This need not appear strange, for the records show that the chiefs were not a unit on the subject. The oldest spelling I have seen is that recorded by Stoddardt in his *Scottish Arms* (Vol. II., p. 284), where Gilleain's son's name, Gillemore Makilyn, occurs as having swore fealty to Edward I. of England, in 1296. In the account of the constable of Tarbart, rendered in 1325, the name is spelled McGilhon (*Excheq. Rolls Scot.*, Roll II., Vol. I., p. 57). In an account rendered at Scone, in 1327, it is also McGilhon (*Ibid.*, Roll XI., p. 201). Also the same in an account rendered in 1329 (*Ibid.*, Roll XII., p. 238). In the charter granted by Donald, Lord of the Isles, to Lachlan MacLean of Duard, in 1390, the name is spelled Makgilleone. Two other charters were granted at the same time and place, and in all the name is uniform (*Reg. Mag. Sig.*, Lib. XIII., No. 300).

The fifteenth century presents no less than twelve different ways of recording the name. In 1405 Ector McGillane is witness to a charter in favor of James Kennedy (*Reg. Mag. Sig.*, Lib. IV., No. 56). In 1409, dated at Ardtornish castle, Donald, Lord of the Isles, gives Hector Makgilleon, lord of Doward, certain privileges in Coll (*Ibid.*, Lib. XIII., No. 300). The same method is pursued in a charter, confirmed in 1478 by the king, of the earl of Crawford to David Lindsay of Buky. To this Lachlan MakGilleon of Doward and Hector Makgilleon of Loichbowe are witnesses. It is probable that this was their own signature (*Ibid.*, Lib. IX., No. 15). Also, in 1493, the king confirms a charter to his esquire John MakGilleon of Lochboye (*Ibid.*, Lib. XIII., Nos. 114, 115, 116). In 1409 a charter was granted by John, Lord of the Isles, to his brother Hugh, in which it is affirmed that Lachlan McGilleon of Doward, and others, gave their advice; but when this charter was confirmed in 1495 by the king, we find the following witnesses with a different spelling; Lachlan McGilleoin, lord of Doward, John McGilleoin of Lochboyg, Lachlan, young McGilleoin, Master of Doward, John of Lachlan, McGilleoin of Colla (*Ibid.*, Lib. XIII., No. 168.) August 1, 1492, John, Abbot of Iona, witnessed a charter by John, Lord of the Isles, in favor of John McGilleon, Lord of Lochbuy (MacLean's "*Iona*," p. 58). In 1496 the act of legitimation to Lauchlan McGilleon, son natural to Hector McGilleon, is recorded (*Reg. Sec. Sig.*, Vol. I., fol. 29). At same time and record same is the precept for charter of resignation to said Lauchlan Makgillane, or, failing heirs, to Donald McGillan, brother of said Hector, bearing the arms and surname of McGillan. This document spells the name two different ways. In a charter given in 1462 by John of the Isles to his brother Celestine, the name of Lachlan McGilleone of Dowart occurs. In the year following, Lachlan McGilleone of Doward and John of Hector McGilleone witness a charter (*Reg. Mag. Sig.*, Lib. VI., No. 116). Lachlan Makgilleone, Master of Doward, in 1495, witnesses a charter for the castle of Strome confirmed by the king to Donald Duff, Captain of the Clan Cameron (*Ibid.*, Lib. XIII., No. 203). In 1463 Lachlan McGilleoin, lord of Doward, and Lachlan McGilleoin, his son, are witnesses to a charter confirmed by the king to Thomas, younger of Dingwall (*Ibid.*, Lib. VI., No. 116). Among the witnesses to a charter confirmed by the king, in 1476, to John Davidson, are Rolland Makclane of Dowart and Hector McClane of Carnlochboy (*Ibid.*, Lib. VIII., No. 1). Rolland Maklane of Dowart is witness, in 1480, to a charter confirmed by the king, in favor of John Davidson (*Ibid.*, Lib IX., No. 30). In a charter confirmed by the king, in 1495, in favor of Makneill, of the island of Barra, the name of Ferchard MakGilleoin occurs. The witnesses to this charter are Lachlan McGilleoin, lord of Doward, John of Murchard, MakGilleoin, Terlet of Ferchard Makgilleoin (*Ibid.*, Lib. XIII., No. 188). In 1499 John McClan of Lochbo received a respite for "herschipp" (*Reg. Sec. Sig.*, Vol. I., fol. 29). At the same time Lachlan McClean of Doward, John McClean of Coil, and Donald McClean "Eym" to the said Lachlan, received respites (*Ibid.*, Vol. I., fol. 115) The ancient Gaelic MS of 1450 writes the name Clann Gilleain (*Collectanea de Rebus*, p. 358).

The public documents and histories of the sixteenth century afford innumerable references to the MacLeans, and only a small proportion of these can be given. Among these it will be noticed there are twenty-seven different modes of writing the name. Some of these are abortive, but in the confusion system is seen gradually to evolve. Regarding them in their order the oldest submitted is Maklane, and so spelled, in 1505, in a remission t

Lachlan Maklane of Dovarde for various faults (*Reg. Sec. Sig.*, Vol. III., fol. 1) in the "tack to Lauchlan Maklane of Doward of the king's lands of Mull and Murwerne" for 11 years, in 1516 (*Ibid.*, Vol. V., fol. 100); in 1516, signed by "Lachlane Maklane of Doward wt. my hand on ye pen," in the famous petition, previously quoted in full (*Acta Dom. Con.*, Vol. XXIX., fol. 77). In this document, with the answer also to the earl of Argyle, the following various spellings are found in this order: McClane of Dowald, McClane of Doward, Makclane of Dowald, Makclanis desiris of Dowfart, Donald Makalane, and Johne Makclane of Lochboy—all of which was probably written by James Wischard, an advocate. Maklane occurs, in 1559, in a contract between the fifth earl of Argyle and Tormod MacLeod, in which Hector Maklane of Doward, as guardian of the latter, gives his consent (*Collectanea de Rebus*, p. 91). Makgilleon appears, in 1505, in a letter to Lauchlane Makgilleon of Doward, charging him not to intromit with the kirk rents (*Reg. Sec. Sig.*, Vol. III., fol. 36); and, again, in 1542, in a charter to Murdock Makgilleon of lands in Molorows, etc. (*Acta Dom. Con.*, Vol. XVI., fol. 43). In 1508, a permit to Lacklane Makgillane to sell certain lands in Badenoch (*Reg. Sec. Sig.*, Vol. III., fol. 208). In 1508, a protection to Lady Agnes McGillane, charging Lauchlan McGillane of Dowart and John McGillane of Lochboy not to trouble said Agnes (*Ibid.*, Vol. III., fol. 209); and in 1510 a letter of safe conduct to Lauchlan McGillane, his kinsmen and servants, to come to the king's presence at Stirling (*Ibid.*, Vol. IV., fol. 38). In 1510, a charter of apprising to Duncan Stewart of Appin, over the lands and castle of Dowart, apprised from Lachlan McGilleon of Dowart (*Ibid.*, Vol. IV., fol. 72); in 1537, confirmation of lands to Murdac McGilleon, natural son of John MacGilleon of Lochboy (*Ibid.*, Vol. XI., fol. 47); and, admission to the nunnery of Lady Mary McGilleon (*Acta Dom. Con.*, Vol. XXII., fol. 37). A respite, in 1516, to Lachlane Makclane of Doward for beseiging Carneboy (*Reg. Sec. Sig.*, Vol. V., fol. 12); in 1516, general remission to Lauchlan Makclane of Doward, Donald Makclane, Lauchlane Makclane of Ardgowr, and others (*Ibid.*, Vol. V., fol. 101); same year, same to John Makclane of Lochboy (*Ibid.*); same year, gift of lands in Tiree to Lauchlane Makclane of Doward (*Ibid.*); in 1531, remission to Hector Makclane of Doward for burning houses in Lennox, etc. (*Ibid.*, Vol. IX., fol. 18); in 1538, presentation to Charles Makclane to the rectory of Kilmore (*Ibid.*, Vol. XII., fol. 19); in 1542, charter to John Makclane, younger of Coll, of lands of Coll (*Ibid.*, Vol. XVI., fol. 19); in 1567 renunciation of Maister Lauchlane Makclane in favor of bishop Carswell, also Macklane (*Collectanea de Rebus*, p. 5); in a lengthy Latin document of 1587, containing a charter for the island of Iona, and many other lands, granted by James VI. to Hector MacLean, son of Lachlan MacLean of Duard, we have Makclane used once, and McClane nine times (*Collectanea de Rebus*, pp. 161-71); and in the complaint of Lachlan MacLean of Coll, against Sir Lachlan Mór, Makclane is used once, and McClayne three times (*Reg. Privy Coun.*, Vol. V., p. 354). In 1516, a respite is given to Alexander Makillan of Dufard to come to Edinburgh (*Reg. Sec. Sig.*, Vol. V., fol. 80). Among the numerous instances of McClane, the following are given: in 1516, Donald of the Isles makes redress to John MacIan of Ardnamurchan for injuries done by Lachlan McClane of Doward (*Acta Dom. Con.*, Vol. XXVII., fol. 206); in 1539, gifts to Allan McClane, brother of Hector McClane of Dowart, of the non-entry maills of Geya, Terbert, and other lands (*Reg. Sec. Sig.*, Vol. XIII., fol. 16); in same year, general charter of the lands to Hector McClane of Dowart (*Ibid.*, fol. 43); in same year, general respite for all crimes past to Hector McClane of Dowart (*Ibid.*, fol. 54); in 1542, presentation to Sir Charles McClane of the rectorage of Killindyke (*Ibid.*, Vol. XVI., fol. 19); in same year, charter to Hector McClane of Doward, the lands of Kilmichell and More in Islay (*Ibid.*, fol. 77); in 1547, legitimation to Hector and John McClayne, bastard sons of Allan McClayne, brother german of Hector McClane of Dowart (*Ibid.*, Vol. XXI., fol. 28); same year, gift to Patrick McClane of the temporality of the Isles (*Ibid.*, fol. 29); in 1548, charter to Hector McClane of Doward, of the lands and barony of Argour (*Ibid*, Vol. XXIII., fol. 37); in 1551, gift to Hector, son natural of the deceased Alan McClane, brother of Hector McClane of Dowart, of the non-entry of Geya, etc., in Kyntire and Islay (*Ibid.*, Vol. XXIV., fol. 120); in 1553, charter to Hector McClane of Doward, of lands in the shire of Terbert (*Ibid.*, Vol. XXV., fol. 84); in 1557, charter by Hector McClane to Janet Campbell of lands in Knapdale and Lochaber (*Ibid.*, Vol. XXIX, fol. 15); in 1558, gift of Coll to Hector McClane, brother and heir of the deceased John McClane of Coll (*Ibid.*, Vol. XXIX., fol. 28); in 1559, charter for Coll to Hector, son and heir apparent of Hector McClane of Coll (*Ibid.*, fol. 79); same year, gift to Lachlan McClane of the rectory of Nahayif in Lewis (*Ibid.*, fol. 88); in 1566, gift to Marian McClane of the nunnery at Ycolmkill, vacant by decease of Agnes McClane (*Ibid.*, Vol. XXXVI., fol. 22); in the "Description of the Isles," written between 1577 and 1595, McClane occurs fifteen times (*Skene's Celtic Scotland*, Vol. III., pp. 428-40); in 1580, in the contract between Sir Lachlan Mór MacLean and the bishop of the Isles, McClane occurs ten times. Jhone McLane Baillie of

Morvern is a witness, and Sir Lachlan's name is appended as a witness, and is written Lauchlane McClane of Dowart (*Gen. Reg. Deeds*, Vol. 19; *Collectanea de Rebus*, pp. 15–18). I notice, however, Sir Lachlan signs his name differently, for in his letter of July, 1595, to Sir Robert Cecil, he writes it " Lauchlane Mclane off Doward." Cecil indorses it " Macklane to me " (*State Papers of Scotland, Elizabeth*, Vol. LVI., No. 26). He uses the same signature to Bowes, same month and year (*Ibid.*, No. 27). It will, however, be noticed that his servitor, John Achinross,* writes it " McClayne of Doward ; " in 1581, in the gift of the escheit of sundry Islesmen to the bishop of the Isles, we have Murdoche McClane of Lochbuye, Lauchlane McClane of Doward, and others (*Reg. Sec. Sig.*, Vol. XLVIII., fol. 29); and in 1587, in the roll of the names of the landlords of the Isles, appears McClane of Dowart and Makclayne of Lochbuy (*Collectanea de Rebus*, p. 37). In 1527, a letter of protection to Hector Makgilleoun of Doward, son and heir of the late Lachlan McGilleoun of Doward, against the earl of Argyle and his brother, John Campbell of Calder (*Reg. Sec. Sig.*, Vol. VI., fol. 66). In 1542, in John Elder's proposal to Henry VIII. to unite Scotland and England, the name is written Mak Yllean (*Collectanea de Rebus*, p. 28). We have the name Alan McLean in 1546 (*Reg. Sec. Sig.*, Vol. XX., fol. 86). Dean Monro, who wrote his " Description of the Isles " in 1549, was out at sea and made some wild guesses, for he writes it MacGullayne, McGellayne, McGillayne, but gives the preference to McGillayne, and so writes it twelve times. Once he is moved to speak of the " twa Clan Lynes with their lynage." In 1567, is Lauchlan Macklane's renunciation in favor of bishop Carswell (*Collectanea de Rebus*, p. 5); and in 1596, Lauchlane Macklane of Dowart becomes principal surety in twenty thousand merks (*Reg. Privy Council*, Vol. V., p. 740). In 1573, the legitimation of Alan Maclane Hectorson, bastard son of said Hector, Charles Maclane Alaneson, bastard son of Alan, John and Donald, John Durache's sons, McClayne bastards of said John Durache (*Reg. Sec. Sig.*, Vol. XLI., fol. 79). The contract of 1580 between Lauchlane McClane of Dowart is witnessed by Jhone McLane, Baillie of Morverne (*Collectanea de Rebus*, p. 18). The obligation of Angus MacDonald of Dunnyveg to the bishop of the Isles, given in 1580, refers to Lauchlane McClayne of Doward (*Gen. Reg. Deeds*, Vol. 19); in the action of the bishop of the Isles against the Islesmen in 1580 are found the names of Murdo McClayne of Lachebowie and Lauchlane McClane of Dowart (*Collectanea de Rebus*, p. 13); in 1587, the king charges

---

* See Appendix, Note B.

Angus McConeill of Dunnyveg, to deliver out of his hands, and into the hands of the erll of Ergyll, those he held in captivity, Hector McClayne, son of Lauchlane McClayne of Dowart, Allane McClayne, sone to Ewin McClayne of Ardgowir, Donald McClayne, sone to Hector McClayne, constable of Carnyburgh, and others (*Reg. Privy Council*, Vol. IV., p. 159). In 1588, action was taken against Lauchlane McClayne of Dowart for ravaging Canna, Rum, and Eig (*Ibid.*, Vol. IV., fol. 341-2); in 1589, Lauchlane McClayne of Dowart is appointed one of the commissioners against the Jesuits and seminary priests (*Ibid.*, p. 463); in 1592, Lauchlane McClayne of Dowart was required to give obedience to certain acts of parliament (*Ibid.*, p. 129); and 1597, Aula McCawlay becomes surety for Lauchlane McClayne of Coill to give up the house of Brekoch when required by the king (*Ibid.*, Vol. V., p. 678). In 1586, Alexander McClene is a witness to certain obligations of Coline McKenzie of Kintaill that he shall cease fishing in the waters of Conane (*Ibid.*, Vol. IV., p. 69). In 1592, among others, the following were relaxed from the horn: Lauchlane McGillane of Dowart, McGillan of Lochboy, McClaine of Coll, Chairlis McGilleane, tutor of Ardgour, Johnne Oig McGillane of Ardnamurcho, Allane McGillane, bailie of Morveane, and Johnne McGilleane, bailie of Rosie (*Ibid.*, Vol. V., p. 54). In 1598, Herbert McKie gives security not to harm Gilbert McClein and others (*Ibid.*, Vol. V., p. 690). In the roll of the broken clans of 1594, that of Clangillane occurs (*Collectanea de Rebus*, p. 39).

Doubtless some of the diversity of the spelling shown in the sixteenth century is due to carelessness on the part of transcribers, as well as a want of knowledge of the true significance of the name itself. The seventeenth century presents nine different ways, showing a tendency toward a uniformity of the method. Added to the contract between the earl of Argyle and Lachlan McKinnon, given in 1601, among others as witnesses are those of Hectour McClayne of Doward, and Charlis McClayne, tutor of Ardgoure (*Collectanea de Rebus*, p. 202); and in the act of the privy council, in 1609, annulling a private proclamation prohibiting trade with Mull and other Isles, Hector McClayne of Dowart is mentioned (*Ibid.*, p. 153). In the bond of the nine principal Islemen, in 1609, declaring their religion, occurs the names of McClane of Dowart, McClane of Cole, and McClane of Lochbowy (*Ibid.*, p. 118); and in the act denouncing MacDougal of Dunolly for levying tolls on cattle crossing from Mull to Lorn, is found the name of Hector McClane of Dowart (*Ibid.*, p. 154). Subscribed to the famous "Statutes of Icolmkill," enacted in 1609, are Hector McCleane of Dowart, Lauchlane McCleane of

Coill, Hector McCleane of Lochbowie, and Lauchlane and Allane McCleanes, brothers germane to the said Hector McClane of Dowart (*Ibid.*, p. 119). In the report of Thomas Knox, bishop of the Isles, in 1626, we have this diversity: Hector M^{c}leane of Dowart, Hector M^{c}lean of Dowart, Hector M^{c}leane of Lochbowie, Lachlane M^{c}lean of Coill, McLeane of Dowart, McLene of Lochbowie, and Hew M^{c}leane (*Ibid.*, p. 124); in 1631, Murdoch M^{c}leane of Lochbowie gives an obligation to Martine McIlvora (*Ibid.*, p. 126); in the letter of Charles I., addressed, in 1635, to Sir Lachlan MacLean, we find mention made of Hectour McCleane (*Ibid.*, p. 185); in the same year, the same king directs the payment of the grant to Icolmkill, from amounts due from Sir Lauchlane McCleane (*Ibid.*, p. 188); and in the precept, granted in 1631, conferring the title of Baronet on Lachlane M^{c}cleane, the name is so spelled. In the report of the commissioners, in 1634, on the fisheries, mention is made, among others, of Sir Lauchlane M^{c}laine of Morverne, Murdoch M^{c}laine of Lochbuy, and Lauchlane M^{c}laine of Coill. To the document, among other subscribers, are L M^{c}lane of Morverne and Lauclane McClane of Coill (*Ibid.*, pp. 109, 110); and in the proclamation, in 1635, regarding the fisheries, the name of McClaine of Coill is found (*Ibid.*, p. 111). The MacVurich *Book of Clanranald*, written in 1647, for Hector MacLean of Duard, has Eachduinn MacGiolla Eoin, Lord of Dubhard (Skene's *Celtic Scotland*, Vol. III., p. 402). Browne, quoting from parliamentary records of 1689, mentions Jo. McLeane, Jo. MacLeane, H. McLean of Lochbuye, Sir John McLean, and Alexr. Maclaine (*History Clans*, Vol. II., p. 183).

It is not necessary to refer to the official documents of the eighteenth century, because enough documents remain in the form of letters from the MacLeans themselves. Confining myself wholly to a few of the characteristic letters in the Lochbuie Charter Room, I find the following, given without any special arrangement, and showing seven methods of spelling: Hector MacLean, justice of the peace in Torloisk, Mull, May 20, 1752, makes out a list of female scholars attending the spring school, eight of whom have the surname of McLean. A letter from Allan MacLean of Coll, December, 1750, written to Lochbuy. In the voluminous correspondence of Hugh MacLean of Kingerloch to John McLean of Gruline, the names occur as above. Sir Allan MacLean, under date of Inch, March 26, 1755, writes to John McLean of Lochbuy. Gillean MacLaine of Scallastle writes September 15, 1779. Murdoch Maclaine, July 4, 1779; but October 20, 1766, and January 16, 1766, signs his name McLaine. John McLean of Gruline, in 1790. John MacLain of Lochbuy, dated Moy, October 24, 1763. Hugh MacLeane of Coll writes

October 12, 1785. John McLain of Muck to John McLaine of Gruline, 1770. Letitia Macleane to the laird of Kingerloch, April 12, 1742. McLaine of Lochbuy, June, 1717. Hector MacLean of Coll, June 21, 1750. In a letter to Mr. Edgar, from Sir Hector, dated at Paris, January 24, 1750, the signature is simply Macleane (Browne's *History High. Clans*, Vol IV., p. 67).

The nineteenth century presents the family of Lochbuie spelling the name either MacLaine or Maclaine, and the Duard family MacLean or Maclean; but nearly all the branches or cadets of Lochbuie follow the Duard family. The earliest date of the Lochbuie family changing the spelling of the name I can find is that of MacLaine of Lochbuy in June, 1717, and since then has fluctuated more or less. March 20, 1801, Jane Maclaine addresses her father as Mr. Mclaine of Lochbuy. There is no correct etymology for the final letter *e* attached to the name. It also does violence to write the name as one word. The present century sees the name written MacLean, McLean, MacLaine, McLaine, McLain, McClean, McClain, McLane, MacLane, and possibly other forms; but with regard to the necessary changes which have taken place since the name was MacGillean, it should be distinctly affirmed that there should now be but one way, and all should agree to that of MACLEAN.

CHAPTER XXXVII.

DR. SAMUEL JOHNSON AND THE MACLEANS.

The visit of Dr. Samuel Johnson to the Hebrides in the year 1773 became celebrated through his own meagre description and the interesting narrative given by James Boswell. Johnson professed great anxiety to inquire into the mysteries of second sight, in which he was a believer, and investigate whether or not there were genuine Ossianic manuscripts, of which he was a violent opposer. During this trip he fell in with some of the MacLeans, of whom he makes some mention; but concerning whom Boswell gives valuable information. On Thursday, September 23, 1773, on the island of Skye, the party fell in with Donald MacLean, son and heir to Hugh, thirteenth of Coll, who, at that time, had arrived there; but obligingly retraced his steps in order to be of service to the distinguished guests. They describe Donald as a young man of middle stature, universally popular, very obliging, intelligent, and, among other varied accomplishments, an active and skillful mariner. He had been in England in order to study the science of farming, and worked while there at the principal operations of agriculture, in order that he might become thoroughly proficient. This was done for the purpose of improving the value of his father's extensive estates, without oppressing his tenants, or losing the ancient Highland fashions. Donald proposed that the party should visit Eig, Muck, Coll, and Tiree. Having been detained in Skye on account of the weather, the party were unable to leave until October 3d, when, under the care and direction of young Coll (Donald MacLean), they set sail in a small vessel for Iona; but the wind failing, they attempted to make Tobermory, in Mull; however, on account of a storm, they were again disappointed, and were forced to put into the harbor of Lochiern in Coll. On this island they were detained by storm until October 14th. On landing they repaired to the home of Captain Lachlan MacLean, who had acquired a small fortune in the East Indies. Hugh, proprietor and laird, at this time, was living in Aberdeen, in order to superintend the education of his children, and had left Donald to govern the estates with the full power of a Highland chief. From Captain MacLean's the party started for Grissipol, and on the way stopped with Hector MacLean, parish minister of Coll and Tiree, who lived in a house of one floor, and not inelegantly furnished. At this time the minister was seventy-seven years old, but not infirm, with a look of venerable dignity, dressed in a suit of black clothes, and a black wig, and, withal, a man of deep learning, and possessed of a valuable library. There was no public edifice for the exercise of his ministry, and the only place on the island then used was his own residence for divine service. The chapels erected prior to the reformation were allowed to decay, unused and uncared for. In his theology, Mr. MacLean was of the pronounced orthodox type of the reformation. In the conversation which ensued the dogmatism of Johnson was met by the equally dogmatic MacLean. "Neither of them heard very distinctly; so each of them talked in his own way and at the same time. Mr. MacLean said he had a confutation of Bayle, by Leibnitz. Johnson: 'A confutation of Bayle, sir! What part of Bayle do you mean? The greater part of his writings is not confutable; it is historical and critical.' Mr. MacLean said: 'The irreligious part;' and proceeded to talk of Leibnitz's controversy with Clarke, calling Leibnitz a great man. Johnson: 'Why, sir, Leibnitz persisted in affirming that Newton called space *sensorium numinis*, notwithstanding he was corrected, and desired to observe that Newton's words were *quasi sensorium numinis*. No, sir, Leibnitz was as paltry a fellow as I know. Out of respect to queen Caroline, who patronized him, Clarke treated him too well.' During the time that Dr. Johnson was thus going on, the old minister was standing with his back to the fire, cresting up erect, pulling down the front of his periwig, and talking what a great man Leibnitz was. To give an idea of the scene would require a page with two columns; but it ought rather to be represented by two good layers. The old gentleman said Clarke was very wicked for going so much into the Arian system. 'I will not say he was wicked,' said Doctor Johnson; 'he might be mistaken.' MacLean: 'He was wicked to shut his eyes against the Scriptures; and worthy men in England have since confuted him to all intents and purposes.' Johnson: 'I know not who has confuted him to all intents and purposes.' Here, again, there was a double talking, each continuing to maintain his own argument without hearing exactly what the other said."*

HECTOR MACLEAN AND DR. JOHNSON.

From Grissipol the party passed to Breachacha, where they were entertained in a pleasant new house, built by Lachlan, twelfth laird of Coll, and which was neatly furnished. The travelers early took a view of the castle, the vault in the second story then used for a prison. In one corner of this vault was a hole, then filled up, which had been used as a place of confinement for greater criminals. Near the castle was a hut in which dwelt a poor family, upon whom Johnson bestowed alms. Dr. Johnson speaks very highly of the government of the island, and is loud in his praise of the kindness of Coll to the eight hundred inhabitants. So well satisfied were they with their landlord that no inducement would cause them to emigrate. The custom of

---

* Boswell's *Tour to the Hebrides*, p. 227.

fosterage still remained in Mull and Coll. This consisted in the laird sending his child to some distant friend to be cared for. The terms of fosterage varied. In Mull the father sends with the child a certain number of cows, to which the fosterer adds the same number, the father furnishing the pasture. When the child returns to its father, it brings with it the original herd with half the increase. The period of fosterage was six years. Donald, younger of Coll, was fostered by MacSweyn, a tenant in Skye. When MacDonald raised the rents in Skye, MacSweyn removed to Coll, and was given land at Grissipol.

The storm having abated, the travelers, still under Coll's guidance, on October 14th, set sail for Tobermory, and after arriving there all repaired to the residence of Dr. Hector MacLean, a physician, and a man of some celebrity, who lived about a mile from the town. Dr. MacLean was not at home, but his wife and daughter entertained them with due hospitality. About the year 1768, Dr. MacLean had made a collection of poems, forty-eight being of ordinary length, and several short ones. This manuscript fell into the hands of John MacLean, known as Am Bard MacGilleain, and from him to Rev. A. MacLean Sinclair. He also wrote a history of the Clan MacLean, but the manuscript is now lost. Johnson was greatly pleased with the hospitality shown him, and spoke highly of Miss MacLean, declaring that she was the most accomplished lady he had found in the Highlands; for she knew French, music, and drawing, sews neatly, makes shell-work, can milk cows, and, in short, can do every thing. Miss MacLean entertained the company by reading and translating some Gaelic poetry, and gave several tunes on the spinnet which had been composed in 1667. The prospects of this accomplished young lady were certainly very bright, but, unfortunately, she conceived an attachment for one Duncan MacKenzie, who was greatly her inferior. In deference to her father's feelings, she remained single until his death, when, in 1786, she married MacKenzie, and lived in reduced circumstances in Tobermory until 1808, when she was left a childless widow, and became a pensioner on the bounty of the laird of Coll, until her death in 1826. She is interred at Kilmore, near Tobermory, but no stone marks her grave.

On October 16th, all set out for Inch Kenneth, hoping to spend the night there with Sir Allan MacLean, but were unavoidably detained at Ulva, and did not arrive at their destination until next day. The only inhabitants of the island were Sir Allan and his two daughters, with their servants, who lived in elegance and with plenty. The chieftain met the *voyageurs* at the landing, and accompanied them to his residence, where they were welcomed with genuine Highland hospitality. It being Sunday, Sir Allan informed his guests that it was his custom on that day to have prayers. Miss MacLean read the evening service, in which all responded. Dr. Johnson not only declared it was the most agreeable Sunday he had ever passed, but the impression made on his mind was so great that he immortalized the scene in a Latin sonnet.* Having seen the travelers safely in the hands of his chief, young Coll took his departure, having been of great service to them. Sir Allan was solicited to give them protection and accompany them to Icolmkill, for which place they set out October 19th. They coasted along the shore of Mull by moonlight, and after a sail of forty miles, including various turnings, they arrived in sight of the village of Icolmkill. Upon hearing of the arrival of Sir Allan, the inhabitants, who still considered themselves as the people of MacLean, ran eagerly to meet him, and received him with all the reverence due their chieftain. It was told to Sir Allan that one of the MacGinnises (a branch of the MacLeans) had refused to send him some rum, which threw the knight into a state of great indignation. "You rascal!" said he, "don't you know that I can hang you if I please? Refuse to send rum to me, you racal! Don't you know that if I ordered you to go and cut a man's throat, you are to do it?" "Yes, ant please your honor," demurely replied MacGinnis, "my own, too, and hang myself, too." By way of upbraiding him, Sir Allan said: "I believe you are a Campbell." The poor fellow denied that he had refused the rum, and afterward declared, "Had he sent his dog for the rum, I would have given it; I would have cut my bones for him."

A part of the 20th was given to viewing the ecclesiastical ruins which the island afforded, besides some natural curiosities along the shore. When the tourists were ready to leave, the islanders gathered about the boat, and with the union of many hands pushed it down the beach; every one thinking himself happy in being useful to his chief. The same evening the party landed on Mull, and were entertained for the night at the house of Rev. Neil MacLeod. The next day, having been furnished with horses, they started for Loch Buy. On the way they dined at Dr. Alexander MacLean's, another physician in Mull. Between seven and eight o'clock that night, still under the supervision of Sir Allan, they arrived safely at the residence of John MacLean of Lochbuie. Of John MacLean and his lady, Boswell remarks: "We had heard much of Lochbuie's being a great, roaring braggadocio, a kind of Sir John Falstaff, both in size and manners; but we found that they had

---

* See Appendix, Note C., No. 18.

swelled him up to a fictitious size, and clothed him with imaginary qualities. Coll's idea of him was equally extravagant, though very different: he told us he was quite a Don Quixote; and said he would give a great deal to see him and Dr. Johnson together. The truth is, that Lochbuie proved to be only a bluff, comely, noisy old gentleman, proud of his hereditary consequence, and a very hearty and hospitable landlord. Lady Lochbuie was sister to Sir Allan MacLean, but much older. He said to me: 'They are quite antediluvians.' Being told that Dr. Johnson did not hear well, Lochbuie bawled out to him, 'Are you of the Johnstons of Glencoe, or Ardnamurchan?' Dr. Johnson gave him a significant look, but made no answer; and I told Lochbuie that he was not Johns*ton*, but Johns*on*, and that he was an Englishman." * Boswell does not finish the story, which has been preserved, and is still current in Mull. When Lochbuie listened to Boswell's explanation, he blurted out, "Then he must be a bastard!" As he did not belong to the MacIans of Ardnamurchan or Glencoe, the old laird concluded that Johnson was an illegitimate.

For October 22d, Boswell continues the narrative as follows: " Before Dr. Johnson came to breakfast, Lady Lochbuie said, ' He was a *dungeon* of wit;' a very common phrase in Scotland to express a profoundness of intellect, though he afterward told me that he had never heard it. She proposed that he should have some cold sheep's-head for breakfast. Sir Allan seemed displeased at his sister's vulgarity, and wondered how such a thought should have come into her head. From a mischievous love of sport, I took the lady's part, and very gravely said, 'I think it is but fair to give him an offer of it. If he does not choose it, he may let it alone.' 'I think so,' said the lady, looking at her brother with an air of victory. Sir Allan, finding the matter desperate, strutted about the room and took snuff. When Dr. Johnson came in, she called to him, ' Do you choose any cold sheep's-head, sir ?' ' No, madam,' said he, with a touch of surprise and anger. ' It is here, sir,' said she, supposing he had refused it to save the trouble of bringing it in. Thus they went on at cross purposes, till he confirmed his refusal in a manner not to be misunderstood; while I sat quietly by, and enjoyed my success." † The same day Sir Allan and Lochbuie accompanied Dr. Johnson and Boswell to the ferry, where they bade them adieu.

---

* *Tour to the Hebrides*, p. 270.   † *Ibid.*, 271.

CHAPTER XXXVIII.
THE CLANSMEN AFTER CULLODEN.

The defeat of the Highland army at the battle of Culloden was far reaching in its consequences. The misery did not alone consist in the butchery of unarmed, defenseless, and wounded men, the burning of houses, the slaughter of cattle, and the raping of inoffensive women by the brutal English soldiery under the direction of the more brutal duke of Cumberland; but parliament set to work to complete the desolation by an ingenuity and an inhumanity unsurpassed for diabolical malignity, even in the records of savagery.

Of these acts it is only necessary to notice two: The act abolishing the Highland garb, and the taking away the heritable jurisdiction of the proprietors, and vesting the same in the crown. The first act declared that no man or boy in Scotland, except officers and soldiers, " shall, on any pretense whatsoever, wear or put on the clothes commonly called Highland clothes, that is to say, the plaid, philebeg, or little kilt, trouse, shoulder belts, or any part whatsoever of what peculiarly belongs to the Highland garb; and that no tartan or partly colored plaid or stuff shall be used for great coats, or for upper coats." * By the depredations of the English soldiery, the people, for the most part, were impoverished, and their chieftains exiles. Their clothing, for the most part, was made in the national habit. The act simply stripped them of their clothing at a time when they had been deprived of the resources for replenishing their garments. The act has been justly termed " an act for the uncivilization of the Highlands, and the profit of cloth workers." No steps, whatever, were taken to re-supply these poor people with clothing, although a severe winter was coming upon them.

The history of the Highlands proves conclusively that the clans were the owners, in common, of the soil of their native districts, and elected their own clan or local rulers. The clans, down to the day of Culloden, enrolled themselves under the native chiefs, recognized by themselves, or the feudal nobility of their respective districts, just according as they themselves preferred the one or the other. No king of ancient Caledonia ever possessed or attempted the power to expatriate the people of any given district. The people were

---

* Act George II., 1747.

generally regarded as having certain inherent rights in the lands; although chiefs might hold charters from those high in authority, whether lords of the Isles, or the monarch on the throne. The Acts of George II. confiscating the lands of the chiefs, and the Acts of George III. restoring the same to the heriditary chief, fully and completely neglected the rights of the people. In the presence of these two electors of Hanover, the common people had no rights that they were bound to respect. The result might have been easily foreshadowed. There came a class of landlords, who had no appreciation of the services of the clansmen, and, perhaps ignorant of the fact, that without their heroic conduct, the young scions of aristocracy would never have risen above the commonalty. The time came when the heritable proprietors desired to get rid of the natural lords of the soil. Eviction's fearful crimes dawned upon the Highlands of Scotland. The duke of Athol was the first to engage in this infamous work, which he commenced in the year 1784. The contagion spread over the Highlands; and for inhumanity, cunning and hardheartedness reached its culminating point on the estate of the duchess of Sutherland, where fire, fagot, and other refined engines of cruelty were practiced without stint upon fifteen thousand defenseless people. A human monster was employed, who appears to have gloated in his work. The feelings of the reader will not here be harrowed by a recital of the wrongs and sufferings of these down-trodden people. The facts have been fully set forth by Alexander MacKenzie in his *Highland Clearances*. The poor, persecuted, homeless sufferers turned to the ministers of religion for advice and consolation. But these creatures held their positions not by the will of the people, but their livings were given them by those in power. They asked of them bread and received a stone; they asked for an egg and received a scorpion. "The clergy, indeed, in their sermons, maintained that the whole was a merciful interposition of Providence to bring them to repentance rather than to send them all to hell, as they so richly deserved." * Of course all the clergy were not so destitute of humanity; neither did all the lairds engage in evictions. But so heartless was the process carried on that the humane in all lands raised the voice of protest.

The question of the Highland evictions must necessarily be confined, in this discussion, to its bearing on the clan MacLean. I have searched diligently for all the facts; but the returns are very meagre, and it is more than probable the bottom has not been reached; but if there was any thing severe

---

* *Highland Clearances*, p. 31.

the watchful eye of the editor of the *Highland Clearances* long since would have detected it. Such as they are, I give without favor and without stint.

The greater portion of the MacLean estates and the most populous were forfeited during the chieftainship of Sir John MacLean. To have the chief dispossessed and an obnoxious landlord placed over them, was very galling to the proud and warlike MacLeans. The dissatisfaction thus engendered could only result in the gradual dispersion of the clansmen, who would migrate into the domains of favorable chieftains, or else remove to the Lowlands, or seek a home in a foreign land. This is not only true of those directly on the Duard estates, but also true of the other leading branches, Lochbuie, Ardgour, and Coll. As early as 1724, John MacLean of the family of Lochbuie had settled in the city of New York; and a very strong migration, not only of MacLeans, but of other clans, took place, looking toward America, many years before evictions took place on Highland estates. This migration was almost wholly due on account of the oppressive laws enacted by the English parliament. During this period of emigration, the MacLean landlords appear to have been very lenient with their tenants, and endeavored to promote their welfare. There appears to have been no dissatisfaction on the part of the one with the other. Oppression did not commence on the ancient estates until after the commencement of the nineteenth century; and only one MacLean proprietor is mentioned as being concerned in it. The population of Mull in 1821 was 10,612, which, in 1881, was reduced to 5,624, or about half which exhibits a very unfavorable state of affairs. The crofters and cotters who have been ejected from their holdings, have moved to Tobermory, and are given in the above enumeration. Hence the distress is much greater than the figures imply. The duke of Argyle has been the most remorseless of the proprietors of these ancient estates, mention of which need only be made of Kilfinichen and Bunessan in Mull, and also Iona and Tiree. The crofters and cotters were warned off the district of Kilfinichen; some were stripped of their small possessions and reduced to pauperism. Twenty-six emigrated to America, and many removed to Kinloch. In Bunessan, the Ross of Mull, the relief committee of 1849 advanced £128 for procuring provisions for a number of emigrants leaving this point for America. The population of Iona has been reduced from 500 in 1848 to 243 in 1881. Tiree, in 1821, contained 4,181, reduced to 2,733 in 1881. The population of Coll, in 1755, was 1,193; in 1771, 1,200; in 1801, 1,162; in 1821, 1,264; in 1841 1,409; in 1849, 1,235. The relief committee of that year, in speaking of Coll, say: "Mr. MacLean (Hugh, fifteenth of Coll), the principal proprietor always acted most liberally when he had it in his power to do so, but, unfortunately, he has no longer the ability." * Soon after, the estates passed out of his hands, and in 1881, the population fell to 643, and the inhumanity and cruelty practiced upon the poor of Coll beggars description. A private letter I received from a responsible man living there states: "There are just ninety-six MacLeans now living in Coll, counting young and old, but some of these are not of the old natives. There are only seven of the old natives occupying land on the Coll estate, whereas, at one time, before MacLean sold it, there were over a hundred families. The whole of these were cleared off by the factor who bought it, and the land turned into sheep-walks, and large tacks occupied by Lowlanders. Sixteen of the Coll people were thrown overboard out of one ship on their way to Tasmania, when they were driven off by the rapacious landlord. These were all respectable and God-fearing people, and about the best law-abiding that could be found in the world. The vessel in which they emigrated was a government one, and they are proverbial for outbreaks of epidemics on account of insanitation." Morvern contained in 1801 a population of 2,000, which, in 1881, was reduced to 714. These figures are very distresing. All the ejected were not MacLeans, but a large proportion were. In 1849, Rev. Dr. MacLachlan of Edinburgh made the following charge: " MacLean of Ardgour and Lochiel bring up the rear of the black catalogue, a large body of people having left the estates of the two latter, who, after a heartrending scene of parting with their native land, are now on the wide sea on their way to Australia." † I submitted this statement to the present MacLean of Ardgour, and asked for an explanation. He replied very promptly, under date of November 7, 1888, saying : " I have looked through my grandfather's letters to my father from 1820 to 1845, and in them is no mention of evictions. In 1850, he made an address to his crofters and tenants, in which he reviewed his dealings with them at the beginning of the century, and stated it would have given him great pain had they emigrated instead of taking their holdings he had established on the sea coast. This was in 1790, and they did not take up the new holdings until 1802. For these he offered leases, but they were satisfied without them. My aunt, aged 85, writes me there were no evictions; for she would have known it, because she was with him until the end of his life. The old game-keeper, who knows all about the old history, gives me the same account. In 1843, he got rid of two families, but soon after brought one back,

---

* *Highland Clearances*, p. 356.   † *Ibid.*, p. 367.

and they are here now." In a conversation I had with Ardgour, July 14, 1887, he informed me that his grandfather used no force in getting the crofters out of the glens and establishing them on the coast. He showed to them it would be better for them, and they removed peaceably. As to changes in population, I have no figures.

Unfortunately, I am forced to record the name of a MacLean evictor—not a landlord, but a tool in the hands of MacLeod of MacLeod. I know nothing of his history, only as I find it in MacKenzie's *Isle of Skye* (p. XX.) Dr. MacLean cleared two townships of twelve families. He was not long in possession before he began to remove the people. When he found a crofter's sheep on his farm, and the owner was not prepared to pay half a crown on the spot for it, he would have the ears of the sheep cut off close to the skull This unwarranted cruelty was certainly very unworthy of his forbears.

Among the MacLeans who have been singled out individually as having suffered from these evictions and oppressions, I find the following: Murdo MacLean testified before the Crofter Commission, that on lord MacDonald's estate every crofter was compelled to give ten days' work at spring and harvest time, and all the wages received for it was abusive language; the labo was so severe that it required the strongest people to stand it; they wer compelled to render the service at any time when wanted; even my wife wa compelled to do the landlord's work when required; she even could not ge leave to come home and prepare food for me.* Donald MacLean testified they were forced to work ten days a year, a man or woman from each croft under danger of eviction. They had to buy hooks from the proprietor t shear his own corn, and when they did not attend to his labor were charge 2s. 6d. a day, but when they worked for payment received from 1s. to 1s. 6d per day.† Donald MacDonald, factor of Lord MacDonald, used libelous an defamatory language concerning Donald MacLean, a single man, living wit his father at Lochcarron. MacLean prosecuted, and received over £22 dam ages; because of this, his father, aged eighty-one, bed-ridden and on his deatl bed, was evicted, although for sixty years he had not failed to pay his rent o the appointed day. His father, grandfather, and great-grandfather occupie the same place, and so did their ancestors before them. "It was most pitiabl to see the aged and frail human wreck as I saw him that day, and to hav heard him talking of the cruelty and hard-heartedness of those who took ac

---

* *Isle of Skye*, p. XIII. † *Ibid.*, XIV.

vantage of the existing law to push him out of the home which he had occupied so long, while he is ready on the brink of eternity." *

On account of her extortions, lady Matheson, in the year 1888, gained for herself a most unenviable reputation. Her acts became so notorious that the Crofter Commission was forced to hold a session on her estates, in order to adjust the rents. The decisions of the Commission are given in the *Scottish Highlander* for December 27, 1888, and January 3, 1889. These tables are very long, and only what relates to the MacLeans is given. These refer to the isle of Lewis. Isabella MacLean, charged £18 18s., reduced to £3; Janet MacLean, reduced from £33 18s. to £3; Donald MacLean, reduced from £3 5s. to £1 1s.; Norman MacLean, reduced from £6 12s. to £2 12s.; Donald MacLean, reduced from £13 9s. to £6; Norman MacLean, from £15 3s. to £2 10s.; Donald MacLean, from £17 6s. to £14 17s.; both John and Neil had their arrears canceled; Donald MacLean from £19 19s. to £2 16s.; Alexander MacLean, from £20 8s. to £4; John MacLean, from £11 13s. to £1 10s.; Donald MacLean, from £13 13s. to £1 15s.; Malcolm MacLean, from £7 14s. to £1 2s.; Angus MacLean, from £8 16s. to £2; Alexander MacLean, from £6 4s. to £1 10s.; widow Marian MacLean, from £14 2s. to £1 10s. Lachlan MacLean, £8 5s. to £3. In the 607 cases in the Lewis, lady Matheson charged an annual rental of £1,784 9s. 4d., which the Commission reduced to £1,146 11s., or an average reduction of 36 per cent. She had charged against her crofters £8,056 0s. 2d. arrears, of which the Commission canceled £6,398 6s. 2d., or an average of 80 per cent.

In this chapter, a paragraph should be devoted to martyrdom. How many MacLeans have suffered martyrdom, I do not know. Doubtless, many should be remembered in that list. At the city of York, England, for the part they took in the revolution of 1745-6, twenty-two persons suffered martyrdom. One of these was John MacLean, who was executed on the 8th of November, along with eight others. "All these unhappy individuals are said to have behaved, throughout the last trying scene, with a degree of decent firmness which surprised the beholders. Every one of them continued till his last moment to justify the cause which had brought him to the scaffold, and some even declared that, if set at liberty, they would act in the same way they had done. They all prayed in their last moments for the exiled royal family, particularly for Prince Charles, whom they concurred in representing as a

---

* *Highland Clearances*, p. 329.

pattern of all manly excellence, and as a person calculated to render the nation happy, should it ever have the good fortune to see him restored."*

Of the many other forms of oppression only one instance will be given. It is taken from the *Celtic Magazine* (Vol. VII., p. 549), copied from the *Boston Traveler* in 1858. The press-gangs employed by the English, for the purpose of forcing men into the army, were composed of desperate characters. They were the terror of all poor men, but well supported by the government and its officers. The infamy of the navy had reached Mull, for half a dozen maimed seamen who had been impressed lived there, and had told of their sufferings. William MacLean and his sons, Ranald and Roderic, were successful fishermen in Mull. One night the father, in company with other fishermen, prepared to smuggle some whisky from a neighboring island to the mainland. On reaching the beach they were terrified by the arrival of two boats that belonged to a ship of war in the offing, and had come for the purpose of impressing the fishermen along the coast. MacLean counseled his friends to warn at once all the fishermen to meet him at a given place to devise means for protection. He went to his own house and armed his two sons with broad-swords, and repaired to the trysting-place, where fifty men and boys were assembled. MacLean, whose terror had given place to indignation, counseled to cut off the gang, which numbered thirty men, fully armed, and led by a lieutenant. "It is well said," replied one of his neighbors. "You lead us, William." Boys gave the report that the gang had broken into a house, and were terrifying women and children. The fishermen, led by the undaunted William, crawled upon their hands and knees, and gradually surrounded the house. At a given signal, the fishermen sprang to their feet, and in less than half an hour annihilated the entire gang. The fishermen retired to the hills, and William called upon the old laird, an old soldier, and told him what had taken place. The laird was not at all displeased, but, being apprehensive of the consequences, advised William to leave the island with his family, and gave him money to bear his expenses. Next morning the brig signaled for the return of the boats. The commander landed, and was soon informed by Sir Archibald MacLean of the fate of the press-gang. "I'll shoot every one of the murderers!" exclaimed the commander. "So you may," replied Sir Archibald, coolly, "if you can catch them." "I'll land my whole ship's company, and hunt them to the death." "How many men have you, sir?" "A hundred." "You will require a thousand," responded Sir Archibald. "The

---

* Chamber's *History Rebellion* 1745-6, p. 465.

whole island is in arms, and mind, sir, these men are Highlanders, men who would rather fight than eat at any time." "Are there no civil officers here?" "None. When a man does not behave himself he is expelled the island, and if he returns he is killed and no questions asked." "How can you live in such a community? What safeguard have you for your life or property?" "Safeguard enough. These wild folks are my kinsmen; there is not one of them who would not risk his life to serve me." "If such be your influence, then, in the king's name, I command you to produce the murderers of my boats' crews." "Name, them, sir, and so I will." This was the last attempt at impressment in Mull during that war with Napoleon. Taking the advice of Sir Archibald, William embarked his wife and two sons in a fishing boat, and, after much privation, landed on the island of Pomona, the mainland of the Orkneys. Here he settled upon a small farm, and changed his name to Bruce. He went upon several whaling expeditions, and was quite successful. On the return voyage of the last one, he and all the rest of the crew were impressed by a frigate. He was then forty-five years of age. His wife, when this fresh disaster befell her, cursed the house of Hanover as the cause of her bereavement, and told her sons if the Stuarts were on the throne their father would not have been dragged away like a thief. In less than a year her two sons were torn from her and impressed into the service. They possessed good natural endowments, and by their daring and exemplary conduct arose to the rank of lieutenants. Their father filled the office of gunner. As all three were separated, they were ignorant of each other's fate for five years; but all three were careful to send money to Mrs. Bruce, the name by which she was known. In 1801, the fleet was sent to Egypt to act in concert with the land forces. Seamen were frequently employed on shore in order to cover the advance of the troops. In one of these operations a boat's crew, consisting of fifteen belonging to the admiral's ship, was surrounded by a French force of two hundred. The sailors, cutlass in hand, threw themselves violently upon the French, and made great havoc. Conspicuous among the sailors was the gunner; his every blow brought a man to the ground, and in whatever direction he turned he made a broad path for himself. When the French fled, the gunner continued the pursuit far ahead of the rest, and actually ran down twenty of the enemy and made them prisoners. Sir Sidney Smith witnessed the heroic daring of the gunner, and sent his lieutenant to inquire his name. "My brave fellow," said the lieutenant, slapping him familiarly over the shoulder, " Sir Sidney Smith wishes to know your name, that he may report you to the admiral." "My name," replied the gunner, "is William Mac-

Lean; no, avast there, I'm adrift, its Bruce." The lieutenant started back; he could not believe his eyes; his father stood before him, and knew him not. "Bruce, did you say? and from the Orkneys?" The gunner raised his eyes; he knew his son, his first born, Ranald, at a glance, and in a moment they were locked in each other's embrace. Sir Sidney Smith hastened to the spot, and congratulated them. The father was promoted to be sailing master of one of the ships, and by the close of the war the father and both sons attained post rank and retired to the Orkneys. Notwithstanding the wealth and honor which the young men had acquired, they never forgave the press-gang that impressed them. All concerned in it they publicly kicked and horsewhipped. The bitterness of their feelings when dragged from home had never been forgotten.

CHAPTER XXXIX.
DISTINGUISHED MacLEANS.

Major-General Francis MacLean was the son of Captain William, who was the son of William, who was the grandson of Lachlan, the first of the family of Blaich, and second son of John Crubach, eighth MacLean of Ardgour. As soon as he was able to carry arms, Francis obtained a commission in the same regiment with his father. He was at the siege of Bergen op-Zoom in 1747, when the French, after a siege of two months, took the place by storm. "Lieutenants Francis and Allan MacLean (third son of Torloisk), of the Scotch brigade, were taken prisoners, and carried before general Löwendahl, who thus addressed them: 'Gentlemen, consider yourselves on parole. If all had conducted themselves as you and your brave corps have done, I should not now be master of Bergen-op-Zoom.'"* He was detained prisoner in France for some time; and on his release was promoted to a captaincy, and entered the Forty-second Royal Highlanders. At the capture of the island of Guadaloupe, Francis was severely wounded, but owing to his gallant conduct was promoted to the rank of major, and appointed governor of the island of Marie Galante. In the Canadian war, he commanded a body of troops under general Wolfe, and participated in the capture of Montreal. He returned to

---
* Keltie's *Highland Clans*, Vol. II., p. 452.

Great Britain, and embarked with the expedition for reducing the island of Belleisle, on the coast of France. Here he had his right arm shattered, and was taken prisoner. On being exchanged, his bravery was rewarded by promotion to a lieutenant-colonelcy. In 1762, he was sent to aid the Portuguese against the combined attack of France and Spain. He was made commander of Almeida, a fortified town on the Spanish frontier, which he held for several years; and on being promoted to the rank of major-general, was nominated to the government of Estremadura and the city of Lisbon. On leaving Portugal in 1778, the king presented him with a handsomely mounted sword, and the queen gave him a valuable diamond ring. On his return to England, he was immediately dispatched with a corps of the army for America, and appointed to the government of Halifax in Nova Scotia. During the month of June, 1779, with a part of his army, General MacLean repaired to the Penobscot, and proceeded to erect defenses. The patriot army under General Lovel, from Boston, appeared in the bay on July 28th, and began to erect batteries for a siege. On August 13th, commodore Sir George Collier entered the bay with a fleet and raised the siege. General MacLean returned to Halifax, where he died, in the year 1781, in the sixty-fourth year of his age, and unmarried.

General Allan MacLean was the third son of Donald, fifth MacLean of Torloisk. He obtained a lieutenant's commission, and, as already noticed, was at the siege of Bergen-op-Zoom. After leaving the Dutch service, he became, in 1757, a captain in Montgomery's Highlanders. In 1759, he raised the One Hundred and Fourteenth Highland Regiment. In that year he was with the expedition under General Wolfe for the conquest of Canada, and at the battle of Ticonderoga was severely wounded; and in the action immediately preceding the surrender of Niagara was dangerously wounded. On the conclusion of the war, he returned to England, and by the government was granted "letters of service" for embodying a battalion of six hundred men, with the privilege of nominating the officers. When the American War of Independence broke out, he was promoted to the rank of colonel, with command of the Highland Emigrant regiment. It was his unwearied zeal and ability that caused the defeat of the patriots at the storming of Quebec. By forced marches, Colonel MacLean entered Quebec on November 13, 1776. Arnold reduced the garrison to great straits. "He next turned the blockade into a siege, and having erected batteries, made several attempts to get possession of the lower town; but Colonel MacLean, to whom the defense of the place had been intrusted by General Guy Carlton, the commander-in-chief, defeated him at every point. After these failures, General Arnold raised the siege and evacuated Canada." * At the conclusion of the war, he retired from active military life, and returned home with the rank of brigadier-general. He married Janet, daughter of Donald MacLean of Brolass, and sister to General Sir Fitzroy Jeffreys Grafton MacLean. He died without issue, in London, in the month of March, 1797. He appears to have been comparatively poor, judging from the contents of many letters, directed to Lochbuie, and now preserved in the charter room of that family.

Lieutenant-General Sir Hector MacLean, K. C. B., was the third son of Hugh, thirteenth MacLean of Coll. In 1775, he was an ensign in the Fifth Native infantry, and was engaged in the expedition against the rajahs to the northward of Arcott. In 1778, he was at the siege of Pondicherry; and as a lieutenant, was in active service against Hyder Ali, and in the reduction of the Dutch fort of Policat. In 1786, was appointed a captain in the First European regiment, and to the command of Cuddalore and its defenses. In 1792, was present at the siege of Seringapatam. In 1795, he was major in the Eighth regiment of native infantry, and in 1798 became lieutenant-colonel and appointed to the command of a native corps at Ceylon. In 1803, he commanded a brigade, and distinguished himself at the capture of Asseer-Ghurr and Gowel-Ghurr, and at the battle of Argaum. After this, and until 1805, he commanded the forces in the vicinity of Hyderabad, having, in September, 1804, been promoted to the rank of colonel. In June, 1811, he was raised to the rank of major-general. In February, 1815, he was created a knight commander of the Order of the Bath; and on October 10, 1821, was promoted to the rank of lieutenant-general. On retiring from the army, he took up his residence in London, where he died in 1849, aged ninety-four.

Lieutenant-General Sir Joseph MacLean, K. C. H., was son of Allan, son of Donald, son of Allan, son of Lachlan Og, the seventh son of Allan, seventh MacLean of Ardgour. Joseph entered the military academy at Woolwich in 1779, and in 1781, was a lieutenant of artillery, and afterward assigned to the command of a detachment of artillery at Brighton. In 1794, he became captain, and in the expedition to the Helder served as aide-de-camp to the general commanding the artillery. In 1800, he was elected to the Irish parliament, and at the same time was a brigade major to the artillery in Ireland. In 1812, he became assistant adjutant-general, which he held until 1821, when he removed to Woolwich, having been appointed chief fire-

---

* Keltie's *Highland Clans*, Vol. II., p. 565.

master to the royal laboratory. In 1825, he was made major-general, and in 1832, appointed to the command of the artillery in Ireland, being next in command to the chief military officer. In May, 1834, he removed from Ireland on being appointed to the command of the royal artillery at the headquarters of the corps. On receiving the command of the artillery at Woolwich, the king conferred upon him the honor of knighthood, with the insignia of a knight commander of the royal Guelphic Order. Sir Joseph was in the active service of Britain for over fifty years. Was promoted lieutenant-general, June 28, 1838. Died at Woolwich, September 19, 1839. In January, 1797, he married Charlotte, daughter of General Sir William Congreve, and had issue, Allan, William Congrieve, Margaret, Julia, Anne, and Caroline.

Lieutenant-General Sir John MacLean, K. C. B., K. C., K. T. S., was the son of John, who was of the MacLeans of Dochgarroch. Sir John's military career commenced April 30, 1794, as ensign of the Royal Scots, and the following day became lieutenant in the Gordon Highlanders. In 1797, he arose to the rank of captain, and served in the whole of the campaign in Holland, and in the action near Alkman, October 2, 1799, received the first of his numerous wounds. He served in the whole of the Egyptian campaign, which ended in the expulsion of the French, with such honor that the sultan conferred on him the order of the Crescent. He next served in Ireland, and in 1808, was made lieutenant-colonel in the Twenty-seventh regiment, and from that time until the close of the war, in 1814, Sir John was a constant sharer in the achievements of Wellington against Napoleon. During the Peninsular war, he was four times severely wounded, and in two battles had his horse killed under him. In 1814, the king of Portugal conferred on him the order of the Tower and Sword, and in the same year, promoted to a colonelcy. In January, 1815, he was created knight of the Order of the Bath. He was made lieutenant-general in   , and died   . On January 26, 1819, he married Sarah, daughter of Benjamin Price, and had issue, a son, who died in infancy.

General Sir Archibald MacLean was the second son of Gillian of Scallasdale of the family of Lochbuie. Sir Archibald was born January 13, 1777, and commenced his career in what was then known as the Scotch brigade. He is best known for his gallant defense of Matagorda, near Cadiz, in 1810, when a captain in the Ninety-fourth. Matagorda was a post deemed of more than ordinary importance in the lines defending Cadiz. For this important post, General Graham selected Sir Archibald with his company of the Ninety-fourth, and a party of the Royal British artillery. For several weeks the post was nobly defended, during a part of the time withstanding the fire of twenty pieces of heavy artillery. Although the brave commander personally exposed himself by day and by night on the battery, he was fortunate enough to escape unharmed. Every man in the little fort aided in pouring incessant shot into the enemy. The band staid immovable, even when every spot was destroyed where they could find shelter; and when they were withdrawn by the British fleet, the spot where Matagorda stood was only a heap of ruins. For this heroic defense, he was promoted to the rank of major in the Eighty-seventh. Subsequently, he became lieutenant-colonel of the Seventh West India regiment, and then general. He received knighthood in the Order of the Bath. In 1823, he married Elizabeth Brydges. He died March 9, 1861.

Lieutenant-General Allan Thomas MacLean was the second son of Archibald, second MacLean of Pennycross. He entered the army as cornet in 1809, in the thirteenth dragoons, and was present in every action in which his corps took part in the Peninsular campaign. He was commended for his bravery at Ronces Valles, on July 25, 1813, and for his courage and military skill at the passage of the Gáve d'Oleron, in February, 1814. At the battle of Orthes, he was wounded and taken prisoner. Colonel MacLean commanded the Thirteenth at Waterloo, where he collected the troops before the battle, to do which he covered thirty miles of ground totally unknown to him, and during a very dark night. For this service he was selected by Wellington, and personally received his instructions. He spent thirty-two years in India without returning home. For his bravery he had the Waterloo medal, and those for the Peninsular war. He was appointed major-general in 1854, and lieutenant-general in 1861. He married, in 1843, Agnes Forlong, and left issue, Arthur Henry, died in 1847, Agnes, Alicia, and Margaret, who is the present Baroness de Pallandt.

Major-General John Hector Norman MacLean was the second son of Hugh, fifteenth MacLean of Coll. He was born January 17, 1829, and entered the army in 1846; obtained a lietenancy in 1849; promoted to a captaincy in 1859; a major in 1866; a lieutenant-colonel in 1872; a colonel, January 26, 1877, and a major-general in 1880. For some time he was commander of the First Madras cavalry, and served in the Nagpoor Province, where he helped intercept the natives under Tantia Topee, from November, 1858, to the following year. In 1859 he served with a column of observation on the banks of the Wurdah river for the suppression of disturbances in the Nizam's dominions, in conjunction with a column under Sir John Rose.

Retiring from the army, he took up his residence in St. Michael's Place, Brighton, where he died August 29, 1882. January 17, 1854, he married M. Roe, a daughter of Robert Roe, and had issue, Emily Agnes, born 1855; Florence Maude, 1856; Isabel Annie, 1862, and Norman, 1863, who died three days later.

Harry MacLean, commander-in-chief of the army of the Sultan of Morocco, is the eldest son of surgeon-general MacLean of Kew, who is the fifteenth offspring of Donald of the MacLeans of Drimnin. Harry enjoys the title of "Chief Kaid," and is well known for his knowledge of military science, as well as his fearlessness, which has been displayed on several occasions. Great honor has been bestowed upon him in Morocco. He has entirely reorganized the Moorish army.

The glory surrounding military renown too often places deeds of kindness and philanthropy in the background. The name of Lieutenant-Colonel Alexander MacLean deserves honorable mention, and his act of philanthropy is worthy of imitation. He was a descendant of Donald, who fought valiantly at Sheriffmuir, and a son of John Og of Dochgarroch. In 1857, Alexander executed his last will and testament, in which he set aside £20,000 to be administered by the magistrates and Kirk Session of Glasgow for the support and education of a certain number of boys of the name of MacLean.

Governor George MacLean was the son of Rev. James MacLean, a minister of Urquhart, and nephew of Major-General Sir John MacLean of the family of Dochgarroch. In the year 1829, was made President of the Council and Governor-in-chief of the British forts on the Gold Coast of Africa. The invaluable service he there rendered is best set forth by the inscription on a costly testimonial presented to him in 1836 by the merchants of London. Among other things, it states, "He found the country in a state of warfare and confusion, alike afflicting to humanity and destructive to trade; human victims were sacrificed almost in sight of the castle walls, where one of the most barbarous of the neighboring chiefs made the life and property of both Europeans and natives the sport of his ferocity and the prey of his cupidity. By bravery, zeal, and humanity, aided by ability, prudence, and firmness, during the seven years that he directed the affairs of these settlements, Mr. MacLean succeeded in restoring the blessings of peace, in promoting the prosperity of trade, in vindicating the rights of humanity, and in laying the foundations of future civilization. By these services Mr. MacLean earned the lasting esteem and gratitude of every friend of African improvement." On his return to England, he married, June 7, 1838, Letitia Elizabeth

Landon, who had gained for herself a reputation in the world of letters. With his wife he returned to the Gold Coast as Governor, where, on October 15, 1839, his wife died from an overdose of prussic acid. Of the subsequent history of Governor MacLean I know nothing, save that he died at Cape Coast Castle.

The history of man is better known by the wars engaged in than by the arts of peace. It is a pleasure to contemplate that all the achievements of the MacLeans have not been with the sword. In the time of the clan system we catch glimpses of nobler pursuits than that of war or of feuds. Unfortunately but little of their history has been preserved, for it was not of such a nature as to dazzle the mind. Many entered the clerical profession, and in their humble way did good service to the human race. The *Fasti Ecclesiæ Scoticanæ*, gives a list of thirty-seven MacLeans settled as clergymen, which by no means includes all. Among those living two are here appended.

Rev. Dr. John MacLean was born at Portsoy, Banffshire, in 1828; studied at the University of Aberdeen; became curate at London, Ontario, in 1853; archdeacon of Manitoba, and professor of divinity in St. John's College in 1866, and bishop of the new diocese of Saskatchewan in 1873. He died in 1886.

Rev. Dr. John MacLean, recently called (1889) to St. Columba's Church, Glasgow, was born on the island of Tiree; graduated at the University of Glasgow, where he carried off several of the prizes; one of the translators of the new edition of the Gaelic Bible, and a noted Hebrew scholar, as well as a man of profound learning.

Mention should be made of Hector MacLean, the greatest Keltic scholar of his name. On his father's side he is a descendant of the family of Shuna, a branch of the MacLeans of Ross, and from his mother he received the blood of the MacLeans of Kingerloch. Nearly all his life has been spent in school-teaching. In 1837, he attended the Normal school in Edinburgh; at the university he devoted much time to mathematics and philosophy; in 1840, entered the class in natural sciences; devoted several years to analyzing ores of lead, copper, and manganese, found in Islay; in 1846, became tutor of J. F. Campbell, the compiler of *West Highland Tales*, to which he made valuable additions; assisted in the compilation of the same author's *Gaelic Heroical Ballads*, published in 1872; in 1860, wrote the *London Times* editorial review—a leader of three columns—of *Dean of Lismore's Book;* contributed to the Anthropological Society of London, and the Anthropological Institute of Great Britain and Ireland; and for twenty-seven years corresponded with

Dr. John Beddoe, who, in his *Races of Britain*, refers to Hector MacLean's researches. Hector MacLean is nearly six feet in height, and carries with ease the weight of seventy-one summers. He lives at Ballygrant, Islay.

It is impossible to follow the descent in the female line. If such an attempt were made, all of Scotland would have been embraced. It may be said with truth, that every distinguished Scottish family, especially of Highland origin, has MacLean blood in its veins. This blood has also gone out into other nationalities. It should here be recorded that the mother of Adam Clarke, the distinguished biblical commentator, was a MacLean, and her great-grandfather was Sir Lachlan Mór MacLean. She had a brother, Rev. J. MacLean, who possessed incredible strength. "He could bend iron bars with a stroke of his arm; roll up large pewter dishes like a scroll with his fingers; and when traveling through Bovagh wood, a place through which his walks frequently lay, he has been known to pull down the top of an oak sapling, twist it into a withe by mere strength of his arms and fingers, and thus working it down in a spiral form to the earth, leave it with its root in the ground, for the astonishment of all that might pass by. One day, dining at an inn with two officers, who, perhaps, unluckily for themselves, wished to be witty at the parson's expense, he said something which had a tendency to lessen their self-confidence. One of them, considering his honor touched, said: 'Sir, were it not for your *cloth*, I would oblige you to eat the words you have spoken.' Mr. MacLean rose up in a moment, took off his coat, rolled it up in a bundle, and threw it under the table, with these fearful words: 'Divinity, lie

HECTOR MACLEAN.

thou there; and MacLean, do for thyself!' So saying, he seized the foremost of the heroes by the cuff of the neck and by the waistband of the breeches, and dashed him through the strong sash window of the apartment, a considerable way on the opposite pavement of the street. Such was the projectile violence, that the poor officer passed through the sash as if it had been a cobweb."* Adam Clarke's rugged mind and manhood unquestionably were largely inherited from his mother.

It is not the intent to speak of distinguished men whose mothers were MacLeans; but the rule will be broken in two more instances, and a short account is added of Colin A. MacVean and Alexander MacLean Sinclair, both of whom have taken a deep interest in this history, and every request made of them has been cheerfully and promptly complied with. Mr. MacVean furnished the sketches of Inch Kenneth, Sir Allan MacLean's tomb, the coat-of-arms on Duard Castle, and the MacLean Leug, illustrations of which have already been given. He is the son of Rev. Donald MacVean, by Susan, daughter of Dugald, son of Hector, son of John, son of Donald MacLean of Killean, of the family of Ross. On his father's side, he is a direct descendant of the chief of the Clan MacVean, or MacBean, which was a sept of the Clan Chattan. Mr. MacVean was born on Iona; educated at Edinburgh; served on the Admiralty Survey of the Hebrides; on the engineering staff of the Varna and Rustchuk railway; on the government railway surveys in Wallachia; in 1868, was one of the engineers for the erection of light-houses in Japan; in 1870, was surveyor-in-chief of Japan; is a F. R. G. S. and F. R. P. S. of Edinburgh, and a member of the N. H. S. of Glasgow. He has traveled extensively in the United States and Canada. At present, with his family, he resides at the southern foot of Ben More, in Mull.

Rev. A. MacLean Sinclair is a grandson of John MacLean, the Gaelic poet, by his daughter Christy, who was well versed in Scottish lore, and from memory could recite one hundred and nineteen poems. Mr. Sinclair has inherited much of his grandfather's poetic genius. He was born in Glenbard, Nova Scotia, March 1, 1840; was educated at Pictou and the college at Halifax; commenced to preach in 1866; in 1869, traveled through the British Isles; speaks, reads, and writes both English and Gaelic with equal facility; devotes much time to ethnology, comparative philology, and Keltic history, and is more intimately acquainted with Gaelic poetry than any other person. He resides at Belfast, Prince Edward's Island.

---

* Clarke's *Life of Adam Clarke*, Vol. I., p. 13.

CHAPTER XL.

MacLEAN POETS.

So far as my own knowledge extends, all MacLean poets, save one, wrote in Gaelic. This consequently not only narrowed their influence, but limited their reputation. For the list of them, I am almost wholly indebted to Rev. A. MacLean Sinclair's *Clarsach na Coille*.

Hector MacLean, commonly called Eachunn Bacach, or Hector the Cripple, was born about the beginning of the seventeenth century, and was poet to Sir Lachlan MacLean of Duard. It is said that he had eight brothers killed at the battle of Inverkeithing, where he was wounded, from the effects of which he was ever afterward lame. He was a poet of great ability. Four of his poems have been published, and eight preserved in manuscript. Two occur in *Beauties of Gaelic Poetry*, and one in *Clarsach na Coille*.

John MacLean, known as Iain MacAilein, or John son of Allan, was born in Mull, about the year 1670. He was highly esteemed and lived in comfortable circumstances, and obtained great celebrity as a bard, and is entitled to high rank as a poet. His elegy on Sir John MacLean is a poem of great beauty. His poems abound in lamentations over the downfall of the MacLeans; but there is no trace of imprecations against the Campbells. His residence was near Aros; and his poems, twenty-eight in number, were taken down by Dr. MacLean, and preserved in his manuscript. Twenty of these were published in 1888, in Rev. A. MacLean Sinclair's *Glenbard Collection*, and two in the *Beauties of Gaelic Poetry*. He belonged to the Ardgour family, and died about 1760.

Captain Andrew MacLean of Knock, eldest son of Bishop Hector MacLean, was known as Anndra Mac-an-Easbuig, or Andrew son of the Bishop. Five of his poems occur in *Clarsach na Coille*.

Rev. John MacLean, known as Iain MacGilleain, was the son of Ewen, ninth MacLean of Treshnish; was minister of Kilninian in Mull; and married Isabella, daughter of Charles MacLean in Tiree. Three of his poems are in Dr. MacLean's collection; one appears in Pattison's *Gaelic Bards*, and one in *Clarsach na Coille*.

Hector, fourth MacLean of Coll, has previously been mentioned as a highly accomplished scholar, a man of piety, and devoted to literature. He composed poems both in Latin and Gaelic. Two of the Gaelic poems appear in *Clarsach*, one of them being his "War Song of Ailein nan Sop."

Catherine MacLean, or Catriona nighean Eòbhain Mhic Lachainn, was born about the year 1650, on the island of Coll, where she spent her life. She was an excellent poetess, and her productions show much tenderness of feeling. She wrote quite a number of songs, two of which appear in *Clarsach*.

Margaret MacLean, or Margaret MacDonald, called Mairearad nighean Lachainn mhic Iain mhic Lachain, was a MacDonald, but her mother was a MacLean. She married and had a large family, all of whom died before herself. She lived to an extreme old age, and nursed many of the MacLeans of Duard. She composed not less than twenty-five poems, one of which is in *Beauties of Gaelic Poetry*, one in *Clarsach*, and several in Turner's collection.

Alexander MacLean, known as Am Cùbair Colach, or the Cooper of Coll, was an expert seaman, a cheerful companion, and well respected. About fifty years ago, he emigrated with his family from Coll to Australia. His poem on his "Journey to America" appears in *Clarsach*.

Archibald MacLean, known as Gilleaspuig Làidir, or Archibald the Strong, was a native of Tiree. He was a high spirited and passionate man, which frequently embroiled him with others. However, his influential friends always came to his rescue. Notwithstanding his rashness, he was greatly respected. He died about the year 1830. Three of his poems are in John MacLean's manuscript, and one published in *Clarsach*.

John MacLean, known in Scotland as Bàrd Thighearna Chola, and in America as Am Bàrd Mac-Gilleain, belonged to the Treshnish branch of the Ardgour family, was born on the island of Tiree, January 8, 1787, and the last bard to the laird of Coll; married Isabel Black in 1808; published a volume of poems in 1818; emigrated to Nova Scotia in 1819; and died January 26, 1848. In his songs he sang the praises of the Laird of Coll, and the glories of Scotland; and in his hymns the praises of the Savior and the blessedness of the promised land. His secular poems, forty-four in number, were published in 1881 by his grandson, Rev. A. MacLean Sinclair, in *Clarsach na Coille*, and his hymns, forty-seven in number, in 1880, under the title "Dain Spirodail."

Donald MacLean, a brother of the above John, was commonly called Dòmhnull Cùbair, or Donald the Cooper, was by trade a cooper. He died in Tiree, in 1868, in the ninety-eighth year of his age. He composed several songs, one of which appears in *Clarsach*.

Charles MacLean, known as Tearlach MacGilleain, son of the above John MacLean, was born in Tiree, July 24, 1813, and died June 27, 1880. He inherited his father's sound principles, and some of his poetic talent. Two of his poems appear in *Clarsach*.

The late Rev. Duncan MacLean of Glenorchy was the last of the great religious bards of the Highlands. All of his productions are pervaded by a keenly æsthetic spirit. He is exceedingly rich in poetic illustration, and very profound in his lines of thought, but entirely too analytical for the popular taste. He was a man of wide general culture; and the fruits of it he brought into the sphere of Gaelic poetry. In 1868, a small volume of his poems was published in Glasgow, entitled *Laoidhean agus Dain*. It contains seventy-nine poems, all of a religious nature, besides fourteen translations and six elegies.

Miss Mary MacLean of Franklin, Massachusetts, is an illustration of inherited genius. She is a granddaughter of Am Bàrd MacGilleain, and daughter of Archibald MacLean. She has written many short poems which have been commended by competent judges. She was born March 28, 1856, in Marshy Hope, Nova Scotia, and in 1881, removed to her present home.

Malcolm MacLean, who died about the year 1764, was a native of Kinlochewe, in Ross-shire. When a young man, he enlisted in the army, and there formed that habit which made him a bacchanalian of the first magnitude. On returning home, he was granted a small pension, and occupied a small piece of ground at the foot of Ben Fuathais. His wife was remarkable for her patience and resignation, and was well worthy being styled the sister of Job. He was the author of one of the most popular songs of Scotland, entitled " Calum a Ghlinne;" or, Malcolm o' the Glen.* The occasion of the song was as follows: MacLean had an only child, a daughter of uncommon beauty and loveliness; but owing to her father's drinking habits, she was unwooed, unsought, and, for a long time, unmarried. The father, in his exordium, portrays the charms and excellent qualities of his daughter, dealing some excellent side-blows at fortune-hunters, but taking a reasonable share of blame to himself for depriving her of the bait necessary to secure a good attendance of wooers. The song has many excellent qualities, and its terseness

---

* See Appendix, Note C., No. 8.

and comprehensiveness are such that two standing proverbs have been deducted from it. It occurs in *Beauties of Gaelic Poetry*.

CHAPTER XLI.

MacLEAN AUTHORS.

It is possible that all the MacLean authors are not given in this list. I have endeavored to search all out, and preserve their names in this chapter. I have taken a wider range than that adopted in other chapters, and have included those of America. Pamphlets and magazine articles are not here given. To enter into that line would require entirely too much labor, which would result in but little profit. A short review of each book I have in my library is given, and a sketch of the author when I have been able to give it.

Lachlan MacLean, who was a merchant in Glasgow, about 1840, gained quite a reputation as an author, and a writer to the *Gaelic Messenger*—An Teachdaire Gaidhealach. All of his works are now difficult to obtain, and one of them at least is a literary curiosity—*Adhamh agus Eubh*. This work, of 107 pages, was published in Edinburgh in 1837. He attempts to prove that Adam and Eve spoke the Gaelic, or, in other words, the Gaelic was the language of Eden. While the body of the book is in Gaelic, the notes are mostly in English. In 1840, he enlarged the work, and printed it in the English tongue, under the title of *The History of the Celtic Language*, in which he claimed that the language was based upon natural principle, and cotemporary with the infancy of the race. The book is a mass of facts showing great research, but not always leading to his conclusions. The book contains 288 pages, and was published in London. In 1841, he published, in Oban, his *Historical Account of Iona*, a really valuable work of 135 pages. Whoever is interested in the history of Iona, or of the MacLeans, can not afford to be without it. His *Sketches of St. Kilda*, and the work on *Etiquette*, I have never seen, having been unable to procure copies. Lachlan MacLean was born on Coll, but I have been unable to learn his history.

John MacLean, known as the Inverness Centenarian, lived to the great age of one hundred and six years, and died in the year 1852. He was of the Dochgarroch family. From his infancy he gave a greedy ear to the recital of old stories. He was gifted with health and a remarkable memory, and by means of the latter many historic incidents of the country have been preserved from oblivion. The stories he recited were published in a local paper in 1842, and then gathered into book-form, under the title *Reminiscences of a Clachnacuddin Nonogenarian*. This was republished in Inverness in 1886. The work contains 110 pages, consisting of tales concerning Inverness and the immediately surrounding country. In 1848, was published at Dingwall another work, entitled, *Historical and Traditional Sketches of Highland Families and of the Highlands*, containing 128 pages. Both works are of great local value, and of interest to the general reader.

Finley, son of John MacLean, the Inverness Centenarian, was a large, stout man, while his father was tall and thin. For many years he was foreman in the *Herald* (Inverness) office. He had a ready pen, and was a man of ability. It was considered that he was the author of his father's *Reminiscences*. He wrote a history of Inverness. He was married, left a family, and died about 1857, aged fifty.

Evils of Quarantine Laws, by C. MacLean. No farther information.

A novel was written by Neil MacLean. No farther information.

John MacLean was born at Kilmarnock, Scotland, October 30, 1851; learned the trade of bootcloser, and at the same time studied Greek and Latin; removed to Rodney, Ontario, in 1873, and the following year entered the ministry of the Wesleyan Methodist Church; in 1877, matriculated at Victoria college; in 1880, married Sarah A. Barker, and the same year commenced to labor as a missionary among the Blackfoot Indians; received degree of A. M. in 1887, and Ph.D. in 1888; became correspondent for British Association in 1884; in 1882 published *Lone Land Lights;* edited the *Methodist Annual* in 1885; in 1889, published *The Indians: Their Manners and Customs*, containing eighteen illustrations; has in MSS, *A Grammar of the Blackfoot Language; A Dictionary of the Blackfoot Language*, and *A History of the Blackfoot Confederacy*, besides being engaged in many other enterprises. He lives at MacLeod, Alberta, Canada.

Illustrations of Teething, by R. MacLean. No farther information.

The Coming of the Princess, by Kate S. MacLean. No farther information.

Donald MacLean, M.D., of Ardchattan, published a work on the diseases of the nerves. No further information.

Sermons on the Christian Life, preached at St. Margaret's Chapel, Bath, by Rev. Arthur J. MacLean. Published in 1855. No farther information.

The More Priests, the More Crime, by Rev. Alexander MacLean. Published in Toronto, 1854. The writer was born in North Uist, in 1827, and died at Morriston, Ontario, in 1864.

Sir John MacLean was born in 1811, and entered the ordnance department in 1837, and deputy auditor at the war office in 1865; resigned on a pension, and was knighted in 1871. He is the author of *Life and Times of Sir Peter Carew* and *Letters of Sir Robert Cecil to Sir George Carew*. Residence, Hammersmith, Middlesex, Eng.

Rev. Archibald MacLean was born May 1, 1733, at East Kilbride. He was the fourth in descent from Brolass, son of MacLean of Duard. He learned to speak Gaelic in Mull, where he was sent at the age of eight, and afterward studied Latin, Greek, and Hebrew. In 1746, he engaged as a printer in Glasgow; in 1767, went to London, and continued in the printing business; in June, 1768, became pastor of the Baptist church, in Edinburgh, and so continued until his death, on December 21, 1812. His literary remains consist of six volumes. Vol. I. of his miscellaneous works—tenth edition, published in Elgin, in 1847—contains his biography. The works consist of sermons and essays, save two, which are devoted to a commentary on Hebrews. The volumes are uniform, and all told contain 2,111 pages. The sermons are of a doctrinal cast, exhibiting the tenets of his church.

Rev. Dr. Archibald MacLean resided at The Hague. In 1764, he published his translation of Mosheim's *Ecclesiastical History*, which has been reprinted in America in two volumes.

John MacLean, in 1849, published, in London, in two volumes, a work entitled *Notes of a Twenty-five Years' Service in the Hudson's Bay Territory*. No further information.

John MacLean, LL.D., was born in Morris County, New Jersey, March 11, 1785; moved in early childhood to Warren County, Ohio; worked on a farm until sixteen; commenced the study of law in 1803, and admitted to the bar in 1807; served in Congress from 1813 to 1816, when he became one of the supreme judges of Ohio; postmaster-general of the United States in 1823; and in 1829, was elevated to the Supreme Court of the United States; and there continued until his death, April 4, 1861. In the famous "Dred Scott" case, he dissented from the opinion of the court, and rendered a minority decision, in which he held that slavery had its origin in force and not in right. He was remarkable for his ability, possessing a clear and comprehensive mind, and noted for his eloquence. In 1856, he was the principal competitor against General Fremont in the Republican convention that nominated the latter for president. He also received votes in the convention of 1860, that nominated Abraham Lincoln. He is the author of two volumes of *Reports of the United States Circuit Court*, published in 1829–42.

Rev. John MacLean, D.D., LL.D., was born in Princeton, New Jersey, March 3, 1800; graduated at the College of New Jersey in 1816; also at Princeton Theological Seminary in 1821; professor of mathematics in the College of New Jersey in 1823; professor of ancient languages and vice-president in 1829; president in 1853, from which he retired in 1868. After his retirement, he wrote his *History of the College of New Jersey, from its Origin, in* 1746, *to the Commencement of* 1854, which was published in two volumes in Philadelphia, in 1877. In 1868, he was appointed one of the regents of the Smithsonian Institution, and so continued until his death, which occurred August 10, 1886.

W. W. MacLean, D.D., published in Philadelphia, in 1883, a work entitled, *The Cross in the Light of To-day*. No further information.

Sallie Pratt MacLean was born in Simsbury, Connecticut, July 3, 1855. She is a daughter of Dudley B. MacLean, and a granddaughter of Rev. Allan MacLean, who for over fifty years was pastor of the Congregational church in her native town. She is a direct descendant of Lachlan, sixth MacLean of Coll. In 1887, she was married to F. L. Greene. As a novelist, she has been remarkably successful, but in no way appears to be elated over it. The most popular of her productions is *Cape Cod Folks*, which has reached its twenty-third edition. It was first published in 1881, in Boston, and contains 327 pages. *Towhead; The Story of a Girl*, appeared in 1882, in Boston. It contains 303 pages. It has reached its fifth thousand. *Some Other Folks* was published in 1884. It contains 287 pages. At this writing she has another work in the press entitled *Lastchance Junction*.

Mary Webster MacLean, daughter of Rev. William MacLean, son of Joseph, son of John, was born in 1842. She early showed a disposition to engage in literary work. Her novels were not written for publication, but for her own amusement. When her father read them, he at once saw their merit, and had them published. Although I tried diligently to procure a a copy of each, I have failed in all save *The Italian Girl*, published in 1869, in Philadelphia. The story is laid in Washington and founded on fact, as I understand; so are all the rest. The work contains 180 pages. The other works are *Bearing Our Burdens*, Boston; *Broken Idols*, same; *Daisy Ward's Work*, same; *Jeanie Darley*, same, *Keeping Open House*, same; *Lifting the Veil*, New York; *Wedding Garments*, same. She has removed from Washington to New York City, where she has made quite a reputation as a portrait painter.

Pennel; or, Face to Face with God, by Alexander MacLean. No further information.

George N. MacLean is the author of *The Curtain Lifted* and the *Rise and Fall of Anarchy*.

John J. MacLean was born in Kirkham, Lancashire, England, May 18, 1848. His father, born in the north of Ireland, died when John was ten years of age. At the age of seventeen, emigrated to America; studied the classics at St. John's College, Annapolis, Maryland; graduated in law in same city; practiced in Washington for two years; in a bank one year, and then entered the signal service, and volunteered to the station at Sitka, Alaska; devoted leisure moments to the collection of ethnological specimens; spent two years in compiling a *Klingit Chinook and English Vocabulary*, consisting of fifteen hundred words. This is to be published by the Smithsonian Institution.

J. P. MacLean.

John Patterson MacLean, son of James, son of William, son of John, was born in Franklin, Warren county, Ohio, March 12, 1848; removed with his parents to a farm, three miles distant, in 1852; attended country school until sixteen years of age, when he entered the National Normal University, at Lebanon, Ohio, where he graduated in the classics and sciences in 1867; two months later, entered the divinity department of St. Lawrence University, Canton, New York, and graduated in 1869; in 1873 entered the Eclectic Medical Institute of Cincinnati, Ohio, where he took a course in medicine and surgery; after leaving college, devoted some time to comparative anatomy and geology; then entered upon an investigation of anthropology, spending some time in the languages, as well as in the study of physical man; in 1875, published *A Manual of the Antiquity of Man*, which has gone through nine editions, a book of 153 pages; in 1878, the *Mastodon, Mammoth, and Man*, a work of 84 pages, appeared, three editions of which have been published. This work, besides summing up all the facts concerning the two great proboscidians, shows that man has been their cotemporary from the earliest times; in 1879, appeared *The Mound Builders*, a work of 233 pages, which treats of the ancient monuments of the Ohio and Mississippi Valleys, and the people who erected them—five editions published. All these works are electrotyped and illustrated, and published by Robert Clarke & Co., Cincinnati, Ohio.

In 1838 appeared the first published history of the Clan MacLean, a work of 358 pages, to which is added a list of one hundred and forty-one subscribers, taking in all two hundred and thirty-three copies—the chief of the clan, with commendable zeal, subscribing for forty copies. The name of the author is concealed under the title of Seneachie, but published at the expense of Charles Hope MacLean of Ardgour. The work has been severely criticised. *The Monthly Review* for April, 1838, contains a lengthy, but bitter notice of it. MacAulay * animadverts on the severity of the language employed in the history. With all its faults, its bigotry, its narrowness, and its fulsome flattery, there is much in it that is commendable. With the resources at his command, and the opportunities then offered, it is to be deplored that a more complete history was not published. Charles Hope MacLean was persuaded into its publication by the author and against the will of his father. The name of the author has long been kept a secret by the Ardgour family, but in 1879 was revealed by the publication, at Columbus, Ohio,† of a short account of the life of the author. It would also appear that the "Duart MS" alluded to in the work was none other than the Ardgour MS. The author was related to the Clan MacLean through his wife, who was of both the Brolass and Kingerloch families. Rev. John Campbell Sinclair, the author, was born in Tiree in the year 1800; in 1822, married Mary Julia MacLean; emigrated to Nova Scotia in 1838; to the United States in 1852, and in 1878 died at Wheeling, West

---

* *History of England*, Vol III., p. 291. † This pamphlet fell into my hands after this work was in the hands of the printer and much of it published.

Virginia. The book belonged to a new era in Scottish history, and was a pioneer in setting forth the operations of the clans. The work was certainly deserving of more credit than it has received.

In 1865, appeared the *History of Clan Tarlach O'Buie*, by Lieutenant-Colonel Charles Maxwell MacLean, second son of William MacLean of Dochgarroch, who served forty-seven years in the Seventy-second Highlanders, and retired from the service in 1852. For this long service, all he had to show for his monarch's appreciation was a war medal and the rank of lieutenant-colonel. He died December, 1864, in the 73d year of his age, and before his book had passed through the press. Only a very small edition was published, intended wholly for private circulation. It contains 190 pages, and relates almost wholly to the MacLeans of Dochgarroch. Many of his conclusions, in regard to the early history of the clan, will not bear critical analysis.

In 1872, *A Brief Genealogical Account of the Ffamily of MacLean* was published at the expense of Alexander, fourteenth MacLean of Ardgour. He died while the work was passing through the press. Only twenty-five copies were struck off, and these were intended solely for private circulation. The manuscript from which it was taken is in the handwriting of Alexander, thirteenth MacLean of Ardgour. The MS is preserved at Ardgour House, and exhibits great age. It was compiled while Sir Allan MacLean was still chief of the clan. Only the family of Duard and its various branches are given. No mention, only incidentally and where necessary, is made of the Lochbuie family and its cadets. The work contains 108 pages.

The Pennycross MS and the Ardgour MS are derived from the same source. I do not think one is a copy of the other, but both compiled from an older MS. The genealogical account is the same, but the Pennycross MS is much fuller in several essential particulars. Greater care has been bestowed upon it. It is in the handwriting of Archibald, second MacLean of Pennycross.

There is a short MS history of the MacLeans in the Advocate's Library, Edinburgh, attached to the MacFarlane MS.

It is said there is a MS history, also, in the Vatican, at Rome.

In the April number of the *Celtic Magazine*, 1888, Rev. A. MacLean Sinclair commenced a series of historical sketches of the clan MacLean. The series was concluded in the *Scottish Highlander* for January 10, 1889, the *Celtic Magazine* having in the meantime been merged into the other periodical.

It is probable there are other MSS. In the account given by "Seneachie," in 1838, reference is made to the "Duard" and the "Coll" MSS; but, after diligent inquiry, I have failed to obtain a trace of them. It is also affirmed that Lieutenant-Colonel Murdoch Hector MacLean, of the Seventy-seventh regiment, wrote a history of the MacLeans of Lochbuie, and that the MS was in the charter room of that family in 1839. It was not there in 1887, and I failed to obtain any trace of it.

It will be noticed that a strange fatality appears to follow those engaged in publishing the history of the MacLeans. Charles Hope MacLean died within a year after the publication of his *Account of the Clan MacLean;* Charles Maxwell MacLean died while his *Clan Tarlach O' Buie* was in the printer's hands, as likewise did Alexander MacLean, with his *Ffamily of McLean.*

CHAPTER XLII.

THE FAMILY OF JOHN MacLEAN.

Sixteen thousand MacLeans still live in Scotland, but very few on the ancestral estates; although they are to be found in Ireland, England, India, the Gold Coast of Africa, the West Indies, Canada, and the United States. Canada and the United States contain not far from twenty thousand of the name. In the directory of the city of Philadelphia are recorded the names of two hundred, probably representing not less than five hundred. New York adds one hundred and thirty, representing about four hundred. To give an account of the MacLeans of America would require a volume nearly as large as the present one. They have flourished in the arts, sciences, and the elements of civilization in this country, surpassing those left on the native soil. All of the various walks of life have been adorned by those of the name. They have attained eminence in statesmanship, diplomacy, civil law, divinity, medicine, invention, literature, and the fine arts. When MacLeans were assisting George III. in his oppression of the American Colonies, we find other MacLeans battling for freedom, and winning renown not only for daring, but for a patriotism born inherent in human rights. To speak of those whose voices have been heard in the halls of Congress, or the acts of those who have held cabinet positions, or sat in governors' chairs, or rendered decisions from the Supreme Court, or engaged in the diplomatic service, or arousing and instructing the people from the editor's chair, or spoken words of wisdom and consolation from the pulpit, or gave sound medical advice, would be great pleasure, but would require a large volume. The name has been fully identified in the geography of the United States. Illinois has a McLean county, containing 1,155 square miles, with a population of 75,000. In that county is a post village of the same name. McLeansborough is the county seat of Hamilton county, same state. One of the counties of Western Kentucky is named McLean. It contains 325 square miles, and a population of 7,500. There is a McLean county in Dakotah. Minnesota has a McLean township in Ramsey county. Ohio has a McLean post-office in Fayette county, and a McLean township in Shelby county. Tompkins county, New York, has a McLean post-village. McLain is the name of a post-office in Harvey county, Kansas. McLane is a post-office in Erie county, Pennsylvania; and in Crawford county, same state, is McLean's Corners. McLeansville, a post-office in Guilford county, North Carolina. McLeansville, a village in Jackson county, Tennessee. McClains, a post-office in Wirt county, West Virginia.

Space is herewith given to record the genealogy of one American family—that of John MacLean. The evidence points that he belonged to the MacLeans of Killran, in Argyleshire, a cadet of the family of Lochbuie, and probably of the Kingerloch branch or sept. John was born about the year 1738, and about 1760 left his native country for the north of Ireland. Here he became acquainted with and married Margaret Lynn. The name is an Irish one, and is the same as Flynn, or O'Flynn. In 1765, he emigrated to America, and settled on a farm on Goose Creek, in Loudon county, Virginia. Here he lived until all his children were born and grown to the years of maturity; then removed to the vicinity of Uniontown, Pennsylvania; and in 1807, to Monroe, in Butler county, Ohio. In August, 1813,* he purchased 120 acres of land, situated in the south-west corner of section 12, Lemon township, on which he then lived, for $900. In April, 1814, he added 18 acres of contiguous land for $135.† In October, 1817, in ascending the stairway of his house, he slipped and fell to the bottom, from the effects of which he died, January 4, 1818, and is buried in the graveyard near Monroe. His last will and testament is dated October 8, 1817, and probated February 11, 1818. In this will, he properly remembers all his offspring, and makes them equal heirs. He remembers an old faithful servant in the family, and his brother James. The estate was appraised at $3,486.56. His name is attached to the will in two places, and is spelled "John Mclean." He was known as a man of kindness of heart and generous impulses, and swayed by the principle of

---

* Book D., p. 23, of Records of Butler Co., O.   † *Ibid.*, p. 253.

justice. He was a member of the Old School Presbyterian Church, called Dick's Creek, now extinct. Tradition says he had another brother besides James, who emigrated with him, named Robert, who left John in Virginia and went to South Carolina. I have been unable to find any trace of him. The changing of residence to Uniontown, Pa., was probably governed by the removal of his son John there; and also being the residence of another John MacLean, who left Killran in 1775, and had settled there about 1778. The relationship of the families was kept up after they removed to Ohio, one branch going to Ross county, and a branch of the other family to Ripley, Brown county. The evidence also shows that John's brother James was a constant companion of his removals. John had issue, and enumerated in his will in the following order: Sarah, John, Margaret, Stephen, Elizabeth, William, Joseph, Mary, and James.

I. Sarah was married to a man by the name of Moore, and was left a widow, with a daughter, Margaret. She was her father's housekeeper in his latter years, her mother having died soon after reaching Ohio. After her father's death, she moved on her brother Joseph's farm. She died at Addison. Margaret married Abraham Baker.

II. John was born November 13, 1777; early learned the millwright's trade; moved to Uniontown, Pa., and from there to Ripley, O.; was the inventor of cup-elevators used in mills; was a successful business man; married Rachel Robinson, and had issue: James Robinson, Narcissa Lynn, Amanda, Mary, William Wylie, Rachael Marquis, Harriet Newell, Joshua Milton, and John Scott. John died at Ripley, Ohio, June 11, 1833, aged 56.

James Robinson MacLean was born March 13, 1807, near Brownsville, Pa., and was first married, December 10, 1829, to Hannah, daughter of Rev. James Gilliland, and had issue: Jane Gilliland, born 1830; and Cary, born 1832. He was a second time married to Nancy, daughter of Robert Anderson, June 15, 1843, and has issue: Nelson Wylie, born 1844; Henry Zwingli, born 1846, now professor of Greek in Wabash College, Crawfordsville, Ind.; Mary Tenny, born 1849, died March 25, 1852; John Scudder, born 1853; twins, born 1856, died September, 1856; William White, born 1858, died (from accident) October 2, 1874. James Robinson MacLean lives at Kendall, Illinois. By strict industry and economy, he amassed considerable wealth, which he has divided among his children. He has grandchildren, but I have no account of them.

Narcissa Lynn was born December 16, 1808; married James Gilliland, of Ripley, Ohio, and had issue. She died July 10, 1881.

Amanda, born March 6, 1811; married ——, 1834; and died in 1837.

Mary, born January 13th, died August 24, 1814.

William Wylie, born September 15, 1815; graduated at Hanover College, Ind., 1836; Western Theological Seminary, Alleghany, Pa., 1839; ordained to the Presbyterian ministry, 1840; died at Mt. Pleasant, Pa., November 10, 1855, aged 40.

Rachel Marquis, born July 14, 1817; married Archibald Hopkins; died at Kendall, Ills., October 1, 1887.

Harriet Newell, born February 27, 1820; married Jackson Stivers; died at Ripley, Ohio, in 1851.

Joshua Milton, born April 14, 1824; graduated at both Marietta College and Oberlin Theological Seminary, Ohio; and died at Placerville, California, 1873.

John Scott, born May 25, 1827; died May 20, 1847.

III. Margaret, daughter of John, married James Karr, and left issue. She died the same day her father died, viz., January 4, 1818.

IV. Stephen was probably one of the youngest. He never married. After the death of his father, in 1818, he was unlike himself. He soon after lost most of his property, and then dealt in horses. He died in Urbana, Ohio, about 1840.

V. Elizabeth was married twice: first to —— Rogers, and had issue, James and Benjamin; second time to —— Hanna, and had issue, Emas and Harriet Newel. She died prior to her father.

VI. William was born about the year 1772; removed with his father to Uniontown, and from there, in 1807, to Butler County, Ohio. He was a millwright by trade, and afterward engaged in mercantile pursuits. He succeeded in amassing a small fortune; but believing that all men were honest, he lost all, a greater part by a brother-in-law. He was a little above medium height, clear grey eyes, and a good conversationalist. Before leaving Uniontown, he courted Margaret Clarke, who died September 25, 1835; but she married a man by the name of Currie, who was killed by his horse, while hunting, running at full speed against a tree. With one son, she removed to Rising Sun, Indiana. William, now forty years old, sought her out and married her, about 1812, and had issue, Narcissa, James, William, Margaret, and Alpheus. William died at the residence of his son James, April 25, 1855, and is buried in Franklin, Ohio.

Narcissa was born about the year 1813, and was twice married; first, to Decatur Housel, and had issue, Margaret Olive; second, to Jacob Whallon, and had issue, Alice, John, and Frances. She died in 1873, and is buried at Sharonville, Ohio.

James was born October 13, 1815, in Middletown, Ohio; saw the first shovel of dirt thrown out of the Miami and Erie canal; the first to swim it (in winter time); drove the first boat, the Lady Jackson, and the first to drive the Oliver from Middletown to Cincinnati; learned the saddler's trade; commenced married life on nothing; worked very hard; twice broken up by placing too much confidence in pious scoundrels; in 1852, purchased a farm near Franklin, Ohio; and afterward added an adjoining farm; gave all his children a good start in life, either in goods or education; January 20, 1836, married Rachael, daughter of Rev. Isaac Dearth, and has issue, Isaac Parry, William Currie, George Washington, Mary Elizabeth, Henry Clay, Harriet Jane, John Patterson, and Anna Eliza. James MacLean still lives on the farm purchased in 1852. The sons were all brought up on the farm and learned the trade of broom making. All were born in the village of Franklin, Ohio.

JAMES MACLEAN.

Isaac Parry, born May 8, 1837, bred to farming and broom making, has continued in those occupations; married first in 1859, and has issue, Clarence Wilbur, 1860, died from burns accidentally received about a year later; James Scott, born 1863, married Sallie E. Johnson, 1884, and has issue, Bessie Anneke, born 1885; and Eva, born 1886. Isaac was again married to Emma Craig, 1885, and has issue, Rachael Edna, born 1886.

William Currie, born October 25, 1838, follows farming and broom making; married Rachael Caldwell, September 9, 1874, and has issue, Thaddeus, born 1876; Hubert, born 1879; and Oakley, born 1883.

George Washington, born January 18, 1840; engaged in livery business; accumulated three farms and other property, and retired about 1878; married Emily, daughter of Joseph Winters, January 1, 1862, and has issue, Joseph Winters, born 1863, died 1864; Wilbur Roy, born 1864; married Josephine Corwin, September 14, 1885; issue, Emily Louise, born 1887; killed by the cars, June 14, 1888, aged 24; Schuyler, born 1867, died 1868; Carrie E., born 1872; and Edward, born 1877.

Mary Elizabeth, born September 30, 1841; married Robert S. Robinson, October 21, 1863; and has issue, Howard, born 1864; Tirza, born 1866; Daisy, born 1871; Emma, born 1874; and John, born 1877.

Henry Clay, born August 26, 1843; died January 2, 1845.

Harriet Jane, born December 15, 1845; married Miley W. Ammons, April 4, 1876. No issue.

John Patterson, born March 12, 1848; married Helen, daughter of Rev. J. H. Cleveland, September 12, 1872, and has issue, Helen, born 1873, died August 10, 1874; Lyell Parker, born 1875; and Eugene Herbert, born 1882.

Anna Eliza was born February 2, 1850; married Blake Wales Barrows, April 15, 1873, and has issue, Louise, Stanley, and Ernest.

William was born in the year 1823; a broom-maker by trade; August 31, 1861, enlisted in Company B., Second Regiment Ohio Volunteer Infantry, for three years, or during the civil war; discharged September 22, 1862, on surgeon's certificate of disability; came home and died November 15, 1862, of disease contracted in the army. Never married.

Margaret was born in the year 1819; married to Daniel H. Clutch; no issue; died March 16, 1849.

Alpheus was born about the year 1826; followed the trade of broom-making; first married in 1846 to Margaret Brown; again married to Elizabeth Zimmermann in 1849, and has issue, John Zimmermann; James, born March 31, 1853, drowned in the Miami canal, December, 1855; and Ella, born April, 1856.

John Zimmermann was born March 16, 1850; broom-maker, carpenter, and engineer; married Emma R. Shuder, January 19, 1873, and has issue, Bertha C., born 1873; Mabel S., born 1877; Ina P., born 1879; Carl D., born 1882; a baby born 1885, died July 13, 1885; and Alpheus, born 1886.

VII. Joseph was born September 21, 1775; removed with his father to Pennsylvania; from there to Monroe, Ohio, and finally settled on a farm near

Urbana, Ohio; May 10, 1799, married Elizabeth Runyan; died on his farm April 30, 1834, leaving issue, John, Stephen, James, William, Sarah, Richard, and Jane.

John was born in 1800, married Rebecca Dowing in 1831, and died in 1836, leaving issue, Emily, who married Niles Wilson, and Jane.

Stephen, born June 16, 1801; married Nancy Dunlap, Janary 8, 1824, and died at Jacksonville, Ill., September 12, 1844, leaving issue, Calvin Washington, Minerva Jane, Joseph, born February 14, 1830, died May 12, 1835, Sarah Elizabeth, born June 28, 1832, died September 14, 1843, and Amelia Dunlap.

Calvin Washington was born December 12, 1825; July, 1861, was lieutenant in Merrill's Horse; captain October, 1862, and afterward major and acting colonel of the regiment; fought at the battle of Springfield, Mo.; engaged in subduing predatory bands; present at the capture of Little Rock, Ark.; in 1864 co-operated with General Banks in the Red River expedition; helped drive General Price out of Missouri, capturing large numbers of prisoners, artillery, and supplies, and one day marching seventy miles; February, 1865, reported to General Thomas at Nashville, Tenn., and soon after stationed at Chattanooga; has been twice married, first to Maria Isabella Hall, September 16, 1852, and again to Ada Eva Clarke, October 23, 1865, and has issue, Harry Allen, born 1871.

Minerva Jane was born March 5, 1828; married Alfred Brown, August 2, 1854, and has issue, Anson, Minnie, Alfred, and Charles.

Amelia Dunlap was born November 20, 1834; married Dr. E. Dayton, October 18, 1866, and has issue, Freddie and Clifford.

James was born in 1804; married Jane Wilson in 1836; accumulated six hundred acres of land near Urbana, Ohio; retired from farming and removed into Urbana in 1880; known as an active, industrious, and honorable man. He has eleven children. Although I have called on him at his residence, obtained nearly all the information I possess concerning the history of his grandfather, and have written him several times, yet have failed to receive even the names of his children. He has added a middle letter (A) to his name, on account of his mail being in former years mixed with that of his Uncle James.

William was born 1806; married Louisa Mosby in 1837, and died in 1837. He was a clergyman of the Presbyterian church. I visited one of the daughters, Mary, and have written several times to the other, Lizzie, but failed utterly to obtain any information whatever. I gained some information from the aunt, Sarah Gill. William left issue, William Mosby, born 1838, died 1874; Lizzie, born 1840; Mary Webster, born 1842; Louis Randolph, born 1846, and John Speed, born 1848. John Speed is a successful physician living in Washington City; and Louis is a consulting engineer and contractor at Ozark, Alabama. None ever married.

Sarah was born April 26, 1809; married Rev. J. H. Gill, April 20, 1840, and had issue, Heber.

Richard, born 1803, died 1833.

Jane, born 1816; married —— Hamilton in 1835; died in 1840, leaving one daughter.

VIII. Mary was married to —— Robinson, near Uniontown, Pa. She was living in 1817, and had two sons. No farther information concerning her.

IX. The remaining son, James, I judge was born about 1770; married Deborah, sister of Elizabeth, and daughter of John Runyon; owned land near Urbana, Ohio, where he died, leaving issue, five daughters: Mary, born about 1808, married to Zebulon Cantwell, settled in Illinois where both died; Margaret, born about 1810, married Smith Minturn, moved to Illinois; Sarah, married first Robert Andrew, and secondly to —— Gilliland, one issue; Elizabeth, married John Earson, no issue; and Deborah, married Robert Earson, died near Urbana, Ohio, and left issue.

Both John and James MacLean were married when they arrived in this country. Robert was single, went south, and married a wealthy lady. John settled on the forks of Goose creek in Virginia, and James, a shoemaker, in a village hard by. In their old age the two brothers loved to talk about the pleasant times they had in Scotland. Of the descendants of John (probably three hundred all told), I have been able to collect the following facts: All have been industrious and hard working, and most of them economical; none given to the use of intoxicants, save three, but not habitual drunkards In politics, all were whigs, and afterward republicans; in religion, all were presbyterians, save a branch of the family of William (James) who espoused universalism; the tendency was toward ultra-calvanism; in the more recent descendants liberal views in theology are mostly maintained. The older stock were well made, compactly built men, slightly above medium, brown hair and light gray eyes. All the descendants, save the house of William, invariably spell their name "McLain." As already noted, John signs his will Mclean but I notice in a promissory note * given to his son John, dated November 26, 1811, spells it Mclain ; in a letter of conveyance to his son John, September 30, 1812, the same ; in a note given to his daughter Sarah Moore, September 11, 1811, the same. This is attested by his son Stephen, who spells his name Mclean. In a due-bill given June 25, 1817, he writes it McLain. These notes are all written in a strong hand, and evidently not that of an old man. After comparing them with the signature of Sarah Moore, I conclude all are in her handwriting. This is farther proved from the fact that the note to her is witnessed by Stephen. The signature to the will is that of a very feeble man. Whether this was signed before or after his fall down stairs I can not determine. William, as one of the executors of the will, invariably writes his name McClean. His son James invariably writes his own McLane, as do all his descendants, save the writer.

---

* All these notes are on file in the Probate Court of Butler County, Ohio, with the final settlement of his estate.

APPENDIX.

NOTE A.
AN ACCOUNT OF THE FLORIDA.

In the traditions of Mull, and in the state documents of Scotland, the vessel de stroyed by Donald Glas MacLean is always referred to as "The Florida;" but in the lis of vessels belonging to the Armada, the name of "Florida" does not occur. It, however does appear that a vessel called the "Florencia," commanded by Pereija, was in the fleet. The names are certainly significant of those which have been preserved by the people of Mull. In the Italian contingent, there was a vessel called the Galleon of the Duke of Tuscany, or the "Florentine Galleon," that joined the fleet at Lisbon, and in September, 1588, was at Santander, having its masts refitted. It does not appear to have survived the expedition. If this is the same vessel that was destroyed in Tobermory she was one of the most important in the fleet; and it is possible that the tradition tha affirms there was a lady of rank on board has a foundation in fact. After the vessel wa destroyed, Ashley wrote to Walsingham that it was one of the largest in the whole fleet and commanded by a grandee of the first rank, and was always served in silver.

The vessel early excited the cupidity of the Argyle family. On February 5, 1641, the marquis of Argyle obtained a gift of the vessel, by consent of Charles I., provided h paid to the duke of Lennox and Richmond the one-hundredth part of the ships, afte deduction of expenses. March 20, 1665, the earl of Argyle entered into a contract wit one James Mauld, wherein the latter agrees to give the former one-fifth part of all tha shall be recovered from the ship of the Armada, lost beside Tobermory. This contrac was to be good for three years. May 10, 1676, the earl of Argyle entered into a contrac with one John St. Clare, to last three years, in which it is stipulated that the earl shoul have one-third of all that should be recovered from the lost ship the first year, and on half that should be recovered during the remaining two years. On July 29, 1676, th contract was made over to Hans Albricht van Treileben. December 26, 1676, the earl Argyle makes a contract, good for three years, to Adolpho E. Smith and Treileben, fo the recovery of the lost vessel and its treasure, in which it is stipulated that the ea shall have £100 sterling worth of the first brass or copper obtained, and that before an division; the third part of all copper and brass afterward recovered; £3,000 sterlin worth of the first silver and gold recovered, out of the whole stock before division; an the half of whatever gold, silver, jewels, etc., should thereafter be recovered. In a dra of 1677, it is affirmed that several cannon had been raised. In another draft of the san year, it is asserted that the Spanish wreck was the "Admiral of Florence," belonging the Armada of 1588, having fifty-six guns and thirty millions of money; that it w burnt and so blown up that two men standing on the cabin were cast safe on shore; th it lies in a little bay in the isle of Mull, about ten fathoms at high water, and eight ground ebb; that the fore part of the ship is quite burnt; that search has been mad but nothing found but a great heap of cannon balls about the mainmast, and son kettles and tankards of copper, and such like, in other places. About the same tim the right of the earl to the vessel was disputed by the government; hence the draft particulars. Another memorandum of the same year says that the fore part of the sh was burnt, leaving no deck; the hull was full of sand, and where the cabin was there a heap of great timber; the cannon lay at some distance from the wreck; in 1666, tv brass cannon of large caliber and a great iron gun were raised; and afterward, six cann

---

* For this account and those that follow, see *Sixth Report Royal Commission Hist. MSS*, part I., pp. 625

were recovered. In 1678, while Captain Smith was at work on the wreck, he was threatened by Hector MacLean, brother of Torloisk, if he did not desist, he would be fired upon. In 1680, the earl of Argyle engaged to pay Archibald Miller £40 Scots monthly to work in the recovery of the wreck. In 1694, a contract was made with Alexander Campbell, younger of Calder. In 1730, a very fine bronze gun was recovered, bearing the founder's mark of R. and G. Phillips, 1584, with a crown and E. R. On the fore part of the gun are the F.'s and *Fleurs de Lis* of Francis I. There were also recovered some gold and silver coin.

NOTE B.
LETTERS OF JOHN ACHINCROSS AND SIR LACHLAN MÓR MacLEAN.

State Papers of Scotland, Elizabeth, Vol. LV., No. 61.—" Pleis it zour lo. that my Maister M^cclayne haifing to do heir in court directet me to my lord erle of ergyill to the effect that his lo. might travell vith ye Kingis Maiestie in his advis qrin also he comandit me to speck zour lo. anent the rebellious doing of the erle of teireone sumtym stylit barronn oneill, Odonill and otheris thair assistaris in yreland aganis the qwenis maiestie of Ingland, quha mynde vith yair forces thair haifing the assistance of the Clandonill and vyiris in Scotland to mak gret insurrection aganis hir g. this odonill hes vritten diverss tymes to M^cclayne craifand his assistance in yis actioun and Donnald gorm m^cconneill heir in Scotland vith ye nuber of sevin or anigh hunder men vith him vas in yreland this last Zulii and august at qlk tyin he haifand comission of Angus m^cconnneill quha remanit in Scotland for him self and for angus maid band vith ye erle and vith odonill, and sen his return to Scotland ar bandit vith ye erle of hwntly. Zit the Clandonill dow notht pless^r Huntly heir in Scotland, nather dow thay leife Scotland to ye assistance of ye erle of teireone and odonill vithout thay first contract pace vith M^cclayne ffor obtenyng q^r of thay haif offerit to M^cclayne to obteyn ye libertie of his sonne and vyiris his playges gevin be him to ye Kingis Md^{tie} and be his g. gevin to ye erle of huntly in custodie quha pat thame in McRaynsil's hande vpon bond to redelyuir thame to his lo. vndir ye pane of xx thowsand mark, and also thir clandonill offeris to M^cclayne the land y^t vas in debat betwix thame, and for fardwr securitie desyiris that M^cclayne sonne mary angus m^cconnill his dochtir as also ye McAngus m^cConnill his sonne mary m^cClaynis dochtir. all this vith vyir propynis is offerit for m^cclaynes assistance. Quhairof M^cclayne thocht guid to adwerteis zour lo. vith this his opinioun for recisting of hir Maiesties rebelles in yreland that hir hienes imploy my Lord erle of ergyill and m^cclayne to stay thir Scottismen from passing to yreland, and also haifand his lo. and m^cclayne on hir syid. that my lord direck of his men vith m^cclayne to yreland quha sall psew hir enemeis, and rebellis thair on ye ane syid, and hir hienes army and force in yreland to psew thame at y^t tym as ye sam salbe appunctid on ye vyir syide. This is the reddiast vay to expell hir g. rebellis and to mak thame to perreis in this thair consait procedit of ane hie counsall moyun and draucht for trubilling of hir hienes stacht and aucte in yreland. I think zour lo. hes hard of ye oppressioun and vrang done to hir hienes subiectis in yreland be ye erle of teireone and odonill in februar last qlk is bot small in respect of thair hie intent. Atto^r gif hir Maiestie imploy the erle of ergyill and m^cclayne in hir service hir hienes vaid direct thre or four schippis furnisit vith sum viwiris and this schippis to be appunctit for keiping of m^cclaynes galayes the tym of his landing in yreland qll his return to thame. the Clandonill of Scotland vith samong as thay dow mak as to be in yreland in Maii nixt. M^cclayne hes na guidvill to ye erle of teireone becaus y^t vith his avin hande he hangit hew oneill quha haid apprehended his man vith certane voittis direct from, him to Spaynartis and feiring ye reveilling thairof be ye said Hew vsit sik moyan that he gat him betrayit. As also m^cclayne vndirstandis y^t be his moyan art oneill vas slayne efter his and odonellis breking hir hienes vard in Duphlyn thir twa

gentilmen to vit Hew oneill and art oneill var brethir gottin be Schaan Vyirvayes namit Johnne oneill on Katherein m^cclayne countissa of ergyill and fader sister to this m^cclayne. Lat nocht ye erle of ergyill nor nane vyir heir in Scotland knaw y^t this consait vas mevifit by M^cclayne quha is reddy to do hir g. service efter his power throw zour lo. absence heir being in Conferance vith Zour servitor george Nycolsone thocht guid to comwnicat to Zour lo. be yis tre my Maisteris comissioun direct to zour lo. and schew to zour lo. said servand ye sam comissioun vndir ye subscriptioun of my maister. Sa efter puting of my humill service vnto zour lo. comittis zour lo. to the protectioun of the almyte god.
ffrom Ed. the xxv of Marche 1595
     Zor lo. humill servitour
         Johnne Achinross servitour
           to McClayne of Doward."

State Paper of Scotland, Elizabeth, Vol. 56, No. 26.—" Efter my humill comendationis I thender maist hartly thankis to zor lo. for the gret fawowr Schawin be zour lo. to my marchand Johnne Cunynghame burges of Ed^r. In sik sart y^t zour lo. hes place to comaund me as one of zour avyn I hard zour lo. comissioun q^rin I haif ens^rit at length in my tre direct to my lord bowes quha vill gif zour lo. inspectioun thairof. Sa resting on new adwertecsment as zour lo. finde occasioun efter puting of my humill service vnto zour lo. Comittis zour lo. in the protection of god. ffrom Castell Carrik the ferd of Zulii 1595.
     Zo^r Lo. verry lovying freind reddy to be imployit.
         Lauchlane Mclane off Doward."

[Endorsed] " July 1595
  Macklane to me.
To the right vorschipfull
Sr Robert Cecill Knyght
ane of hir maiesties moist
honorable previe counseill."

State Papers of Scotland, Elizabeth, Vol. 56, No. 27.—" My Lord efter my very hartly comendationis hes ressaint zour lo. tre fra my michand Joh. Cuynghame burges of Ed^r quha hes schawin to me how ze convoyit him to Sr. Robert Cecill Knicht one of hir maiesties maist hono^ble privie counseill, quho vith speciall fawour at large conferrit vith him in suche matteris and to suche effect as he maid me knawin. Undirstande how my guidvill and dewotiouns haif beyn imbraced. Schew me also that Sr. Robert leit him to vndirstand that materis of trubill in yreland var alreddy tane vp and obedience offerit to the qwenis maiestie, nochtyeless thocht me vorthie of thankis for my goodvill offerit desyrit to know of me quhom I micht stay from passing to yreland ffor anss^r I may stay my self my friende and dependars in the ylis. and also I know y^t nane ptenying to ye erle of ergyill vill pas thair aganis me nar by my counsell this mekill I may assure and ans^r for. Throw the conferrance y^t hes past betwix vs be voilt I haif done mair hes refusit gret offeris maid to me be Donnald gorm m^cconnill and angus m^cconnill fawooares a assista^rs of the erle of teirone and for staying of thame from his aide and assistance in yreland I sustenit sax hunder men lyand in garisoun thir thre monethis only mvif thair stay and to mak thame to feir the vrak of thair lande throw leifing ye samyn. Bot seing y^t thair appeirit na neid of me in hir hienes service sen y^t I vas nocht imployit thairin as I preparit and luikit for. thocht nocht guid to put me ony langar to extraordinar expenss hes dissolvit this nuber and force and be ye des^t of my cousing ye erle of ergyill am now cuin in his bounde of ergyill g^r I attend on his cuing from cowrt. In this meyntym Donnald gorm m^cconnill and angus m^cconnill seavd y^t I haif dissolvit thir forces and apperantly maenis na thing bot pace ar convenand their forces an purpose to pas to yreland and mynde to haif in thair cupanie M^ccloid Lewis, M^ccloid Herreis quha ar my

freinde and men quha hes beyn in my service aganis thame bot being zoung men of ane
hie spreit desyrus to acqwent them in veiris and being mekill advancit be ressait of gret
gaines ar pswadit to pas vith thame this veyage seing the sam vas mocht aganis me
q^{r}in I sall schaw guidvill be craft and moyan to stay thame all or ane gret p^t of thame,
am vsand all maenis to y^t effect. Sen it vas the comissioun direct vith Johnne be Sr.
Robert and zou, and gif thay stay nocht sall mak haistie adwerteisment to zor servand
george Nycolsoun, in sik form that I being imployit be hir maiestie sall suddanlie caus
thame return hame to Scotland. Or elles vse ye meyn that thay sall lois be thair passing to yreland, and mak ye convoy y^t be hir Maiesties servande sik vescheallis as trans-
portit thame to yrelande salbe brok in thair qlk salbe thair vrak to the qlk doing gif occasioun beis offerit, it is necess^r that thair be thre or fo^r pynnages vith twa schippis veill
appunctil to cum on the coist of yreland to this turn. gif I var hir maiesties bund servand I sould gar thay pynnayes be my moyan and convay and foirsicht in haifing of
yame heir in Scotland neir my place of Doward gif thame ane gret skaith, seing y^t neir
my place the meist p^t of this force man pas by ye sam, be ye qlk I ever cink my avyn
vantage of thame in tyme of trubill betwix o^r selfis. I vill requeist zo^r lo. to speak Sr.
robert hereanent and to resolwe me v^t expeditioun of hir Maiestie and counsillis mynd
towarde me heirin in sik sovit y^t gif I be imployit in hir service y^t I may pvyd for the
sam. Or vthirvayes y^t I may be exonerit honestlie of- sik as hes pcedit betwix vs. qlk I
haif done only vpon ane zeill and fawour y^t I had to hir maiesties service be quhais
moyan I miegt ressaif fawour of my avin prince, and also I haid ane gret mislyiking of
ye erle of teireone and his fauors as my serwand Johnne achinros did first vryilt to zo^r
lo. be the qlk and my avyn tre sensyne I haif reveillit to zor. lo. my haill mynd vithout
ony dissimolation, and knawes nocht be zour tre of zo^r ressait of myn. Johnne Cunyghame
hes schawin me that zour servand george hes spokin ye kingis maiestie and ye erle of
ergyill quha at home ciding vill tomunicat the mater to me for as zit I keip all secreit.
Zo^r lo. salbe sa guid as to present this vyir tre of thankis gifing to Sr. robert for the
fawowr y^t he schew to my m chand and I haid me gretwinly addettit to zour lo. for zo^r
guidvill and freindly doinge. In my tre to Sr. robert I refer the haill mater to yis zo^r lo.
lcttir q^r of zo^r lo. vill gif him inspcotioun, and as occasioun beis offerit I am reddy to
follow out the cowrs of guid service to his Maiestie. Comittis zour lo. in ye ptectioun of
ye almyte god.
ffrom Castell carrik the ferd of Julii 1595.
Yo^r lo. verry loving friend
Lauchlane M^{c}lane
[Endorsed] "Julii 1595 off Doward."
Macklane from Carickford
to Mr Bowes."

State Papers of Scotland, Elizabeth, Vol. 56, *No.* 66.—" Guid brother george I ressavit
zowr tre accordingly and thankis zow for the interteinment my man haid of zow, and
for zour guidvill offerit as ze sall knaw be my nixt tre qlk now I continew throw vncer-
taintie of your ressait heirof sen the ressait of my guid lord zour Maisteris tre and comissioun direct yv^t be Sr. Robert Cecill vith Johnne Cunnyngham. My Maister findand
him self fardar desyirit vith ye stay of thir Scottismen from yreland quhom he stayit for
ane certaine space as he did vryitt at qlk tym he saw thame reddy to pas fordvart at
thae tym unabill to him to stay thame, thairfoir offerit the nixt remeid to compell
thame to return to Scotland thocht the sam var mair daingerus to him, and efter ye
passing south by him of ane gret nuber of thame as vas vrittin to zow be me, he con-
venit of his fyne men thre hunder to remayn vith him in hoshald and yarde, ane hunder of thaime in armor of coit of mailze as ve vse vith twa handit sward and heidpiece
of yrun and vyir hunder of fyirmen and ane hunder of bowmen. In yis tym thair restit
be o^r knawlege the nuber of nyn hunder vith mony principallis to follow on the rest quha

come fordvart, and be ye vay tuik landing in ane lytill yle on ye coist of oʳ gret yle of
Mull, callit the Callow, thair to rest the nycht tym, being very all the day be sey. My
Maister heirand of thair landing qlk vas in the evenyng neir ye nycht, tuik pùrpois to
psew thame in the mornyng and to use sik coast and hardie convoy as he ducht, first
to be maister of their veschellis qlk vas galayes, birlingis, and boitlis, than to haif na
dout of thame selfis for gif ony defence vard be offerit be thame, his haill men vard
conveyn to thair psuit. As he dwysit and tuik the interpryis in hand, sa god of his
mychtie power hes concludit, and all the said nuber tane captives the principallis qʳof
ar thir as followes.—The capitan of Clanrenill and thre of his fader brether, the laird
of Kneydort, the laird of ardinvich, Donnald gormes broder, and mony principallis and
gentilmen of quhom he hes detenit and comittit to vard in his castellis as lyckit him,
on quhom he has spairit na yrnes to mvis thame the bettir to tak eis in patience and
hes ferriit the rest out of his land to the maynlad of Scotland narrest their duellingis.
I knew that this vas to be interprisit affoir my vritting to my guid lord zour maister as
also vthir turnes yᵗ is in hande and in virking. Many vaid nocht vryit bauldly thairof
except of one thing to comfort zour maister and vtheris oʳ guid freinde thair, that my
Mʳ vas bissie, qlk now I may say is sein and hard of, as I vait. ze vill heirof in court to
oʳ honoʳ. ze sall misknow the same. My maister is acqwentit vith thir prattie onsettis
vithout respect to nuber findand vantage, for diwers tymes he plaid this dance heir
aganis his enemeis. I assuir zow thir men yᵗ ar tane and in captivitie ar the maist douttit
and abil men in ye ylis and all thayis quho knawis thame vill say ye same. Lat zoʳ guid
Mʳ. and Sʳ. Robert confort thame vith this guid luke done be ane vailzeat man of veir
and ane man of honor in begynnyng of hir maiesties service, and as hir hienes and
counsell lyikis to employ him vith ye grace of god he sall schaw guidvill to accomplische
all yᵗ ever ve vritt. I continew the rest qlk aucht to follow and begin the mater in vritt
and vthirvayes, to ye visedome of sik honorabill psonis thair quhamto ye mater apperteins, as I did vryitt in my formar tre to zʳ guid Mʳ according to quhais ansʳ is god villing
ve sall do on oʳ pt. for thir materis being of gret importance vaid be condiscendit on and
concludit be vritt qlk my maister linkis for as is contenit in my forme lre to zʳ guid Mʳ.
The rest of hir maiesties vnfriende heir and assistaris of ye erle and odonill vill raige
aganis my Mʳ, bot ve vndirstand throw the guid confort yᵗ god of his miehtie power hes
gevin vs in this veyaige sik speciall men being in hande and oʳ avyn habilitie thairvith
that thay man on force oʳ sie all yᵗ is done heir in Scotland, and as oʳ service beis desyirit
in yreland man oʳ sie vs to do the vrak of ye erle and of odonill also. qlk I hoip in god
salbe done to ye confort and honor of all sik honorabill and vorschipfull pronis quhair-
vith ve ar in doing and quhom to the mater apperteins. ffor all the guddis ressavit be
yir Scottismen angus McConnill and Donald gorm and their assistaris from ye erle and
Odonill, this mornyg veyaige sall mak thame to render na service nor confort to ye erle
thairfair qʳ of I vill assuir zʷ and sa the dessʳ of Sʳ. Robert and zour guid Mʳ is obtein-
perit follows nixt thair doing to my mʳ. The pclamatioun vas pclamit heir for staying
of all furnising from thir psonis, as ye heir in court ye allowance and miscontment heirof
mak me acqwentit thairwith qlk ve regaird nocht only his hienes guid and princlie
countenance to vs being except for thayis quha ar in hande man rest quhair they ar,
and I think his Maiestie sould esteym of this as of guid service, spair nocht to send this
lre to zoʳ Mʳ for farder informatioun of thayis yᵗ ar thair. Lat this lre haif my dewtie of
service rememberit to the right vorschipfull Sʳ. robert cecill and zoʷ to zoʳ guid Mʳ nocht
forgetting my comendacionis to zour self comittis zow all in the protectioun of god.
ffrom Dumbertane the last of Julii.

                                              Zoʳ loving broder and guid ffreind.
                                                       Johnne Achinros."

[Endorsed]   "To my loving brother and
              guid ffreind
                 George Nycolsoun."

NOTE C.
POETRY ON OR ABOUT THE MacLEANS.

Gifted with poesy as are the Highlanders, and given to the praise of their country and their leaders, it would be expected that many poems would still be extant concerning the MacLeans and their ancestral dominions. To present this question properly requires a wide acquaintance with Gaelic poetry, both published and unpublished manuscripts. The probability is that the greater part of this literature has never been published. In Rev. A. MacLean Sinclair's manuscript collection, entitled *Clarsach nan Eileinean*, are sixty-six poems either by or else about the MacLeans, only seven of which have ever been in print. I find others exist in volumes which I do not have access to. I enumerate the following known to me: first, from the *Glenbard Collection*, published in 1888. This contains two by Iain Lom, eleven by Iain MacAilein, five by Mairerad nighean Lachairm, one by Mairi Nic-Phail, and one by Domhnall MacGillemhoire.

Iain Lom, or John MacDonald, born about 1620 and died in 1709, was one of the most celebrated of Gaelic poets. His poems are numerous, but have never been published in a collected form. On page 18 is his poem on Sir Lachlan MacLean, first Baronet of Duard, containing 15 verses of three lines each; followed on page 20 by one on "MacLean of Duard," of twelve verses, each also containing three lines. This appears to have been composed when Brolass was guardian of Sir John. It mentions Sir Lachlan Mór, Hector Roy, and MacLean of Brolass. This poem also occurs in *Clarsach na Coille*, on page 244.

Of the poems of Iain MacAilein, given under notices of the poets, the first occurs on page 55, and is on Sir John MacLean of Duard. It contains six verses of four lines each. This is followed by another on Sir John (p. 57), of nineteen verses of four lines each; followed immediately by two others on Sir John, one containing eleven verses of eight lines each, and the other fifteen verses of seven lines each. The next is the "Battle of Alfort," a dialogue of seventeen verses of four lines each. This is founded on a six weeks' session of a court of justice held at Aros, Mull. The following MacLeans figure in the poem: Murdoch Og of Lochbuie, Donald of Coll, MacLean of Brolass, Doidim Dana of Ardgour, and Lachlan of Calgary. On page 89, thirty-two lines of the poem on Colonel Charles MacLean of Drimnin (who fell at Culloden) are given. It is found in Stewart's *Highland Bards* and in *Beauties of Gaelic Poetry*. This is followed by three more, on Charles of Drimnin: the first containing six verses of eight lines each, the second, five verses of eight lines each, and the last (p. 97) eight lines. On page 101 is a poem of three verses of eight lines on the "Blessing of a House," which belonged to a MacLean who is called the "grandson of Charles the son of Allan." On page 102 is a poem of sixteen verses, entitled "The Migration of MacLean of Treshnish."

Mairearad, mentioned among the poets on page 105, has a lament of twenty verses of eight lines each on Allan, brother of Donald, third MacLean of Brolass. This Allan was an officer in the army, and died in Stirling, in 1722. The next (p. 110) is a lament for Lachlan MacLean, containing eleven verses of five lines each. Just who this Lachlan is, the poem does not clearly reveal. This is followed by two poems on Sir John, and one on Sir Allan MacLean. The first (p. 112) contains nine verses of four lines each; the second, six verses of eight lines each; and the third, eight of four lines each.

Mairi Nic-Phail, or Mary Mac-Phail, whose history I am ignorant of, on page 117 has a lament on Hector MacLean, consisting of nine verses of five lines each. The poem does not reveal what Hector this was.

Domhnall MacGillemhoire, or Donald Morrison, appears to have been a native of

Coll, but lived in Tiree. On page 119, he has a poem of thirteen verses of three lines each on Hector, eleventh MacLean of Coll.

The second book of poems is called *Clarsach na Coille*, and contains thirteen by Am Bard MacGilleain, one by Eachunn Bacach, one by Mairearad Nighean Lachainn one by Anndra Mac-an-Easbuig, one by Domhnull Bán MacGilleain, one by Eachunn MacIain, two by Catriona Nic-Gilleain, one by Aigeannaich, one by Niall MacLaomuinn, one by Gilleaspuig MacGilleain, one by Alastair MacIonmhuinn, one by Domhull MacGilleain, one by Iain Camshron, and one by Alastair MacDhomhnuill.

Am Bard MacGilleain, or John MacLean, is duly noticed in the chapter on poets. The book opens with a poem of eighteen verses of eight lines each on Alexander, fourteenth MacLean of Coll; followed, on pages 119, 125, by two more, one of twenty-one verses of eight lines each, and the other twenty-two of eight lines each. To these must be added five more ascribed to the Laird of Coll. The first (p. 7) has twelve verses of eight lines each; the second (p. 11), the same; the third (p. 15), seventeen of eight lines each; the fourth (p. 20), ten of seven lines each; and the last (p. 23) contains eleven verses of seven lines each. We also have two poems addressed to the "Younger Laird of Coll," which was Hugh, fifteenth. The first (p. 26) contains eleven verses of eight lines each, and the other (p. 30) eleven of sixteen lines each. On page 40 is a sonnet of fourteen verses of four lines each, addressed to Rev. John MacLean of Coll. Page 58 is a poem on the "Loss of Neil MacLean," who was drowned in 1809. It contains fifteen verses of eight lines each. The lament on Archibald MacLean of Scour (p. 81) contains thirteen verses of eight lines each.

Eachunn Bacach, or Hector MacLean, the poet to Sir Lachlan of Duard, has been mentioned under poets. His song to Sir Lachlan (p. 193) contains fourteen verses of three lines.

Mairearad Nighean Lachainn has a song of eleven verses of six lines each, dedicated to Sir John MacLean. It occurs on page 204.

Dhomhnull Ban MacGilleain, or Donald MacLean, the fair-haired, was a poet of Mull. His song (p. 207) on Donald, third MacLean of Brolass, contains seventeen verses of six lines each.

Eachunn MacIan, or Hector, son of John, or Hector, fourth MacLean of Coll, had the honor of composing what afterward proved to be the song of the MacLeans. It is entitled "The War Song of Allan nan Sop." It is composed of twelve verses of four lines each. See page 215.

Catriona Nic-Gilleain, or Catherine MacLean, mentioned under poets, composed a song to Lachlan, eighth MacLean of Coll. It contains (p. 217) seven verses of eight lines each.

Aigeannaich, called in Gillie's collection Nighean Dhòmhnuill Ghuirm, composed a poem (p. 223) of twelve verses of eight lines each, on Donald, tenth MacLean of Coll.

Niall MacLaomuinn, or Neil Lamont, was a native of Tiree. When the Montgomery Highlanders went to America in 1757, he composed (p. 233) a song to Sir Allan MacLean. It contains nine verses of three lines each.

Ghilleasbuig MacGilleain, or Archibald MacLean, previously noticed, composed (p. 238) a song of ten verses of seven lines each on Archibald MacLean of Kilmoluaig.

Alastair MacIonmhuinn, or Alexander MacKinnon, born in 1770, and died in 1814, addressed a song (p. 257) to the noble of the Clan Gilleain. It contains nine verses of four lines each.

Domhnull MacGilleain, or Donal MacLean, has a song (p. 258) of thirteen verses of four lines each, addressed to Dr. Allan MacLean of the Ross of Mull.

Iain Camshron, or John Cameron, who died in Antigonish, Nova Scotia, in 1858, inscribes an elegy (p. 231) of fourteen verses of seven lines each, to Am Bard MacGilleain, or John MacLean, the poet.

Alexander MacDonald, a native of Moidart, but living in Antigonish, also writes an elegy to Am Bard MacGilleain. It contains (p. 335) eight verses of eight lines each.

MacKenzie's *Beauties of Gaelic Poetry*, in two volumes, was published in 1841 and 1845. It contains one by Iain Dubh MacIain 'Ic-Ailein, three by Eachunn Bacach, one by Iain MacAilein, and one by Calum a Ghlinne.

Iain Dubh MacIain 'Ic-Ailein, or John MacDonald, was of the Clanranald family, and born about the year 1665. His elegy on Sir John MacLean (p. 70) is partly given, viz., fifteen verses of sixteen lines each.

Eachunn Bacach, or Hector MacLean, above mentioned, has three poems: The first (p. 77), an elegy on Sir Lachlan MacLean, of eighteen verses and one hundred and thirty-seven lines. The verses contain eight, seven, and six lines. This poem attracted the attention of Sir Walter Scott, who published a free translation of it. A song to Lachlan Og (p. 79), of eleven verses of eight lines each. The last (p. 386) is put down as anonymous. It is an elegy on the death of Sir Hector Roy MacLean, composed of fourteen verses of eight lines each.

Calum a Ghlinne or Malcolm MacLean, noticed under poets, composed a song (p. 365) of nine verses of eight lines each, on his daughter, whom he calls his "Nighean dubh Thoggarach." This has been put into English by Professor Blackie, and given as No. 8 of this note.

In many Gaelic poems not devoted to the MacLeans, reference is made to the Clan Gilleain. To hunt these up and make particular reference to them would result in no particular advantage. Those which have been translated into English may be of some interest. Some of these are contained in Hogg's *Jacobite Relics*, in two volumes, published in 1874. In the first volume are five references. In song II., "The Haughs of Cromdale," composed of sixteen verses, the thirteenth is as follows:

"MacLeans, MacDougals, and MacNeils,   And made their enemies to yield,
So boldly as they took the field,   Upon the haughs of Cromdale."

Song XVI., "Three Good Fellows ayont yon Glen," contains five verses, the fourth being:

"There's Skye's noble chieftain,   Reoch, Bane Macrabach,
Hector, and bold Evan,   And the true MacLean."

Song XVII., "The Battle of Killiecrankie," contains seven verses, the fifth as follows:

"Sir Evan Dhu, and his men true,   The true MacLean, and his fierce men,
Came linking up the brink, man;   Came in amang them a', man;
The Hogan Dutch, they feared such,   Nane durst withstand his heavy hand,
They bred a horrid stink then.   A' fled, and ran awa' then."

Song XC., "The Chevalier's Muster-roll," contains five verses, the second being:

"Borland and his men's coming,   Ilka Dunywastle's coming,
Cameron and MacLean's coming,   Little wat ye wha's coming,
Gordon and MacGregor's coming,   MacGillivray's and a's coming."

In Vol. II., or second series of *Jacobite Relics*, song CVIII., "On the Restoration of the Forfeited Estates," containing six verses, the fourth reads:

"MacLeod, MacDonald, join the strain,   Whose generous bounty richly pours
MacPherson, Fraser, and MacLean;   The streams of plenty round your shores,
Through all your bounds let gladness reign,   To Scotia's hills their pride restores,
Both prince and patriot praising,   Her faded honors raising."

Sir Walter Scott, in his *Lord of the Isles*, makes mention of the MacLeans. In Canto I. and Section XV. we read:

"Full many a shrill triumphant note
Saline and Scallastle bade float
Their misty shores around ;

And Morvern's echoes answer'd well,
And Duard heard the distant swell,
Come down the darksome Sound."

In that scene so terrifically portrayed in Canto II., Sections XVI. and XVII, when the attempted assault is made in Ardtornish castle, by the lord of Lorn and mainland chiefs, upon Bruce, among those who rally to the defense of the latter is the lord of Duard:

"Brave Torquil from Dunvegan high,
Lord of the misty hills of Skye,
MacNeil, wild Barra's ancient thane,
Duard, of bold Clan Gillian's strain,
Fergus, of Canna's castled bay,
MacDuffith, lord of Colonsay,

Soon as they saw the broad-swords glance,
With ready weapons rose at once,
More prompt, than many an ancient feud,
Full oft suppress'd, full oft renew'd,
Glow'd 'twixt the chieftains of Argyle,
And many a lord of ocean's isle."

Again, in Canto IV., Section XI.:

"They left Loch-Tua on their lee,
And they waken'd the men of the wild Tiree,
And the chief of the sandy Coll;

* * * * *

Lochbuie's fierce and warlike lord
Their signal saw, and grasp'd his sword."

No. 1.—The Isle of Mull.
By Dugald MacPhail.

[Dugald MacPhail was born in Torosay, Mull, in the year 1818, and afterward became surveyor in Glasgow. The poem is taken from Blackie's *Language and Literature of the Highlands*.]

O the island of Mull is an isle of delight,
With the wave on the shore and the sun on the height,
With the breeze on the hills, and the blast on the Bens,
And the old green woods, and the old grassy glens.

Though exiled I live from the land of my race,
In Newcastle, a grey and a grimy old place,
My heart, thou fair island, is ever with thee,
And thy beautiful Bens with their roots in the sea!
　　　　　　　O the Island, etc.

There was health in thy breeze, and the breath of thy bowers
Was fragrant and fresh 'neath the light summer showers,
When I wandered a boy, unencumbered and free!
At the base of the Ben 'neath the old holly tree!
　　　　　　　O the Island, etc.

Where the Lussa was swirling in deep rocky bed,
There the white bellied salmon, with spots of the red
And veins of dark blue, in young lustihood strong
Was darting and leaping and frisking along!
　　　　　　　O the Island, etc.

And a deft-handed youth there would gallantly stand

With a triple-pronged spear, smooth and sharp in his hand,
And swiftly he pounced, like a hawk, on his prey—
And glancing and big on the bank there it lay!
　　　　　　　O the Island, etc.

And the red hen was there 'neath the wood's leafy pride,
And the cock he was crooning and cooing beside;
And though forest or fence there was none on the Ben
The red deer were trooping far up in the glen!
　　　　　　　O the Island, etc.

O then 'twas my joy in the pride of the May
To list to the sweet-throated birds on the spray,
And to brush the cool dew from the low-winding glen,
When the first ray of morning streamed down from the Ben!
　　　　　　　O the Island, etc.

Bright joys of my youth, ye are gone like a dream,
Like a bubble that burst on the breast of the stream;
But my blessing, fair Mull, shall be constant with thee,
And thy green-mantled Bens with their roots in the sea!
　　　　　　　O the Island, etc.

No. 2.—The Last Harper o' Mull.

By Tannahill.

[The last harper of Mull was Murdoch MacDonald, harper to MacLean of Coll, who retired in 1734 to Quinish in Mull, where he died. I take this poem from the Pennycross MS, and know nothing of its composer.]

When Rosie was faithfu' how happy was I,
Still gladsome as simmer the time glided by.
I played my harp cheery, while fondly I sang
O' the charms o' my Rosie the winter nichts lang;
But now I'm as waefu' as waefu' can be,
Come simmer, come winter, it's a' ane to me;
For the dark gloom o' falsehood sae clouds my sad soul,
That cheerless for aye is the Harper o' Mull.

I wander the glens and the wild woods alone,
In their deepest recesses I make my sad moan:
My harp's mournfu' melody joins in the strain,
While sadly I sing o' the days that are gane.

Tho' Rosie is faithless she's no' the less fair,
And the thocht o' her beauty but feeds my despair.
Wi' painfu' remembrance my bosom is full,
An' weary o' life is the Harper o' Mull.

As slumbering I lay, by the dark mountain-stream,
My lovely young Rosie appeared in my dream;
I thocht her still kind, and I ne'er was sae blest
As in fancy I clasped the dear Nymph to my breast.
Thou fause fleetin' vision, too soon thou wert o'er;
Thou wak'd'st me tae tortures, unequalled before.
But death's silent slumbers my grief soon shall lull
An' the green grass wave o'er the Harper o' Mull.

No. 3.—Chieftain MacLean.

By Evan MacColl.

[Evan MacColl, known as the Bard of Lochfyne, was born near Inverary in 1803. He now lives at Kingston, Ontario. The poem is taken from *Poetic Works*, second Canadian edition. The poem was written for a festival of the Kingston St. Andrew's Society, over which Professor Donald MacLean of the Lochbuie family presided.]

Up, bonnet and feather! Up, thistle and heather!
St. Andrew's good advent is on us again:
What Scotsman, revering in its mem'ries endearing,
Would not make a night o't with Chieftain MacLean!

When Noah turned seaman, most people agree, man,
MacLean of that day had "a boat o' his ain;"
A clansman less famous, though ev'ry inch game, is
Our own gallant chieftain—the other MacLean.
Up, bonnet and feather! etc.

Away with your grumblers whom nothing but tumblers
Of punch and a haggis can tempt to fall in!
The fair happy faces that here fill their places
Most proud of by far must be Chieftain MacLean.
Up, bonnet and feather! etc.

Old Scotland's grand story, so pregnant of glory,
The ballads that cheered her in days that have been,
Her songs so heart touching, all hearers bewitching,
O, who would not feast on with Chieftain MacLean!
Up, bonnet and feather! etc.

From Ossian and Sehna to Lucknow and Alma,
Such triumphs are linked to the war-pipe's proud strain
That fellows who'd hear it, its music to sneer at,
Had best shun the sight of our Chieftain MacLean!
Up, bonnet and feather! etc.

Let pinks of perfection, themselves verily vexing,
A good Scottish reel call a pastime profane;
The worst I wish for them would be "Tullochgorum"
To dance till they sweated with Chieftain MacLean.
Up, bonnet and feather! etc.

O, Scotland, dear Scotland! alas that there's not land
Enough in thy bounds all thy sons to contain!
Else not this far west one, but thy own dear breast on,
Our joys would be perfect with Chieftain MacLean.
Up, bonnet and feather! etc.

No. 4.—MacLean's Child.

A Legend of Lochbuie.

[This poem I find in the Pennycross MS. I do not know who the author is. The legend, told in this and the three following ones, is very popular. The scene is supposed to have taken place at a headland on the east coast of the Ross of Mull, at a place called Malcolm's Point. The bluff at that point is a thousand feet in height. Malcolm Garry was a henchman of MacLean of Lochbuie.]

The sun rose fair on distant Mull,
Where ocean heaves its billows high,
And o'er Loch Buy the white sea-gull
Winged its way 'tween wave and sky;

The wild pipes uttered their pibroch shrill
And clansmen came from hut and heather,
With belted kilt and waving feather
To chase the deer on the misty hill.

MacLean was there with his haughty bride
And his only boy in his nurse's arms,
And the chieftain looked with love and pride
On his infant hope and his lady's charms.
"And now," he cried, "thou'lt see what cheer
MacLean's dark hills can yield thee here.
We'll touch not now the timorous hare,
That croucheth low in the shady glen,
Nor whistling plover nor bonny moor hen,
But stir the fawn from its dewy lair
And drive in herds the antlered deer."

And straight his clansmen round were spread,
Or fleet like winds of winter sped
The ground to beat both far and near,
And drive together the startled deer,
Where the chieftain's lady with ease might trace
The gathering herds and headlong chase.

Young Ian, the pride of his native glen,
The love of maids and boast of men,
Was placed alone to guard with care
A pass that ope'd a refuge where
The deer might 'scape the waiting fare.

They came and swept the youth away,
As a tempest scatters the foaming spray.
An angry man MacLean was then
As he saw the fleet herd pass the glen,
And the youth came on with head hung low,
With shame but not with fear, I trow.

"Go, seize the dog," the chieftain said,
"And tear the plume from his dastard head;
Strip his coward shoulders bare,
Why should the tartan flutter there?
Go quickly, bind and scourge the wretch,
We'll see what blood the rod can fetch;
Or whether his mother's milk in part
Still lingers about his childish heart."
No words they spoke, but stifled sighs
Might tell what dimmed the clansmen's eyes,
And why a shudder went round and round
As the lash fell on the deepening wound.

No shriek nor groan nor stifled sigh
Was heard to come from Ian's breast,
Nor tear was seen in his fiery eye,
But pale his cheeks with the chill of death.
His eyeballs strained and his lips compressed,
And his nostrils bled with his laboring breath.
At length the scourge away is cast,
The thongs are cut that bound him fast,
And Ian started bleeding there
And wildly seized the chieftain's heir,
And fast away to a cliff he sped,
That far o'er the boiling billows hung;
And he waved the infant high o'erhead,
And laughed till the rocks around him rung.

Oh wildly look the chieftain then
As shriek and shout filled all the glen;
And with clasped hands and bended knee,
He cried, "Oh save my only child!"
While Ian danced and shrieking wild
Answered thus with fiendish glee,
"Come, strip thy back, and let me see
The wolfish blood that flows in thee,
And then thy gory arms may hold
The infant chief that crows so bold."
The chieftain stripped and the red drops fell,
For the clansmen urged the strokes full well;
"And now," he cried, "my infant give,
And thou, I swear, in peace shall live."
"Aha," he shrieked, "go, get thee now,
And see in every clouded brow
A blushing friend or a biting foe,
Or follow thy boy to hide thy name,
And wash thy back and brow from shame
In the boiling waves where now we go."
And away he sprung, still laughing wild,
The bleeding youth with his chieftain's child.

They rushed to the brink of the rocky steep,
But the sea had covered its bosom deep,
And they heard but the sound of the billows sweep
As they seemed to lull their charge asleep.
And the sailors still as they pass the shore
With shuddering look on cliff and sea,
And tell how oft when the wild winds roar,
And their boats on the foaming billows flee,
An infant's wail they seem to hear;
Or, loud and shrill on the startled sea,
The clansman's shriek and fiendish glee.

No. 5.—MacLean's Child.
By Charles MacKay.

[Charles MacKay, born in Perth in 1812; traveler, editor, author, poet, and philosopher. This poem is taken from his *Poetical Works*.]

"MacLean, you've scourged me like a hound;
You should have struck me to the ground,
You should have play'd a chieftain's part—
You should have stabbed me to the heart.

"You should have crush'd me into death;
But hear I swear with living breath,
That for this wrong which you have done
I'll wreak my vengeance on your son—

"On him, and you, and all your race!"
He said, and bounding from his place,
He seized the child with sudden hold—
A smiling infant three years old.

And, starting like a hunted stag,
He scaled the rocks, he clomb the crag,
And reach'd o'er many a wide abyss
The beetling seaward precipice.

And, leaning o'er its topmost ledge,
He held the infant o'er the edge.
"In vain thy wrath, thy sorrow vain,
No hand shall save it, proud MacLean!"

With flashing eye and burning brow
The mother followed, heedless how,
O'er crags with mosses overgrown,
And stair-like juts of slippery stone.

But midway up the rugged steep,
She found a chasm she could not leap,
And, kneeling on its brink, she raised
Her supplicating hands, and gazed.

"Oh, spare my child, my joy, my pride,
Oh, give me back my child!" she cried;
"My child! my child!" with sobs and tears,
She shriek'd upon his callous ears.

"Come, Evan," said the trembling chief,
His bosom wrung with pride and grief,
"Restore the boy, give back my son,
And I'll forgive the wrong you've done."

"I scorn forgiveness, haughty man!
You've injured me before the clan,
And naught but blood shall wipe away
The shame I have endured to-day."

And as he spoke he raised the child,
To dash it 'mid the breakers wild,
But at the mother's piercing cry,
Drew back a step, and made reply:

"Fair lady, if your lord will strip,
And let a clansman wield the whip
Till skin shall flay and blood shall run,
I'll give you back your little son."

The lady's cheeks grew pale with ire,
The chieftain's eyes flashed sudden fire;
He drew a pistol from his breast,
Took aim, then dropped it, sore distrest.

"I might have slain my babe instead.
Come, Evan, come," the father said,
And through his heart a tremor ran,
"We'll fight our quarrel man to man."

"Wrong unavenged I've never borne,"
Said Evan, speaking loud in scorn;
"You've heard my answer, proud MacLean.
I will not fight you—think again!"

The lady stood in mute despair,
With freezing blood and stiffening hair;
She moved no limb, she spoke no word,
She could but look upon her lord.

He saw the quivering of her eye,
Pale lips, and speechless agony—
And doing battle with his pride,
"Give back the boy—I yield," he cried.

A storm of passion shook his mind,
Anger, and shame, and love combined;
But love prevailed, and, bending low,
He bared his shoulders to the blow.

"I smite you," said the clansman true;
"Forgive me, chief, the deed I do!
For by yon Heaven that hears me speak,
My dirk in Evan's heart shall reek."

But Evan's face beamed hate and joy;
Close to his breast he hugg'd the boy:
"Revenge is just! revenge is sweet!
And mine, Lochbuie, shall be complete."

Ere hand could stir, with sudden shock
He threw the infant o'er the rock;
Then followed with a desperate leap,
Down fifty fathoms to the deep.

They found their bodies in the tide;
And never till the day she died
Was that sad mother known to smile—
The Niobe of Mulla's isle.

They dragg'd false Evan from the sea,
And hang'd him on a gallows tree;
And ravens fatten'd on his brain,
To sate the vengeance of MacLean.

No. 6.—WILD REVENGE.
By Thomas Nimmo.

[This poem and the one following I find in a brochure published in 1884 by MacLean of Lochbuie. No account of Thomas Nimmo is given.]

'Tis morning. O'er Hebridean Isles,
  Which dot the surface of the deep,
The orb of day returning smiles,
  The spirits of the water sleep.

Oh! sweet's the breath of early morn,
  And bright the glow of eastern sky,
And fair the flowers whose tints adorn
  Mull's wild and rugged scenery.

But brighter far than nature's light
  Is woman's pure and pensive eye,
While watching through the dreary night
  The innocence of infancy.

And fairer than the fairest flower
  That decks the mead or mountain wild
Are smiles, which, in a mother's bower,
  Play o'er the features of her child.

The matins in Lochbuie's halls
  Are said: MacLean, the doughty chief,
With haughty mein his henchman calls,
  And gives command in language brief.

"Go; let the pibroch of the clan
  The gathering, both loud and clear,
Be sounded from the bartizan,
  MacLean to-day will hunt the deer.

"His child, Lochbuie's son and heir,
  His wife, the Lady Isabel,
Will with himself be present there,
  Hence! Quickly go, thy message tell."

The henchman sped, the staghounds bay,
  The fiery steeds impatient rear,
The vassals in their tartan gay,
  With gladsome faces soon appear.

The chief with bow and buglehorn
  Rides foremost with his island queen,
The nurse and child aloft are borne
  Within their wicker palanquin.

The thrilling bagpipes gayly play
  As from their drones the streamers fly,
The merry clansmen bound away
  And shout in wildest ecstacy.

And now they reach the forest green
  Of pine trees with their scaly cone,
Where turning round the proud MacLean
  Keen marks his followers every one.

Each gorge and pass he fenced with care,
  And strictest vigilance enjoined
In order that the quarry there
  No outlet for escape might find.

Twelve men of might and stature tall,
  Well armed with lance and studded shield,
Form quickly at their chieftain's call
  To tend their Lady on the field.

A little higher ground to gain
  They onward mov'd, and many a prayer
Is muttered as they cross the plain,
  For Isabel so bland and fair.

The bugles sound, the startled deer
  Fly fleetly as the viewless wind,
The shaggy hounds in full career
  Pursue and leave the woods behind.

The bowmen with their weapon bent
  Concealed behind the rocks remain,
With sinews braced and eyes intent,
  To lance the barb with deadly aim.

But quicker still the red deer flew,
  The warders' shouts were given in vain,
As nearer to the pass they drew
  Their course to change or speed restrain.

With bounding spring and antlers reared
  In air this furious rush; anon
The hard and narrow gorge they've cleared,
  The hunting of that day is done!

Exerted hope can rarely brook
  The sting of disappointment keen;
So told the dark and angry look
  And flashing eye of proud MacLean.

"Seize, bind the slave!" he madly cried;
  "A cur dog's death his doom shall be;
All hope of mercy is denied;
  Diavual: hang him on the nearest tree.

"But no! a refuge in the grave
  From sneering scorn the coward finds;
Misfortune's bitter blast to brave
  Belongs alone to noble minds.

"So let him live; the knotted lash—
  Instead of death—his flesh shall tear
Till blood spurt out from every gash,
  Which stains his craven shoulders bare."

With lips compressed and dauntless breast
   The Gaël his stripes unflinching bore,
No change of countenance confess'd
   The pain that thrill'd through every pore.

"Enough!" the chieftain call'd aloud;
   The victim's cords were quick untied;
And, slowly followed by the crowd,
   Lochbuie to meet his lady hied.

Like sunbeam peering o'er the fells
   Through musky clouds which sudden roll,
She sweetly smiles, and soon dispels
   The moody umbrage of his soul.

With kindly glow his bosom warms,
   And, stooping low upon the plain,
He raised the infant in his arms
   And kissed him o'er and o'er again.

As if by force of magic's power,
   The clansmen, in their transports wild,
Join in the greetings of the hour,
   And bless the lady and her child.

The cheetah in the jungle trail
   Creeps stealthy forward as he goes,
And, if observed, he sweeps his tail
   And clouds of dust around him throws.

As, thus concealed, he crouching lies,
   The doe no longer looks behind;
Reliev'd from dread of all surprise
   She feeds and thinks 'twas but the wind.

But, creeping nearer, with a bound
   The cheetah fixes on his prey,
Which, felling on the tangled ground,
   He paws and tears with savage play.

So Callum Dhu with felon aim
   His direful purpose to conceal
Shouts with the crowd in loud acclaim,
   As if disgrace he could not feel.

But, sudden as the lightning's flash,
   He from the nurse the child has torn,
And up the cliff, with frenzied dash,
   The infant on his arm has borne.

He never stopp'd till, clamb'ring high,
   The fearful peak at last he gained;
And thence he scowled with glaring eye
   On those who far below remained.

He quickly drew his dagger blade,
   And o'er his heart he placed the child;
He wrapped it in his tartan plaid,
   And stood erect, and grimly smiled.

The chief was powerless and appall'd,
   The pale and frenzied Isabel
Wild shrieked, and for her infant called,
   As prostrate on the earth she fell.

Seem'd as if wakening from a trance,
   'Twas only then, the clansmen knew
By instinct, or by dint of chance,
   The vengeful act of Callum Dhu.

Infuriate, madden'd, forth they bound
   To scale the steep and narrow path,
Which up the cliff so slippery wound,
   From which to swerve were certain death.

"Move but a step," he hoarsely cried,
   And on this dagger's hilt, I swear,
Its blade shall red in blood be dyed,
   Of innocence—take heed! beware!"

The chieftain, with uplifted hands,
   Looks heav'nward on the voiceless sky,
And tremblingly imploring stands,
   Rack-torn with fiercest agony.

"One-half my lands I'll freely give.
   All! all!" he cried, in accents wild,
"So that the innocent may live.
   Oh! save my wife, and spare my child."

"Lochbuie!" Callum Dhu replied,
   "Gold can never indemnify
For loss of honor, nor can hide
   The stains of open infamy.

"Me wantonly you have disgrac'd,
   Ay me, altho' full well you knew
Your confidence was ne'er misplaced
   When giv'n in trust to Callum Dhu.

"To me your life you once have owed;"
   And opening his chequer'd vest,
He with his finger proudly showed
   A cicatrice upon his breast.

"To you your angel wife is dear,
   To me more dear than life and light
Is Flora * who with soul sincere
   Her maiden troth to me did plight.

---

* Flora was the laird's sister. It is also related that the laird, suspecting that an attachment existed between the two, caused Malcolm to be maimed. Malcolm swore vengence, and declared to his mother that the laird's seed should not rule in Lochbuie. His demand was that the laird should be likewise maimed. They tried to pass off the maiming of a sheep upon Malcolm, but he demanded to know just how and where the pains he felt. When this was accomplished, he destroyed both the child and himself.

"And am I then so abject now
  As not to dare her smiles to greet?
Yes! I absolve her from her vow:—
  Revenge alone to me is sweet!

"Yet listen! If on bended knee
  You do now publicly confess
How deeply you have injured me
  And sorrow and regret express:—

"And farther, if you shall consent
  To bare your shoulders to the scourge
And suffer what I underwent,
  These, these, perhaps, the stain may purge."

"Yes! yes! thy purpose to recall,
  I here confess on bended knee,
In presence of my vassals all,
  That I have deeply injured thee.

"Stripes, torture, death itself I dare,"
  Exclaimed aloud the stricken chief,
"So that my only child you spare,
  And thus assuage his mother's grief."

Th' astonished clansmen murmured loud,
  But quailed as them their chieftain eyed,
Who in the center of the crowd,
  The agonizing lash defied.

'Twas over, tho' he could not speak,
  He, breathing deep, look'd wistfully
Toward the cold and dreary peak
  Which topped the rugged cliff so high.

Oh! horror! with outstretched arm
  The desp'rate man held up the child
As if he meditated harm;
  His looks were haggard, dark, and wild.

One moment more! With demon glare,
  He bent his arm the child to kiss,
Then vaulting into empty air,
  Both sank into the dark abyss!

Oh! who can paint a scene so dread,
  The howling and the dismal yell
Enough to rouse the sleeping dead
  And scare the very fiends of hell?

But whence those other sounds of woe
  Which now assail the wearied ear,
So mournful, plaintive, wailing low,
  Like moaning winds in autumn sere?

Has some illusion of the mind,
  Some airy phantom of the brain,
A dream of fancy undefin'd,
  Awakened up such doleful strains?

Ah, no! the accents sad of grief;
  The passing knell have mournful knolled
And warned the childless, widowed chief,
  That Isabel in death lies cold.

How vain, alas! is human pride—
  In youth, impatient of control;
It swells like ocean's raging tide,
  And saps the barriers of the soul.

In after years, as death draws near,
  Its waves begin to retrograde;
While we lament with many a tear,
  And mourn the mocks which they have made.

The morn had seen Lochbuie proud
  Ride forth, the idol of his clan;
The evening hears him sob aloud,
  A lone and broken-hearted man.

For closed in dullness is that ear
  Which mercy never sued in vain;
And dim's that eye which wont to cheer,
  And make the wretch forget his pain.

No longer shall the infant gem
  Of innocence endearing smile;
Cut off before its beauteous stem
  It sleeps beside Mull's mournful isle.

Poor Flora in fantastic weeds
  Wild wanders on the lonely shore,
And muttering mournful tells her beads
  She ne'er shall see her Callum more!

Lochbuie's halls are silent now;
  Within Iona's cloister'd pile
The chief to heaven his life did vow,
  And never more was seen to smile.

No. 7.—MacLean's Child.
By Marquis of Lorn.
[John George Edward Henry Douglass Sutherland Campbell, or Marquis of Lorn, born in 1845.]

Part I.

Dark with shrouds of mist surrounded
  Rise the mountains from the shore,
Where the galleys of the islemen
  Stand updrawn, their voyage o'er.

Horns this morn are hoarsely sounding
  From Lochbuie's ancient wall,
While for chase the guests and vassals
  Gather in the court and hall.

Hounds, whose voices could give warning
  From far moors of stags at bay,
Quiver in each iron muscle,
  Howl, impatient of delay.

Henchmen, waiting for the signal
  At their chief's imperious word,
Start, to drive from hill and corrie
  To the pass the watchful herd.

Closed were paths as with a netting,
  Vain high courage, speed or scent;
Every mesh a man in ambush
  Ready, with a cross-bow bent.

"Eachann, guard that glade and copsewood,
  At your peril let none by!"
Cries the chief, while in the heather
  Silently the huntsmen lie.

Shouting, by the green morasses,
  Where the fairies dance at night,
Yelling 'neath the oak and birches,
  Come the beaters into sight.

And, before them, rushing wildly,
  Speeds the driven herd of deer,
Whose wide antlers, tossed like branches,
  In the winter of the year.

Useless was the vassal's effort
  To arrest the living flow,
And it passed by Eachann's passage,
  Spite of hound, and shout, and blow.

"Worse than woman! Useless caitiff!
  Why allowed you them to pass?
Back! No answer! Hark, men, hither!
  Take his staff and bind him fast."

Hearing was with them obeying,
  And the hunter's strong limbs lie,
Bound with thongs from tawny oxen,
  'Neath the chieftain's cruel eye.

"More than two-score stags have passed him,
  Mark the number on his flesh
With red stripes of this good ashwood,
  Mend me thus this broken mesh!"

Ah! Lochbuie! Faint and sullen
  Beats the heart, once leal and free,
That had yielded life exulting,
  If it bled for thine and thee.

Deem'st thou that no honor liveth,
  Save in haughty hearts like thine?
Think'st thou men, like dogs in spirit,
  At such blows but wince and whine?

Often, in the dangerous tempest,
  When the winds before the blast,
Surging, charged like crested horsemen
  Over helm, and plank, and mast,

He, and all his kin before him,
  Well have kept the clansman's faith,
Serving thee in every danger,
  Shielding thee from harm and skaith.

'Mid the glens and hills in combat,
  Where the blades of swordsmen meet,
Has he fought with the Campbells,
  Mingling glory with defeat.

But, as waters round Eorsa,
  Dark and deep, then blanch in foam,
When the winds, Ben Mór has harbored,
  Burst in thunder from their home,

So the brow, fear never clouded,
  Blackens now, 'neath anger's pall,
And the lips, to speak disdaining,
  Whiten at revenge's call!

Part II.

Late, when many years had passed him,
  And the chief's old age begun,
Seemed his youth again to blossom,
  With the birth of his fair son.

Late, when all his days had hardened
  Into flint his nature wild,
Seemed it softer grown and kinder,
  For the sake of that one child.

And again a hunting morning,
  Saw Lochbuie and his men,
With his boy, his guests, and kinsmen
  Hidden o'er a coppiced glen.

Deep, within its opened thickets,
  Ran its waters to the sea;
On the hill the chief lay careless,
  While the child watched eagerly.

'Neath them, on the shining ocean,
  Island beyond island lay,
Where the peaks of Jura's bosom,
  Rose o'er holy Oronsay.

Where the greener fields of Islay
  Pointed to the far Kintire,
Fruitful lands of after ages,
  Wasted then with sword and fire.

For the spell, that once had gathered,
  All the chiefs beneath the sway
Of the ancient royal scepter
  Of the Isles, had passed away.

Once from Rathline to the southward,
  Westward to the low Tiree,
Northward, past the Alps of Coolin,
  Somerled ruled land and sea.

Colonsay, Lismore, and Scarba,
  Bute and Cumrae, Mull and Skye,
Arran, Jura, Lew's, and Islay,
  Shouted then one battle-cry.

But those Isles that still united
  Taught at Harlaw Scotland's might,
Broken by their fierce contentions,
  Singly waged disastrous fight.

And the teaching of forgiveness
  Grey Iona's creed became,
Not a sign for men to reverence,
  But a burning brand of shame.

Still among the names, that ruin
  Had not numbered in her train,
Lived the great clan, proud as ever,
  Of the race of strong MacLean.

And his boy, like her he wedded,
  Though of nature like the dove,
Showed the eagle spirit flashing
  Through a heritage of love.

Heir of all the vassals' homage,
  Rendered to the grisly sire,
He had grown his people's treasure,
  Fostered as their heart's desire.

Surely safety guards his footsteps,
  Enmity he hath not shown;
Yet who stealthily glides near him,
  Whose the arm around him thrown?

It is Eachann, who has wolf-like
  Seized upon a helpless prey!
Fearlessly and fast he bears him!
  Where a cliff o'erhangs the bay.

There, while sea-birds scream around them,
  Holding by his throat the boy,
Eachann turns, and to the father
  Shouts in scorn and mocking joy:—

"Take the punishment thou gavest,
  Give before all there a pledge
For my freedom, or thy darling
  Dying falls from yonder ledge.

"Take the strokes in even number,
  As thou gavest, blow for blow,
Then dishonored on thine honor,
  Swear to let me freely go."

Silent in his powerless anger,
  Stood the chief with all his folk,
And before them all the ransom
  Was exacted stroke for stroke.

Then again the voice of vengeance
  Pealed from Eachann's lips in hate,
"Childless and dishonored villain,
  Expiation comes too late!

"My revenge is not completed!"
  And they saw in dumb despair
How he hurled his victim downward
  Headlong through the empty air.

Then they heard a yell of laughter,
  As they turned away the eye;
And they gazed again, where nothing
  Met their sight but cliff and sky.

For the murderer dared to follow,
  Where the youthful spirit fled
To the throne of the avenger,
  To the Judge of quick and dead.

No. 8.—CALLUM O' THE GLEN.

By MALCOLM MACLEAN.

[Malcolm MacLean is noticed under Poets. This poem refers to his daughter. What follows is a translation from the Gaelic. I find it in Blackie's *Language and Literature of the Highlands.*]

My bonny dark maid,
  My precious, my pretty,
I'll sing in your praise
  A light-hearted ditty;
Fair daughter whom none
  Had the sense yet to marry;
And I'll tell you the cause
  Why their love did miscarry,
    My bonnie dark maid!

For sure thou art beautiful,
  Faultless to see;
No malice can fasten
  A blot upon thee.
Thy bosom's soft whiteness
  The sea-gull may shame,
And for thou art lordless
  'Tis I am to blame.
    My bonnie dark maid, etc.

And indeed I am sorry,
  My fault I deplore,
Who won thee no tocher
  By swelling my store;
With drinking and drinking
  My tin slipped away,
And so there's small boast
  Of my sporan to-day.
    My bonnie dark maid, etc.

While I sit at the board,
  Well seasoned with drinking
And wish for the thing
  That lies nearest my thinking,
'Tis the little brown jug
  That my eye will detain,
And when once I have seen it,
  I'd see it again!
    My bonnie dark maid, etc.

The men of the country
  May jeer and may gibe,
That I rank with the penniless,
  Beggarly tribe;

But though few are my cattle,
  I'll still find a way
For a drop in my bottle,
  Till I'm under the clay.
    My bonnie dark maid, etc.

There's a grumpy old fellow,
  As proud as a king,
Whose lambs will be dying
  By scores in the spring,
Drinks three bottles a year,
  Most sober of men,
But dies a poor sinner
  Like Callum o' Glen.
    My bonnie dark maid, etc.

When I'm at the market,
  With a dozen like me,
Of proper good fellows
  That love barley-bree,
I sit round the table,
  And drink without fear,
For my good-wife says only,
  "God bless you, my dear!"
    My bonnie dark maid, etc.

Though I'm poor, what of that?
  I can live and not steal,
Though pinched at a time
  By the high price of meal.
There's good luck with God,
  And he gives without measure;
And while he gives health,
  I can pay for my pleasure.
    My bonnie dark maid, etc.

Very true that my drink
  Makes my money go quicker;
Yet I'll not take a vow
  To dispense with good liquor;
In my own liquid way
  I'd be great among men,—
Now you know what to think
  Of good Callum o' Glen.
    My bonnie dark maid, etc.

No. 9.—Inch Kenneth.
By Prof. J. S. Blackie.

[Prof. John Stuart Blackie was born in Glasgow in 1809. He is a noted classic scholar, professor of Greek in the University of Edinburgh, poet, and author. This and the following poem are taken from his *Altavona*.]

Nay, spur not so! he wastes no time who tarries
  A moment here to spell the old grey stones,
Where high-renowned MacLeans and stout
    MacQuarries
Rehearse their glories, and preserve their
    bones.
Here think thee back a thousand years or more,
  And ask how tonsured monks were mighty
    then
From gray Iona's granite-girdled shore
  To tame the souls of rude rough-hearted men.
No feeble race were they who chose to dwell
  In the green refuge of this wave-lashed nook,
But strong in love, and the all-conquering spell
  Of death-defying cross, and peaceful crook,
And armed with law divine more strong than
    steel,
To bend the staff, and make the proud man kneel.

No. 10.—Nine Noted Chiefs of MacLean.
By Prof. J. S. Blackie.

[The last referred to is Lachlan Catanach. Prof. Blackie admitted to Sir Fitzroy D. MacLean, that had he known, before he wrote this, the other side of the story, he would not have been so severe.]

When the king of Norway came,
  Our Alexander's crown to claim
    At Largs with pomp and pride there!
Gill MacGillean seized the villain,
  And drowned him in the Clyde there!

Red Hector slew, I tell you true,
  The laird of Drum, and all his crew,
    At Harlaw on the heather there;
But there the slain the slayer slew,
  And both lay dead together there!

At Flodden field stout Hector stood,
  With all the best of Scottish blood,
    Till swooping ruin found him there!
And man for man his faithful clan,
  Were heaped in death around him there!

Big Lachlan from his rocky hold
  Right wisely ruled his clansmen bold,
    That owned the stout command there,
But stained with gore green Islay's shore,
  Cut down by traitor hand there!

At Inverlochy on the foes
  Sir Lachlan rained a shower of blows,

A true and loyal knight there;
  While false Argyle, removed a mile,
    Looked on, and then took flight there!

Sir Hector Roy, the stout MacLean,
  Fought one to ten, but all in vain,
    His broad claymore unsheathing;
Himself lay dead 'mid heaps of slain,
  For Charles at Inverkeithing!

O good Sir John, hadst thou been wise
  To read the times with prophet eyes,
    Nor propped the falling Stuart then,
The false Argyle, with all his wile,
  Had not set foot in Duard then!

On dark Culloden's bloody heath
  Drimnin's claymore leaped from its sheath,
    Prince Charlie to deliver there!
But vain the fight; in pitchy night
  His star went down forever there!

When Lachlan's soul to Ifrinn sped,
  The fiends below rejoiced, and said,
    "If Satan should resign here,
This bad MacLean in hell shall reign,
  And drink red blood for wine here."

No. 11.—War-Song of Lachlan, High Chief of MacLean.
From the Gaelic. By Sir Walter Scott. 1815.

[Sir Walter appends this note: "This song appears to be imperfect, or, at least, like many of the earl: Gaelic poems, makes a rapid transition from one subject to another; from the situation, namely, of one o the daughters of the clan, who opens the song by lamenting the absence of her lover, to an eulogium ove the military glories of the chieftain. The translator has endeavored to imitate the abrupt style of the original." Sir Walter Scott, the great novelist and poet, was born in Edinburgh, in 1771; died at Abbotsford, in 1832. The following is taken from his *Poetical Works*.]

A weary month has wandered o'er
Since last we parted on the shore;
Heaven! that I saw thee, Love, once more,
Safe on that shore again!
'Twas valiant Lachlan gave the word:
Lachlan, of many a galley lord:
He called his kindred bands on board,
And launch'd them on the main.

Clan Gillian is to ocean gone,
Clan Gillian, fierce in foray known;
Rejoicing in the glory won
In many a bloody broil:

For wide is heard the thundering fray,
The rout, the ruin, the dismay,
When from the twilight glens away
Clan Gillian drives the spoil.

Woe to the hills that shall rebound
Our banner'd bag-pipes maddening sound;
Clan Gillian's onset echoing round,
Shall shake their inmost cell.

Woe to the bark whose crew shall gaze,
Where Lachlan's silken streamer plays!
The fools might face the lightning's blaze
As wisely and as well!

No. 12.—Coronach on Sir Lachlan, Chief of MacLean.
From the Gaelic. By Sir Walter Scott.

[Of this Sir Walter says: "The following is a lamentation literally translated from the Gaelic. The tune is so popular that it has since become the war-march, or Gathering of the clan." It is a part of Eachann Bacach's Elegy on Sir Lachlan MacLean, one of the songs given in *Beauties of Gaelic Poetry*. This translation is taken from "The Lady of the Lake."]

Which of all the Senachies
Can trace thy line from the root up to Paradise,
But MacVuirih, the son of Fergus?
No sooner had thine ancient stately tree
Taken firm hold in Albion,
Than one of thy forefathers fell at Harlaw.
'Twas then we lost a chief of deathless name.

'Tis no base weed—no planted tree,
Nor a seedling of last Autumn;

Nor a sapling planted at Beltain;
Wide, wide around were spread its lofty branches
But the topmost bough is lowly laid!
Thou hast forsaken us before Sawaine.

Thy dwelling is the winter house:—
Loud, sad, sad, and mighty is thy death-song!
Oh! courteous champion of Montrose!
Oh! stately warrior of the Keltic Isles!
Thou shalt buckle thy harness on no more!

No. 13.—The Lady of Duard's Vengeance.
By Charles MacKay.

[From MacKay's *Poetical Works*. The poem is a legendary incident of the Florida, of the Invincible Armada.]

"Weird woman, that dwellest on lofty Ben Mor,
Give ear to my sorrow, and aid, I implore.
A lady has come from the green sunny bowers
Of a far southern clime, to the mountains of ours;
A light in her eyes, but deceit in her heart,
And she lingers, and lingers, and will not depart.

"Through darkness and danger, 'mid tempest and rain,
She has sail'd to our shores from the vineyards of Spain,
Forsaking her country, her kindred, her home,
Abroad through our cold Western Islands to roam,
To find a young lover as fair to her sight
As a vision she saw in the slumbers of night.

"And hither by stars inauspicious convey'd,
She has come, in her gems and her beauty array'd,

With a tongue full of sweetness—a heart insincere,
And fixed her bright eyes on the chief of MacLean.
To toy with his heart, and bewilder his brain.

"And I, who was once the delight of his soul,
Ere she like a blight on my happiness stole,
Now wander through Duard, neglected and lorn,
Of a stranger the scoff—of my maidens the scorn;
With a grief in my bosom that gnaws at the core,
And a fire in my brain that will burn evermore:

"Unless thou wilt aid me with charm and with spell,
To gain back the heart I have cherish'd so well,
And rid me of her who with art the most vile
Has poison'd my peace with her glozing and guile—
I hate her with hatred intense as despair!
Yet murder's a guilt that my soul can not bear."

"Be calm, craven spirit! On me be the guilt.
No poison shall rack her, no blood shall be spilt.
Till my hair has turn'd gray, and my blood has
 grown thin,
I have dwelt on Ben Mor with the spirits of sin;
And have learn'd by their aid without weapons to
 kill,
And can blast by a look, and destroy by my will.

"Were the good ship, the Florida, far on the seas,
I'd whirl her and toss her, like chaff on the breeze,
And far on some cliff, where the storms ever roar,
And aid could not reach them, I'd drive them
 ashore;
And the wanton I'd seize by her long raven locks,
And drag her to death at the foot of the rocks.

"But safe from all danger of winds and of tides,
In calm Tobermory at anchor she rides;
But peril may come 'mid security deep,
And vengeance may wake when the world is
 asleep;
And strong though her timbers—her haven secure,
The hand of revenge, though unseen, shall be
 sure."

Serene was the night, and unruffled the bay,
Not a breath stirred the deep where the Florida lay;
Her broad azure pennant hung breezeless on high,
And her thin taper masts pointed clear to the sky;
And the moonlight that fell on the breast of the
 deep
Appear'd like the charm that had lull'd it to sleep.

The cabin-boy dream'd of the vineyards of Spain,
Or roam'd with a maiden at sunset again;
The sailor, in fancy, was dancing afar,
In his own native land, to his graceful guitar;
Or bless'd with a household, in sleep, was restored
To the children he loved, and the wife he adored.

The fair Spanish lady in visions was blest:
She dream'd that, escaped from the isles of the
 West,
Her young Highland chief had consented to roam
To her far Andalusia in search of a home;
That together they dwelt in her own sunny clime,
Where life was no effort, and love was not crime.

None dream'd of the danger that round them might
 lurk;
But in darkness and silence a spell was at work.
Conceal'd in the waters, at poop and at prow,
The agents of evil were busy below;
And noiseless their labor, but certain their stroke,
Through her strong copper'd hull, and her timbers
 of oak.

And long ere the morning, a loud sudden shriek
Was heard o'er the bay, "Sprung a leak! sprung a
 leak!"
Oh! then there was gathering in tumult and fear,
And a blanching of cheeks, as the peril grew near;
A screaming of women—a shouting of men,
And a rushing and trampling, again and again!

No time for leave-taking—no leisure to weep!
In roll'd the fierce waters, and down to the deep,
Down, down fifty fathoms, with captain and crew,
The Florida sank, with the haven in view—
Down, down to the bottom, escaping but one,
To tell the sad tale of the deed that was done.

And he, as he battled for life with the tide,
Beheld the fair lady of Spain by his side,
And a lank, skinny hand, that came up through
 the spray,
And twined in her tresses, as floating she lay,
And heard the loud laughter of fiends in the air,
As she sank 'mid the waves with a shriek of des-
 pair.

No. 14.—BURIAL OF SIR LACHLAN MÓR MACLEAN.

By Thomas Pattison.

[Thomas Pattison's mother was a MacLean, and in consequence he was much interested in the history of the clan. He studied for the Church of Scotland, but died young, a few years ago. By his own request his remains were brought back to Islay and buried in Kilarrow church-yard. The poem is taken from his *Gaelic Bards*.]

Slowly, from the field of slaughter,
 Do they bring Sir Lachlan Mór;
Slowly, o'er the weary moorland,
 From the damp and deadly shore.

Slowly, and in bitter sorrow,
 Through a rough and rugged way,
With the yellow beams upon it
 Of the sickly setting day.

Ah! how lowly lies the leader;
 See how pale his face is now;
Never in the hall or highway—
 Never on the mountain brow—

Shall his step be laid majestic;
 Shall his stately form be seen;
Shall his voice inspire the council,
 Or the fight his manly mien.

Never shall his clan behind him
 Gather in the joy of fight;
Never draw their cold blue weapons—
 Hard and deadly—glancing bright.

Poorly now's the chief attended,
 Rudely now the hero's led;
Yet he wakes not from the slumber
 Of yon red and mossy bed.

For the sad stamp's on his features
  Which Dubh Shee's hard arrow bore;
On the moor Clan Gillian reddened
  With their brave and boiling gore.

Only two are with the driver
  On a rolling, rocking car,
Stretch'd whereon the dead man's carried
  From the fiery field of war.

Two that walk in silent sorrow—
  Ladies of his kindred are—
Mourning, to the field of slaughter
  Come to seek him from afar.

As they drive him slowly onward,
  O'er the bad and broken way,
His head, with all its matted tresses,
  Nodded where he lifeless lay.

Then the driver laugh'd who saw him,
  Large and massy lie along,
Senseless, soulless—him so lately
  Foremost in the martial throng.

Laugh'd! and quicker drove him onward,
  Yet again to see the head
Nodding, without will or reason,
  With its light of manhood fled.

Nodding at the boor who jeered him
  With that mean, malicious scorn,
Nursed in secret by the envy
  In the vulgar spirit born.

Then the ladies hastened forward—
  Not a word the younger said,

While the tears rained down in anguish
  On the wan face of the dead.

But the elder damsel answered:
  "Laugh'st thou at my fallen chief?
May thy own vile carcass, caitiff,
  Fill thy mother's heart with grief!"

Out she drew the chieftain's dagger,
  As she hurled this angry cry
At the boor who gloomed before her,
  With his dull and threatening eye.

And she struck him down and left him
  Stretched beneath the sunbeams there,
Like a wild fowl by the falcon
  Swept from out the fields of air.

Then, alone, their dead they carried,
  While one nursed the manly brow—
Nursed it on her bosom gently,
  Like a holy, heavenly vow.

And one—tenderly she drove him
  To the sad and solemn ground,
Where the hero's dust reposes
  With the moldering ashes round.

Soft and slowly there we leave them—
  Chieftain! may thine ashes rest,
Peaceful as the voice of prayer
  From a calm, untroubled breast!

Long as sound the breezes o'er them,
  Sound the voice of psalms beside;
And spread Christ's peace-speaking gospel
  From thy green sod far and wide!

No. 15.—The Battle of Knockbreck.

[This poem is an English translation of a lost epic poem written in Latin, and called the Grameis. The original was composed by Phillipps of Amryscloss, a zealous Jacobite. This version is taken from *Account of Clan MacLean*.]

Meantime Lochbuie from the stormy isle
Of warlike Mull advanced to join Dundee;
Three hundred brave MacLeans composed his train,
A generous, loyal clan, whose faithful blood
Untainted filled his veins. Quick he marched along
The banks of Spey in silence of the night.
The royal camp unknown, a stranger he,
And unacquainted with the gloomy shade,
Upon a hostile troop of Belgic horse—
The advanced guard, whom he believed his friends—
Erroneous fell. "Stop!" the hoarse sentry bawled
In horrid Dutch, and straight upon them fired;
The rest alarmed, a thundering peal of shot
Discharged, and tore the air with fire and smoke.

The brave MacLeans their compliment returned,
And scattered flaming death among the foe.
Then forming in a wedge, their thickest lines
They pierced, and through the furious squadron broke
With sword in hand; nor halted they until
They gained a neighboring eminence, a rock,
Whose frowning top, among the clouds concealed,
Shewed all its battered sides with rugged stones
And fragments huge perplexed, and took its name
From blood which their impervious surface stained;
Where, as with ramparts fenced, secure they lodged,
superior to the foe.
Thither, in haste, and with collected strength of different lands,
Germans, Dutch, English, rebel Scots, and Danes,
The adverse troop pursue. Oft did they aim
With fire and sword to storm the rugged camp,
But all in vain. With spears, and darts, and stones,
And rocks, which tumbling down with hideous din,
O'erwhelm'd both horse and man, they headlong drove

Th' insulting foe; who with their mangled limbs,
And brains, and blood, the ragged flints besmeared.
Their leader, daring, haughty, fierce, and proud,
In war delighted, and with keenest rage
His foe pursued; Great Britain's southern shore
His boasted clime,—the English horse and rough
   Batavian troops
His stern command obeyed.
His shining neck a golden collar graced,
And from his shoulder hung a scarlet sash
O'er a purple robe, conspicuous far,
With golden lace and rich embroidery shone.
Enraged to see his baffled troops repelled,
And scatter'd 'mongst the rocks their mangled
   limbs,
He gnash'd his teeth, and mad with fury bawl'd
"Come down, ye thieves; ye barbarous crew descend,
And on the equal plain your courage prove,

Nor lurk behind those rocks, if ye be men."
Then, as if impelled by rage, of all delay
Impatient, furious he commands his troops
The precipice to gain and drive them down,
Or leave their batter'd carcasses a prey
To wolves and dogs, and fearless leads them on.
But, undismay'd, the brave MacLeans beheld
Th' audacious foe, and with firm hearts resolved
By manly deeds to answer boasting vain;
And, quick as thought, to his unerring eye
His thund'ring piece a warrior bold applied,
Whence, as from fate, a whizzing bullet flew,
With fire and sulpur wing'd, and at the mouth
Of the proud boaster ent'ring, pierced his lungs
With rapid force, and at his back
Its passage made. Down to the earth he fell,
And rolling round his languid eyes, his soul,
Forth issuing with his blood, dissolved in air.

No. 16.—MacLean's Welcome to Prince Charlie.

[This poem is from the Gaelic. It is here taken from Hogg's *Jacobite Relics*, second series, where it may be found set to music.]

Come o'er the stream, Charlie, dear Charlie, brave
   Charlie,
Come o'er the stream, Charlie, and dine with MacLean;
And though you be weary, we'll make your heart
   cheery,
And welcome our Charlie and his loyal train.
We'll bring down the track deer, we'll bring down
   the black steer,
The lamb from the breckan, the doe from the glen;
The salt sea we'll harry, and bring to our Charlie,
The cream from the brothy, and curd from the
   pen.

Come o'er the stream, Charlie, etc.
And you shall drink freely the dews of Glen Sheerly,
   That stream is the star-light when kings do not
   ken;

And deep be your meed of the wine that is red,
   To drink to your sire, and his friend the MacLean.

Come o'er the stream, Charlie, etc.
O'er heath-bells shall trace you the maids to embrace you,
   And deck your blue bonnet with flowers of the
   brae;
And the loveliest Mari in all Glen MacQuarrie
   Shall lie in your bosom till break of the day.

Come o'er the stream, Charlie, etc.
If aught will invite you, or more will delight you,
   'Tis ready, a troop of our bold Highland men
Shall range on the heather with bonnet and feather,
   Strong arms and broad claymores three hundred
   and ten.

No. 17.—Gathering of the Clan.
By Mary Ross.

[Miss Ross was a lady of rare accomplishments. She was born in Edinburgh. Her mother was Juliana, daughter of Gillean MacLean of Scallasdale. Miss Ross dedicated this ballad to the clan. The poem is taken from *Account Clan MacLean*. It is a ballad of the Forty-five.]

Banners are waving o'er Morvern's dark heath,
Claymores are flashing from many a sheath.
Hark! 'tis the gath'ring! On! onward! they cry;
Far flies the signal, "To conquer or die."
   Then follow thee! follow! a boat to the sea!
   Thy Prince in Glen Moidart is waiting for thee;
   Where war-pipes are sounding and banners are
   free;
   MacLean and his clansmen the foremost you'll see.

Wildly the war-cry has startled yon stag,
And waken'd the echoes of Gillean's lone crag;
Up hill and down glen each brave mountaineer
Has belted his plaid and mounted his spear.
   Then follow thee! follow! etc.

The signal is heard from mountain to shore.
They rush like the flood o'er dark Corry-Vohr;
The war-note is sounding loud, wildly, and high;
Louder they shout, "On! to conquer or die."
   Then follow thee! follow! etc.

The heath-bell at morn so proudly ye trod,
Son of the mountain, now covers thy sod;
Wrapt in your plaid, 'mid the bravest ye lie;
The words as ye fell, still to conquer or die!
   Then follow thee! follow! a boat to the sea!
   Thy Prince in Glen Moidart is waiting for thee;
   Where war-pipes are sounding and banners are
   free;
   MacLean and his clansmen the foremost you'll see

No. 18.—THE ISLE OF INCH KENNETH.

BY DR. SAMUEL JOHNSON.

[Dr. Johnson, the noted English philosopher and writer, was born in 1709, and died in 1784. The Sunday he passed on Inch Kenneth made such an impression on his mind that he afterward wrote in Latin a sonnet called "Insula Sancti Kennethi." Afterward, he made various alterations in it. It may be said to have been dedicated to the amiable Sir Allan MacLean and his accomplished daughters. It was translated into English by Sir Daniel K. Sandford, formerly professor of Greek in the University of Glasgow. The original Latin and the English version may be found in Boswell's *Tour to the Hebrides*.]

Scarce spied amidst the west sea foam,
Yet once religion's chosen home,
Appears the isle whose savage race
By Kenneth's voice was won to grace.
O'er glassy tides I thither flew,
The wonders of the spot to view;
In lonely cottage great MacLean
Held his high ancestral reign,
With daughters fair, whom love might deem
The Naiads of the ocean stream;
Yet not in chilly cavern rude
Were they, like Danube's lawless brood,
But all that charms a polished age,
The tuneful lyre, the learned page,

Combined to beautify and bless
That life of ease and loneliness.
Now dawned the day whose holy light
Puts human hopes and cares to flight,
Nor mid the hoarse waves' circling swell
Did Worship here forget to dwell.
What though beneath a woman's hand
The sacred volume's leaves expand,
No need of priestly sanction there,
The sinless heart makes holy prayer!
Then wherefore further seek to rove,
While here is all our hearts approve—
Repose, security, and love?

No. 19.—A LAY OF CLAN MACLEAN.

[This poem was furnished me by Mrs. Helen MacLean Wotherspoon of the city of New York, accompanied by the following note: "I send you a copy of some poetry that was read at the birthday dinner of Herr MacLean in Berlin some years ago. This Herr MacLean held a very important position in the German government, and was much esteemed while he lived. I do not know who wrote the poetry. It was received at the dinner with enthusiasm." It reached me too late for insertion in the proper place.]

PROLOGUE.

With pen and ink and eke pen-wiper,
  A clerk would fain indite a song;
He would he were a Highland piper,
  To blow a bagpipe loud and long.

About the Clan MacLean of Duard,
  The Archies, Lachlans, Hughs and Johns;
As good a clan as royal Stuart,
  And better than the German "Vons."

The clerk himself is come of Japhet,
  Though neither "Mac" nor "Von" he be.
In ancestry there's naught to laugh at;
  Who mocks, no grandfather had he!

The men who venerate their fathers,
  Desire their sons should do the same,
'Tis thus a race its essence gathers,
  'Tis thus ennobled is a name!

SONG.

The Isles that stud the stormy waters
  Of Caledonia's rugged strands,
Send warlike sons and gentle daughters
  To brace the blood of tamer lands.

They leave the islands of the far West,
  The cradle of the iron Gaël—
For scanty is the Highland harvest,
  Too many mouths—too little kale.

No purple grapes, but oats and barley
  Give nerve and blood to the MacLeans,
Yet loyal blood that flowed for Charlie
  Still circles in their children's veins.

Their fathers supped oatmeal and whisky,
  Their beds were made of fragrant heath,
Their heads were cool, their legs were frisky,
  Their hearts like fires the plaids beneath.

Their limbs were free in nature's leather,
　As Greeks rejoiced their gods to mold;
The Phrygian cap with eagle's feather
　Adorned the head and braved the cold.

The kilt! the tunic of the Roman!
　The plaid, the drapery of the Greek!
When were such sons of mortal woman,
　Whose very dress had tongues to speak?

Heroic men in vain one preaches—
　The prosy race of moderns find
'Tis decenter to wear the breeches,
　A tile, and coat with tails behind.

But fancy Staffa's glorious columns
　Draped with the creepers of Sulu!
A Highlander in what d'ye call ems,
　The things his fathers never knew.

But never mind, you'll always find him
　As warm in heart as leal in bone—
He graced the kilt he leaves behind him,
　He honors what he now puts on.

They leave the land of sombre beauty
　Of mountains, rock and sandy shore,
But full of love, of faith, and duty,
　Where ere they go they love it more.

Dear land, tho' o'er thy hills, the heaven
　May lack Morea's lustrous skies
To thee a freedom has been given
　Which in yon dazzling climate dies.

As these gray hills of rock and heather
　Draw down the clouds in misty rain,
So draw them by a mystic tether,
　The exiled Highland heart again.

Their memory warms at old tradition
　Of Mull, and Coll, and dark Lismore,
Old Fingal deeds, Columba's mission,
　The Duard towns, and Aros shore.

How proud are they of clannish tartan!
　How dear to them the bonnet blue!
The Gaëls' descendants set their heart on
　The colors of their fathers true.

In later, as in older story
　Of battle-field, the Clan MacLean
Has borne a greater share of glory
　Than tamer races of the plain.

Schooled as of old the warrior Spartan,
　To live and die for home and fame,
With steel, in blood, these men in tartan
　On honor's shield have graved a name.

In war, MacLean is brave in battle!
　In peace, a credit to his clan!
In office, trade, or feeding cattle,
　In love, or friendship, he's your man.

Then blow the pibroch o'er the waters
　We'll dance a reel with might and main,
Long live the name, the sons, and daughters,
　At home, abroad, of Clan MacLean!

No. 20.—COURTSHIP OF HECTOR MACLEAN.
By WILLIAM ALLAN.

[William Allan was born in Dundee in 1837. He resides in Sunderland, England. He has published two volumes of poetry. The following poem was originally published in the *Celtic Magazine*, entitled the "Doom of Dunolly." It is here taken from his volume of poems entitled *Rose and Thistle*. In sending permission to insert the poem with accompanying cut, Mr. Allan also added: "I had no direct foundation for the plot. Being at Oban one summer for a holiday, I was one day lying amid the ruins of Dunolly Castle, musing on the departed glory of the MacDougalls. Duard Castle loomed away in the distance on the Mull shore; so I mentally planned the poem, and worked it out as you have it.]

I.

The night clouds are falling,
　The curlew is calling,
Maid of Dunolly I come unto thee!
The grey mists are sleeping
　On Cruachan Ben,
The red deer are keeping
　Their watch in the glen—
Light of my darkness, come! come unto me:
　Come, gentle spirit! we part and forever,
Come, my lone star, see! my skiff's in the bay;
　Sunbeam of morning, alas! we must sever,
Maid of Dunolly! we part, and for aye.

The past I shall cherish,
My love can not perish,
Maid of Dunolly, oh! why did we love?
The wrath of thy father
　Is winter's cold breath,
Around me fast gather
　Weird visions of death;
Soul of my dreamings! thy home is above.
Come drooping floweret, I've dared thy brave kinsmen,
　Come lonely dove to thy warrior true;
Shadow of heaven! and pride of thy clansmen,
　My heart goes to thee in my lingering adieu!

Ere died the echoes of the lay,
An oar-song swept across the bay;
Ere turned the youth his skiff to reach,
Swift footsteps ran along the beach:
Before him came MacDougalls dread,
Returning from an island raid;
Behind him came MacDougalls wild,
Aroused to guard their chieftain's child.
Their startling yells of rage were flung,
And back from grey Dunolly rung.
The oarsmen heard the well-known cry,
And fiercer far pealed their reply;
Their stalwart arms out sternward went,
Their lithe backs forward lowly bent,
To simultaneous motion prone,
Their oars arose and fell as one.
Impelled with danger's vigor new,
Swift o'er the bay each galley flew;
Like arrows shot from full-drawn bows,
On sped the billow-cleaving prows,
Till driven on the shingle nigh,
The oaken keels arose on high.
With sudden bound unto the shore,
Each clansman leapt with drawn claymore,
Bare-armed, unbonneted they ran,
To join the members of their clan
Ranged round a stalwart youth, who stood
Bold-fronted 'mid the savage brood.
At every point the thirsty brands
Around him flashed in angry hands.
With eagle eye, and undismayed,
The stranger drew his trusty blade,
And tighter grasped his studded shield,
And firmer stood upon the field,
And watchful as a wolf at bay,
His lightning eye did them survey;
Nor quailed, nor flinched, tho' well he saw
The gathering horde still closer draw.
No coward heart within him beat,
Nor sought he safety in retreat;
Unequal tho' the contest seemed,
Defiance on his features gleamed.
One hurried glance he flung above,
Where dwelt the maiden of his love—
A pale face from a window peered,
A sigh upon the wind careered,
A whisper trembled in the air,
As if an angel breathed a prayer.—
Undaunted all, and scorning death,
He faced his foes and held his breath,
With back against King Fingal's rock
He boldly met their onset shock,
And flung his haughty looks of scorn
Upon MacDougall, Chief of Lorn.

II.

O! Isles of the West, lovely Isles of the West,
As emeralds set in the blue ocean's breast,
The birth-place of clansmen war-nurtured and brave,
The home where the tempest king rides on the wave,
Where thunders roll on in their terrible might,
And keen lightnings dance on each peak with delight;
Where Morning's dawn-rays o'er the mountain-crests run,
And gloaming descends as a sigh from the sun;
Where pale ghosts career on the mist-shrouded hills,
And heard are their wails in the songs of the rills;
Where beauty is shrined in each lone, grassy vale,
And wee flowerets laugh to the voice of the gale;
Where unfettered peace as a heaven presides,
And Nature's sweet loveliness ever abides;
Where maidens and youths, round their dim cottage fires,
Exultingly tell of the deeds of their sires;
Or sing with emotion the grand battle lays
Of heroes who fought in the far-away days
For king and for chieftain, for honor and love,
For aught that would valor or dignity prove.
O! Isles of the West, ever bosomed in song,
My Highland harp whispers—the sound I'll prolong;
Speak on! my dear harp; list! it trembles again,
Its theme—The MacDougall and dauntless MacLean!

The sun-rays had fled from the mountains of Lorn,
And kissed the cloud peaks looming jagged and riven,
That westward were trailing as wanderers forlorn
Upon the broad heaths of the night-tinted heaven.
Peace clothed the green valleys, the hills, and the isles,
The strange sounds of silence seemed wondrously clear—

Unbroken, save when, with his chase-laden spoils,
Arose the loud shout of a brave mountaineer,
Which woke the weird echoes of corrie and cave,
And startled the lord of the clouds in his dreams,
Who raised his proud head and defiantly gave
His fierce challenge back in his shrill-sounding screams.
The distant bell-notes slowly rung from Lismore,
And fluttered with joy o'er the fast-ebbing tide
Which bore them with love unto Morvern's far shore,
Where 'mid its blue mountains they whispered and died.
Sweet o'er the dark waters the vesper hymn stole,
In cadences kissed by the gloaming's soft breath;
Monks poured their orisons, with joy-dwelling soul,
And hied to their cells in the fullness of faith.—
Who knelt with the Abbot? Who joined in his prayer?
Whose voice in devotion fell soft as a sigh?
MacDougall's fair daughter was worshiping there!
MacDougall's fair daughter was heard in reply.
Why lingered she thus as the sun-rays depart?
Dunolly was far! and the dark sea her path;
What recked she! she bore in her bosom a heart
That feared not the swift-rushing tide in its wrath—
A child of the forest, a child of the chase,
Accustomed to danger, to hardship inured;
Descended from chiefs of a warrior race,
Whose titles and acres were held by the sword.
The blood of the valiant flowed pure in her veins,
She loved to behold the brave clansmen in arms,
The bright, flashing steel, and the pibroch's wild strains,
Gave light to her dark eyes and grace to her charms.

Tho' nurtured 'mid war's stirring clangor and din,
Her heart was a woman's in all which endears;
The fountain of tenderness welling within,
For children had smiles, for the dying had tears.
Her dark-flowing locks hung unfettered and free,
And waved in the wind as a banner love-driven;
Her brow, gently kissed by the sun in his glee,
Reflected the beauty of summer-fraught heaven;
Her eye-brows as fringes of darkness arose,
In soft, glossy silkiness fading to naught,
While 'neath their love-shadows, in tender repose,
Her dreamy eyes rippled in soul-light of thought,
Which brightly illumined her features, and lent
Ineffable witchery to the sweet smiles
Oft throned on her lips, with a gracefulness meant
To beautify Nature's pure innocent wiles.
In symmetry faultless, in tartan arrayed,
She moved as a sylph in her artless attire;
When heard were the songs of Dunolly's fair maid,
The clansmen wept great tears of grief, joy, or ire.—
The grey-headed Abbot stalked down to the shore,
And blest the young maiden, and bade her adieu;
She launched her light skiff, waved her hand, seized the oar,
Then off with the tide for Dunolly she flew.

III.

Away, and away! with the speed of the wind,
Each headland, each creek, and each cranny she knew;
Lismore's verdant island was left far behind,
And distant Dunolly loomed darkly in view.
The tide-rush of Etive she battled with might,
'Twas vain! to the westward she swiftly was hurled,
Strong eddies, wild sweeping, hissed hoarse with delight;
As oft her frail skiff in their vortex was whirled.*

---

* Under certain conditions of the wind, the ebb from Loch Etive is irresistible. The phenomenon of a tidal *bore* is often seen here. It is supposed to be the "roaring Lora" of Ossian.

Undaunted and tireless she pulled at the oars,
　Undaunted and fearless the breakers' deep song
She heard, 'mid Kerrera's wild, treacherous shores,
　But watchful and wary she darted along.
She saw with dismay that Dunolly she passed,
　She saw its dark tower swiftly gliding astern;
As gloaming gave place to night's darkness at last,
　The landmarks, erst known, she could dimly discern.—
The lone herald star of the evening appeared,
　In pale, silvern modesty's beauty serene;
While down in the east o'er the cloud edges peered
　The halo that ushered Night's full-beaming Queen;
Then leapt every star from its holy repose,
　As choristers sweet in the heavens above
Their bright, joyous anthems of glory arose
　In soft, trembling beauty, in homage of love.
On, on! and still on! to the westward she sped,
　And cold-dawning fear filled her bosom with awe—
That awe which unnerves us and fills us with dread,
　And makes us poor slaves to its pitiless law.
The night mists descended from lofty Ben More,
　And rolled as a cloud on the breast of the deep.
Weird sounds rose anon—now behind, now before,
　And floating sea-gulls wildly screamed in their sleep.
The conflict of currents hissed loud to the skies,
　And heightened the waves that in anger arose
Around her frail skiff, their wan, death-gleaming eyes
　Oft peered at the maiden and laughed at her woes.
The terror of death filled her soul with despair,
　She trembled and wept as a motherless child;
She gazed to the heavens, she shrieked a heart-prayer
　In accents of agony fearfully wild.
Hark! hark! .o'er the deep came a sound; could it be
　Her prayer was answered? that succor was nigh?
The harsh creak of oars on the mist-laden sea
　Came nearer! came clearer! and filled her with joy.
A voice from the darkness was heard! she replied,—
　The moments seemed hours that would ne'er have an end;
She marked through the mist a boat's faint shadow glide,
　And heard the "Halloo!" of a fast-nearing friend.
Invisible hands flung unerring a rope,
　Its swift-gliding folds seemed the answer she craved,
'Twas clutched with the frenzy of fast-dying hope,
　And consciousness fled as the maiden was saved!
MacDougall's grim chieftain was restless this night,
　He stood on his ramparts, he watched, and he mourned;
His henchman and clansmen, with fleet-footed might,
　Had sought her afar, but despairing returned:
They sought her in chamber, they sought her in cot,
　They searched Etive's shore, they scoured valley and heath;
Their slogan pealed far, but an answer came not,
　And filled was each breast with forebodings of death.
MacDougall's grim chieftain stalked thro' his lone halls,
　Despair's moody silence o'ershadowed his face,
The voice of the night-wind in ominous calls
　Seemed chanting a dirge for the doom of his race.
He started, he wept, then he laughed, then he scowled,
　Then sullenly motionless stood on the floor,
And quivered with terror as dismally howled
　The stag hound that kept his night-watch at the door.
Mysterious footsteps he heard as they moved,
　Strange beings appeared but to vanish again;
Ah! little he knew that the daughter he loved
　Was safe in the halls of his foe, the MacLean!

IV.

There was a time, a long, long time ago,
When Duard's halls resounded to the flow
Of minstrel harmony, of dance, and song,
Of mirth, and glee, from clansmen old and young;
When Duard's chief could muster at his word
A thousand doughty champions of the sword,
A thousand plaided men whose only faith
Was—Love the chief, and fear no foe or death.
No other aspirations filled them then,
Save to be reckoned as heroic men;
Their hearts were fraught with burning warlike zeal,
Their frames were iron and their sinews steel.
On simple fare as hardy men they grew,
Nor luxury's effeminacy knew;
Their cots and fields were theirs, rude comfort reigned,
They felt not want, and healthful years maintained.
They loved their chief for honor and for name,
And freely shed their blood to guard his fame.
The chief loved them with patriarchal care,
Knew all their sorrows, heard each plaint or prayer,
And, as a father 'mid his children dear,
He lived beloved, and honored without fear.
Untainted thus, with no ambition's pride,
In Nature's happiness they lived and died.
See Duard now! its shapeless ruins gloom
In the sad grandeur of a shivered tomb.
Time's silent chisels have fell havoc spread,
A wreck is here, cold, desolate, and dead.
The moaning sea around the headland sweeps,
And o'er the rocks in fretful surges leaps,
Or wanders mournfully around the bay,
Where oft the black-prowed oaken galleys lay;
The eerie wind within the ruin raves,
And shrilly whistles o'er the warriors' graves;
The grasses bend 'neath the uncertain blast,
As Nature's mourners for a glorious past.
No sound is heard, no wandering footstep seen,
Decay's weird silence lords it o'er the scene;
The night bats dart from out the chinky walls,
And ghostly owlets own the roofless halls;
The gloomy spirits of a valiant race
Seem stalking ever round the lonely place,
Or 'neath the full moon's wan, unearthly light,
Seem mustering as of yore for raid or fight,
Unto the mournful pibroch of the wind,
That dies, and leaves a deeper hush behind.

'Twas here the Hector of my tale
Drew his first breath, and poured his infant wail;
Here his young lips drew with a lover's zest
His future valor from his mother's breast;
Here his young eyes beheld with fond delight
The shining, steely panoply of fight.
His chubby hands oft vigorously essayed
To lift, with shouts, the old paternal blade.
A dirk and shield were his infantile toys,
Their rattling din the source of childish joys.
The ancient dame, endowed with second-sight,
Foretold his future as a chief of might;
The hoary bards would on him wondering gaze,
And croon to him their stirring battle lays;
The smiling clansmen would, with loving scan,
Applaud the antics that bespoke the man,
And gathering round their fair-haired future lord,
They taught him early how to wield a sword,
And bend a bow with steady hand and eye,
Until the shafts would all unerring fly;
To scale the rugged heights devoid of fear,
And track with wary steps the watchful deer;
To pull an oar, or tend a shortened sail,
When burst the fury of a sudden gale.
Beneath tuition such as this he grew,
Skilled in the various arts the clansmen knew,
Till daring Hector stood unmatched at length,
For feats of arms, agility, and strength.
The wolf that roamed the shores of Golla Dhu,
He tracked unto his lair and singly slew.
He fought the eagle on the giddy crest,
And conquering, bore the eaglets from their nest;
The prowling foe, on sudden, nightly raid,
Was vanquished oft beneath his foremost blade;
In skirmishes upon the mainland shore,
His skillful prowess oft the victory bore;
His doughty deeds were whispered far and wide,
And bards and maidens sang of them with pride,
Till 'mid the Isles his warlike name was spread,
And foemen feared the men by Hector led.
Proud was the father of his chief-like boy,
The gentle mother's only hope and joy;
His well-knit frame of perfect, manly mold,
At once the leader and the warrior told.
A calm determination lit his face,
And gave his mien an awe-commanding grace;

In judgment cool, in wary caution skilled,
His looks and gestures confidence instilled;
His eye, in peace, beamed with a kindly glow,
But fiercely flashed when told a tale of woe;
The heart that beat within his tartaned breast
Was swift to help the weak or the oppressed.
Untouched as yet by Love's absorbing flame,
It felt not aught save the parental claim,
As 'mid his clansmen's homes he freely roved,
The maidens gazed, and as they gazed they
    loved.
Thus Hector lived, and spent his youthful
    years,
A lordly prince amid his mountaineers;
By all who knew him loved, adored, revered,
By every foeman in encounter feared.—
Not so his hereditary foe,
MacDougall's chief, who longed his hate to
    show;
Incensed to hear of Hector's rising fame,
His breast was filled with jealousy and shame.
Long in the west as Lorn's unconquered lord,
He awed the chieftains by his cruel sword:
In raid or foray, or in deeds of blood,
His wild and lawless clan the foremost stood;
Nor could he brook to know some chiefs had
    sued
Alliance with the clan he had subdued.
To guard his power, which seemed upon the
    wane,
His dark heart planned a conflict with Mac-
    Lean.

V.

The full-browed moon leapt from her shrouds,
Leaving behind the darkening clouds,
And flung o'er mountains, hills, and braes,
The softened splendor of her rays;
O'er Cruachan Ben they nimbly crept,
On dark Loch Awe they gently slept,
And westward far she sent her smiles,
Till silver-bathed appeared the Isles.
The moon was up! then wide and far
Arose MacDougall's cry of war;
From Etive's shore, from sweet Bonaw,
To Kilninver and gray Kintraw;
It wildly pealed on Avich's side,
Dalmally and Kilchurn replied,
And gloomy Brander's echoes rung,
As speedy clansmen rushed along
Thro' tangled brake, o'er stretching heath,
And poured their startling cry of death,
Which summoned from each distant cot
The clansmen to the mustering spot.
Ere reached the moon her half-way mark,
From mountain-side, from gorges dark,
From heath, from hill, from every glen,
Rushed forth full-armed, stout, plaided men,
Whose distant forms were oft revealed
As flashed the moonbeams on each shield;
Obedient to the call they flew,
Nor aught of toil or fear they knew.
As singly some careered along,
They lowly hummed a battle song,
The distance lessening 'neath the lay,
Which cheered them on their lonely way,
Till on Dunolly's tower they gazed,
Upon whose northern walls still blazed
The beacon's fitful, lurid light,
Betokening danger, foes, or fight.
Around the walls were gathered then,
Two hundred of MacDougal's men,
Wild, unkempt, shaggy warriors grim,
Broad-chested, strong in arm and limb;
From youth to ceaseless warfare trained,
A terror far their names remained;
Before their chief in armed array,
The horde stood ready for the fray.
"Swift, to the galleys, swift!" he cried,
"We must away ere falls the tide."
Ten oaken, broad-beamed galleys lay,
Rocked with the tide, in Oban's bay,
Now from their moorings soon they danced,
As oars upon the waters glanced.
And 'neath their chieftain's eye and word,
The clansmen nimbly sprang on board,
Four brawny arms seized every oar,
And soon the fast receding shore
Was left behind, and fainter grew,
As past Kerrera's isle they flew.
MacDougall led; the course was west;
In whispers low his clansmen guessed
That, ere the morning sun arose,
Their swords would smite some island foes—
As huntsmen steal with caution near
The browsing, unsuspecting deer,
As wild-cats crouch and trailing creep,
Before they make their deadly leap,
As eagles circle in the sky
Ere on their prey they downward fly,
So stealthily the waters o'er,
MacDougall neared the hazy shore,
Where Duard's keep, hushed in repose,
In frowning grandeur looming rose.
Calm, standing on his galley's prow,
With anxious glance and cloudy brow,
The chieftain led the dubious way,
And sought the sheltered, western bay,
Whose shelving shore gave footing meet
For landing, or for safe retreat.
Tho' steering in the hazy band

Which hugged the confines of the land,
He cleared the rocks that girt the shores,
And Duard passed with muffled oars.
Ah! wot he not the warder there,
Skilled in the night sounds of the air,
Had heard with ready, well-trained ear,
Oar-echoes softly stealing near,
Which all too measured, faint, and slow,
Betokened some advancing foe?
Quick from the ramparts, quick, he sped,
And roused young Hector from his bed—
"Up, Hector, up! a foe is near,
Their galleys 'neath the walls appear;
Arm! arm! they seek the bay,
Their coming brooks of no delay."
Up from his couch bold Hector leapt,
And o'er his startled countenance crept
A smile of joy, which seemed to show
His readiness to meet the foe.
"Wake, Malcolm, our retainers all,
Who slumber in the banquet hall,
Then speed thee on, ere dawns the day,
To Auchnacross and Torosay;
Away! away! rouse every man
Who owes allegiance to our clan;
With lightning footsteps tireless go,
We must and shall repel this foe!"—
Devoid of bonnet, hose, or plaid,
He snatched his shield and glittering blade;
With eye that flashed red battle-fire,
And step that told of rising ire,
With lips compressed till void of blood,
He sought the hall where ready stood
Scarce thirty stalwart clansmen leal,
Whose hearts and arms were like their steel.
"No sound! no word! Men, follow me,
A foe comes on us from the sea;
The lark pipes now its morning strains;
Come on! it rouses the MacLeans!"

VI.

The morn was calm; bright in the east afar,
As a lone sentinel, the morning star
Glimmered its welcomes in the deep-hued blue,
As o'er the high-banked clouds the monarch threw
His scepter-gleams of living, glowing gold
Which vanquished Night, and, space illuming, rolled
In all the grandeur of a conqueror's might;
Whose path is victory, whose throne is light.
The sullen shadows fled from mountain-crests,
And scowling sought the gorges in their breasts,
Their lingering footsteps in the trailing mist,

The airy smiles of light with fondness kissed,
Till grandly lone, with broad, uncovered brows,
As hoary worshipers each mountain rose.
The wonder-chorus of each stream was heard,
And joyous trillings rose from every bird.
Adown each glen the messengers of dawn
Danced merrily o'er forest, heath, and lawn,
Swift o'er the heaving bosom of the sea
They lightly flew with love-inspiring glee,
And kissed the pale lips of the wavelets cold,
Till gleamed their foam-flowers with the hues of gold;
They wooed the haze, that wrapt the slumbering isles,
Which gently rose beneath their chastening wiles,
But ere it faded from the shores away,
The sounds of battle burst in Duard's bay.
MacDougall led the van, and well had steered
Into the bay, where on each side appeared
Brown, sea-washed rocks, whose unseen, stretching arms
Broke the wild fury of the northern storms.
Thus guarded from the ocean's wildest rage,
It gave a safe and sheltered anchorage.
His ready henchman, with inverted spear,
Probed the still depths, and found the shore was near,
Then passed a whispered signal to each crew;
To right and left the boats in order drew,
With silent skill the oars were placed on board,
And every clansman seized his shield and sword.
In line abreast the galleys forward went,
As, from the stern, they shorewards swift were sent;
No word was uttered, and arose no sound,
Save when the hard keels creaked upon the ground.
The chieftain first leapt nimbly on the sand,
Then followed fast his fierce and warlike band.
The shore was still, no foe their landing barred,
No Hector stood his island home to guard,
No clansmen rushed impetuous to th' attack,
To drive with might the wild invaders back.
Where! where is Hector's deathful arm and blade?
Where! where has valiant Hector's prowess waned?
Alas! has valiant Hector's prowess waned?
His foes, unchallenged, have a footing gained.
Hark! hark! now pealed an agonizing yell,
As in the sea MacDougall's henchman fell,
Pierced by an arrow that still quivering swayed

Within the wound its brazen point had made.
Again! again! again! with deadly aim,
The messengers of death loud whizzing came
From daring men unseen amid the haze,
Who crouched with Hector on the furzy braes.
The feathered shafts from full-drawn bows were sprung
And 'mid the startled foes their challenge flung;
Brave warriors fell, and writhed upon the sands,
And wildly drew the barb with dying hands;
Yea, vainly strove in agony to stay
The pulsing stream of life which ebbed away;
And sodden sands the hot blood greedy drank,
Staining the spot wherein it bubbling sank;
Full well MacDougall knew, without dismay,
That Hector and his men around him lay!
Oblivious to the thickening, arrowy storm,
His looks betrayed no fear nor dire alarm,
His ringing voice its chief-like orders gave,
Which cheered the heart of each desponding brave—
"Down! down, men! down, until the fading haze
Flies from MacLean's safe ambush on the braes."
Obedient all, they sank upon the shore,
And o'er their heads their shields aloft they bore,
Against whose sloping fronts the arrows rung,
And curving, far into the ocean sprung.
Then Hector knew, as clear that voice was borne,
His foeman was MacDougall, Chief of Lorn;
Undaunted, undismayed, yea, rather glad
To measure swords with one who ofttimes had
In other years with devastation dire
Ravaged the lands and clansmen of his sire;
Outnumbered now, no rash onslaught he tried,
His skillful tactics numbers well supplied.
The dread confusion of attack on flanks
He early learned, and on the grassy banks
He placed his little but determined force
In two divisions 'mid the sheltering gorse,
Where, leading steeply downward to the bay,
The rugged, bouldered path between them lay,
Which thus commanding, with advantage great,
Their foemen's charge they anxiously did wait;
Nor waited long, for, as the sun arose,
The haze evanished, and they saw their foes.
Now as the dark tide-wave on Etive's shores
Rears its high crest and forward rolling roars,
Or as a pent-up spate, with mighty force,

Rushes upon its broad, resistless course,
So rose MacDougall's men, and forward dashed,
And brightly in the sun their weapons flashed,
Swift-footed o'er the sands with yelling wrath,
They sought the only upward-tending path;
O'er rocks and stones disorderly they flew,
And to the ridge in breathless hurry drew.
MacDougall led them on, and upward pressed,
To reach the gap upon the grassy crest;
Unswerving, unfatigued, he scaled the height,
And gazed around, but saw no foe to fight.
When suddenly from out each shady bush
The valiant Hector and his men did rush,
And loud arose their startling battle-yell,
As on the clambering foe they fiercely fell,
Who staggering, beheld the maddening grief,
MacLeans between them and their warrior chief.
Swords rung on swords, fire flashed from every blow,
Blood rushed in streams unto the sands below;
Forward, and forward still, MacDougalls rushed,
The foremost fell, to be by kinsmen crushed.
Upon the quivering corses of the slain,
They fighting came, and strove the ridge to gain,
But as a compact phalanx stood their foes,
Who mercilessly showered their deadly blows,
Which crashing clave each high-raised shining shield,
And smote the man beneath, who downward reeled.
Still on they came, in wild despairing might,
Unyielding stood the braves who held the height;
Not all MacDougall's warlike numbers now
Could backward drive the thirty from that brow,
Who spoke not, quailed not, but resolved to give
Their dearest blood for liberty to live.

VII.

MacDougall's chieftain-breast with anger burned,
And swiftly on the foe he fiercely turned,
But ere he could his sudden stroke bestow,
A readier sword met the descending blow.
'Twas nimble Hector's, on whose features played
A smile of triumph, as he quickly weighed
The issues of a fight with Lorn's dread lord,
Who now had raised his yet untarnished sword,

And backward drew a pace, then scowling
   glared
Upon the half-clad youth who thus had dared
To thwart his onset, and to turn aside
The blade which had the royal Bruce defied.*
With sudden bound he on the stripling
   dashed,
Whose quicker weapon like a sunbeam flashed,
And kissed with joy MacDougall's baffled
   steel,
Which now, for once, an equal match did feel.
His groaning clansmen roused his ireful heart,
Again on Hector did he fiercely dart,
To be repelled with skillful blow or guard,
And backward hurled upon the dewy sward.
Ill could he brook defiance thus disclosed,
And with the youth in deadly conflict closed;
Now rung their blows upon each guardian
   shield,
And rugged dents their angry might revealed.
With equal skill the contest wildly raged,
Each knew a worthy foe he had engaged,
Tho' round them played the steely gleams of
   death,
They thrust and struck with unabated breath.
Each lightning eye was fixed, each sparkling
   gleamed,
Each marked the point where an advantage
   seemed,
And as each willing blade the opening sought,
The sudden guard made sudden efforts nought;
And victory, wavering 'tween such sons of
   fame,
Withheld the laurels that each well could
   claim;
Till youthful Hector's unabated strengh
Proclaimed him victor in the fight at length,
For fast MacDougall's furious ire decayed,
And feeble blows his waning pow'rs betrayed—
Pale grew his face, his watchful eyes grew dim,
Less swift to guard, he shook in every limb,
Fast heaved his breast with ever lessening
   breath
And as he struck he reeled upon the heath—
Defeat's dark demon raged within him now,
Its withering shade sat scowling on his brow,
And fanned the feeble flame of hope in vain,
Which mocked the hero as his strength did
   wane;
But Hector, tireless still, the conflict sought,

And by a subtle cut MacDougall smote
Upon the sword arm, which all pow'rless
   hung,
Then fell the blade which he in valor swung;
Triumphant o'er his foe young Hector stood,
Nor sought he now to shed defenseless blood.
"Yield thee, MacDougall, yield!" he hoarsely
   cried.
"And who art thou, bold youth?" the chief
   replied.
"Hector MacLean, of an illustrious line!
Yield thee, MacDougall, now thy life is mine;
Behold thy clansmen unto these succumb,
To foil aggression, see, our kinsmen come!
Back to their galleys now thy men will be
Driven with the vengeance born of victory!"
Now rushed MacLeans along the grassy fileds,
And loudly struck their swords upon their
   shields,
With wild impetuosity they sought
The ridge whereon their dauntless kinsmen
   fought,
Nor checked their speed, but thro' the thin
   rank dashed,
And on the foe with headlong fury crashed,
Who, baffled, fled across the sands, and sought
Safety on board their galleys still afloat.
Out from the bay with terror's speed they
   drew,
While in their midst thick showers of arrows
   flew;
Eastward they sped, with favoring tide and
   wind,
And left their wounded and their chief behind,
Who, 'midst a throng of savage Islesmen stood
Unmoved, although they clamored for his
   blood.
Now Hector spoke, and hushed was every
   voice—
"Clansmen, MacDougall's fate must be my
   choice;
No deed of wanton blood shall stain our name,
Unsullied victory is our highest fame.
Whoe'er the foe, whate'er the battle-cause,
We triumph best when ruled by honor's laws;
MacDougall's chief, thy life I now bestow,
Back to Dunolly, vanquished, thou must go;
Be thou the bearer of thy wounded men,
And war no more unjustly 'gainst MacLean."
The generous impulse stilled the angry band,

---

* The MacDougalls defeated Bruce in the battle of Dalree, at the head of Loch Tay. One of the MacDougalls seized the king by the plaid, which was fixed across his breast by a large brooch. The king killed his assailant, but left the plaid and brooch in the grasp of the clansman. His brooch was long kept in the family of the MacDougalls.

Who loved the virtue in their chief's com-
    mand;
With tender grasp the dying and the dead
Within the galley of the chief were laid,
The wounded next fraternal care received—
Such love from foes their hearts had ne'er
    conceived.
Now ready all, between the conquering clan
MacDougall marched, a stern and gloomy man,
And as he, frowning, slowly stepped on board,
Hector, with princely grace, returned his sword.
The proffered gift with haughty grasp he took,
And thanked the donor with a threatening
    look;
Then, as the blood-fraught galley seaward
    drew,
He kissed the blade, and waved its dark adieu!
Undying hatred, and revenge combined,
Stood warders at the portals of his mind,
And filled his heart with their demoniac fire,
Till the strange madness of their one desire
Reigned as the lord of his embittered life,
And chained him slaved unto its fearful strife—
The visions of his hate-disturbed brain
Were bloody specters muttering "MacLean!"
In horror's dreams he saw a ghastly train,
Which, passing, whispered in his ear, "Mac-
    Lean!"
Lone on Dunolly's ramparts every day
His restless eyes were fixed on Duard's bay;
No light of joy illumined his vengeful state,
His life was now unfathomable hate.
His lovely daughter's smiles had lost their
    charm,
Her soothing voice no more his heart could
    warm,
Her constant fondnesses, her tears, her sighs,
Changed not the fierce gleam of his loveless
    eyes,
MacDougall dreamt not that ere long her love
Would of his conqueror the conq'ror prove—
Decreed by heaven to meet her father's foe,
They loved, 'was death, their death her father's
    woe.

VIII.

Bewitching, mild-eyed nature bright,
Woke when her misty veil of night
Had left her vernal bosom bare,
And vanished in the sun-souled air.
The lark had risen from its nest,
The deer had sought the mountain crest,
The sea had lost its nightly hue,
The flowers had parted from their dew,
The streamlets poured their wanton lays,
The lambkins frisked upon the braes,

The hinds had yoked their oaken ploughs,
The rosy maids had milked the cows,
The clouds, in smiling beauty high,
Sailed o'er the blue deeps of the sky,
When from her sudden slumber yoke,
MacDougall's dark-haired daughter woke,
And gazed around the chamber strange,
While memory, with contracted range,
From dreamy retrospection sought
The flickering truths of dawning thought
Which ushered in with stern delight,
The horrors of the former night.—
The door was ope'd and forward came,
A stately, gentle-featured dame,
Whose mother-looks, and smiles and voice,
Were such as made the heart rejoice.
The wondering maid she fond caressed,
And clasped her to her joyous breast;
She kissed der cheek, and kissed her brow,
And welcomed her awakening now—
" Daughter of warriors," she said,
" I joy to find my care repaid."
Dunolly's maid, half-rising, sighed,
And strove the welling tears to hide,
Her eyes beamed thro' her love's surfeit,
Her voice was tremulously sweet.
"Tell me, good mother, tell me true,
To whom my life and thanks are due?
Where am I now? Whose home is this?
Where dwells such Christian tenderness?"
"Child of the waves! calm the unrest
Which lingers in thy anxious breast,
Within our bosoms kindness reigns,
Know we are friends, although MacLeans.
My Hector was by heaven decreed
To save thee in thy hour of need;
Start not! no harm to thee shall come,
Our clansmen shall convey thee home—
Unto Dunolly's warrior lord
His daughter shall be safe restored."
The tearful maiden warmly kissed
The chieftain-mother, whom she blessed,
Then from her couch she lightly rose,
At peace, though in the halls of those
'Gainst whom her father erstwhile fought,
On whom his wild revenge was sought,—
The morn's repast was quickly spread,
And by the chieftain's lady led,
The blushing maiden entered then
The hall where sat the chief, MacLean,
Who rose and gave, with kindly smiles,
A lordly welcome to the Isles.
His hair, touched by Time's silvern spell,
Adown his shoulders streaming fell;
Of kindred hue his flowing beard

In snowy, furrowed waves appeared,
And gave a charm unto his face,
Which glowed with patriarchal grace,
His eyes beamed with the soul-repose
Which years of happiness disclose;
His broad brow showed in sundry scars
The valor-emblems of his wars;
His countenance was calm, benign,
His smile was fatherly, divine.
Of stalwart mien unbowed by years,
His voice dispelled the maiden's fears,
And as she heard his gentle tone,
She gazed with reverence upon
The hoary chief, the island lord,
Who welcomed her unto his board.
Ere seated round the table all,
Young Hector strode into the hall,
One hurried bow he gave the maid,
Whose simultaneous glance betrayed
The strange confusion, unexpressed,
Which bodes a maiden's feelings best,
As on her savior she gazed
Love's tumult in her bosom blazed,
Her meed of thanks refused to come,
Her eyes spoke now, her lips were dumb,
She heard of Hector as of one
Blood-thirsty, cruel, scarce a man,
Who drove her father from the shore,
In battle, nigh two months before;
Her father's ire she deemed unjust,
She saw in Hector one to trust.
As Hector gazed upon the maid,
His heart from every theme was swayed,
His morning meal before him lay
Untouched, save in a listless way,
A feast of fire o'erfilled him now,
He knew not why, he felt not how.
With truthful eye the chief divined
The thoughts which racked the maiden's mind,
And ere the simple meal was o'er,
He sent his henchman to the shore
To launch his boat, to bend the sail,
To spread his banner to the gale.
"Sweet Maid of Lorn, thou must away,
Though welcome here, thou must not stay;
Thy father's grief none can reveal,
Thou can'st alone his anguish heal;
Hector shall steer thee o'er the sea,
And thy deliverer shall be.
Farewell, sweet maid, our prayers are thine,
May future joys around thee shine!"

IX.

Right well MacLean had read her heart,
The maid was anxious to depart;
Her earnest gratitude of soul,
O'erpowering rushed beyond control;
She sobbing bade them all adieu!
And from the castle slowly drew.
Young Hector lightsome led the way,
Where in the cove the galley lay;
Then as a gallant courtier lord
He placed the weeping maid on board.
With skillful hands he plied the oars,
And shot beyond the sheltering shores;
Then hoisted up the broad, brown sail,
Which filled unto the gentle gale,
With favoring tide and favoring wind,
Grey Duard soon was left behind.
Right merrily the boat sped on,
And now they felt they were alone.
They spoke! 'neath Hector's voice the maid
The hidden mystery obeyed—
Her world, erst fair, seemed fairer now,
Her eyes beheld life's heaven below;
And yielding to the conqueror's sway,
They pledged eternal love that day.—
There is a music in the sea,
An everlasting melody,
An earnest chant of throbbing love,
An echo of God's voice above,
Which gives unto our hearts the peace
That bids our mutual loves increase.
The little dancing waves rejoice
To hear a maiden's love-fraught voice;
They leap with frenzied mirth and glee,
As fall her vows of constancy.
And fain their foamy crests would bless,
Affection's sacred, primal kiss.
They sang with joy when Hector brave
His heart unto the maiden gave;
They leapt with smiles on every crest,
To hear the maiden's vow expressed.
With hand in hand, eye fixed on eye,
The lovers kissed, and seemed to die
'Neath the enraptured bliss divine,
Which springs when Love's great fountains join.—
They neared Kerrera's rocky shore,
And round its northern headland bore;
Swift for Dunolly's curving bay,
The galley bounded on its way.
They saw upon the glistening sand
One solitary warrior stand,
Who marked MacLean's dread banner fly
Upon the nodding mast on high—
A whistle loud and shrill he blew,
Then from the cliffs MacDougalls flew;
But ere they bent a single bow,
He spied his daughter on the prow;

His hatred wilder, fiercer rose,
To mark her 'mid his deadly foes.
Ere slid the galley on the sand,
Hector beheld the threatening band,
Then lowered his sail, and seized the oar,
And slowly neared the dreaded shore.
One word of love he gave the maid,
Whose gestures all their vengeance stayed;
One look of hope beamed in her eye,
Which seemed to say "I all defy!"
Impatient now his child to free,
The chieftain rushed into the sea:
Before the keel had touched the sand,
He grasped again his daughter's hand,
Then in his frenzied, powerful arm,
He bore ashore her lovely form.
Hector he saw, and darkly flung
A scowl of hate from vengeance wrung.
Bold, standing with an oar in hand,
Before MacDougall's gathering band,
He forced th' unwilling boat astern,
And sadly could the maid discern
Amid the throng of clansmen, wild
With joy at finding thus their child.
Remembering their hateful foe
They ceased their cries, and from each bow
Discharged a shower of darts which fell
Harmless into the ocean's swell.
Far o'er the sea on southern tack,
Hector with wistful eye looked back,
A ceaseless longing o'er him stole,
A darkness settled on his soul.
The brightness of the morn had fled,
And left him gloomy fears, instead.
The dawn-rise of Love's cheering ray
Had vanished all to soon away,
The golden charm of hope's bright goal
Seemed fading from his saddened soul,
And as he neared his native shore
One burning wish alone it bore.
MacLean received with joy his son,
As if a victory he had won;
But Hector's heart was far away,
His Duard's charms seemed to decay—
Unrest's remorseless, cruel ban,
Had made him now an altered man.
He sought the shores in darkest night,
And ne'er returned till morning's light.
They watched, but none the paths could name,
Or how he went, or whence he came.
Ah! in his skiff he stole away
Across the Sound to Oban's bay,
Where, by King Fingal's rugged stone,

MacDougall's maid he met alone—
Renewed their vows, re-pledged their faith,
And kissed unswerving love till death.

X.

Not all a daughter's love assuaged the hate
Which in MacDougall's bosom burned elate,
Not all her soft expostulations sweet
Could the dread demon of revenge defeat;
Unmoved, and coldly calm he heard her prayer,
For well he knew that Hector was her care.
His trusty warder oft in midnight hour
Saw two mysterious forms beneath the tower,
And oft of late had heard the sound of oars
Receding in darkness from the shores.
To crush her love, to overcome his foe,
His clansmen nightly watched the beach below;
And when they heard her Hector's parting song,*
They swiftly stole by secret paths along,
And rushed upon the youth, whose ready blade
Gleamed but an instant, and their onslaught stayed—
With sudden swoop, and straight-delivered thrust,
Three warriors fell before him in the dust.
His light steel shield with cunning motion flashed,
And on its front their blows descending crashed.
Forward! and forward still they pressed combined,
Struck but one blow, and, wounded, reeled behind;
On every hand his sword appeared to see
Their covert cuts of dark ferocity,
And instantly his ready guard essayed
To foil each stroke that fell and notched his blade.
Around him lay, in groaning, helpless rows,
The prostrate forms of his remorseless foes;
Some glared revenge; some cursed with dying breath;
Some strove to strike him in the throes of death;
Some drew their dirks in anguish of despair,
Upraised their arms, and, dying, struck the air;
Some tore, in agony, while life remained,
The clotted grass their own life-blood had stained.

---

* See First Canto.

Unwounded all, the youth unconquered stood,
Starred with the red drops of his foemen's blood;
Fired with the madness springing from defeat,
They blindly rushed, and struck, but to retreat.
Then forward stood amid the stiffening slain,
MacDougall's chief, who fiercely hissed "Mac-Lean!"
Awed by their chief, the clansmen ceased to fight,
And viewed the combat with intense delight.
Revenge imbued his unaffected powers,
His blows descended on the youth in showers,
Who stood unwavering, and the onset foiled—
Yea, smote the chief, who, wounded, back recoiled.
Implacable, and heedless of his wound,
He rushed on Hector with a sudden bound,
Whose sword hand, swol'n with conflict, filled the hilt,
And now, for once, he weakening Nature felt.
While waged the strife, loud from the cliffs above
A cry arose of agony and love:
The watching clansmen gazed in wild dismay:
Down from each crag, upon her headlong way,
MacDougall's daughter rushed, with frantic cries,
As Hector, wounded, fell no more to rise.
Swift through the silent horde she madly fled,
Oblivious to the dying and the dead;
And stooped o'er Hector, who, with fitful breath,
Smiled still his love, and whispered low "In death!"
Upon his dripping blade MacDougall leant,
As o'er the youth his weeping daughter bent,
Who kissed his blood-stained lips, and wildly cried,
"Cursed is the blade that pierced my Hector's side!"
Then strangely gazed around, below, above!
And falling, died upon her only love.
MacDougall gazed, nor thought his daughter dead;
Till stooping, gently raised her lovely head:
Her cold, pale face, too truly told the tale.
Then burst a father's deep, heart-rending wail.
Her eyes were closed, and silent now her tongue;

Bright on her pallid cheeks her last tears clung,
The gentle hands, which oft had stroked his brow,
Clenched in their death-grasp Hector's bosom now;
The lips which oft had sung in joyous mood,
Bore the red imprint of his trickling blood.
With groans of terror, anguish, pain, and grief,
The clansmen gathered round their stricken chief,
Who gazed in silence on his daughter's corse,
While o'er her fell his tears of deep remorse.
"Warriors!" he cried, "Behold my daughter—dead!
No more around us will her light be shed:
Heaven wars with me; oh! that I had but felt
The depth of love which in her bosom dwelt.
Here let the lovers lie, no more to part,
In dust united, slumbering heart to heart;
'Neath Fingal's stone let them be gently laid,
To rest forever in its storied shade.
In coming years the warriors of our race
Will stand uncovered o'er their resting place,
And breathe the tale of how MacDougall's maid,
Loved unto death, and, dying, love obeyed.
The mighty stone, untouched by Time, shall tell
In voiceless whisperings, *'Here Hector fell'*"
With folded arms, in stern and lowering mood,
MacDougall's chieftain meditative stood;
While trembling, weeping clansmen dug the grave
For all he loved, and for her Hector brave.
No song of woe burst from the anguished crowd
When both were laid within their earthy shroud;
The reddened sods they laid with care above,
And all was hid from eyes of grief and love.
The chief in dreamy silence strode away,
Unto unutterable woe a prey.
Revenge and hate had from his bosom fled,
He longed for love, but all of love was dead.
No joy or peace within his halls remained,
To Hell's unrest he felt forever chained;
While Conscience, with red-burning beak and claws,
Consumed the heart which broke its Maker's laws.

APPENDIX.

E'en coming foes, led on by Scotland's King,* Stirred not his soul, nor could war's pleasure bring—

His sword was sheathed, his path was toward the tomb, And Brander's battle pealed Dunolly's Doom!

* Bruce.

DUNOLLY CASTLE AND FINGAL'S STONE.
"*Here Hector Fell.*"

No. 21.—GLENARA.

By Thomas Campbell.

[Thomas Campbell was born in Glasgow in 1777, and died at Boulogne in 1844. This poem has reference to Lachlan Catanach exposing his wife on the rock. It is taken from *Poetical Works*.]

Oh, heard ye yon pibroch sound sad in the gale,
Where a band cometh slowly with weeping and wail?
'Tis the chief of Glenara laments for his dear;
And her sire, and the people, are call'd to her bier.

Glenara came first with the mourners and shroud;
Her kinsmen they follow'd, but mourn'd not aloud;
Their plaids all their bosoms were folded around;
They march'd all in silence,—they look'd on the ground.

In silence they reach'd over mountain and moor,
To a heath, where the oak tree grew lonely and hoar:
"Now here let us place the gray stone of her cairn:
Why speak ye no word?" said Glenara the stern.

"And tell me, I charge you! ye clan of my spouse,
Why fold ye your mantles, why cloud ye your brows?"
So spake the rude chieftain:—no answer is made,
But each mantle unfolding, a dagger display'd.

"I dreamt of my lady, I dreamt of her shroud,"
Cried a voice from the kinsmen, all wrathful and loud;
"And empty that shroud, and that coffin did seem:
Glenara! Glenara! now read me my dream!"

O! pale grew the cheek of that chieftain, I ween,
When the shroud was unclosed, and no lady was seen;
When a voice from the kinsmen spoke louder in scorn,
'Twas the youth who had loved the fair Ellen of Lorn:

"I dreamt of my lady, I dreamt of her grief,
I dreamt that her lord was a barbarous chief;
On a rock of the ocean fair Ellen did seem;
Glenara! Glenara! now read me my dream!"

In dust, low the traitor has knelt to the ground,
And the desert revealed where his lady was found;
From a rock of the ocean that beauty is borne—
Now joy to the house of fair Ellen of Lorn.

No. 22.—THE LADY OF THE ROCK.

By Emily Pfeiffer.

[Emily Pfeiffer is the author of quite a number of different books, and the composer of many poems. During a visit to Duard castle, in 1883, she conceived the plan of the following poem, and published it, with observations, in 1884, calling it "The Rhyme of the Lady of the Rock."]

Part I.

Rose-red for the banner of love,
 And a blush for the cheek of the bride;
To the valleys and hills of fair Loch Fyne
 The word went far and wide:
They will marry this day, and marry to death,
Our flower of ladies, Elizabeth.

On through the valleys, and down from the hills,
 As the gathering cry of the clan
Had called them forth, through the moithering mist
 The lieges rode or ran
To meet at the foot of the runic cross,
And wring out the heart of their wrong and loss.

And there met them here and there on the breeze,
 Faint as a word of shame,
The sound of a bell, but they knew not well,
 As dubiously it came,
Or whether it chimed, or whether it tolled,
But they thought a knell had been more bold.

And they questioned the wind as it rose and fell
 Above and about Loch Fyne—
The wind that lashed at the shrinking wave,
 And harried the grove of pine—
Is your cry as the cry of her love on the rack,
Or only our lady's coronach?

But when they had come to the cross, and thence
 Peered over the castle wall,
And beheld the rout that was thronging the court,
 And the train that swarmed out of the hall—
With the banners that flaunted beside the door,
And the dog and the ship that the banners bore—

And saw by the fiery beard and eyes,
 And the motions cold and dull,
That the man who was leading the bartered bride
 Was MacLean of Duard in Mull,

Then they knew they had married to worse
    than death
Their flower of ladies, Elizabeth.

Rose-red is the banner of love,
    But this bride is pale, snow-pale,
And she grows snow-cold as he helps her to
    horse,
As the touch of the groom were bale;
But she proudly follows the lead of fate,
Nor once looks back when she passes the gate.

Some tuneless souls will meet, and make
    No answering music here,
But keep in our low, reverberate air,
    The peace of the outer sphere,
And passing, mix with the silent dead
And leave the word of our life unsaid.

But not Glenara's falls at "spate,"
    With their lusty voice for praise,
And not the vocal heart of spring
    That beats in its covert ways—
Not stream, or merle, or 'plaining dove
Went ever so near to utter love

As twain who under the "marriage-tree"
    Once heard their voices all,
And sent a confluent answer back
    To the cuckoo's double call,—
A sudden note so piercing sweet,
    It drowned the waterfall,—
Till with the primrose she grew pale,
He, wakeful with the nightingale.

For all as wise as their hearts had been
    To know and to claim their own,
They saw how oft by the felon world
    Love's dues are overthrown :
The world that knows not thine or mine,
But snatches a treasure from off a shrine.

And so it fell from the deep Argyle
    Had a bargain he would make,
And his sister must be the seal of it,
    Should it burn her heart or break.
Thus he married her to the slow, the dull,
Red-bearded tyrant, the chief of Mull.

The clansmen saw her where she came
    In the hold of the red MacLean,
Who once had ridden more free than free
    With love at her bridle-rein,
And passing left them for lingering trace
The smile that had flowered on every face.

They let her go with never a word—
    Was never a word to say;

MacCallum Mór was lord of all,
    And his will must have its way;
Though the heart of the speechless bride was
    wrath
As the torrent roaring beside her path.

But when to Cladich ferry they came,
    And the chief had called a halt,
While his shaggy train on bite and sup
    Were making swift assault,
She lighted down, and knelt beside
An image of the crucified.

There, overborne with the stroke of fate,
    As droopingly she sunk,
She had not known how near her heart
    There knelt a cowled monk,
Till he took her hand and whispered low,
And she felt it riven with joy and woe.

Here was the voice in all the world,
    For her the only voice—
The hand whose touch in face of death
    Had made her sense rejoice;
And for these hearts with love so rife,
One moment but of common life!

"Up, love, and fly!" For one heart-beat
    Love had and held his own :
They mingled breath, they mingled tears—
    A word and he had flown,
Had carried her over ford and dyke
From Campbells and MacLeans alike.

She strove with him, she clasped the cross :
    "Let pine," she said, "or die,
But never from this fore-front of fate
    Tempt me to fail or fly;
It has not been laid upon any man,
But on me to suffer and save the clan.

"MacCallum Mór has spared to meet
    MacLean as in open fight,
So awake or asleep in his island keep
    I must face him day or night;
For a true Argyle is but one thing sure :
The will and the word of MacCallum Mór."

They looked to right, they looked to left :
    O fair and cruel world!
Where tender firstlings of the spring
    On gusts of March are hurled,
The wild wind bent the pine-tops tall,
It rent the folded leaves, and small;—
The mocking sun laughed down on all.

They looked to left, they looked to right,
    And lo, through the cloven mist,

Loch Awe, that laughed to the laughing sun,
  As stormily they kissed.
"Cold sun," she said, "and bitter bliss,
Dear love, be witness: never kiss
Of man shall mar the print of this!"

A heavy freight bore down that day
  The Cladich ferry-boat,
And one that saw it had liefer seen
  It founder, I think, than float.
"Better a bride so foully wed
Were bedded here in the lake," he said.

But the lake would none of them, bride or groom,
  Or scurvy train, and tossed,
'Twixt Cladich ferry and Brander Pass,
  The boat that crossed and crossed;
And the eyes that hung on the throat of the pass
Saw, blocking the way of love, the mass

Of dark Ben Cruachan, or ere they turned
  In wrath from the path of men;
And the way-worn bride, by forest and flood,
  Through moss and reedy fen,
Went, forced on her way in the teeth of the wind
By the men of Mull who were trooping behind.

They crossed the sound; the dim isle seems
  Adrift in the wind and rain,
As cold in the shadow of Castle Duard
  Its sodden shore they gain,
But the iron click of the stanchioned gate
Rings home like the closing jaws of fate.

Her bower-maidens had busked the bride,
  The feast was long and loud,
But she scarce had sat at the board more still
  Had she sat there in her shroud.
And her courage failing for wearihead:
"'Tis a far cry to Loch Awe," she said.

Part II.

The wassail had reached its stormy height,
  The feast was over in hall,
When there came and stood at the lady's side
  A gloomy seneschal;
As he pointed the way to a turret near
She knew that it led to the bride chambère.

And she that was rose of fair Argyle—
  A white rose she was then!—
Stood up and waited no second sign,
  But bowed to the roystering men,
And passed with her bower-maids out of the hall
I' the lead of the wordless seneschal.

Then some who noted her proud and pale
  Bent laughing over the board:
"She is white as a widow's callant," they said,
  "Who should whet a maiden-sword."
And in sooth the Lady Elizabeth
Had blithelier followed the feet of death
Than the form which, fronting the torch's glare,
Cast a giant shade on the turret stair.

And when she stood in her bridal bower,
  She turned to her maidens twain:
"No hand but this of mine may dress
  The bride of the red MacLean;
So lend me but your prayers this night,
And fare ye well till the fair daylight."

She cast her garments one by one,
  Alone as she stood there;
She was to sight no summer flower
  But a woman deadly fair,
When forth she drew the golden comb
  And loosed the golden hair
Which sheathed her body to her knee,—
A ringed and burnished panoply.

Then, as a swimmer, with her arms
  The amber flood she spurned
To either side, and in her hand
  She took a gem that burned—
That rose and fell upon her heart
As a thing that bore in its life a part.

'Twas a golden dragon in jewelled mail
  That lay betwixt breast and breast
Over that gentle lady's heart,
  Couched as a lance in rest;
And that cunning sample of goldsmith's work,
It was the handle of a dirk.

She drew it forth of its leathern sheath,
  And she felt its steely edge,
Then gave some drops of her quick young blood
  To its point, as if in pledge,
Ere she wound her hair in a silken thong,
And the dirk in that golden chain and strong.
She laid the dragon again to sleep
  In its balmy place of rest:
O God, that a home so soft and fair
  Should harbor such a guest!

Then her winsome self she re-arrayed,
And fell on her trembling knees and prayed.

She muttered many an Ave then,
　And told off many a bead,
Till her passion sealed her lips, for words
　But mocked so sore a need;
Then she stopped and listened beside the breeze,
And only waited upon her knees.

And as she listened, the distant sound
　Of wassail ceased, and all
Her soul rushed armed into her ears
　At sound of a dull foot-fall
Which wound its way to the topmost tower
Where was the lady's bridal bower.

The wind was piping through lock and loop,
　But of nothing was she 'ware,
There was no sound in all the world
　But that foot upon the stair;—
And as she listened, and heard it rise,
Her soul rushed armed into her eyes.

She stood up white in her snowy pall,
　A breathing image of death,
The torch-light crowning her radiant hair,
　Her sombre face beneath.
"As I am a virgin pure this night,
So keep me, God, through dark to light;
As I am a child of the deep Argyle,
Souls of my fathers! teach me wile."

The iron door on its hinges turned
　And closed on the married twain,
And redder yet from his deep carouse
　There stood the red MacLean;
And their four eyes met, and no word was said
Till his glance fell off on the vacant bed.

Then she: "I have prayed of Mary's grace
　That she would us assoil
For that this day with lips forsworn
　We sought to cut the coil
Of mortal hate that has ever lain
Betwixt the Argyle and MacLean."

Then low he laughed: "To kneel and pray,
　Lady, beseemeth thee,
But to make of our false oath a true
　Is the task that fitteth me;
My word, before the morrow's sun,
You shall avouch the work well done."

He moved a step to where she stood,
　And she recoiled a pace;

His wandering eyes again were set
　In wonder on her face.
They paused, they made a mutual stand;
His breath fell hot upon her hand.

"You are a lord of the Isles," quoth she,
　"And the Islemen's mood is light,
But I am a child of the firm mainland,
　And I change not in a night.
There is nought of me that a man may win
And I think not to overlay sin with sin.

"Now nothing could hap that would make us twain
　But false as woman and man,
Yet by grace of God we may still be true
　Each to our name and clan,
And each to each in a sidelong way
True to the bond we have sealed this day.

"You asked for a gage of my feudal chief,
　But of me nor word nor smile;
You sought but to better the strength you had
　With the strength of the deep Argyle;
You shall have your due but no more of me,
Than a contract's seal and warranty."

He laughed in his beard: "Ay, many have tried,
　But all have tried in vain,
To mete with a measure that was not his
　The due of the red MacLean;
Still with iron hand he has held his right,
But never so close as he will this night."

She set herself as a hind at bay,
　She straightened her back to the wall;
"I that am come as a hostage here,
　Would you use me as a thrall?"
"Not so," quoth he, "but by limb and life,
I'll use you as my wedded wife."

"I am an earl's daughter," she said,
　"And my oath is worth a knight's,
And I swear by the health of my mother's soul,
　That the kiss which first alights
On me as we two lie in bed,
Shall have the force to strike me dead."

"You are an earl's daughter," he said,
　"And a maid without a stain;
But as you are here in Castle Duard,
　And I the red MacLean,
That oath shall no more be your screen
Than if you were the veriest quean."

She shrunk as into the granite wall,
　She parried his rude embrace;

His fierce eyes glowed like the autumn fern,
  His breath was hot on her face;
Her heart seemed knocking against the stone,
  It beat as it would burst her zone.

She cried a cry, but it fell still-born,
  It died in her throat for fear,
Though the meaning ablaze in the dauntless
    gaze
Of her flame-blue eyes was clear;
And it was that the Lady Elizabeth
Was ready to give as to take of death.

Her hand bore hard on her heaving breast,
  And he knew whereto it clung,
And saw how her eyes on the turn of his,
  Two deadly warders, hung;
Then his caitiff soul succumbed to hers,
  He let her go, and sprung
Back with the cry of a ravening beast
Baulked on the eve of a gory feast.

Twice already that tyrant chief
  Had seen th' accusing steel
Cleaving the way to his savage heart
  In a victim's last appeal;
And he hated more the better he knew
The flash of that lightning cold and blue.

He glanced at the dagger's golden string,
  And his sodden wit grew clear;
" Wear to, wear to, I will stalk this maid,
  As we stalk the Highland deer."
The fumes of wassail that left his brain
  Had left it free to fear;
"She is yet too wild," he said, " and deep
To be taken waking or asleep."

He spoke her fair: " You have journeyed far,
  By mountain and by flood,
And to you of all that life hath dear,
  Sleep only seemeth good;
So you shall taste untroubled rest
This night as 'twere a stranger guest."

Her left hand sheathed the shining dirk,
  She gave to him her right;
" Now lay your sword betwixt us two,
  As you are a belted knight.
Then God be watch and ward," she said,
And stretched herself by the sword in bed.

And hourly, as the night wore on,
  She lay in the deepening gloom,
Her two hands folded upon her breast
  Like a statue on a tomb;
But she seemed to feel the dirk beneath
Her fingers tingling in its sheath.

And the moon came softly out of a cloud
  I' the midmost of the night,
And through the loop-hole gazed at her,
  She lying still and white
Beside the castle's lord, who slept
While she her weary vigil kept.

But when the morning's face rose pale
  O'er the shoulder of Cruachan-ben,
She stole from out the bride chambère,
  A joyful woman then;
And alone in face of the risen sun
She dared to weep: the day was won!

PART III.

When the morning board with the rests of the
    feast
  Was set, and the martial kin—
The vassals in chief of the castle's lord—
  Still heavy with sleep dropped in,
They found a smiling chatelaine
Threading her keys on a silver chain.

And still when her lord, like a thunder-cloud
  Full-charged, came louring down,
With her own white hand she served to him
  The prime of the venison;
So tending him in the downward eyes,
It 'hoved him not to speak or rise.

Thus every morning she was meek
  As a loving wife might be,
And full of service and soothfastness
  As a lady of high degree:
In house and hall a guiding power,
A gracious presence in lady's bower.

At eventide she graced the feast
  With a face of merry cheer,
And her voice to the harp when the harp went
    round,
  As the laverock's note was clear;
So "she singeth in the night, they say,
As a bird that singeth in the day."

And seeing her so amenable
  And lovely in daylight hour,
Her lord would follow as time might serve
  For dalliance in lady's bower,
Where sitting apart on the window stone
They parleyed together as if alone.

And once, she making the shuttle fly,
  Her maidens spinning near,

He seized her fluttering hands, and laughed:
 "They are captives, white with fear."
"Nay, call them rather," she laughed back,
 "Pale victims, faithful on the rack."

And seeing her frail, as she was fair,
 He measured with thievish eye
The length of the dirk which clove her breast,
 And thought where the hilt might lie;
But he saw no way through her silken suit,
Which clipt her close as the rind the fruit.

And seeing her fair, as she was frail,
 In the sting of a new-born need,
His tuneless voice for once rang true,
 His fierce tongue learnt to plead.
Then her daylight face was in eclipse,
The shadow of night on her eyes and lips,

As she answered him: "While the stars endure
 You will get no more of me
Than what you hold at my brother's hand,
 For a gift is of the free:
That hour which made us two handfast,
The time to win as to woo, was past."

"You are haggard, dame, as a hawk," he said,
 And he gave her hands reprieve,
"But we tame the wildest tercelet
 That ever we let live."
Then he rose and left the bower in wrath,
And the stones cried out upon his path.

"Craft is the strength of Argyle; she knows
 Our heads are under one hood,
But that hood shall be cover for mine alone,
 If ever meseemeth good;
The sleuth-hound in vain, if he failed of that,
Had been held in leash with the mountain cat.

"*Now* is better than *then;* good brother Argyle,
 New love is like new wine;
I will put to the proof this brotherly shield,
 Before it is worn too fine,
And see when my hand has done a thing,
How you make it good in the eye of the king."

He called aloud to his namesmen all,
 As they loitered about the court;
"Come, rouse ye, men, for a bloody raid,
 And I warrant ye good sport;
The better that we by night shall stoop,
And seize our prey in a silent swoop.

"And some of your band must go by land,
 And some shall come by sea;
And those shall ride with Malcolm Mór,
 And these shall sail with me;

Our meeting-place Glengarry Bay:
The boats, there needs no more to say."

Then some to horse, and some to ship,
 Some sailed, some rode or ran;
While shrill at their head the pipers played
 The gathering of the clan;
The work was death, the road was rough,
They knew no more, it was enough.

But when they came to Loch-na-kiel,
 Nor pipe nor voice was heard,
You might have caught, as you brushed the ling,
 The cry of a brooding bird,
And a league or ever you reached the shore,
Have steered by the dull Atlantic roar.

Then warily they at Glengarry Bay
 Make sign to the waiting boat,
And the word goes round whereto they are bound,
 As they silently get afloat;
And they steal upon Cairnburg's island keep,
Where it lies in the cradling surf asleep.

Then little they heard of the scared sea-bird
 Or the near Atlantic roar,
For the fierce war-clang of the crossing swords
 As led by Malcolm Mór.
They stormed the keep, and its keepers slew,
 Or laid in irons before;
MacLean with his merry men sailed in,
Safe to conquer and bold to win.

He passed the body of Cairnburg's lord
 With its gaping wounds and red,
And he spurned it from him with his foot—
 He did not fear the dead;
Then he filled a horn and gave a toast
"We'll drink," quoth he, "to our silent host."

The thirsty crews swarmed up, they left
 The dead men and the bound,
And, drunk with blood, in wassail deep
 Their reeling senses drowned.
The captive's groans, the victor's glee,
The lashing of the ruthless sea,
Made up the wild world's harmony.

O loving God, whom all men loved
 When hating most their kind,
They lifted bloody hands in prayer,
 Now all are stricken blind,—
And we never more may see the sun
Till all men's eyes and hearts are one!

The red MacLean set his signet seal
  On the castle's garnered store,
Then he filled his pouch with its gold, and gave
  The keys to Malcolm Mór,
Whom he left in charge, bold man and true,
While himself took ship with his jolly crew.

And he thought: "To this frost-bound maid of mine,
  When I come red-handed in,
Will the ice of her virgin pride break up,
  Shall I come as I came, to win?"
But the spirits that wrought for him by day,
Were nought at night; and she held her way.

Then he fell in longing by day and night
  As the sick man longs for health;
And he longed for her by night and day
  As the beggar longs for wealth,
As one who hung over the pit of hell
Might clutch at a star-beam ere he fell.

And his stricken thought turned round on himself,
  And his dim low-lying soul
Caught a shadowy glimpse of a fairer way,
  As he deemed, to a fairer goal;
So a heavier stone on his heart was flung,
Which helped but to sink him where he hung.

He dreamed of tortures of rare device
  As to give his passion ease,
And once in his dire extremity
  He sued her upon his knees;
But alone, without her Campbell shield,
Who knows to die, needs not to yield.

For bulwark and for last defense
  She had the strength of steel:
The sword betwixt them was a sign,
  The dagger was a seal;
And each fine hair that wound about
The dagger's hilt, a watchful scout.

But sitting alone on the window stone,
  Though still was the summer air,
She heard a whispering on the sea,
  A moaning she knew not where;
Then she looked to the hills where the two winds meet,
And saw them wrestle together, and beat
Each against each, and pant and smoke
Like beasts that fret in unequal yoke.

And she said: "O love that I knew so fair,
  Whoever had thought of thee
That thy summery breath could raise the storm,
  And the wreck— whose shall it be?
Were the end but death, would it now were here,
And a white fringed pall on my maiden bier."

Part IV.

As the red MacLean went to and fro
  'Twixt Duard and Cairnburg tower,
One day he chanced to spy a rose;
  It seemed a single flower
With an open eye, but in some close part
The bud was shaping a double heart.

And this flower grew up so fresh and fair
  On land that was held in fief,
The Treshnish Isles, which her father owned
  Of MacLean, a vassal chief,
And this fair maid, having a vassal soul,
Of her beauty paid the tyrant toll.

And his galled spirit found ease in her
  From the bond of the proud Argyle,
And his famished pride rose up full-fed,
  And rampant beneath her smile,
That he laughed his laugh: "I will take this flower
And plant as a thorn in my lady's bower."

So he took the maiden with him in croup,
  And to Castle Duard they came,
Where my lady looked her through and through,
  Without or pity or blame:
"Would God," she thought, "this flower would twine
And stablish herself in this place of mine!"

So she let it be, and it wound and wound,
  It was so soft and young,
So lithe as the green shoots felt their way,
  But they hardened where they clung,
Till they bent the stake the way they chose;
For this plant it was a climbing rose.

And the red MacLean, the chief of the clan,
  To her was the chief of men,
And she thought in her pride, "Could I win to his side,
  As the mists upon Cruachan-ben,
My matron coif would be borne so high
It would shine the first in the great world's eye."

Now MacLean in the strength of others is waxed
  So proud that nought avails,

But the ships that traverse the Sound of Mull
   Must lower their topmost sails,
When of Duard they come within gun-shot—
Still the woman who called him lord, bent not.

She looked from the seeming single flower
   That twined until, none knew how,
The tender shoot that had clasped a twig,
   Had all but bent a bough,
To her baffled lord, for his changed desire
Had held her safe in its counter-fire.

And he who noted her morning face
   Grow clearer and yet more clear,
Beheld her the only untamed thing
   Of all that came him near;
And his longing was as the thirst for blood,
   His hate was the hate of fear;
And the fear and longing so grew and grew,
That together they rove his heart in two.

And still he saw her the bond that bound
   Clan Campbell to his name,
And knew the issue between them, one
   That for very pride and shame,
In his strong walls filled with his vassal kin,
His hand unholpen must lose or win.

The round world spinning about the sun
   Appeareth a two-fold arc;
It nothing knoweth of high or low,
   But only of light and dark:
That many, dreaming they climb a height,
Are boring deep in the pitchy night.

So the wilding rose it crept and crept,
   It was so soft and fair,
That it wound till it reached the chamber door
   At the top of the turret stair;
As its sweetness weighted the air within,
She thought, "One night he will tirl the pin.

"He will open and put my lady forth,
   And will set me by his side."
And so it fell; and my lady rose
   And past in her virgin pride
From out of the chamber adown the stair
With a foot as light as a bird o' the air.

Then the fierce MacLean, when as chatelaine
   She greeted him from her place,
And he caught the tenser tone of her voice,
   The light on her morning face,
Was hounded as by the devils in hell
To quench the spirit he could not quell.

And his limmer, striking deeper root,
   Still darkly wound her way,
For she hated, who only reigned at night,
   The woman who ruled by day;
And at Castle Duard the fiends full fain
Went up and down betwixt these twain.

Then the limmer made an image of wax,
   Alike in every part
To my lady's self, and when all was done,
   She stuck it through the heart:
"Dwindle and dwine in shade and shine,"
She said, "till all of thine be mine."

And ever beside the waxen shape
   In the gloaming of the day,
With folded hands she crooned the curse
   As a troubled soul might pray:
"Dwindle and dwine in shade and shine,
Till all be mine that now is thine."

In an evil hour the baffled chief
   Looked in as she crooned the spell;
He plucked the shroud from the waxen shape:
   "You have wrought this passing well;
My lady's face, and the smile thereof;
Here hate hath done the work of love.

"My lady's face as she lives—not so;
   My lady's face," he said,
"Not as she lives to flout us two,
   But as—*she might lie dead*."
Then each glanced up as in vague surprise,
And shrunk at the light in the other's eyes.

For the wish that was quick in the woman's breast
   Had mothered the thought of the man,
And he said: "Ay, harry this work of wax,
   And the woman you would ban
Shall feel the sting in her heart of stone."
But his laugh rang hollow, and died a groan.

He seized the knife, he struck it anew
   And turned in the wounded wax:
"Take heed of this bloodless beauty," he said,
   "That thereof nothing lacks;
We will keep this saint as in a shrine;
She may be worth your life and mine."

He led his limmer forth, and turned
   The key ere he went his gait:
"If hate can do the work of love,
   So love the work of hate."
Then his fierce heart surged in its beaten pride
As the great waves surged in the high spring-tide.

Part V.

My lady sat in her bower, and span
From a newly plenished creel;
She loved the wild sea noise that drowned
 The droning of her wheel,
Nor feared to hear the low winds race
Through the tall spear-grass to their meeting-
 place.

But the restless wind awoke her heart
 Where her love was laid asleep,
And it rose up wild like a startled child,
 It waked like a child to weep;—
O world forlorn in the wan grey weather,
And young heart weeping and wailing to-
 gether!

For the wrestling wind recalled a time
 When the grey wan world was green,
When the sun was high, her lost love nigh,
 And the sting of love so keen
In the stroke that cleft her heart in twain,
She knew not if it were joy or pain.

The wind, the waves, the droning wheel,—
 No new sound thrilled the air,
But her flesh made motion that some strange
 thing,
 Some loathly to life, stood there.
She stopped her wheel, the fine thread broke;
It was her lord, he laughed, he spoke:
"Would'st give your thought in my thought's
 stead,
You'd win by the exchange," he said.

She turned from him, she locked her hands
 And laid them athwart her breast;
She feared belike his questing gaze
 From sanctuary might wrest
A name she knew the faintest breath
Betraying, would betray to death.

"Put by your wheel and spin no more,
 Come, lady, and come with me;
You ever have loved the singing wind,
 You love the dancing sea;
My biorlin is on the shore,
Leave flax and fancies, spin no more."

His voice was soft, his words were smooth,
 His eye had a feline glow,
You seemed to see it burn more bright
 That the light was waxing low.
He smiled, repeating as before:
"Leave flax and fancies, spin no more."

She left her wheel, she left her bower,
 She followed the false MacLean,
The piper piped them to the shore,
 He piped a doleful strain:
The pibroch of Macrimmon Môr:
"The way you go you'll come no more."

The chieftain's foster-brethren twain
 Hung on the shallop's side,
That shook in the breeze as a courser shakes
 Ere he steadies himself in his stride;
The lady barely brooked their help,
 In her strength of youth and pride;
They back the boat through the blown sea-
 scurf
And board her all in the boiling surf.

The helm was ta'en of the red MacLean,
 The oars of Donald Dhu,
And Shamesh, he of the bloody hands—
 And they were a grisly crew;
But my lady's spirit rose bold and free
'Twixt the singing wind and the dancing sea.

O youth, what art thou for gallant stuff?
 Well known to the fiend Despair,
Of him you haply will take of Death
 But never will doff to Care;
A gleam of sun, a breath of brine,
Will mount your pulses as brisk new wine.

The good boat breasted the creaming waves,
 She rose in the teeth of the breeze,
She charged again as a fiery steed
 When stricken aback by the seas.
The mountains seemed to soar and dive;
The dim world heaved as yet alive.

The Norse-built keep of Castle Duard,
 That one while, gaunt and bare,
Looked glowering from its stony height,
 Melted as smoke in air;
As faint from that dissolving shore
The pibroch wailed, "You'll come no more,"

But where the two winds meet, the drift
 Had loosed a lurid cloud
Which floated up as the tide went down—
 In fashion as a shroud,
Or liker to a woman drowned,
With arms outspread, and hair unbound.

As the rowers caught in the lady's eyes
 A shadow of vague affright,
They turned about on their laboring oars,
 To question the waning light;

And deep in the downdraught of one thought
  A moment those four souls were caught.

Then looked at her with wolfish eyes
  And fierce, the red MacLean;
Then looked at her with conscious eyes
  And keen, those gillies twain;
Their meeting glances quelled her breath,
They seemed to smite, and deal her death.

The pibroch's note was heard no more,
  The pallid mist had spread
O'er all the world a winding-sheet
  For all the world seemed dead;
The wind and the waves upon its track
Shrieking the lost world's coronach.

But broadening over their bows they see
  A line of angry foam
That hard on a bare, nigh-sunken rock
  With maddened haste beats home;
And all the woe that was no more,
The dead world's woe, was in its roar.

The lady heard, and she rose up pale,
  In the quivering boat upright;
It was but the blind young blood that rose,
  Alas! what hope in flight,
What hope of any help might be
Betwixt the dead world and the sea?

And looking ahead where the breakers struck
  The black, low-lying shore,
'Twas a man's hoarse voice that smote her ear—
  Smote through the deafening roar:
"There one in love with death," it said,
"Might have white sheets for a marriage-bed."

Then not for tumult of wind or wave
  That lady's heart beat high,
It swung with the dead, dull weight of lead,
  It struck as for danger nigh
A wild alarum, whereat each sense
Doubled the force of its frail defense.

And, served by the drift of the landward seas,
  The boat makes straight for the rock;
She shoots the waves, and in the trough
  Lies stunned as if with the shock;
Then rights herself as fearing more
The helmsman than the deadly shore.

Dumb 'mid the thunder of wind and surge,
  That savage helmsman steers,
The world in lapsing from out their sight
  Is clamoring at their ears;
But through the tumult they can feel
The shingles grind a quivering keel

And swept ashore on a towardly wave,
  They haul the good boat in,
And without a word the brethren fall
  To work in the 'wildering din:
Some deadlier task, and still to come,
Would seem to hold those brethren dumb.

Then swift as strokes of the stormy sea,
  More rude than the raging wind,
The lady is 'ware of two sudden arms
  That seize her body and bind,
And knows from its beating that dull way
The heart her dagger had kept at bay.

The red MacLean! none other than he,
  He has her in hand at last,
And oh, ye smoldering fires of hell!
  This time he holds her fast;
The teeth of the dragon beneath her vest
Are buried deep in her bleeding breast.

He stood with his bride on that trampled shore—
  They two, and they alone—
And with brackish kisses he pressed and pressed
  As one who would make his own
Her shuddering lips; then he cast her down
As a man might cast a stone,
And the rock that was all that was left of the world
Seemed sinking with that light weight so hurled.

He turned where the tattered fringe of the sea
  Lighted the falling night;
That face, that face on the brown sea-ware
  Had shown so ghastly white!
He dares the foaming wrath of the surge,
  He boards his boat as in flight,
He shouts: "Haste, brothers, make for the large!"
The waves are roaring a countercharge.

The foster-brothers they heave their hearts
  Loud beating against the prow,
But in face of the countervailing sea
  The labor of man is slow;
And somewhat white hangs on to the boat,
Forbearing the shallop to get afloat:

Ah! what but the swift young blood again,
  Uprisen as with a cry—
The voice of its still-aspiring life
  "Not yet is it time to die,"
Has sent my lady in this wild way
With grappling hands to plead and to pray?

He struck her off, the caitiff MacLean—
　The very breakers had fled
To let her kneel—but there be lost men
　And damned or ere they be dead.
"Kneel, woman, kneel," said the red MacLean,
"And kneel as once I knelt—in vain!"

The sea in its sovereign strength returned
　And took the maid to its breast,
Then arched itself—a triumphant wave—
　And bore her high on its crest,
To lay the face so ghostly fair
Unharmed again on the brown sea-ware.

My lady rose in the strength of her pride,
　She saw herself there alone—
She rose and blest the sundering sea,
　The islet was all her own;
She rose and rose to its topmost ledge—
　She made thereof a throne;—
She cried: "MacLean of Duard, farewell!
We're parted now as heaven and hell!"

No blot on the shrouding mist, MacLean
　With his whole dark world seemed dead,
All, even to the very hate of him,
　Gone like a knotless thread,
So that behind, as about, above,
Was nothing left her but Death and Love.

Then she wept for ruth of her maiden truth:
　"O Love, have I waked for thee
By day and night, but to face thee now
　With this loathed stain on me?
Come, ocean, and with your bitter brine
Sweeten these ravished lips of mine!"

The hydra heads of the western waves
　Broke, parted to north and south,
They lipped the shore, commixed, and closed
　As one vast, foaming mouth
That hungered for her evermore,
That all but slew her with its roar.

And still she called upon Love: "False Love,
　To think thy summery breath
Should drive a soul that trusted thee
　On this wild way of death!"
The foam-fringed rock was wearing small,
Scarce bigger now than a maiden's pall.

The clamoring surges formed and fell,
　Pressed nearer and yet more near,
Then plunged and quivered in pale recoil
　Of pity, or eke of fear.
They broke, they wandered round her seat—
They went, they came, they licked her feet.

And still she cried and still she clung:
　"O treacherous sea, and slow,
Come take my life and make an end,
　Since death will have it so!"
The mad sea melted at her commands,
Came back and kissed her clinging hands.

The charging waves come on, fall off,
　Rise, sheer as a wall, and steep—
O Christ, must the whole dead world go down,
　Entombed in the charnel deep?
The strong tide lays her bosom bare,
She feels it dragging her tangled hair.

Her hands have ceased to clasp and cling,
　She has shaken her spirit free,
She will strive no more, she will make no
　moan,
　She will go with the clamoring sea.
The waves ring only against the rock,
But it feels as yielding beneath the shock.

And still the breakers lift their crests,
　"O maiden Mary," she cries,
"Who will tell my lover my heart was true,
　Who will right me in love's eyes?"
But the hydra heads have come and gone,
And in face of death she still lives on.

But they come no more, dear God, so nigh
　They come not again, they fall
And trample the rock beside her feet,
　Fierce monsters, but held in thrall,
Tamed in their very pride's excess
To this turbulent show of humbleness.

The battle-front of the daunted sea,
　Though the waves still chop and churn,
Is in forced retreat, the wavering tide
　Has trembled long on the turn;
Then one white wave came back and surged
About her—and her lips were purged.

And she lay there washed as for the grave,
　And purer than virgin snow,
Her beauty seemed as a conquering power
　In this its overthrow;
Her eyes were blinded, choked her breath,
Her ears were open gates of death.

A panic seized on the routed waves:
　They fled to the sandy shelves,
They writhed, they foamed, they broke, they
　turned,
　And foundered upon themselves;
But in that maiden was no stir;
Great Love had had his will of her.

The terror deepened upon the sea,
  The stillness grew on the wind;
They fled together, these fierce allies,
  And left their spoil behind—
The one sole thing that glimmered white
And pure in all that world of night.

Part VI.

Two shapes passed over the sobbing sea
  To land at Dunolly bay;
One passed at sunrise, one at noon
  Of the new-created day.
The first was a work of God undone;
The second, a devil's but ill begun.

And both were silent as outer space,
  Both white as the upper air;
As one mask lay to the rising sun,
  And one to the noon-day bare,
Broke from the first a gasping breath.
Shone on the second the beads of death.

So the first was laid on the yellow sands
  To catch the coming of day,
And the second was covered up close as night
  To hide from the noon away;
And light of life came into the first,
But the second sweltered, a thing accurst.

Through the standing floods, by the lonely ways,
  In the tracks which the sheep had worn,
By Shamesh, he of the bloody hands,
  That spotless lady is borne;
But her sleeping sense of his care is fain,
And his bloody hands leave never a stain.

He had sighted her soul when it rose and sued
  To his chief at her wild, wide eyes;
And the sea and the shore through the live-long night
  Had been ringing as with her cries;
And they drew him whether he would or no
With the cords of a man, and he had to go.

So he found her there where the sea had laid
  And left her, but not a sound
There breathed from her body, as mournfully
  The waves fell sobbing round;
Then a stainless lily, alive or dead,
He gathered her up in his hands, and fled.

Then as bloody Shamesh was making the shore,
  And laying that white ladye
In the sun's warm bed on the yellow sands,
  MacLean was putting to sea
With the waxen shape that in hate of hell
His limmer had molten and made so well.

But or ever the seeming widower
  Had come with the seeming dead
To Dunolly Bay, that first true twain
  Were well on their journey sped,—
Ben Cruachan behind them, frowning above
And blocking the way of the foes of love.

Then they hail the ferry, and lightly go
  Where heavily erst she came,
And the jubilant song of Glenara fall
  Sets her frozen blood aflame,
And she lights at the gate, and she seems to win
Her way like a chartered ghost within.

And she glides to her place by the arras screen,
  And faces her kinsmen all,
For a wandering breath that told of her death
  Had called them together in hall:
"You must open your hearts as of yore to me,
For you get me back at the gift of the sea!"

They opened their hearts, and they lent their ears
  To her tale, but on every dirk
A hand was locked in a fast embrace
  And with promise of wilder work
Than ever had been in the age-long reign
Of hate 'twixt Clan Campbell and Clan MacLean.

Then the women swarmed round her and bore her away,
  As a leaf on a stream at flood,
They shrieked wild curses, but eased their hearts
  With tears, while they talked of blood;
And my lady who heard was resolving it all
In the call of the cuckoo, the song of the fall.

But when, brave and sweet, from her maiden bower
  She issued again, they had done;
And the whole clan rose to the queen of the feast,
  And she faced them, and saw but one,
Till her thought was drawn to that vanished shore
By the ghost of the dirge of Macrimmon Mór

Faint as a traveling spirit of sound
  It came and went on the breeze,

Now low in the valley, now high on the hill,
  Now lost in the leaves of the trees;
But ever emerging, and ever more near,
  As men clutched their dirks and bent forward to hear,
For they knew of the thing that was like to appear.

A lie will be loud in its own defense,
  As a fearsome heart will be bold;
And in every clachan the thing went through,
  The lie had been told and told,
And the dool of the lady lamented o'er
In the wild death-song of Macrimmon Mór.

Now it wails, it shrieks, it is passing the cross,
  It has entered the gate, and the beat
Grows loud and louder, the steady ground-tone
  Of an army of tramping feet;
Then the great hall fills with a funeral train,
And in weeds of mourning the false MacLean

Steps warily close to an open bier,
  With one downward fiery eye
That has found a way through his folded plaid
  Fast fixed on the waxen lie;
Then he lifts his hand and he stops the march
Of the train in the favoring gloom of an arch.

And one clan halts in the cavernous shade,
  One stands in a bright half ring
By the torch-lit board, each man in his place,
  But alert, and ready to spring
If damnable treason for once overbore
The bloodless craft of MacCallum Mór.

Then from out the darkness a hollow voice
  Comes deep as the gloom and dull,
And the Campbells are fretting like hounds in leash,
  While the tortuous lord of Mull
Pours the tale of his loss and his dole in their ears
While his false eyes verily shed false tears.

"Abide, my brothers!" MacCallum Mór
  Has taken his sister's hand,
And adown the hall in their Campbell pride
  They pace together, and stand
In a halo of light by the open bier,
  He waving a burning brand
In the false dead face which wears flat in the flare,
As the falser living shrinks back from the glare.

But the lady has fronted the men of Argyle,
  And though never a sign gave she,
Her heart on another's made silent call,
  And the twain were suddenly three,
She holding inward with her maiden might
The armed right hand of her own true knight.

The mourner has turned in his ghastly fear
  From that deadlier image than death,—
And lo, on the topmost stair, as of life,
  Sees the Lady Elizabeth,
And the radiant vision had all but slain,
As with effluent being, that caitiff MacLean.

His lieges are thronging in hall and court,
  And many bold men and true,
But in view of that lady who dazzles their eyes
  They cower and tremble too:
'Tis an unkenned sight, and a weird, to see
A spirit stand clear of its own bodie.

Now MacLean lies bleeding and overthrown
  In his recreant haste to fly;
But MacCallum Mór had foreseen his gain
  In the life of his false ally,
Though his fiercer namesmen had all but broke
From his cautious hold, when his sister spoke.

She spoke in her tolerant scorn: "This chief
  Has suffered some wrong of me,
Which failing to right, he went near to avenge
  In the strength of his fere the sea.
I stand here victor: let no man dare
To take from the vanquished the life I spare!"

She seized the brand, and tossed it alive
  On the waxen shape where it lay,
And the full-fed leaped up to the roof,
  And the night was a brighter day.
Then red MacLean, who, dabbled with gore,
And abject with terror, fled out of the door,
To his whilom lady became no more.

And she spoke again to her own true love,
  None hearing but only he:
"Forgive that a traitor in love's despite
  Once dared in sight of the sea—
But only once—high God He knows—
  To touch the lips of me,
Sith the great white wave that broke from above
Hath made them meet now for death or for love."

Then she turned in her pride to her feudal lord,
Said, "Brother, now give me shrift;
I was offered to shame, I was offered to death;
As I hold at the sea's free gift
My life and love, I will hold them fast,
Or find me a grave with the true at last."

But her brother has taken and joined their hands,
And so soothfast was the kiss—
So dear love's due to her lips so true—
She had like to have died of bliss;
Then over her cheek as she drooped her head,
Loves banner at last rose red, rose red.

No. 23.—The Family Legend.
By Joanna Baillie.

[Joanna Baillie was a distinguished poetess, born in 1762, at Bothwell, in Lanarkshire, Scotland, and died February 23, 1851. Her genius was greatly admired by her literary contemporaries. Sir Walter Scott was numbered among her principal friends. "The Family Legend" was written in 1805, and the second edition, dedicated to Sir Walter Scott, was published in Edinburgh in 1810.]

PROLOGUE.
Written by Sir Walter Scott.

'Tis sweet to hear expiring summer's sigh,
Through forests tinged with russet, wail and die;
'Tis sweet and sad the latest notes to hear
Of distant music, dying on the ear;
But far more sadly sweet, on foreign strand,
We list the legends of our native land,
Linked as they come with every tender tie,
Memorials dear of youth and infancy.

Chief, thy wild tales, romantic Caledon,
Wake keen remembrance in each hardy son;
Whether on India's burning coasts he toil,
Or till Acadia's* winter-fettered soil,
He hears with throbbing heart and moisten'd eyes,
And as he hears, what dear illusions rise!
It opens on his soul his native dell,
The woods wild-waving, and the water's swell;
Tradition's theme, the tower that threats the plain,
The mossy cairn that hides the hero slain;
The cot, beneath whose simple porch was told
By grey-hair'd patriarch, the tales of old,
The infant group that hush'd their sports the while,
And the dear maid who listen'd with a smile.
The wanderer, while the vision warms his brain,
Is denizen of Scotland once again.

Are such keen feelings to the crowd confined,
And sleep they in the poet's gifted mind?
Oh no! For she, within whose mighty page
Each tyrant passion shows his woe and rage,
Has felt the wizard influence they inspire,
And to your own traditions tuned her lyre.
Yourselves shall judge—whoe'er has raised the sail
By Mull's dark coast, has heard this evening's tale.
The plaided boatman, resting on his oar,
Points to the fatal rock amid the roar
Of whitening waves, and tells whate'er to-night
Our humble stage shall offer to your sight;
Proudly preferr'd, that first our efforts give
Scenes glowing from her pen to breathe and live;
More proudly yet, should Caledon approve
The filial token of a daughter's love.

ACT I.

Scene I.—*Before the gate of MacLean's castle in the Isle of Mull: Several Highlanders discovered cross-*

* Nova Scotia.

ing the stage, carrying loads of fuel, whilst Benlora *is seen on one side, in the background, pacing to and fro, and frequently stopping, and muttering to himself.*

1st High. This heavy load, I hope, will be the last:
My back is almost broken.
2d High. Sure am I,
Were ev'ry beeve in Mull slain for the feast,
Fuel enough already has been stow'd
To roast them all: and must we still with burdens
Our weary shoulders gall?

[Enter Morton.]

Mor. Ye lazy lubbards!
Grumble ye thus?—Ye would prefer, I trow,
To sun your easy sides, like household curs,
Each on his dung-hill stretched, in drowsy sloth.
Fy on't! to grumble on a day like this,
When to the clan a rousing feast is giv'n,
In honor of an heir born to the chief—
A brave MacLean, still to maintain the honors
Of this your ancient race!
1st High. A brave MacLean indeed! vile mongrel hound!
Come from the south, where all strange mixtures be
Of base and feeble! sprung of varlet's blood!
What is our race to thee?
2d High. (To Morton). Thou'lt chew, I doubt not.
Thy morsel in the hall with right good relish,
Whether MacLean or Campbell be our lord.
Mor. Ungracious surly lubbards! I say,
And bring your burdens quicker. And, besides,
Where is the heath and hare-bells, from the glen,
To deck my lady's chamber?
2d High. To deck my lady's chamber!
Mor. Heartless hounds!
Is she not kind and gentle? Spares she aught
Her gen'rous stores afford, when you or yours
Are sick, or lack relief? Hoards she in chests,
When shipwreck'd strangers shiver on our coast,
Or robe or costly mantle?—All comes forth!
And when the piercing shriek of drowning mariners
Breaks through the night, up starting from her couch,
To snatch, with eager haste, the flaming torch,
And from the tower give notice of relief,
Who comes so swiftly as her noble self?
And yet ye grumble.
1st High. Ay, we needs must own,

That, were she not a Campbell, fit she were
To be a queen, or ev'n the thing she is—
Our very chieftain's dame. But, in these towers,
The daughter of Argyle to be our lady!
  Mor. Out! mountain savages! is this your spite? Go to!
  2d High. Speak'st thou to us? thou Lowland loun!
Thou wand'ring pedlar's son, or base mechanic!
Com'st thou to lord it here o'er brave MacLeans?
We'll carry loads at leisure, or forbear,
As suits our fancy best, nor wait thy bidding.
(Exeunt Highlanders grumbling, and followed by MORTON.)
(Manet BENLORA, who now comes forward, and after remaining some time on the front of the stage, wrapt in thought, not observing LOCHTARISH, who enters behind him.)
Heigh ho! heigh ho, the day!
  Loch. How so? What makes Benlora sigh so deeply?
  Ben. (Turning round). And does Lochtarish ask? Full well thou know'st,
The battles of our clan I've boldly fought,
And well maintained its honor.
  Loch. Yes, we know it.
  Ben. Who dared, unpunish'd, a MacLean to injure?
Yea; he who dared but with a scornful lip
Our name insult, I thought it feeble vengeance
If steed or beeve within his walls were left.
Or of his holds one tower unruined stood.
  Loch. Ay; who dared then to brave us?
  Ben. Thus dealt Benlora ev'n with common foes;
But in the warfare of our deadly feud,
When rung the earth beneath our bloody strife,
And brave MacLeans brave Campbells boldly fronted.
(Fiends as they are, I still must call them brave),
What sword more deeply drank the heated blood
Than this which now I grasp—but idly grasp?
  Loch. There's ne'er a man of us that knows it not,
That swears not by thy valor.
  Ben. Until that fatal day, by ambush ta'en,
And in a dungeon kept, where, two long years,
Nor light of day, nor human voice e'er cheer'd
My loneliness, when did I ever yield,
To ev'n the bravest of that hateful name,
One step of ground upon the embattled field—
One step of honor in the banner'd hall?
  Loch. Indeed thou hast our noble champion been;
Deserving well the trust our chief deceased,
This chieftain's father, did to thee consign.
But when thou wert a captive, none to lead us,
But he, our youthful lord, yet green in arms,
We fought not like MacLeans; or else our foe,
By fiends assisted, fought with fiend-like power,
Far—far beyond the Campbells' wonted pitch.
Ev'n so it did befall:—we lost the day:—
That fatal day!—Then came this shameful peace.
  Ben. Ay, and this wedding; when, in form of honor
Conferr'd upon us, Helen of Argyle
Our sov'reign dame was made,—a bosom worm,
Nursed in that viper's nest, to infuse its venom
Through all our after race.
        This is my welcome!

From dungeon freed, to find my once-loved home
With such vile change disgraced; to me more hateful
Than thraldom's murkiest den.—But to be loosen'd
From captive's chains to find my hands thus bound!
  Loch. It is, indeed, a vile and irksome peace.
  Ben. Peace, say they! who will bonds of friendship sign
Between the teeming ocean's briny broods,
And say, "Sport these upon the hither waves,
And leave to those that farther billowy reach?"
A Campbell here to queen it o'er our heads,
The potent dame o'er quell'd and beaten men,
Rousing or soothing us, as proud Argyle
Shall send her secret counsel! hold, my heart!
This, base degenerate man!—this, call ye peace!
Forgive my weakness: with dry eyes I laid
My mother in her grave, but now my cheeks
Are, like a child's, with scalding drops disgraced.
  Loch. What I shall look upon, ere in the dust
My weary head is laid to rest, heaven knows,
Since I have lived to see Benlora weep.
  Ben. One thing, at least, thou ne'er shalt live to see—
Benlora crouching, where he has commanded.
Go, ye who will, and crowd the chieftain's hall,
And deal the feast, and nod your grizzled heads
To martial pibrochs, played, in better days,
To those who conquer'd, not who woo'd their foes;
My soul abhors it.—On the sea-beat rock,
Removed from ev'ry form and sound of man;
In proud communion with the fitful winds
Which speak, with many tongues, the fancied words
Of those who long in silent dust have slept;
While eagles scream, and sullen surges roar—
The boding sounds of ill:—I'll hold my feast,—
My moody revelry.
  Loch. Nay, why so fierce?
Think'st thou we are a tame and mongrel pack?
Dogs of true breed we are, though for a time
Our master-hound forsakes us.—Rouse him forth
The noble chase to lead: his deep-toned yell
Full well we know: and for the opening sport
Pant keenly.
  Ben. Ha! is there amongst ye still
Spirit enough for this?
  Loch. Yes, when good opportunity shall favor.
Of this, my friend, I'll speak to thee more fully
When time shall better serve.
        MacLean, thou know'st,
Is of a soft, unsteady, yielding nature;
And this, too well, the crafty Campbell knew,
When to our isle he sent this wily witch
To mold, and govern, and besot his wits,
As suits his crafty ends.—I know the youth:
This dame or we must hold his will in thraldom:
Which of the two.—But softly: Steps approach.
Of this again.
  Ben. As early as thou wilt.
  Loch. Then be it so: Some staunch determined spirits
This night in Irka's rocky cavern meet;
There must you join us. Wear thou here the while
A brow less cloudy, suited to the times.

(Enter GLENFADDEN.)
See, here comes one who wears a merry face;
Yet, ne'ertheless, a clansman staunch he is,
Who hates a Campbell, worse than Icolm's monks
The horned fiend.
  Ben. Ha! does he so?
        (Turning graciously to GLENFADDEN.)
                    Glenfadden!
How goes it with thee?—Joyous days are these—
These days of peace
  Glen. These days of foul disgrace!
Com'st thou to cheer the piper in our hall,
And goblets quaff to the young chieftain's health,
From proud Argyle descended?
  Ben. (Smiling grimly.) Yes, Glenfadden.
If ye will have it so; not else.
  Glen. Thy hand—
Thy noble hand!—thou art Benlora still.
(Shaking Benlora warmly by the hand, and then
            turning to Lochtarish.)
Know ye that banish'd Allen is return'd—
Allen of Dura?
  Loch. No; I knew it not.
But in good time he comes.—A daring knave:
He will be useful.   (After considering.)
                    Of MacLean we'll crave
His banishment to cancel: marking well
How he receives it. This will serve to show
The present bent and bearing of his mind.
              (After considering again.)
Were it not also well, that to our council
He were invited at a later hour,
When of our purpose we shall be assured?
  Glen. Methinks it were.
  Loch. In, then; now is our time.
  Ben. I'll follow thee, when I a while have paced
Yon lonely path, and thought upon thy counsel.
(Exeunt LOCHTARISH and GLENFADDEN into the
castle, and BENLORA by the opposite side.)

SCENE II.—*An Apartment in the Castle.*
(Enter MORTON and ROSA, speaking as they enter.)
  Rosa. Speak with my lady privately?
  Mor. Ay, please ye:
Something I have to say, regards her nearly.
And though I doubt not, madam, your attachment—
  Rosa. Good Morton, no apology: thy caution
Is prudent; trust me not till thou hast proved me.
But oh! watch o'er thy lady with an eye
Of keen and guarded zeal! She is surrounded—
              (Looking round the room.)
Does no one hear us?—O, those baleful looks
That, from beneath dark surly brows, by stealth,
Are darted on her by those stern MacLeans!
Ay; and the gestures of those fearful men,
As on the shore in savage groups they meet,
Sending their loosen'd tartans to the wind,
And tossing high their brawny arms, where oft
In vehement discourse, I have, of late,
At distance marked them.—Yes; thou shakest thy
  head:
Thou hast observed them, too.
  Mor. I have observed them oft. That calm Lochtarish,
Calm as he is, the growing rancor fosters:
For, fail the offspring of their chief, his sons
Next in succession are. He hath his ends,
For which he stirs their ancient hatred up;
And all too well his dev'lish pains succeed.
  Rosa. Too well indeed! The very bed-rid crones
To whom my lady sends, with kindly care,
Her cheering cordials,—could'st thou have believed it?
Do mutter spells to fence from things unholy,
And grumble, in a hollow smother'd voice,
The name of Campbell, as unwillingly
They stretch their wither'd hands to take her
  bounty.
The wizards are in pay to rouse their fears
With dismal tales of future ills foreseen,
From Campbell and MacLean together join'd,
In hateful union.—Ev'n the very children,
Sporting the heath among, when they discover
A loathsome toad or adder on their path,
Crush it with stones, and, grinding wickedly
Their teeth, in puny spite, call it a Campbell.
Benlora, too, that savage, gloomy man—
  Mor. Ay, evil is the day that brings him back.
Unjustly by a Campbell hath he been,
The peaceful treaty of the clans unheeded,
In thralldom kept; from which but now escaped,
He like a furious tiger is enchafed,
And thinks Argyle was privy to the wrong
His vassal put upon him. Well I know
His bloody, vengeful nature: and MacLean,
Weak and unsteady, moved by ev'ry counsel,
Brave in the field, but still in purpose timid,
Oft times the instrument in wicked hands
Of wrongs he would abhor,—alas, I fear,
Will ill defend the lovely spouse he swore
To love and cherish.
  Rosa. Heavy steps approach.
Hush! see who comes upon us! sly Lochtarish,
And his dark colleages.—Wherefore come they
  hither?

(MORTON retires to the bottom of the stage, and enter LOCHTARISH, BENLORA, and GLENFADDEN.)
  Loch. We thought, fair maid, to find the chieftain
here.
  Rosa. He is in these apartments.
  Loch. Would it greatly
Annoy your gentleness to tell his honor,
We wait to speak with him upon affairs
Of much concernment?
  Rosa. My service is not wanted; to your wish
See, there he comes unwarn'd, and with him too
His noble lady.
              (Retiring to the bottom of the stage.)
  Loch. Ha! there they come! see how he hangs
          upon her,
With boyish fondness!
  Glen. Ah, the goodly creature!
How fair she is! how winning!—See that form;
Those limbs beneath their foldy vestments moving,
As though in mountain clouds they robed were,
And music of the air their motion measured.
  Loch. Ay, shrewd and crafty earl! 'tis not for
          nought
Thou hither sent'st this jewel of thy race.
A host of Campbells, each a chosen man,
Could not enthrall us, as, too soon I fear,
This single Campbell will. Shrewd, crafty foe!
  Ben. Hell lend me aid, if heaven deny its grace,
But I will thwart him, crafty though he be!

Loch. But now for your petition: see we now
How he receives your suit.

(Enter MacLEAN and HELEN.)

Ben. (Eyeing her attentively as she enters.) A
potent foe it is; ay, by my faith,
A fair and goodly creature!
Mac. Again, good morning to ye, gallant kinsmen:
Come ye to say, I can with any favor
The right good liking prove, and high regard
I bear to you, who are my chiefest strength,—
The pillars of my clan?
Ben. Yes, we are come, MacLean, a boon to beg.
Loch. A boon that granted, will yourself enrich.
Mac. Myself enrich?
Loch. Yes; thereby wilt thou be
One gallant man the richer. Hear us out.
Allen of Dura, from his banishment—
Mac. False reaver! name him not.—Is he return'd?
Dares he again set foot upon this isle?
Ben. Yes, chief; upon this isle set foot he hath:
And on nor isle nor mainland doth there step
A braver man than he.—Lady, forgive me:
The boldest Campbell never saw his back.
Hel. Nay, good Benlora, ask not my forgiveness:
I love to hear thee praise, with honest warmth,
The valiant of thy name, which now is mine.
Ben. (Aside.) Ha! good Benlora! this is queenly pride.
(Aloud.) Madam, you honor us.
Hel. If so, small thanks be to my courtesy,
Sharing myself with pride the honest fame
Of every brave MacLean.—I'll henceforth keep
A proud account of all my gallant friends:
And every valiant Campbell therein noted,
On the opposing leaf, in letters fair,
Shall with a brave MacLean be proudly matched.
(BENLORA and GLENFADDEN bow in silence.)
Loch. Madam, our grateful duty waits upon you.
(Aside to BENLORA.) What think'st thou of her, friend?
Ben. (Aside to LOCHTARISH.) What think I of her?
Incomparable hypocrite!
Loch. (Aloud.) But to our suit: for words of courtesy
It must not be forgotten.—Chief, vouchsafe:
Benlora here, who from his loathly prison,
Which for your sake he hath endured,
Begs earnestly this grace for him we mention'd,
Allen of Dura.
(Aside to BENLORA.) Kneel, man; be more pressing.
Ben. (Aside to LOCHTARISH.) Nay, by my fay! if crouching pleaseth thee,
Do it thyself. (Going up proudly to MacLEAN.)
MacLean, thy father put it into these hands
The government and guidance of thy nonage.
How the trust fulfill'd, this castle strengthen'd
With walls and added towers, and stored, besides,
With arms and trophies, in rough warfare won
From ev'n the bravest of our western clans,
Will testify. What I in recompense
Have for my service earn'd, these galled wrists
(Pushing up the sleeve from his arm.)
Do also testify.—Such as I am,
For an old friend I plainly beg this grace:
Say if my boon be granted or denied.

Mac. The man for whom thou pleads't is most unworthy:
Yet let him safely from my shores depart:
I harm him not.
Ben. (Turning from him indignantly). My suit is then denied.
(To LOCHTARISH and GLENFADDEN.) Go ye to
Dura's Allen; near the shore
He harbors in his aged mother's cot;
Bid him upon the ocean drift again
His shatter'd boat, and be a wanderer still.
Hel. (Coming forward eagerly). His aged mother.
(To MACLEAN.) Oh! and shall he go?
No, no, he shall not! On this day of joy,
Wilt thou to me refuse it?
(Hanging upon him with looks of entreaty, till, seeing him relent, she then turns joyfully to BENLORA.)
Bid your wanderer
Safe with his aged mother still remain,—
A banish'd man no more.
Mac. This is not well; but be it as thou wilt;
Thou must prevail'd, my Helen.
Loch. and Glen. (Bowing low.) We thank thee, lady.
(BENLORA bows slightly, in sullen silence.)
Mac. (To BENLORA.) Then let thy friend remain; he has my pardon.
(BENLORA bows again in silence.)
Clear up thy brow, Benlora; he is pardon'd.
(Pauses, but BENLORA is still silent.)
We trust to meet you shortly in the hall;
And there, my friends, shall think our happy feast
More happy for your presence.—
(Going up again, with anxious courtesy, to BENLORA.)
Thy past services,
Which great and many are, my brave Benlora,
Shall be remember'd well. Thou hast my honor,
And high regard.
Hel. And mine to boot, good kinsman, if the value
You put upon them makes them worth the having.
Ben. (Bows sullenly and retires; then muttering aside to himself as he goes out.) Good kinsman! Good Benlora! gracious words
From this most high and potent dame, vouchsafed
To one so poor and humble as myself.   (Exit.)
Loch. (Aside to GLENFADDEN.) But thou forgettest—
Glen. (Aside to LOCHTARISH.) No: I'll stay behind,
And move MacLean to join our mighty meeting.
Loch. Yes, even so: then will we be prepared.
        (Exit.)
Glen. (Returning to MACLEAN.) Chieftain, I would some words of privacy
Speak with you, should your leisure now permit.
Mac. Come to my closet then, I'll hear thee gladly.
        (Exeunt MACLEAN and GLENFADDEN.)
Hel. (To ROSA, who now comes forward.) Where hast thou been, my Rosa? With my boy?
Have they with wild flowers deck'd his cradle round?

And peeps he through them like a little nestling—
A little heath-cock broken from its shell,
That through the bloom puts forth its tender beak,
As steals some rustling footstep on his nest?
Come, let me go and look upon him. Soon,
Ere two months more go by, he'll look again
In answer to my looks, as though he knew
The wistful face that looks so oft upon him,
And smiles so dearly, is his mother's.
                      Think'st thou
He'll soon give heed and notice to my love?
  Rosa. I doubt it not: he is a lively infant,
And moves his little limbs with vigor, spreading
His fingers forth, as if in time they would
A good claymore clench bravely.
  Hel. A good claymore clench bravely! O! to see him
A man!—a valiant youth!—a noble chieftain!
And laying on his plaided shoulder, thus,
A mother's hand, say proudly, "this is mine!"
I shall not then a lonely stranger be
'Midst those who bless me not. I shall not then—
But silent be my tongue.   (Weeps.)
  Rosa. Dear madam, still in hope look forward cheerly.
  (MORTON comes from the bottom of the stage.)
And here is Morton, with some tidings for you:
God grant they comfort you!—I must withdraw:
His wary faithfulness mistrusts my love,
But I am not offended.   (Offering to retire.)
  Hel. Nay, remain.   (Beckoning her back.)
Say what thou hast to say, my worthy Morton,
For Rosa is as faithful as thyself.
  Mor. This morning, lady, 'mongst the farther cliffs,
Dress'd like a fisher peasant, did I see
The lord of Lorn, your brother.
  Hel. Ha! say'st thou,
The lord of Lorn, my brother?—Thour't deceived.
  Mor. No, no; in vain his sordid garb conceal'd him:
His noble form and stately step I knew
Before he spoke.
  Hel. He spoke to thee?
  Mor. He did.
  Hel. Was he alone?
  Mor. He was; but, near at hand,
Another stranger, noble as himself,
And in like garb disguised, amongst the rocks
I mark'd, though he advanced not.
  Hel. Alas, alas, my brother! why is this?
He spoke to thee, thou say'st—I mean my brother:
What did he say!
  Mor. He earnestly entreats
To see you privately; and bids you say
When this may be. Meantime, he lies conceal'd
Where I may call him forth at your command.
  Hel. O, why disguised?—Thinks't thou he is not safe?
  Mor. Safe in his hiding-place he is: but yet
The sooner he shall leave this coast, the better.
  Hel. To see him thus!—O, how I am beset!
Tell him at twilight, in my nurse's chamber,
I will receive him. But be sure thou add,
Himself alone will I receive—alone—
With no companion must he come. Forget not
To say, that I entreat it earnestly.
  Mor. I will remember this.

  Hel. Go to him quickly then; and, till the hour,
Still do thou hover near him. Watch his haunt,
Lest some rude fisherman or surly hind
Surprise him.—Go thou quickly. O, be prudent!
And be not for a moment off the watch.
  Mor. Madam, I will obey you: trust me well.
                                        (Exit.)
  Hel. (Much disturbed.) My brother on the coast; and with him too,
As well I guess, the man I must not see!
  Rosa. Mean you the brave Sir Hubert?
  Hel. Yes, my Rosa.
My noble brother in his powerful self
So strong in virtue stands, he thinks full surely
The daughter of his sire no weakness hath;
And wists not how a simple heart must struggle
To be what it would be—what it must be—
Ay, and, so aid me, heaven! what it shall be.
  Rosa. And heaven will aid you, madam, doubt it not.
Though on this subject still you have repress'd
All communing, yet, ne'ertheless, I well
Have mark'd your noble striving, and revered
Your silent inward warfare, bravely held;
In this more pressing combat firm and valiant,
As is your noble brother in the field.
  Hel. I thank thee, gentle Rosa; thou art kind—
I should be franker with thee; but I know not—
Something restrains me here.
                (Laying her hand on her breast.)
I love and trust thee;
And on thy breast I'll weep when I am sad;
But ask not why I weep.   (Exeunt.)

ACT II.

SCENE I.—*An apartment in twilight, almost dark; the door of an inner chamber, standing a little ajar, at the bottom of the stage.*

(Enter JOHN OF LORN and SIR HUBERT DE GREY, disguised as peasants.)

  De Grey. Nay, stop, I pray; advance we not too far?
  Lorn. Morton hath bid us in this place to wait.
The nurse's chamber is adjoining to it;
And, till her light within give notice, here
Thou may'st remain; when I am call'd, thou'lt leave me.
  De Grey. Till thou art call'd! and may I stay to hear
The sweetness of her voice—her footstep's sound;
Perhaps snatch in the torch's hasty light
One momentary vision of that form—
The form that hath to me of earthly make
No fellow? May it be without transgression?
  Lorn. Why should'st thou not? De Grey, thou art too fearful;
Here art thou come with no dishonest will;
And well she knows thine honor. Her commands,
Though we must yield to them, capricious seem;
Seeing thou art with me, too nicely scrupulous;
And therefore need no farther be obey'd
Than needs must be. She puts thee not on honor.
Were I so used—
  De Grey. 'Spite of thy pride, would'st thou
Revere her still the more.—O, no, brave Lorn,
I blame her not. When she, a willing victim,
To spare the blood of two contending clans,

Against my faithful love her suffrage gave,
I blessed her; and the deep, but chasten'd sorrow
With which she bade me—Oh! that word! farewell,
Is treasured in my bosom as its share
Of all that earthly love hath power to give.
It came from Helen, and, from her receiv'd,
Shall not be worn with thankless dull repining.
   Lorn. A noble heart thou hast: such manly meekness
Becomes thy gen'rous nature. But for me,
More fierce and willful, sorely was I chafed
To see thy faithful heart robb'd of its hope,
All for the propping up a hollow peace
Between two warlike clans, who will, as long
As bagpipes sound, and blades flash to the sun,
Delighting in the noble sport of war,
Some fierce opponent find. What doth it boot,
If men in fields must fight, and blood be shed,
What clans are in the ceaseless strife opposed?
   De Grey. Ah, John of Lorn! too keenly is thy soul
To war inclined—to wasteful, ruthless war.
   Lorn. The warlike minstrel's rousing lay thou lov'st:
Shall bards i' the hall sing of our fathers' deeds
To lull their sons to sleep? Vain, simple wish!
I love to hear the sound of holy bell,
And peaceful men their praises lift to heaven:
I love to see around their blazing fire
The peasant and his cheerful family set,
Eating their fearless meal. But, when the roar
Of battle rises, and the closing clans,
Dark'ning the sun-gleam'd heath, in dread array
Are mingled; blade with blade, and limb with limb,
Nerve-strain'd, in terrible strength; yea, soul with soul
Nobly contending; who would raise aloft
The interdicting hand, and say: "Be still'd?"
If this in me be sin, may heaven forgive me!
That being am not I.
   De Grey. In very deed
This is thy sin; and of thy manly nature
The only blemish worthy of that name.
More peaceful be, and thou wilt be more noble.
   Lorn. Well, here we will not wrangle for the point.
None in th' embattled field who have beheld
Hubert de Grey in mailed hauberk fight,
Will guess how much that knight in peace delights.
Still burns my heart that such a man as thou
Was't for this weak, unsteady, poor MacLean—
   De Grey. Nay, with contempt, I pray thee, name him not.
Her husband, and despised! O, no, no, no!
All that pertains to her, ev'n from that hour,
Honored and sacred is.
   Lorn. Thou gen'rous heart! more noble than myself!
I will not grieve thee.—I'll to Helen go,
With every look and word that might betray
Indignant thoughts, or wound her gentle spirit,
Strictly suppressed: and to her ear will give
Thy gen'rous greetings, and thy manly words
Of cheering comfort;—all most faithfully
Shall be remembered.
   De Grey. Ay, and my request.
   Lorn. To see the child?
   De Grey. Ev'n so: to look upon it;—

Upon the thing that is of her; this bud—
This seedling of a flower so exquisite.
          (Light is seen in the inner chamber.)
Ha! light is in the chamber! moves the door?
Some one approaches. O! but for a moment
Let me behind thy friendly tartans be,
And snatch one glance of what that light will give.
(Conceals himself behind LORN, who steps some
   paces back, setting his hand to his side, and
   tilting his plaid over his arms to favor him;
   while the door of the inner chamber opens,
   and HELEN appears, bearing a lamp, which she
   afterward sets upon a stone slab as she advances.)
Her form—her motion—yea, that mantled arm,
Press'd closely to her breast, as she was wont
When chilly winds assail'd.—The face—O, woe is me!
It was not then so pale.
   Lorn. (To him in a low voice.) Begone: begone.
   De Grey. Blest vision, I have seen thee! Fare thee well!   (Exit in haste.)
   Hel. (Coming forward alarmed.) What sound is
that of steps that hasten from us?
Is Morton on the watch?
   Lorn. Fear nothing; faithful Morton is at hand:
The steps thou heard'st were friendly.
   Hel. (Embracing LORN.) My brother! meet we
thus,—disguised, by stealth?
Is this like peace? How is my noble father?
Hath any ill befallen?
   Lorn. Argyle is well;
And nothing ill, my sister, hath befallen,
If thou art well and happy.
   Hel. Speak'st thou truly?
Why art thou come? Why thus upon our coast?
O take it not unfriendly that I say,
"Why art thou come?"
   Lorn. Near to the opposite shore,
With no design, but on a lengthen'd chase,
A lusty deer pursuing from the hills
Of Morvern, where Sir Hubert and myself
Guests of the social lord two days had been,
We found us; when a sudden strong desire
To look upon the castle of MacLean,
Seen from the coast, our eager fancy seized,
And that indulged, forthwith we did agree
The frith to cross, and to its chief and dame
A hasty visit make. But as our boat
Lay waiting to receive us, warn'd by one
Whom well I knew, (the vassal of a friend,
Whose word I could not doubt,) that jealous rancour,
Stirr'd up amongst the vassals of MacLean,
Who, in their savage fury, had been heard
To utter threats against thy innocent self,
Made it unsafe in open guise to venture,
Here in this garb we are to learn in secret
The state in which thou art.—How is it then?
Morton's report has added to my fears:
All is not well with thee.
   Hel. No, all is well.
   Lorn. A cold constrained voice that answer gave;
All is not well.—MacLean—dares he neglect thee?
   Hel. Nay, wrong him not; kind and affectionate
He still remains.
   Lorn. But it is said, his vassals with vile names
Have dared to name thee, even in open clan,

And have remain'd unpunished. Is it so?
(Pauses for an answer, but she is silent.)
All is not well.
Hel. Have I not said it is?
Lorn. Ah! dost thou thus return a brother's love
With cold reserve?—O speak to me, my Helen!
Speak as a sister should.—Have they insulted thee?
Has any wrong—my heart within me burns
If I but think upon it.—Answer truly.
Hel. What, am I questioned then? Think'st thou to find me
Like the spoil'd heiress of some Lowland lord,
Peevish and dainty; who, with scorn regarding
The ruder home she is by marriage placed in,
Still holds herself an alien from its interest,
With poor repining, losing every sense
Of what she is, in what she has been? No.—
I love thee, Lorn; I love my father's house:
The meanest cur that round his threshold barks,
Is in my memory as some kindred thing:
Yet take it not unkindly when I say,
The lady of MacLean no grievance hath
To tell the lord of Lorn.
Lorn. And has the vow,
Constrain'd, unblest, and joyless as it was,
Which gave thee to a lord unworthy of thee,
Placed thee beyond the reach of kindred ties—
The warmth of blood to blood—the sure affection
That nature gives to all—a brother's love?
No, by all sacred things! here is thy hold:
Here is thy true, unshaken, native stay:
One that shall fail thee never, though the while,
A faithless, wavering, intervening band
Seems to divide thee from it.
(Grasping her hand vehemently, as if he would lead her away.)
Hel. What dost thou mean? What violent grasp is this?
Com'st thou to lead me from my husband's house,
Beneath the shade of night, with culprit stealth?
Lorn. No, daughter of Argyle; when John of Lorn
Shall come to lead thee from these hated walls
Back to thy native home,—with culprit stealth,
Beneath the shades of night, it shall not be.
With half our western warriors at his back,
He'll proudly come. Thy listening timid chief
Shall hear our martial steps upon his heath,
With heavy measured fall, send, beat by beat,
From the far smitten earth, a sullen sound,
Like deep-dell'd forests groaning to the strokes
Of lusty woodmen. On the watch-tower's height,
His straining eye shall mark our sheathless swords
From rank to rank their lenghten'd blaze emit,
Like streams of shiv'ring light, in hasty change,
Upon the northern firmament.—By stealth!
No! not by stealth!—believe me, not by stealth
Shalt thou these portals pass.
Hel. Them have I enter'd
The pledge of peace; and here my place I'll hold
As dame and mistress of the warlike clan
Who yield obedience to their chief, my lord;
And whatsoe'er their will to me may bear,
Of good or ill, so will I hold me ever.
Yea, did the lord of Lorn, dear as he is,
With all the warlike Campbells at his back
Here hostile entrance threaten; on these walls,

Failing the strength that might defend them better,
I would myself, while by my side in arms
One valiant clansman stood, against his powers,
To the last push, with desp'rate opposition,
This castle hold.
Lorn. And would'st thou so? So firm and valiant art thou?
Forgive me, noble creature!—Oh! the fate—
The wayward fate that binds thy gen'rous soul
To poor unsteady weakness!
Hel. Speak'st thou thus?
Thus pressing still upon the galled spot?
Thou deal'st unkindly with me. Yes, my brother,
Unkindly and unwisely. Wherefore hast thou
Brought to this coast the man thou knowest well
I ought not in mysterious guise to see?
And he himself—seeks he again to move
The hapless weakness I have strove to conquer?
I thought him generous.
Lorn. So think him still.
His wishes tend not to disturb thy peace:
For other are his thoughts—He bids me tell thee,
To cheer thy gentle heart, nor think of him
As one who will in vain and stubborn grief
His ruin'd bliss lament,—he bids me say
That he will even strive, if it be possible,
Amongst the maidens of his land to seek
Some faint resemblance of the good he lost,
That thou may's hear of him with less regret,
As one by holy bands link'd to his kind.
He bids me say, should ever child of his
And child of thine—but here his quivering lip
And starting tears spoke what he could not speak.
Hel. O, noble gen'rous heart! and does he offer
Such cheering manly comfort? Heaven protect,
And guide, and bless him! On his noble head
Such prosp'rous bliss be pour'd, that hearing of it
Shall, through the gloom of my untoward state,
Like gleams of sunshine break, that from afar
Look o'er the dull dim heath.
Lorn. But one request—
Hel. Ha! makes he one?
Lorn. It is to see thy child.
Hel. To see my child! Will he indeed regard it?
Shall it be bless'd by him?

(Enter MORTON in haste.)

Mor. Conceal yourself, my lord, or by this passage (Pointing off the stage.)
The nearest postern gain: I hear the sound
Of heavy steps at hand, and voices stern.
Hel. Off my brother! Morton will conduct thee.
(To MORTON.) Where is Sir Hubert?
Mor. Safe, he is without.
Hel. Heaven keep him so!
(To LORN.) O leave me! I, the while,
Will in, and, with mine infant in mine arms,
Meet thee again, ere thou depart'st.—Fly! fly!
(Exeunt HELEN into the inner chamber, putting out the lamps as she goes, and LORN and MORTON by a side passage.)

SCENE II.—*A cave, lighted by flaming brands stuck aloft on its rugged sides, and shedding a fierce glaring light down upon the objects below.* LOCHTARISH, BENLORA, GLENFADDEN, *with several of the chief vassals of* MACLEAN, *are discovered in a recess, formed by projecting rocks, at the bottom of the stage, engaged in earnest discourse, from which they move forward slowly, speaking as they advance.)*

Loch. And thus, ye see by strong necessity,
We are compelled to do this.
   1st Vas. Perhaps thou'rt right.
   Loch. Say'st thou *perhaps?* Dost thou not plainly see
That ne'er a man amongst us can securely
His lands possess, or say, "My house is mine,"
While under tutorage of proud Argyle,
This beauteous sorceress our besotted chief
By soft enchantment holds?
            (Laying his hand on the first vassal.)
My brave Glenore,
What are thy good deserts, that may uphold thee
In favor with a Campbell?—Duncan's blood,
Slain in his boat, with all its dashing oars
Skirting our shore, while that his vaunting piper
The Campbell's triumph play'd? Will this speak
   for thee?   (Turning to second vassal.)
And, Thona, what good merit pleadest thou?
The coal black steed of Clone, thy moonlight plunder,
Ta'en from the spiteful laird, will he, good sooth!
Neigh favor on thee?   (To 3d vassal.)
         And my valiant Fallen,
Bethink thee well if fair-hair'd Flora's cries,
Whom from her native bower by force thou took'st,
Will plead for thee.—And say ye still *perhaps—*
Perhaps there is necessity?
   1st Vas. Strong should it be, Lochtarish; for the act
Is fell and cruel thou would'st push us to.
   Glen. (To 1st Vas.) Ha, man of mercy! are thy lily hands
From bloody taint unstain'd? What sights were those
Thou look'dst upon in Brunock's burning tower,
When infants through the flames their wailings sent,
And yet unaided perish'd?
   Loch. (Soothingly.) Tush, Glenfadden!
Too hasty art thou.
   (To the vassals.) Ye will say, belike,
"Our safety—our existence did demand
Utter extinction of that hold of foes."
And well ye may.—A like necessity
Compels us now, and yet we hesitate.
   Glen. Our sighted seers the fun'ral lights have seen,
Not moving onward in the wonted path
On which by friends the peaceful dead are borne,
But hov'ring o'er the heath like countless stars,
Spent and extinguish'd on the very spot
Where first they twinkled. This too well foreshews
Interment of the slain, whose bloody graves
Of the same mold are made on which they fell.
   2d Vas. Ha! so indeed! some awful tempest gathers.
   1st Vas. What sighted man hath seen it?
   Glen. He whose eye
Can see on northern waves the found'ring bark,
With all her shrieking crew, sink to the deep,
While yet with gentle winds, on dimpling surge
She sails from port in all her gallant trim:
John of the Isle hath seen it.

   Omnes. (Starting back.) Then hangs some evil over us.
   Glen. Know ye not
The mermaid hath been heard upon our rocks?
   Omnes. (Still more alarmed.) Ha! when?
   Glen. Last night, upon the rugged crag
That lifts its dark head through the cloudy smoke
Of dashing billows, near the western cliff.
Sweetly, but sadly, o'er the stilly deep
The passing sound was borne. I need not say
How fatal to our clan that boding sound
Hath ever been.
   3d Vas. In faith thou makest me quake.
   2d Vas. Some fearful thing hangs o'er us.—
   1st Vas. If 'tis fated,
Our clan before our ancient foe shall fall,
Can we heaven's will prevent? Why should we then
The Campbells' wrath provoke?
   Ben. (Stepping up fiercely to 1st Vassal).
Heaven's will prevent!—The Campbells' we provoke!
Is such base tameness utter'd by the son
Of one, who would into the fiery pit
Of damned fiends have leapt, so that his grasp
Might pull a Campbell with him?
               Bastard blood!
Thy father spoke not like thus.
   Loch. (Soothingly.) Nay, brave Benlora,
He means not as thou think'st.
   Ben. If heaven decrees
Slaughter and ruin for us, come it then!
But let our enemies, close grappled to us,
In deadly strife, their ruin join with ours.
Let corse to corse, upon the bloody heath,
MacLean and Campbell, stiff'ning side by side,
With all the gnashing ecstasy of hate
Upon their ghastly visages impress'd,
Lie horribly!—For ev'ry widow's tear
Shed in our clan, let matron Campbells howl.
   Loch. Indeed, my friends, although too much in ire,
Benlora wisely speaks.—Shall we in truth
Wait for our ruin from a crafty foe,
Who here maintains this keenly watchful spy
In gentle kindness masked?
   Glen. Nor need we fear,
As good Lochtarish hath already urged,
Her death will rouse Argyle. It will be deem'd,
As we shall grace it with all good respect
Of funeral pomp, a natural visitation.
   Loch. Ay, and besides, we'll swear upon the book,
And truly swear, if we are call'd upon,
We have not shed her blood.
   Ben. I like not this.
If ye her life will take, in open day
Let her a public sacrifice be made.
Let the loud trumpet far and near proclaim
Our bloody feast, and at the rousing sound,
Let every clansman of the hated name
His vengeful weapon clench.—
I like it not, Lochtarish. What we do,
Let it be boldly done.—Why should we slay her?
Let her in shame be from the castle sent;
Which, to her haughty sire, will do, I ween,

Far more despite than taking of her life.—
A feeble woman's life!—I like it not.
(Turning on his heel angrily, and striding to the bottom of the stage.)
 Loch. (Aside to GLEN.) Go to him, friend, and sooth him to our purpose.
The fiery fool! how madly wild he is!
(GLENFADDEN goes to the bottom of the stage, and is seen remonstrating, in dumb-show, with BENLORA, while LOCHTARISH speaks to the vassals on the front.)
 Loch. My friends, why on each other look ye thus
In gloomy silence? Freely speak your thoughts.
Mine have I freely spoken: that advising
Which for the good—nay, I must say existence,
Of this our ancient clan most needful is.
When did Lochtarish ever for himself
A separate 'vantage seek, in which the clan
At large partook not? Am I doubted now?
 2d Vas. No, nothing do we doubt thy public zeal.
 Loch. Then is my long experience o' the sudden
To childish folly turn'd?
         Think'st thou, good Thona,
We should beneath this artful mistress live,
Hush'd in deceitful peace, till John of Lorn,
For whom the office of a treacherous spy
She doth right slyly manage, with his powers
Shall come upon us? Once ye would have spurn'd
At thoughts so base; but now, when forth I stand
To do what vengeance, safety, nay, existence,
All loudly call for; even as though already
The enemy's baleful influence hung o'er ye,
Like quell'd and passive men ye silent stand.
 1st Vas. (Roused.) Nay, cease, Lochtarish! quell'd and passive men
Thou know'st we are not.
 Loch. Yet a woman's life,
And that a treacherous woman, moves ye thus.
Bold as your threats of dark revenge have been,
A strong decisive deed appals ye now.
Our chieftain's feeble undetermined spirit
Infects you all: ye dare not stand by me.
 Omnes. We dare not, say'st thou?
 Loch. Dare not, will I say!
Well spoke the jeering Camerons, I trow,
As past their fishing boats our vessels steer'd,
When with push'd lip, and finger pointing thus,
They call'd our crew the Campbell-cow'd MacLeans.
 Omnes. (Roused fiercely.) The Campbell-cow'd MacLeans!
 2d Vas. Infernal devils!
Dare they to call us so?
 Loch. Ay, by my truth!
Nor think that from the Camerons alone
Ye will such greetings have, if back ye shrink,
And stand not by me now.
 Omnes. (Eagerly.) We'll stand!—We'll stand!
 2d Vas. Tempt us no more:—there's ne'er a man of us
That will not back thee boldly.
 Loch. Ay, indeed!
Now are ye men! Give me your hands to this.
         (They all give him their hands.)
Now am I satisfied.   (Looking off the stage.)

The chief approaches.
Ye know full well the spirit of the man
That we must deal withal; therefore be bold.
 Omnes. Mistrust us not.

(Enter MACLEAN, who advances to the middle of the stage, while LOCHTARISH, BENLORA, GLENFADDEN, and all the other vassals gather round him with stern, determined looks. A pause; MACLEAN eyeing them all round with inquisitive anxiety.)
 Mac. A goodly meeting at this hour convened
         (A sullen pause.)
Benlora; Thona; Allen of Glenore;
And all of you, our first and bravest kinsmen;
What mystery in this sullen silence is?
Hangs any threaten'd evil o'er the clan?
 Ben. Yes, chieftain; evil, that doth make the blood
Within your gray-haired warriors' veins to burn,
And their brogued feet to spurn the ground that bears them.
 Loch. Evil, that soon will wrap your tower in flames,
Your ditches fill with blood, and carrion birds
Glut with the butcher'd corses of your slain.
 Glen. Ay; evil, that doth make the hoary locks
Of sighted men around their age-worn scalps
Like quickened points of crackling flame to rise;
Their teeth to grind, and strained eye-balls roll
In fitful frenzy, at the horrid things
In terrible array before them raised.
 1st Vas. The mermaid hath been heard upon the rocks;
The fatal song of waves.
 Glen. The northern deep
Is heard with distant moanings from our coast,
Uttering the dismal bodeful sounds of death.
 2d Vas. The funeral lights have shone upon our heath,
Marking in countless groups the graves of thousands.
 Ben. Yea, chief; and sounds like to thy father's voice
Have from the sacred mold wherein he lies,
At the dead of night, by wakeful men been heard
Three times distinctly. (Turning to GLENFADDEN.)
Said'st thou not thrice?
 Glen. Yes; three times heard distinctly.
 Mac. Ye much amaze me, friends.—Such things have been.
 Loch. Yea, chief; and think'st thou we may lightly deem
Of coming ills, by signs like these forewarn'd?
 Mac. Then an it be, high heaven have mercy on us!
 Loch. (In a loud solemn voice.) Thyself have mercy on us!
 Mac. How is this?
Your words confuse and stun me.—Have I power
To ward this evil off?
 Omnes. Thou hast! thou hast!
 Mac. Then God to me show mercy in my need,
As I will do for you and for my clan
Whate'er my slender power enables me.
 Omnes. Amen! and swear to it.
 Mac. (Starting back.) What words are these?

With such wild fierceness uttered? Name the thing
That ye would have me do.
   Ben. (Stepping from the rest.) Ay, we will name it.
Helen the Campbell, foster'd in your bosom,
A serpent is, who wears a hidden sting
For thee and all thy name; the oath-bound spy
Of dark Argyle, our foe; the baleful plague
To which ill-omen'd sounds and warnings point,
As that on which existence or extinction—
The name and being of our clan depend;—
A witch of deep seduction.—Cast her forth.
The strange, unnatural union of two bloods
Adverse and hostile, most abhorred is.
The heart of every warrior of your name
Rises against it. Yea, the grave calls out,
And says it may not be.—Nay, shrink not, chief,
When I again repeat it.—Cast her off.
   Mac. Art thou a man? and bid'st me cast her off,
Bound as I am by sacred holy ties?
   Loch. Bound as thou art by that which thou regardest
As sacred holy ties; what tie so sacred
As those that to his name and kindred vassals
The noble chieftain bind? If ties there be
To these opposed, although a saint from heaven
Had bless'd them o'er the cross'd and holy things,
They are annull'd and broken.
   Ben. Ay, Lochtarish,
Sound doctrine hast thou uttered. Such the creed
Of ancient warriors was, and such the creed
That we their sons will with our swords maintain.
(Drawing his sword fiercely, whilst the rest follow his example.)
   Mac. Ye much confound me with your violent words.
I can in battle strive, as well ye know:
But how to strive with you, ye violent men,
My spirit knows not.
   Lorh. Decide—decide, MacLean: the choice is thine
To be our chieftain, leading forth thy bands,
As heretofore thy valiant father did,
Against our ancient foe, or be the husband,
Despis'd, forsak'n, curs'd, of her thou prizest
More than thy clan and kindred.
   Glen. Make thy choice.
Benlora, wont in better times to lead us
Against the Campbells, with a chieftain's power,
Shall, with the first blast of his warlike horn,
If so he wills it, round his standard gather
Thy rous'd and valiant vassals to a man.
   Mac. (Greatly startled.) Ha! go your thoughts to this? Desert me so?
My vassals so desert me?
   Loch. Ay, by my faith, our very women too:
And in your hall remain, to serve your state,
Nor child nor aged crone.
   Mac. (After great agitation.) Decide, and cast her off!—How far the thoughts
To which these words ye yoke, may go, I guess not.
(Eagerly.) They reach not to her life?
(Pauses and looks at them anxiously, but they are silent.)
Oh, oh! oh, oh! that stern and dreadful silence!

   Loch. We will not shed her blood.
   Mac. Then ye will spare her.
   Loch. Commit her to our keeping: ask us not
How we shall deal with her.
   Mac. Some fearful mystery is in your words,
Which covers cruel things. O woe the day.
That I on this astounding ridge am poised!
On ev'ry side a fearful ruin yawns.
(A voice heard without uttering wild incoherent words, mixed with shrieks of horror.)
What frenzied voice is that?

(Enter FOURTH VASSAL, as if terribly frightened.)
   Loch. (To 4th Vassal.) What brings thee hither?
   4th Vas. He fixes wildly on the gloomy void
His starting eye-balls, bent on fearful sights,
That make the sinews of his aged limbs
In agony to quiver.
   Loch. Who didst thou say?
   4th Vas. John of the Isle, the sighted awful man.
Go, see yourselves: i' the outer cave he is.
Entranced he stands; arrested on his way
By horrid visions, as he hurried hither
Inquiring for the chief.
   (Voice heard without as before.)
   Loch. Hark! hark, again! dread powers are dealing with him.
Come, chieftain—come and see the awful man.
If heaven or hell have power to move thy will,
Thou canst not now withstand us.
(Pausing for him to go.) Hear'st thou not?
And motionless!
   Mac. I am beset and stunn'd,
And every sense bewildered. Violent men!
If ye unto this fearful pitch are bent,—
When such necessity is press'd upon me,
What doth avail resistance? Woe the day!
Ev'n lead me where ye will!
(Exit MACLEAN, exhausted and trembling, leaning on LOCHTARISH, and followed by BENLORA and GLENFADDEN and vassals; two inferior vassals alone left upon the stage,)
   1st Vas. (Looking after MACLEAN.) Ay, there he goes; so spent, and scared, and feeble!
Without a prophet's skill, we may foretell,
John of the Isle, by sly Lochtarish taught,
Will work him soon to be an oath-bound wretch
To this their fell design!—Are all things ready?
   2d Vas. All is in readiness.
   1st Vas. When ebbs the tide?
   2d Vas. At early dawn when in the narrow creek
Near to the castle with our trusty mates,
Our boat must be in waiting to receive her.
   1st Vas. The time so soon! alas, so young and fair!
That slow and dismal death! To be at once
Plunged in the closing deep many have suffered,
But to sit waiting on a lonely rock
For the approaching tide to throttle her—
But that she is a Campbell, I could weep.
   2d Vas. Weep, fool! think soon how we'll to war again
With our old enemy; and, in the field,
Our good claymores reek with their hated blood:
Think upon this, and change thy tears to joy.
   (Exeunt.

SCENE III.—*The bed chamber of* MACLEAN. *Enter* MACLEAN *followed by* HELEN.

Hel. Ah! wherefore art thou so disturbed? the night
Is almost spent: the morn will break ere long,
And rest hast thou had none. Go to thy bed:
I pray thee, go.
Mac. I can not: urge me not.
Hel. Nay, try to rest: I'll sit and watch by thee.
Mac. Thou'lt sit and watch! O woe betide the hour!
And who will watch for thee?
Hel. And why for me?
Can any harm approach? When thou art near,
Or sleeping or awake, I am secure.
Mac. (Pacing to and fro distractedly.) O God! O God!
Hel. Those exclamations! (Going up to him, while he avoids her.)
Turn'st thou from me thus?
Have I offended? dost thou deny my faith?
Hath any jealous thought—I freely own
Love did not make me thine: but, being thine,
To no love-wedded dame, bound in the ties
Of dearest sympathy, will I in duty—
In steady, willing, cheerful duty yield.
Yea, and though here no thrilling rapture be,
I look to spend with thee, by habit foster'd,
The ev'ning of my days in true affection.
Mac. The ev'ning of thy days! alas, alas!
Would heaven had so decreed it!
(Pulling away his hand from hers.)
Grasp me not!
It is a fiend thou cling'st to. (A knock at the door.)
Power of heaven!
Are they already at the chamber door!
Hel. Are those who knock without unwelcome?—hush!
Withdraw thyself, and I will open to them.
(Goes to the door.)
Mac. O go not! go not!
(Runs after her to draw her back, when a vassal, rushing from behind the bed, lays hold of him.)
Vas. Art thou not sworn to us? Where is thy faith?
Mac. I know, I know? the bands of hell have bound me.
O fiends! ye've made of me—what words can speak
The hateful wretch I am!
Hark! hark! she cries!
She shrieks and calls on me!
(HELEN'S cries heard without, first near and distinct, afterward more and more distant as they bear her away; while the vassal leads MACLEAN forcibly off the stage by the opposite side, he breaks from him, and hastens toward that by which HELEN went out.)
Vas. Thou art too strong for me. Do as thou wilt;
But if thou bring'st her back, even from that moment
Benlora is our leader, and thyself,
The Campbell's husband, chieftain and MacLean
No more shalt be. We've sworn as well as thou.
(MACLEAN stops irresolutely, and then suffers the vassal to lead him off by the opposite side.)

ACT III.

SCENE I.—*A small island, composed of a rugged craggy rock, on the front of the stage, and the sea in the background. Enter two vassals dragging in* HELEN, *as if just come out of their boat.*

Hel. O why is this? Speak, gloomy, ruthless men!
Our voyage ends not here!
1st Vas. It does: and now,
Helen, the Campbell, fare thee—fare thee well!
2d Vas. Helen, the Campbell, thy last greeting take
From mortal thing.
Hel. What! leave me on this rock,
This sea-girt rock, to solitude and famine?
1st Vas. Next rising tide will bring a sure relief
To all the ills we leave thee.
Hel. (Starting.) I understand ye.
(Raising her clasped hands to heaven.)
Lord of heaven and earth;
Of storms and tempests, and th' unfathomed deep;
Is this thy righteous will?
(Clasping the hands of the men imploringly.)
Ye can not mean it!
Ye can not leave a human creature thus
To perish by a slow approaching end,
So awful and so terrible! Instant death
Were merciful to this.
1st Vas. If thou prefer'st it, we can shorten well
Thy term of pain and terror: from this crag,
Full fourteen fathoms deep thou may'st be plunged.
In shorter time than three strokes of an oar
Thy pains will cease.
2d Vas. Come, that were better for thee.
(Both of them take her hands, and are going to hurry her to the brink of the rock, when she shrinks back.)
Hel. O no! the soul recoils from swift destruction!
Pause ye a while. (Considering for a moment.)
The downward terrible plunge!
The coil of whelming waves!—O fearful nature!
(Catching hold of a part of the rock near her.)
To the rough rock I'll cling: it still is something
Of firm and desp'rate hold—Depart and leave me.
(Waving her hand for the vassals to go, whilst she keeps close hold of the rock with the other.)
1st Vas. Thou may'st still live within a prison pent,
If life is dear to thee.
Hel. (Eagerly.) If life is dear!—Alas, it is not dear!
Although the passing fearful act of death
So very fearful is.—Say how, even in a prison,
I still may wait my quiet natural end.
1st Vas. Whate'er thou art, such has thy conduct been,
Thy wedded faith, e'en with thy fellest foes,
Sure and undoubted stands:—Sign thou this scroll,
Owning the child, thy son, of bastard birth:
And this made sure, Lochtarish bade me say
Thy life shall yet be spared.
Hel. (Pushing him away with indignation as he offers her the scroll.)
Off, off! vile agent of a wretch so devilish!
Now do I see from whence my ruin comes:
I and my infant foil his wicked hopes.

O harmless babe! will heaven abandon thee!
It will not!—No; it will not!
　　　　　　(Assuming firmness and dignity.)
Depart and leave me. In my rising breast
I feel returning strength. Heaven aids may weakness:
I'll meet its awful will. (Waving them off with her hand.)
　1st Vas. Well, in its keeping rest thee: fare thee well, Helen the Campbell.
　2d Vas. Be thy suff'ring short!
　　　　　　(Aside to the other.)
Come, quickly let us go, nor look behind.
Fell is the service we are put upon:
Would we had never ta'en that cruel oath!
　　　　　　(Exeunt vassals.)
　Hel. (Alone, after standing some time gazing around her, paces backward and forward with agitated steps, then, stopping suddenly, bends her ear to the ground as if she listened earnestly to something.)
It is the sound; the heaving hollow swell
That notes the turning tide.—Tremendous agent!
Mute executioner, that, step by step,
Advances to the awful work of death.—
Onward it wears: a little space removed
The dreadful conflict is.
　(Raising her eyes to heaven, and moving her lips, as in the act of devotion, before she again speaks aloud.)
Thou art i' the blue coped sky—th' expanse immeasurable:
I' the dark roll'd clouds, the thunder's awful home:
Thou art i' the wide-shored earth,—the pathless desert;
And in the dread immensity of waters,—
I' the fathomless deep thou art.—
Awful but excellent! beneath thy hand,
With trembling confidence, I bow me low,
And wait thy will in peace.
　(Sits down on a crag of the rock, with her arms crossed over her breast in silent resignation; then, after a pause of some length, raises her head hastily.)
It is a sound of voices in the wind?
The breeze is on the rock: a gleam of sunshine
Breaks through those farther clouds. It is like hope
Upon a hopeless state.
　　　　(Starting up and gazing eagerly around her.)
I'll to that highest crag and take my stand:
Some little speck upon the distant wave
May to my eager gaze a vessel grow—
Some onward wearing thing,—some boat—some raft—
Some drifted plank.—O hope! thou quit'st us never!
(Exit, disappearing amongst the rugged divisions of the rocks.)

SCENE II.—*A small island, from which the former is seen in the distance, like a little pointed rock standing out of the sea.*
(Enter SIR HUBERT DE GREY, followed by two fishermen.)
　De Grey. This little swarded spot that o'er the waves,
Cloath'd in its green light, seem'd to beckon to us,
Right pleasant is: until our comrades join,
Here will we rest. I marvel much they stand
So far behind. In truth, such lusty rowers
Put shame upon their skill.
　1st Fish. A cross-set current bore them from the track,
But see, they now bear on us rapidly.
　(Voices without.) Hola!
　2d Fish. They call to us.—Hola! hola!
How fast they wear: they are at hand already.
　De Grey. Right glad I am: the lord of Lorn, I fear,
Will wait impatiently: he has already
With rapid oars the nearer mainland gain'd,
Where he appointed us to join him.—Ho!
　　　　　　(Calling off the stage.)
Make to that point, my lads. (To those near him.)
Here, for a little while, upon the turf
We'll snatch a hasty meal, and, so refreshed,
Take to our boats again.

(Enter three other fishermen, as from their boat, on the other side of the stage.)

Well met, my friends! I'm glad you're here at last.
How was it that you took that distant track?
　3d Fish. The current bore us wide of what we wist;
And, were it not your honor is impatient
Mainland to make, we had not come so soon.
　De Grey. What had detained you?
　3d Fish. As near yon rock we bore, that o'er the waves
Just shews its jetty point, and will, ere long,
Beneath the tide be hid, we heard the sound
Of feeble lamentation.
　De Grey. A human voice?
　3d Fish. I can not think it was:
Far on that rock, sea-girt, and at high tide
Sea-cover'd, human thing there can not be;
Though, at the first, it sounded in our ears
Like a faint woman's voice.
　De Grey. Perceived ye aught?
　3d Fish. Yes; something white that moved, and, as we think,
Some wounded bird that there hath dropt its wing,
And can not make its way.
　4th Fish. Perhaps some dog,
Whose master, at low water, there hath been,
And left him.
　3d Fish. Something 'tis in woeful case,
Whate'er it be. Right fain I would have gone,
To bear it off.
　De Grey. (Eagerly.) And wherefore did'st thou not?
Return and save it. Be it what it may;
Something it is, lone and in jeopardy,
Which hath a feeling of its desperate state,
And therefore doth to woe-worn, fearful man,
A kindred nature bear.—Return, good friend:—
Quickly return and save it, ere the tide
Shall wash it from its hold. I to the coast
Will steer the while, and wait your coming there.
　3d Fish. Right gladly, noble sir.
　4th Fish. We'll gladly go:
For, by my faith! at night I had not slept
For thinking of that sound.

DeGrey. Heaven speed ye then! Whate'er ye bring to me
Of living kind, I will reward ye for it.
Our different tracks we hold; nor longer here
Will I remain. Soon may we meet:
  God speed ye! (Exeunt severally.)

SCENE III.—*A fisherman's house on the mainland.*

(Enter JOHN OF LORN and SIR HUBERT DE GREY.)

Lorn. Then wait thou for thy boat; I and my men
Will onward to the town, where, as I hope,
My trusty vassals and our steeds are stationed.
But lose no time.

De Grey. Fear not; I'll follow quickly.

Lorn. I must unto the castle of Argyle
Without delay proceed; therefore, whate'er
Of living kind, bird, beast, or creeping thing,
This boat of thine produces, bring it with thee;
And, were it eaglet fierce, or wolf, or fox,
On with us shall it travel, mounted bravely,
Our homeward cavalcade to grace. Farewell!

De Grey. Farewell, my friend! I shall not long delay
Thy homeward journey.

Lorn. (Calling off the stage.) But ho! good host and hostess!
(To DE GREY.) Ere I go
I must take leave of honest Duncan here,
And of his rosy wife.—Ay, here they come.

(Enter the host and his wife.)

(To Host, etc.) Farewell, my friends, and thanks be to ye both!
Good cheer, and kindly given, of you we've had.
Thy hand, good host. May all the fish o' th' ocean
Come crowding to thy nets!—And healthy brats,
Fair dame, have thou! with such round rosy cheeks
As brats of thine befit: and, by your leave,
  (Kissing her.)
So be they kiss'd by all kind comers too!
Good luck betide ye both!

Host. And, sir, to you the same. Whoe'er you be,
A brave man art thou, that I will be sworn.

Wife. Come you this way again, I hope, good sir,
You will not pass our door.

Lorn. Fear not, good hostess;
It is a pleasant, sunny, open door,
And bids me enter of its own accord;
I can not pass it by.—Good luck betide ye!
  (Exit, followed to the door by SIR HUBERT.)

Host. I will be sworn it is some noble chieftain,
Though homely be his garb.

Wife. Ay, so will I: the lord of Lorn himself
Could not more courteous be.

Host. Hush! hush! be quiet!
We live not amongst the Campbells, wife.
Should some MacLean o'erhear thee—hush, I say.
  (Eyeing DE GREY, who returns from the door.)
And this man, too; right noble is his mien;
He is no common rambler.
(To DE GREY.) By your leave,
If I may be so bold without offending,
Your speech, methinks, smacks of a southern race.
I guess at least of Lowland kin ye be.
But think no shame of this; we'll ne'ertheless
Regard thee: thieves and cowards be not all
Who from the Lowlands come.

Wife. No; no, in sooth! I knew a Lowlander,
Some years gone by, who was as true and honest—
Ay, and I do believe well-nigh as brave,
As though, with brogued feet, he never else
Had all his days than muir or mountain trod.

De Grey. Thanks for your gentle thoughts!—It has indeed
Been my misluck to draw my earliest breath
Where meadows flower, and corn-fields wave i' the sun.
But let us still be friends! heaven gives us not
To choose our birth-place, else these wilds, no doubt,
Would be more thickly peopled.

Host. Ay, true it is, indeed.

Wife. And hard it were
To quarrel with him too for his misfortune.
  (Noise heard without.)

De Grey. Ha! 'tis my boat return'd.

(Enter FIRST FISHERMAN.)

1st Fish. Yes, by my faith! but neither bird nor beast.
Look there, my master. (Pointing to the door.)

(Enter HELEN, extremely exhausted, and almost senseless, wrapped closely up in one of their plaids, and supported by the other two fishermen.)

De Grey. A woman! heaven in mercy! was it then
A human creature there exposed to perish?

1st Fish. (Opening the plaid to show her face.)
Ay, look, and such a creature!

De Grey. (Starting back.) Helen of Argyle!
O God! was this the feeble wailing voice!
(Clasping his arms about her knees, as she stands almost senseless, supported by the fishermen, and bursting into tears.)
Could heart of man so leave thee? thou of all
That lovely is, most lovely.—Woe is me!
Some aid, I pray ye. (To host and his wife.) Bear her softly in,
And wrap warm garments round her. Breathes she freely?
Her eyes half-open are, but life, alas!
Is almost spent, and holds within her breast
A weak uncertain seat. (HELEN moves her hand.)
She moves her hand:—
She knows my voice.—O heaven in mercy save her!
Bear her more gently, pray ye:—Softly, softly!
How weak and spent she is!

1st Fish. No marvel she is weak: we reach'd her not
Until the swelling waters laved her girdle.
And then to see her—

De Grey. Cease, I pray thee, friend,
And tell me not—

2d Fish. Nay, faith, he tells you true:
She stood above the water, with stretched arms
Clung to the dripping rock, like the white pinions—

De Grey. Peace, peace, I say! thy words are agony:—
Give to my mind no image of the thing!
(Exeunt, bearing HELEN into an inner part of the house.)

ACT IV.

SCENE I.—*A small Gothic hall, or ante-room, in* ARGYLE'S *castle; a door at the bottom of the stage, leading to the apartment of the earl, before which is discovered the piper, pacing backward and forward, playing on his bagpipe.*

(Enter DUGALD.)

Dug. Now, pray thee, piper, cease! That stunning din
Might do good service by the ears to set
Two angry clans; but for a morning's rouse,
Here at an old man's door, it does, good sooth,
Exceed all reasonable use. The earl
Has pass'd a sleepless night: I pray thee now
Give o'er, and spare thy pains.

Piper. And spare my pains, say'st thou?—I'll do mine office,
As long as breath within my body is.

Dug. Then mercy on us all! if wind thou mean'st,
There is within that sturdy trunk of thine,
Old as it is, a still exhaustless store.
A Lapland witch's bag could scarcely match it.
Thou could'st, I doubt not, belly out the sails
Of a three-masted vessel with thy mouth:
But be thy mercy equal to thy might!
I pray thee now give o'er: in faith the earl
Has pass'd a sleepless night.

Piper. Think'st thou I am a Lowland, day-hired minstrel,
To play or stop at bidding? Is Argyle
The lord and chieftain of our ancient clan,
More certainly than I to him, as such,
The high hereditary piper am?
A sleepless night, forsooth! He's slept full oft
On the hard heath, with fifty harness'd steeds
Champing their fodder round him;—soundly too.
I'll do mine office, loun, chafe as thou wilt.
(*Continuing to pace up and down, and play as before.*)

Dug. Nay, thou the chafer art, red-crested cock!
The lord of Lorn has spoilt thee with indulging
Thy willful humors. Cease thy cursed din!
See; here the earl himself comes forth to chide thee. (*Exit.*)

(Enter ARGYLE, *attended, from the chamber.*)

Arg. Good morrow, piper! thou hast roused me bravely:
A younger man might gird his tartans on
With lightsome heart to martial sounds like these,
But I am old.

Piper. O no, my noble chieftain!
It is not age subdues you.

Arg. No; what else?

Piper. Alack! the flower and blossom of your house
The wind hath blown away to other towers.
When she was here, and gladsome faces brighten'd
With looking on her, and around your board
Sweet lays were sung, and gallants in the hall
Footed it trimly to our varied measures,
There might, indeed, be found beneath your roof
Those who might reckon years fourscore and odds,
But of old folks, I warrant, ne'er a soul.
No; we were all young then.

Arg. (*Sighing deeply.*) 'Tis true, indeed,
It was even as thou say'st. Our earthly joys
Fly like the blossoms scattered by the wind.

(Enter a servant.)

Ser. Please ye, my lord,
Some score of vassals in the hall attend
To bid good morrow to you, and the hour
Wears late: the chamberlain hath bade me say
He will dismiss them, if it please your honor.

Arg. Nay, many a mile hath some of them, I know,
With suit or purpose lurking in their minds,
Rode o'er rough paths to see me; disappointed
Shall none of them return.—I'm better now.
I have been rather weary than unwell.
Say, I will see them presently. (*Exit servant.*)

(*Re-enter* DUGALD *in haste.*)

(*To* DUGALD.) Thou comest with a busy face: what tidings?

Dug. The lord of Lorn's arrived, an' please your honor;
Sir Hubert too, and all their jolly train;
And with them have they brought a lady, closely
In hood and mantle muffled: ne'er a glimpse
May of her face be seen.

Arg. A lady, say'st thou?

Dug. Yes; closely muffled up.

Arg. (*Pacing up and down, somewhat disturbed.*)
I like not this.—It can not surely be—
(*Stopping short, and looking hard at* DUGALD.)
Whence comes he?

Dug. He a hunting went, I know,
To Cromack's ancient laird, whose youthful dame
So famed for beauty is; but whence he comes
I can not tell, my lord.

Arg. (*Pacing up and down, as he speaks to himself in broken sentences, very much disturbed.*)
To Cromack's ancient laird!—If that indeed—
Beshrew me, if it be!—I'd rather lose
Half of my lands, than son of mine such wrong,
Such shameful wrong, should do. This sword I've drawn
Like robb'ry to revenge, ne'er to abet it:
And shall I now with hoary locks—No, no!—
My noble Lorn! he can not be so base.

(Enter LORN, *going up to* ARGYLE *with agitation.*)

Arg. (*Eyeing him suspiciously.*) Well, John, how is it? Welcome art thou home,
If thou return'st, as well I would believe,
Deserving of a welcome.

Lorn. Doubts my lord
That I am so returned?
(*Aside to* ARGYLE, *endeavoring to draw him apart from his attendants.*)
Your ear my father.—
Let these withdraw: I have a thing to tell you.

Arg. (*Looking still more suspiciously upon* LORN *from seeing the eagerness and agitation with which he speaks, and turning from him indignantly.*)
No, if by this honest blade! if wrong thou'st done
Thou hast no shelter here. In open day,
Before th' assembled vassals shalt thou tell it;
And he, whom thou hast injured, be redress'd,
While I have power to bid my Campbells fight
I' the fair and honor'd cause.

Lorn. I pray, my lord—
Will you vouchsafe to hear me?
Arg. Thoughtless boy!
How far unlike thy noble Lorn I thought thee!—
Proud as I am, far rather would I see thee
Join'd to the daughter of my meanest vassal,
Than see thy manly, noble worth engaged
In such foul raid as this.
Lorn. Nay, nay! be pacified!
I'd rather take, in faith, the tawny hand
Of homeliest maid, that doth, o'holidays,
Her sun-burnt locks with worsted ribbon bind,
Fairly and freely won, than brightest dame
That e'er in stately bower or regal hall
In graceful beauty shone, gain'd by such wrong—
By such base treachery as you have glanced at.
These are plain words: then treat me like a man
Who hath been wont the manly truth to speak.
Arg. Ha! now thy countenance and tone again
Are John of Lorn s. That look, and whispering
voice,
So strange appear'd, in truth I liked it not.
Give me thy hand.—Where is the stranger dame?
If she in trouble be—
Lorn. (Aside.) Make these withdraw,
And I will lead her hither.
(Exit while the earl waves his hand, and DUGALD
and attendants, etc., go out: presently re-enter
LORN, leading in HELEN, covered closely up in
a mantle.)
Lorn. This is the dame who, houseless and deserted,
Seeks shelter here, nor fears to be rejected.
Hel. (Sinking down and clasping ARGYLE'S
knees.) My father!
Arg. That voice!—O God! Unveil—unveil, for
mercy!
 (Tearing off the mantle that conceals her.)
My child! my Helen! (Clasping her to his heart,
and holding her there for some time, unable to
speak.)
My child! my dearest child!—my soul! my pride!
Deserted!—houseless!—com'st thou to me thus?
Here is thy house—thy home: this aged bosom
Thy shelter is, which thou shalt quit no more.
My child! my child!
(Embracing her again: HELEN and he weeping
upon one another's necks.)
Houseless! deserted!—'neath the cope of heaven
Breathes there a wretch who could desert thee?—
Speak,
If he hath so abused his precious trust,
If he—it makes me tear these hoary locks
To think what I have done!—Oh thoughtless
father!
Thoughtless and selfish too! (Tearing his hair,
beating his forehead with all the violent gestures
of rage and grief.)
Hel. Oh, oh! forbear! It was not you, my father;
I gave myself away: I did it willingly;
We acted both for good; and now your love
Repays me richly—stands to me instead
Of many blessings.—Noble Lorn, besides—
O, he hath been to me so kind—so tender!
(Taking her brother's hand, and pressing it to her
breast; then joining her father's to it, and
pressing them both ardently to her lips.)
Say not I am deserted: heaven hath chid me—

Hath chid me sorely; but hath bless'd me too,—
O, dearly bless'd me!
Arg. Hath chid thee sorely!—how I burn to
hear it!
What hast thou suffer'd?
Lorn. We will not tell thee now. Go to thy
chamber,
And be a while composed. We have, my father,
A tale to tell that will demand of thee
Recruited strength to hear.—We'll follow thee.
(Exeunt LORN, supporting his father and HELEN
into the chamber.)

SCENE II.—*The garden of the castle.*
(Enter ARGYLE, LORN, and SIR HUBERT DE GREY,
speaking as they enter.)

Lorn. A month!—A week or two!—No, not an
hour
Would I suspend our vengeance. Such atrocity
Makes e'en the little term between our summons
And the dark crowding round our martial pipes,
Of plumed bonnets nodding to the wind,
Most tedious seem; yea, makes the impatient foot
To smite the very earth beneath its tread,
For being fix'd and ertless.—
Arg. Be less impatient, John: thou canst not
doubt
A father's keen resentment of such wrong:
But let us still be wise: this short delay
Will make revenge the surer; to its aim
A just direction give.
De Grey. The earl is right:
We shall but work in the dark, impatient Lorn.
If we too soon begin.
Arg. How far MacLean
Hath to this horrible attempt consented,
Or privy been, we may be certified,
By waiting silently to learn the tale
That he will tell us of his lady's loss,
When he shall send to give us notice of it,
As doubtless soon he will.
De Grey. If he, beset and threatened, to those
fiends,
Unknowing of their purpose, hath unwillingly
Committed her, he will himself, belike,
If pride prevent him not, your aid solicit
To set him free from his disgraceful thraldom.
Lorn. And if he should, shrunk be this sinew'd
arm,
If it unsheath a weapon in his cause!
Let ev'ry ragged stripling on his lands
In wanton mock'ry mouth him with contempt!
Benlora head his vassals; and Lochtarish—
That serpent, full of ev'ry devilish wile,
His prison keeper and his master be!
De Grey. Ay; and the keeper also of his son,
The infant heir.
Lorn. (Starting.) I did not think of this.
Arg. Then let thy head-strong fury pause upon it.
Thanks to Sir Hubert's prudence! thou as yet
Before thy followers hast restrained been;
And who this lady is, whom to the castle,
Like a mysterious stranger, ye have brought,
From them remains conceal'd.—My brave De Grey!
This thy considerate foresight, join'd to all
Thy other service in this woeful matter,
Hath made us much thy debtor.

De Grey. I have, indeed, my lord, considered only
What I believed would Helen's wishes be,
Ere she herself could utter them; if this
Hath proved equivalent to wiser foresight,
Let it direct us still; let Helen's wishes
Your measures guide.
   Arg. Ah, brave De Grey! would they had ever done so!
I had now—
      (Taking Sir Hubert's hand with emotion.)
Forgive me, noble youth!
Alas, alas! the father's tenderness
Before the chieftain's policy gave way,
And all this wreck hath been.
   Lorn. 'Tis even so,
That cursed peace; that coward's shadeless face
Of smiles and promises, to all things yielding
With weak, unmanly pliancy, so gained you—
Even you, the wise Argyle!—It made me mad!
Who hath no point that he maintains against you,
No firmness hath to hold him of your side:
Who can not sturdily against me stand,
And say, "Encroach no farther," friend of mine
Shall never be.
   De Grey. Nay, Lorn, forbear!—forbear!
Thine own impetuous willfulness did make
The other's pliant mind more specious seem;
And thou thyself did'st to that luckless union,
Although unwittingly, assistance lend.
Make now amends for it, and curb thy spirit,
While that the earl with calmer judgment waits
His time for action.
   Lorn. Beshrew me, but thy counsel strangely smacks
Of cautious timid age! In faith, De Grey,
But that I know thy noble nature well,
I could believe thee—
   Arg. Peace, unruly spirit!
Bold as thou art, methinks, with locks like these,
Thy father still may say to thee, "Be silent!"
   Lorn. (Checking himself, and bowing very low to Argyle.)
And be obeyed devoutly. O forgive me!
Those locks are to your brows a kingly fillet
Of strong authority, to which my heart
No rebel is, though rude may be my words.
(Taking Sir Hubert's hand with an assured countenance.)
I ask not thee, De Grey, to pardon me.
Resistance here with gentleness is join'd,
Therefore I've loved thee, and have laid upon thee
The hand of sure possession; claiming still
A friend's endurance of my froward temper,
Which, froward as it is, from thee hath borne
What never human being but thyself
Had dared to goad it with.
   De Grey. It is indeed
Thy well-earn'd right thou askest, noble Lorn,
And it is yielded to thee cheerfully.
   Arg. My aged limbs are tired with pacing here;
Some one approaches: within that grove
We'll find a shady seat, and there conclude
This well-debated point. (Exeunt.)

Scene III.—*A court within the castle, surrounded with buildings.* Enter Dugald *and a vassal, two servants at the same time crossing the stage, with covered dishes in their hands.*

   Vas. I'll wait until the earl shall be at leisure;
My business presses not. Where do they carry
Those cover'd meats? Have ye within the castle
Some noble prisoner?
   Dug. Would so it were! but these are days of peace.
They bear them to the stranger dame's apartment,
Whom they have told thee of. There, at her door,
An ancient faithful handmaid of the house,
Whate'er they bring receives; for none besides
Of all the household is admitted.
   Vas. Now, by my fay! my purse and dirk I'd give
To know who this may be.—Some chieftain's lady
Whom John of Lorn—
   Dug. Nay, there, I must believe,
Thou guessest erringly.—I grant, indeed,
He doffs his bonnet to each tacks-man's wife,
And is with every coif amongst them all,
Both young and old, in such high favor held,
Nor maiden, wife, nor beldame of the clan
But to the earl doth her petition bring
Through intercession of the lord of Lorn;
But never yet did husband, sire, or brother,
Of wrong from him complain.
   Vas. I know it well.
   Dug. But be she who she may,
This stranger here; I doubt not, friend, ere long,
We shall have bickering for her in the field
With some fierce foe or other.
   Vas. So I trust:
And by my honest faith! this peace of ours
Right long and tiresome is.—I thought, ere now,
Some of our restless neighbors would have tres pass'd
And inroads made: but no; Argyle and Lorn
Have grown a terror to them: all is quiet;
And we ourselves must the aggressors be,
Or still this dull and slothful life endure,
Which makes our men of three-score years an ten
To fret and murmur.

(Enter Rosa, *with a servant conducting her.*)
   Ser. (To Dug.) A lady here would see my lord of Lorn.
   Dug. Yes, still to him they come.
      (Looking at Rosa
Ha! see I rightly—
Rosa, from Mull?
   Rosa. Yes, Dugald; here thou see'st
A woeful bearer of unwelcome tidings.
   Dug. What, hath thy lady sent thee?
   Rosa. Alas, alas! I have no lady now.
   Dug. Ha! is she dead? Not many days ago
She was alive and well.—Hast thou so soon
The castle quitted—left thy lady's corse?
   Rosa. Think'st thou I would have left her?—(the night
When, as they say, she died, I from the castle
By force was ta'en, and to mainland conveyed;
Where in confinement I remain'd, till chance
Gave me the means of breaking from my prison
And hither am I come, in woeful plight,
The dismal tale to tell.
   Dug. A tale, indeed.
Most dismal, strange, and sudden.

Rosa. How she died
God knows; but much I fear foul play she had.
Where is the lord of Lorn? for first to him
I wish to speak.
Dug. Come, I will lead thee to him.—Had foul
play!
Vas. Fell fiends they are could shed her blood!
If this
Indeed hath been, 'twill make good cause, I wot;
The warlike pipe will sound our summons soon.
(Exeunt DUGALD and ROSA, etc., as ARGYLE and SIR
HUBERT enter by the opposite side.)
Arg. And wilt thou leave us then, my noble
friend?
May we not still for some few days retain thee?
De Grey. Where'er I go, I carry in my heart
A warm remembrance of the friendly home
That still within these hospitable walls
I've found; but longer urge me not to stay.
In Helen's presence now, constrained and strange,
With painful caution, chasing from my lips
The ready thought, half quiver'd into utterance,
For cold corrected words, expressive only
Of culprit consciousness,—I sit; nor ev'n
May look upon her face but as a thing
On which I may not look; so painful now
The mingled feeling is, since dark despair
With one faint ray of hope hath temper'd been.
I can no more endure it. She herself
Perceives it, and it pains her.—Let me then
Bid you farewell, my lord. When evening comes,
I'll under favor of the rising moon,
Set forth.
Arg. Indeed! so soon? and must it be?
De Grey. Yes; to Northumberland without delay
Fain would take my road. My aged father
Looks now impatiently for my return.
Arg. Then I'll no longer urge thee. To thy father.
The noble baron, once, in better days,
My camp-mate and my friend, I must resign thee.
Bear to him every kind and cordial wish
An ancient friend can send, and—
(A horn heard without.)
Hark,—that horn!
Some messenger of moment is arrived.—
We'll speak of this again.—The moon to-night
Is near the full, and at an early hour—

(Enter a messenger, bearing a letter,)
Whose messenger art thou, who in thy hand
That letter bear'st with broad and sable seal,
Which seems to me to bring some dismal tidings?
Mes. From Mull, my lord, I come; and the MacLean,
Our chief, commissioned me to give thee this,
Which is indeed with dismal tidings fraught.
(ARGYLE opens the letter, and reads it with affected
surprise and sorrow.)
Arg. Heavy, indeed, and sudden is the loss—
The sad calamity that hath befallen.
The will of heaven be done!
(putting a handkerchief to his eyes, and leaning,
as if for support, upon SIR HUBERT; then, after
a pause, turning to the messenger.)
How didst thou leave the chieftain? He, I hope,
Permits not too much sorrow to o'ercome
His manhood! Doth he bear his grief composedly?

Mes. O no, it is most violent! At the funeral,
Had not the good Lochtarish, by his side,
Supported him, he had with very grief
Sunk to the earth.—And good Lochtarish, too,
Was in right great affliction.
Arg. Ay, good man;
I doubt it not.—Ye've had a splendid funeral?
Mes. O yes, my lord! that have we had. Good
truth!
A grand and stately burial has it been.
Three busy days and nights through all the isle
Have bagpipes played, and sparkling beakers
flowed;
And never corse, I trow, i' th' earth was laid
With louder lamentations.
Arg. Aye, I doubt not,
Their grief was loud enough.—Pray pass ye in.
(To attendants at a distance.)
Conduct him there; and see that he be treated,
After his tedious journey, as befits
A way-tired stranger.
(Exeunt all but ARGYLE and SIR HUBERT.)
This doth all hope and all belief exceed.
MacLean will shortly follow this his notice,
(Giving SIR HUBERT the letter.)
To make me here a visit of condolence;
And thus within our power they put themselves
With most assured blindness.
De Grey. (After reading it.) 'Tis Lochtarish,
In all the arts of dark hypocrisy
So deeply skill'd, who doth o'ershoot his mark,
As such full often do.
Arg. And let him come!
At his own arts we trust to match him well.—
Their force, I guess, is not in readiness,
Therefore, meantime, to stifle all suspicion,
This specious mummery he hath devised;
And his most wretched chief, led by his will,
Most wretchedly submits.—Well, let us go
And tell to Lorn the news, lest too unguardedly
He should receive it. (Exeunt.)

SCENE IV.—*An apartment in the castle. Enter* SIR
HUBERT, *beckoning to* ROSA, *who appears on the
opposite side.*

De Grey. Rosa; I pray thee, spare me of thy
leisure
Some precious moments; something would I say;
Wilt thou now favor me?
Rosa. Most willingly.
De Grey. As yet thy mistress knows not of the
letter
Sent by MacLean, announcing his design
Of paying to the earl this sudden visit—
This mockery of condolence?
Rosa. No; the earl
Forbade me to inform her.
De Grey. This is well;
Her mind must be prepared. Meantime I go,
And thou art here to comfort and attend her;
O do it gently, Rosa! do it wisely!
Rosa. You need not doubt my will.—Go ye so
soon;
And to Northumberland?
De Grey. So I intended,
And so Argyle and John of Lorn believe;
But since this messenger from Mull arrived,
Another thought has struck me.—Said'st thou not

The child—thy lady's child, ta'en from the castle,
Is to the keeping of Lochtarish's mother
Committed, whose lone house is on the shore?
  Rosa. Yes, whilst in prison pent, so did I hear
My keeper say, and much it troubled me.
  De Grey. Canst thou to some good islander commend me,
Within whose house I might upon the watch
Conceal'd remain?—It is to Mull I go,
And not to England. While MacLean is here,
Attended by his vassals, the occasion
I'll seize to save the infant.
  Rosa. Bless thee for it!
Heaven bless thee for the thought! I know a man—
An aged fisherman who will receive you;
Uncle to Morton; and if he himself
Still in the island be, there will you find him,
Most willing to assist you.
  De Grey. Hush, I pray,
I hear thy lady's steps.
  Rosa. Near to the castle gate, ere you depart,
I'll be in waiting to inform you farther
Of what may aid your purpose.
  De Grey. Do, good Rosa,
And make me much thy debtor. But be secret.
  Rosa. You need not doubt me.

(Enter HELEN, and DE GREY goes up to her as if he would speak, but the words falter on his lips, and he is silent.)

  Hel. Alas! I see it is thy parting visit;
Thou com'st to say "farewell!"
  De Grey. Yes, Helen; I am come to leave with thee
A friend's dear benison—a parting wish—
A last—rest ev'ry blessing on thy head!
Be this permitted me:
        (Kissing her hand with profound respect.)
            Fare thee well!
Heaven aid and comfort thee! Farewell! farewell!
(Is about to retire hastily, whilst HELEN follows to prevent him.)
  Hel. O go not from me with that mournful look!
Alas! thy gen'rous heart, depress'd and sunk,
Looks on my state too sadly.—
I am not, as thou think'st, a thing so lost
In woe and wretchedness.—Believe not so!
All whom misfortune with her rudest blasts
Hath buffeted, to gloomy wretchedness
Are not therefore abandoned. Many souls
From cloister'd cells, from hermits' caves, from holds
Of lonely banishment, and from the dark
And dreary prison-house, do raise their thoughts
With humble cheerfulness to heaven, and feel
A hallowed quiet, almost akin to joy;
And may not I, by heaven's kind mercy aided,
Weak as I am, with some good courage bear
What is appointed for me?—O be cheered!
And let not sad and mournful thoughts of me
Depress thee thus.—When thou art far away,
Thou'lt hear, the while, that in my father's house I
I spend my cheerful days, and let it cheer thee.
I too shall ev'ry southern stranger question,
Whom chance may to these regions bring, and learn
Thy fame and prosperous state.
  De Grey. My fame and prosperous state, while thou art thus!

If thou in calm retirement liv'st contented,
Lifting thy soul to heaven, what lack I more?
My sword and spear, changed to a pilgrim's staff,
Will be a prosperous state; and for my fame,—
A feeble sound that after death remains,
The echo of an unrepeated stroke
That fades away to silence,—surely this
Thou dost not covet for me.
  Hel. Ah, I do!
Yet, granting here I err, didst thou not promise
To seek in wedded love and active duties
Thy share of cheerful weal?—And dost thou now
Shrink from thy gen'rous promise?—No, thou shalt not.
I hold thee bound—I claim it of thee boldly.
It is my right. If thou, in sad seclusion,
A lonely wanderer art, thou dost extinguish
The ray that should have cheer'd my doom: thou makest
What else had been a calm and temper'd sorrow,
A state of wretchedness.—O no! thou wilt not!
Take to thy gen'rous heart some virtuous maid,
And doubt not thou a kindred heart will find.
The cheerful tenderness of woman's nature
To thine is suited, and when joined to thee,
Will grow in virtue:—Take thou then this ring,
If thou wilt honor so my humble gift,
And put it on her hand; and be assured
She who shall wear it,—she whose happy fate
Is link'd with thine, will prove a noble mate.
  De Grey. O there I am assured! She whose fate
Is link'd with mine, if fix'd be such decree,
Most rich in every soft and noble trait
Of female virtue is: in this full well
Assured I am—I would—I thought—forgive—
I speak but raving words:—a hasty spark,
Blown and extinguish'd, makes me waver thus.
Permit me then again,   (Kissing her hand.)
        High heaven protect thee!
Farewell!
  Hel. Farewell! and heaven's good charge be thou!
(They part, and both turn away to opposite sides of the stage, when SIR HUBERT, looking round just as he is about to go off, and seeing HELEN also looking after him, sorrowfully, eagerly returns.)
  De Grey. Ah! are those looks—
(Going to kneel at her feet, but immediately checking himself with much embarrassment.)
        Alas! why came I back?
Something there was—Thou gavest me a ring:
I have not dropped it?
  Rosa. (Coming forward.) No, 'tis on your finger.
  De Grey. Ay, true, good Rosa; but my wits are 'wilder'd;
I knew not what I sought.—Farewell! farewell!
(Exit DE GREY hastily, while HELEN and ROSA go off by the opposite side.)

ACT V.

SCENE I.—ARGYLE's *castle, the vestibule, or grand entrance; a noise of bustle and voices heard without, and servants seen crossing the stage, as the scene opens.*

(Enter DUGALD, meeting first servant.)

  Dug. They are arrived, MacLean and all his train;
Run quickly, man, and give our chieftains notice.

1st Ser. They know already: from the tower we spied
The mournful cavalcade: the earl and Lorn
Are down the stair-case hasting to receive them.
Dug. I've seen them light, a sooty-coated train,
With lank and woeful faces, and their eyes
Bent to the ground, as though our castle gate
Had been the scutcheon'd portal of a tomb,
Set open to receive them.
2d Ser. Ay, on the pavement fall their heavy steps
Measured and slow, as if her palled coffin
They followed still.
Dug. Hush, man! Here comes the earl,
With face composed and stern; but look behind him
How John of Lorn doth gnaw his nether lip,
And beat his clenched hand against his thigh,
Like one who tampers with half-bridled ire!
2d Ser. Has any one offended him?
Dug. Be silent,
For they will overhear thee.—Yonder, too,
    (Pointing to the opposite side of the stage.)
Come the MacLeans: let us our stations keep,
And see them meet.
    (Retiring with the other to the bottom of the stage.)

(Enter ARGYLE and LORN, attended, and in deep mourning; while, at the same time, by the opposite side of the stage, enter MACLEAN, BENLORA, LOCHTARISH, and GLENFADDEN, with attendants, also in deep mourning; ARGYLE and MACLEAN go up to one another, and formally embrace.)

Arg. Welcome! if such a cheerful word as this
May with our deep affliction suited be.
Lochtarish, too, and brave Benlora, aye,
And good Glenfadden also,—be ye all
With due respect received, as claims your worth.
    (Taking them severally by the hand as he names them. MACLEAN then advances to embrace LORN, who shrinks back from him, but immediately correcting himself, bends his body another way, as if suddenly seized with some violent pain.)
Arg. (To MACLEAN.) Regard him not: he hath imprudently
A recent wound exposed to chilling air,
And oft the pain with sudden pang attacks him.
Loch. Ay, what is shrewder? We have felt the like,
And know it well, my lord.
Arg. (Bowing to LOCHTARISH, but continuing to speak to MACLEAN.)
Yet, ne'ertheless, good son-in-law and chieftain,
Believe thou well that with a brother's feelings,
Proportion'd to the dire and dismal case
That hath befallen, he now receives you; also
Receiving these your friends with equal favor.
This is indeed to us a woeful meeting,
Chieftain of Mull.
    (Looking keenly in his face, while the other shuns his eye.)
I see full well the change
Which violent grief upon that harrow'd visage
So deeply hath impress'd.
Mac. (Still embarrassed and shrinking from Argyle's observation.)
Ah! ah! the woeful day!—I can not speak.
Alas, alas!
Arg. Alas, in truth,
Too much the woeful widower's alter'd looks
Upon thy face I see.
Loch. (To ARGYLE.) You see, my lord, his eyes
    with too much weeping
Are weak, and shun the light. Nor should we marvel:
What must to him the sudden loss have been,
When even to us, who were more distantly
Connected with her rare and matchless virtue,
It brought such keen affliction?
Arg. Yes, good Lochtarish, I did give her to ye—
To your right worthy chief, a noble creature,
With every kindly virtue—every grace
That might become a noble chieftain's wife:
And that ye have so well esteem'd—so well
Regarded, cherish'd, and respected her,
As your excessive sorrow now discloses,
Receive ye from me a grateful father's thanks.
Lochtarish, most of all to thy good love
I am beholden.
Loch. Ah! small was the merit
Such goodness to respect.
Arg. And thou, Benlora;
A woman, and a stranger, on the brave
Still potent claims maintain; and little doubt I
They were by thee regarded.
    (BENLORA steps back, frowning sternly, and remains silent.)
And, Glenfadden,
Be not thy merits overlook'd.
Glen. Alas!
You overrate, my lord, such slender service.
Arg. Wrong not, I pray, thy modest worth.—But here, (Turning again to MACLEAN.)
Here most of all, from whom her gentle virtues,—
And so, indeed, it right and fitting was,—
Their best and dearest recompense received,
To thee, most generous chieftain, let me pay
The thanks that are thy due.
Mac. Oh, oh! alas!
Arg. Ay, in good sooth! I see thy grief-worn eyes
Do shun the light.
But grief is ever sparing of her words.
In brief, I thank you all: and for the love
Ye have so deeply shewn to me and mine,
I trust, before we part, to recompense ye
As suits your merit and my gratitude.
Lorn. (Aside to ARGYLE.) Ay, father; now ye
    speak to them shrewd words;
And now I'm in the mood to back you well.
Arg. (Aside to LORN.) 'Tis well thou art; but
    check those eager looks;
Lochtarish eyes thee keenly.
    (Directing a hasty glance to LOCHTARISH, who is whispering to GLENFADDEN, and looking suspiciously at LORN.)
Lorn. (Stepping forward to MACLEAN, etc.)
Chieftain, and honor'd gentlemen, I pray
The sullen, stern necessity excuse
Which pain imposed upon me, and receive,
Join'd with my noble father's, such poor thanks
As I may offer to your loving worth.
Arg. Pass on, I pray ye; till the feast be ready,
Rest ye above, where all things are prepared
For your refreshment.   (*Exeunt.*)

POETRY ON OR ABOUT THE MACLEANS.

SCENE II.—*A narrow arched room or closet, adjoining to a gallery.*

(Enter LOCHTARISH and GLENFADDEN.)

Loch. How lik'st thou this, Glenfadden? Doth the face
Argyle assumes, of studied courtesy,
Rouse no suspicion?
Glen. Faith, I know not well!—
The speech, indeed, with which he welcomed us,
Too wordy, and too artificial seem'd
To be the native growth of what he felt.
Loch. It so to me appear'd: and John of Lorn,
First shrinking from MacLean, with sudden pain,
As he pretended, struck, then stern and silent,
Till presently assuming, like his father,
A courtesy, minute, and over-studied.
He glozed us with his thanks:—
Didst thou not mark his keenly flashing eye,
When spoke Argyle of recompensing us
Before we part?
Glen. I did indeed observe it.
Loch. This hath a meaning.
Glen. Faith, I do suspect
Some rumor must have reach'd their ear; and yet
Our agents faithful are; it can not be.
Loch. Or can, or can it not, beneath this roof
A night I will not sleep. When evening comes,
Meet me again. If at this banquet, aught
Shall happen to confirm our fears, forthwith
Let us our safety seek in speedy flight.
Glen. And leave MacLean behind us?
Loch. Ay, and Benlora too. Affairs the better
At Mull will thrive, when we have rid our hands
Of both these hind'rances, who in our way
Much longer may not be. (Listening.)
 We're interrupted.
Let us into the gallery return,
And join the company with careless face,
Like those who have from curiosity
But stepp'd aside to view the house.—Make haste!
It is Argyle and Lorn.

(Exeunt, looking to the opposite side, alarmed, at which enter ARGYLE and LORN.)

Lorn. Are you not now convinced? his conscious guilt
Is in his downcast and embarrass'd looks.
And careful shunning of all private converse
Whene'er aside you've drawn him from his train,
Too plainly seen: You can not now, my lord,
Doubt of his share in this atrocious deed.
Arg. Yet, Lorn, I would, ere further we proceed,
Prove it more fully still. The dinner hour
Is now at hand. (Listening.) What steps are those,
That in the gallery, close to this door,
Like some lone straggler from the company
Withdrawn, sound quickly pacing to and fro?
Look out and see.
Lorn. (Going to the door, and calling back to ARGYLE in a low voice.)
It is MacLean himself.
Arg. Beckon him hither then.—Thank heaven for this!
Now opportunity is fairly given.
If that constrainedly he cloaks their guilt,
To free him from their toils.

(Enter MACLEAN, conducted by LORN.)

Arg. (To MACLEAN.) My son, still in restraint before our vassals
Have we conversed; but now in privacy—
Start not, I pray thee:—Sit thee down, MacLean:
I would have close and private words of thee:
Sit down, I pray; my aged limbs are tired.
(ARGYLE and MACLEAN sit down, whilst LORN stands behind them, with his ear bent eagerly to listen, and his eyes fixed with a side-glance on MACLEAN.)
Chieftain, I need not say to thee, who deeply
Lament'st with us our sad untimely loss,
How keenly I have felt it.—
And now indulge a father in his sorrow,
And say how died my child.—Was her disease
Painful as it was sudden?
Mac. It was—alas! I know not how it was.
A fell disease!—Her end was so appointed.
Lorn. (Behind.) Ay, that I doubt not.
Mac. A fearful malady! though it received
All good assistance.
Lorn. (Behind.) That I doubt not either.
Mac. A cruel ill!—but how it dealt with her,
My grief o'erwhelm'd me so, I could not tell.
Arg. Say—wert thou present? didst thou see her die?
Mac. Oh, oh! the woeful sight, that I should see it!
Arg. Thou didst not see it then!
Mac. Alack! alack!
O would that I had seen—O woe is me!
Her pain—her agony was short to mine!
Lorn. (Behind impatiently.) Is this an answer, chieftain, to the question
Argyle hath plainly ask'd thee—wert thou present
When Helen died? didst thou behold her death?
Mac. O yes; indeed I caught your meaning lamely;
I meant—I thought—I know not certainly
The very time and moment of her death,
Although within my arms she breathed her last.
Lorn. (Rushing forward eagerly.) Now are we answered.
(ARGYLE, covering his face with his hands, throw himself back in his chair for some time without speaking.)
Mac. (To ARGYLE.) I fear, my lord, too much have distress'd you.
Arg. Somewhat you have, indeed.—And further now
I will not press your keen and recent sorrow
With questions that so much renew its anguish.
Mac. You did, belike, doubt of my tenderness.
Arg. O no! I have no doubts.—Within your arm
She breath'd her last?
Mac. Within my arms she died.
Arg. (Looking hard at MACLEAN, and then turning away.)
His father was a brave and honest chief!
Mac. What says my lord?
Arg. A foolish exclamation.
Of no determined meaning. (Bells sound without
 Dry our tears:
The hall-bell warns us to the ready feast;
And through the gallery I hear the sound
Of many footsteps hastening to the call.
Chieftain, I follow thee.
 (Exeunt ARGYLE and MACLEAN

Lorn. (Alone, stopping to listen.) The castle,
  thronged throughout with moving life,
From every winding stair, and arched aisle,
A mingled echo sends.
Ay; light of foot, I hear their sounding steps
A-trooping to the feast, who never more
At feast shall sit, or social meal partake.
O wretch! O fiend of vile hypocrisy!
How fiercely burns my blood within my veins
Till I am matched with thee! (Exit.)

SCENE III.—*The great hall of the castle, with a feast set out, and the company already placed at table, with servants and attendants in waiting, who fill the stage in every part:* ARGYLE *is seated at the head of the table, with* MACLEAN *on his left hand, and a chair left empty on his right.*

Arg. (To MACLEAN, etc.) Most worthy chief,
  and honored guests and kinsmen,
I crave your pardon for this short delay;
One of our company is wanting still,
For whom we have reserved this empty place;
Nor will the chief of Mull unkindly take it,
That on our better hand this chair of honor
Is for a lady kept.
  Omnes. A lady! (A general murmur of surprise is heard through the hall.)
  Arg. Yes;
Who henceforth of this house the mistress is;
And were it palace of our Scottish king,
Would so deserve to be.
  Omnes. We give you joy, my lord.
  (A confused murmur heard again.)
  Mac. We give you joy, my lord, your age is bless'd.
We little thought, in these our funeral weeds,
A bridal feast to darken.
  Lorn. No, belike.
Many who don their coat at break of day,
Know not what shall befall them, therein girt,
Ere ev'ning close. (Assuming a gay tone.)
The earl hath set a step-dame o'er my head
To cow my pride—what think ye brave MacLean?
This world so fleeting is and full of change,
Some lose their wives I trow, and others find them.
Bridegrooms and widowers do, side by side,
Their beakers quaff; and which of them a heart
Most glad or sorry is, the subtle fiend,
Who in men's hollow hearts his council holds
He wotteth best, though each good man will swear,
His, *lost or found*, all other dames excell'd.
  Arg. Curb, Lorn, thy saucy tongue: MacLean himself
Shall judge if she—the lady I have found,
Equal in beauty she whom he hath lost.
In worth I'm sure she does.—But hush! she comes.
A great commotion through the hall amongst the attendants, etc.)
  Omnes. It is the lady.
  Arg. (Rising from his seat, and making signs to the attendants nearest the door.)
Lo there! make room, and let the lady pass.
(The servants, etc., stand apart, ranging themselves on every side to let the lady pass; and enter HELEN, magnificently dressed, with a deep white veil over her face; while LORN, going forward to meet her, conducts her to her chair on ARGYLE'S right hand.)

Arg. (To the CAMPBELLS.) Now, fill up a cup of welcome to our friends.
  Loch. (To MACLEAN.) Chieftain, forgettest thou to greet the lady?
  Mac. (Turning to ARGYLE.) Nay, rather give, my lord, might I presume,
Our firstling cup to this fair lady's health,
The noble dame of this right princely house.
And though close veil'd she be, her beauty's lustre
I little question. (Fills up a goblet, while LOCHTARISH, BENLORA, etc., follow his example, and, standing up, bows to the lady.)
  Your health, most noble dame.
(HELEN, rising also, bows to him, and throws back her veil: The cup falls from his hands; all the company start up from the table; screams and exclamations of surprise are heard from all corners of the hall, and confused commotion seen every-where. MACLEAN, LOCHTARISH, and GLENFADDEN stand appalled and motionless; but BENLORA, looking fiercely round him, draws his sword.)
  Ben. What! are we here like deer bay'd in a nook?
And think ye so to slay us, crafty foe?
No, by my faith! like such we will not fall,
Arms in our hands, though by a thousand foes
Encompass'd.—Cruel, murderous, ruthless men,
Too good a warrant have ye now to think us,
But cowards never!—Rouse ye, base MacLeans!
And thou, whose subtlety around us thus
With wreckfull skill these cursed toils hast wound,
Sinks thy base spirit now? (To LOCHTARISH.)
  Arg. (Holding up his hand.) Be silence in the hall!
MacLeans, ye are my guests; but if the feast
Delight ye not, free leave ye have to quit it.
Lorn, see them all, with right due courtesy,
Safely protected to the castle gate.
  (Turning to MACLEAN.)
Here, other name than chieftain or MacLean
He may not give thee; but, without our walls,
If he should call thee murderer, traitor, coward,
Weapon to weapon, let your fierce contention
Be fairly held, and he, who first shall yield,
The liar be.—
  Campbells! I charge ye there,
Free passage for the chieftain and his train.
(MACLEAN and LOCHTARISH, etc., without speaking, quit the hall through the crowd of attendants, who divide, and form a lane to let them pass. HELEN, who had sunk down almost senseless upon her seat, seeing the hall cleared of the crowd, who go out after the MACLEANS, now starts up, and catches hold of ARGYLE with an imploring look of strong distress.)
  Hel. O father! well I know foul are his crimes,
But what—O what, am I, that for my sake
This bloody strife should be?—O think, my lord!
He gave consent and sanction to my death,
But thereon could not look: and at your gate—
Ev'n on your threshold, must his life be ta'en?
For well I know the wrath of Lorn is deadly.
And gallant Lorn himself, if scaith should be,—
O pity! pity!—O for pity stay them!
  Arg. Let go thy hold, weak woman: pity now!
Rosa, support her hence. (Committing her to ROSA, who now comes forward, and tears him-

self away. HELEN runs after him and endeavors to catch hold of him.)
Hel. O be not stern! beneath the ocean rather
Would I had sunk to rest, than been the cause
Of horrid strife like this. O pity! pity!
(Exeunt, she running out after him distracted.)

SCENE IV.—*Before the gate of the castle: a confused noise of an approaching crowd heard within, and presently enter, from the gate,* MACLEAN, BENLORA, LOCHTARISH, *and* GLENFADDEN, *with their attendants, conducted by* LORN, *and followed by a crowd of* CAMPBELLS, *who range themselves on both sides of the stage.*

Lorn. (To MACLEAN.) Now, chieftain, we the gate have pass'd,—the bound
That did restrain us. Host and guest no more,
But deadly foes we stand, who from this spot
Shall never both with life depart. Now, turn,
And boldly say to him, if so thou darest,
Who calls thee villain, murd'rer, traitor, coward,
That he belies thee. Turn then, Chief of Mull!
Here, man to man, my single arm to thine,
I give thee battle; or, refusing this,
Our captive here retain thee to be tried
Before the summon'd vassals of our clan,
As suits thy rank and thine atrocious deeds.
Take thou thy choice.
Mac. Yes, John of Lorn, I turn.
This turf on which we tread my death-bed is;
This hour my latest term; this sky of light
The last that I shall look upon. Draw thy sword:
The guilt of many crimes o'erwhelms my spirit;
But never will I shame my brave MacLeans,
By dying, as their chief, a coward's death.
Ben. What! shalt thou fight alone, and we stand by
Idly to look upon it? (Going up fiercely to LORN.)
Turn me out
The boldest, brawniest Campbell of your bands;
Aye, more than one, as many as you will;
And I the while, albeit these locks be grey,
Leaning my aged back against this tree,
Will show your youngsters how, in other days,
MacLeans did fight, when baited round with foes.
Lorn. Be still, Benlora; other sword than these,
Thy chief's and mine, shall not this day be drawn.
If I prevail against him, here with us
Our captives you remain. If I am conquer'd,
Upon the faith and honor of a chieftain,
Ye shall again to Mull in safety go.
Ben. Spoke like a noble chieftain!
Lorn. Ye shall, I say, to Mull in safety go.
But there prepare ye to defend your coast
Against a host of many thousand Campbells;
In which, be well assured, swords as good
As John of Lorn's, to better fortune join'd,
Shall of your crimes a noble vengeance take.
(LORN and MACLEAN *fight; and after a combat of some length,* MACLEAN *is mortally wounded, and the* CAMPBELLS *give a loud shout.*)
Mac. It is enough, brave Lorn; this wound is death:
And better deed thou couldst not do upon me,
Than rid me of a life disgraced and wretched.
But guilty though I be, thou see'st full well,
That to the brave opposed, arms in hand,
I am no coward.—Oh! could I as bravely,

In home-rais'd broils, with violent men have strove,
It had been well: but there, alas! I proved
A poor, irresolute, and nerveless wretch.
(After a pause, and struggling for breath.)
To live, alas! in good men's memories
Detested and contemn'd:—to be with her
For whom I thought to be—come, gloomy grave!
Thou cover'st all!
(After another painful struggle, every one standing in deep silence round him, and LORN bending over him compassionately.)
Pardon of man I ask not,
And merit not.—Brave Lorn, I ask it not;
Though in thy piteous eye a look I see
That might embolden me.—There is above
One who doth know the weakness of our nature,—
Our thoughts and conflicts:—All that e'er have breathed,
The bann'd and bless'd must pass to Him: My soul
Into his hands, in humble penitence,
I do commit.   (Dies.)
Lorn. And may heaven pardon thee, unhappy man!

(Enter ARGYLE, HELEN, *attended by* ROSA, *following him.*)
Lorn. (To attendants.) Alas, prevent her! (Endeavoring to keep her back.)
Helen come not hither:
This is no sight for thee.
Hel. (Pressing forward, and seeing the body.)
Oh! oh! and hast thou dealt with him so quickly,
Thou fell and ruthless Lorn?—No time allow'd!
(Kneeling by the body.
O that within that form sense still were lodged!
To hear my voice,—to know that in my heart
No thought of thee—Let others scan his deeds,
Pitied and pardoned art thou here.
(Her hand on her breast.
Alas!
So quickly fell on thee th' avenging stroke,
No sound of peace came to thy dying ear,
No look of pity to thy closing eyes!
Pitied and pardoned art thou in this breast,
But canst not know it now.—Alas! alas!
Arg. (To attendants.) Prepare speedily to mov the body.
Meantime, our prisoners within the castle
Secure ye well. (Other attendants lay hold LOCHTARISH *and* GLENFADDEN, *but* BENLOR drawing his sword, attacks furiously those wh attempt to seize and disarm him, and they, clo ing round and endeavoring to overpower hir mortally wound him in the struggle.)
Ben. Ay, bear me now within thy prison walls:
Alive indeed, thought ye to bind me? No.
Two years within your dungeons have I lived,
But lived for vengeance: closed that hope, t earth
Close o'er me too! Alive to bind Benlora! (Fall
Lorn. (Running up to him.) Ha! have ye sla him?—Fierce and warlike spirit!
I'm glad that thou hast had a soldier's death,
Arms in thy hands, all savage as thou art.
(Turning to LOCHTARISH *and* GLENFADDE But thou, the artful, base, contriving villain,
Who hast of an atrocious, devilish act

The mover been, and this thy vile associate,
Prepare thee for the villain's shameful end,
Ye have so dearly earn'd. (Waving his hand for
 the attendants to lead them off.)
 Loch. Be not so hasty, Lorn.—Think'st thou in-
deed
Ye have us here within your grasp, and nought
Of hostage or security retain'd
For our protection?
 Lorn. What dost thou mean?
 Loch. Deal with us as ye will:
But if within a week, returned to Mull,
In safety I appear not, with his blood,
The helpless heir, thy sister's infant son,
Who in my mother's house our pledge is kept,
Must pay the forfeit.
 Hel. (Starting up from the body in an agony of
 alarm.)
O horrible, ye will not murder him?
Murder a harmless infant!
 Loch. My aged mother, lady, loves her son
As thou dost thine, and she has sworn to do it.
 Hel. Has sworn to do it! Oh! her ruthless nature
To well I know.   (To LORN eagerly.)
 Loose them, and let them go.
 Lorn. Let fiends like these escape?
 Arg. (To HELEN.) He does but threaten
To move our fears: they dare not slay the child.
 Hel. They dare! they will!—O if thou art my
 father!
If nature's hand e'er twined me to thy heart
As this poor child to mine, have pity on me!
Loose them and let them go!—Nay, do it quickly.
O what is vengeance! Spare my infant's life.
Unpitying Lorn!—art thou a brother too?
The hapless father's blood is on thy sword,
And wilt thou slay the child! O spare him! spare
 him!
(Kneeling to ARGYLE and LORN, who stand irreso-
 lute, when enter SIR HUBERT DE GREY, carry-
 ing something in his arms, wrapped up in a
 mantle, and followed by MORTON. On seeing
 SIR HUBERT, she springs from the ground, and
 rushes forward to him.)
Ha! art thou here? in bless'd hour return'd
To join thy prayers with mine,—to move their
 hearts—
Their flinty hearts; to bid them spare my child! .
 De Grey. (Lifting up the mantle, and showing a
 sleeping child.)
The prayer is heard already: look thou here
Beneath this mantle, where he soundly sleeps.
 HELEN utters a cry of joy, and holds out her arms
 for her child, but at the same time sinks to the
 ground, embracing the knees of SIR HUBERT.
 ARGYLE and LORN run up to him, and all their
 vassals, etc., crowding round, close them about
 on every side, while a general murmur of exult-
 tation is heard through the whole. LOCHTARISH
 and GLENFADDEN, remaining on the side of the
 stage with those who guard them, are struck
 with astonishment and consternation.)
 Arg. (To those who guard LOCHTARISH, etc.,
 stepping forward from the crowd.)
ead to the grated keep your prisoners,
here to abide their doom. Upon the guilty
ur vengeance falls, and only on the guilty.
o all their clan besides, in which I know

Full many a gallant heart included is,
I still extend a hand of amity.
If they reject it, fair and open war
Between us be: and trust we still to find them
The noble, brave MacLeans, the valiant foes,
That, ere the dark ambition of the villain,
For wicked ends, their gallant minds had warp'd,
We heretofore had found them.
 O that men
In blood so near, in county, and in valor,
Should spend in petty broils their manly strength,
That might, united for the public weal,
On foreign foes such noble service do!
O that the day were come when gazing southron,
Whilst these our mountain warriors, marshall'd
 forth
To meet in foreign climes their country's foes,
Along their crowded cities slowly march,
To sound of warlike pipe, their plaided bands,
Shall say, with eager fingers pointed thus,
" Behold those men!—their sunn'd but thoughtful
 brows;
Their sinewy limbs; their broad and portly chests,
Lapp'd in their native vestments, rude but grace-
 ful—
Those be our hardy brothers of the North;—
The bold and generous race, who have, beneath
The frozen circle and the burning line,
The rights and freedom of our native land
Undauntedly maintain'd."
 That day will come,
When in the grave this hoary head of mine,
And many other heads, in death are laid;
And happier men, our sons, shall live to see it.
O may they prize it, too, with grateful hearts!
And, looking back on these our stormy days
Of other years, pity, admire, and pardon
The fierce, contentious, ill-directed valor
Of gallant fathers, born in darker times.

EPILOGUE.
WRITTEN BY HENRY MACKENZIE.

Well! here I am, those scenes of suff'ring o'er,
Safe among you; "a widowed thing" no more;
And though some squeamish critics still contend
That not so soon the tragic tone should end,
Nor flippant Epilogue, with smiling face,
Elbow her serious sister from the place;
I stand prepared with precedent and custom,
To plead the adverse doctrine—Won't you trust 'em?
I think you will, and now the curtain's down,
Unbend your brows, nor on my prattle frown.
You've seen how, in our country's ruder age,
Our moody lords would let their vassals rage,
And while they drove men's herds, and burnt their
 houses,
To some lone isle condemn'd their own poor
 spouses;
Their portion—drowning when the tide should
 serve;
Their separate aliment—a leave to starve.
And for the Scottish rights of *Dower* and *Tierce*,
A deep-sea burial, and an empty hearse.
Such was of old the fuss about this matter;
In our good times, 'tis managed greatly better;
When modern ladies part with modern lords,

Their business no such tragic tale affords;
Their "Family Legends," in their *Charter-chest*,
In deeds of ink, not deeds of blood, consist;
In place of ruffians ambushed in the dark,
Comes, with his pen, a harmless lawyer's clerk,
Draws a long—bond, my lady packs her things,
And leaves her mate to smooth his ruffled wings.
   In the free code of first enlighten'd France,
Marriage was broke for want of *convenance;*
No fault to find, no grievance to tell,
But, like tight shoes, they did not fit quite well.
The lady curt'sied, with "*Adieu, Monsieur,*"
The husband bow'd, or shrugg'd, "*de tout mon coeur!*"
"*L'affaire est faite;*" each partner free to range,
Made life a dance, and every dance a change.
   In England's colder soil they scarce contrive
To keep these foreign freedom-plants alive;
Yet in some gay parterres we've seen, ev'n there,
Its blushing fruit this frail exotic bear;—

Couples make shift to slip the marriage chain,
Cross hands—cast off—and are themselves again.
But, soft, I hear the Prompter's summons rung,
That calls me off, and stops my idle tongue;
A Sage, our fair and virtuous Author's friend,
Shakes his stern head, and bids my nonsense end;—
Bids me declare, she hopes her parent land
May long this current of the times withstand,
That here, in purity and honor bred,
Shall love and duty wreathe the nuptial bed;
The brave, good husband, and his faithful wife,
Revere the sacred charities of life;
And bid their children, like their sires of old,
Firm, honest, upright, for their country bold,
Here, where "Rome's eagles found unvanquished foes,"
The Gallic vulture fearlessly oppose,
Chase from this favored isle, with baffled wing,
Bless'd in its good old laws, old manners, and old king.

ALPHABETICAL LIST OF SUBSCRIBERS.

Abernethy, Mrs. Charles, 39 West 56th St., New York, N. Y. (Gilt edges.)
Ackers, Mrs., Moreton Hall, Cheshire, Eng.
Aitkin, Dr., F.S.A., Scot., Asylum House, Inverness, Scot.
Ammons, Mrs. Harriet McL., Franklin, Ohio.
Belcher, Mrs. E. J., Cherry Valley, N. Y.
Botfield, Mrs. W. E. Garnett, The West Bishop's Castle, Shropshire, Eng.
Cameron, Dr. J. A., 10 Salisbury Road, Edinburgh, Scot.
Campbell, J. L., Esq., 5 Victoria Place, Broughty Ferry, Scot. (Gilt edges.)
Cushing & Bailey, Booksellers, Baltimore, Md. (Gilt edges.)
Dana, Emily W., Falmouth, Me.
Dickinson, Mrs. R. M., Rockville, Conn. (Gilt edges.)
Fraser-Macintosh, Charles, Esq., M.P., F.S.A., Scot., of Drummond, Inverness, Scot. (Gilt edges.)
Gifford, H. L., Esq., Attorney at Law, Hamilton, Ohio.
Greeley, Mrs. Wm. H., Lexington, Mass. (Gilt edges.)
Griffith, Mrs., Glenmâkra, Upper Norwood, London, Eng.
Hamilton-Dundas, Mrs., Glenmâkra, Upper Norwood, London, Eng. (Gilt edges.)
Henniker, Mrs. Lillias G., Charlottetown, P. E. I., Canada.
Hibbard, Mrs. Susan W., Plano, Ill.
Homan, William Maclean, Esq., Christiania, Norway. (Gilt edges.)
Hood, Lady, 19 Queen's Gate Place, London, Eng.
Innes, Charles, Esq., Ballifeary, Inverness, Scot. (Gilt edges.)
Leath, Mrs. Margaret MacLean, Burkeville, Va.
Lockhart, Lady Macdonald, The Lee, Lanarkshire, Scot.
Macdonald, D. T., Esq., Red Jacket, Mich. (Gilt edges.)
Macdonald, T., Esq., Skeabost Bridge, Skeabost, Scot. (Gilt edges.)
Mackay, William, Esq., Solicitor, Inverness, Scot.
Mackenzie, John, Esq., Airdlair, Spylaw Road, Edinburgh, Scot.
Mackenzie, Nigel B., Esq., British Linen Bank, Fort William, Scot.
Mackenzie, Wm., Esq., Ardgowan, Inverness, Scot.
Maclean, Alexander, Esq., Drynachan, Invergarry, Scot. (Gilt edges.)
Maclean, Archibald John, Esq., of Pennycross, Tiroran House, Pennyghael, Mull. (3 copies.)
Maclean, A. Macdonald, Esq., Langbank, Scot. (Gilt edges.)
Maclean, Andrew, Esq., 7 Hamilton Crest, Partick, Glasgow, Scot. (Gilt edges.)
Maclean, Colonel Sir Fitzroy D., of Duard and Morvern, Chief of MacLean, 15 Hyde Park Terrace, London, Eng. (10 copies.)
Maclean, D., Esq., M.D., 7 Newton Place, Charing Cross, Glasgow, Scot.
Maclean, Don., Esq., Arilead, Isle of Coll, Scot. (Gilt edges.)
MacLean, Donald A., Argyle Shore, Prince Edward's Island, Canada.
MacLean, Eugene H., Urbana, Ill. (Gilt edges.)
MacLean, F. P., M.D., Chemist and Chief Examiner, U. S. Patent Office, Washington, D. C. (2 gilt edges.)
MacLean, Hector, Bridgetown, Annapolis, Nova Scotia. (Gilt edges.)

Alphabetical List of Subscribers.

Maclean, Henry, Esq., 19 Maresfield Gardens, South Hampstead, London, N. W., Eng. (Gilt edges.)
Maclean, Hugh, Esq., Brecklarach, Tarbert, Loch Fyne, Scot.
Maclean, Hugh, Esq., Camphill, Uddingston, Glasgow, Scot.
Maclean, John, 1123 Penn Ave., Pittsburg, Pa. (Gilt edges.)
MacLean, John Waters, 315 Genesee St., Utica, N. Y. (Gilt edges.)
Maclean, K. T., Thomasville, Ga.
Maclean, Lowry Cole, Esq., Bencraig, Sevenoaks, Kent, Eng.
MacLean, Lyell P., Urbana, Ill. (Gilt edges.)
MacLean, Malcolm, Ogalalla, Neb. (Gilt edges.)
Maclean, Miss, of Coll, Glenmâkra, Upper Norwood, London, Eng. (6 copies, 2 gilt edges.)
Maclean, Miss, 82 Great King St., Edinburgh, Scot. (Gilt edges.)
Maclean, Miss E. F. H., West Cliff House, Folkestone, Eng.
Maclean, Mrs., Aros House, Upper Norwood, London, Eng.
MacLean, Mrs. Helen Cleveland, Urbana, Ill. (Gilt edges.)
MacLean, Professor George Edwin, University of Minnesota, Minneapolis, Minn.
MacLean, Rev. Charles, Pembina, North Dakota.
Maclean, Rev. Duncan, Strontian, Lochsunart, by Ardgour, Scot. (Gilt edges.)
MacLean, Rev. Thomas W., Bay City, Mich. (Gilt edges.)
Maclean, Robert, Esq., Advocate, 19 Queen's St., Edinburgh, Scot.
Maclean, Sir Andrew, Viewfield House, Partick, Scot.
Macrae, John, Esq., 42 Royal Highlanders, Kames Castle, Rothesay, Scot. (Gilt edges.)
Malcolm, George, Esq., Factor, Inverary, Scot. (Gilt edges.)
Martin, Henry MacLean, N. E. Cor. Cala. and Taylor Sts., San Francisco, Cal. (Gilt edges.)
McIntyre, Allan, Lake Linden, Mich.
McClain, Ephraim, M.D., Lawrenceburg, Tenn.
McClain, E. L., Greenfield, Ohio. (Gilt edges.)
McClain, T. B., New Palestine, Ind.
McClean, Charles B., Towson, Md.
McClean, George C., M.D., Springfield, Mass.
McClean, Hon. William, Prest. Judge 42d Judicial District, Gettysburg, Pa. (3 gilt edges.)
McClurg & Co., Booksellers, Chicago. Ill. (5 copies, 3 gilt edges.)
McLain, A. O., National Bank, Newton, Kan. (Gilt edges.)
McLain, John Speed, M.D., 1924 N St., Washington, D. C. (7 copies, 4 gilt edges.)
McLain, Louis Randolph, C. E., Ozark, Ala.
McLain, Major Calvin W., 13 33d St., Chicago, Ill.
McLain, Miss Lizzie, 1924 N St., Washington, D. C.
McLain, Professor Henry Z., Wabash College, Crawfordsville, Ind. (Gilt edges.)
McLain, W. D., Esq., 200 Oakwood Boul., Chicago, Ill. (Gilt edges.)
McLane, Charles A., Laredo, Tex.
McLane, Edward A., Chicago, Ill.
McLane, James, Franklin, O. (Gilt edges.)
McLean, Alexander D., Esq., Wallingford, Conn. (2 copies, 1 gilt edges.)
McLean, Arthur Elliot, Norfolk, Conn. (Gilt edges.)
McLean, Allan Oswald, Lethbridge, Alberta, Canada. (Gilt edges.)
McLean, Archibald, Bradford, Pa.
McLean, Charles N., American Mills Co., Rockville, Conn.
McLean, Colin, Esq., 42 Royal Highlanders (Malta). (Gilt edges.)
McLean, Colin Campbell, Janesville, Wis. (Gilt edges.)
McLean, D. A., De Funiak Springs, Fla.

Alphabetical List of Subscribers.

McLean, Daniel, 106 Timson St., Lynn, Mass. (Gilt edges.)
McLean, Daniel E., Walton, N. Y.
McLean, David, Esq., The Crooks, Coldstream, Scot. (Gilt edges.)
McLean, D. G., De Funiak Springs, Fla.
McLean, Duncan R., Bellows Falls, Vt.
McLean, Donald, Esq., Attorney at Law, 170 Broadway, New York, N. Y.
McLean, Francis, 507 A, S. E., Washington, D. C.
McLean, Francis J., Esq., Attorney at Law, Menomonie, Wis.
McLean, George, Lethbridge, Alberta, Canada. (Gilt edges.)
McLean, George C., Jr., 208 Centre Ave., Janesville, Wis.
McLean, H. & H., Dickinson, N. C. (Gilt edges.)
McLean, Hector, 14 Gardner Ave., Roxbury, Boston, Mass.
McLean, Hon. Daniel, Washington C. H., O. (Gilt edges.)
McLean, Hon. George P., Simsbury, Conn. (Gilt edges.)
McLean, Hon. John R., Editor and Proprietor "Cincinnati Enquirer," 1500 I St., Washington, D. C. (Gilt edges.)
McLean, J. A., De Funiak Springs, Fla.
McLean, James, Esq., 94 Dundas St., Glasgow, Scot. (Gilt edges.)
McLean, J. D., M.D., Health Officer, Spokane Falls, W. T.
McLean, James L., Winfield, West Va.
McLean, James M., Esq., Prest. Manhattan Life Ins. Co., 156 Broadway, New York, N. Y. (Gilt edges.)
McLean, James W., M.D., Fayette, Iowa.
McLean, John, Froebel School, Chicago, Ill.
McLean, John, West Hartford, Conn. (Gilt edges.)
McLean, John, M.D., Morehead, Minn.
McLean, John Hall, San Francisco, Cal.
McLean, John J., Palmyra, N. Y.
McLean, John J., U. S. Signal Service, Red Bluff, Cal.
McLean, John R., Evanston, Ill.
McLean, John W., 42 State St., Chicago, Ill. (Gilt edges.)
McLean, L. A., Editor "Herald," Urbana, Ill.
McLean, Lester, Esq., Attorney at Law, Elyria, O.
McLean, Lieut. T. C., U. S. N., Asst. Inspector of Ordnance, U. S. Torpedo Station, Newport, R. I. (Gilt edges.)
McLean, Miss Mary, Franklin, Mass. (2 copies.)
McLean, Miss Mary E., South Glastonbury, Conn. (Gilt edges.)
McLean, Mrs. Allan, Litchfield, Conn. (Gilt edges.)
McLean, Mrs. Charles B., Wethersfield, Conn. (14 copies, 13 gilt edges,)
McLean, Mrs. Edward, Los Angeles, Cal. (Gilt edges.)
McLean, Mrs. Susan A., 3402 Wabash Ave., Chicago, Ill. (Gilt edges.)
McLean, N. A., Esq., Attorney at Law, Lumberton, N. C.
McLean, Norman, 29 Monroe St., Lynn, Mass. (Gilt edges.)
McLean, Professor John B., Simsbury, Conn. (Gilt edges.)
McLean, R. B., Nashville, Tenn.
McLean, Robert C., of Kingerloch, 10 Mariana St., Lynn, Mass. (Gilt edges.)
McLean, Rev. Calvin B., Newfield, N. J. (Gilt edges.)
McLean, Rev. James D., Gainesville, Ala.
McLean, Rev. J. K., 520 13th K. W., Oakland, Cal.
McLean, Rev. John, Vernon, Mich.
McLean, Rev. John, M.A., Ph.D., Macleod, Alberta, Canada.
McLean, Sarah A. Thorne, Chicago, Ill.
McLean, Thomas Alexander, Charlottetown, P. E. I., Canada. (Gilt edges.)

Alphabetical List of Subscribers.

McLean, W. A., Adjuster of Fire Losses, 172 La Salle St., Chicago, Ill.
McLean, W. C., De Funiak Springs, Fla.
McLean, William, Merchant, Evansville, Ind. (Gilt edges.)
McLean, William, Druggist, Albion, Neb. (Gilt edges.)
McLean, William Clark, 2705 Hamilton St., Omaha, Neb.
McLean, Wm. K., Esq., Barrister at Law, Guelph, Ontario, Canada.
McLean, William Murdock, 14 Boylston St., Boston, Mass. (Gilt edges.)
McLean, William S., Esq., Attorney at Law, 21 S. Franklin St., Wilkesbarre, Pa. (Gilt edges.)
McLean, William Stevenson, Lethbridge, Alberta, Canada. (Gilt edges.)
McLean, Thomas Neil, M.D., 1144 East Broad St., Elizabeth, N. J.
McLeod, Roderick, Esq., 20 Greenhill Gardens, Edinburgh, Scot. (Gilt edges.)
Minnesota Historical Society, St. Paul, Minn.
Moss, Mrs. William Lathrop, Chicago, Ill.
Munsell, Joel's Sons, Publishers, Albany, N. Y.
Nevill, The Honorable Mrs. Ralph, Birling Manor, Maidstone, Eng.
Pallandt, Baroness de, Seymour St., Portman Square, London W., Eng.
Pennsylvania State Library, Harrisburg, Pa.
Phillipps, Mrs. Mary Frances, 28 Cromwell Grove, West Kensington, London, Eng.
Public Library, Boston, Mass.
Reed, Rev. Julius A., Cor. Brady and Locust Sts, Davenport, Iowa.
Richards, Mrs. Sarah M., 394 Union St., Allentown, Pa. (Gilt edges.)
Rolls, Mrs., of The Hendre, Monmouth, Eng.
Scripps, E. W., Esq., Journalist, West Chester, O. (Gilt edges.)
Sinclair, Rev. B. D., Newburyport, Mass. (Gilt edges.)
Stockard, Samuel McLean, Springfield, Mo.
Thin, James, Bookseller, Edinburgh, Scot. (29 copies, 18 glt edges.)
Tyler, F. E., Esq., Kansas City, Mo.
University Library, Aberdeen, Scot.
Wailey, Frances Dyaz, Stangorse House, Prince's Park, Liverpool, Eng.
Watson, Sereno, M.D., Cambridge, Mass.
Wilkinson, Mrs. Henry W., 92 Bowen St., Providence, R. I.
Windham, Miss, Glenmâkra, Upper Norwood, London, Eng. (Gilt edges.)
Windham, Mrs., Glenmâkra, Upper Norwood, London, Eng.
Wotherspoon, Mrs. William Wallace, 119 West Eleventh St., New York, N. Y. (Gilt edges.)
Wyllie & Co., Aberdeen, Scot.

FULLNAME INDEX

----, Ailean Nan Sop 284 312 321 Alexander 279 Alexander Of Dunvegan 77 Alexander Of Glengarry 78 Alexander Of Lochalsh 51 237 Alexander Son Of Ross 43 Alexander Third Lord Of The Isles 283 Allan 336-337 Allan Nan Sop 265 336 Andrew Lord Stewart Of Ochiltree 146 Angus 120 256 Ann Daughter Of John Laird Of Lehire 276 Anne Princess 280 Archibald 162-163 Archibald Earl Of Argyle 111 Archibald Earl Of Ergyle 126 Barabel 338-340 Bristi Son Of Gilleain 33 Catrina 338 Celestine 353 Colquhoun 32 Conchatha 32 Conduiligh 32 Consithe 32 Cucatha Son Of Raingee 32 Cuduilig Son Of Raingee 32 Cusidhe Son Of Raingee 32 David Earl Of Crawford 49 236 Donald 26 69 Donald Lord Of The Isles 299 327 352 Donald Of The Isles 355 Donald Second Lord Of The Isles 251 Douglas 256 Dubh-chal 300 Duncan 54 Edward 35 Ewen 166 Fionnaghal 49-50 Gamail Lord Of Carrick 35 George Elector Of Hanover 207 Gilhon 36 Gilireamhack 48 Gille-calum 35 Gille-eoin Son Of Rath 32 Gille-iosa 35 Gille-iosa Second Chief 33 Gilleain 29 31-33 Gilleain Na H'airde 32 Gilleain Na Tuaighe 33 Gilleain Son Of Rath 32 Gilleain The First Chief Of Maclean 33 Gillebridge Son Of Gilleain 33 Gilleownan Of Roderic 50 Gillespie 53 Godred 28 Hugh 96 352 Hugh Of Rose Baron Of Kilravock 255 James 110 307 John Abbot Of Iona 353 John Duke Of Lauderdale 184 John Laird Of Lehire 276 John Lord Of The Isles 352-353 John Of The Isles 299-300 John Second Earl Of Hopetoun 271 John Son Of Gilhon 36 Lady Catherine Daughter Of Roderick Of The Isles 252 Macgillebride Sombairle Mor 32 Macrath Son Of Niall 32 Magnus Barefoot 34 Malcolm 34 Maol-calum 35 Maoliosa Son Of Gilleain 33 Margaret Daughter Of The Earl Of Mar 45

---- (cont.) Marian Daughter Of The Chief Of Duard 174 Mary 199 Mary Daughter Of James V 78 Mary Of Guise 25 Mary Princess 280 Neil Son Of Gilhon 36 Nial Mor 285 Niall Mor 285 Niall Son Of Cuduiligh 32 Old Dougall Of Scone 32 Old Dougall Son Of Fearchar Abraruadh 32 Old Dougall Son Of Mocche 32 Raingee Son Of Old Dougall 32 Rath 33 Rath Son Of Niall 32 Reginald Lord Of The Isles 318 Rioghnach Daughter Of Gamail 35 Roderick Of The Isles 252 Ross 43 Ruari Mor 120 Somerled 28 32 Thomas Younger Of Dingwall 353
ABERNETHY, Charles 477 William 42
ACHESON, 158 Archibald 156 159 Isabella 159
ACHINCROSS, John 402
ACHINROS, Johnne 405
ACHINROSS, 122 124 John 120-121 239 356 Johnne 403
ACKERS, Constance Marianne 232 George Holland 232 Mrs 477
AGHLINNE, Calum 408
AIGEANNAICH, 407
AIRLEY, Lord 171
AITKEN, James 311
AITKIN, Dr 477
ALANESON, Charles Maclane 356
ALCOYNE, Margaret 314 Spencer Joshua 314
ALEXANDER, Earl Of Huntly 61 Earl Of Mar 44 Lord High Steward 34 Lord Of The Isles 50 57 Of Islay 76 Third Lord Of The Isles 44
ALEXANDER III, 34 Of Scotland 33
ALEXR, Erle Of Huntlie 25
ALI, Hyder 306
ALLAN, William 425
ALLANSON, Alan 56 Ewen 56 Ewin 56-57 68 237
ALLEIN, Na Sop 46
ALLEN, William 22
ALLOID, Mhic 30
ALLOIL, Erin Mhic 31
AM, Bard Mac-gilleain 383

AM (cont.)
  Bard Macgilleain 384 Cubair Colach 383
AMMONS, Harriet Jane 397 Harriet Mcl 477 Miley W 397
ANDERSON, 133 Nancy 394 Robert 394
ANDREW, Robert 399 Sarah 399
ANGUS, Dhu 41 Earl Of Scotland 114
ANGUSSON, Donald 56-57
ANNDRA, Mac An Easbuig 326
ANNE, Queen 206-207 213 225 302 308
ANTHONY, Susan 307 William Banks 207
AONGAS, Tuirmeach Teamhrach 31
AONGHAS, Turmhi Teamhrach 30
AONGHUS, Fairmhic Jeam Mhic 31
APNADULL, 75
APPIN, 209 216
ARDCHATTAN, 156
ARDGOUR, 212
ARESKINE, George 121
ARGILE, Lord 113
ARGYLE, 24-25 49 51 58 64 68-70 72 74-76 80-81 94 116-119 121-123 140 142-143 155-156 161-162 165 167-170 173-174 176-178 183-188 190 192-198 200 205-206 210 213 225 237 239 242 268 299 303 401 Catherine 81
ARMIDALE, Lord 227
ARNOLD, 374 Gen 375
ARRAN, 59 75
ASHLEY, 401
ATHOL, 51 171
ATHOLE, 64 75
AUCHENDOWN, 116
AUCHINBRECK, 207
AUCHINROS, Johnne 126
AUSTIN, Alvin 263 Emma Eliza 263
BACACH, Eachunn 407
BAILEY, Bookseller 477
BAILIE, Charles 296 Marian 296
BAILLIE, 168 170 Jannet 258 Joanna 71 452 Of Dochfour 260 William 258
BAINBRIDGE, Phoebe 274
BAKER, Abraham 394 Margaret 394
BALHADY, 222
BALIOL, Edward 299
BALLACH, Donald 45
BALLIOL, Edward 28
BALLOCH, Donald 44 48
BAN, Ranald 45
BANKS, Gen 398
BAOGHAIN, Mhic 30
BARD, Thighearna Chola 383
BARKER, Sarah A 386
BARRA, 48
BARROWS, Anna Eliza 397 Blake Wales 397 Ernest 397 Louise 397 Stanley 397
BARTON, Robert 58

BEATON, 26 John 30
BEDDOE, John 380
BELCHER, E J 477
BERFAET, Magnus King Of Norway 318
BERKLEY, George 202
BETON, Donald 323 John 321 323
BIRREL, 133
BISCHOP, Jhon 328
BISHOP, John 230
BLACK, Isabel 383 William 311
BLACKIE, 409 418 J S 311 John Stuart 22 419 Professor 408
BLAIR, 222 Maggie 222
BLEAU, George 222 Mr 223
BORLUM, 253-254
BORRERAY, 273
BOSWELL, 227 244-245 363-364 424 James 359
BOTFIELD, W E Garnett 477
BOTHWELL, 64
BOWES, 113 121 123-124 356 404 R 122 Robert 120
BOYD, Jane 326 Thomas 326
BRAE, Of Lochaber 193
BREADALBANE, 209-210 290 295
BRIADALBANE, 75
BROWN, Alfred 398 Anson 398 Charles 398 George 231 John 179-180 Lennox 311 Margaret 397 Minerva Jane 398 Minnie 398
BROWNE, 118 161 340 343 358-359
BRUCE, 22-23 372-373 409 433 David 28 36 Edward 35 Mrs 372 Robert 28 35 346 Robert King 299
BRUDE, 317
BRYDGES, Elizabeth 377
BUCHAN, 204
BUCHANAN, 42 180
BURGHLEY, Minister 120
BURNETT, Catherine 296 Daniel 296
BUTT, 75
BUY, Anne 238 Sorley 238
CAILENKERHEILM, Eliza 315 Maj 315
CAIRBRE, Chromachinn Mhic 30 Ffuinmhov Mhic 30 Riad Mhic 30
CAIRIBRI, Ffuinmhov Mhic 30
CAITHNESS, 64
CALDER, 143 156
CALDWELL, Rachael 397
CAMBPELL, Jannet 106
CAMERON, 35 38-39 44 56-57 59 77 115 138 144 153 169 178 193 199 207-209 219 237 254 257 268 279 283-284 305 327 Alan 267 Allan 126 269 289-290 Anne 270 Catherine 269 290 Christianna 290 Donald 253 270 278 Ewen 169 176 194 197 203-204 266 270 304 Hector 305 Helen 305 Hugh 263 309 Isabella 176 303 J A 477

CAMERON (cont.)
Jannet 301 305 Jean 290 John 301 407
John Of Callart 303 John Of Erracht
303 Margaret 263 Mary 303 309 Of
Lochiel 88 200 Samuel 253 Sibella 289
Una 87 304
CAMPBELL, 24-25 32 35 56 63 100 155-
156 165 167-169 177 185 197-198 207
275 277 332 363 382 Alexander 194
289 402 Angus 269 Anna 346 Anne 243
269 298 Archibald 57 71 76 80 83 87
115 119 142-143 154 161 166 171-172
176 183-184 193 196 200 204 213 300
306 308 Archibald Of Auchinbreck 75
Archibald Of Inveraw 313 Archibald
Of Skipnish 75 Archibald Of
Sunderland 313 Capt 173 248 305
Catherine 49 87 273 300 305 313 Colin
49 66-67 70 74-75 77 93 194-195 205
241-242 270-271 289 307 Colin Earl Of
Argyle 72 Domald 259 Donald 126 174-
175 178 243 248 270 273 289 294 305-
306 313 315 Dugald 73 287 Duncan 64
194 214 276 312-313 Duncan Of
Glenurchy 75 Duncan Of Ilangerig 75
Elizabeth 71 248 Emilie Guillaumine
249 Florence 287 Frederick 249 Helen
315 Hugh 194 241 243 Isabella 273-
274 289 306-307 J F 379 J L 477
James 194 208 214 Jane 248 305 Janet
81 83 105 Jannet 306 313 355 Jean
289 308 John 72-74 77 79 172 195 205
208 227 237 248 274 278 301 305-306
313 356 John George Edward Henry
Douglass Sutherland 416 John Gorm
240 300 Johne 162 Julian 241 Marellia
72 Margaret 73 241-242 258 300-301
305 Marian 312 Mary 278 289 301
312-313 Neil 298 Neill 186 194 197 Of
Ardkinglass 124 Of Argyle 208 Of
Calder 123 Of Cawdor 200 Of
Duntroon 80-81 Of Glendaruel 208 214
Of Inverawe 193 Of Lochgoilhead 94
Of Lochnell 115 Of Strond 274 Robert
241 301 Susanna 273 Susannah 306
Thomas 439
CAMPBLE, Archibald 328 Jhone 328
CAMPION, Frances 230 Henry 230
CAN, Cailean 32
CANNON, 204 Col 201 Gen 203
CANTWELL, Mary 399 Zebulon 399
CARBRE, Chromchinn Mich 30
CARLISLE, 215
CARLTON, Guy 374
CAROLINE, Queen 361
CARRACH, Alastair 251
CARRICK, 75
CARSWELL, Bishop 354 John 326 328
CASSILLIS, 64

CASTELLAR, 327
CATRIONA, Nighean Eobhain Mhic
Lachainn 383
CEALLI, Mhic 30
CECIL, 124 133 R 124 Robert 120-123 356
CECILL, Robert 403
CELESTINE, Lord Of Lochalsh 57
CHAMBERS, 219
CHARLES, 165 171 179 251 King 196 297
Prince 216 243 260 370 Sir 252 The
First 315
CHARLES I, 135 163 258 358 401 King
161 176 329
CHARLES II, 161 176 178 184 330 348
CHARLIE, Prince 222
CHATTAN, 25 44 52 56 65 68
CHISHOLM, 207 331 Thomas 267
CHLAN-ILLEAIN, 352
CINE, Mhic 30
CINTA, Mhic 30
CLANDONALD, 50 82 101 104
CLANDONNALD, 84
CLANIAN, 96 108
CLANLEAN, 104
CLANLEOD, 96 101
CLANN-GHILLEAIN, 352
CLANQUHATTANE, 25
CLANRANALD, 48 96 107-109 115 158
Marian 254
CLANRANNOLD, 46
CLARK, George 314
CLARKE, 360-361 Ada Eve 398 Adam
380-381 Margaret 395 Robert 390
CLARSAIR, Eoin Macmhurchaidh 289
Murdoch 289
CLEPHANE, Anna Jane 314 Douglas 314
Margaret 314 Marianne 314 Wilmina
Marianne 314
CLEVELAND, Helen 397 J H 397
CLUNY, 216
CLUTCH, Daniel H 397 Margaret 397
COLE, J W 298
COLLIER, George 374
COLLS, Mium Mhic 30
COLQUHOUN, 143 Of Luss 45
COLUMBA, St 24 232
COMYN, 28
CONDUELI, Mhic 30
CONGREVE, Charlotte 376 William 376
CONOIR, Mhic 30 Mhoir Mhic 30 30-31
COPE, John 215
CORWIN, Josephine 397
COTTINGHAM, Hannah Barbara 295
CRAIG, Emma 396 Margaret Anne 264
Thomas 126 William 264
CRATH, Mhic 30
CRAWFORD, 64 Alexander 305 Isabella
305
CREIGHTON, William 254

INDEX

CROMWELL, 161 178-180 183
CROTTACH, Alastair 47
CUBBAGE, James 293
CUDDALORE, 375
CUDUILIG, Son Of Raingee 30
CUMBERLAND, 200 221
CUMMING, 35 Lord Of The Braes Of Lochaber 37
CUMYN, Farquhar 252
CUNNINGHAM, 75 121 124 John 120-123 Margaret 95 137 William 94 137
CURRIE, Margaret 395
CUSHING, Bookseller 477
CUTLER, Elizabeth 263 Robert M 263
DACRE, 64
DALL, Rory 289
DALLAS, Jannet 259 William 259
DALRYMPLE, Helen Jane Hamilton 271 John 271
DANA, Emily W 477
DARI, Dormhor Mhic 30 Dornmhor Mhic 30
DARNLEY, Lord 83
DAVID, King 287
DAVIDSON, John 50 353 Robert 42
DAYTON, Amelia Dunlap 398 Clifford 398 E 398 Freddie 398
DEADHE, Mhic 31
DEADHI, Mhic 31
DEARTH, Isaac 396 Rachael 396
DENNISTOUN, James 291 Jannet 291
DENORMAN, Wilhelm Baron 314 Wilmina Marianne 314
DHU, Donald 58-59 62
DICKEN, Selina Philippa 272 William S 272
DICKINSON, R M 477
DICKSON, John 229 Mary 229
DIEHL, Patricia S 13
DOMHNULL, Cubair 383
DONALD, Gorm Of Sleat 158 Of The Isles 25
DONNELL, 121
DOUGLAS, 48 240 James 35
DOWARDIUS, Lauchlanus Maclanus 135
DOWING, Rebecca 398
DRIMNIN, 262
DRUMMOND, 35 John 216 221-222 Miss 306
DUARIS, Fortunatus 307 Maria 307
DUBH, Donald 59 78-80 89-90 237-238 255 John 24
DUFF, Donald 353
DUGAL, King 34
DUGALL, 38
DUIRACH, Anne 306 Donald Maceachann-vic-ian 306
DUNBAR, Patrick 34
DUNCAN, David 315 Maria 315

DUNDAS, George 292 Jane Albane 292
DUNDEE, 200-203 258-259 Viscount 199
DUNLAP, Nancy 398
DUNOON, Hugh 263
DUNSTAN, Emilie Fordyce 298 W R 298
DURACHE, Donald 356 John 356
EACHAN, Mhac Ailean Nan Sop 300
EACHDUINN, Macgiolla Eoin Lord Of Dubhard 358 Son Of Lachlan 30
EARNALI, Mhic 31
EARSON, Deborah 399 Elizabeth 399 John 399 Robert 399
EDGAR, Mr 223 359
EDIR, Sceoil Mhic 31 31
EDWARD I, Of England 352
EDWARD IV, 48 300
ELCHO, Lord 222
ELDER, John 356
ELIZABETH, Queen 121-124 134 Queen Of England 113 120
ENOCHI, Tuamhil Mhic 30
EOCHA, Mhic 30
EOCHI, Anureamhair Mhic 30 Bunream Hair Mhic 30
EODNIN, Mhic 31
EOGHANN, A' Chinbhig 332 A' Chinn Bhig 237
EOGHM, Mhic 31
ERAN, Or The 75th Monarch Of Ireland Vide Peter Welsh 31
ERC, 31 Irish Chieftain 30
ERGILE, 69
ERI, Mhic 30-31 No Hior Mhic 31
ERROL, 64 116-117
ERROLL, 115 Earl Of Scotland 114
ERSKIN, George 126
ERSKINE, 222 John 208
ESCHE, Mhic 30
FALSTAFF, John 363
FAREIJA, Capt 108 Don 107 109
FARQUHARSON, 216
FEACHRA, Mhic 30
FELEMLAMDOID, Mhic 30
FELIM, Lamdoid Mhic 30
FERADICH, Mhic 31
FERCHAR, Fiarvain Mhic 31
FERGHIE, Mhic 31
FERGHUIS, Abhraruoidh Eadhorn Righ Alba 30 Mhic 30 30
FERGO, Mhic 31
FERGUIS, Mhic 30
FERGUS, I King Of Scotland 30
FERQUARD, Bishop 90
FHRAINE, Mhic 30
FISHER, Adelaide Owen 298 Edward H 298 Mr 290
FITZROY, Charles 226
FLYNN, 393
FORBES, Gen 293 President 220 289

INDEX.

FORLONG, Agnes 377
FOWLER, Baillie 259 Margaret 259
FRACHRI, Fravray Mhic Aonghuis 31
FRANCIS I, 402
FRASEE, Miss 263
FRASER, 35 51-52 209 219 258 Agnes 258
   David 307 Farquhar 287 305 Florence
   305 Isabella 283 Jannet 287 Mary 307
   Of Lovat 283 The Kings Herald 116
FRASER-MACINTOSH, Charles 477
FREMONT, Gen 387
FRENCH, Miss 306
FUINDUIN, Mhic 30 30
GARBH, Charles Ian 281 Mary 281
GARRY, Malcolm 410
GEORGE I, 303
GEORGE II, 202 221 366 King 215
GEORGE III, 246 366 392
GEORGE, King 207-208
GIBSON, Murdoch 45
GIFFORD, H L 477
GIGGIE, Dr 311
GILL, Heber 399 J H 399 Sarah 399 399
GILLEAIN, 351-352 Mac 30 Na Tuaidh
   351
GILLEAN, 160 301 Mary 301
GILLEASPUIG, Laidir 383
GILLEEOIN, Son Of Macrath 30
GILLIAN, 22 Of Scallasdale 376
GILLIE, 407
GILLILAND, ---- 399 Elizabeth 399
   Hannah 394 James 394 394 Narcissa
   Lynn 394 Sarah 399
GLENCAIRN, 64
GLENGARRY, 223
GORDON, 116 119 209 216 Anna
   Margaret 315 Gen 210 George 198 Of
   Gicht 117 Patrick 116 R 133-134
GORM, Donald 79
GRAHAM, 319 326 Gen 376 James 161
   166 199
GRANT, 35 56 115 207 257 Alexander 307
   Colquhoun 305 Lillian 305 Margery
   257 Of Frenchie 252
GRAY, Capt 116
GREELEY, Wm H 477
GREENE, F L 388 Sallie Pratt 388
GREGORSON, Angus 264 Donald 248
   John 248 Marjory 264 Mary 248
   Phoebe 248
GREGORY, 70-71 74 90 117 132-133 143
   351
GREVILLE, Marian 261
GRIEVE, Mackenzie 279 Mary Anna 279
GRIFFITH, Elizabeth 291 Mrs 477 Walter
   291
GRUAMACH, Donald 75
GRUCHY, Peter 263 Sophia 263
GUNSTON, William 271

GUORI, Mhic 30 30
HACO, King 34
HALL, Maria Isabella 398
HAMILTON, ---- 399 Catherine 315
   James 291 Jane 399 Malcolm 315
   Margaret 291
HAMILTON-DUNDAS, Mrs 477
HANNA, ---- 395 Elizabeth 395 Emas 395
   Harriet Newel 395
HANOVER, 207
HARFAGR, Harald 28
HASTING, 203
HAWLEY, Gen 215
HAY, Alexander 143 James 146
HECTORSON, Alan Maclane 356
HENDERSON, Elizabeth 260 Thomas 261
HENNIKER, Lillias G 477
HENRY IV, King 40
HENRY VIII, 238 356
HEREIS, Lord 126
HIBBARD, Susan W 477
HOBART, George Vere 291 Jannet 291
HOBEG, 158
HOGG, 423
HOLBURN, 179-180
HOLLINGSHED, 40
HOMAN, William Maclean 477
HOME, Lord 67
HOOD, A W A 230 Fanny Henrietta 230
   Lady 477
HOPKINS, Archibald 395 Rachel Marquis
   395
HOUSEL, Decatur 395 Margaret Olive
   395 Narcissa 395
HOUSTON, Alexander 271 Elizabeth 271
HOWE, William 247
HUCHONSON, John 56
HUGHSON, John 56
HUNTER, Alexander 291 Maria 291
HUNTLY, 58 63-64 68 115-120 140 145-
   146 209 256 Earl Of Scotland 114 Lord
   25
HUTTLESTON, Henry 298 Mary 298
HYDER, Ali 375
ILLIS, Donald 70
ILVURRICH, 43
INAGHUISVALICH, Be Mhic 30
INNES, 43 Charles 477
INOGHUIS, Valaich No Inaghuis Fiar
   Mhic 30
IRUEN, Mhic 31
IRVINE, 43 Alexander 42
IRVING, 41
JAMES, 63-64 115 121 123 200 206-207
JAMES, King 111 114 134 139 144 157
   201 205 210 258
JAMES I, King 29 43-44 46
JAMES II, 45 198-199 207 213 215 242
   252 279 284

INDEX.

JAMES III, 207-208
JAMES IV, 62 66 236 256 King 29 55 325
JAMES V, 77-78 256 King 73 284
JAMES VI, 22 82 118 136 145 148-149 152 238 355 King 92 328
JAMES VII, 268 330
JOHN, Fourth Lord Of The Isles 23 Of Logan 36 Son Of Malcom 30
JOHNSON, 135 360 362 Dr 135 227 361 363-364 Sallie E 396 Samuel 226 245 359 424 Secretary Of State For Scotland 206
JOHNSTON, 364 Dr 228
JUDD, J W 311
JULIUS III, Pope 326
KARR, James 395 Margaret 395
KAY, Catherine 73 Patrick 73
KEITH, 90
KELTIE, 61 118 143 200 343
KENNEDY, 253 Dr 30 James 39 352
KEPPOCH, 217 341
KIDD, Charles 230
KINCAID, Jacobus 328 James 328
KINLOCH, Francis 280
KITTEACH, Col 300
KNOX, Andrew 146 152 Thomas 162 240 358
KYLE, 75
LACHAINN, Mairearad Nighean 407
LACHAIRM, Mairerad Nighean 406
LACHLAN, Oir Mhac Dhonil Mhic Neil 301 Son Of Eachduinn 30 Son Of Hector 30 Son Of John 30
LADY, Of Duard 174
LAMBERT, 179-181 Gen 179
LAMBY, 273 John 302
LAMONT, Neil 407
LAMOTTE, French Ambassador 64
LANDON, Letitia Elizabeth 379
LAUDERDALE, 185-187
LEAN, 22
LEATH, Margaret Maclean 477
LEE, Baillie 260 Marjory 260
LEIBNITZ, 360-361
LENNOX, 64 78-79 140
LESLEY, 41
LESLIE, 174 David 172-173
LINCH, 308
LINCOLN, Abraham 388
LINDSAY, David 236 352
LIVINGSTON, Thomas 204
LIVINGSTONE, Capt 210
LOCHIEL, 126-127 138-139 169 207 209 216 239 284
LOCHNELL, 207 242
LOCKHART, Lady Macdonald 477
LOGHAIRNE, In Hoir Mhic 30 Mar Mac 30
LOM, Iain 406

LONG, Anne 274
LORN, Lord 162-163 194 227
LORNE, A 164
LOUP, 292
LOVAT, 216 258 Lord 254 283 Margaret 254
LOVEL, 41 Gen 374 James 42
LOVETT, Lord 79
LOWTHER, Barbara 246
LUIG, Alltach Mhic 30
LYNN, Margaret 393
MAC, Mhic Allan 267 Mhic Eachainn 261 Mhic Eachiann 263 Mhic Eoghainn 126-127 Mhic Eoghiann 266
MAC-AN-EASBUIG, Anndra 407
MAC-GHILLE-ATHAIN, 351
MAC-GHILLE-EION, 351
MAC-GHILLEAIN, 352
MAC-GHILLEOIN, 352
MAC-GILLE-SHEATHAIN, 351
MAC-ILLEAIN, 352
MAC-ILLEAN, 352
MAC-MHIC-ALLEIN, Charles 278
MAC-PHAIL, Mary 406
MAC-VIC-EWIN, John 151
MACADAM, Isabella 302
MACAILEIN, Iain 406
MACALISTER, Rory 79
MACALLAN, Charles 303 305-306 Donald 148 154 Ranald 59
MACALLASTER, 128 144 Gorrie 127
MACALLEN, John 266
MACALLISTER, 96 101 Finovola 285 Godfrey 285 Johne 79
MACARTHUR, Duncan 307 Jannet 307
MACAULAY, 199-200 242 390
MACBEAN, 381
MACBETH, 319
MACCHARLES, Allan 197 Donald 197 Hector 197 Hugh 197 Lachlan 197
MACCOLL, Evan 410
MACCOLLA, Raonuill 100
MACCONEYLLIS, 78
MACCORMICK, Jane 263 John 263
MACCOUL, 173
MACDONALD, 23-24 38 45 47 52-53 83 102-103 105-107 109 113-114 126 134 141-142 152 199 203 209-210 217 219 239 258 267-268 280 285 292 294 301 308 319 337 362 Aeneas 340 Alexander 66 74 87 168 171 173-174 287 289 289-290 295 308 313 408 Alister Mac-ian-chathanaich 285 Allan 295 336 341 Angus 49-51 91-93 95 97-101 104 110-111 123 125 127-128 132-133 143-144 146-148 150 300 356 Angus Og 28 35 147 299 Anna 308 Anne 302 Archibald 145 194 Barbara 313 Catherine 307 Celestine 50 Colla-kittoch 173 D T 477

MACDONALD(cont.)
 Donald 29 39-41 67-68 87 124 156-157
 195 202 204 207 209 274 307 312 369
 Donald Gallda 66 Donald Gorm 92 95-
 97 101 110 120-123 148 154 158 238
 240 Fionnaghal 49 Florence 274 295
 Hugh 237 273 348 James 78-80 82 89
 89 97-99 127-133 138-139 143 155-156
 286 294 313 Janet 88 Jannet 287 John
 28-29 35 37 39 48-50 50-51 55 57-58
 159 237 275 291 341 406 408 Lady 98
 Lady Margaret 38-39 Lord 186-187
 193-195 197 369 Malcolm 290
 Margaret 41 51 289 295 383 Marian
 290 312 Marjory 305 Mary 87 91 95
 294 300 Meve 284 Murdoch 289 410 Of
 Dunyveg 153 Of Glencoe 200 Of
 Glengarry 200 207 Of Glengary 341 Of
 Islay 59 89 Of Keppoch 88 200 207 341
 Of Largie 59 144 Of Sleat 125 153 209
 Ranald 97 302 Randall 156 Samuel
 274 T 477 Una 301 William 275
MACDONNELL, Aeneas 160 Margaret
 160
MACDOUGAL, 357
MACDOUGALL, 38 207 267 332 425 433
 Duncan 126 243 Isabel 241 Isabella
 243 John 160 Of Dunolly 34 Of Lorn
 35
MACDUFFIE, Jannet 302 Malcolm 302
MACDUGALL, Donald 248 Margaret 248
MACEACHAINN, Ailean 333 Allan 280
MACFADYEAN, 235
MACFARLANE, 35 391
MACFIRBIS, 30
MACFLAIN, Blathmac 318
MACGHILLEAIN, 32
MACGHLASRAICH, 267
MACGILIVRA, Florance 301 Martin 301
MACGILL, David 106
MACGILLEAIN, 352 Am Bard 362 407
 Domhnull Ban 407 Gille-moire 35 Iain
 382
MACGILLEAN, 259 359 Gillise 35
MACGILLEMHOIRE, Domhnall 406
MACGILLEON, John 354
MACGILLEOUN, Hector 239
MACGILLIMORE, 252
MACGILLIVRAY, 219 Alexander 306 309
MACGILLIVRAY Isabel 312 Julian 302
 Martin 241 302 312 314 Neil 302 Una
 306 309
MACGINNIS, 363
MACGREGOR, 35 115 143 242 Lieut-col
 204
MACGULLAYNE, 356 Of Douard 84
MACHLEAN, Murdoch Gearr 264
MACIAIN, Eachunn 407
MACIAN, 56 58 67 100 107-108 127 178

MACIAN (cont.)
 267 286 294 336 364 Alexander 75
 Allaster 106 Angus 106 Anne 292
 Donald 126 Eachann 300 Hector 300
 John 57 105 110 355 Margaret 300 Of
 Ardnamurchan 45 58 144 151 Of
 Arnamurchan 121 Of Glencoe 144
MACIAN'IC-AILEIN, Iain Dubh 408
MACIANDY, Allan Cameron 153
MACILDUY, Neill 148
MACINNES, 299-300 331
MACINNON, Ewin 79
MACINTOSH, 25 35 41-42 62 115 207
 216-217 219 253-254 286 337
 Alexander 260 Brigadier 303 Duncan
 56 Farquhar 56 255 Isabel 255 Jannet
 259-260 Malcolm 259 Malcolm Beg 254
 Margaret 254 Marjory 260 William
 255 259
MACINTYRE, Mr 291
MACKAY, 35 51 201-204 255 258 337
 Charles 411 420 Donald 77 Gen 200
 288 William 332 477
MACKENZIE, 35 51 56 61 67 78 123 141-
 143 169 207 256 319 348 369 408
 Alexander 273 366 Ann 273 Cailean
 Cam 159 Comneach 32 Dr 248 Duncan
 52-53 362 Elizabeth Henrietta 248
 George 330 George Of Tarbet 198
 Gilleain 32 Henry 474 Janet 159 John
 303 352 477 Kenneth 51-53 126
 Kenneth Og 56 Margaret 51 Nigel B
 477 Of Dunachnahard 257 Of Kintail
 257 Sir George 198 Wm 477
MACKEYN, Alexander 79
MACKINNON, 37-38 80 101 103 138 153
 319 337-338 Alexander 306 407 Anne
 306 Catherine 287 Finovola 292 John
 287 Lachlan 100 157 159 176 Margaret
 38 Mary 176 Neill 100
MACKLANE, 356 403-404 Lauchlan 356
 Lauchlane 71 126 356 Rolland 50
MACLACHLAN, 207 219 313 Alexander
 297 Allan 270 Margaret 297 Marjory
 270 Rev Dr 368
MACLAIN, John 358 Lord 79
MACLAINE, 193 Alexr 358 Gillean 358
 Hector 247 Jane 359 John 244 247
 Murdoch 240 358
MACLALLISTER, 292
MACLANE, 359 Alane 79 Donald 79
 Hector 79 Jhone 79 79 Murdoch 79
MACLAUCHLAN, 219
MACLAURIN, 227
MACLEAH, Hector Og 224
MACLEAIN, Neil Ban 266 Somerled 39
MACLEAN, 21-22 24-26 31 33 49 52 55 63
 81 118 121 136 149 152 161 178 180
 187 190-191 194 196 199-201 203 205

488 INDEX.

MACLEAN (cont.)
209-210 215 217 220 228 251 317 319 323-325 330 342-344 359 366 406 409 --- 242 257 295 349 A Macdonald 477 Abolla Sophia 315 Ada Eve 398 Adelaide Owen 298 Adeline Travers 298 Agnes 252 258 377 Ailean 88 Ailean Na Sop 73 Ailean Nan Sop 80 88 92 Aithbric 36 Alexander 71 197-198 201-202 204 245 248 252 254 257-260 271 273 275 277 277-278 280-281 290-291 297-298 305-306 306-310 313-314 327 363 370 378 383 386 389 391-392 407 477 Alexander Campbell 298 Alexander Henry Herbert 298 Alexander John Hew 272 Alexander Of Calgarry 278 Alexander Of Coll 292 Alexander Of Otter 327 Alexander Of Torloisk 308 Alexander Thomas 272 Alicia 264 306 309-310 313-314 377 Allan 88-89 100 102 137 156 166 176 182-185 188-189 192 194 196-198 204 226-229 241-246 248 248 254 258 260-261 264 267-270 273 275-276 278 280-281 285 289-290 292 294-298 300 300-306 308 312-314 327 329 331-334 340 358 362-364 373-376 381 388 391 406-407 424 Allan Brother Of Kingerloch 307 Allan Charles 280 Allan Fitzroy 311 Allan Macintosh 261 Allan Na Sop 346 Allan Nan Sop 89 276 Allan Non Sop 407 Allan Of Ardgour 225 279 297 303 Allan Of Ardtornish 269 309 Allan Of Brolass 224 Allan Of Coll 277 Allan Of Drimnin 225 Allan Of Gormony 224 Allan Of Grulin 305-307 309 Allan Of Inverscadell 278-279 Allan Of Killean 279 Allan Of Killintyn 197 Allan Of Lochbuie 306 312 Allan Of Torloisk 279 303 Allan Of Totaranald 297 Allan The Elder 303 306 Allan The Younger 303 306-307 Allan Thomas 309 377 Allan Thomas Lockhart 310 Alpheus 395 397 Amanda 394-395 Amelia Dunlap 398 Andrew 305 309 326-327 382 477-478 Angus 252 260 264 270 301 308 326-327 370 Ann 212 273 273-274 276-278 281 292 295 295-297 305 307 314 Anna 225 271 307-308 313 315 346 Anna Eliza 396-397 Anna Mactearlach 324 Anna Margaret 315 Anna Prioress 323 Anna The Prioress 325 Annabella 258 273 Anndra Mac-an-easbuig 382 Anne 238 243 263 269-270 274 292 296-298 302-305 305-306 306 309 376 Annie 252 259 261 Annie Travers 298 Antoine 249 Archibald 182 198 227 234 246-247 264 266 269 269-271 273-276 279 294 296 305-306

MACLEAN (cont.)
306-309 313 371-372 376-377 383 384 387 391 407 Archibald Donald 309-310 Archibald John 310 477 Archibald Of Hyscer 278 Archibald Of Kilfinichin 278 Archibald Of Pennycross 306 Arthur Henry 377 Arthur J 386 Barbara 246 260 273-274 278 313 Beatag 36 Beatrice 36 212 Bertha C 397 Bessie Anneke 396 Betty 274 313 Black John 37 Breadalbin 291 Bridget 258 Buadan 349 C 386 Calvin Washington 398 Cameron Travers 298 Capt 244 Carl D 397 Caroline 376 Carrie E 397 Cary 394 Catharine 297 302 Catharine Marianna 250 Catherine 49 81 87 225 246 248 252 269 273-274 274 277-278 280-281 287-288 290-291 294-297 300 302 305 305-307 309 312-313 315 351 383 407 Catherine 2d 87 Catherine Cameron 291 Catherine Helen Dalrymple 272 Charles 137 182 197 216 227 231 236 239 251-252 254 257-260 262 267-270 273 273 276-279 287 292 300-302 302-303 303-309 313 315 325-327 349-350 382 384 406 478 Charles Alexander Hugh 311 Charles Durell 307 Charles Fitzroy 230 Charles Hope 271 390 392 Charles James 309 Charles Lachlan 232 Charles Maxwell 260 391-392 Charles Of Achat 251 Charles Of Coll 296 Charles Of Hynish 296 Charles Of Inverscadell 278 Charles Of Kilis 302 Charles Of Kilunaig 306 Charles Shrieve 263 Charlotte 310 376 Charlotte Amelia 260 Charlotte Brodie 310 Charlotte Margaret 271 Christian 301 Christiana 269 307 313-314 Christianna 290 301 Christina 236 248 263 278 281 297 305 Christina Sarah 249 Christopher 306-307 Christy 381 Clarence Wilbur 396 Col 374 Colin 263 305 Colman 349 Colquhoun 305 Constance Marianne 232 D 477 David 259 315 Deborah 399 Diarmad 36 Doidim Dana 406 Domlig 349 Don 477 Donal 407 Donald 36 45-46 100 159 166 168 179 182-183 195-197 214 224 229-230 236 246 248-249 252-254 257-259 262-263 266-267 269-271 273-276 278-281 287-290 292 294-296 296-298 302-306 306-307 309 312-314 325 333 359-360 362 369-370 374-375 378 381 383 386 406-407 410 Donald A 477 Donald Glas 108-109 300-301 331 401 Donald Mactearlach 324 Donald Of Brolass 224-225 270 281 304 Donald Of Coll 225 Donald Of Kingerloch 287

MACLEAN (cont.)
Donald Of The Isle Of Muck 281
Donald Of Torloisk 229 313-314
Donald Of Treshnish 275 279 Dr 369
Dr Hector 305 Dudley B 388 Dugald
381 Dugall 281 Duncan 306 384 478
Eachann 73 76 Eachann Mor 159
Eachann Og 81 87 90-91 137 Eachann
Reaganach 37 234 Eachann Ruadh 176
Eachann Ruadh Nan Cath 39
Eachuinn Ni Num-bristion 50
Eachuinn Odhar 50 Eachunn Bacach
382 408 Edith Jane 250 Edmund
Henry 298 Edward 397 Eliza 261 315
Elizabeth 71-72 248 257 260 262-263
271 291 293 302 313-314 377 394-395
397-398 Elizabeth Henrietta 248
Elizabeth Margaret 271 Ella 397 Elsie
Una 311 Emilie Fordyce 298 Emilie
Guillaumine 249 Emily 397-398 Emily
Agnes 378 Emily Frances Harriet 230
Emily Louise 397 Emma 396 Emma
Austin 263 Emma Eliza 263 Emma R
397 Eoghan Uaibhreach 279 Eugene H
477 Eugene Herbert 397 Eva 396 Evan
292 Ewen 168 182 236 239 241 252
254-255 266-268 270 273 275-277 279-
281 283 296 302-303 308 312 382
Ewen Dubh 278 Ewen Of The Little
Head 321 332 Ewen Of Treshnish 182
Ewen The Elder 269 Ewen The
Younger 269 Ewen Uaibhreach 275
Ewin 100 F P 477 Fannie 263 Fanny
Henrietta 230 Farquhar 252 254 256-
259 Feradach 349 Ferchard 349
Finovala Marianne Eleanor 232
Finovola 285 292 Finvola 350
Fionnaghal 45 283 Fitzroy 232 Fitzroy
D 419 477 Fitzroy Donald 72 230-231
Fitzroy Holland 232 Fitzroy J G 230
Fitzroy Jeffreys Grafton 229 375
Fitzroy Jeffries Grafton 305 Flora 247
264 272 276 281 Florance 159 229 301
Florence 224 273 273-274 277 286-288
294-297 303 305 308 327 Florence
Maude 378 Frances 230 Francis 280
373 Francis George 263 Gabriel 307
Gen 374 George 271 314 378 George
Edwin 478 George Francis 298 George
N 389 George Washington 396-397
Georgina Marcia 230 Gilleain 349
Gilleain Na Tuigahe 32 Gillean 137
246 264 423 Gillespig 266 Gillian 225
Gov 379 Gunston 271 Gustavus 315
Hannah 394 Hannah Barbara 295
Harriet 230 248 Harriet Jane 396-397
Harriet Newell 394-395 Harry 378
Harry Allen 398 Hattie Elizabeth 263
Hector 32 38-39 41 43 49-50 53 56-57

MACLEAN (cont.)
75-76 78 90-93 100 125 127 137-138
140-142 144 146-148 150 154 156 158-
159 176 178-183 188-189 192 194-195
197 200 212 214 216 221-226 228-229
235-237 239 241-247 252 257-258 261
261 263-264 267 267-271 273-275 275-
276 278-281 283-285 287-290 292 294-
295 301 303 303 305-310 312-315 326-
328 333 345 348-351 355 358 358-360
362 375 379-382 402 406-407 407-408
477 Hector Ailean Nan Sop 93 Hector
Buie 252-254 256 262 266 Hector Coll
298 Hector Fitzroy 232 Hector George
298 Hector Mor 73 76-77 80 83-85 87-
90 92 95 105 159-160 224 300 309 315
336 341 Hector Odbar 51 Hector
Odhar 59-62 65 240 336 Hector Of
Blaich 275 Hector Of Coll 89 239 269-
270 277 302 312 Hector Of Grulin 270
Hector Of Isle Of Muck 287 301 Hector
Of Kilmory 281 306 Hector Of
Kinlochaline 276 312-313 Hector Of
Knock 277 Hector Of Lochbuie 239
Hector Of Lochbuy 157 183 Hector Of
The Island Of Muck 305 Hector Of
Torloisk 241 269-270 287 301 Hector
Of Torren 243 306 309 Hector Of
Torrestan 204 305 Hector Of
Treshnish 277 302 Hector Og 90 129
132-133 140 143 156-157 159 197 229
276 287 301 Hector Oig 285 Hector
Reaganach 236 251-252 349 Hector
Reaganeach 347 Hector Roy 39-40 42-
43 46 54 62 91 156 176 181-182 265
285 287-288 294-295 308 406 408
Hector Rufus 176 Hector Rufus
Bellicosus 39 Hector Son Of
Kingerloch 204 Hector The Cripple 382
Hector The Stern 37 234 Hector The
Swarthy 50 Helen 242 261 305 315 397
Helen Cleveland 478 Helen Frasier
263 Helen Jane Hamilton 271 Henry
293 296 478 Henry Clay 396-397
Henry Dundas 271 Henry Travers 298
Henry Zwingli 394 Hubert 397 Hugh
172 182 194 197 244 261-264 270-271
274 278 281 287-292 294-297 302 308
326 349 351 359-360 367 375 377 478
Hugh Of Ardgour 263 Hugh Of Carnae
197 Hugh Son Of Maclean Of
Treshnish 274 Iain Ghanbhaur 276
Iain Macailein 382 Iain Odhar 275 Ian
300 Ian Dubh 37 Ian Gauld 286 Icrath
349 Ina P 397 Isaac Parry 396 Isabel
241 244 246 255 312 383 Isabel Annie
378 Isabel Juliet 311 Isabella 159 176
212 225 243 261 270 273-274 277-278
280 283 288-289 294-295 298 302-307

MACLEAN (cont.)
312-313 346 370 382 Isabella
Alexandrina 310 Isabella Sibella 291 J
380 Jacob 315 James 257-258 270 280
293 306 378 389 394-398 400 James
Charles 271 James I 399 James
Robinson 394 James Scott 396 Jane
248 263 292 305 326 398-399 Jane
Albane 292 Jane Gilliland 394 Janet
81 88 91 91 105 159 224 229 269 295
370 375 Jannet 106 255 258-260 283
285 287 289 291 296 301-302 305-308
312-313 Jean 289-290 305 308 Jennet
277 281 Jessie 261 297 Jessie Marian
261 John 32 36-37 39 69 73 75 90 101
172 182 185-186 194-195 198 200-202
204-210 212-213 221 224-225 229 234
236-237 241-244 246-248 255-258 260-
263 269-270 273 273-275 275-276 278-
281 283-286 289-290 293-298 301-310
313-315 327 349-350 362-363 367 370
376 378-379 381-388 393-395 398 400
406-408 478 John Abrach 255 283
John Aldolphus Count 315 John
Archibald 270 John Ban 258 John
Campbell 248 John Crubach 269 279
303 373 John Dalrymple 272 John
Diurach 182 302 John Diuriach 312
John Dubh 39 43 45 87 90 93 99-101
105 108 137 159 235 265 285 300 302
309 312 John Garb 284 John Garbh
45-48 159 172 224 277 283 285 287-
288 296 300 302 312 350-351 John
Garbh Second 301 John Glennich 267
John Hector Norman 292 377 John
Hugh 271 John J 389 John Lachlan
298 John Marsham 232 John Mor 238-
239 326 John Of Achanasaul 287 John
Of Ardgour 196-197 267 312 John Of
Borreray 295 298 John Of Coll 57 John
Of Drimnin 305 John Of Duard 259
John Of Grulin 246 263-264 326 John
Of Guirdhill 296 John Of Inverscadell
227 John Of Killean 303 John Of
Kilmore 296 John Of Kingston 307
John Of Kinlochaline 182 196-197 287
John Of Langmull 303 307 John Of
Lochbuy 225 227 John Of Mull 274
John Of Pennygoun 306-307 John Of
Tarbert 306 313 John Of Totaranald
269 287 305 John Of Totteronald 182
John Of Treshnish 267 274-275 295
John Og 53 77 236 258-259 264-265
332 378 John Patterson 389 396-397
John Roy 239 John Ruadh 266-267
John Scott 394-395 John Scudder 394
John Speed 399 John Teomachd 283
John The Younger 269 277 John
Waters 478 John Zimmerman 397

MACLEAN (cont.)
Joseph 375-376 388 394 397-398
Joseph Winters 397 Josephine 397
Joshua 307 Joshua Milton 394-395
Julia 297 376 Julian 87 185 241 243
294 301-302 306 312 Julian Archibald
311 Juliana 264 309 423 Juliet 292 K
T 478 Kate S 386 Kathlein Emilie 250
Keanlochallan 197 Kenneth Douglas
Lorn 250 Kenneth John 263
Kingerloch 204 Lachainn Lubanach 37
Lachainn Odhar 333 Lachiann
Lubanah 39 Lachlainn Macthearlaich
53 Lachlan 29-30 38-39 43-44 53 60-61
64-65 67 70 72-74 93-95 97 99 106 108-
111 114 124-126 128-129 132-133 137-
138 148 158-160 162-163 165-166 168
170-176 182 188-189 192 194 206 222-
225 227 229 235 239-240 242 247 258
260 262-263 267 273-274 276-281 285-
286 288 292-297 299 301 303-305 305-
307 309-310 313-314 328-329 333-334
348-350 352 355-356 358 360-361 370
373 382 385 388 406-408 420 Lachlan
Barrach 133 Lachlan Bronnach 43 45-
47 62 65 262 266 280 283 350 Lachlan
Catanach 60 65-69 71 73 76 88 90 237
252 312 419 439 Lachlan Cattanach
326 Lachlan Cattanch 275 Lachlan
Fionn 275 Lachlan Lubanach 39 39 45
347 Lachlan Mor 23 32 88 91-92 95-96
98-99 101 103-105 112 117 119-120
122 127 130-131 134-135 137 140 198
239-241 258 267-269 276 280 292 300-
301 312 315 331 333 355 380 402 406
Lachlan Odhar 182 280-281 334
Lachlan Of Ardgour 196 Lachlan Of
Brolass 185 196 224 313 Lachlan Of
Bunessan 306 Lachlan Of Calgary 198
269 295 303 305 Lachlan Of Coll 157
159 198 295 Lachlan Of Duard 327
Lachlan Of Grisiboll 296 Lachlan Of
Grulin 307 Lachlan Of Lochbuie 243
269 307 312 Lachlan Of Torloisk 157
159 185 197-198 225 243 Lachlan Og
45 48-49 62 65 129 131 137 269 276
279 301-302 312 314 327 350 375 408
Lachlan Perceval 298 Lachlan The
Wily 37 Laclan Of Calgary 294 Lady
47 Lauchlan 193 Lehire 265 Lether
265 Letitia Elizabeth 378 Lilian Gray
298 Lillian 305 Lillias 248 Little
Murdoch 238 Lizzie 398-399 Lochlan
Of Brolass 197 Louis Randolph 399
Louisa 212 305 398 Louisa Marianne
230 Lowry Cole 298 478 Lyell P 478
Lyell Parker 397 M 378 Mabel Julia
250 Mabel S 397 Mac-mhic-eachainn
Chinnghearloch 45 Macian Abrach 283

INDEX. 491

MACLEAN (cont.)
Maelsig 349 Malcolm 35-36 236 370 384 408 418 478 Malise 36 Maol-calum 36 Maoliosa 36 Marellia 72 Margaret 38-39 43 45 73 95 137 160 229 240-242 246 248 254 258-259 263 270-277 279 285 287 289 291-292 295 295-297 300-302 302-303 305-308 308 312 312 314 376-377 383 393-395 395 397 399 Margaret Anne 264 Margaret Gavine 298 Margaret Maxwell 248 Margery 257 Maria 227 264 291 305 307 315 Maria Isabella 398 Marian 73 87-88 91 176 236 254 261 269 275 275 281 285 287-288 290-291 294-297 302 305-306 308 312 329 370 Marian Palmer 248 Marianna 309 Marianne 248 298 313-314 Marion 257 Marjory 260 264 270 279 305 Martha 264 Mary 87 91 95 137 176 206 212 229 241-243 248 257 259 263-264 269-270 273-274 277-281 289 294-297 297-298 300 302-307 309-310 312-313 384 394 394-395 398-399 Mary Ann 306-307 Mary Anna 279 Mary Elizabeth 298 396-397 Mary Julia 390 Mary Kate 298 Mary Tenny 394 Mary The Elder 301 Mary The Younger 301 Mary Webster 388 389 Master Lachlan 93 Meve 284 Minerva Jane 398 Miss 362-363 478 Miss E F H 478 Morgan 298 Morvern 99 Mr 311 Mr Of Coll 289-290 Mrs 478 Murchadh Gearr 237 Murchadh Scalasdail 264 Murdo 369 Murdoch 182 236-237 240 242-243 246-249 263 273 280-281 305 346 349 Murdoch Gearr 238 Murdoch Gillian 249 Murdoch Hector 250 392 Murdoch Mor 240 Murdoch Of Scallasdale 237-238 Murdoch Og 241 406 Muriel 311 Nancy 394 398 Narcissa 395 Narcissa Lynn 394 Neachtan 349 Neil 39 45-46 89 182 254 265 273-278 280-281 287-289 292 295-297 302 312 333-334 338-340 350-351 370 386 407 Neil Ban 273 Neil Of Drimnacross 273 295 Neill 189 349 Nelson Wylie 394 Nial Ban 273 Niall 36 46 Niall Ban 266 274 Norman 263 290 370 378 Norman Henry 311 Norman Plaice 263 Oakley 397 Of Ardgour 23 66 182 193-195 198 368-369 Of Borreray 102-104 182 Of Brolass 187 195 198 214 406 Of Coll 23 81-82 178 182 282 321 351 368 410 Of Dochgarroch 253 Of Drimnin 182 219 303 Of Duard 23 26 30 33 51 56 59 68 77 81-82 116 121 123 153 155 158 216 237 318 321 335 337-338 341 Of Garmony 229 Of Glenevis 258

MACLEAN(cont.)
Of Grulin 321 Of Inverscadell 182 Of Kingerloch 45 154-155 166 178 193 197 258 266 Of Kinlochaline 166 198 Of Langmull 297 Of Lochbiue 312 Of Lochbuie 321 335 337-338 Of Lochbuy 23 53 56 59 66 68 77 139 174 193 198 201 207-208 229 234 261 Of Lochiel 368 Of Morvern 104 176-177 Of Ross 181-182 321 351 Of The Isle Of Muck 182 Of Torloisk 182 187 194-195 198 Of Treshnish 102 108 168-170 Old Dugall 349 Patrick 73 79 88 90 302 326 Peggie 244 246 Peter 271 305 315 Phineas 260 Phoebe 248 274 R 386 Rachael 396-397 Rachael Edna 396 Rachel 394 Rachel Marquis 394-395 Ranald 371 373 Rebecca 398 Red Hector Of The Battles 39 Richard 398-399 Riognach 35 Robert 271 394 399 478 Robert Cutler 263 Roderic 371 Roderick 90 257 290 292 297 Ronald 292 Ronald Gillian 250 Rosa Elizabeth 249 Rosalie Abbe 298 Ruingr 349 Sallie E 396 Sallie Pratt 388 Sarah 376 394 398-400 Sarah A 386 Sarah Amelia 260 Sarah Elizabeth 398 Schuyler 397 Selina Philippa 272 Sibella 227 279-280 289 291 302 Simon 252 263 Sliochd Iain Ghairbh 292 Sophia 263 Stephen 394-395 398 400 Suan 349 Susan 307 381 Susanna 273 281 Susannah 306 Swarthy Hector 240 Sween 252 Tarlach 252 Thaddeus 397 Thomas 236 271 307 Thomas W 478 Una 87 226 287 289 301 304 306-309 Violet 311 W W 388 Wallace Stanley 263 Wilbur Roy 397 William 259-260 262 271 275 279 292 371-373 388-389 391 394-395 397-400 William Congrieve 376 William Currie 396 396 William Mosby 399 William Murdoch 263 William Thomas Henderson 261 William White 394 William Wylie 394-395 Young Lachlan 48 Zeiretta 308
MACLEANE, 223 359 Hugh 358 Jo 358 Letitia 359
MACLEIR, 315
MACLEN, Alexander Of Sollose 293
MACLEOD, 49-50 63 67 80 97 122 138 149 155 158 207 216 319 337 341 350-351 369 Alastair Crotach 236 Alexander 66 69 75 79 100 274 Allaster 148 Catherine 288 291 297 Christina 236 Donald 289 294 Fionnaghal 45 283 Florence 286 288 Isabella 288 294 Janet 91 Jannet 289 306 John 75 185 198 288-289 306 Julian 185 Maj 291 Malcolm 236

MACLEOD (cont.)
  Margaret 160 274 Marian 87 236 288
  Mary 176 289 Neil 274 281 363
  Norman 87 286 288 Of Dunvegan 58
  68 Of Harris 58-59 68 123 153 283 350
  Of Lewis 38 104 Roderick 91-92 160
  176 297 Rorie 240 286 Rory 276 286
  288 292 Rorye 79 Ruari 77 148 154
  156-157 159 159 Susanna 281 Tormod
  354 Torquil 58-59 William 45 100 236
MACMARTIN, 275
MACMASTER, 266 Chief Of Ardgour 46
MACMHULOINIGH, 283
MACNAB, 35
MACNACHTEN, Alexander 238 Anne 238
  John 238
MACNAUGHTAN, Alexander 242
MACNAUGHTON, 204
MACNEIL, 26 48-49 73 103 138 289 Ann
  274 Catherine 312 Flora 276 Hector
  274 Janet 224 John 312 Margaret 301
  Neil 301 Of Barra 47 104 224 312 350
  Rory 276
MACNEILL, 50 59 80 96 101 115 149 168
  201 Gilleonan 56 Gilliganan 79 John
  100 Lachlan 293 Murdo 100 Neill 154
  Of Barra 88 229 Ruari 100 153
MACONNILL, Angus 79 Archibald 79
MACPHAIL, Dugald 409
MACPHEE, 96 101 Of Colonsay 104
MACPHERSON, 25 35 115 207 252
  Aeneas 206 212 Mary 206 212
MACQUARRIE, 35 59 80 101 103 168 319
  ---- 296 Alexander 308 Alicia 314 Ann
  276 Catherine 287 307 Donald 240 306
  308 Flora 247 Florence 308 Hector 197
  296 Isabella 212 John 197 309 Lachlan
  247 287 314 Margaret 240 308 Maria
  264 Marian 308 Of Ulva 197 Una 306
MACQUEEN, Angus 258 Bridget 258
MACQUORRE, Jhone 79
MACRAE, John 478
MACRANALD, 144
MACRATH, Son Of Maolsruthain 30
MACRUARI, Ailean 337 Allan 56-57 336
  Neill 148
MACRUARRIE, Allan 46
MACSWEYN, 362
MACTHEARLAICH, 55 Lachlan 54
MACVEAN, Colin A 228 335 381 Donald
  381 Susan 381
MACVURICH, 30 358
MADCOUGALL, 39
MAIREARAD, Nighean Lachainn Mhic
  Lachain 383
MAITLAND, Frederick 230 Harriet 230
  John 196
MAK, Yllean 356
MAKALANE, Donald 354

MAKCLANE, 354-355 Charles 354
  Donald 71 354 Hector 354 John 71 354
  Johne 354 Lachlane 70 354 Lauchlan
  71 Lauchlane 354 Luachlan 354
  Rolland 353
MAKCLANIS, 354 Lauchlane 68
MAKCLAYNE, 356 Hector 90-91 John
  Dow 91
MAKCLOID, Alexander 71 Alister 70
MAKCURA, Dwnsleif 68
MAKGILLANE, Donald 61 325 Hector 60
  Lacklane 61 354 Lady Agnes 61 325
  Lauchlan 353
MAKGILLEOIN, Ferchard 50 353 John
  Of Murchard 353
MAKGILLEON, Hector 29 236 352 John
  352 Lachlan 352 Lauchlane 61 354
  Murdock 354
MAKGILLEONE, 352 Lachlan 29 353
MAKGILLEOUN, Hector 356 John 237
MAKILLAN, Alexander 71 355
MAKILYN, Gillemore 352
MAKKENZIE, Kenneth 126
MAKKYNNA, Neil 71
MAKLANE, 353 Hector 354 Lachlan 61
  354 Lachlane 69 Lauchlan 354
  Lauchlen 70 Rolland 353
MAKMAKNELE, Donald Makalane
  Gillonan 68
MAKNEIL, Gillenwin 71
MAKNEILL, 353 Roderic 50
MAKRORY, Alan 325 Ranold 325
MAKWIDY, Dulleis 71
MAKYNNON, Nele 68
MALCEAN, Donald Of Killean 281
MALCOLM, George 478
MALCOM, Son Of Maoiliosa 30
MALEAN, David 258
MANI, Mhor Mhic 31
MANIMHOIR, Mhic 31
MAOILIOSA, Son Of Gilleeoin 30
MAOLSRUTHAIN, Son Of Neill 30
MAR, 41-42 44 208-210 212 214 350
MARGARET, Queen 319
MARSHALL, Sarah Amelia 260
MARSHAM, Emily Eleanor 230 Jacob 230
MARTIN, Henry Maclean 478
MARY, Queen 89 257 262 326
MASSERENE, Lord 293
MASSEY, Eyre 247
MATHESON, Lady 370
MATHEWS, Elizabeth 293 Philip 293
MAULD, James 401
MAULE, 41 Robert 42
MCALLANE, Donald 150
MCCARLYCH, John 83
MCCARTHOUR, Patrick 328
MCCAWLAY, Aula 357
MCCHARLES, Lauchlane 163-164

INDEX. 493

MCCLAIN, 359 E L 478 Ephraim 478 T B 478
MCCLAINE, 357-358 Lauchlane 164 358 Lauchlane Of Coill 163-164 Lauchlane Of Morverne 163 Murdoch 163-164 358 Of Coll 114
MCCLAN, John 237 353
MCCLANE, 239 355 Agnes 326 355 Alan 355 Allan 355 Charles 355 Hector 50 83 160 284 327 353 355 357-358 Jhone 328 John 284 355 L 358 Lachlan 355 355 Lauchlane 25 25 69 328 356 358 Marian 326 355 Mary 327 Murdoche 356 Of Cole 357 Of Dowald 354 Of Doward 112-113 354 Of Lochbowy 357 Of Lochbuy 112-113 Patrick 90 355
MCCLAYNE, 355-356 403 Allan 355 Allane 357 Charlis 357 Donald 357 Ewin 357 Hector 140 152 355 357 Hectour 357 John 355 Johnne 239 Lauchlane 111 125 136 356-357 Lauchlane Of Coill 357 Murdo 356 Rory Beg 125
MCCLEAN, 359 Charles B 478 Donald 60 353 George C 478 Hectoris 262 John 60 353 Lachlan 113 353 Lachlan Mor 100 Lachlane 162 358 William 478
MCCLEANE, Donaldus 262 Hector 240 357-358 Hector Of Doward 150 Hector Of Dowart 162 Hector Of Lochbowie 150 162 Hectour 329 358 Hew 162 358 Lachlane 358 Lauchlane 150 Murdoch 358 Murdochi 240
MCCLEANES, Allane 150 358 Lauchlane 150 358
MCCLEIN, Gilbert 357
MCCLENE, Alexander 357
MCCLEOD, Johne 163 Rorie 164
MCCLOYD, Rorie 150 Tutor Of Harrick 114
MCCLURG, Booksellers 478
MCCONEILL, Angus 111 152 357
MCCONNEILL, 112
MCCORREY, Hector 114
MCCRANNOLD, J 164
MCDONALD, Alexander 166 Donald 70 Donald Gorme 150 Jhone 328
MCDONELL, Jhone 328
MCDONNALD, Donald 164 Donnald 163
MCDOUGALL, 22 Isabel 244 John 160
MCEWIN, Lauchlane 68
MCFIE, Donald 150
MCFINGOUN, Lauchlane 114
MCGELLAYNE, 356 Of Kinlochbuy 84
MCGILHON, 352 Donald 36
MCGILLAN, 357 Donald 60 353 Of Lochbuy 114
MCGILLANE, Allane 114 357 Ector 352 John 325 354 John Oig 114

MCGILLANE (cont.)
Johnne Oig 357 Lady Agnes 354 Lauchlan 61 325 354 Lauchlane 114 357
MCGILLAYNE, 356 Of Doward 84 Of Dowarde 85 Of Lochbuy 85
MCGILLEAIN, Lachlan 50
MCGILLEAN, John 237 Murdac 237
MCGILLEANE, Allane 357 Chairlis 114 Johnne 114 357
MCGILLEAWNE, Capt Of Carnybreigh 114
MCGILLECALLUM, Neil 114
MCGILLEOIN, Hector 236 John 236 353 Lachlan 353 Murdac 236
MCGILLEON, Ferquard 326 Hector 60 353 John 353 Lachlan 61 352 Lady Mary 326 354 Lauchlan 353 Lauchlane 60 Murdac 354
MCGILLEONE, Finvola 50 Hector 353 John 353 Lachlan 50 353
MCGILLEOUN, Lachlan 356 Murdoch 239
MCGILLIAN, John 246
MCGILLON, Neil 36
MCILLURA, Martine 162
MCILVORA, Martine 358
MCINTYRE, Allan 478
MCIVOR, Flora 22
MCKANE, Allaster 107 Angus 107 Johnne 106-107
MCKENZIE, Allister 126 Coline 357 Johnne 126 Rory 160
MCKIE, Herbert 357
MCKINNON, Lachlan 357 Lachlane 162
MCKYNNOUN, 84 Lauchlane 114 150
MCLAIN, 399 A O 478 Calvin W 478 Henry Z 478 John 359 400 John Speed 478 Lizzie 478 Louis Randolph 478 Murdoch 243 Stephen 400 W D 478 William Allan 185
MCLAINE, 358 Hector 240 John 242 359 Mr 359
MCLANE, Charles A 478 Edward A 478 James 400 478 Jhone 328 355-356 John Dow 91 Lauchlane 356 403-404
MCLEAN, 359 Alan 356 Alexander D 478 Allan 479 Allan Oswald 478 Ann 227 Archibald 195 478 Arthur Elliot 478 Calvin B 479 Charles B 479 Charles N 478 Colin 478 Colin Campbell 478 D A 478 D G 479 Daniel 479 Daniel E 479 David 479 Donald 479 Donald Of Brolass 182 Duncan R 479 Edward 479 Francis 479 Francis J 479 George 479 George C Jr 479 George P 479 H 358 479 Hector 177 241 479 Hector Mor 81 162 Hugh 358 J A 479 J D 479 J K 479 James 479 James D 479 James L 479

MCLEAN (cont.)
James M 479 James W 479 John 358 358 479 John B 479 John Hall 479 John J 479 John R 479 479 John W 479 L A 479 Lachlan 100 107 Lachlan Catanach 74 Lachlan Mor 24 115 Lester 479 Mary 479 Mary E 479 Murdoch 241 N A 479 Norman 479 R B 479 Robert C 479 Sarah A Thorne 479 Susan A 479 T C 479 Thomas Alexander 479 Thomas Neil 480 W A 480 W C 480 William 280 480 William Clark 480 William Murdock 480 William S 480 William Stevenson 480 Wm K 480
MCLEANE, Hector 358 Jo 358 Lauchlanus 241 Murdochi 241
MCLENE, 358
MCLEOD, Alastair 47 J 164 Malcolm 47 Roderick 480 William 47
MCMILLAN, Niniane 162
MCNEILL, Neil 163 Neill 164 Of Barry 114
MCNELE, Malcolm 90
MCQUEINE, Hector 114
MCQUIRIE, Gillespie 150
MCRANNALD, Johne 163-164
MEAN, Mary 306
MENTEITH, 75
MENZIES, 35 Col 242
MHAC-GILLEAIN, 352
MHAC-GILLEOIN, 352
MHAC-ILLEAN, 352
MHAOLSUTHIN, Mhic 30
MHIC, Eri Mhic 30 Jeril Duerbh Mhic 30
MHIC-GHILLEAIN, 352
MHOR, Ian 67
MHUREHUIDSH, Mhic 30
MILLER, Archibald 402
MINTURN, Margaret 399 Smith 399
MISE, Lachin Mhac Gilleoin 312
MOGNA, Laimhe Mhic 30
MONK, Gen 200
MONKTON, Gen 293
MONRO, Donald 84
MONROE, Daniel 246
MONTGOMERY, 270 305 374 407 Maj 291
MONTROSE, 64 161-162 166-172 175 183 188-189 197 258 276-277 294 296
MOORE, 394 Margaret 394 Sarah 394 400
MOR, Duncan 53
MORAY, 41 Thomas 42
MORE, Maccollum 200
MORRISON, Donald 406
MORTON, 64
MORUERNE, L Mcclane 164
MOSBY, Louisa 398

MOSHEIM, 387
MOSS, William Lathrop 480
MOYDERTACH, John 75 78
MUDDOCK, 187
MUGACH, Domhnall 285
MUIDAIRTEACH, John Dubh 288
MUIDAIRTECH, Marian 288
MUNCH, Professor 38
MUNOE, Andrew 258 Annabella 258
MUNRO, 35 Anne 50 Dean 228 351 356 Robert 50
MUNSELL, Joel 480
MURCHISON, Roderick I 311
MURDOCH, 333 Archibald 290
MURRAY, David 144 Earl 196 Gen 295 301 315 George 216-217 John 222 Lord 201 Of Tullibardine 117
NABOB, 293
NAPOLEON, 372 376
NAVE, John 173
NEACHDUIN, Mhic 30
NEAVES, John 173
NEIL, Mhic 30 Of The Thumbs 265
NEILL, Son Of Cuduilig 30
NEVILL, Louisa Marianne 230 R P 230 Ralph 480
NEWTON, 360
NIC-PHAIL, Mairi 406
NICHOLSON, 121-122 133
NICOLSON, George 121
NIKILLEAN, Mary 327
NIMMO, Thomas 413
NIO-GILLEAIN, Catriona 407
NOONAN, Miss 263
NYCOLSOUN, George 405
O'DOCHTRIE, Shayne 94
O'DONNELL, 122-123 276 Calvagh 87 Julian 87
O'FLYNN, 393
O'NEIL, 276
O'NEILL, Julian 87 The Great 87
O'ROURKE, 113
OCHILTREE, Lord 147-148
OGILVIE, Brigadier 209
OGILVY, 216 Alexander 41 George 42
OLD, Dougall Of Scone 30
OLLOIL, Mhic 31
OLLOILERM, Mhic 31
ORAN, 319
OSBORNE, Martha 264 William 264
PALLANDT, Baroness De 480
PANMURE, 209
PARK, Elizabeth 314 James 314
PATTISON, 382 Thomas 421
PAULSON, Maj 303
PENNANT, 326
PENNYCROSS, 65 72 119 135 140 212
PEREIJA, 401
PFEIFFER, Emily 439

INDEX. 495

PHILIP, 331 Of Spain 114 225
PHILLIPPS, Of Amryscloss 422
PHILLIPS, 242 G 402 Mary Frances 480 R 402
PRICE, Benjamin 376 Gen 398 Sarah 376
QUICKELBERRY, Anna 315
QUIXOTE, Don 364
RAINGEE, Son Of Old Dougall 30
RAMSAY, David 193
RANALD, 121 200
RANALDSOUN, Alexander 79 Angus 79
RANNOCH, 75
REAY, Lord 255
REED, Julius A 480
RICHARDS, Sarah M 480
ROBERT, Duke Of Albany 40 Sir Of Peblis Chamberlain Of Scotland 36 The Bruce King 33
ROBERT II, 37
ROBERT III, 37
ROBERTSON, 35 Jane 292
ROBINSON, ---- 399 Daisy 397 Emma 397 Howard 397 John 397 Mary 399 Mary Elizabeth 397 Rachel 394 Robert S 397 Tirza 397
ROE, M 378 Robert 378
ROGERS, ---- 395 Benjamin 395 Elizabeth 395 James 395
ROLLS, Georgina Marcia 230 John A 230 Mrs 480
ROOKE, George 201
ROSE, 258 John 377
ROSS, 35 46 Annie 259 James 259 Juliana 264 Mary 423 Thomas 264
ROTHES, 64
ROTHM, Mhic 31
ROTHREUN, Mhic 31 31
RUARRIE, Allan 283
RUNYAN, Elizabeth 398
RUNYON, Deborah 399 Elizabeth 399 John 399
SACHEVERELL, William 198
SAINT, Columba 335 Kilda 335 Oran 335
SAINTCLARE, John 401
SAINTCOLUMBA, 317 324
SAINTJOHN, William 147
SANDFORD, Daniel K 424
SANDS, Marian Palmer 248
SCHWABE, Catharine Marianna 250 Salis 250
SCOTT, ---- 248 Dred 387 J L 298 Jane 248 Margaret Gavine 298 Sir Walter 419-420 452 Walter 22 88 118 340 408-409
SCRIPPS, E W 480
SCRYMGEOUR, 42 James 41
SEAFORTH, 178 209
SEATON, Lord 231
SENEACHIE, 65 391

SHAW, Dubh-sith 131
SHEAN, Dughaill Scoinne 30
SHELBURNE, Lord 293
SHERIDAN, Thomas 222
SHINE, Mhic 31
SHOAR, Gillespie Macian 178
SHUDER, Emma R 397
SIMON, Isabella Alexandrina 310
SINCLAIR, 35 A Maclean 352 362 381-383 391 406 Alexander 306 Alexander Maclean 381 B D 480 Catherine 306 315 David 315 John Campbell 390 Mary Julia 390
SKENE, 22 24 29 29 37 111 348-349 358
SKINNER, Donald 263 Mary 263
SMITH, Adolpho E 401 Capt 402 Margaret 314 Richard 314 Sidney 372-373
SOMERLED, 23
SOMERSET, Henry 271
SPOTTISWOODE, 90 118 Archbishop 97
STANLEY, 64 Edward 63
STEWART, 35 144 209 238 264 267-268 406 Alan 44 Alexander 43 Allan 287 Ann 305 Capt 305 312 Catherine 87 302 Dorothea 94 Duncan 61 287 354 Harriet 248 John 87 248 Lady Margaret 43 Margaret 287 312 Mary 263 Of Appin 200 Una 287 William 126
STIRLING, 41 Alexander 42
STIVERS, Harriet Newell 395 Jackson 395
STOCKARD, Samuel Mclean 480
STODDARD, 342
STODDARDT, 352
STRACHAN, 258
STRAITON, 41 Alexander 42
STUART, 219 223 258-259 262 372 Charles Edward 215 Prince Charles 215 219 305 Roy 216
SURREY, 64
SUTHERLAND, 35
SWEETLAND, Elizabeth 263 John 263
SYMSON, Mary 296 Mr 296
TALLISKER, 289
TANNAHILL, 410
TARBAT, Viscount 200
TEARLACH, Macgilleain 384 Macneill Bhain 273-274 Mor Na Sgurra 274
TERREAGH, Macdonald 96 99
TERRY, Miss 262
THIN, James 480
THOMAS, Gen 398
TOPEE, Tantia 377
TRAQUAIR, 222
TRAVERS, Mary Elizabeth 298
TRUEN, Mhic 31
TUIRMHICH, Teainrich Righ 31

TULLIBARDINE, 209
TURNBULL, Col 306
TURNER, 174 383 James 173 175
TYLER, 133 F E 480
TYRONE, 120-124
TYTLER, 74 120 P F 61
URQUHART, Alexander 52 Elizabeth 257 Walter 257
VALA, Lachlan Maclean 274
VANPLASSEN, Abolla Sophia 315
VANTREILEBEN, Hans Albricht 401
VINCENT, Charles A 249 Emilie Guillaumine 249
WAILEY, Frances Dyaz 480
WALL, James 229 Margaret 229
WALLACE, Capt 288 William 202
WALSINGHAM, 401
WALTER, The Steward Of Scotland 35
WATSON, Sereno 480
WELLINGTON, 376-377
WHALLON, Alice 396 Frances 396 Jacob 395 John 396 Narcissa 395

WHITEHEAD, Dr 248 Flora 248
WILKINSON, Henry W 480
WILLIAM, 200 King 198 205-206 213 Prince Of Orange 199
WILSON, Emily 398 Jane 398 Niles 398
WINDHAM, Ashe 292 Juliet 292 Miss 480 Mrs 480
WINTERS, Emily 397 Joseph 397
WIRTTUS, Capt 287
WISCHARD, James 354
WOLFE, Gen 373-374
WOOD, Alicia 264 Andrew 58 John 264 Louisa 305 Mr 302
WOODROW, 173
WOTHERSPOON, Helen Maclean 424 William Wallace 480
WYLLIE, 480
YORK, Cardinal 223
YOUNGER, Thomas 45
ZIMMERMAN, Elizabeth 397

www.ingramcontent.com/pod-product-compliance
Lightning Source LLC
Chambersburg PA
CBHW050132240426
43673CB00043B/1641